THE OPERAS OF MOZART

WILLIAM MANN

The Operas of Mozart

New York

Oxford University Press

1977

This book is for

DOMENIQUE
ELISABETH
MADELEINE
MIRABELLE

and their mother

ERIKA

CONTENTS

FOREWORD

This book is indebted to many people. First to Evelyn Waller, an elderly, large and comforting friend for a little boy: she was not less devoted to the arts than my parents except that she loved opera more than they, and she took me to my first opera, *The Magic Flute* at the Old Vic in the late 1920s and introduced me to her friend Joan Cross who, for several years, remained for me the only possible Pamina, Countess Almaviva, Donna Anna and Fiordiligi. It was Norman Del Mar, now my brother-in-law, who made me listen to Mozart's operas in the original language and think about the influence of vowels and consonants, and order of words, on the music given to them by the composer. All the operas I had seen in the theatre were sung in English: Norman taught me about opera in the language set by the composer; languages were already one of my passions, so I was an easy convert. In 1947 the Vienna State Opera visited London and performed several operas by Mozart (in German translation), bringing me under the spell of Julius Patzak and Richard Tauber, Irmgard Seefried, Sena Jurinac, and Ljuba Welitsch, Erich Kunz and Georg Hann, but signally Elisabeth Schwarzkopf whose singing has taught me more about Mozart than anyone else, except her husband Walter Legge. I would like to thank Arthur Hammond, Charles Mackerras and Maurits Sillem for much help, over many years, on points of Mozartian vocal style. Some debts are unforgotten though the creditors at the moment cannot be remembered and thanked. Chiefly I am indebted to Peter Branscombe who read the whole typescript and commented acutely on some of its deficiencies; Christopher Raeburn also read several chapters and gave much helpful advice about long-forgotten singers and historical details. Anthony Besch, Haydn Rawstron and Eric Spragett kindly read some chapters and commented helpfully. Times Newspapers gave me sabbatical leave to complete the book. David Ascoli commissioned it for Cassell's. Giles Hewlett-Cooper drew the music examples after reducing them himself from full score. He used the New Mozart Edition wherever possible; other sources are to be found in the Bibliography. Much help in research came from the British Library. Marcella Barzetti gave valued assistance in problems about the Italian language. Harry Moon typed some chapters, my wife and daughters the rest. They helped me to complete this large, I hope useful book. That is why it is dedicated to them rather than the other persons gratefully acknowledged heretofore.

Brighton–Aldeburgh–Salzburg–Wimbledon 1966–1976   W S M

THE OPERAS OF MOZART

INTRODUCTION

Three-quarters of our way through the twentieth century, opera appears to be more popular than ever. Opera companies and opera festivals, schemes for the training of operatic performers, courses for opera-goers, all proliferate continually, and standards of performance seem to rise with them. Yet opera, as a living art, has been in a decline for several decades. I am not postulating a decline in the art of singing: connoisseurs in reminiscent mood have been doing that in every generation, certainly since Samuel Burney in 1789, probably back to the time when Miriam took the timbrel and gave the first performance of 'Sing ye to the Lord' while an aged bystander muttered that there were no good singing teachers these days.

In 1976 there are plenty of excellent opera singers about; many can look the parts they are engaged to play, some can even act as convincingly as Thespians of the playhouse. The decline is in a steady flow of new operas apt to present-day taste, a fair proportion quickly taken up elsewhere with general enthusiasm, as regularly happened in former generations and until Richard Strauss's *Der Rosenkavalier* (1911) and Puccini's *Turandot* (1925). Living composers since then have been encouraged by others, and commissioned, to write new operas: sometimes the results were widely acclaimed, and every potential success was hungrily exported. Berg's *Wozzeck* and *Lulu*, Einem's *The Trial* and *The Visit*, Gershwin's *Porgy and Bess*, Britten's *Peter Grimes*, several works by Henze (notably *The Bassarids*), Stravinsky's *The Rake's Progress*, Prokofiev's *War and Peace*, Poulenc's *The Carmelites* are some examples; yet we cannot claim that any of these is at present as good news to the box office as *Turandot* or *Rosenkavalier*, let alone *La traviata* or *Fidelio* or *Die Meistersinger*.

Society, taste, thought have all evolved. Opera composers, the more imaginative, are not content to rehash old ideas for the sake of a commercial success: when a composer as masterly as Walton in *Troilus and Cressida*, or Barber in *Antony and Cleopatra*, writes a traditional opera it has proved no more successful internationally than more progressive and less popularly designed new operas. The public which once flocked to see Verdi's new *Aida* now flocks, not to Nono's *Intolleranza* or Zimmermann's *Die Soldaten*, but to . . . *Aida* again. Astrologers explain that our world has moved from the age of Sagittarius to that of Aquarius, which will give rise to new, valid, progressive and widely acclaimed art-forms. The new Aquarian music-theatre will surely take some time to throw up popular masterpieces of topical relevance; at present rock-opera (*Hair*, *Tommy*, *Jesus Christ Superstar*—the last shamelessly backward-looking in content) provokes the real world-wide interest, not the new straight operas.

As a result, and for some decades, operatic taste has been largely directed to the revival of old operas, long ignored, by composers either great or of historical interest. We have rediscovered Monteverdi, Handel, Gluck, Verdi, investigated Cavalli, Haydn, Mercadante, Giordano, and operatic composers of lesser artistic importance but attractive none the less from a historical point of view—as museum exhibits.

Among these rediscovered masters of operatic history Mozart is acclaimed higher than ever before. During his lifetime his stage works were praised and then dropped, like pop songs nowadays. When Lorenzo da Ponte proposed *Le nozze di Figaro* to the Austrian Emperor Joseph II, that cultured monarch objected that Mozart had previously composed only one opera, *Die Entführung aus dem Serail* (he forgot that he had commissioned *La finta semplice* and, very recently, *Der Schauspieldirektor*). Kaiser Joseph was unaware of the thirteen stage works, and three others incomplete, which had led to *Die Entführung*, some of them commissioned by, and performed before, his own family. They were not known any more, though *La finta giardiniera* and *Zaide* (perhaps in more complete form than we possess), and *König Thamos* too, were being constantly performed by travelling companies in Austria and Germany. Cultural memory was short. Eventually Mozart died and was survived by his last six major operas, from *Die Entführung* onwards and including *La clemenza di Tito*, this last enjoyed by conservative audiences for some decades (it was the first Mozart opera to be staged in England).

The nineteenth century, which still clung to the theory that music had progressed qualitatively from earlier times until the perfection of the present day, did not ignore Mozart (or Handel or Haydn), but reactivated his music in its own image. It was taken for granted that some musical and dramatic changes would have to be made for current taste, including interpolated numbers. We may nowadays shudder at the thought that the sacred score of *Figaro* was profaned by extra numbers specially composed by Sir Henry Bishop.

They will not have sounded incongruous because Mozart's music had been re-aligned for the taste of the time, so that Mozart was admired for his up-to-dateness. We would hate a tenor or female soprano Don Giovanni, a Vitellia who sang Sextus's music, a Susanna who rejected Mozart in favour of a new solo by Bishop. But Mozart was always aware of such habits and himself composed many additional arias, from boyhood until death, to be added to existing operas.

The nineteenth century loved Mozart as we do now, but needed to appreciate him as an old-fashioned composer whose work miraculously suited the modern taste of the time. His operas continued to be performed in Britain (in Italian), in France (heavily adapted), and in Germany where singing grew romantically blowzy and drove away Mozart's careful concern for florid divisions, ornamentation and cadenzas. The cult of the inviolate printed text set in; deviation from it (natural to all eighteenth-century singers, expected by the composer) became anathema and the real nature of Mozart's operas was subsumed into 'hovering Hellenic grace' (Schumann's phrase) and doll-like stylization. German detestation of eighteenth-century accepted gracing in Mozart dates from this period, though some singers went on decorating (as we hear in records by Patti, Lilli Lehmann, Frida Leider and others). Even *Idomeneo* was tried out for impact several times during the nineteenth century.

By the time that Hermann Levi and Richard Strauss in Munich began to reinstate *Così fan tutte* into the Mozart repertory, in about 1896, the notion of virtuoso vocal improvisation and agility had more or less disappeared. Rapid runs were almost impossible to a singer whose voice was chiefly used in loud, passionate romantic music accompanied by a big orchestra. The banishment of gracing, in favour of literal adherence to the printed text (however inaccurate), enabled potential Brünnhildes to wobble away more or less acceptably in Mozart as in Wagner—East European audiences still prefer wobbly singing, and find the clean-pitched style unemotional.

By these developments Mozart's operas, some of them, remained current in the repertory, though the music was sung heavily as if by Brahms. Our own century has come to value Mozart even more highly. Strauss, Mahler and Beecham, to go no farther, taught singers to respect Mozart's notes and rhythms and something of his eighteenth-century style. Later generations have concentrated on clean runs, expressive and musical enunciation of words, legato line, and attention to the un-noted code of vocal embellishment, in Mozart as vital to the spirit of the music (he always planned for it) as to the success of the individual singer. Our stage-directors and audiences everywhere are much more appreciative of dramatic context and detail in Mozart's operas—but only because Mozart himself took such pains to get all these factors to his satisfaction (as his letters constantly show).

We know from his letters (especially about *Idomeneo* and *Die Entführung*) how much he thought about words and situations and characters before he composed the music for them. We know how many libretti he read and rejected, in the years between *Die Entführung* and *Figaro*, how many he started setting and then despaired of.

Leopold Mozart, an excellent musician who quickly recognized his son's unusual promise, is often castigated for exploiting Wolfgang's youthful genius, but must be credited with giving him as complete a musical education as any musician ever received. Wolfgang Mozart toured western Europe in his boyhood and automatically imbibed the musical styles of France, Germany and Italy, the major influences on the Continent. Daines Barrington's report, quoted in my first chapter, describes Mozart's spontaneous response, at the age of eight, to a request for operatic music in several moods. Singing lessons at the same age (too soon for modern theory), with a starry male soprano (Manzuoli), had by then implanted in Mozart an appreciation of *bel canto* and individual quality which he went on developing all his life.

We will admire Mozart's diverse, scrupulous orchestration (when to use flutes, when cors anglais, when high horns, when prominent bassoons, when clarini, when *not* to divide violas as, in youth, he almost always did). We will watch him link movements or sections together, for dramatic effect (as early as *Ascanio in Alba*), and repeat movements for the same purpose, observe how he learned to abbreviate, coherently and purposefully, the aria forms he was brought up on, so that they would be less lengthy and repetitive, more inventive.

Best of all, this detailed survey of all Mozart's operas will show how early he understood the dramatic purpose, as well as the musical pleasure, of the vocal ensemble, a sort of music treated circumspectly by his Italian colleagues in *opera buffa* and reckoned unsuitable in *opera seria*. Mozart understood otherwise, perhaps because he had been brought up on French, German and Italian opera, perhaps because he vaguely foresaw how serious and comic Italian opera could be blended—at first, rather stiffly, in *La finta giardiniera* (which lists, separately, serious and comic roles), later in the da Ponte operas which are the operatic equivalent of Shakespeare's serio-comic amalgam. *Die Zauberflöte* is even more drastic, since it mingles the comic pleb with the loftiest divinity, religious and secular life on equal terms, something that no author has managed so persuasively.

The late and famous operas have never needed propagation. *Figaro, Giovanni,* and *Flauto magico* were all well known to our grandparents or great-grandparents (who regarded all good opera as Italian). *Così fan tutte* gradually won admirers, more recently *Idomeneo.* The Mozart revival during the last twenty years or more has bought into common appreciation not only *Tito* but *Mitridate* and *Il rè pastore,* and indeed at one time or another all the works discussed in this book.

Mozart was never short of commentators: Stendhal in 1812 is still worth reading, like Hoffmann, Berlioz, Shaw and others. There have been major books on Mozart and his operas, required reading for all students. The most important were by Otto Jahn and Hermann Abert, Edward J. Dent, and Alfred Einstein, classic volumes all of them.

I have ventured to explore the same territory as these great scholars, most unscholarlylike, because (unlike them) I have seen all but one of these stage works by Mozart, and have known them all from the music, many from records, for a quantity of years. As they flooded back into the theatre, to my delight, it seemed sensible to pass on to others basic information about each of them, derived from the music and stage directions, or from seeing a production and thinking about it. The great Mozart commentators of the past had not seen most of these operas (even curtailed and unseemly non-decorated, as often now, let alone poorly sung without a shred of elegant gracing). If they had, they would have hurried into new editions.

My book is strictly a guide, based on theatrical as well as score experience. The reader needs to know the genesis of each opera by Mozart (including, I decided, the dramatic oratorios and the incidental music, very typical, for *König Thamos*), exactly what words and music are contained in each musical number, of course a commentary on the whole dramatic action as it develops, as well as a critical consideration of each work.

Because stage producers tend to ignore authentic instructions for their own ideas, I have included the original ones, just as I have given all the musical information. The musical commentary is designed to suggest how Mozart used music to convey character or mood, and how the early works are reflected in the best known late ones. Mozart's musical language developed, from first to last, but he was not an innovator, only a masterly synthesizer whose achievement was to bring together musical elements (e.g. duets, ensembles, choruses) that had been exiled from standard opera in his immediate past. What Mozart achieved will not generally be acknowledged until the contemporary operas by Paisiello, Martín, Jommelli, Hasse, and so on, are performed—unfortunately they are not good box-office material. I do know that Mozart put more humanity into his operas, at any level.

Mozart was a great actor in his composition, a great humanist: he brought back good old ideas into his operas, when everyone else had forgotten them. He was, above all, a musician of his time and so one must view his stage works in context, as he wrote them. I have paid attention to his orchestra (in Austria significantly different from Italy), to his scoring everywhere, have given an English translation of every solo aria, and its pace and orchestral requirements. Tonality, the key involved, was most important to Mozart, and I have written an interchapter on this subject, as on other general subjects to do with Mozart's operas. In the analyses I spend much time on dramatic motivation because Mozart did.

I hope it will help newcomers to enjoy Mozart's operas more fully; even the early ones are fascinating. I could not survey all the original details: the New Mozart Edition is not yet completely published, and many of the autograph scores were stolen by Russia in 1945 and are being kept hidden in Poland. This secrecy is pointless: the scores must be made available to scholars. The main point of this book is to show that Mozart is an international composer of operas that belong to the whole world.

I DIE SCHULDIGKEIT DES ERSTEN GEBOTES

DIE SCHULDIGKEIT DES ERSTEN GEBOTES

Part I of a Sacred Drama by IGNAZ WEISER

K. 35

GERECHTIGKEIT (Justice)	SOPRANO
CHRISTGEIST (Christianity)	TENOR
BARMHERZIGKEIT (Mercy)	SOPRANO
EIN LAUER UND HINNACH EIFRIGER CHRIST (A lukewarm, afterwards zealous Christian)	TENOR
WELTGEIST (Worldliness)	SOPRANO

Wolfgang Mozart's career as a composer of operatic music can be traced back to 1765, during his extended visit to London with his parents and sister Nannerl. At some time in this year the nine-year-old boy composed an aria for tenor, *Va, dal furor portata* (Köchel-Verzeichnis 19 c), which the singer Ciprandi included in a performance of Metastasio's poetic drama *Ezio* given at the King's Theatre, Haymarket, in *pasticcio* form, i.e. with music by many different composers. During the same visit Wolfgang received some singing lessons from the famous castrato Manzuoli.* In June 1765 he spent some time with the Hon. Daines Barrington, F.R.S. (1727–1800), an eccentric lawyer, antiquary and enthusiastic polymath who, among many other papers, wrote one about musical prodigies, including Mozart.

One passage in the report which Barrington sent to the Royal Society in 1769 is worth quoting. Barrington was attempting scientifically to examine Mozart's prowess as a musician:

Happening to know that little Mozart was much taken notice of by Manzoli [*sic*], the famous singer, who came over to England in 1764, I said to the boy, that I should be glad to hear an extemporary Love Song, such as his friend Manzoli might choose in an opera.

The boy on this (who continued to sit at his harpsichord) looked back with much archness, and immediately began five or six lines of a jargon recitative proper to introduce a love song.

He then played a symphony which might correspond with an air composed to the single word, *Affetto*.

It had a first and second part, which, together with the symphonies, was of the length that opera songs generally last: if this extemporary composition was not amazingly capital, yet it was really above mediocrity, and shewed most extraordinary readiness of invention.

Finding that he was in humour, and as it were inspired, I then desired him to compose a Song of Rage, such as might be proper for the opera stage.

The boy again looked back with much archness, and began five or six lines of jargon recitative proper to precede a *Song of Anger*.

This lasted also about the same time with the Song of Love; and in the

---

* Giovanni Manzuoli (1725–c. 1780) was a Florentine male soprano. He left home for Madrid in 1763, then appeared in London (1764–5) where the Mozarts heard him and made his acquaintance. Manzuoli sang in Vienna in 1765, then returned to Florence with a court appointment. Mozart saw a good deal of him in 1770 during the visit to Italy and in 1771 the title role of *Ascanio in Alba* was expressly designed for Manzuoli. He was an ungainly actor, popular nevertheless among opera-goers for the power and sweetness of his voice, and for the tasteful musicianship of his singing.

middle of it, he had worked himself up to such a pitch, that he beat his harpsichord like a person possessed, rising sometimes in his chair.

The word he pitched upon for this second extemporary composition was, *Perfido.*

Leopold Mozart's catalogue of his son's compositions shows that Wolfgang wrote fifteen Italian arias while he was in London and the Hague in 1765–6; only two of them have survived. We know that during his tour he attended several operas, and studied the scores of others. From Barrington's account it is clear that he had absorbed the idea of opera as a heightening of words and situations by musical setting.

Soon after the family returned to Salzburg on 29 November 1766 Leopold's master, Sigismund Schrattenbach, the Archbishop of Salzburg, celebrated the anniversary of his consecration in this post (it was more secular than religious in significance), and for this occasion Mozart composed a recitative and aria in Italian operatic style, called a *Licenza*, as congratulatory music. It was a tenor piece, *Or che il dover . . . Tali e cotanti* (K. 33i), and was sung at the end of an operatic performance on the appropriate day, 21 December.

The success of this *Licenza* and of a symphony performed shortly afterwards established Mozart at the age of eleven as one of Salzburg's leading composers, and so it is that we find him collaborating with Michael Haydn (leader or concert-master of the court orchestra, and brother to Joseph Haydn) and Cajetan Adlgasser (organist of the cathedral) in a three-part oratorio *Die Schuldigkeit des ersten und fürnehmsten Gebotes*, which was performed during Lent when operatic representations were not permitted. The text of the oratorio was by the merchant and councillor Ignaz Anton von Weiser (1701–85), a future burgomaster of Salzburg and an old friend of the Mozart family.* He may have recommended that Mozart should contribute.

Daines Barrington writes: 'I am also informed that the prince of Saltzbourg, not crediting that such masterly compositions were really those of a child, shut him up for a week, during which he was not permitted to see anyone, and was left only with music paper and the words of an oratorio.' Until lately it was assumed that *Die Schuldigkeit* was the work referred to; O. E. Deutsch, following Einstein, thought it likely that the oratorio was the *Grabmusik* (K. 35a). The autograph of *Die Schuldigkeit* (now in Windsor Castle, having been acquired by Prince Albert) is hurriedly written, with many a blot and scratch consistent with the conditions related by Barrington. But there are additions and improvements, as well as text-underlaying, in Leopold Mozart's hand: they may have been made after the Archbishop had been satisfied that his young prisoner had fulfilled his task unaided. It is more likely that for this test Mozart would have been given a less complicated libretto than that of *Schuldigkeit*; the *Grabmusik* is shorter and has only two singing roles.

Mozart's composition had its première on 12 March at 6.30 p.m. ('after dinner', the university register notes) in the Knights' Hall of the archiepiscopal palace, and was repeated on 2 April. The work is subtitled *geistliches Singspiel*, or sacred

---

* He is identified as author in the diary of Beda Hübner, a Benedictine priest who was also friendly with the Mozarts.

music-drama (the arias are connected, it will be seen, by secco recitative and not, as we tend to assume in *Singspiel*, by spoken dialogue), and the librettist declared in his preface that its aim was 'entertainment and edification', all of which may lead us to suppose that it was staged with scenery and costumes, as so often in oratorio performances of the day—though contemporary references to the event mention only singing and the music. Herbert Klein points out that for theatrical performances the *Theatersaal* in the palace would obviously have been more suitable, and that Archbishop Schrattenbach's pious scruples would have prevented theatrical shows even of a religious nature during Lent.

The singers were leading members of the Archbishop's choir: Joseph Meissner (Christian)★; Anton Franz Spitzeder (Christianity), an industrious and versatile musician; Maria Anna Fesemayer (Worldliness), who later married Adlgasser, the composer of this oratorio's third part; Maria Magdalena Lipp (Mercy), who married Michael Haydn; and Maria Anna Braunhofer (Justice). They all subsequently took part in the first performance of *La finta semplice*. Note that the sopranos were females, not castrati.

2

A word of warning perhaps. Mozart at eleven years old was a well travelled and musically experienced child prodigy, but it must not be expected that his early works will show the divine sparks which flash at us in *Figaro* and *Giovanni*, or even in the violin concertos of 1778. He was writing music in the traditional idioms which he had learned to accept as suitable for the sort of works he was asked to compose. Soon he would manipulate conventional clichés to unusual inventive purpose, and eventually begin composition with ideas that were in themselves unique and momentous. In these early stage works I am only concerned to state what happens, and (where appropriate) show how it connects with the musical language of the adult Mozart. An example is his use of an orchestra including divided violas (1 and 2) as well as divided violins. In his youthful works Mozart, himself a viola player, adopted this practice which he had learned from J. C. Bach and other contemporaries, to obtain richer texture or some semblance of string antiphony. We find it often in these first stage works. Later Mozart learned to vary his string texture and to reserve the two-viola effect for special occasions. Yet the boy is well aware in *Schuldigkeit* precisely how divided violas affect the music, and his recourse to them, even if over-lavish, always makes the instrumentation more attractive.

Violas are already divided in the *Sinfonia* or overture to *Die Schuldigkeit*, which uses the full woodwind complement of two oboes, two bassoons, two horns, and strings. (Later numbers will find flutes substituted for the oboes, and an alto trombone will be added.) The key is C major, the tempo *allegro*. The overture opens naïvely with a brief, primitive subject contrasting soft and loud. The second subject contrasts upper and lower strings to evoke dialogue effects.

★ Misleadingly described as a bass singer in Deutsch's *Documentary Biography*.

The first subject, rather curiously but not redundantly, now reappears in the dominant, as if acting as a transition to the short, more animated coda subject. After a development which involves all three themes the second, dialoguing tune returns in C major and is followed by the first subject, doing double duty as itself and as part of the coda group.

The scene discloses a pleasant garden with a small forest in the neighbourhood. The protagonist, Lukewarm Christian, is asleep on a flowery knoll. Around him stand three angelic figures, the spirits who are discussing his destiny in secco recitative. Christianity (tenor) has evidently been pleading for time in which to alert Christian to his spiritual responsibilities. Justice (a soprano) is touched by the plea but has no intention of sparing this lazy churl, since it is the prime function of Justice to distinguish good from bad by dispensing either reward or punishment. Christianity therefore turns to the third spirit, Mercy (another soprano), and begs her to help him save mankind from the wiles of Worldliness, who tempts whole crowds to follow him down the primrose path to the infernal abyss. He expands on this theme in **No. 1, Aria,** Christgeist, *Mit Jammer muss ich schauen*, C major, *allegro*, horns and strings (bassoons would double on the bass line in numbers involving other wind instruments).

> With distress I have to watch countless precious souls choose downfall in my enemy's claws, unless your wondrous power brings them health and salvation.
>
> Their unbridled senses, like rivers in torrent that froth and flood, carry them away by the thousand.

The orchestral introduction clearly portrays the 'breite Blumenstrasse' that leads to the everlasting bonfire.

Mozart, according to E. J. Dent, did not show much interest in counterpoint until after his studies with Martini. But Leopold had kept him busy at exercises since their return home, and the invertible counterpoint in Ex. 2 is one of the rare indications in *Schuldigkeit* that polyphony had taken root in his compositional processes. The other idea in this introduction involves a great plunge (into the *Höllenschlund*) that is even enhanced when it is sung by Christianity.

nicht Heil, nicht Ret ——tung   schafft.

Christgeist cannot do much about singing the quaver theme of Ex. 2, so Mozart either gives him the horn's tonic pedal note or a free vocal line above these quavers which readily assume the contours of an Alberti bass.

There is a short *andante* middle section in F major, 'Ihr zügelfreier Sinn', which involves plentiful rushing figures for strings to depict the comparison between Man's uncontrolled sensuality and rivers bursting forth. This section ends in A minor whereupon the main section of the aria is repeated. The exit convention is not observed in this sacred work.

Mercy, in a recitative, finds the situation lamentable but is in no doubt that mankind deserves what it gets. These humans regard the First Commandment as nothing but a burden. Justice is appalled that humanity does not naturally obey the commandment out of gratitude for God's gift of life and health. But the glitter of false gods, splendour, selfishness, lust and pseudo-honour draw men more. If Mercy's call goes unheeded neither Mercy nor Justice can lend assistance.

No. 2, Aria, Barmherzigkeit, *Ein ergrimmter Löwe brüllet*, E flat major, *allegro*, oboes, horns, strings (with continuo bassoons).

A gruesome lion roars, filling the forest with fear as he searches around for spoil.
But the huntsman wants to sleep longer, lays down his gun and dagger, cares not for protection or help.

There is an extended introduction of twenty-eight bars, beginning with a crescendo on held semibreve unisons that then charge away in pouncing phrases over a rapid ostinato figure in semiquavers, and later with clawing trills. The semiquaver figure remains under horn calls (hunting!) answered by oboes (which also mean hunting in the finale of symphony 34), and the ritornello ends with a growl in menacing octaves up the scale of E flat. Mercy's vocal line is brilliantly explosive, in the vein we associate with such later heroines as Constanze and Fiordiligi, with florid runs and leaps that obviously evoke the ravaging lion even though they are actually set to the word 'Wald', meaning 'forest'. The furious string writing is evocative as well. It collapses, rather lamely, without intervening pause, into a short C minor *andante* middle section about the sleepy huntsman, sensitively written especially in the descending scales at 'achtet Schutz' which seem typical of Mozart's German heroines in moments of unhappiness.

13

ach————tet Schutz und Hel—fer nicht,

After this cadence in G minor Mozart effects one of his tense, dimly lit modulations back to E flat, and we expect a straightforward *da capo*. But it does not happen. The resumed *allegro* now tends towards the flat side of the tonic, as if the end were approaching. The 'Wald' is newly decorated, the vocal writing gains expressiveness, and we begin to realize that this is not the conventional rounding off of an *a-b-a* aria. Back comes the *andante*, now in A flat major with new runs on 'schlafen', nicely suggestive of yawning Little Boy Blue (father Leopold added some questionable improvements to the second set of runs). The section returns to E flat and the orchestra concludes with the end of its original allegro ritornello, turning at once into C major, rather awkwardly, for the resumption of the recitative dialogue for the three angels.

Mercy and Justice are not much touched by compassion for the sinner who sinned by his own will. But Christianity wonders if a really vivid representation of infernal torment might shock their sinner into a change of heart. Promptly the full orchestra (including divided violas) joins in to depict the horrors of eternal damnation. This was Mozart's major opportunity to show his powers, and he seized it. The passage opens with repeated triplet triads over an oscillating bass tonic pedal (forecasting a famous moment in Beethoven's 7th symphony, though not unprecedented even so). But after Christianity's first vocal phrase creative imagination springs up in an extremely chromatic passage of two-part counterpoint, abounding in excruciating false relations—it needs harmonic filling-in at the keyboard.

This terrible vision (which E. J. Dent assumed must have been shown visually, though Salzburg practice seems to contradict it) will without doubt, Christianity suggests, awaken the sleeping laggard to his responsibility. Mercy agrees, but Justice insists that the call to spiritual zeal must not be made by extravagant pressure: Christian must himself want to be good. Justice is, however, willing to awaken him.

No. 3, Aria, Gerechtigkeit, *Erwache, fauler Knecht*, A major, *andante*, strings only. Here again the initial impression is conventional, but the structure is unusual.

> Awake, lazy vassal! You have jeopardized the glorious prize by wasting so much time, though you were born for hard, zealous work. Awake and await stern justice.
>
> Hell and death are calling: you will have to give an exact account of your life to the judge, your God.

The introduction is rather sensuous and charming with a good deal of triplet movement and *galant* snaps, as well as a melody in beguiling thirds—not very imperative! Mozart's feeling for A major is already apparent but contextually unhelpful, most of all when Justice launches on an epicurean division in triplets on the word 'erwarten': expectations could hardly be more optimistic! Justice's wooing manner changes for the middle section to a stern *allegro* with warnings of Hell and death, but moves at once into a melancholy F sharp minor *adagio* full of repeated triplet chords for strings. The earlier *allegro* figuration returns to Justice's cries of 'Erwache!' Then the initial *andante* is resumed, with some changes of bass figuration and of melody for a few bars, after which Mozart is at last content to duplicate conventionally what went before.

Christian shows signs of awaking, and all three spirits conceal themselves.

Recitativo stromentato, Christ, *Wie, wer erwecket mich?*, C major, 2 bassoons, 2 horns, strings with divided violas. Christian awakes from his terrifying vision into a serene pastoral landscape: the music sounds accordingly bland, touched with a gentle inner intensity; first violins and basses, later with bassoons, are in imitation. Christian wonders if his vision was truth or a practical joke. At once an emotional *allegro* in D major bursts in, 'Tod, Hölle', with sudden tempo switches and rushing strings that remind Christian how vivid his nightmare was.

A new character comes to meet him. This is Worldliness who counsels him not to worry, and whom he is delighted to meet, though Christianity (hidden close by, presumably behind a tree) expresses concern at this encounter with his enemy. Worldliness tries to reassure Christian that his bad dreams were no more than meaningless imagination. But Christian still hears the dreadful call: 'Awake, lazy vassal . . . you will have to give an exact account of your life'—and at this the orchestral strings (*allegro*) momentarily intercede with a semiquaver figure from No. 3, and (*adagio*) a grave appeal by the alto trombone (the German equivalent of our Last Trumpet). Worldliness finds nothing in all this that should cause alarm.

No. 4, Aria, Weltgeist, *Hat der Schöpfer dieses Leben*, F major, *allegro grazioso*, oboes, horns, strings.

> Since the Creator has given us life and a free run of the world, we had best be glad of the gift, and treat bad dreams with the contempt they deserve.
>
> Go and enjoy the bushes, fields, hedgerows; and ecstasy will find a home in your troubled heart.

This is a thoroughly frivolous, galant piece, perfectly suited to the character with its bouncing rhythms, trills, antiphony (oboes, horns, for example) dummy accompaniment figures, extreme dynamic contrasts, and runs on the word 'lache' rising to B flat. The main body of the aria is in extended binary form. A contrasted minuettish middle section in B flat major, 'Dein Ergötzer', is rather more chromatic in line. The introduction to the reprise is abbreviated.

Christian has been too upset by his nightmare to dismiss it at once. He answers Worldliness in a recitative with muted string accompaniment full of tonal affinities with Justice's dream-sequence (A major, G minor, E flat minor), though not direct quotations, as he tells just how clear its memory still is, how his mind and body have been affected.

No. 5, Aria, Christ, *Jener Donnerworte Kraft*, E flat major, *andante un poco adagio*, alto trombone and strings (with two violas).

> The words of thunder, which oppress my soul, warn me of judgement.
> In their echoes my anxious ear already hears the last trumpet.

So the voice of the 'letzte Posaune' is obbligato in this aria, looking forward to the 'Tuba mirum spargens sonum' in the *Requiem* where its role is somewhat similar—otherwise listeners might be bewildered by its unsolemn trills and florid running semiquavers. The music is in itself perfectly dignified and mellow, even staid. Christian's first entry shows dramatic understanding in the change of harmony from tonic to diminished seventh, and his vocal line is full of the big leaps that we associate with Fiordiligi and nervous excitement; in the same vein is the prominence of first viola, almost as persistent as solo trombone. The middle section is in C minor, 'Ja mit ihrem Widerhall', in which Christian explicitly refers to the sound of the Last Trump, and has one of those picturesquely hesitant runs (including a leap from low C to top G) on the word 'bange'. An access of triplets for trombone and viola leads back to the reprise.

Worldliness is now sure that the nightmare was the work of her and Christian's indefatigable enemy, a fly-catching, unsociable, joyless, hair-splitting, puritanical peacock, not to be named but easily recognizable. This vivid and entertaining description not only wounds the hidden spirit of Christianity but convinces him that, if he is to get his way, he must adopt some disguise. He removes himself, while Worldliness gives a fuller description of the foe Christian must guard against: **No. 6, Aria**, Weltgeist, *Schild're einen Philosophen*, G major, *allegro*, flutes, horns, strings (with bassoon as above mentioned).

> Imagine a philosopher with gloomy eyes, shy and pale; there you have this enemy to the life.

The first subject is dry and didactic with long notes and a stiff dummy accompaniment; second subject is off-beat, with flute dialogue and a tendency towards D major. Third subject brings out the horns and, for benefit of Worldliness rather than the subject of the aria, cheerful violins. But these are to set in focus Worldliness's enactment of the pompous killjoy, which must surely follow the music in involving some caricature acting, especially at the vocal division on 'Angesicht' which takes the soprano up to top D. The *andante* middle section, also in G, 'Dann hast du ein Bild getroffen', reveals the latent Despina in this allegorical character; it is so brief as to seem more like a refrain than a true middle section. The return to 'Schild're einen Philosophen' is in D major, as if the second part of a binary-form half, and it ends on rather than in the dominant so that 'Dann hast du' can be unambiguously tonic in feeling. The aria concludes with a brief orchestral reference to the first-section material.

Worldliness now observes a stranger loitering on the edge of the forest and suspects that he may be the deadly enemy. But he is seen to be an apothecary of sorts, busy gathering herbs for medicines. Neither of them recognizes Christianity behind this disguise, and Christian quickly asks this medico if he has suitable cures for his ailments. Oh yes, answers the apothecary, I work for the best doctor in the world. Worldliness senses that this medical consultation will last some time, and goes off to breakfast, muttering that Christian's symptoms would be best treated by doses of sex, food, drink, sport and sessions at the gaming-table.

Christian prefers to consult this professional man who demands his full attention and a complete report, concealing nothing.

No. 7, Aria, Christgeist, *Manches Übel will zuweilen*, B flat major, *allegro*, oboes, bassoons, horns, strings (with divided violas). A long-winded but fluent, cheerful *da capo* aria.

> Many diseases cannot be healed with medicine until scalpel, forceps and diathermy* have been employed.
> That summons which awoke you, that voice which frightened you, was needful and good for you.

Edward Dent happily remarked on the closing 'cadential shake on the scissors'. The middle section in G minor points to the salubrious effect on Christian of the voice that awoke him. Mozart later transferred this aria, after some abbreviations, to *La finta semplice* where it is sung, in a completely different context (see p. 43), by the foolish lovesick Don Polidoro—a part taken in the Salzburg première by Spitzeder who had previously sung Christgeist here.

Christian is rather surprised to learn that this total stranger knows about his dream, but is even more anxious to be rid of his anxiety. Christianity presents him with a prescription with full details of its curative properties (but aside he indicates that they all refer to spiritual and moral ailments). Worldliness, well breakfasted, returns to conduct Christian to a jolly party and is relieved when Christian begs the doctor to excuse him on grounds of politeness, promising due reward if the potion is efficacious. Christianity lets him go, ruefully reflecting that the enemy is more popular than himself, sensual liberty preferred to pious words.

Now Mercy and Justice return, Mercy taunting Christianity with his incompetence, Justice smugly assuring them that Christian will certainly serve her if not them. Christianity, however, promises to persevere with this weak character so that all three of them may be satisfied. Mozart's part in the oratorio ends with an amenable ensemble for the three spirits: **No. 8, Terzetto**, Barmherzigkeit, Gerechtigkeit, Christgeist, *Lasst mir euer Gnade Schein*, D major, *un poco andante*, oboes, horns, strings (divided violas, bassoons with cellos).

* Orig. *Messer, Scher und Glut*.

Never let your goodwill fail me and I shall gain fresh courage. Our goodwill shall not be lacking if that man does his share.

Christianity's bland solos are repeated by Mercy and Justice in fluent thirds and sixths; there is a certain amount of block harmony, but also some simple imitative writing, such as the following:

6

to remind the audience that Mozart knew about composition in the old style.

The central section is a solo for Christianity, *andante grazioso* in G major.

Ever will I aspire and think how to win precious souls for my creator. That must be my task.

The libretto set Mozart a problem here in the irregular length of the second line. Mozart, who had been brought up on well proportioned classic musical phrases, either naïvely or pugnaciously did what the verse suggested, and wrote a four-bar phrase followed by a five-bar phrase.

7

There are some chromatic feints at D minor and B minor, following a long run of triplets on the word 'trachten'. Then the first part is resumed, and Mozart's contribution to the oratorio ends. Those of Michael Haydn and Adlgasser have not survived.

3

'The two childish entertainments,' wrote Edward Dent in 1913, 'may be dismissed at once.' 'Nor,' Alfred Einstein confirmed in 1944, 'need we occupy ourselves with the analysis of other dramatic works of Mozart's youth.' Despite these deliberate blackballs by two outstanding Mozart scholars of the twentieth century I thought it right to describe in some detail the contents of these early works. Partly because a book about Mozart's stage music must take every item into account if readers are to arrive at an estimation of the total value—composers are to be assessed by their failures as well as their masterpieces—partly because, at a time when performances of the obscurer Mozart stage works may be more easily encountered than detailed descriptions or critical essays about them, it is helpful to offer readers a book which will contain fairly comprehensive information about the less familiar works (the magnificent Jahn–Abert volumes have never been translated into English and some of their copious information is by now outdated) as simple preparation for a scheduled performance—I write these words only a few days before a staged performance in London of *Die Schuldigkeit* and, remembering an earlier concert performance at the Royal Festival Hall in 1952 (with Elisabeth Schwarzkopf as an enchanting Barmherzigkeit and Adèle Leigh as an irresistible advocate of Worldliness), am fairly confident that, after this book is published, other performances will occasionally happen and their audiences wish to know in advance what goes on.

To attempt a critical summing-up of *Die Schuldigkeit* is neither appropriate nor just nor even easy. From the foregoing analysis it will be clear that Mozart set his given text (in itself quite vivid and amusing at times) carefully and often imaginatively, sometimes with the misunderstanding or ignorance of a child, usually according to familiar models (Eberlin, Leopold Mozart, J. C. Bach) as may be expected, without the scrupulous economy and point-making of his adult music (strings with divided violas are his norm). The youthful *da capo* arias are long, following Salzburg taste, though a few are structurally imaginative. The dramatic characterization of Weltlichkeit is altogether delightful, that of the other dramatis personae more dependent on serendipity. Mozart responded to dramatic atmosphere in recitatives with a sense of mood and moment that to us seems extraordinarily vivid, though his ideas (apart from the vision of judgment) are more conventional than the moments where he applies them. His vocal music is floridly quite exigent and technically knowledgeable, often musically inspired. Dent affirmed that Mozart showed no feeling for counterpoint until after 1770: the contrapuntal passages of *Die Schuldigkeit* are simple and scarce but they are there and make creative, not merely copybook-student, effects. The careful elaboration of the music (e.g. in No. 5) gives one to doubt that this score could have been completed under the cloistered, time-restricted circumstances mentioned by Barrington. Equally the vivid musical invention alluded to, and sometimes quoted, above may suggest that, despite Dent* and Einstein, *Die Schuldigkeit* is not for the dustcart—though it contains few passages of Mozart's adult dramatic

---

* Dent wrote an enthusiastic, quite detailed analysis of the work for the 1952 performance; I have raided it shamelessly, though also out of piety to his memory. He changed his mind as every critic must hope to do.

technique. The biggest inference one may draw is perhaps the boy's predilection for the character of Worldliness in her brief appearance, his response to the vision of damnation, and his restricted but bravura use of the trombone as soloist.

MOZART'S CHOICE OF KEYS

Commentators have often remarked on Mozart's regular recourse to certain keys for the expression of particular emotional states. E. J. Dent drew attention to G minor and E flat major, Alfred Einstein to the significance of other keys in Mozart; Hermann Abert compared key-meaning *passim* in his two monumental volumes. Only Einstein attempted to formulate what each key meant to Mozart, and his fascinating chapter does not go far enough. It may be interesting, perhaps enlightening, to take their findings a stage or two further.

Choice of key for a late eighteenth-century composer depended on instrumental practicability—which notes could without difficulty or distortion be played by which instruments in which key. Einstein noted that Mozart was usually content with plain keys up to two sharps or flats, major or minor, three accidentals more rarely, four very seldom; he did not publicly experiment with very sharp or flat keys, as Haydn and some others had done. Having chosen the home-key for a work he would respect its tonal near-neighbours and not travel far beyond them.

Thus in D major he would find key contrast in the tonic minor, D minor, rarely the relative B minor, mostly the dominant A major, and the subdominant G major; sometimes the minor mediant, F major (or minor) and submediant B flat major would be involved. In a D major work he will sometimes put a section into geographically propinquent C major or E flat major for special purposes. But heavy key-content seems not to have been necessary to him: in a strong tonic situation a simple mediant switch acts like a thunderbolt.

The home tonic will determine most of the other keys used for contrast. Nevertheless there are certain keys which Mozart preferred for particular situations; and the greater the number of accidentals, the more loaded the emotional ambience. He does not use C sharp or D flat major, except incidentally (e.g. No. 17a in *Tito*) or C sharp minor except in an E major context, E flat minor only in an E flat major climate, e.g. *Don Giovanni* (No. 10, recitative). F sharp major, a favourite Haydn key, occurs as rarely as B major in Mozart; A flat minor is only for moments of transition.

For Mozart **C major** is a basic key; most of his operas are based on C or D major—*Bastien* in G and *Zauberflöte* in E flat are special cases. Some early operas end in other keys; at that time Mozart did not yet believe in permanent tonal centres. C major was a bland, open key, as it is to everyone. It might have majestic overtones as in the piano concerto K. 503, it could be bluff as in Figaro's *Non più andrai*, tender as in Zerlina's *Vedrai, carino*, mysterious as at the start of the first act finale in *Die Zauberflöte*. Many a great work by Mozart is in C major; usually the line is open and human, as in the overture to *Così* or the start of the Jupiter Symphony or the piano concerto K. 467; it is a *donnée* from which more intriguing ideas are extracted.

C minor has more varied but consistent connotations: Mozart used it carefully and memorably. We may think of it as the key of the solemn incomplete Mass K. 427, and of the Promethean piano concerto K. 491. As early as *La Betulia liberata* Mozart adopted it for distressful prayer, as he had done for the K. 47a Mass (two movements only), and would do again for the chorus *Pietà, numi, pietà* in *Idomeneo*. A stronger expression of this hieratic solemnity is found in the chorus *O voto tremendo* from the same opera, as well as in the chorale-prelude of the two men in armour from *Die Zauberflöte* and the (also contrapuntal) fugue for two keyboards (K. 426) or string quintet (K. 546) and of course in the unfinished Mass. Ritual C minor informs the Masonic Funeral Music K 479a, and opens No. 2 of the *König Thamos* music with the Masonic three chords; thereafter the music is concerned with conspiracy, as is C minor in the last appearance of the Queen of Night (*Zauberflöte* Act II Finale)—do not the cries of 'Dir, grosse Königin der Nacht' look back to *O voto tremendo*?

At a secular level, Mozart's C minor may convey plain anger or frustration, as in *Il rè pastore* No. 12, or *La finta giardiniera* No. 26 or, best of all, Electra's final outburst *D'Oreste, d'Ajace* in *Idomeneo*; Ferrando's *Tradito, schernito* perhaps belongs in this pigeonhole, together with K. 491 and the wind serenade K. 384a. But in these works the anger is more heroic, defiant, what I called Promethean just now. This is the C minor which Mozart chose for *Mitridate* No. 22 and *Lucio Silla* No. 22, bravery in the face of death; we may connect this mood with the aria of K. 272 *Ah lo previdi*, and with the piano fantasy (K. 475) and sonata (K. 457). As heroic despair it opens *Die Zauberflöte* with Tamino's pursuit by the serpent. Sometimes C minor is simply a key of melancholy, as in *La finta semplice* No. 24 and *La finta giardiniera* No. 21, two lost and distressful ladies—here deriving, maybe, from the affective C. P. E. Bach C minor which inspired the gentle melancholy of the slow movements in the E flat piano concertos KK. 271 and 482 and in the violin–viola Sinfonia concertante K. 364. It is from this hieratical pole that we should approach Colas's No. 10 in *Bastien et Bastienne*, a charlatan peasant weaving spells of mystery.

D major was Mozart's key of pomp, military or heroic glory, or aristocratic self-confidence, traditionally associated with trumpets and drums. As such it figures handsomely in *Mitridate, Ascanio, Il sogno di Scipione, Silla, Idomeneo, Don Giovanni*—and also *Figaro* because of Count Almaviva. There is another sort of D major characteristic of Mozart but less conventional. Its music is chromatic and intimate in tone: the motet *Ave verum corpus* may be its finest example though we hear this same aspect in the minuet for piano K. 576b and at the end of Leporello's *Madamina*.

D minor is a key of human anxiety, chromatically expressed, the key of the piano concerto K. 466, the string quartet K. 421, the Requiem Mass; operatically of the overture to *La Betulia liberata*, of the melologue No. 2 in *Zaide*, of the chorus *Corriamo, fuggiamo* in *Idomeneo* and the missing slow section of the *Figaro* overture; more grandly of the Commendatore's entrance in the overture and second finale of *Don Giovanni*, of the first duet, *Fuggi, crudele, fuggi* (noble but abject distress), from that opera, and of the Queen of Night's second, furious aria in *Die Zauberflöte*, similarly for Electra's No. 4 in *Idomeneo*. Mozart had been using it as a pathetic foil for F major or D major from his boyhood, and for church music—the chromatic *Kyrie* K. 368a is a fairly mature example. In maturity he used it circumspectly, for special purposes even as the tonic or relative minor of a home key, and even though it has only one flat in the key-signature.

For Neapolitan opera composers in Mozart's time **E flat major** meant solemnity. He used it so in *Die Zauberflöte* and other masonic works (e.g. symphony 39), but also for varied purposes: in his horn and some piano concertos (for practical reasons) where cheerful, convivial music tends to succeed nobility; in *L'amerò* from *Il rè pastore* for constant, dedicated love—whence, perhaps, its relevance to dedicated Donna Elvira, or to Ilia's *Se il padre perdei* in *Idomeneo*, or Countess Almaviva's *Porgi, amor*, or the quintet, *Sento o dio*, in *Così fan tutte*. E flat major for Mozart was a key for emotional contrasts, frequently yet precisely employed as early as *Scipio* and *Silla*.

Mozart used **E major** quite rarely in his instrumental works, more often and consistently in his operas. For rococo composers as for the baroque E major was a bland key, apt to pastoral music and the contemplation of nature: so Apollo disguised as a shepherd introduces himself, and Zaide looks forward to freedom, and Ilia contemplates the garden where she will meet her lover, and the chorus in *Idomeneo* gazes thankfully at the calm sea. This is the mood of the slow movement in the A major violin concerto, and the finale of the piano trio K. 542 (the first movement is emotionally more complex).

E major seems also to be for Mozart a key of apology: so Rosina, in *La finta semplice*, asks the cupids not to wound her heart; Amital in *La Betulia* asks forgiveness for her unpatriotic behaviour; Ascanio regrets that he cannot join the girl he adores; Leporello begs the Statue's pardon for the supper invitation he is obliged to give; Fiordiligi tells the absent Guglielmo how she regrets her thoughts of infidelity. Two other instances have to do with explanation or teaching: Don Alfonso assures his soldier friends that female constancy is a figment of the imagination; and Sarastro teaches Pamina the non-vengeful philosophy of the Sun's initiates.

E minor is very rare in Mozart. There is a forlorn two-movement violin sonata, K. 300c; and the final chorus of *La Betulia* begins in a grand, almost baroque E minor, inclined towards G major because of the plainchant quoted in it. The slow movement of an early G major string quartet, K. 134b, two numbers from the *Gelosie del Seraglio* ballet, some movements in church works, are in E minor. For some reason Mozart avoided it.

F major is a cheerful, open-hearted key, so used much by Mozart to best effect. More interesting are its chromatic possibilities as explored by the boy Mozart (how much helped by Father?) in the first minuet of the F major violin sonata K. 13; its undertones of sadness in No. 9 of *Così fan tutte* and No. 23 of *Tito*, of nobility at the start of Act II in *Die Zauberflöte*, likewise in the temple scene of *Idomeneo*. Their music is not finer than the F major of *Figaro* Nos. 18 and 27, *Don Giovanni* Nos. 1, 6, and 13 and indeed the more uplifted No. 25, or No. 23 in *Così*, or Papageno's No. 20.

F minor is the key of Barbarina's none-too-serious lament for the lost pin, and of Don Alfonso's fake melancholy in *Vorrei dir*. With them we may perhaps link Charmis's fine aria No. 15 in *La Betulia*, describing (not without *Schadenfreude*) the groans and cries of the defeated enemy outside. Wholly serious is the F minor of the Commendatore's death trio in No. 1 of *Don Giovanni*. This is also, indeed, the key in which, momentously, two of the *Orgelwalze* works, KK. 594 and 608, begin.

For every Mozartian, **F sharp minor** is the key of the sublime *adagio* in the piano concerto K. 488, a wonderful vehicle for Mozart's pathos—but he used it nowhere else though greatly addicted to its relative, A major. There is a fine **G flat major** episode in the first finale of *Tito*.

G major is open-hearted, like F and C. It opens *Figaro* and *Così*; it conveys the excitement of Zerlina and Masetto in *Giovinette che fate al amore*, the good-humoured anger of Guglielmo in *Donne miei* (much less enraged than Figaro's E flat major in a similar context). It introduces vivacious Elisa in *Il rè pastore*—her more thoughtful but still cheerful lover made his entry in F major. Einstein pointed to the multifarious moods of G major in the first ritornello of K. 453. Almost as much can be found in the violin concerto K. 216, a synthesis in *Das Veilchen*.

Dent regarded **G minor** and E flat major as the most personal Mozart keys. I am trying to suggest that other keys had special significance for him also. G minor is certainly one. He uses it for anger in the symphony 25 K. 173dB, in Arminda's No. 13 of *La finta giardiniera*; and in Zaide's *Tiger, wetzet nur die Klauen*, also in the first movement of the K. 478 piano quartet and the middle section of the romanze in K. 466. A particular usage is the comic entry song of Osmin, *Wer ein Liebchen*, in *Die Entführung*; there is a hint of sarcastic comedy in the finale of the 40th symphony K. 550, I sometimes think. Mostly G minor is, for Mozart, the nonpareil key for melancholy or pathos—Pamina's *Ach ich fühl's*, the first movement of K. 550 at least, Giunia's prayer to her father's ghost in the first finale of *Silla*, Ilia's *Padre, germani*, Constanze's *Traurigkeit*. Sometimes the sadness is a superficial melancholy, as in Mme Herz's *Schon schlägt die Abschieds-stunde* or *Bastien* No. 14, or the slow movement of the B flat piano concerto K. 456. It can be satirical, like the fake suicide in *Così*, or the Queen of Night's feigned self-pity in *Zum Leiden*. Mozart was composing music in G minor from K. 9 in 1764 onwards, at first unemotionally but soon (e.g. K. 15p for piano) in terms of drama. Oebalus's No. 7 in *Apollo* ends its middle section in a G minor that combines both rage and pathos. Here and again in *Mitridate* No. 4 he already expresses the dolorous possibilities which were to be emotionally extended whenever he used this key. Consistently he brought a flat second and flat sixth into his G minor melodies: it is tempting to deduce an archetypal G minor pattern—but it may be found in his C minor and D minor themes too.

A flat major with four accidentals in the key-signature, is an advanced key for Mozart, but he used it frequently, as early as the andante K. 15dd sketched as a symphonic movement in London. In his operas the key is associated only with the Brindisi canon, *È nel tuo, nel mio bicchiero*, in the second act finale of *Così fan tutte*; but it is also the key of the charming song *Dans un bois solitaire*, and of numerous instrumental movements, notably the andante of symphony 39 K. 543.

Mozart inherited **A major** as a pastoral key favoured by J. C. Bach, his contemporaries and immediate predecessors. Initially its implications for Mozart are bland. In maturity he increasingly found sensuous appeal in its three sharps, especially when clarinets were involved (it is the simplest key for the clarinet in A). Examples are noted throughout these chapters: the reader need only observe the difference between bland A major (e.g. the piano concerto K. 414 and symphony 29 K. 186a) and tender A major (e.g. Don Giovanni's *La cì darem*, Cecilio's *Pupille amate*, Ferrando's *Un aura amorosa*). Very often, for the expression of magnanimity, Mozart in maturity begins an A major piece on the fifth degree, E (cf. *Così* No. 4, *Don Giovanni* No. 16, the piano concerto K. 488, the clarinet concerto and quintet, the string quartet K. 464); this was surely a fingerprint for Mozart in A major.

A minor, simple key without key-signature, was Mozart's first attempt at a symphony in a minor key (the lost K. 16a). Later he associated it with exoticism★ (*Rondo alla turca*, finale interlude in K. 219, *Gelosie delle seraglie*, and *Entführung*— perhaps the first subject of the piano sonata K. 300d is relevant here) but also with loneliness as in the rondo of K. 300d, the intensely melancholy keyboard work K. 511, Almaviva's *Crudel! perchè finora*, and Sandrina's No. 22 in *La finta giardiniera*. There is a psychological link between all these pieces, as well as a connection with A major.

B flat major in Mozart is often for physical movement at walking pace: Ferrando's *Ah, lo veggio*, Elvira's *Non ti fidar*, Figaro's *Se a caso Madama*, Papageno's discontented *Hm, hm, hm, hm*; perhaps also the hunting rondos in this key. It is also a key of animated brilliance, as witness Giovanni's *Fin ch'han dal vino* and Constanze's remembered bliss in *Ach, ich liebte*. In many large works by Mozart it is the home-tonic conveying brightness and energy.

B flat minor occurs in the second minuet of K. 8, and the *Viaticum* in the K. 125 Litanies, not, except incidentally (e.g. *Entführung* Quartet No. 16, *Tito* No. 14), in the operatic works—five flats were too many for most musicians. **B minor** turns up in several instrumental works by Mozart, as foil to D major, for melancholy effect—e.g. the *Agnus Dei* of the mass K. 186h. In his operas it was the original but rightly rejected key for the Armoured Men's chorale in *Die Zauberflöte*, and is the ambiguous key of Pedrillo's Act III serenade *Im Mohrenland* (though this veers modally towards D major).

It must be emphasized that the recourse to any particular key, for a composer of Mozart's time, was motivated by no whim but by the tonal context. Mozart could rove audaciously—in *Figaro* he set his extended second act finale a semitone (E flat major) above the opera's tonic (D major). When he wanted, at a particular moment, to dwell on a particular mood, he could not always jump into a favourite key, but might have to find a promising substitute—and it must fit the available orchestral musicians. Some of his most evocative uses of keys are to be found, for a moment, in a mid-passage of recitative or one section of an aria—this too should be stressed because I am here dealing with tonal generalizations. Mozart's appreciation of key-character was surely as strong as that of any tonal composer in history.

★ Abert confused this with 'eroticism' and deduced that A minor was a key of sexuality for Mozart.

2   APOLLO ET HYACINTHUS

APOLLO ET HYACINTHUS

Latin Intermezzo to a school play:
CLEMENTIA CROESI by RUFINUS WIDL

K. 38

OEBALUS, King of Sparta	TENOR
MELIA, his daughter	TREBLE
HYACINTHUS, his son	TREBLE
APOLLO, his guest	ALTO
ZEPHYRUS, Hyacinthus's friend	ALTO
TWO PRIESTS, acolytes of Apollo	BASSES

I

At Salzburg University the tradition of presenting a Latin school play at least once a year went back to 1617 and survived until 1796. The annual play was given in August or September immediately before Prizegiving; at other times in the year individual forms occasionally acted a play. In 1661 a stage had been built next to the Great Hall of the University for this purpose and was elaborately equipped with theatrical machinery. Any incidental music required was customarily provided by a local composer. Michael Haydn and Adlgasser (see *Die Schuldigkeit*) were two who had obliged in this way.

Such a theatrical work was performed there on 13 May 1767. It was *The Clemency of Croesus* (*Clementia Croesi*) written by Father Rufinus Widl, the Benedictine monk (1731–98) who was Professor of Syntax to the third-year students. Unusually for this time of year, but 'by desire', it was performed by students from several forms; such at least was the case in the *intermedium* which Widl had interpolated, in the classical manner, between the acts of his play. The *intermedium* was set to music in the manner of an Italian opera and called for voices and musicianship which the Syntax class evidently could not supply. Recourse was therefore had to boys from other classes, and in one case to a choirboy who was not due to enter the university until the following year.

Clementia Croesi is based on Herodotus's tale of the King of Lydia who took the exiled Phrygian prince Adrastus into his household (Adrastus had inadvertently killed his own brother) and put him in charge of the education of his son Atys. While on a boarhunt Atys was slain by a spear misthrown by Adrastus who, stricken by grief, killed himself on his pupil's grave. Father Widl changed the story, for educational purposes, to show Adrastus being forgiven and welcomed home by the generous Croesus: his scenario begins when Atys is already dead, and spends five acts over discussions between Croesus and his court as to whether retribution should or should not be taken. Widl also imported love-interest into the tale, in the form of Adrastus's sister who is betrothed to Atys.

For his musical *intermedium* Widl selected the myth of Apollo and Hyacinthus, as related by Pausanias and Ovid. There were many apt similarities in the two stories: an exile made welcome by a foreign king and entrusted with the royal prince's education; a fatal sporting accident; the father's anger softened into forgiveness. There was one snag for Father Widl: the crux of the legend is that Hyacinthus was killed deliberately by the West Wind Zephyrus who loved him and, jealous of his rival Apollo, took advantage of a discus-throwing lesson to divert Apollo's throw so that the discus struck Hyacinthus on the head. It was clearly undesirable to represent rivalry in male homosexual love in an educational play for students of an all-male university. Father Widl's solution was to give Hyacinthus a sister, Melia (famed in Greek mythology as one of Apollo's brides, though her true father was Oceanus, not Oebalus as here), who is shown to be loved by Apollo and Zephyrus—here incarnate as Hyacinthus's school-chum.

Widl's libretto does not convincingly explain why or how Zephyrus was moved to slaughter Hyacinthus: if he was human and jealous, why not Apollo? There are still veiled suggestions in the text that Hyacinthus is the person in whom Apollo and Zephyrus are interested. And, since female parts were always played by young boys, Father Widl's bowdlerization of the myth would not significantly banish homosexual fancies from the minds of actors or audience.

The *intermedium* was cast in three acts, classically entitled *Prologus*, *Chorus I*, and *Chorus II*. *Prologus* preceded Act I of *Clementia Croesi*. *Chorus I* was sung between Acts II and III of the play, *Chorus II* between Acts IV and V. The accepted modern title of the *intermedium* as *Apollo et Hyacinthus* is not definitely authentic since it appears nowhere in the printed textbook or programme (both extant in Salzburg's archives) of the performance. We owe it to Nannerl Mozart, Wolfgang's sister, who in 1799, about to sell the catalogue of Wolfgang's early compositions which their father had kept, wrote the title into the appropriate place. If the piece was ever referred to by name we can well believe that the family called it *Apollo et Hyacinthus* since this is what it is about.

Wolfgang Mozart, as Chapter 1 shows, had returned to his native Salzburg the previous November as the musical miracle of Europe, and had even managed to convince his fellow-citizens that his musical talent at the age of eleven deserved their respect. He had played and improvised on public occasions, conducted his works from the harpsichord and composed two oratorios and two concert arias to commission. It may be that his father, who had several pupils attending the University, put forward Wolfgang's name as composer for the Syntax play; Leopold Mozart was not backward at pushing his son's gifts. But in this moment of sustained *réclame* (the Passion Cantata or *Grabmusik*, K. 35a, was probably performed on 17 April, Good Friday, in Salzburg Cathedral) Wolfgang may well have been a reasonable choice on the estimation of the university authorities. At any rate he composed the required nine numbers and connecting recitative together with a short overture. Chronicles do not say whether he conducted the performance on the afternoon of 13 May (it may have been taken for granted), though the Salzburg Gymnasium minutes relate that 'at night [which means in the early evening after dinner which followed the performance] he gave us notable proofs of his musical art on the harpsichord'. The records show that much rehearsal time had been allowed: several classes were postponed and on the morning of the performance there was 'short schools on account of phlebotomy' —one hopes that the singers were not leeched before singing. The excuse could well cover a final extra rehearsal or time to put the scenery and costumes in order: they had been lent to an Italian troupe in Salzburg who returned them only after threats of force, and then in atrocious condition. Time may have been sought for final attention to the music which is difficult for young performers though Mozart composed in the manner and spirit of the appropriate music known to him, notably that of his elder Salzburg colleague Eberlin.

The cast of the *intermedium* included two members of the Syntax class: Joseph Vonterthon who at seventeen was still able to undertake the alto role of Zephyrus; and Jacob Moser, aged sixteen, who sang the small part of the second priest. The other alto part of Apollo had to be given to a twelve-year-old choirboy, Johann Ernst. Christian Enzinger, the Hyacinthus, was of the same age and a choirboy too though he had joined the junior Rudiments class of the University. The travesty soprano part of Melia went to Felix Fuchs, aged fifteen, a member of the second-year Grammar class though still a choirboy; the most expert Mozart sopranos of our day would be hard pressed to sing Melia's music efficiently. A fourth-year student, Joseph Bruendl, aged eighteen, sang First Priest. The tenor role of Oebalus was given to the oldest singer, 'the most illustrious and learned Master Mathias Stadler (Scholar in Theology, Morals and Law)', aged twenty-three, who later played the violin obbligato in the Salzburg performance of *Die Entführung* and became a good friend of the Mozarts, replacing Leopold Mozart as violin teacher to the Salzburg choirboys. Vonterthon became a monk and later wrote a libretto for Michael Haydn in the year of Mozart's death. An otherwise unidentified Fuchs was listed in 1778 as a *basso* of the German opera company in Vienna, but Fuchs is a common name, and in 1778 Felix Fuchs was still named as a choral vicar in Salzburg. Because they sang music by Mozart at its first performance these boys have passed into history, but their own subsequent careers seem fairly uneventful.

2

The first act, or *Prologus*, of *Apollo et Hyacinthus* begins with a short overture or *Intrada, allegro* in D major. The orchestra consists of oboes, horns and strings (the violas are divided—see previous chapter for a comment on this feature of Mozart's early works). This is a spirited movement with curt gestures and rapid figuration in Mozart's youthful style. The second subject involves spicy Scotch snaps passed between violins and violas over spiky running figures; the closing section is more graceful, the development section short.

The curtain rises to discover Hyacinth and his friend Zephyr (their names as yet mean nothing). Outside Apollo's temple Hyacinth tells his friend that King Oebalus is on his way to wed his daughter Melia to Zephyr. The prospective bridegroom asks which of the many gods commonly revered will be involved. Hyacinth cheerfully reveals that, though all are worshipped here in Sparta, the chief cult is that of Apollo. Zephyr, already perhaps suspecting Apollo's amorous inclinations, blurts out his wish that Hyacinth would fulfil that role for Zephyr. Hyacinth regards this as an extravagant and embarrassing compliment. Father and sister arrive before this seduction can go further, and Melia sees black smoke arising from the temple; but Oebalus dismisses it as a mere sign that the god awaits his unpunctual devotees. They all enter the temple: **No. 1, Chorus** with tenor solo (Oebalus), *Numen o Latonium*, D major, *andante alla breve*, oboes, horns, strings. This is a serene and textually simple prayer for response to the people's invocation; surely it is too square and blunt to be sung simply as written? The violins' antiphony is attractive, as is the switch back from B minor to D major. The Gluck-like (but no doubt Eberlin-derived) atmosphere is intensified in Oebalus's prayer for Apollo's protection, in G major, *tempo moderato* with dummy accompaniment for strings alone. The opening chorus is repeated. The sacrificial flame is ignited, but lightning descends to destroy it and the altar.

Confusion reigns. Hyacinth hazards that Apollo is disturbed by the presence of Zephyr whose words were unfriendly to the god; but Zephyr swears him to secrecy. Hyacinth exhorts his father with the thought that Apollo has harmed none of those present.

No. 2, Aria, Hyacinthus, *Saepe terrent numina*, B flat major, *allegro moderato*, oboes and strings.

> Often the gods cause terror, rise up and threaten, simulate wars which distress us, shoot arrows that do not hit a mark; but after the imitation storms they laugh and joke.
> And with love and fear they coerce their subjects. Sometimes by love, sometimes by threat their authority stands secure.

The main atmosphere of the aria is pictorial but formal and classical, though the string writing is full of purposeful activity. The middle section of this *da capo* aria turns into F major, for a quicker pace and a more factual expressive style.

Oebalus still fears divine wrath but Apollo, who now steps forward, is all charm and friendliness and dressed as a shepherd. He has been exiled, he says, by Jupiter and craves the hospitality of Oebalus's palace. Melia at once showers him with pretty compliments which he reciprocates. Zephyr expresses anxiety at the god's presence, and with reason for Apollo now turns to admire Hyacinth (who remained on stage at the end of his aria; the exit convention is not adopted in this work) and asks for his friendship. Oebalus is delighted to be Apollo's host ('Beata dies!').

No. 3, Aria, Apollo, *Jam pastor Apollo*, E major, *andantino*, horns and strings with divided violas.

> I'm Apollo the shepherd, I guard my flocks, keep watch kneeling over my crook. Sometimes I forsake the meadow and visit kings, sometimes give medicine to mortals.
> Apollo's only concern is to raise up the sorrowful and help the invalid. While I remain here as your friend, you, o King, are more blessed than all kings.

The aria involves charming echo effects between violins and violas, and its principal tune is attractive, though somewhat short-breathed and square. The middle section turns to C sharp minor but returns speedily and cautiously to E; the vocal writing becomes decidedly florid. The reprise is abbreviated to an orchestral repeat of the introduction alone. Here the *Prologus* ends.

3

Act II of the *intermedium*, labelled *Chorus primus*, begins with a recitative in which Oebalus reminds Melia of Apollo's kindness to her (we are to regard the advent of Apollo, or any other god, as an extraordinary blessing but not an incredible visitation—in mythical times the gods moved freely among people; only Jehovah never visited his worshippers in physical person), and proposes that Melia should marry their visitor. She is honoured and delighted at the prospect, and longs to talk with Apollo. Learning that he is engaged in discus-throwing with Hyacinth, Melia is content to wait until he returns.

No. 4, Aria, Melia, *Laetari jocari*, D major, *allegro*, oboes, horns, strings.

> May I not rejoice, be merry, enjoy the honour done me by the god, now that a perfect marriage, with torches and garlands, makes me a blessed bride and causes jubilation?
>
> Now I shall be called a goddess if a god is my lover. I shall rove among the stars and tread on the clouds. Cities and kingdoms will be my devotees; fauns and satyrs will worship me.

A lively, brilliant piece, designed for an agile soprano voice in the baroque tradition. It expresses Melia's comically (and prematurely) status-seeking delight with uninhibited florid passages matched with rushing first violins. The long principal section is relieved by a short G major episode, rather more placid and ending in B minor, before returning to D major for the conventional reprise.

Zephyr now re-enters to announce Hyacinth's death in terms so blunt as to rouse instant suspicions (*Rex! de salute filii est actum, jacet Hyacinthus!*). Zephyr tells how Apollo slew Hyacinth with a discus, how he was witness to the death. Melia's lamentations for her brother slain by her promised bridegroom astound Zephyr who was under the impression that her bridegroom was to be himself. He strongly supports Oebalus's decision to banish Apollo, and proceeds to press his favours upon Melia who responds, to his surprise, unenthusiastically.

No. 5, Aria, Zephyrus, *En! duos conspicis*, A major, *un poco allegro*, strings alone. This is a galant solo in binary form, full of freshness and well suited to a male alto with strong low notes.

> Which of your suitors will you prefer, Apollo who will kill you as he shed your brother's blood, or Zephyr who will love you?

The vocal writing is noticeably unflorid and has written-in appoggiaturas, though the string parts are continually agile; Mozart perhaps feared to overpart his seventeen-year-old alto. The cheerful setting of a sober text also suggest that Mozart may have been in too much of a hurry to read the Latin words carefully or get someone to translate them for him.

Zephyr, having made his appeal to Melia's better feelings, now betrays anxiety and a desire to hide from the god who will surely be angry with them ('timeo ferocem'). Melia finds this attitude unchivalrous ('An ergo me solam objicis?') but it is not unwarranted as she discovers when Apollo enters and berates Zephyr with ferocious abuse as traitor, murderer, and liar, before calling on the winds to carry him off to Aeolus's cave. The continuo for once jumps into action with a rapid scale and Zephyr has time for no more than a 'Quid? Heume!' before he is snatched away, obviously by some marvel of the Aula's seventeenth-century stage machinery.

Melia has not fully grasped the situation; to her it appears that Apollo has murdered first her brother and then the young man who was courting her before Apollo's arrival. Spiritedly she tells him to go away before he does any more mischief.

No. 6, Duetto, Melia and Apollo, *Discede, crudelis*, F major, *allegro*, oboes, horns, strings (with divided violas). A vigorous duet of emotional conflicts, Melia protesting, Apollo reassuring her. The orchestral accompaniment is as notable for its dynamic markings in the rushing scale passages as for its dramatic invention. At first we may assume that this is to be a duet consisting of alternating solos, but eventually Melia breaks in on one of Apollo's avowals of innocence and they sing together, Apollo quite floridly at one moment.

The libretto intended that Melia should now exit, leaving Apollo to end the act with a solo. Mozart, however, insisted on writing it as a *da capo* duet of which Apollo's solo is the middle section. Melia, if we are to honour Father Widl, must now leave the stage. Apollo sings his solo, *Quem coeli premunt inopem*, in B flat, *moderato*, in which he declares his intention of staying here, hiding if necessary ('manebo! latebo!')—the string music remains agitated and equally rich in dynamic contrast. Mozart even modulates boldly to E major, the farthest remove from B flat (perhaps to signify concealment), returning with magical swiftness to F major for the *da capo*. Either the reprise must be restricted to the orchestral interlude (which ends in the same way as the whole duet) upon which the act finishes; or Melia must return, incensed to find Apollo still there. Since the duet is sufficiently vivid to bear repetition, and since ten bars is poor balance for the original 137 bars, the latter course may seem preferable. It gives the producer scope for dramatic ingenuity.

4

Act III of the *intermedium*, or Chorus II as Widl identifies it, begins with Oebalus standing by the bier on which Hyacinth lies. The wounded boy stammers some phrases, enough to reveal that Zephyr, not Apollo, was his killer, then dies. The muted string-accompanied recitative, with its hesitations, fragmentary chords, poignant chromatic harmony and careful dynamics, is precociously sensitive. Oebalus's wretchedness is poignantly underlined by repeated string chords and then by an access of agitation as the father understands the true situation. The tempo increases, strings remove their mutes and launch into purposeful octaves; Zephyr's crime, Hyacinth's death, the calumny against Apollo, all must be revenged.

No. 7, Aria, Oebalus, *Ut navis in aequore*, E flat major, *allegro agitato*, oboes, horns, strings (with *divisi* violas) is a *da capo* piece with an extended binary main section.

> As a ship in surging sea is hurled over crests and troughs of waves, now close to the clouds, now to the gate of hell: so the bile from my bellicose breast rages through my body, veins and limbs.
> I am uplifted by fury, depressed by grief. Anger and revenge together shatter me incessantly.

Violins have rushing scales in dialogue and huge leaps like monster waves. Oebalus is given some precipitous runs on the word 'threatening' ('minante') and his vocal line is often answered effectively by lower strings. The central section in C minor (2/4 *vice* 3/8) begins with soft throbbing strings, turns to declamation, then volatile divisions ('Quassare'), and finishes poignantly with G minor music ('non, non, non'—reiterated as in 'non erit finis' of the eighteenth-century Mass) worthy of a Mozart older then eleven. The first part is repeated.

Oebalus is joined by Melia, who is slowly and carefully told what really happened, and how just and kindly is Apollo. Now she regrets her conduct towards him, and laments that he has left them.

No. 8, Duetto, Melia and Oebalus, *Natus cadit atque Deus*, C major, *andante*, horns and strings (with 2 violas). The muted violin melody with plucked and murmurous accompaniment was drafted into the F major symphony No. 5, K. 43, as its slow movement. Oebalus laments that the god as well as Hyacinth has vanished, that his kingdom cannot survive. Melia echoes these sentiments. Both entreat divine Apollo to return, and as in No. 6 the duetting passages are beautifully contrived—there are more here. The violin line is full of precipitous descents, symbols no doubt of death. The principal tune of the duet is worth quoting for its simple charm, and for its sensitive turn into the tonic minor:

1

No sooner has the orchestra ended this duet, with many another fatal fall and plucked chord, than Apollo reappears, drawn back by his love for Hyacinth, determined to show it by a special blessing.

Horns and strings, *andantino*, G major, give warmth and a semblance of magic to Apollo's **Recitative** spell, *Hyacinthe surge!* The vocal part is recitative, the instrumental theme an old one signifying the descent of heavenly power into mortal beings:

2

This is repeated, a tone higher, after Apollo's prayer that the corpse be turned into a flower, as the miracle occurs. The upward transposition is genuinely dramatic after two intervening bars of dry recitative.

Oebalus and Melia beg forgiveness for their ignorant hostility to Apollo. He, like clement Croesus in the main play, accepts their apologies as well as Melia's hand in marriage. Oebalus begs him to be another Hyacinth to the Spartan family. Apollo promises that future centuries shall resound in praise of Oebalus's clemency. The piece closes with a vocal trio (the university chorus, conventionally but unimaginatively, is not brought back for this concluding number), **No. 9, Trio**, Melia, Apollo, Oebalus, *Tandem post turbida*, G major, *allegro*, oboes, horns, strings (again with *divisi* violas), a conventional galant minuet that gathers pace, or rather agility. Apollo's first entry shows off his lower register; the other singers join him in firmly jubilant harmony, with moments of elementary counterpoint and some running passages in dialogue. After these troubles, they sing, peace and love are restored to their spirits.

5

Mozart wrote *Apollo et Hyacinthus* out of a head filled with music, a dramatic instinct as yet in infancy but already actively alive—the ensembles in *Apollo* show it, as do Hyacinth's terror-inspired No. 2, Melia's Handelian (or Christian Bachian) virtuoso No. 4, and the orchestral music of Oebalus's No. 7. Mozart's melodic invention may be seen from my few music-examples: it is conventional but real. The descriptions in these two chapters should show that even in boyhood Mozart understood the nature of music-drama and was moved to match dramatic event with musical gesture—though less urgently in *Schuldigkeit* than *Apollo*. The obsession with a string orchestra including two violas was to be a lifelong trait which this book will trace as author's pleasure—for the effect enriches all the music which it involves, and it is a peculiarly Mozartian effect. Mozart was not yet a devotee of counterpoint, nor did he yet understand the relationship of words and music that he later expounded in his famous *Entführung* letter. But anyone who watches or hears, or quietly reads, these two first dramatic scores will appreciate that the child was father to the man.

3 LA FINTA SEMPLICE

LA FINTA SEMPLICE

Opera buffa in three acts

Libretto by

MARCO COLTELLINI (after CARLO GOLDONI)

KE 46a = 51

FRACASSO, Hungarian captain, lodging with Cassandro	TENOR
ROSINA, his sister, a Baroness	SOPRANO
CASSANDRO, a tyrannical misogynist	BASS
POLIDORO, his timid brother	TENOR
GIACINTA, their sister, evidently no longer young	MEZZO
SIMONE, Fracasso's batman, in love with	BASS
NINETTA, Giacinta's maid	SOPRANO

Scene: Cassandro's estate near Cremona

From the foregoing it should be clear that Wolfgang Mozart had worked his way under adult supervision to the moment, necessary for prestige, and more or less destined by the nature of his genius, when he would begin to receive commissions for operas.

That moment arrived, in the estimation of father Leopold, during their visit to Vienna, which they reached on 10 January 1768. Wolfgang's genuine musical talent, absurdly precocious as it must have appeared, was thoroughly attested on the evidence of eminent and ungullible people, some musicians, some scientists. But there were still suspicious souls about and, despite the successfully surmounted Salzburg test (described in Chapter 1), Leopold still had to convince Vienna. On 19 January he and Wolfgang were received by the Emperor Joseph II and his mother Maria Theresa. Joseph proposed that Wolfgang should allay scepticism by composing an opera which he would then conduct. The project was settled with the impresario Giuseppe d'Affligio,* recently put in charge of the Burg and Kärntnertor theatres in Vienna, who promised a fee of 100 ducats. The pool of singers in the imperial opera company included able buffo artists but was weak in the serious opera repertory—at about this time Gluck, one of the chief court composers, took exception to the incompetent fashion in which his revolutionary *Alceste* was presented in Vienna (the Mozarts saw it and Wolfgang studied the score), and tried unsuccessfully to prevent further performances. So a comic subject was chosen, Goldoni's *La finta semplice*—it had already been set as an opera in 1764 by Salvatore Perillo and given in Venice. The adaptation for Mozart and the chosen cast (sure to demand new arias) was undertaken by Marco Coltellini, a Tuscan who had studied under Calzabigi, moved to Vienna in 1772 and succeeded Metastasio as Viennese imperial librettist (*poeta cesareo*). He was to provide Mozart with the revised text of *La finta giardiniera*. Mozart was to have the score ready for performance at Easter.

Mozart completed the first of the three acts, and the music was heartily approved by the Cassandro (Francesco Coratoli), the Polidoro (Gioacchino Garibaldi), and the Simone (Domenico Poggi). A few alterations were requested by the singers, but Coltellini was so slow in supplying these that the opera could not be given before the Emperor's departure in mid-April for a visit to Hungary. The première was postponed. Mozart completed the score of 558 pages by June 1768, and rehearsals began. At this time he gave private performances of one or another musical number in the houses of the Viennese nobility, and he performed the whole opera in the house of Baron van Swieten (a music-loving nobleman who figures later in Mozart's biography).

By this time, though, the intrigues had been set in motion, as always in Vienna. It was rumoured that the music had been composed by Leopold Mozart, not his

* Sometimes misspelt Afflisio—he was lampooned in Joseph Haydn's Singspiel *Der neue krumme Teufel.*

twelve-year-old son; Leopold organized a public demonstration at which Wolf-gang set to music the first operatic text by Metastasio that was presented to him. It was rumoured that so young a boy was incompetent to compose and conduct a three-act Italian opera: Leopold persuaded Gluck, Hasse, and Metastasio to approve publicly Wolfgang's abilities. The Emperor returned from Hungary and regularly asked how the opera was going. But by now the performers were becoming anxious lest the opera should be a flop and the blame attached to them. They started to complain, then threatened to abandon the performance, even though they had approved Wolfgang's work on paper and had sung it privately to general applause.

We know a little about the seven principal singers. The Rosina, Clementina Baglioni, was a respectable actress with a silvery, mercurial voice. She had been singing in Vienna since 1762; by 1783, when she was engaged by the Graz company, her voice was reported by Count Rosenberg to be 'autumnally ripe'. We shall meet another Baglioni, Antonio, in *Don Giovanni* and *La clemenza di Tito*. He was Clementina's brother. Burney, in his Diaries, mentions two sisters, Constanza and Rosa Baglioni. One of these will be Mad. Richter *née* Baglioni who was singing at Dresden in 1785. But Clementina's married name was Poggi, so she may have married the Simone in *La finta semplice*. The Ninetta was Antonia Bernasconi *née* Wagele (1741-1803), who had just sung the title role in the première of *Alceste* and was in 1783 to do the same for *Iphigénie en Tauride* (in Italian). We think of these as grand tragic roles but Bernasconi won her fame as a soubrette. In 1781 Mozart reported that she was being paid extra for singing all her solos a semitone or more higher than the original, though he added that her voice was now horrid to hear and her dialogue spoken with a thick Viennese accent. She was to sing Aspasia in Mozart's *Mitridate, rè di Ponto*. The mezzo-soprano role of Giacinta (notated indiscriminately in soprano and alto clefs) fell to a Madame Eberhardi, an affected actress with no gift for trills but a pleasant contralto voice. Fracasso was taken by Signore Laschi, a buffo tenor whose voice was on its way out and who demanded two new arias perhaps because of this; he is chiefly famous as the father of Luisa Mombelli (*née* Laschi), Mozart's first Countess Almaviva in Vienna, and first Zerlina.* The comic tenor part of Polidoro was given to Garibaldi, a ham actor ungifted in florid runs or in slow expressive music; his solos are quite difficult and he approved them, so he must have found the part satisfying, not to say feasible. Coratoli was more actor than singer, but had learned how to put over a role without attempting *bel canto*. Poggi had a well trained voice and was accounted a good as well as popular soloist.

But it all came to nothing. When influential ignoramuses or prejudiced aristocrats have their way (as still happens sometimes) artistic enterprise is booted out and caution, however inartistic, prevails. Affligio found one excuse after

---

* Nowadays we pay much more attention to *Fach* or vocal character than any of our fore-bears did. Who today would ask a leading Iphigénie or *Figaro* Countess to sing Zerlina, or the equivalent Ninetta? In our own century Margarethe Siems was the first Marschallin and then the first Zerbinetta; Rosa Ponselle sang Norma and Carmen. Nowadays though, it is thought extraordinary that Christa Ludwig should sing Carmen and Brünnhilde, or Anja Silja the Queen of the Night and Isolde. Maria Callas has even refused to sing Carmen on stage, because she is a soprano by *Fach*. But in earlier generations such versatility was regarded as by no means curious or unsuitable, indeed very praiseworthy.

another why *La finta semplice* should not be performed, and eventually checked Mozart's importunate father by assuring him that, if a performance was insisted on, he would take care that the reception would be completely hostile. Leopold Mozart protested by letter to the Emperor on 21 September 1768; he feared greatly that his boy would grow up before making an adult success to cap his boyhood triumphs, and would therefore never make a serious career. The two of them stayed in Vienna until 29 December, by which time they had spent all their money, then returned to Salzburg with the untouched score of a new opera. Fortunately the Archbishop Sigismund von Schrattenbach took a kindly interest in Mozart's genial young son, and he commanded a production of *La finta semplice* which took place in his Salzburg palace on the Archbishop's name-day, 1 May 1769 (May Day was also to see the première of *Figaro*), with a completely new cast. Since Mozart did not write the music for these singers one need mention no more than their names: Maria Magdalena Haydn (wife of Michael) as Rosina, Maria Anna Fesemayer as Ninetta, Maria Anna Braunhofer as Giacinta, Joseph Meissner as Fracasso, Anton Franz Spitzeder as Polidoro, Joseph Hornung as Cassandro and Felix Winter as Simone. Several of them had taken part in *Die Schuldigkeit des ersten Gebotes* (Spitzeder even took over one of his arias from that work). The opera was given and then it was forgotten while Mozart wrote new operas, first more able, then more searching. In the Mozart revival of the twentieth century it has been exhumed, as usual played about with to gratify the egotism of somebody who knows better than the little boy who became the most intelligent of all opera composers. The only useful purpose of producing *La finta semplice* nowadays is to show where Mozart started from; to do this it is necessary to perform what he wrote in the order he fixed. To do otherwise is unhelpful as well as disloyal and unprofessional.

2

Goldoni worked inside the long-established frame of the *commedia dell' arte*. His achievement was to give new flesh, bones and personality to Arlecchino, Truffaldino and the rest. The characters of *La finta semplice* are antique, their ancestors noted in my interchapter on *opera buffa*: the sophisticated girl who pretends to be naïve, the ageing woman in search of a husband, the amorous fool, the bully, the wily servants, the noisy duelling soldier. For *commedia dell'arte* audiences they were familiar types. Goldoni turned them into something like real people, and Mozart was lucky to be pitted against them at an age when his idea of the adult world was rather vague. He responded here because his characters had idiosyncrasies that he recognized from precocious experience; not completely (how could he at twelve?) but remarkably.

The overture to *La finta semplice* is in D major, the integral key of the opera. Mozart used three of the four movements of his symphony No. 5, K. 45, written earlier that year, elaborating and improvising here and there. The first section bustles in quavers, *molto allegro*, and places its second subject precariously on, rather than in, the dominant—you might conclude in the dominant's dominant, E major, though the implication is meant to enhance expectation. The central slow section, *andante* in G major, proposes wide-ranging violin phrases and exposes a harmonic chasm (e.g. in bar 3) requiring keyboard filling (Mozart of course conducted from the harpsichord himself; he added woodwind scoring for this operatic version); the final section returns to D major and *molto allegro* and includes triplet movement as contrast to the dotted arpeggiated figuration which already steps up the tension. He changed the symphony's ending so that the overture would run straight into Act I, which is set in Cassandro's house.

No. 1, Choral Quartet, *allegro*, D major. *Bella cosa è far l'amore*, flutes, oboes, horns, strings.

Here are Ninetta, Giacinta, Fracasso and Simone, together praising the delights of love and freedom, separately expounding their own philosophies: Giacinta admits that she is no longer young, Fracasso that he has a hot temper, Ninetta that she is tired of spinsterhood, and Simone that his chosen wife promises to be stubborn. This opening number, rococo opera's substitute, as the ambiguous description *Coro-Quartetto* reminds us, for an initial chorus (which would have been too expensive for the potentate), ends with a quasi-processional minuet section, rather baroque with its Scotch-snaps.

The four characters on stage are connected through the two brothers, Cassandro and Polidoro. They explain that both are fools, the former a bully since his sister-in-law betrayed him, the other terrified of his elder brother's rages. Ninetta proposes that both brothers should be cured by falling in love with Fracasso's sister who is on her way there. Simone is to put her in touch with Ninetta who will advise her how to behave. Ninetta presumably leaves here. Simone grumbles that he and his master should have to go to such trouble in order to get their chosen wives.

No. 2, Aria, Simone, *Troppa briga a prender moglie*, C major, strings alone. A presumably slow 4/4, with declamatory vocal part and hectic patterns for violins:

alternates with an *allegro* in 2/4, more fluent and confidential, a definite foretaste of Leporello and Figaro.

> Too much bother to take a wife—no job for a soldier who wants one cheap or else won't trouble.
> Ladies may be pretty and kind, but they cost a packet. For a pack of cards, a flask of decent wine, two pipes of tobacco, I'll exchange the lot of them, in a bag. I'm no longer interested in marriage.

Fracasso gives his opinion that if guile fails they should use force to gain their brides. But Giacinta takes a passive view. She'd like a husband, but doesn't want to have to work to get him. Her easy-going philosophy is perfectly characterized in the smooth, bonhomous, graceful introduction to her:

No. 3, Aria, Giacinta, *Marito io vorrei*, F major, *allegro grazioso*, oboes, horns, strings.

> I'd like to be married, but without trouble if he suits me, leave him if he's a nuisance. After waiting all these years it's enough if he just kisses my hands.
> All in all I need a man of talent but made of wood so that wherever I put him he'll remain.

The orchestra confirms her decision with a postlude that features wooden baroque snaps. Here are the usual alternating sections, suave 3/4 and more animated 2/4. The 3/4 has charming dialogue for wind and strings.

Her intended, Fracasso, answers that a frigid wife is not at all what he intends. Giacinta does not hear him; she has obeyed the exit-rule after her aria, and departed. We may expect Fracasso to launch into song, as he is alone on stage. But there is a diversion, the entry of the blustering tyrannical Cassandro, incensed to learn that his house is to be invaded by a strange woman, the sister of his lodger Fracasso.

No. 4, Aria, Cassandro, *Non c'è al mondo*, D major, *allegro non molto*, strings alone. This is a short bustling piece without contrasting episodes. According to custom Cassandro's first solo explains what sort of person he is.

> The world is full of women. But be they lovely, be they kind, I do not want to feminize, I don't want matrimony. Servant—yes, master. His sister, that's my worry; she can go and live elsewhere.

A more sophisticated point of reference to the phrasing and texture may be found in Masetto's *Ho capito* in *Don Giovanni*.

Cassandro, having only just entered, is not obliged to leave the stage after his aria. He has to explain his annoyance to Fracasso. He suspects that Rosina is coming to the house for flirtatious purposes. Cassandro is a literary character and lards his recitative with allusions to such historical figures as Lucretia, Mark Antony, Catiline, and Orlando or Roland de Roncesvalles (a lunatic, comments Fracasso). Consistency of character seems here to collapse since the pugnacious soldier Fracasso sings a bland little ditty about the inescapable charms of women: **No. 5, Aria**, Fracasso, *Guarda la donna in viso*, G major, *allegro moderato*, horns and strings; the central section is in G minor.

> Just look at the lady and see if you don't fall in love with her gentle smile, with those pretty eyes of hers. When you weep and suffer, she tells you, I'll comfort you.
> Even when they are unfaithful and thankless, those ladies, after a glance and smile you have to forgive them, whether you will or not.

The principal subject, a scalic one, gains some vitality by being presented imitatively; and the vocal part has some florid moments. But the piece is not much and in fact is a replacement for Mozart's original setting (printed in the GA appendix), a more characterful, diversified and heroic number which the original singer Laschi found too difficult.

Cassandro, for his part, determines that he will treat Fracasso's sister in such a one-upmanlike fashion that she will think him a very Cicero. At this the curtain falls for a change of scene to Cassandro's study. Fracasso's sister Rosina has arrived and now makes her entrance.

2

Bass: A———————————————————————— E——— A—

No. 6, Aria, Rosina, *Colla bocca e non col core*, A major, *andante*, flutes and strings (divided violas) is a sensuous binary number for the prima donna's entrance, with a smoothly flowing melody, perhaps looking forward to Mozart's horn concerto slow movements, and much delightful instrumental detail, carefully nuanced, as well as some lightly florid music for the soprano.

> Anyone can fall in love by talk, not feeling. If you want constancy and love, come and learn from me how, without embarrassment, one can appreciate all men yet love only one.

Ninetta advises her to start on the first brother who comes along. Polidoro, the timid brother, has been drawn by the scent of a lovely woman (*cf.* Don Giovanni!). He comes to meet Rosina, admires her gown, and almost at once proposes marriage. Rosina suggests that whirlwind courtship is not in the best taste; she would prefer a leisurely wooing in the French manner, with genteel visits, pretty presents, and a good many love-letters. But Polidoro does not know French customs and Ninetta has told him that uninhibited frankness is better. He has to change his tune. The visit is occurring now, the presents will follow in prompt order. As to the letters Ninetta reassures him that she can write them for him. Polidoro is still afraid of his brother, who can be heard approaching. But Rosina promises to be faithful to him and to persuade Cassandro.

The ladies leave. Cassandro enters in search of the baroness and is surprised, but not convinced, to hear that Polidoro has already had audience with her and is in love with her. Cassandro warns his brother off. But Polidoro, though consenting to do Cassandro's bidding, has to admit that every woman he sees encourages him to win her. **No. 7, Aria**, Polidoro (external evidence says *allegro*, sentiment adds *moderato*) B flat major, *Cosa ha mai la donna indosso*, oboes, bassoons, horns, strings (again with divided violas).

> Every woman has something about her that gives me pleasure. If I look at her I am enchanted, if I touch her I blush and she makes me turn hot all over. If she has a deformity, such as husbands despise, I'll kiss and cuddle her. Even a poor wife is a blissful wife to me.

The introduction is quite long, with a graceful violin melody nicely sustained by woodwind, music for an ageing gentleman, one might say; some hesitations in the melodic line suggest timidity, as does a descending, syncopated chromatic phrase. The writing appropriately looks forward to the Don Basilio of *In quegli anni*. Surprising then to find that Mozart borrowed the whole number from another work, Christianity's sermon about surgery, No. 7 in *Die Schuldigkeit* (see p. 17). Mozart, finding the aria too long-winded maybe, allowed some cuts in the music; these are quite disastrous (they remove the antecedent of consequents) and later he thought better, so that they are printed in the score. There are rhythmical hints at Papageno's *Hm, hm* in *Die Zauberflöte*.

Polidoro leaves the stage at this point, of course. Cassandro has to admit that he is faintly unnerved. Rosina now returns and Cassandro begins to woo her in exactly the opposite fashion, full of compliments and courtesies and promises of phrases in French and Italian and German. She refuses her age but offers the calendar date 1768. And she repeats Molière's old joke about the difference between verse and prose. But she does not deny that she is willing to be wooed by any man, even Cassandro's brother. She responds to his mild courtship, and begs the gift of the ring on his finger which she so much admires. He admits his attraction but also his deafness to her gold-digging pleas.

No. 8, Aria, Cassandro, *Ella vuole ed io torrei*, F major, *Moderato e maestoso*, strings alone.

> She is willing and I would kill myself if she did not accept me. When we are alone together a glance, a word, will set me sweating, make me blush. I seem to be on fire and feel my blood boil in every vein, bubble, bubble, bubble.
>
> But love will be stopped by purse and ring, and my blood will recover and freeze.
>
> I am like a wild dog, caught between meat and a stick. I stretch out my paw, draw nearer to the stick then, for all my barking and whining, I don't manage to catch hold of the pork.

Violin triplets portray what he describes as the 'blo-blo' of his heart. (Gluck had done something similar in *La rencontre imprévue*, and Mozart was to revive the effect in the *Il core vi dono* duet of *Così fan tutte*.) Cassandro's concern for money and possessions prompts a contrasting section in 3/4 ('Ma l'amor finisce poi'). The sections alternate, and the later half of the aria involves some nice imitations *à la* Vivaldi. In the coda the dog snatches the meat and runs away (Mozart originally inserted some pig imitations here). The orchestral postlude recalls the primitive dramatic music that Mozart had improvised at the keyboard when he was showing Daines Barrington how to write operatic music.

Cassandro makes a formal exit. Rosina is joined by Fracasso and Ninetta. Rosina tells them of her success with both brothers and declares her intention to marry whichever of them suits her best.

No. 9, Aria, Rosina, *Senti l'eco ove t'aggiri*, E flat major, *andante un poco adagio*, with oboe, two cors anglais, two hunting horns, strings. A lovely serene oboe solo prefaces Rosina's initial entry (the mood is similar to that of *Zeffiretti lusinghieri* in *Idomeneo*, but colder so that one might be reminded more of Gluck), and echoes her phrases in the well known eighteenth-century manner prescribed by the aria's text.

43

3
[Andante un poco Adagio]

Rosina: Sen——ti l'eco o————ve t'ag-gi—ri

> Listen to the echo, wherever you wander, whispering through flowers and leaves. But if you cry or sigh, echo gives only that answer which it hears you utter.
> So it must be with lovers: wish well the one who adores you, mock the one who mocks you, give nothing to him who will not give. It is a fair and good custom to do as you are done by, and in love it cannot fail.

When Rosina mentions the murmur of the echo, violins paint the word 'sussurrar' with gentle running semiquavers (as in the *Così* trio *Soave sia il vento*). All this is at a precocious level of expressive invention, as is the scoring with dark-toned English horns★ (notated oddly in C major) and *corni di caccia*, presumably prescribed for their raw, naturalistic tone colour. At the phrase 'che ti senti a ragionar' Rosina launches twice into brilliant roulades, the first time tender, the second more impetuous (because she is arguing alternative tactics, to yield or to fight, according to the mood of the prospective lovers who, of course, are gentle Polidoro and aggressive Cassandro). Now comes the contrasting section, *allegro grazioso*, in which the heart's conclusions are formulated; this is more square and stiff in phraseology—Mozart sensed what was meant, but did not fully understand. The two sections alternate.

Polidoro returns. He wants Ninetta to write for him a *billet-doux* to Rosina, but he doesn't want the embarrassment of her brother Fracasso as eavesdropper to the errand. Fracasso flares up at the request to go, but Polidoro is not distressed by his ill-temper; the letter is his only concern. Ninetta has already written it for him, though she advises Polidoro that oral communication is much more effective than the cleverest letter.

No. 10, Aria, Ninetta, *Chi mi vuol bene*, B flat, *tempo di menuetto*, strings alone.

> Whoever likes me will tell me straight. I don't like taking pains to understand, nor languishing for the sake of politeness.
> All the letters I give her from you are bothersome and stupid. All business is quickest transacted in person.

This is a rather stiff, almost awkward aria, despite some agreeably unconventional touches of harmony. Mozart was playing safe with Mme Bernasconi, for all her fame.

Armed with the *billet-doux* Polidoro prepares to present it and a lover's gift to Rosina in person, confident that these will procure him his bride on the spot.

★ At two points in this aria the old *Gesamtausgabe* draws attention to a vile clash between cors anglais and violins. But a closer look will show that Mozart expected his wind players to take for granted a pair of appoggiaturas that are self-evident in the string writing. Today musicians are still re-learning how to realize old notation, and the interpretation may have to be explained. The clashes are not intentional.

Nobody is about, so he boldly advances upon Rosina's bedroom which, we now realize, leads off Cassandro's study. Rosina comes to the door and intercepts him.

No. 11, Finale, *Dove avete la creanza?* D major, *un poco adagio,* full orchestra. Polidoro's conduct, she declares, is outrageous, and her reactions are reflected in horror-struck upward string scales and a shuddering German sixth. The music at once turns to *allegro.* Fracasso comes out with her, equally furious, ready as ever for a duel. Ninetta joins in, and their dialogue is nicely pointed by chattering string antiphony, full of steep dynamic gradients. Tension rises with the angry duetting of Rosina and Fracasso, and Ninetta advises Polidoro to kneel and beg their pardon; she admits that the letter is her own work. Here any human verisimilitude that we may have felt like accepting vanishes: the dolls are in control, and young Wolfgang, try as he may, can only hold up masks in front of their blank faces, begging us to suspend disbelief even if only for moments at a time. This is the moment at which to remember the *Don Giovanni* finales: they seem quite close but, even if you have not tumbled the puppetry of the *Finta semplice* characters, you must notice that Mozart's music here, compared with that of his adult comic operas, consists of stiff, automatic gestures, string-pulled, reaching as soon as possible for the haven of a cadence. Mature Mozart knows how to postpone those cadential full-stops for as long as the drama demands. You can enjoy this finale by thinking of what was to come when the infant prodigy turned into the colossus of music-drama. But it is more profitable to start with the puppets and be glad that Mozart transforms their fabric into some semblance of flesh and blood.

Cassandro lumbers in, delighted to see his feeble brother on his knees, abject. Polidoro calls on Fracasso for assistance but it is not needed. Cassandro has only to mention a letter, and Rosina is insisting that he must have written it himself. There is a diversion while Fracasso and Rosina open Polidoro's present and express scorn to find that it is money. However, Rosina quickly changes the topic asking Cassandro, as a token of affection, to give her his valuable ring, only for a little while—she will return it. As a hostage for Ninetta's love-letter he is willing to part with the ring.

No sooner has she taken it than Simone appears calling Rosina outside to meet the gallant (a conspiratorial figment) who has asked her to dine with him. Cassandro foresees the disappearance of his ring and in desperation asks the company to sup with him so that he may not lose sight of his property ('così l'anello non sparirà!') They all join in a final *più moderato* ensemble (Giacinta has turned up by now, rather quietly) accepting the invitation in block harmony.

3

The gentlefolk are at dinner with their guests. Ninetta and Simone are waiting on the veranda for them to finish, and Simone wishes they would hurry up since he is hungry (servants had to feed on their masters' leftovers). Ninetta thinks he should be content to be in love, but for Simone the fires of love require regular stoking with food, drink and slumber. This seems ungallant to her: she describes her ideal husband.

No. 12, Aria, Ninetta, *Un marito, donne care*, G major, *andantino*, strings only.

> A good husband, dear ladies, is one who accepts just what we give him when we think best.

Here is the prototype of those lively, resourceful girls Blonde, Susanna and Despina, and Ninetta's music here has much of the same character though it is still rather stiff in this first attempt at the character. The elements of charm are present, all the same, particularly in the sequential phrases which act as orchestral refrains in the aria.

There is a reminiscence here of the Dance of the Blessed Spirits in Gluck's *Orfeo* though Mozart may have come upon the pattern by a different route.

Simone's response to this philosophy is that wives of that kind deserve the stick. But before the argument need be taken further Giacinta hurries out, begging Simone to go and make peace among the two brothers who are squabbling drunkenly across the dinner table. In order to make the required exit Simone has formally to sing an **Aria, No. 13**, *Con certe persone*, D major, *allegro*, oboes, horns, strings.

> When someone won't love you or makes you jealous, it's time to use the stick (*bastone*).

The music for this violent statement of policy is cheery, a swinging 3/8, with plentiful dummy, semi-Alberti accompaniment for violins and violas. If Mozart had been older he would have used the horns prominently for the word 'geloso', as he did in Figaro's *Aprite un po'* and Fiordiligi's *Per pietà*. But the suggestion of cuckoldry was not in his mind yet; for the boy, the outstanding stimulus was obviously the 'bastone', the father's or dominie's cane, and he makes a dramatic ending by having Simone repeat admonishingly, 'Madama bastone' just before the concluding ritornello.

Simone must pass Polidoro in the corridor, for hardly is the servant gone to patch things up before the nervous brother is here to explain to us (Giacinta surely knows already) that the quarrel is about Cassandro's precious ring which Rosina has appropriated. Giacinta's remedy for the squabble is that Polidoro should give Rosina an even more beautiful ring; then she will spurn Cassandro's. But Polidoro has a better present for Rosina: a baby boy (less expensive of course to begin with!), since she has already promised to marry him. Giacinta finds this hard to believe; and, although he tells her his plans for a double wedding, the return of Giacinta as Signora Fracasso to Hungary, and his partition of the mansion here into two houses, one for Cassandro, the other for Polidoro and Rosina, Giacinta can see the flaw: only a madman makes plans that he cannot execute. There is a schizophrenic lacuna here: Giacinta means that Rosina cannot live in the house (however architecturally semi-detached) with her husband and his jealous brother. She goes on to explain how she proposes to keep her husband, in **No. 14, Aria**, Giacinta, *Se a maritarmi arrivo*, A major, *allegro comodo*, flutes, horns, strings. Another of these stupid pieces about how spouse is going to keep spouse to heel.

> If I get married I know just what to do. I shall keep my husband completely tied to my apronstrings.
> He must always be near me to cuddle and learn to flirt, and show me that I am properly married; and I shall let him sing so that nobody steals him.

Mozart treats it as a game, writing sensuous, inventive A major music, with a pretty sequential coda phrase as in the previous number. The aria in 2/4 has a 6/8 middle section in which Giacinta's intention to keep her husband on a chain is reflected in a dominant-bound bass pedal. The sections alternate.

Giacinta exits. Polidoro boasts to Ninetta how he will effectively retain the wife he marries. Ninetta advises him to go quickly to Rosina who is on the point of leaving them for ever because Cassandro has forbidden her to talk to Polidoro. Polidoro asks Ninetta to instruct him in the legalities of marriage. The curtain falls.

The new scene takes place, without orchestral interlude, in a drawing-room that evening. Rosina is discovered alone.

No. 15, Aria, Rosina, *Amoretti che ascosi*, E major (*andante* is suggested by the note-values and moods), bassoons and strings (divided violas).

> Cupids concealed here, flying about and shooting arrows, I pray you do not come and torment my heart.

This is one of the most elaborate numbers in the score, texturally considered, for all that it is fairly short. The very opening, with melody hovering on first violins, murmurous counterphrases drifting from bassoons to violas, plucked basses, and a high dominant pedal on second violins, is pure magic and this is worked again at Rosina's first entry on a sustained B and a baroque effect in a new context. The wonder fades progressively as the aria continues, but the spirit remains.

Polidoro and Ninetta, who have been privately discussing courtship and the etiquette of matrimony, return, and he informs Rosina that, the niceties of gallantry having been observed, the moment for marriage is at hand. But she has still more tests for her prospective bridegroom: he must sing her an aria in French or Tuscan style, dance a minuet, answer questions on etiquette. None of these is quite a Polidoro speciality. Before his studies can get far, Cassandro enters.

No. 16, Aria, Cassandro, *Ubriaco non son io*, C major, *allegro con brio*, strings only, cheerful jerky music with gay Scotch-snap rhythms.

> I am not tipsy, just a trifle merry. But that ring is still mine and I can ask for it back. Since the wine is at last talking through me, let what is mine remain so.

Rosina mutters a promise that she will have some fun with the ring. Cassandro now turns to ridicule and abuse of his brother who claims his share of their inheritance so that he can depart for Hungary with his bride Rosina. Cassandro protests that she has promised to marry him and, when she announces that she wants as many husbands as she can get, calls her stupid ('stolida') to which she responds with a display of injured feelings almost worthy of Donna Anna:

5

Rosina:

lo sto–li–da   guar–da–te

Cont.

Polidoro comforts her, in **No. 17, Aria**, *Sposa cara*, G major, *adagio*, oboes, horns, strings. A binary number, each half of which contrasts three sections:

> Do not weep, dear spouse.

This is slow with a plucked string accompaniment and an affecting, tenderly cosseting melody:

> If you are drunk, sir, go to bed and don't molest her. I am your slave and you can beat and slaughter me as you wish.

This presumably faster, with a triple-time lilt.

> But you must not touch my wife.

This third section is marked *moderato* with rushing string accompaniment. The three sections are repeated with adjustment for the binary return from D to G major.

Polidoro's exit leaves Cassandro worried how to prevent his brother from decamping with half their fortune and the lady to whom he imagined himself betrothed, not to mention his valuable ring. He braces himself to speak sternly to Rosina. However, she tells him he stinks atrociously of wine, and must therefore sit at the opposite end of the room and converse with her in sign-language. Mozart accompanies their mime with muted strings, a vivid duet for first violins and cellos (appropriate to the voice of each converser). Occasionally one or other of them lets fall a sentence as guide to the meaning of the gestures. Cassandro does not understand Rosina's gist and he soon drops off (heavy string chords). Quickly Rosina replaces the ring on his finger, then returns to her seat before he awakes with a start (another loud chord). Their recitative is resumed. He mentions the ring of which he has been dreaming. She pretends total ignorance of the ring and says she is equally fond of both brothers.

No. 18, Aria, Rosina, *Ho sentito a dir di tutte*, F major, *allegro grazioso* alternating with *allegretto*, oboes, horns and strings.

> The prettiest and ugliest of ladies have told me that a large heart will never be content with just one lover.
>
> When there are five or six admirers, if one leaves, another arrives, if one is in a bad mood, another is well disposed, if one is rough, another is loving, and the stupidest of the lot will always fade out eventually.

It has been argued that Mozart was obviously too young to appreciate the niceties of the text here with its sexuality and pretended naïvety, but I doubt whether an adult composer of his time would have made more of it in music. We have a gently swinging *siciliano* deliciously flavoured with oboe thirds and sixths, and then a scurrying *alternativo* in which the contrasted temperaments of the various lovers are briefly but aptly depicted in music.

Cassandro has been taken in; he decides that the Baroness is as much of a booby as his brother. He needs to discuss the situation with Fracasso who appears at this moment. When Cassandro brings up the topic of his ring which Rosina has taken from him, Fracasso at once flares up and insists on avenging his family's honour in a duel with this insulting drunkard. Cassandro boasts of his courage (hurtling scales in the bass depict his comparisons with the hearts of lions, tigers, elephants) but such as he can muster is Dutch courage. In a flash of sudden sobriety he tries to postpone the fight till they have had a smoke. Fracasso taunts him with cowardice and both draw their swords.

No. 19, Duetto, Cassandro and Fracasso, *Cospetton, cospettonaccio*, D major, *vivace*, oboes, horns and strings. Despite Cassandro's show of fantastic bravery he is now reduced to mouse-like terror, and for Mozart the joy of this duet was obviously the physical activity of fighting coupled with the contrast between a bully and another bully who is really a coward. Cassandro produces one excuse after another why the fight should cease: Fracasso's family would not like it; the sun is in Cassandro's eyes; Fracasso's sword is too long. The music is *cliché* but continually vital, very detailed and full of dynamic nuance. It is tempting to suppose that this highly stimulating introduction to the dramatic duet is the source of Mozart's great dramatic ensembles in his mature operas. It will, none the less, be noticed in performance that the weight of eventfulness here falls on the orchestra while the two singers sing their lines to fill-in music without much character of its own; the true Mozart operatic ensemble has as much musical character in the vocal as in the orchestral parts. In later chapters we shall notice this technique evolving; for the moment it is enough to compare the vocal-instrumental invention of this duet with, say, *Eh via buffone* in *Don Giovanni* where the argument is infinitely more vivid even though the two duettists share the same musical material.

Considered purely on its own merit this duet, with its rushing scales and precipitous leaps, the depiction of Cassandro's terror, the violin antiphony (second violins *must* be on the conductor's right, firsts on his left), all bespeak a born musical dramatist.

Just as Cassandro's excuses are running out, Rosina runs in and he can tell her he must vent his pugnacious instincts elsewhere so as to avoid assassinating her own flesh and blood. This leaves Rosina and Fracasso to compare results. Fracasso is sure that the terrified Cassandro will gladly let him marry Giacinta; Rosina senses that it is Cassandro she loves, though she still wants to fan the flames of jealousy between the two brothers.

Here are Ninetta and Simone in time to assist Fracasso's plan, which is that Giacinta should be abducted so as to force Cassandro's hand, with Ninetta to keep her company since Giacinta is such a timid person.

Fracasso expounds his reasons in **No. 20, Aria**, *In voi belle è leggiadria*, B flat major, *andante*, horns and strings.

> Girls are whimsical; they may be totally lazy, but they'll do anything for love.

This eulogy of the fair sex, if read from score without attribution or text, might be taken for one of Ninetta's arias, it is so easy-going and light-hearted. In context we are close here to the world of *Così fan tutte*, but this aria has only to be compared with Guglielmo's *Donne mie* for the distinction to become apparent—though the *allegro* coda does look forward a little to that aria, or to the equivalent section in the *Così* duet *Il core vi dono*.

Ninetta and Simone hastily decide how and where Giacinta is to be hustled out of sight; she is to meet Simone in the garden, and they can then proceed from there. Cassandro, however, is back, chasing and as usual remonstrating with Polidoro. The second act is building towards its close.

No. 21, Finale, *T'ho detto, buffone*, G major, full orchestra. This is a fairly unsophisticated finale, but not unenjoyable since the animation is sustained and the sections well varied and proportioned. Cassandro berates Polidoro for aspiring to marry Rosina; Ninetta, expressing disapproval of Cassandro's boorish behaviour, completes a vocal trio. Rosina re-enters and the music moves into a more dignified 2/4; Rosina pretends to faint at the sight of her betrothed Polidoro's ill-treatment by his crude brother (chromatic harmony and much diversified orchestral texture in the spirit of the great *Don Giovanni* sextet). Rosina revives and announces her determination to leave this disputatious household. Now Mozart creates a helpful structural reprise of the finale as Fracasso bursts in with the news that Giacinta has run away with her family's funds. Without money the brothers cannot marry. Fracasso suggests that Giacinta shall marry whoever brings her home, to which the brothers gladly agree. Now Simone comes running back in with the news that Ninetta has also run away taking all she could lay hands on. Happy opportunity for musical reprise of the brothers' shocked astonishment. Rosina suggests that Ninetta too should marry whoever finds her, viz. Simone who hurries off on his quest. Now it is up to Rosina to choose between the two brothers, so that a triple wedding may take place. Rosina says she has made her decision but will keep the secret. They combine their voices in a lively 3/4 final chorus hoping that the wedding day will shortly come to pass.

4

Act III is unlocated in the full score. We simply discover Simone and Ninetta presumably somewhere in the garden. A bar of orchestral music raises the curtain and then Simone begins this final act with **No. 22, Aria**, *Vieni, vieni, o mia Ninetta*, F major, *un poco adagio*, horns and strings. This is a sturdy buffo aria from which we may gather that Simone is a short-breathed singer, perhaps because he is dynamically so active. A change has come upon him since the opening of Act II: there he was more concerned with eating, drinking and sleeping than with love. Now he has had supper.

> Come, my Ninetta: I'm in a great hurry to wed. I have vowed and promised, I'm a soldier, and now isn't the time to tremble on the brink.

He sings conventional *buffo* patter and the orchestral violins are kept well on the move.

Ninetta learns the master's conditions of rescue, and insists that if she returns she must not suffer recriminations or she will speak her whole mind.

No. 23, Aria, Ninetta, *Sono in amore*, C major, *tempo di menuetto*, flutes and strings.

> I'm in love and I want a husband, even if he were the first passer-by.
> Woe to him if he annoys or maltreats me; I'll make for his eyes like any cat, and use my nails so violently as to leave the marks.

The minuet alternates with a 3/8 *allegro*. Both sections may suggest respectively the Zerlina of *Vedrai, carino* and the Blonde of *Durch Zärtlichkeit* (though the *allegro* here is mostly more rapid in note-values). It is not that Mozart remembered Ninetta when he wrote those later operas, but that by twelve years old he knew these operatic types quite well and knew what music was expected of them, and that he could write it almost in his sleep.

The scene changes, now surely to a secluded part of the garden. Giacinta is here, overcome by anxiety.

No. 24, Aria, Giacinta, *Che scompiglio*, C minor, *allegro*, bassoons, horns and strings.

> What confusion, what calamity, if my brother were to see me; he'd absolutely slay me. No, there's no pity for me.
> I'm all a-tremble with fear, can't control myself, can't breathe. I feel my blood freezing and my spirit swooning.

This is the most advanced, most theatrical music in the whole opera, thematically looking forward to the woodwind serenade in the same key, K. 388, and to the opening number of *Die Zauberflöte*. There are dramatic boil-ups and *tremoli* and significant pauses, there are rushing scales and shattering dynamic contrasts and vocal hesitations.

She is near fainting as the aria ends in G minor, a forward-moving tonal progression. Fracasso joins her and exhorts her to muster her self-control. Giacinta recovers sufficiently to insist that she will not marry Fracasso unless Rosina gets the brother she prefers. Giacinta assumes that Polidoro is the choice, though Fracasso knows otherwise and prefers to keep silent, merely advising her to consult Rosina.

No. 25, Aria, Fracasso, *Nelle guerre d'amore*, D major, *andante maestoso*, flutes. oboes, horns, strings.

> In the wars of love valour is not always valid: jealous rage and innocent deception are better aids to victory.
> If you tire and harry your lovely foe without ever assaulting her, you'll take her prisoner on the battlefield.

This is a big ternary-form aria, all in the same tempo and metre, a chance for Mozart to display his architectural skill (any capable hack can think of two tunes and alternate them). The introduction is very grand and animated, as though introducing the first movement of a concerto. This is because Fracasso is arguing that, in the wars of love, the strongest does not always win (is he encouraging her to favour Polidoro?). The orchestra remains full and active, with plenty of scales, chains of sixths and thirds, and scrubbing for dramatic impetus. The music carries out a short first-movement form. Then we land in a contrasted G major middle section, with prominent dotted rhythms, at 'Chi stanca ed affattica'. It collapses into B minor, the violas seize on the keynote and tonality is diverted back to D for an abbreviated reprise. This middle section had originally been shorter and more demure; Mozart was obviously asked by Laschi for something less vocally taxing, more dramatic, to disguise his failing vocal technique and gratify his expressive powers.

Cassandro joins Rosina and asks again whom she will marry: she evades the question with a joke, but goes so far as to ask Cassandro to hide while she teases Polidoro.

The shy younger brother is all set for his wedding. But Rosina insists that, if they are to eat, he must first have Cassandro's blessing. Polidoro wants Rosina to square Cassandro herself, but this is obviously unpromising while Cassandro is himself madly in love with Rosina. She will not divulge which of the brothers she prefers.

No. 26, Finale, *Se le pupille io giro*, G major, full orchestra. A discouragingly bland and naïve musical beginning, a duet for Rosina and Polidoro about the nature of the love he feels for her. The *andante grazioso* is a moralizing duet about lovers whose kisses plunge them into prison-like restraint. The first tempo is resumed, Polidoro apparently accepted as husband. But Cassandro leaves his hiding-place and claims marital rights, much though Polidoro complains. Ninetta, Giacinta, Fracasso and Simone now return in jubilation (they begin singing off-stage), *allegro non presto*, demanding realization of their promised marriages. They complete the plot ('Fù colpo d'amore'), *un poco adagio* and very expressive—endless parallels with the late Mozart operas. Ninetta and Giacinta entreat Cassandro's pardon in florid patterns of thirds. Cassandro's family are willing to forgive (*allegro*, quasi-D major, 'Che serva, che giova'), and in an *allegro* Cassandro yields. At once Rosina reveals her love for him in warm, florid phrases, and begs pardon for her deception. The brothers are greatly surprised by her admission but accept it. In a final *allegro*, all the characters promise no regrets, in conventional block harmony against lively orchestral writing.

5

La finta semplice was Mozart's first opera. In this book it is discussed after the oratorio *Die Schuldigkeit* and Latin school-intended *Apollo* partly because these, like *La finta semplice*, help us to learn how Mozart acquired his mastery of operatic composition, partly because nowadays either of these early pieces is liable to be performed somewhere, probably on stage (where they belong), and the whole purpose of this book is to provide information for people attending such occasions.

In 1956, the bicentenary of Mozart's birth, *La finta semplice* was unearthed, staged (by an Austrian company which brought the production to London where I saw it) and recorded. The performance was heavy and unstylish. At best it showed that Mozart at twelve was capable of composing attractive and sometimes dramatically vivid music though the play is not comical nor engaging, mostly primitively stupid—we can hardly recognize the skilled, sophisticated hand of Goldoni, nor the Calzabigi pupil and Austrian *poeta cesareo* Marco Coltellini, though there are visible and audible links with the silly, occasionally interesting, and rather similar *Finta giardiniera* which is Calzabigi adapted by Coltellini and made nearly great by Mozart.

La finta semplice would have been rejected out of hand by the grown-up Mozart. For the twelve-year-old genius it was a handy first stepping-stone to operatic accomplishment. The tomfoolery appealed to the boy, as we discover in the duelling Duet No. 19, a childish *lazzo* set by an unusually imaginative child. Loneliness, insecurity, fear are more vivid for a young person, who has not learned to expect them, than for any adult who has often to live with these calamities. Giacinta's No. 24, an expression of just such a state, is the most vivid piece in the opera, and a precious invention, just because young Wolfgang had lived through such a state of mind when he was put to bed and the light blown out, or left waiting for parents who did not meet him punctually. The lively dramatic music for the Finale of Act II excited his interest because the situations were known to him from personal experience of his elders. The most remarkable music in *La finta semplice* is Rosina's No. 15, a woman's plea for freedom from the torments of love, nowhere near the personal experience of a twelve-year-old boy, yet sensuous and greatly appealing to an adult audience.

Wolfgang Mozart was thoroughly trained and widely experienced in the techniques of music and the nature of opera. On all his journeys abroad he saw operas and by the time he sat down to *La finta semplice* he knew what was required. Accordingly he went through the motions. He had no idea yet how to express ambivalent feelings. But the characters of the *Commedia dell' Arte* were quite familiar to him from many an opera he had seen and he was a natural musical mimic. Faced with Fracasso's No. 25 he knew that he must compose something like a potentate's heroic aria in the *serio* vein, and he brought one off, of a sort. He did not, could not, do justice to Rosina as a sophisticated lady playing the Dumb Blonde, nor to Polidoro as a prototypical Albert Herring. He appreciated the drunkenness, and elsewhere the crudity, of Cassandro, the dithering maternal Giacinta, most of all the sparkling charm of Ninetta, an archetype of his later soubrette sopranos; Ninetta has most of the gratifying music in *La finta semplice*, especially in her No. 12.

Chiefly he showed his professionalism in his regard for singers, every aria and every major contribution to an ensemble geared to the special character and qualities of the person assigned to the role. The singers for whom he wrote did not perform the opera, but we can imagine well what sort of singers they were. We will hear them as prototypes of Leporello or some other character in a mature, familiar opera by Mozart. In *La finta semplice* they are less vivid and interesting, but already identifiable human beings even though represented in caricature as near-puppets.

The boy Mozart was not ready to elevate Goldoni's characters into idiosyncratic people. The cast of *La finta semplice* is stiff and stereotyped like the music, almost as if Mozart were thinking of dolls in the nursery from which he was emerging. Now and then he had learned from Gluck, as in the use of *cors anglais*, standard in the Vienna orchestra in place of clarinets, a development from the Purcell *tailles* from whom J. C. Bach must have learned to use them. Knowledge had gone into this opera, and much of it came from Leopold, his father, who corrected all Mozart's early scores.

But the music is clearly Mozart's and some of it is ecstatically lovely. The foretastes of later Mozart are vivid, but *La finta semplice* is already a home-grown opera of delectable charm and vivacity, even if not more brilliant than the operas of Mozart's contemporaries.

4 BASTIEN UND BASTIENNE

BASTIEN UND BASTIENNE

Singspiel in one act

Text by
FRIEDRICH WILHELM WEISKERN
(translated from the French)
Additional lyrics by J. H. F. Müller

K. 46b (formerly K. 50)

BASTIENNE, a shepherdess   SOPRANO
BASTIEN, a shepherd   TENOR
COLAS, village soothsayer and shepherd   BASS

*First performance at the house of Dr Anton Mesmer in the
Landstrasse district of Vienna, autumn 1768*

Disappointment at the non-performance of *La finta semplice* must have been slightly alleviated by another Viennese operatic commission during the same summer of 1768. This came from Anton Mesmer, the doctor who later became famous as the inventor of the hypnotic method called Mesmerism (Mozart and da Ponte allude playfully to his magnet in the Act I finale of *Così fan tutte*). Thanks to a wife with a substantial private income Mesmer, who was thirty-five, kept open house at his home in the Landstrasse district of Vienna. Now he asked Wolfgang to compose a short opera for performance there in September or October. Choice fell on *Bastien und Bastienne*, which had been a popular comedy in Vienna since 1764 when the successful comedian Friedrich Wilhelm Weiskern (1710–68) produced it there.* He had made his own German translation from the French *Les Amours de Bastien et Bastienne* by Harny de Guerville and Charles-Simon Favart (1753),† itself a realistic parody (dirty clothes and hands, coarse acting, etc.) of Jean-Jacques Rousseau's famous arcadian pastoral intermezzo *Le Devin du village* (1752). Rousseau's plot is essentially identical with Mozart/Weiskern except that Rousseau calls his lovers Colin and Colette, the soothsayer has no name, and a chorus is brought on at the end. Weiskern, like Favart, made use of dialect and popular expressions that sent up the elegant language in which Rousseau had made his supposedly bucolic characters speak and sing—though *Le Devin* owed its historic importance to the deliberate avoidance of conventional dramatic rhetoric, and the quest for un-courtly simplicity, the much discussed 'return to nature'. Weiskern's text, which anticipates the characteristic diction of the later German *Singspiel*, was revised here and there for Mozart—perhaps by Johann Müller‡ who wrote verses for three numbers (11, 12 and 13). No programme of the Mesmer première survives, so we do not know exactly when it took place, or who sang (usually so important for the character of Mozart's operatic music). It used to be said that the performance took place in the garden where Mesmer had a little theatre cut out of hedges; but the theatre was not made until after 1768.

After Mozart's return to Salzburg he planned a performance there, began to adapt the part of Colas for an alto, and set the first four of the dialogues as recitatives to texts by Andreas Schachtner,§ the court trumpeter who was to supply the libretto for *Zaide*. The Salzburg performance came to nothing and no more recitatives were written—the extant ones can advantageously be dropped since

* Johann Adam Hiller had already set *Bastien und Bastienne* as an opera before Mozart.
† The latter gave his name to the Opéra Comique in Paris, correctly known as the Salle Favart. Favart's wife Marie, a favourite singer of the day, assisted in the musical arrangement and herself played the part of Bastienne.
‡ Supposedly the Burgtheater actor Johann Heinrich Friedrich Müller, who concocted doggerel verses for the pantomime which Mozart and some friends performed at carnival time in Vienna in 1783, and who was director of the German Singspiel in Vienna in 1778–9.
§ Named by Constanze Mozart's second husband as the reviser of Weiskern's text, on the unsupported assumption that Wolfgang wrote the opera in Salzburg a year earlier.

spoken dialogue is more in keeping with the unpretentious style of this (or any) *Singspiel*. Mozart's *Bastien und Bastienne* has sustained a modest place in the operatic repertory since its Berlin première on 20 October 1890; it reached London (in English) on Boxing Day 1894 at Daly's Theatre; at Covent Garden in German, with Frieda Hempel as Bastienne, in 1907; New York heard it in 1916 in English. It did not arrive home in Salzburg until 6 August 1928 when it was sung in Russian by Leningrad students (the mind boggles). *Bastien* is well suited to student or amateur, or even school, production, and makes an attractive marionette opera. Mozart's plan for Colas as an alto role may encourage schools to entrust all three roles to unbroken voices, but this would cause undesirable part-crossings in the closing duet and trio unless the vocal parts are re-designed, a task that few reputable editors are bold enough to attempt nowadays.

2

Mozart used the standard chamber orchestra of his day: two oboes (exchanged in No. 11 only for two flutes—the same players, we may be sure), two horns, and a string quintet. He would preside from the harpsichord; once or twice the harmony sounds odd if the chords are not filled in.

This little orchestra begins the opera with an *allegro* mini-overture in G major, modestly entitled *Intrada* (like that of *Apollo*). There is only one theme, which does duty for both formal subjects, appearing the second time in D, its contours slightly altered. Some gentle back-modulation (quite dramatic with its dropping sevenths) leads to a reprise, the theme again changed in shape at both repeats; its second subject reappearance is in C from which the music returns a shade abruptly to G (there are many awkward key-switches of this sort in the opera, but little else to betray flaws in the compositional technique of Mozart at twelve). *Bastien* used to be famous (a) as Mozart's first opera, (b) because the theme of this overture is reminiscent. I quote Mozart's third version:

1

This overture was composed two years before the birth of Beethoven, who was almost certainly ignorant of *Bastien und Bastienne* which was neither performed nor published during his lifetime; coincidences are more than possible when composers are inventing themes based on the notes of the common chord. What is more interesting is that, having hit upon the first four notes, both Mozart and Beethoven varied the rest of the theme at each of several appearances.

The scene shows a village with a prospect of meadows where shepherds and shepherdesses tend their flocks. The cottage of Colas is to one side. Bastienne, a shepherdess, has come to ask his advice and is sitting on a bench waiting for him.

Bastienne's **Aria, No. 1**, *Mein Freund hat mich verlassen*, in C major, *andante un poco adagio* with oboes and strings, explains that her sweetheart Bastien has forsaken her.

I can't sleep or pull myself together; the wretchedness is making me weak and likely to die.

The music is slowish in C major, perhaps looking forward a shade to Belmonte's entrance aria in *Die Entführung*. Oboes are discreetly touched in, and there is a sweetly melancholy middle section beginning in G minor—the leaping octave on 'Vor Gram und Schmerz' is another *Seraglio* touch, as if Constanze were complaining through the mouth of Blonde. Again the key-switches, from tonic to dominant and back again, are rather sudden.

In a little passage of spoken soliloquy Bastienne complains that Bastien has forsaken her, and further subjectivizes her wretchedness in **No. 2**, a pretty, *andante* pastoral **Aria** in F major, with horns and strings, *Ich geh' jetzt auf die Weide*.

In the meadows I walk to and fro, impervious to all about me except my lambs. My loneliness brings only sorrow to my heart.

Like several arias in *Bastien* this is in *a-b* form without musical connection between the two halves. Despite the depressing story-line the music is cheerful in its first strain, mostly through the jovial horn punctuation, a hint of baaing sheep, and galant violin snaps. Half-way through there is a pause in the dominant and the metre changes from two to three. The gently wandering violins and static horn pedal, at the third verbal repetition of 'Ach ganz allein', vividly suggest the shepherdess peering into the distance. There are some telling key-changes and a closing galant cadence.

In soliloquy Bastienne remarks the arrival of the shepherd Colas who is also well known as a magician and fortune-teller.

Colas enters accompanied by a short rustic orchestral strain, **No. 3**, in D major which begins with open strings and imitates bagpipes with plentiful drones, arpeggio phrases and a persistent Lydian fourth. It is a moment of typical humour and charm, not a bit arch or patronizing. Mozart had evoked bagpipes in the two Pastorella movements of his quodlibet *Galimathias musicum* composed two years earlier. No speed indication is inscribed, but it is clearly an *allegretto*.

Colas's *allegro* D major entrance **Aria, No. 4**, *Befraget mich ein zartes Kind*, with oboes and strings, follows immediately and suggests a more genial Osmin with its quasi-parlando character, phraseological repetitions, turns into the supertonic minor, busy violin writing, and frequent unison—though his vocal compass is not very low.

When young people ask me to tell their fortunes I can easily read destiny in their lovesick eyes.

This is exactly why Bastienne wants Colas's assistance. He is willing and asks no reward unless perhaps a couple of kisses—but no, she keeps them for Bastien, if only he will return to her. Colas assures her that Bastien loves her well—only he is easily flattered and keen on finery. Bastienne naïvely protests that she has given him endless floral decorations. She expands the point in her G major **Aria, No. 5**, *Wenn mein Bastien einst im Scherze* (horns and strings), a binary-form *tempo grazioso*

59

piece, charming and characteristic of Mozart's simpler Lieder. The vocal line is smooth and shapely, the violin writing full of rhythmic life; the horn parts are somewhat primitive. The first part is in triple time:

> Once my Bastien stole a flower from me as a joke and I was as delighted by the theft as he was. I have always given him everything: why should he now be tempted by presents from others?

The second half moves into 2/4 and its patter style suggests a slightly faster tempo. The musical invention is more sharply defined, with a nicely harmonized sequence at 'jetzt soll ich verachtet werden' (taking the music back to G major rather sooner than necessary), a *ranz des vaches* pattern almost at once, and after a pause (perhaps for cadenza) a phrase that seems typical of Mozart.

2

Soll ich nun ver——ach—tet wer—den,   da ich ihm so viel ge—than?

Bass: C   B   C   E   D   C   D   G

This is cheerful music for a song of protest:

> Gladly I offered him farms, fields, flocks; now he forsakes me though I did so much for him.

The orchestral coda begins to make a learned point, thinks better of it and collapses in activity and (unmotivated) jubilation.

Colas explains that Bastienne is up against formidable competition—no less than the Lady of the Manor who fancies Bastien and has been plying him with costly presents. To which Bastienne replies that she has frequently been offered such things but, being loyal to Bastien, has always refused them.

Mozart's key scheme has, up to this point, remained close to the opera's home tonic of G major. In Bastienne's next **Aria, No. 6**, *Würd' ich auch, wie manche Bühlerinnen*, he moves a little further away to B flat major. This is another binary movement, *allegro moderato* in 2/4 with a (deducibly) quicker second half in 3/4, to which the oboes contribute positively.

> Like many sought-after girls I'd never have enough of compliments from strangers, if I were willing to be conquered easily. But Bastien is the only one for me, and nobody else will win love from me.

The firmly and actively moving bass line and determined, strong melody at the beginning characterize the antithesis, not the thesis, of the text. The flavour (note especially the sharpened fourth in Bastienne's second line) is German rather than French, and a shade old-fashioned. Baroque yields to galant as the aria proceeds. The bouncing octave jumps for first violins at 'doch nur Bastien' expressively suggest Bastienne's leaping of the spirit at the thought of her boy—though for Mozart this was probably a subliminal rather than a conscious emotive response (as a way of giving variety to a vocal line of four repeated notes). After a pause at the end of the first half (vocal flourish expected) she seems to address her unwanted suitors.

> Be off, I say, and learn that even a young shepherdess can be pure-hearted.

Her outburst, 'Geht! Geht!' sets out on the road to the Queen of Night. The music steadily grows more serene and the closing phrases breathe sweet rustic balm.

Colas now advises her to win back Bastien by feigning coldness and provoking his jealousy as the flighty *Bühlerinnen* in town are accustomed to do.

No. 7, *allegro* with horns and strings in F major (still farther away from tonic G), is entitled a **Duetto**, but Colas and Bastienne do not sing together until their very last line. Colas's affinity with Osmin is furthered in the opening phrase, 'Auf den Rat', which may recall *Marsch, marsch, marsch!* in *Die Entführung*, and in the phrase repetitions (typical of *Singspiel* in general rather than any particular specimen).

> COLAS   Pay attention to the advice I've given you.
>
> BASTIENNE I'll do my best, day and night.
>
> COLAS   You'll live to thank me.
>
> BASTIENNE Yes, sir, day and night.
>
> COLAS   O innocence! Look merry, never sad!
>
> BASTIENNE As best I can, sir.

Colas's didactic firmness prescribes the opening theme and the addition of horns, rather than oboes, to strings. Bastienne's first entry adds a touch of levity to the mood, making for C major whence Colas twists to an Osminesque G minor, though not for long; by 'O die Unschuld' we are back in F major and a more serious emotional climate, only dispelled towards the end. The string writing is especially grateful in this duet.

Colas sees Bastien approaching and tells Bastienne to conceal herself.

Bastien enters to **No. 8**, his C major **Aria**, *Grossen Dank dir abzustatten* (the tonality is returning home). This is *allegro*, with strings alone, and might be called Turkish in character (repeated opening note, phrase repetition) if one were not minded to ascribe the traits to popular South German music (Viennese *Gassenlieder*, for instance). Mozart's intention is, I fancy, merely to establish Bastien as a self-assured young man returning from the new love to the old one, convinced that he will be received with open arms. Within a narrow harmonic range the string writing is active and lively; Bastien's part goes up to A but remains modest in technical demands and might well have been sung by a cultivated amateur (like the other two roles) if such were not below the social pretensions of Dr Mesmer.

Bastien has come to thank Colas for wise advice on affairs of the heart.

> My duty is to thank you, Colas, for parting the shadows of doubt by your counsel. I shall choose the bride who will make me happy. Bastienne's love is worth more to me than gold and jewels.

Colas expresses relief that Bastien has returned to his senses; alas, too late, for Bastienne has given him up. He reacts, in his G major *Moderato* **Aria, No. 9**, *Geh! du sagst mir eine Fabel* (horns and strings), with a stiffness that conveys outraged incredulity, perhaps insincere because expected all along (schoolboys adopt this holier-than-thou tone of reproach all the time, so we cannot pretend that Mozart was incapable of expressing it in music).

> Don't tell such stories! Bastienne is incapable of deceit, she's no hypocrite who doesn't speak as she thinks. If she praises my looks it's because she thinks me handsome, and the love that fires her must be ignited by me.

At 'Bastienne trüget nicht' the mood softens to a wheedle, and this sweetly lulling phrase returns for 'welcher anders denkt als spricht', and is transfigured in his last line, 'muss die Glut von mir entstehn'. Both these arias are simple in construction compared with the earlier ones, though **No. 9** is not without emotional subtleties.

Colas explains that Bastienne has acquired a rich and attentive suitor, handsome too. Bastien's confidence is shaken and Colas offers to consult his magic book for omens. His researches are conducted in **No. 10**, a portentously dramatic C minor **Aria**, *andante maestoso*, full of wailing oboes, helter-skelter violins, and shuddering chords. The rustic wisdom of the text is worth quoting:

> Diggi, daggi, schurri, murry,
> horum, harum, lirum, larum,
> randi, mandi, giri, gari, posito,
> besti, basti, Saron froh,
> fatto, matto, quid pro quo.

All a great joke, which Mozart furthers by writing perfectly serious music that would not be out of place in *König Thamos* or for Electra in *Idomeneo*; the whipped chords and descending five-finger exercises make one almost believe, as Bastien believes, in Colas's hocus-pocus. This is the music of magic which scarifies because magic is indeed nonsensical hocus-pocus that is being taken seriously. Mozart, as usual, does not let on or even give us a clue whether he is giggling as he writes or quaking with fear lest Satan jump out of the paper he is writing on before he has time to score the last rests and double-bar. What he does let on is that at twelve he is already a true, and potentially great, opera composer.

The dialogue which follows could be called nursery *Zauberflöte*. Colas, with a solemnity worthy of Sarastro, promises that Bastien shall see his beloved and may even speak to her, but he must, from now on, treat his true happiness with more care. Colas orders him to hide until Bastienne arrives—so that the spirits do not see him.

While he is concealing himself Bastien sings an **Aria No. 11**, *Meiner Liebsten schöne Wangen*, a simple but enchanting *tempo di menuetto* in A major (the tonality begins to move even further away from its central G major, as the drama proceeds to its crisis) in which the oboe-players switch to flutes for the only time in the opera, giving this aria a texture of special tenderness and pliancy.

How glad I shall be to see my darling's pretty cheeks again! I despise gold, rank and treasures, since none of them calms my longing as she does.

Bastien croons these amorous sentiments to gently hypnotic, self-repeating phrases of the utmost sweetness. The pairs of phrases do not here suggest *Entführung* (it is not the fact of repetition that typifies the Turkish music in that opera, but what is repeated and in what manner—these here are simply sequences which stay at the same pitch, if the description is not too fanciful) but frenchified rococo *chanson*. Of all the numbers in this little opera this was the only one to be published separately, with minimally altered words but a new second verse to the same music, in December of the same year (*Daphne, deine Rosenwangen*, K. 46c). The music is so delightful that, given a mellifluous tenor, it would be sensible to include the second verse in performances of the opera—especially since nowadays the two flutes have to be engaged separately. Students of harmony may raise eyebrows at the progression in bars 2 and 4: the consecutive second-inversions create a curious and unidiomatic effect unless harpsichord continuo fills them out; the last 6/3 chord in these bars need an added E, particularly as the third of the chord is doubled. At the end of the song the orchestral introduction is directed to be played one more time; this, not always done, is desirable for structural neatness.

Bastienne re-enters, sees Bastien and affects indifference. She pretends not to know him and refuses to believe that he is her Bastien who was quite a different person.

She describes this other Bastien in **No. 12**, an F major **Aria** of *Siciliano* type, *Er war mir sonst treu*. The pace is *andante*, the accompaniment for horns and strings.

Bastien used to be faithful to me alone, interested in nobody else, however beautiful, pleased only when he could look at me.

The opening melody contains a surprise. After the first bar:

we expect the tune to rise to F or possibly A, but not conceivably to:

The result suggests a demure yodel, not inappropriate, though when Bastienne takes up the tune, the singer may be tempted to ignore the sudden *forte* and whiten the tone so that the sudden leap seems pointless. The *Siciliano* rhythm is nicely sustained, especially at 'Das schönste Bild' which heightens the impression of wistful retrospect.

This is, like Bastienne's earlier solos, an *a-b-a* structure. After a cadence whose bass F sharp twists the music definitely, even forcefully, towards C major a faster middle section ensues, with a vigorous violin part.

> Other women were thrilled by his glances but when they gave him presents he passed them on to me. And now he is quite altered.

This last sentence is sung *adagio* to an affecting and typical Neapolitan cadence. The andante is resumed to different words ('vergebens ist jetzt') and with a varied vocal line.

> Now my love is in vain. My lover has left me and become a flirt.

Bastien explains that he was bewitched into pursuing the Lady of the Manor; Bastienne assures him that she too is under a spell which even Colas's magic is not competent to exorcise. Bastien indicates that independence is a game two can play. The strings (no extras here) strike up a defiant, peremptory E flat theme, *adagio maestoso*, that promises matters of grand and serious moment. But this is only a cover, an introduction to their shared strophic **Aria, No. 13**, *Geh hin!* which proceeds at livelier tempi. Its construction is quite complicated though formal. After the *adagio*, at once there ensues an *allegro* which races away with runs and tremolos for violins, very brilliant and pugnacious; the voice part moves more slowly. Bastien says:

> Off you go! Your stubbornness doesn't scare me. I'll run to the castle and tell Madame my heart belongs entirely to her.

The latter part of this section shifts towards B flat in which key the tempo switches to a 6/8 *Grazioso un poco allegretto*, full of sensuous parallel thirds and vocal slides, and again a lilting Sicilian mood.

> I'll wed her if she'll be as amenable as before.

The first *adagio* is resumed and Bastienne follows with verse 2, to the same music.

> I'm off to the town where suitors are easy to find, and I'll live like a lady with a hundred men in my clutches. If I find a handsome one, I'll marry him.

The second half of this divorce duet imitates the first in manner but begins in B flat, alters the *allegro* tune, and finds E flat in time for the *grazioso* which incorporates pleasant subdominant touches. Again Bastien sings first:

> I'll glitter in gold and silver, my radiant sweetheart will pay for it all, and I won't be coy when the treasures are brought out.

And Bastienne adopts the same music:

> Pretty girls easily acquire valuables in town, so long as they're friendly. I'll always be polite to rich men.

This is Mozart's scheme, better balanced than the recent practice of performing a whole double verse followed by another exactly like it.

Bastienne affects surprise that Bastien has not already gone. He attempts to restrain her: she consents, then quickly changes her mind. Bastien's fury is roused and he bursts out in accompanied recitative, always Mozart's most powerful weapon in the war of the sexes. Mozart supports him with the key of passionate emotional drama, G minor. The recitative of **No. 14** lasts only one sentence, then moves into a quick **Arioso** in G minor, *Wohlan! den Augenblick hol'ich*, with strings.

HE I shall go and please you by stabbing or hanging myself.
SHE Good luck.
HE Or I'll drown myself.
SHE Enjoy your cold bath.

The G minor *gruppetto* figure is touchingly applied, so is the diminished seventh chord on the leading-note in bars 3 and 6 of the *arioso* (after 'Freuden' and on 'Ja!'). Bastienne's sarcastic comments are orchestrally supported by rushes of enthusiasm and galant snaps. At first blush the conflict in this key looks forward to Papageno's hanging scene, but on closer acquaintance it is nearer to the frustrated adolescent rage of the K. 173dB symphony 25. Mozart voices Bastienne's feignedly unfriendly remarks in the crueller tones which Bastien heard in them.

Bastienne twists the knife further: Hasn't he dived in yet? No, says Bastien, I need to talk to you some more before I take the plunge. But Bastienne is now almost at home in her new role.

> Be off, Flanders-heart,* I no longer love you.

This is the beginning of the Finale, though so far only indicated as **No. 15**, a **Duetto** in B flat (with oboes and horns plus strings) for the two estranged lovers. The *allegro moderato* opening theme for strings is florid and dotted and stiff, but the flat seventh in the bass at bar 3 foretells (as commonly in classical music) a musical structure of some size—subdominant implications usually occur in a recapitulation. Another indication of approaching *dénouement* is the use of both oboes and horns, and the horn parts in this duet are unusually, and expressively, high pitched.

Bastien answers fatalistically in an F major second subject (*Wohl, ich will sterben*), interrupted and extended by Bastienne's transitional, petulantly regretful, *Falscher, du fliehst?* Bastien confirms, in a tenderly melancholy F minor, his intention of dying (his solo includes a pause for bravura, after a tearful half-cadence), then excuses her from blame in a bouncing, lightly rhythmic F major consequent. Hope

---

* Flemish lovers were proverbially fickle. One alternative subtitle of *Così fan tutte* was *Die Mädchen sind von Flandern*.

springs eternal, and she calls him back, but quickly resumes her wolf's clothing to taunt him. He begs her to remember former happy days, clinching his plea with an *adagio* half-cadence that needs the most eloquent decoration. They sing in duet, as if totally reconciled, in E flat major. Their avowed corporate desire to remain apart, a bland, precocious musical portrait of total insincerity (confirmed by the key of the flattened supertonic, always indicative of dark clouds before the dawn), is elaborated in an orchestral interlude, then another duet. B flat has been established and turns into its own minor, with much violin dialogue and a middle dominant pedal (suspense!) for oboes and horns, as they postulate pleasanter hypotheses—'if you could, should, might, call me your sweetheart'.

Bastien takes the initiative to reconciliation, she ecstatically seconds him, in tones worthy of Mozart's grown-up heroes and heroines (*Ich bliebe denn allein*, etc.). Then *andantino* they alternately re-plight their troth. The orchestra closes the section, and they complete the number with a moralizing duet, orchestrally punctuated and finishing with a switch from B flat into the dominant of D (like the end of the *Don Giovanni* overture, structurally speaking) for the final **No. 16** in which Colas discovers the happy pair reunited. Breezy dotted figures portray his delight as he addresses them—*Kinder, Kinder!*—with great delight. He launches another, quicker D major section, more pastoral in tone (*Auf, auf*), ordering them to forget the past. An orchestral interlude moves the music back to G, with a fascinating and unconventional comment from oboes (a quite unexpected D sharp), for the final ensemble. First a duet in G for the lovers (*Lustig, lustig*) repeating Colas's first section but elaborating the string parts, then a further reprise of *Auf, auf!* for the happy pair, now praising Colas. He joins in its final reprise, making a vocal trio. A learned point of instrumental imitation and a flurry of violin scales complete the opera.

3

Bastien und Bastienne is the most accessible (three singers, small orchestra, undemanding vocal music) and therefore the most often performed of Mozart's operas before *Idomeneo*. It has further virtues of conciseness (one act), directness of utterance due to a combination of naïf feeling and precociously apt response to situation (a precious virtue that vanishes if performers attempt to sophisticate or patronize or guy the music-drama), and a more than precocious unity of style, combining French, German and Italian elements into a musical style essentially south German, reminiscent sometimes of the *Gassenlieder* that we hear in some of Mozart's later concertos or divertimenti, frequently looking forward to his later German operas. Devotees of Mozart's operas must have noticed how often a passage in an early Mozart opera looks forward to something in one of the last masterpieces. In *Bastien* they are always premonitions of the German operas, whereas the early Italian operas always look forward to the da Ponte operas, seldom to *Entführung* or *Zauberflöte*. It was Mozart's achievement to develop an idiosyncratic musical style which we recognize, in his mature works, as Mozart rather than any of his contemporaries: it was a blend compounded of elements from other contemporaries and predecessors in various countries. But even in the mature vocal music Italian and German styles remain distinct, as they do in *La finta semplice* and

Bastien und Bastienne. Mozart, even as a boy, was sensitive to words and language: the diction of Italian to him suggested vocal phraseology and rhythm quite distinct from those which he set to German words: the words were the springboard for his musical invention. We can hear this in the music and confirm it in the letters which he wrote in other languages, even as a child—I would almost suggest that his greatness as a musical dramatist was assured because he understood what sort of music was implicit in what sort of words. Once this is appreciated we can understand why *Don Juan* in Munich (as I have heard it superbly performed) sounds not quite like *Don Giovanni* with a cast of expert Italian singers (even poor Mozartian stylists such as one may hear in Italian opera companies), and why an English *Don Giovanni*, however good, sounds more like Gilbert and Sullivan than like the German version, let alone the Italian original. In Mozart's vocal music words and melodic line are a perfect fit. If you translate the words the audience might understand more quickly what is going on; but the object understood is altered, as though one were trying to make friends with a married couple when the husband is always accompanied by another lady. He may look the same, but he will behave differently and the nature of his marital relationship will not be revealed. Mozart's relationship with the words he set was not more consistent than the individual behaviour of a man with a woman of his choice. This is the individuality of *Bastien und Bastienne* among the works of Mozart's youth which surround it. In later chapters we may find this opinion confirmed.

MOZART AND THE OPERA SERIA

At the time when little Wolfgang Mozart began to be promoted by his father as a precociously gifted composer his greatest chance of international success was in the field of opera. That chance would most probably come through the approval of court establishments rather than public opera companies: it was obvious that Wolfgang must make himself expert in the composition of the heroic opera, or *opera seria* as it is generally called, which was most favoured at court. So at least it may have appeared to Leopold Mozart, a provincial musician of rising years— particularly since the archiepiscopal Salzburg court had no regular operatic establishment of its own.

Opera seria was a highly codified art-form whose rules were as strict as they were, by the 1760s, beginning to be consistently undermined. Mozart's achievement in opera, not only in *Idomeneo* which is an Italian *opera seria*, but in *Don Giovanni*, an Italian *dramma giocoso* with serious and heroic elements skilfully blended into the comedy, and in *Die Zauberflöte*, a German *Singspiel* which evokes a world embracing low farce and high religious ritual, was the result of his earlier training in all branches of music-drama, and particularly in the discipline of courtly *opera seria*. It will be helpful perhaps to recapitulate the history of this eighteenth-century Neapolitan art-form.

Opera had begun in Italy, just before the arrival of the seventeenth century, as an attempt to revive the imagined splendours of classical Greek drama. The subjects were mythological, the poetic verses declaimed in music close to the inflexions of heightened speech. During the century theatrical spectacle—dancing, scenic transformation, big choruses—rose to popular favour. So did the virtuosity and artistry and fame of the principal singer, especially the male soprano or castrato. Emasculated male singers were singing in church in Florence in 1534, and took to the stage as soon as Florentine and Venetian opera got going around 1590. By 1650 the chorus had lost its importance, but melodious song, the aria, had become important through Cavalli and Cesti. It rapidly found the form of the *da capo* aria whose third portion repeated the first half with more or less profuse extempore decoration by the singer.

By the last decade of the seventeenth century the literary devotees of opera determined to reform the ideals of the medium so that the texts would be as distinguished and important as the music. The most influential body in this enterprise was the Arcadian Academy in Rome, founded in 1692. Among its members were Carlo Goldoni (1707-93), author of heroic as well as the comic operas by which he is now chiefly remembered, Apostolo Zeno (1668-1750) and later Pietro Metastasio (1698-1782)—he had been found as a vagrant boy singer in a Roman street by one of the Academy's members. Zeno formulated and Metastasio perfected the shape and nature of this reformed heroic opera whose ideals were simplicity, beauty, clarity. Mythological subjects were rejected in favour of historical themes, carefully researched by their authors; pastoral stories and oriental or otherwise exotic situations were permitted. Magic, supernatural phenomena, interludes, bombastic language and pompous spectacle, including choruses and ballet, were all banished from the scene. The ideal was the classical French drama of Racine and Corneille. Aristotelian unities of time, place and theme must be preserved, and dramatic action carefully motivated. The lyric drama must be a theatre of morals. The cast of six or eight would represent noble, aristocratic characters from history who would exhibit great virtue (the villain excepted) in the face of tragic reverses; everything would come right in the end, virtue and true love victorious.

The Neapolitan heroic opera devoted itself to 'the Affections'. It was not an art-form which promoted natural behaviour or diction on stage. Naturalness was a quality much despised by well-bred persons: one should react, and express oneself, in polite, sophisticated, suitably unextravagant terms, whatever the situation.

This balance was achieved by a scrupulously observed formula. The various characters entered one by one and conversed in dry recitative* (opportunity for fine poetry in blank verse to be savoured), during which some trait of character or dramatic incident was revealed. After the event had occurred, whatever it was, the most involved person sang an aria which summed up the situation, then left the stage. The aria, which had been carefully designed to exhibit the singer's best vocal qualities, might be one of several kinds, charming, angry, imperious, rapid-patter, brilliant, smoothly wheedling, or some no-man's-land between all of these. The principal characters had to sing one or two arias in each act, the subsidiary persons one or two in the three-act course of the opera. No two successive arias could use the same singer, the same mood, or the same orchestration.

---

* *Recitativo secco*: accompanied by cello and/or double bass with harmony added by harpsichord. *Recitativo stromentato*, used at moments of greater intensity, was accompanied by orchestra.

After the exit of the aria's soloist, those left on stage would continue in secco recitative, perhaps joined by others bearing dramatic news. Other arias would follow, for preference at the end of scenes (i.e. before the entry of the next character), until everyone had sung an aria and made an exit (servants could leave without being granted an aria). There was then a change of scenery and the procedure was resumed. Duets, mostly sung as alternating solos, occurred infrequently, perhaps one at the end of an act. Trios, quartets, and other concerted vocal ensembles were very rare, except in the final number labelled *Coro* when, there being no chorus, all the principal singers would line up and sing a bright, brisk concluding ensemble, usually in block harmony.

The importance of the principal vocalists was not disputed by the literary members of the Roman Arcadian Academy which systematized the eighteenth-century heroic opera. The solo singer was acknowledged as a creative collaborator in any opera, with the librettist and composer, because of his or her important contribution of graces, flourishes and cadenzas not written into the music but improvised during performance, again according to closely defined rules—each cadenza in an aria longer than the preceding ones, each melodic reprise more elaborately embellished. The solo aria was the rock on which *opera seria* was founded, and although regional varieties of taste and the changes of fashion altered Zeno's systematization in the course of the eighteenth century, Mozart accepted the importance of the aria, and the creative contribution of the singer, in every opera he wrote. It is seldom that we can examine one of his stage works without knowing precisely for which particular singers he composed the arias (*La Betulia liberata* is a perplexing exception). Zeno, and after him Metastasio, held the post of Imperial Poet in Vienna whence musical taste filtered slowly to more conservative Salzburg where Mozart grew up. Their libretti, especially those of Metastasio, were continually set to music afresh throughout the eighteenth century by composers all round Europe, because they fulfilled conventional operatic taste, were exquisitely poetic in diction, and scrupulously designed for music by a poet who was also an expert singer and composer as well as keyboard player; he was said to have tested all his lyrics by setting them himself and singing them in private before delivering the words to the destined composer. Mozart, at an early age, was presented with Metastasio's complete works. He set a number to music, thereby learning the established rules of aria and *opera seria*. When he grew older he understood that he needed more flexible libretti, which is why he bullied Mazzolà into adapting Metastasio's *Clemenza di Tito* for Mozartian purposes.

The Metastasian aria consisted of two quatrains, precisely diversified in content for the needs of the *da capo* aria as it had developed in about 1650. The first stanza exposed the principally relevant mood, the second one offered an alternative or contrast; then the first verse was repeated with its original music embellished by the singer (who had to have even more brilliant decoration if the aria was encored). Metastasio's arias are famous for their similes: the singer imagines a tempest, or a caged bird, or a radiant landscape, in the first stanza; then, in the second quatrain, contrasts it with his/her present, or longed-for, emotional state. This worked well for musical structure, and for vocal display, as well as for stage deportment: it was considered appropriate that the singer strike one pose for the first section and hold it unchanged until the middle section when another was adopted, the first being resumed for the *da capo*.

This may have proved effective in the late seventeenth century when *da capo* arias were quite short. After Alessandro Scarlatti, who initiated the lengthening of each section culminating in the extended sonata-form *da capo* aria which Mozart inherited from his Salzburg colleague Eberlin, it became increasingly non-visual in interest, and non-dramatic in the necessity to repeat lines and phrases and even individual words in the individual sections. In Prussia Frederick the Great, a connoisseur of music and able practitioner, objected violently to the unnatural repetitiousness of *da capo* arias, encouraged the briefer cavatina as norm, and himself wrote a more up-to-date libretto *Montezuma* for his court composer Karl Heinrich Graun.

We in the late twentieth century know the *da capo* aria best through Handel's operas and oratorios (though the numbers are often abbreviated because the singers cannot manage progressive embellishment). Mozart did not know much Handel until his last years, when he responded enthusiastically. He learned to compose *opera seria* from later composers, some given to reactionary length, others like Hasse and J. C. Bach inclined to shorten the repeated section or the orchestral ritornellos, or introduce contrast in the main section like a symphonic second subject. Mozart, like his Italian contemporaries, quickly saw the advantage of a return to binary aria structure, on the models of Domenico Scarlatti's keyboard sonatas or J. S. Bach's suite movements: tonic moves to dominant; dominant reshapes first-half ideas so as to move back to tonic—a significant improvement on the mammoth Eberlin construction of tonic orchestral exposition, tonic-to-dominant solo repeat, development and reprise, then middle section followed by the first double-sonata-form all over again.

Mozart was not an innovator, but he was an intelligent magpie, lucky to hear a great deal of opera in many countries while he was still learning his trade. He noted the dramatic premature solo entries, shortened structure, binary forms, and charming moods of his idol J. C. Bach, the concision of Hasse, the dance rhythms outlawed after Scarlatti but returning through Sarti. Slowly he arrived at the value of dance and choruses (hitherto relegated to comic opera), of ensembles and extended finales, of orchestrally accompanied recitatives and the possibility of making secco recitative emotionally committed by violent modulation or keyboard figuration or idiosyncrasy in vocal writing. As a German he could not leave his orchestra inactive, but had to use it for intensity and atmospheric colour—he borrowed many ideas about scoring, including the multiple obbligato accompaniment to an aria, from J. C. Bach who had learned it from Alessandro Scarlatti; and he learned too, from Jommelli and Traetta, to use themes from the opera in its orchestral overture, as well as the unbroken link from overture to opening scene.

Mozart did not invent any procedure in his operas: he was a perfecter, not an innovator. He listened widely, thought, then used each idea for his own, new purpose. When Gluck introduced his operatic reforms, from *Alceste* onwards, Mozart took note and composed *Idomeneo* and *Tito*, turning Gluck's French style into Viennese international. As I write, the musical world knows something about orchestral music in Mozart's formative years, little about the operas which he heard on his travels as a boy and young man. They taught him how to respond musically to standard situations: the tomb scene in *Lucio Silla*, the slumber scene in *Scipione*, the harbour with ships in *Idomeneo*, the portraits in *Zaide* and *Die Zauberflöte*, the prison in *Mitridate*. These were standard situations, like the tower scene (which he would have used in *L'oca del Cairo*), the letter, the ghost, the mirror, and others well known from other operas. Mozart was fully aware of dramatic business, even in his boyhood. His achievement in heroic opera was to endow his characters with personality as well as emotional reaction to incident: not only Sextus and Vitellia, Idomeneo and Electra, are credible, fascinating people, but also Giunia, and Xiphares and Amyntas.

5 MITRIDATE, RÈ DI PONTO

MITRIDATE, RÈ DI PONTO

Dramma per musica in three acts

Libretto by
VITTORIO AMEDEO CIGNA–SANTI

K. 74a (formerly K. 87)

MITRIDATE (Mithridates), King of Pontus and other kingdoms, lover of Aspasia	TENOR
ASPASIA, betrothed to Mithridates, already proclaimed Queen	SOPRANO
SIFARE (Xiphares), son of Mithridates and Stratonica, in love with Aspasia	MALE SOPRANO
FARNACE (Pharnaces), eldest son of Mithridates (by another wife), also in love with Aspasia	MALE SOPRANO
ISMENE, daughter of the King of Parthia, in love with Pharnaces	SOPRANO
MARZIO (Martius), Roman tribune, friend of Pharnaces	TENOR
ARBATE (Arbates), Governor of Nymphea	MALE SOPRANO

First performance: Teatro Regio Ducale, Milan, 26 December 1770

Leopold and Wolfgang Mozart returned home from Vienna, and the aborted première of *La finta semplice*, on 5 January 1769. On 13 December they departed again, this time for a tour of Italy. The Archbishop gave his blessing to the enterprise, as well as 600 florins subsidy; he had taken a lien on the young boy by appointing him third concert master to the Salzburg court. Father and son travelled via Innsbruck to Bolzano, Verona, Mantua, Cremona, then Milan. It was here that they met Count Karl Joseph Firmian, the Governor General of Lombardy, one of whose brothers was Inspector of Court Music in Salzburg and whose uncle had been Archbishop of Salzburg when Leopold Mozart first entered court service there. The Mozarts lunched with Firmian on 7 February 1770, and afterwards Wolfgang (or Amadeo as he was called in Italy) played for the other guests (they included Sammartini) and was presented with the works of Metastasio, complete in nine volumes. Wolfgang performed at two further parties given by Count Firmian in subsequent weeks: they were important to his immediate future, as all his dealings with Count Firmian seem to have been. On 18 February the guests included the Duke of Modena, to whom *Mitridate* was to be dedicated, and his daughter Beatrice Ricciarda for whose wedding festivities he composed *Ascanio in Alba*. On 12 March, when 150 nobles of the district attended, he contributed four new arias to texts by Metastasio which he had composed for the occasion: these were (we learn from a subsequent letter) in the nature of an audition whereby the company would discover whether Mozart at fourteen years old was sufficiently talented to compose an opera for Milan. The possibility must therefore have already been discussed since, on the following day, Leopold Mozart wrote to his wife that Wolfgang had been invited to write the first opera for the forthcoming carnival season in Milan (i.e. beginning at Christmas time and continuing until Shrove Tuesday). Contracts were exchanged by 24 March: Mozart recommended a Metastasio text (Count Firmian's present had already been twice put to good use) and accepted a fee of 100 Gulden (*cigliati*) and free lodging for the duration of his stay in Milan. He was required to arrive by 1 November (the recitatives having been delivered a month earlier) to meet the singers and write their arias. The principal singers were already named at this stage, though only the Cavaliere Guglielmo d'Ettore eventually took part. Manzuoli, an old friend of the Mozarts (see p. 9), was proposed, obviously for the part of Xiphares—he sang Mozart's audition arias when father and son met him in Florence some weeks later, but did not appear in a Mozart opera until *Ascanio in Alba*.

Wolfgang and his father had in any case intended to remain in Italy throughout 1770 (the Milan commission meant for Leopold that he would rejoin his wife and daughter earlier than had been planned). By mid-July they had not been informed what the chosen libretto was to be, nor who (apart from the *primo uomo* and tenor) was definitely to sing it. The text arrived on 27 July, and it was not Metastasio at all but an abbreviated and altered version of a French drama best described as follows. The original was a tragedy by Racine, *Mithridate*, dating from 1673. This had been translated into Italian by Giuseppe Parini (later the librettist of *Ascanio in Alba* and a journalist whose chronicles are quoted *passim* in this book), then turned into an opera libretto for the Abbot Quirino Gasparini (1721–78) by Vittorio Amedeo Cigna-Santi (1725–85). Gasparini's version had been composed in 1767 for Turin, where he and Cigna-Santi were both employed. The libretto was now wished on to Mozart who set the recitatives in a somewhat abbreviated form (occasionally removing important explanatory sentences) and did not put all the arias to music—thus causing one or two problems, to be discussed in due course.

Mozart did not begin composing the recitatives, according to his father's letters, until 29 September, though we learn that earlier in the month he was thinking about them and working hard, as well as reading books, going for walks with a countess, riding a donkey, playing the violin, composing arias, symphonies and a motet, looking incompetently after his indisposed (and evidently hypochondriac) father, and suffering the indignity of voice-breaking which meant that he had only five or six notes left in his voice and could not sing to himself what he had written, as was his custom. This last explains the delay in beginning work on the opera. By 20 October, when the recitatives should have been delivered, he complained that his fingers were aching so much from composing so many recitatives that he could hardly pen a letter: he asked his mother and sister to pray that his work would go well—and often repeated the request in forthcoming months.

The recitatives were late in completion but the Mozarts arrived, by design, early in Milan on 18 October, perhaps to save lodging expenses so their letters let us infer. In November the singers arrived by dribs and drabs. We learn that the *prima donna* Antonia Bernasconi (Aspasia) was beside herself with delight at Mozart's arias for her—so was her singing teacher, the renowned Giovanni Battista Lampugnani who played second harpsichord in the opera's first three performances and thereafter assumed direction of the work.* When operatic intriguers, determined that a boy should not be allowed to inflict his immature (however precocious) ignorance on the theatre now called La Scala, Milan, tried to persuade Bernasconi to substitute Gasparini's arias for those of Mozart, she held out for the virtues of the new ones by the young composer.†

Almost certainly Mozart examined Gasparini's (later he met and became friendly with their composer) and learned how to achieve different, more expressive results without ignoring their good points. But he did have to compose a number of the arias several times before the singers were satisfied with them—the alternative versions, which have survived, will be discussed in due course: and eventually Bernasconi and Pietro Muschietti (the Arbates) each sang one aria not by Mozart to words that he seems not to have set at all.

Most hard to please of all the cast was the principal tenor Guglielmo d'Ettore who was specially imported from the Bavarian Royal Opera (when Dr Burney heard him he noted that Ettore was 'more applauded than all the rest') to sing the title-role. Ettore evidently became a byword in the Mozart family for fussiness.

* He was a fine composer who had spent some years in England, and whose music has been rediscovered and applauded in modern times.
† She may have sung one aria (*Secondi il ciel*) to music by some other composer, perhaps Gasparini.

He only demanded that two of his arias be re-composed, but the first of these, *Se di lauri*, had to be written no less than five times. This importunacy was doubtless what Leopold Mozart referred to as a 'second storm weathered', though the intrigue against Wolfgang was general and continued until rehearsals began and the voices of discontent were silenced by the incontrovertible excellence of the music that the boy had written and was now expertly directing. Mozart had by this time won over the singers (the male soprano Pietro Benedetti, known as Sartorino, declared that he would have himself castrated a second time if his big duet with Bernasconi didn't go well—it did), the orchestra, all the local composers who were full of praise and, particularly important, the copyist who could make good money if an opera became popular, and whose orchestral parts for *Mitridate* proved so accurate that hardly any time at all during the first orchestral rehearsal was needed to correct errors—this was pronounced extremely unusual.

Wolfgang Mozart had been obliged to work very hard indeed throughout November and the first part of December. On 1 December Leopold wrote to his wife: 'If you think the opera is already finished you are very wrong. If it had been up to our son only, two operas would have been completed, but in Italy things are quite crazy. . . . At the time of writing the *primo uomo* has not yet got here.' Mozart could not write his arias or duets before consulting personally with Sartorino, least of all in these unusual circumstances in which the boy had to prove to each performer individually that he was an expert professional musician, not an infant mountebank being exploited by unscrupulous persons (a perfectly natural reaction to child prodigies of all eras). It was, after all, his first opera written for Italy, and his first attempt at *opera seria*.

Rehearsals of recitatives were able to start in early December. The first, prestige-asserting, orchestral rehearsal took place on the 12th: there were five in all, the last three in the Royal Ducal Theatre (now La Scala) where the first performance was given on 26 December (dress rehearsal on Christmas Eve). Father Mozart had been well aware that, even granted the good will of Milan's professional musicians, everything depended on the whim of the public—and the Italian public were in no way to be swayed by official approval. He need not have worried. Contrary to all precedent the opera was enthusiastically applauded, number by number (apart from a few in the second half), one of Bernasconi's arias was (most unusually) encored, and there was much shouting and applause. Never, according to Leopold Mozart after several performances, had any opera which opened the Milan Carnival season been so enthusiastically received. *Mitridate* had twenty-two consecutive performances before the second opera of the season took its place. All houses were full and some encores were usually granted: the work lasted six hours, two of them taken up by the ballets which were the work of Francesco Caselli, not Mozart. This, according to Leopold Mozart, was significant in as much as Milanese audiences were complete individualists who would never give their approval to any opera unless they genuinely meant it. Mozart and his father were able more closely to experience this enthusiasm from the fourth performance onwards when they sat in the auditorium and not only enjoyed the applause but discovered how many spectators felt obliged to shake hands with the composer. Press notices stated that the opera was admired 'as much for its tasteful stage designs [by the three Galliani brothers] as for the excellence of the music and the ability of the actors . . . [Bernasconi's arias] vividly express her passions, and touch the heart', while Mozart's music 'studies the beauty of nature and exhibits it adorned with the rarest of musical graces'. These were the words of Giuseppe Parini, translator of the Racine original.

Apart from Bernasconi, Ettore and Sartorini, the cast included Giuseppe Cicognani, a castrato male alto who was already friendly with the Mozarts and whose beautiful voice and lovely cantabile were praised by Leopold (Cicognani sang Pharnaces); Anna Francesca Varese, the Ismene; Muschietti (Arbates), and Gasparo Bassano the tenor who sang Martius.

Mozart's autograph score of *Mitridate* had disappeared before the first complete Mozart edition began to be prepared. Modern scholarship relies on a copy made for the court opera at Lisbon, much more complete than any other; a score of the principal numbers (now in the British Museum) copied out by the great double-bass player Domenico Dragonetti; the score and precedent sketches now in the Paris Conservatoire Library; and a later but less comprehensive copy in West Berlin. It has always been supposed that *Mitridate* was never subsequently performed until modern times, and two scenes in the first act are nowhere musically extant, as we shall see. But it is curious that no record of a Lisbon performance survives, since this is the fullest and evidently latest version of Mozart's score, and had been commissioned from the Milanese copyist at the time of the première, as Mozart's letters show.

2

In the preface to his *Mithridate* Racine observes that since his hero's name and deeds are so well known it does not seem necessary to cite his sources: 'excepting some events which I have brought a little closer (*rapproché*), by the right which poetry gives, all the world will easily recognize that I have followed history with much fidelity'. The historical Mithridates VII, known as Eupator* or Mithridates the Great (*c.* 135–65 B.C.), had a long and eventful life of plucky fighting against the tyranny of Rome; but very little of history is reflected in Racine's drama. Mithridates did have a concubine named Stratonica (their son Xiphares seems to be an invention) and one named Monime, a Greek princess from Miletus about whom Plutarch gives much information, as well as a son Pharnaces who usurped the throne at which news Mithridates killed himself. Several of Mithridates's concubines were ordered by him to take poison, but not Monime whom he had assassinated by a eunuch. It is related that Mithridates tried to kill himself by poison but failed because he had taken so many antidotes to avoid being poisoned by his enemies. He therefore stabbed himself but the blow was not lethal and he had to request a bystanding Gaul to give the *coup de grâce*. The real Pharnaces gave Julius Caesar the victory which he described in the phrase *veni, vidi, vici*. Racine was simply concerned to construct a tragedy in which filial duty conflicts with infatuated love and rivalry between brothers and father for the same woman. To this end he effected the poetic *rapprochements* of history to which he alludes.

* Alessandro Scarlatti wrote an opera *Mitridate Eupatore* in 1701: its characters include Pharnaces and Stratonica, but the story is quite unhistorical and is indeed recognizably based on the *Electra*.

Cigna-Santi, preparing his operatic libretto from Parini's translation of Racine, converted Monime into Aspasia, removed her confidante and Mithridates's servant Arcas, gave Pharnaces his Roman tribune friend Martius and his eventual bride Ismene as well as his lightning transformation in Act III from villainy to heroism (Racine's Pharnaces is left at the end alive and fleeing with the Romans).

3

Leopold Mozart obligingly left a written record of the Milan orchestra as constituted for the première of *Mitridate, rè di Ponto*. There were two flutes, two oboes, two bassoons, four horns (*corni da caccia*), two trumpets (*clarini* or *trombe lunghe*), two harpsichords (*clavier*), fourteen first and fourteen second violins, six violas, two cellos, six double-basses. Leopold notes that when flutes are not scored for, the oboe parts are played on four oboes—the flutes doubling oboes according to common eighteenth-century practice. Similarly the bassoons, when not scored for, always double the cello part—hence the small number of cellos employed (it was standard for this theatre). Leopold forgets to mention the timpani needed in No. 7.

Mozart abstained from using his full band at the very start, and even from beginning with the sounds of pomp that would have been quite appropriate to the subject of the opera. The overture, in D major (the home-key of the opera), is a charming, quite light-weight Italian *sinfonia* in three well balanced movements scored for flutes, oboes, two horns and strings. Its first movement, *allegro*, contrasts furtive broken-chord figures with faster noisy ones in the first subject. The second group steals in delightfully round a dominant middle pedal-note in A.

1

The viola pedal-point returns in the development section for a delicately coloured idea based on descending thirds, the first of whose top notes is left hanging. The recapitulation touches on subdominant and supertonic counterpoises; the second subject sounds less magical in its reprise form. The middle movement, *andante grazioso* in A major, is scored for flutes and strings alone, and has an enchanting melody, combining Italian and French features, elegantly ornamented, impeccably formed, pure treasure trove for anyone who lights upon it. This short quotation may draw attention to the movement but gives little idea of its full beauty.

2

Oboes and horns return for the triple-time *presto* which rushes forward energetically and with hardly a pause for breath.

The curtain rises for Act I to disclose the square in the Macedonian port of

Nymphaeum.* In the distance is a view through the gates of the city. The younger of Mithridates's sons, Xiphares (Sifare), has returned home from Colchos, of which his father has made him governor, and is being welcomed by the governor of Nymphaeum, Arbates. Both are attended by a retinue, like all principal characters in *opera seria*. The elder brother Pharnaces (Farnace), who had been left in charge of Pontus, has also arrived in Nymphaeum, Xiphares notes with distaste. Arbates asks if Xiphares is annoyed because he was hoping to gain the throne of Nymphaeum now that Mithridates's death in battle has been reported. Xiphares explains that he and his brother are rivals for the love of Aspasia the *bella Greca* left behind by their father. Arbates intimates that Aspasia favours Xiphares and that his own loyalties are to Xiphares also: Pharnaces will have to look elsewhere, while Arbates is governor, for both wife and throne. Arbates and his posse of citizens leave.

Now Aspasia comes to beg Xiphares's assistance against Pharnaces who, not content with unfilial jockeying for power, is seeking to force his odious love upon her. Xiphares offers to keep his brother at bay but asks if Aspasia will not hate her defender as much as the importunate suitor. If he is successful, she answers, he will learn not to accuse her of hard-heartedness.

The orchestra, with oboes, horns and trumpets added to strings, heralds Aspasia's *allegro* **Aria, No. 1**, *Al destin che la minaccia* in C major, vigorous, heroic, grand in scale, rich in vocal display. Like many of the *Mitridate* arias it is a spacious sonata-form (double exposition) movement of 110 bars with a contrasting middle section and a shortened *da capo* starting from the end of the solo exposition (an abbreviation that became necessary in the second half of the century as the main body of the *da capo* aria expanded to near-symphonic dimensions, one that Mozart justifies by continual reshaping of his themes, as here).

Spare my oppressed soul the destiny which menaces it. First let me become myself again, then be angry with me.

Faced with danger how do you want me to obey your decrees? Ah, you know me and the nature of my heart.

Within its restricted emotional range the aria has some enjoyable features: for example the revised vocal version of the first subject, almost a new tune, with tense off-beat violin dummy accompaniment, the new melody superimposed on the fanfare second subject now given to divided violas instead of brass, the exuberant vocal runs going up to top C, the dramatic end of the exposition with a broken diminished seventh chord (so that the development may begin on the dominant of D minor—the whole procedure is repeated at the end of the middle section, when it has a more clumsy effect because the key-progressions have been too much impacted for the spaciousness of the aria as a whole), then perhaps the more sombre and pathetic middle section where Aspasia admits the fallibility of her heart.

---

* I only hazard that Racine meant Macedonian Nymphaeum: Mithridates was at one stage in occupation of Macedonia. Racine may have read the name in Plutarch's life of Sylla (one of his sources for the play), liked the sound of it, and *rapproched* it as an imaginary capital city of some Mithridatean territory—not Pontus, since Mithridates chides Pharnaces for being in Nymphaeum instead of Pontus.

The earlier version of this aria (without trumpets) was similar in structure but less grand, more gentle in manner; we might think more expressive, but Bernasconi may have wanted to make a stronger impression in her first solo of the evening. There can be no suggestion that the first version was unsatisfactory as a specimen of musical composition; it simply did not provide the *prima donna* with the initial triumph that she, and the young composer's new opera, needed for success.

As Aspasia goes Xiphares reflects, in a recitative accompanied by strings with a vivid emotional picture of each sentiment he utters, on the new revival of hope in his dejected breast, spurred by his beloved's words. He must delay no longer, and hopes to deserve the reward she seemed to promise, even if he does not obtain it. All of which leads to his first **Aria, No. 2**, *Soffre il mio cor* in B flat major, *allegro*, doggedly determined in character, bright and radiant in colouring (high horns in B flat, biting oboes, the clarion ring of a male soprano). There is more of effect than thematic invention: the main tunes are ordinary and repetitious, but the singer's first entry (after a lengthy orchestral ritornello) on a sustained top-of-stave F, soon followed by an octave leap up to top B flat, is startling; his new second subject is nicely shaded in the string accompaniment, and his florid divisions have great rhythmic bravura.

> My heart will peacefully suffer the tyranny of a beauty, but will not tolerate a rash man's pride.

The very short, gentler, middle section elegantly varies the same sentiments in buoyant triple time, whereafter the *da capo* resumes from the development section, as in No. 1.

The scene changes to the Temple of Venus. The altar is burning, and the place is decorated with myrtles and roses. Priests stand near the altar. Pharnaces, attended by a section of his troops, is once again urging Aspasia to become his wife, here in this temple which is prepared for the ceremony. She explains that filial devotion to her father, who was slaughtered by the Romans, prevents her from giving her hand to such a friend of Rome as the vile Pharnaces. He responds with force, dragging her to the altar. Xiphares and his soldiers punctually come to Aspasia's aid and Pharnaces releases her, with a sneering comment that doubtless she prefers Xiphares. The brothers quarrel and are about to draw their swords and fight when Arbates enters hurriedly announcing the arrival in the harbour of Mithridates, and telling them all to stop their squabble and go out and greet him.

Unfortunately this last passage of recitative, from Aspasia's 'friend of Rome, vile Pharnaces', is missing from all the extant scores; Luigi Tagliavini, editor of the New Mozart Edition of the opera, surmises that the passage was composed hurriedly on separate sheets which were never pasted into the finished copy (but surely the copyist would have got the missing passage from somebody when he made the copy to be sent to Lisbon). The opera cannot be performed without this scene; it is dramatically essential. However, Mozart's secco recitatives in this work are not of special character or excellence and anyone who decides to revive *Mitridate* has only to get the gap filled in by a capable Mozart scholar.

The extant score continues with Arbates's **Aria, No. 3**, *L'odio nel cor*, in G major accompanied by strings.

> Cease this hatred. Show respect for your father who will not condone it. If you are not friendly he will rightly be stern.

This is a concise ternary-form aria on three subjects, the third prefigured rhythmically in the transition from first to second. The thematic working is cogent and consistent, giving strong unity to the piece. The mood is debonair and easy-going, the vocal music low-lying and only mildly taxing. It suggests that Muschietti may have been elderly, restricted in compass and agility. It is the only aria that Mozart certainly composed for him; the later one is thought to be unauthentic.

Arbates hurries to the harbour. Pharnaces is nonplussed, Xiphares unrepentant. But Aspasia sees in Mithridates's return the end of love's dream. Her exit **Aria, No. 4**, *allegro agitato* with oboes, horns and strings, is a highlight of the whole score, an urgent piece whose initial D minor chord breaks into the end of the recitative, achieves its tonic key of G minor by a two-bar wrench, and breaks into panting, shuddering string chords over which Aspasia at once voices her grief (*Nel sen mi palpita*) with heartbreaking chromatic music in Mozart's characteristic *agitato* G minor vein (at fourteen!), not angry as in K. 173dB but anguished as in Ilia's *Padre, germani, addio* and the G minor piano quartet and the first movement of K. 550.

> My grieving heart throbs in my breast. My grief calls me to weep: I cannot remain.
>
> But if my eyelids are wet with tears, believe me your peril is the only, terrible cause of my suffering.

The marvellously affecting vocal phrases, eloquent instrumentation, dovetailing of themes and sections, bold harmony, are combined at white heat from first to last—the orchestral postlude is as thrilling as anything that has gone before. For these couple of minutes, at least, *opera seria* is not a dead duck, and *Idomeneo* is within earshot.

Aspasia's tone of voice is not lost on Pharnaces. When Xiphares opposes his suggestion that they close the city gates against their father, Pharnaces advises his brother to keep quiet about what has been going on, since they both have something to hide. Xiphares assures him that he will equally behave as a loyal brother and loyal son. His A major **Aria, No. 5**, *Parto: nel gran cimento*, accompanied by strings, is in *a–b–a* form where *a* contrasts *andante adagio*, dignified with florid violin commentary, against a more conventional but not inexpressive *allegro* which includes some brilliant agile divisions.

> I go. In the great test I shall be brother and son.
>
> My fate will match your danger. Use your skill; you will never see me wanting in constancy.

A respectable but not outstanding aria. Gasparini's setting at this point had an aria for Xiphares to another text.

Now Pharnaces is alone, licking his wounds. Martius, his Roman friend, comes to tell him that Rome is on the point of demonstrating actively its interest in his cause. If, says Pharnaces, I can enlarge the Roman empire, I shall die revenged.

His **No. 6 Aria**, *allegro andante* in F major with oboes, horns and strings, *Venga pur, minacci*, is another of the long, stiff, plodding arias that make one appreciate why for long after 1770 nobody bothered with *Mitridate*, and why E. J. Dent dismissed it as 'more heroics than humanity' (though No. 4 has shown the other side of the coin). It begins with a show of energy, but soon the activity of the bass sinks back into the stagnant monotone of ordinary galant music. The ideas are unremarkable and hardly contrasted in character, the vocal writing kept low for Cicognani's alto voice—but his best qualities are not called on here, which is perhaps why the aria sounds so dull.

> Let my father storm and threaten: I will not yield.
> Let him respect and fear the Roman in me, less savage and less strict; other-
> wise his anger will make me more cruel or more proud.

Interest revives in the *andante* middle section where the low-lying vocal phrases have a dark, glinting grandeur, nicely set off by the violins' burst of fury. There is a short new lead-back to the abbreviated *da capo* with a curt and indecisive unison ending (like Figaro's *Non più andrai*).

The scene changes again to the sea harbour showing two fleets at anchor (those of Pharnaces and Xiphares) and a prospect of the city. The orchestra plays a **March, No. 7**, *maestoso* in D major with oboes, horns, trumpets, drums and strings, which Mozart borrowed from K. 62, the elaborate, strongly characterized march written a year earlier for a cassation K. 62a (formerly K. 100) performed at a party given in Salzburg Gymnasium in honour of Father Widl (librettist of *Apollo et Hyacinthus*). Here it is (in the Lisbon copy) more fully scored and accompanies the arrival of a third fleet, that of Mithridates who disembarks with Ismene and his retinue, and is met on the beach by Arbates with his attendants, while remaining troops line up behind them. *Mitridate* was not designed for a pocket-handkerchief stage.

The march ends in D, and at once the oboes, horns and strings break into the martial, equestrian *andante* strains of **No. 8**, Mithridates's entrance solo, *Se di lauri*, which is entitled **Cavata** (an old-fashioned title by 1770 denoting a short aria, perhaps Mozart's excuse for not giving his hero something more extensive here, though I wonder if he was thinking of *Cavalcata*, for the equestrian motif occurs in all the sketches and doubtless was suggested by the captious Cavalier). The violas, rocking-horse triplets, and choppy dotted rhythms are not particularly appropriate to the text of the *Cavata*.

> Though not crowned with laurels, I come home without disgrace. I lost the
> battle but my heart is still courageous.

At the *andante* tempo prescribed, and indicated by the orchestral detail, this aria cannot help sounding faintly absurd, as if the great hero Mithridates was still searching for his land-legs and had his helmet askew. Perhaps Mozart did it deliberately: in performance he seems to have cut the viola triplets (as well as three bars later on) though they are thematically indispensable. Ettore evidently demanded immediate attention to his two-octave range and his ringing top Bs of which there are an unwarrantable quantity.

THE OPERAS OF MOZART

Mithridates apologizes to Arbates for having been defeated by Pompey (this replaces the lengthy and vivid scene in Racine where he describes his escape and long period of travelling in exile). Ismene asks concernedly after his sons: we gather that she, a Parthian princess, has for some time been the betrothed of Pharnaces. Arbates indicates the boys' arrival. Xiphares warmly embraces his father who asks why they have left their posts in Colchis and Pontus. Pharnaces narrates their anxiety at reports of Mithridates's death and relief at seeing him here. Ismene reproaches Pharnaces (to his discomfiture) for showing no delight at seeing her again; Mithridates promises that they will soon be wed and tells his sons to conduct her into the city. Ismene doubts if she is going to be happy here, and expands this sentiment in an **Aria, No. 9**, with strings in B flat major, of some length (and repetitiousness) for a *seconda donna*. *In faccia all'oggetto*, a bland jog-along *allegro*, is reasonably exhibitionistic but otherwise not greatly interesting, nor notably relevant to its text—

> I should feel glad to see my beloved, but feel sad and do not know why.
> Silent lips, frigid eyes tell me I am going to suffer.

—save in the G major middle section. It replaced a longer, slower, rather bouncier setting, even less appropriate and doubtless not so flattering to the singer.

To Arbates Mithridates confesses concern about his sons. The governor reveals Pharnaces's designs on Aspasia and the throne, but tells the king that Xiphares's mind is bent only on revenge and war against the Romans. Arbates is told to keep a watch on Pharnaces and departs full of mental turmoil. And Mithridates begins an accompanied recitative (strings only) full of instrumental illustration—perfectly standard in *opera seria* of this period—as he expresses his pleasure at Xiphares's loyalty, his scorn at Pharnaces's behaviour. The act ends with his **Aria, No. 10**, *allegro* in D major, *Quel ribelle*, with oboes, horns, trumpets and strings.

> Would I might see this thankless rebel bleed to death at my feet, I know I
> would avenge more than one misdeed with that vile blood.

The music is chiefly remarkable for the quantity of soft, furtive music, and the emphasis on expressive singing without any bravura at all. Again Mozart was spared the long *da capo* aria for the Cavalier Ettore; perhaps he was not a long-distance vocalist but one who preferred to captivate his audience quickly and intensely.

4

Act II begins with Ismene and Pharnaces in what are described as 'apartments'. She rebukes him for his fickle-heartedness and threatens to tell Mithridates. Pharnaces counters that his father already detests him, and in any case nothing can fan an extinct flame. In his *allegro* G major **Aria, No. 11**, *Va, l'error mio palesa*, with horns and strings, he dares Ismene to disclose his misdeed.

> My misdeed is known and my punishment approaches. But revenge may
> cost you dear, and you will recognize your own guilt.

This is a dramatic number, demonstrative of Cicognani's vocal accomplishment, and enhanced with a purposeful bass line to support the busy upper string parts.

He leaves and Mithridates comes to console Ismene, promise Pharnaces's death as soon as further proof is forthcoming, and suggest that she be married to Xiphares. But he is not the man I love, she wails as she goes out. (We may expect an aria for Ismene here, but she is not sufficiently important to be allowed another just yet.)

Now Aspasia appears and is told they will be married today since Mithridates returns to sea tomorrow. Despite her willingness he accuses her of infidelity and calls Xiphares not, as she fears, to accuse him but to bid him wait on Aspasia and bolster her morale. This is the burden of **No. 12**, the alternately *adagio* and *allegro* **Aria**, *Tu che fedel* in B flat major with oboes, high horns and strings.

(*to Xiphares*) You who are loyal to me, O God, may your heart serve me.
(*to Aspasia*) Ungrateful woman, let my scorn come to fruition.

An aria addressed to two people is almost like an ensemble, inasmuch as it involves three characters rather than two or one—this is especially dramatically vivid in an *opera seria* in which even duets are rarities. This one may seem prodigal of invention (I am thinking of the springing violin theme in bar 7, an excellent idea which never reappears) but in fact is quite closely worked, as may be observed in the contrast between the *adagio* Xiphares theme, a scalic descent from the fifth to the tonic (B flat)—this is mooted in several ways during the orchestral introduction—and the Aspasia *allegro* theme which is most striking rhythmically but also preserves the contours of its melodic outline. Mithridates's huge vocal jumps (not quite two octaves) are emotionally telling, so is the key-swerve up a tone when *adagio* changes to *allegro*. A tiptoe theme makes helpful contrast, and when Xiphares is addressed, in the second *allegro*, with the *adagio* theme at quicker tempo, violins add a new wheedling countersubject that momentarily heightens tension.

He leaves Xiphares and Aspasia alone. She admits that she is in love with him. Her confession is interrupted by Arbates who summons them both to a conference in the court with Mithridates. Before Arbates's exit the London copy of the score shows an aria for him, *D'un padre l'affetto*, which is regarded as unauthentic and does not appear in the Milan libretto, though the text was included in Gasparini's setting. The absence of this aria renders Arbates's interruption musically un-motivated by the strict standards of *opera seria* (the only standards that make sense of it) since after his departure the same two characters are left on stage. She tells him that he must go away for ever, painful as this will be for them both, since her duty to Mithridates is clear and, therefore, his duty too. Only so can they both retain their self-respect.

The emotional stress of the moment draws string orchestral accompaniment into the recitative, though it is still in dialogue. Xiphares finds it impossible to obey her command while she still acts so kindly towards him. She entreats him to see reason and behave nobly. He apologizes and bids her farewell. But before departing he sings **No. 13**, the **Aria** *Lungi da te*, an *adagio cantabile* in D major which has the signal enhancement of a glorious and virtuoso horn obbligato, as well as oboes and two *ripieno* horns plus strings.

> I will go far away, if you so desire, and forget the pains I have caused you.
> Farewell, beloved; if I remain here I shall forget my duty entirely.

The aria begins almost lazily, with a soporific undulating accompaniment that renders the musical texture reminiscent of German romantic horn music in the time of Schubert and Weber—fifty years later. The mood is prolonged throughout the later, freely ranging stages of the movement, though this combination of voice and instruments becomes less beguiling because Mozart is thinking more about compositional technique than about artistic vitality. In the middle section, a dull 3/8 *andante* episode, the horn is silent and its return in the shortened *da capo* works all the more gratifyingly. The combination of mellifluous horn and blazing male soprano voice (granted a compass from low B to high B and an agile florid technique) must in this aria have been unforgettable. Evidence, alas, suggests that it may never have been heard by an audience since, in the score regarded as representing what happened in the première and afterwards, the aria is given in a version without horn obbligato, with extended orchestral interludes, but with the identical vocal music—since Sartorini could not be expected to re-learn the aria differently whereas, it is surmised, the Milanese principal horn found his solo impracticable. Sketches show that Mozart worked hard at this aria and textual collation suggests that in any modern performance the version with horn obbligato should unhesitatingly be preferred though, pending the reintroduction of castration, a new and as yet unprefigurable type of soprano will be required to present this music as it should sound.

The accompanied recitative returns for Aspasia's soliloquy after Xiphares's departure. Thank God he's gone, she murmurs. The music switches from *andante* to *allegro* as she recalls how violently she has treated her beloved. She had better try, however hopelessly, to forget him. Her F major **Aria**, *Nel grave tormento* (a new text since Gasparini), **No. 14,** with flutes, oboes, horns and strings, is again an alternation between *adagio* and *allegro*, no longer a novelty, almost becoming a mechanical solution for textual dichotomy.

> My bosom is tormented, my peace is gone.
> Duty and love are at war in my soul.

The musical dichotomy is justified. The *adagio* begins with a glorious melody. The change from slow to quick tempo is bravely done and the dovetailing of contrasted sections bespeaks the masterly young craftsman, spirited as well as clever. Her second *allegro* outburst, in G minor, is especially stirring, and the orchestral postlude is full of spirit.

Now the scene changes to Mithridates's headquarters in a pavilion surrounded by trees. Mithridates is complimenting Ismene on the benefit of her presence, and the perilous position of Pharnaces as potential traitor. Arbates conducts the two sons before their father who announces his departure for an assault on Rome, Pompey and the Capitol. He dispatches Pharnaces with Ismene to set up their throne in Asia beyond the Euphrates. Pharnaces reveals his desire to remain in Nymphaeum and conclude a truce with Rome, whose terms Martius now arrives to dictate. This man is the proof that the king has sought. He imprisons Pharnaces and with appropriate threats sends Martius back to his own people. Ismene, called to confess her blushes for this unworthy son of Rome's great enemy, admits that she is blushing for an unworthy son of this king. She exhorts him in her **Aria No. 15**, *So quanto a te*, accompanied by strings alone (with continuo, of course), an *allegro* shortened *da capo* aria, with *andante* middle section. The main *allegro* is characteristic A major music of Mozart's youth; the key had not yet acquired for him those special qualities of eloquence that we shall discover later. The tunes are galant, bland, unassuming, the basses rather static, the textures quite plain, the vocal line supple and nicely fluent, with arpeggio divisions and galant snaps.

> I know how much you are displeased by the sins of an ungrateful son; but you must preserve your peace of mind.

The middle section in A minor is very short, pleasing, well contrasted, and propounds a simile on the lines of Metastasio:

> A transplanted branch will often flourish away from the trunk whence it sprang.

Having repeated part of her *allegro* Ismene leaves, with her retinue. Pharnaces now protests that he is not the only guilty party: Xiphares is as much to blame as himself. His **Aria** in D major, **No. 16**, *Son reo; l'error confesso*, with oboes, horns and strings, extends the confession with alternating sections of *adagio maestoso* and *allegro*. As in the earlier No. 12, the singer addresses two characters alternately.

> (*To Mithridates*) I am guilty, I admit; but Xiphares is no less to blame.
> (*To Xiphares*)   You should weep at my grief, not laugh.

The *adagio* is declamatory—it even begins with unaccompanied voice—the *allegro* more cantabile in character. The musical invention though fairly conventional is quite lively. Mozart's earlier version, longer and with trumpets in the orchestra, seems preferable, less polished perhaps but more interesting. At its conclusion Pharnaces is led away by Arbates and his guards.

Now Mithridates tells Xiphares to hide while he questions Aspasia: on this interview both their lives will depend. When she enters, Mithridates tells her how old and undesirable a husband he would be for her. He suggests instead that she should marry Xiphares; when she protests her duty to Mithridates he taunts her with her presumed infatuation for Pharnaces and her love of Rome. His cruel mockery pushes her into admitting that her only real affection is for Mithridates's more admirable son, Xiphares. The king now calls Xiphares from his hiding-place, declares himself betrayed, and promises revenge on them both in his angry *allegro* C major **Aria No. 17**, *Già di pietà mi spoglio*, with oboes, horns and strings.

> There is no pity in my breast for you, ungrateful creatures, only unbridled rage. As father and as lover I must have revenge.

This is a stirring concise *a-b-a* with rushing scales for strings, sudden fortes, slashed chords; the square phrases and lack of orchestral introduction give the music strong impetus, and harmonic contrast is provided in the *b* section with tremolo

87

unison excursions into minor keys. 'Perfidi!' Mithridates twice exclaims, hurling the word into the air with tragic impact before returning to the material of section *a*. Florid divisions are usually a feature of the *furibondo* aria but not when sung by Ettore.

Away he storms. Aspasia asks Xiphares to punish her guilt now with his sword, but he begs her to live, marry Mithridates and ascend his throne, leaving Xiphares to expiate their guilt with his own blood. In a recitative now accompanied by strings she refuses to wed the monster who could wish to slaughter his own son and the man she loves. Then, Xiphares proposes, let us die together. The orchestra, oboes, four horns and strings, launches into the A major **Duet, No. 18**, *Se viver non degg'io* which is to end the second act, and which prompted Sartorini's improbable wager. It consists of a balmy *adagio* in which each sings a verse alone, their voices only overlapping at the end; then follows an *allegro* in which they sing together in thirds and sixths and echo one another's mellifluous runs. You would hardly guess from the music that the lovers were discussing whether or not they should die together, or lamenting that cruel destiny is killing them with too much grief; but the duet makes an effective finish to the act and offers plentiful scope for a contrast of vocal virtuosity which is the real purpose of a duet in opera of this period. It was perhaps for this reason that Mozart scrapped an earlier setting of the duet which was longer (*adagio—allegro—adagio—allegro*) and had more shapely melodies but less bravura for the voices.

5

The third act begins in the Hanging Gardens of the palace. Mithridates is raging against his sons who shall both die, first Xiphares then Pharnaces. Aspasia hurries in and throws to the ground the crumpled fragments of the royal diadem, much to the king's surprise. Ismene, who has followed her, explains that Aspasia has attempted to strangle herself with the coronet but that the clasp broke.* She entreats Mithridates to forgive Aspasia as Ismene forgives Pharnaces. Ismene expounds her philosophy of clemency and long-suffering patience in a pleasant G major **Aria, No. 19**, *Tu sai per che m'accese*, accompanied by strings and marked *allegro* though (as Tagliavini points out) the music itself suggests an *andante*; these phrases, for example, are reminiscent of the *andantes* in Mozart's divertimenti:

* Racine borrowed this incident from Plutarch's description of the death of Monime, but made her confidante Phoedime the only witness. The scene, which opens Racine's Act V, immediately precedes the one in which Mithridates sends the cup of poison to her. Cigna-Santi's reordering of events may be thought advantageous to the shaping of this last act. It is more dramatic, too, to make her throw the diadem at the feet of the man who gave it to her. There is no particular gain in making Ismene tell the tale except that she is due another aria.

After all I have suffered, I still love him. You can punish him, but I bear with his offences and do not despair of conquering his heart.

The middle section (second sentence above) is a shade more chromatic and finds its way to E minor. In the reprise—all in the tonic—Ismene's runs are more elaborate than before, and even more surely demand a steady tempo.

Aspasia asks if Xiphares has already died. No, answers the king; and you can assure his survival by giving yourself to me. But even threats cannot change Aspasia's heart. Mithridates refuses to believe in Xiphares's innocence; they shall both be victims of his revenge.

At this moment Arbates enters announcing that the Roman army has landed and is at the city gates; the Nymphaean forces have been routed. Mithridates must escape or fight. The king sends Arbates back to the defences and bids Aspasia farewell: she shall not live to see him defeated. His last **Aria, No. 20**, *Vado incontro*, in F major, *allegro*, is a martial one, though scored without trumpets (oboes, horns and strings), and is a straightforward binary form structure,* full of dramatic vocal leaps and ringing top Cs.

> I go to meet my fate. But meanwhile an ungrateful soul shall precede me to the grave.

The first theme is fanfare-like, the second almost bouncy, the third sinuous and chromatic for 'l'ombra mia' (a rare instance of word-painting in *Mitridate*) though the same phrase of text is repeated almost at once for the most brilliant of the leaping passages.

This setting replaced a shorter, more energetic, less dignified version that slightly recalls Colas's *Diggi, daggi* in *Bastien und Bastienne*. Here already we find big leaps at 'l'ombra mia' but not the Cavalier's essential top Cs.

Aspasia is left alone, attempting to muster courage to meet her death. A Moor enters and presents her with a cup of poison to which she reacts with **No. 21**, a tripartite structure beginning with an orchestrally accompanied *allegro* **Recitative**, *Ah ben ne fui presaga*. This moves immediately from C to E flat major for a grand defiant musical gesture with a shudder at the end: the importance of the occasion is signalled by the momentary inclusion of oboes and horns (*recitativi accompagnati* in early Mozart are usually with strings only).

> Here is Mithridates's last gift to me. Are you afraid, my hand, to take the fatal goblet? No, take it and thank the giver who restores me my freedom in the grave.

The strings' commentary on these phrases is as apt as elsewhere and twice something more exceptional, in the C minor violin solos after the first sentence, and the soft,

---

* A second verse of text was not set by Mozart.

mysterious sustained chords during the last words. The orchestra moves from here directly into an *andante* for her **Cavatina**, *Pallid' ombre*, whose firmly shaped melody unfolds slowly and with real dignity from a low-lying first phrase to the climax on repeated high A flats.

> You wan shades of Elysium that know my ills, give me back all the good that I have lost.

The nobility of the vocal line, the aptness and pathos of the oboes' interjections, the delicately judged touch of E flat minor at bar 67, all denote a master of opera. As the cavatina ends the accompanied recitative is resumed.

> Come, drink it! Alas, what ice restrains my hand? [*Here Mozart asks for* tremolando *string chords.*] Perhaps even now Xiphares is drinking his death? [*The C minor sobbing recurs in a varied form, with added oboes and horns.*] No, it cannot be true; the gods always favour innocence and will defend so great a hero.

As she prepares to drink the poison Xiphares rushes in and dashes the goblet to the ground (in Racine's play it was Arbates). He is off to fight at his father's side and has brought soldiers to guard her during the battle. Let the gods ordain their destinies afterwards. Aspasia proclaims him a son worthy of a better father, and leaves with the soldiers—though the Milan libretto shows that first she sang an aria *Secondi il ciel* which Mozart seems not to have set; here Bernasconi may have drawn on Gasparini, though the extant key-scheme does not fit.

Xiphares remarks on the conflict within him between love and duty, and his desire to end a worthless life, at least dying the death of an innocent man. His **Aria, No. 22**, *Se il rigor d'ingrata sorte* is an *allegro agitato* in C minor with oboes, bassoons; horns and strings, a more heroic but still emotionally eloquent counterpart to Aspasia's G minor No. 4.

> If fate casts doubts on my loyalty, at least death will reveal the purity of my soul. I am tired of a life that makes me bear charges of perfidy.

The structure is ternary; all three sections use the same sinuous, darkly chromatic, syncopated material. By this stage in the composition Mozart was ceasing to write long formal *da capo* arias; this one is a mixture of *da capo* and sonata form, yet more concise than either.

The scene changes to the interior of a tower on the city walls. Here Pharnaces has been imprisoned, and is discovered in chains, sitting on a boulder. (And here Cigna-Santi diverges radically from Racine, inventing freely.) He laments the apparent failure of his fair hopes, then hears sounds of battle. A gap appears in the wall, and through it stream some Roman soldiers led by Martius, who unchains Pharnaces and gives him weapons. This, says Martius, is the Roman pact he had promised. Today Pharnaces will be made king of Nymphaeum. Martius now gets his **Aria, No. 23**, *Se di regnar*, a spirited military G major *allegro* in *a-b-c-b* form where *b* and *c* are variants of *a*. The accompaniment is for strings only. Martius has plenty of jolly bravura in his one moment of glory, and the vocal tessitura lies consistently high. Gasparo Bassano may have been a junior singer but Mozart must have admired him.

> If you want to rule, your wish is granted. You can decide if you want revenge for your wrongs.

The Romans run off to fight elsewhere. Pharnaces, in an accompanied recitative, now undergoes a change of heart: voices of nature stir within him, recalling him to his loyalties, banishing impious thoughts. 'Aspasia, Romans,' he cries, 'I detest you.' For this last **Aria, No. 24**, *Già dagli occhi* in E flat major with oboes, horns and strings, Mozart did observe a *da capo* scheme, though the middle section and partial reprise are missing in some sources and were probably omitted in performance.

> The veil is torn from my eyes. Vile impulses, I abandon you, and listen only to the dictates of my heart.

The orchestral texture is rich, chiefly for strings alone in the vocal sections, the vocal writing smooth and dignified (*Andante ma adagio*, says one copy), attentive to Cicognani's admired low register. The *allegretto* middle section, in which Pharnaces dwells on the path of glory and honour that he has chosen, helpfully introduces a change of pace, but does not achieve such inspiration that one would hesitate to adopt the shorter version.

The scene changes for the last time to show the courtyard of the palace with a porch through which can be seen the Roman fleet burning at sea in the distance. Mithridates lies wounded on a pallet constructed from shields; Xiphares, Arbates and soldiers are with him.

Mithridates wants no lamentation. If he dies, he dies victorious, and no other man's sword has wounded him (he has stabbed himself). He has, furthermore, witnessed the bravery of his faithful son Xiphares. Aspasia comes forward and is greeted tenderly by the dying king who gives her to Xiphares and regrets his past unkindness to her. Xiphares's first desire is to take vengeance on Pharnaces. But at this moment Ismene runs in with Pharnaces, absolving him of all guilt, explaining to Mithridates that it was Pharnaces who ensured victory by setting fire to the Roman fleet. The king embraces this son too, declares his joy, and is carried away by soldiers while the five remaining singers, all of them sopranos or altos, sing a brief concluding **Chorus** of 40 bars in block harmony, **No. 25**, *Non si ceda al Campidoglio* in which, *allegro* in D major, with oboes, horns, trumpets and strings, they affirm their resolve to pursue their war against the Romans.

6

The history of the composition of *Mitridate, rè di Ponto* is extensive and interesting as a well chronicled account of how an eighteenth-century opera was created. It must be doubted that Hasse was submitted to such labour, calumny and intrigue as befell Mozart in Milan; but every composer had to satisfy his principal singers, every newcomer show his audiences that he was worthy of his commission. The various preliminary versions of musical numbers give a fascinating demonstration of the young genius trying out different methods of flight, attempting to satisfy his singers as well as himself; in at least one number the earlier version is artistically more successful by modern standards.

There is an understandable proportion of dead wood in *Mitridate*, conventional galant or even old baroque music in it. But the greater freedom of *da capo* formulation shows Mozart working towards the untrammelled structural delights of his later, quite informal musical numbers: Nos. 4, 13 and 22 are particularly happy in their invention. Florid divisions are sparingly used, not automatically as earlier. And Aspasia's accompanied recitatives in No. 21 are altogether remarkable.

The score is uneven, the characterization spasmodic, and the music incomplete. No wonder *Mitridate* lacks performance in an age that busily exhumes the neglected works of great, and lesser, composers. But it could be performed* and, though no *Idomeneo*, would certainly give some pleasure if the singers were technically and artistically convincing. Granted expertise in florid technique the female roles and that of Mithridates (Martius too) are performable. A gifted young male alto can manage Pharnaces, though he needs a seamless vocal scale, strong in the low register, and a real legato technique. The male soprano parts, particularly that of Xiphares, cannot properly be represented by tenors or female sopranos in breeches. Mozart was writing for another sort of voice entirely, a brightly singing clarion instrument of infinite flexibility and agility that would vie successfully with any obbligato instrumentalist (e.g. the horn soloist in No. 13). Imagine the most brilliant counter-tenor you ever heard, transpose his vocal compass up at least a fifth in your mind, and you will guess at the stunning sounds Sartorini must have produced. It is not the agility but the timbre that modern singers cannot rival. Yet there are some normal male voices that can encompass this register and might, with practice, achieve euphonious results in male soprano music while the singer is still young. Perhaps it may happen within the lifetime of this book, and readers may yet savour the joys of *Mitridate* without the cruel work of the *coltello*.

* Since this chapter was written *Mitridate* has been produced in Salzburg and Düsseldorf/ Duisburg.

6 LA BETULIA LIBERATA

LA BETULIA LIBERATA

Azione Sacra in two parts

Text by

GIOVANNI METASTASIO

K. 74c (formerly K. 118)

OZIA (Ozias), son of Micah, Governor of Bethulia	TENOR
GIUDITTA (Judith) widow of Manasses, daughter of Merari	ALTO
AMITAL, a noble Israelite woman	SOPRANO
ACHIOR, Prince of the Ammonites	BASS
CABRI (Chabris) son of Gothomiel ⎱ rulers of Bethulia with Ozias	SOPRANO
CARMI (Charmis) son of Melchiel ⎰	SOPRANO
Bethulians	CHORUS

The text commissioned by Emperor Karl VI in 1734
The music commissioned by the Prince of Aragon in 1771

On their return journey to Salzburg from Milan after *Mitridate* Leopold and Wolfgang Mozart spent the day of 13 March in Padua, where Wolfgang played music in two houses and was commissioned by Don Giuseppe Ximenes, Prince of Aragon, to compose an oratorio for the forthcoming Lent season in Padua. Leopold told his wife that the commission could be executed at Wolfgang's leisure. It was decided that Mozart would use the old (1734) and popular oratorio libretto by Metastasio on the apocryphal subject of Judith and Holofernes. It will be remembered that Wolfgang had been given the complete works of Metastasio by Count Firmian. On 19 July, after their return to Salzburg, Leopold wrote to Count Pallavicini in Bologna that 'my son is composing an oratorio of Metastasio for Padua. . . . I shall send this oratorio, when we pass through Verona, to be copied in Padua, and later return from Milan to Padua to hear the rehearsal.'

The Mozarts left Salzburg on 13 August and passed through Verona. But they had no time to visit Padua on their return journey and indeed the oratorio seems not to have been performed. At Padua in the 1772 Lent season *La Betulia liberata* ('The Liberation of Bethulia') was indeed given; but the libretto published for the occasion names the composer as Giuseppe Callegari, a local musician—whose name, however, is crossed through in the city's surviving copy. The Prince of Aragon was a native Italian whose noble family had left Spain several generations earlier: he was one of those music-lovers, rare and eccentric for his time though nowadays in a majority, who adored the music of the past and promoted concerts devoted to it, but could not abide the music of his own time—he referred to contemporary works as *Tamburate* (drum-beating) and their composers, apart from some Germans, as deficient in knowledge of counterpoint. Perhaps he found Mozart's oratorio too modern in style, and hastily ordered the substitute by Callegari.*

Alfred Einstein supposed that Mozart's *Betulia liberata* was more likely performed in Salzburg—a sensible suggestion, but unconfirmed by local evidence (which is fairly copious about the music of Mozart).

The real enigma in the whole story is this: for which singers was Mozart writing? Vocal music, as earlier chapters in this book have shown, was always tailored to the individual accomplishments and artistic specialities of the singers engaged. Before embarking on the composition of arias (there are 12 in *La Betulia*) Mozart customarily met his singers, talked to them and heard them sing. Only then could he know what sort of music to write. Nor was oratorio a special case: for Mozart it meant Neapolitan oratorio, the tradition of Alessandro Scarlatti and Leonardo Leo, the best modern practitioner of which was the German composer

---

* We cannot rule out the possibility that Mozart had not completed the music by the time he reached Verona, but did so in Milan while waiting for the *Ascanio* libretto (we know he was composing on the day before it arrived). The Prince of Aragon, fearing that the commission would not be fulfilled in time, could have countermanded it at this time. But it is curious that the Mozarts' letters do not mention *La Betulia liberata*.

J. H. Hasse—strong, rather sensational subject-matter, a bare minimum of theological precept, but a good number of choruses (not too difficult) and carefully detailed orchestral writing. Ensembles were favoured, and orchestral recitatives; but the musical brunt fell upon virtuoso arias in contrasted moods—just as in *opera seria*. Mozart followed this plan (rather than the Salzburg-type oratorio of Eberlin which had been his model in *Die Schuldigkeit*—he was alas to discover Handel too late to revive that epic style of oratorio) though he shunned duets and trios in favour of the Gluck-derived chorus with solo interludes, as in Nos. 4, 6 and 16 of *Betulia*. We can only guess what vocal personalities he envisaged when composing the arias in *La Betulia liberata*. The only realistic suggestion I can make is that he composed in terms of a Salzburg cast which he could readily assemble for a performance on his return from Italy.

Mozart did not forget *La Betulia liberata*. In July 1784 he wrote to his sister from Vienna asking for the score, some parts of which he thought he could use again for a performance of the same work which he had been asked to compose anew for the *Wiener Tonkünstlersozietät*. The whole idea sounds curious and unpractical, and once again no performance seems to have taken place—or at least not in Vienna, Leopold Sonnleitner was careful to specify when questioned about it. But after Mozart's death his widow offered the publisher André two texts for numbers added by her husband to *Betulia*—they were an opening chorus *Qual fiero caso* and a vocal quintet version of Achior's *Te solo adoro* (no. 13—Beethoven also set these words three times).*

Music for these added movements has not survived; and significantly Mozart mentioned nothing about them in his *Verzeichnis meiner Werke*, as he otherwise did when he added to existing works. There exists in Vienna a copy of Metastasio's libretto as set by Florian Gassmann, with manuscript alterations for a performance in 1786 which the then owner Heinrich Henkel (an André *protégé*) claimed were made by Metastasio himself for Mozart. But Metastasio died in 1782. Once again we are up a *cul de sac*. The only unblocked road is Mozart's autograph score which exists and proves that the oratorio is authentic.

2

The story of *La Betulia liberata* is most readily to be found in the Apocrypha of the Bible, as the Book of Judith which was written in the second century B.C. Nebuchadnezzar, king of Assyria in 350 B.C., had declared war on anyone who would not accept his divinity. His armies did great damage under Holofernes, chief captain of his host. But the children of Israel in Judea held out and, taking to the mountains, prepared for siege. Holofernes, learning of this, demanded information about this enemy. So Achior, 'the leader of all the children of Ammon', told him the history of the Israelites, with special reference to their troubles with Pharaoh in Egypt. 'And whilst they sinned not before their God, they prospered because God that hateth iniquity was with them. But when they departed from the way which he appointed them, they were destroyed in many battles very sore. . . . And now they are returned to their God. . . . If there is any error in this people,

---

* Metastasio's text was also set by many other composers, e.g. Jommelli, Anfossi, and Salieri.

and they sin against their God, we will go up and overcome them. But if there is no lawlessness in their nation, let my Lord now pass by, lest their Lord defend them, and we shall be a reproach before all the earth.'

Holofernes regarded this as defeatist propaganda, offensive to the accepted Assyrian notion 'Who is God but Nebuchadnezzar?' So he 'commanded his servants . . . to take Achior . . . to Bethulia and deliver him into the hands of the children of Israel'. Achior was made welcome by the children of Israel in Bethulia and their rulers, 'Ozias the son of Micah, of the tribe of Simeon, and Chabris the son of Gothoniel, and Charmis the son of Melchiel'. Holofernes then began an assault on Bethulia and, acting on good advice, began by getting possession of the fountain which supplied Bethulia with water. The Israelites in Bethulia began to die of thirst or lose heart and told Ozias that they should surrender. But Ozias said, 'Brethren, let us yet endure five days in the which space the Lord our God shall turn his mercy unto us.'

This, in brief, is the background to the oratorio, as noted in the Book of Judith to which Metastasio's text remains, except in one trifling respect, scrupulously faithful. He sets the action of the drama entirely within Bethulia.

3

Mozart's setting begins dramatically and dynamically with an (assumable) *allegro* in D minor, the first of the **Overture**'s three sections (it is an Italian *sinfonia*). Some have claimed this as his first characteristic use of a key later to be one of his favourites. It is scored for oboes, bassoons, four horns (two in D, two in F) trumpets (no drums) and strings. There is certainly a spine-chilling quality of urgency about the opening theme—if it is taken at the proper *allegro* suggested by the crochet and quaver movement (otherwise it plods disastrously), especially when one can hear the awesome contributions of horns and trumpets and the anguished wailing thirds of oboes, as well as the quaver scrubbing of lower strings below this tune:

1

This can be recognized as the mood in which K. 466, the D minor piano concerto, opens, the mood of *Corriamo, fuggiamo* in *Idomeneo*, of the *Don Giovanni* overture and the Statue's arrival at dinner.* Mozart had already composed some different but equally striking D minor music, especially in No. 11 of *Galimathias musicum* and in the second trio of the minuet of K. 7; already he knew the meaning of D minor as he had inherited it from his predecessors. After the phrases quoted above, the music of the overture becomes rather stiff, indeed baroque in manner. At bar 17 the horns keep the interest alive as the music moves towards F major, only, however, to relapse, without an intervening second subject into E major (a surprise) on the way back to D minor for a reprise. There are some spectacular leaps for

* Does it not also suggest the beginning of Mendelssohn's violin concerto, a tone higher in E minor?

violins (from bar 57). The cadence is interrupted to bring forward a slower section still in D minor with a theme imitatively exposed (to gratify the Prince?), passing to one of Mozart's typically declamatory phrases of the *Tradito!* type, then to a weaker consequent. The music swerves to F minor, suitably, but much too quickly swerves back; this happens again with feints at B flat minor and C minor— the keys are suggested but not established—Mozart did not think it correct to bring out such intense keys more prominently. We are kept on tenterhooks but are never grabbed. There are some nice touches of syncopation in the reprise which leads directly into the overture's final section, a *presto*, again in D minor, and thematically linked to Ex. 1. Again there is no new second subject and the presentation of the main theme is rather clumsy but its consequent (bar 116) is vivid, like a duet, and there is some development. The theme remains active through the overture's closing bars, giving weight to the formal cadence which accordingly sounds more than usually involved with what has just been going on. Mozart was only fifteen and this is striking music for a boy of his age.

Ozias begins his first recitative at once, the orchestra's D minor brightening to the continuo's D major which accompanies him. He tells his subjects to abandon the fear expressed in the overture; where there is doubt there can be no faith nor positive action. He expands on this, *allegro aperto* in B flat major, in **No. 1**, his first **Aria**, *D'ogni colpa*, with two oboes, two horns, and strings.

> The greatest guilt of all is an excess of impious fear, an insult to God's compassion.
>
> Without hope one cannot love or have faith. For faith, hope and love are three torches which blaze together; none of them shed light if all are not lit.

This is a spacious, heroic aria in the abbreviated *da capo* form standard for this type of music and necessary because many of the first sections are themselves sonata movements with double exposition (as in concerto first movements). So here we have a swaggering, almost strong first subject, perhaps inspired by Ozias's previous sentence ('to the despairing steersman every storm, however slight, is fatal')—

2

a cunningly detailed consequent (much variety of movement and a tinge of B flat minor), a gentler second subject which leans towards G minor and C minor, and a flamboyant coda group full of trills and galant slashes (miscalled Scotch Snaps) such as we find in concerto coda groups (e.g. K. 364 for violin and viola). Ozias manages to turn Ex. 2 into a singable theme; there is a new, technically felicitous transition to the second subject (bars 29–38). He has a long and splendid florid passage in the coda group, lying robustly above the stave and presupposing a tenor of strength as well as precision. The development section does develop, beginning with a new, furtive idea in F minor and ending on the verge of C minor. The reprise is drastically and inventively achieved: it includes more brilliant divisions and a cadenza. All this has taken 135 bars. The middle section of the aria begins in E flat as though in accompanied recitative, with rocketing violin arpeggios that refer to the 'three torches' mentioned above. Soon, however, a sense of stagnation begins to protrude; but this section is worth including for the spicy orchestral return to the *da capo* which begins with the recapitulation of the second subject.

The despairing Bethulians now voice their complaints through the voices of Chabris (a male soprano) and Amital★ (a female soprano, later to emerge as the negative, pessimistic counterpart of heroic Judith). They sing, in recitative, of the hunger, looting, exhaustion and general fatalism in the city.

Chabris reminds us that this is an improving moral entertainment by philosophizing on the motives of present anxiety. *Ha quel virtù*, his **Aria, No. 2** with strings only, is short but impressive.

> The fiercest heart must be humbled to see such misery.
> Compassion demands that we grieve to see others pale-faced and weeping.

The urgent triplet quavers in the bass and uneasy G minor tune suggest a quicker tempo than *moderato*, something more like the mood of the overture than like Barbarina's Pin Aria in *Figaro*—the violin trills and scales suggest anger, the singer's big leaps express passion, the turn to B flat minor at bar 28 conveys intensity. The phrases sound short-breathed if the tempo is slow.

Ozias replies with a reminder of the Lord's goodness to the Children of Israel. For Chabris this is less considerable than the fact that the city's water-supplies have been dried up by Holofernes. (Chabris presumably leaves the stage at this point.) Amital presses their cause more subjectively: she is a mother and must watch her children die because Ozias insists on prolonging an unnecessary war.

Amital's **Aria, No. 3** in E flat major, *Non hai cor*, with oboes, bassoons, horns and strings, may be considered a female companion-piece to its predecessor.

> Everyone, even our enemies, must weep to see how we suffer.

This short *allegro* aria, with *andante* middle section and shortened *da capo*, is more declamatory and formal. The repeated cries of 'Non hai cor' communicate vivid passion, and in the middle section the syncopatory metrical dislocations of the second violins perfectly suggest despair and exhaustion (C minor moves towards G minor). But Mozart is audibly less moved than Metastasio's Amital—she is not, until much later, an interesting character.

From such barbarous foes Ozias hopes for no peace; Amital proposes that living coexistence is better than certain death, and claims that she voices the will of all Bethulia (the chorus supports her with a cry 'To arms'). Ozias only asks that surrender be deferred for five days, and calls his subjects to prayer.

Mozart, in **No. 4**, a C minor *adagio* **Prayer** for Ozias and Chorus, seems to invoke the example of Gluck.

> Have pity, Lord, if you are angry. You punish the guilty, but when your
> devotees suffer, the ungodly ask where is their God?

★ Not a biblical personage.

Pietà se irato sei is formally and inventively superb music, precociously so in the inspiration of the offbeat second violins at the beginning, the votive atmosphere of the chords for oboes, horns and divided violas, in the melancholy of the cadences, in the *pizzicati* for Ozias's solo entry, the heart-stopping interrupted cadence at 'Dov'è?', and in the rightness of the block-harmonic choral writing (not dull but deeply imposing). The effects are unoriginal, the effect sublime.

Chabris enters asking who is the intruder now approaching. Amital recognizes Judith by her dishevelled hair and dark widow's weeds; she has been indulging herself in four years' mourning, but has interrupted them because of the crisis. Judith breaks momentously into the discussion. Although her clothing is dark and dingy the radiance of her presence is proclaimed by the halo of string tone which surrounds her words. Her importance is the more unmistakable since she is a female alto, rare in Mozart's day (when elsewhere he wrote for a lady in that register she was—*pace* Dorabella—elderly and, for politeness' sake, was still referred to as soprano). Judith is young, beautiful, rich and indomitably courageous. At once she begins to berate the Bethulians for cowardice, and Ozias for promising a term to their defence of the city. The thought of these five paltry days pulls the strings back to *andante* and a plangent tune, imitatively continued as her diatribe proceeds. When she scolds Ozias the music turns *allegro*, rather cheerfully—she warms to her task, but measures the pace of her denigration to *andante* for later outbursts. A formidable female indeed—she had to be a contralto and probably an eighteenth-century Clara Butt.*

Disappointing therefore to hear the suave introductory strains *andante* in F major of her (shortened *da capo*) **Aria No. 5**, *Del pari infeconda*, with flutes, horns and strings, for they are devastatingly bland. The suave opening tune is doubled by dulcet flutes (their only appearance), the second subject serenely aqueous with its gentle middle voice, the vocal divisions purposeful rather than brilliant. The middle section, *Si acquista baldanza*, has a pleasant, popping violin figuration that looks forward to the first appearance in *Così fan tutte* of the frivolous Dorabella. But this is not the great mother figure of Judith. Metastasio's text is a simile.

> The bank of a river is equally barren if it is flooded or dry. Over-confidence is as dangerous as excessive timidity.

Ozias is much impressed by Judith's divinely inspired wisdom, and Chabris admits his error. When Ozias asks God's forgiveness Judith tells her compatriots to trust in Him and suffer what must be. She explains that this is how Abraham, Isaac and their other forebears found favour with the Lord; the others suffered horrible deaths. She herself has conceived a grand design for the salvation of them all. She will not reveal it, but tells Ozias to meet her at the city gate when the sun sets.

---

* Brigid Brophy, in an interesting article entitled 'The Young Mozart' (contributed to *Opera 66*) which throws out, Catherine-wheel-fashion, a quantity of incendiary and illuminating sparks (many of them characteristically irrelevant), claims that Judith, Mozart's only heroic contralto role, is a *figura* of the Virgin Mary. All available evidence indicates that, on the few occasions when Mozart thought musically about Our Lady, he conceived her as a soprano. Judith is neither blessed nor a virgin: she is a predatory tigress fighting for her young. If Mozart wrote for a Salzburg cast he may aptly have designed the part of Judith for Maria Anna Braunhofer who had sung Justice in *Die Schuldigkeit*, a similar part, as well as Giacinta in *La finta semplice*.

Meanwhile they must all pray for God's help, which they do in **No. 6**, a repeat of **No. 4**.

Chabris announces Charmis's arrival (Amital characteristically deplores his absence from watch on the city walls). Charmis (another male soprano) has found one of the enemy, the Prince Achior, tethered to a tree by the hostile force. Achior explains that Holofernes has condemned him to this fate for having dared to suggest that throughout history the children of Israel have been sheltered and protected by their God. Holofernes, who knows no God but Nebucchadnezzar, promptly banished him to share the Bethulians' fate. Asked if Holofernes can be so cruel, Achior describes him in his C major **Aria, No. 7**:

> He is terrible to look at and barbarous in behaviour, yet he regards himself as a god.

This aria, *Terribile d'aspetto*, includes parts not only for oboes, horns and strings but also for the old-fashioned clarini which Mozart alas uses dully. The pace of the music is a gawky *allegro*, full of dynamic contrast, with a fanfare-like first subject and a stealthy second group. Back-knowledge suggests that at this point we are not to take Achior at more than face-value; for the moment he is an unsophisticated heathen who has had enough of his ex-boss.

Ozias nevertheless offers hospitality to Achior, then dismisses his companions since Judith is approaching.* We have now descended to the city gates. Ozias is astonished to see her dressed in her most sumptuous clothes, decked with rich jewels, generously perfumed and exquisitely hair-styled. To his horror she announces that she intends to leave the city unattended (later we discover that, as in the Apocrypha, she takes a female servant with her). Ozias, trusting her, wishes her a safe journey and return.

Judith bids the city farewell in **No. 8**, an *allegro* **Aria** in G major with oboes, horns and strings, *Parto inerme e non pavento*.

> I go unarmed and unafraid. God will accompany me and I shall be victorious.

This is a busy, rushing aria, full of semiquaver runs for the violins, with an expressive G minor-minded second subject. Judith's first entry is splendidly dramatic, on a sustained *mesa di voce* (as if for Manzuoli). Again the vocal part, though quite agile, is not supplied with written-out divisions. The *adagio* middle section uses oboes to suggest the twilight atmosphere, and is melodically generous. There is a clumsy key-switch to the da capo which begins from half-way.

As Judith leaves, the chorus begins **No. 9** (presumably off-stage), *Oh prodigio!* This **Chorus**, *allegro* in E flat major, with oboes, horns and strings, is grandly imagined, with its momentous dotted rhythms for violins and syncopations (majesty in the vein of K. 503), and its plunging or soaring melodic leaps.

> How astonishing that a woman should assume public responsibility, and not tell our ruler what she is doing; should dress herself so splendidly yet nobody doubts her virtue.

* Miss Brophy makes much of Mozart's 'brilliant' response to the sunset scene. It consists of plain, formal common chords. She must be thinking of the middle section in No. 8.

The choral writing is unadventurous, yet the piece is sublime—the harmony and dramatic timing see to this. There is a superb pause near the end at 'di tai portenti'.

4

Part Two begins with an extended theological discussion between Achior and Ozias. Metastasio had evidently realized how little his oratorio had to do with religious instruction, and therefore made up for previous shortcomings in this recitative scene which the less godly could abbreviate if they wished. Ozias, we infer, has just made some rude remark about polytheists and this, in the context of his general kindness and culture, has surprised Achior. Ozias explains his inflexibility as zeal: Achior respects Jehovah but so intelligent a person must not be allowed to rest until he actually worships Him as the only God. Ozias expounds the historical tradition of Jehovah-worship but this means nothing to a man from another culture—a sympathetic, broadminded stroke by Metastasio. Ozias now takes the Socratic standpoint, appealing to reason: there is clearly a motivating power behind everything in creation, therefore it must be what we call God, and equally therefore perfect, unique, limitless in capacity and understanding, and so one God, not many as Achior suggests—if there were many gods, each distinguished by special abilities, then none would be perfect, so none would be venerable.

Achior grants the skill of this argument but not the cogency of its corollary. How can anybody worship a God whose nature is unimaginable? Ozias counters that a conceivable deity is automatically imperfect; he can be described as good without reference to quality, great without reference to quantity. But as to His visibility you can no more see Him than the sun's rays which warm you every day. This is as solidly argued a piece of libretto-writing as anybody could find anywhere (Schoenberg devoted *Moses und Aron* to it). Mozart sets it dully, with only a moment or so of *frisson*. Doubtless he perceived the religious importance of the scene, but he was waiting, like us, for the **Aria**.

No. 10, Ozias's *Se Dio veder tu vuoi*, with oboes, horns, and strings marked *andante*, is warm, sensuous, but essentially the young Mozart.

> You can see God in everything, even in your own breast. If you still do not understand where he is, then tell me where he is not.

The A major of the aria is honeyed and galant, mellifluously written for an attractive tenor voice. The middle section in D has a more tranquil atmosphere.

Achior finds these arguments persuasive but not wholly convincing. Ozias explains that he is like a neglected lyre which needs much time and work before it plays in tune again.

We expect an aria at this point but it does not eventuate. Instead Amital enters, worrying once again about morale in Bethulia, yesterday so high, now relapsed into quarrels or silence.

Her *allegro* **Aria, No. 11** with oboes, horns and strings, is yet another Metastasian simile.

> The pilot who, in a big storm, does not sweat or speak is near to shipwreck. The invalid who does not groan is near to death.

Quel nocchier is a good, bold aria in B flat, another heroic piece of the type parodied in *Come scoglio*; the singer's tenuto F at bar 32 is particularly reminiscent. The storm is strongly portrayed in the violins at bar 5, and other felicities will readily be found, such as the sinuous chromatic figurations at the start of the development section, or the urgent string figures in the *andante* middle section, or the vivid gasps on the word 'sospirar' (even if they were all too modish in those days).

Ozias tells her to go on hoping. Amital infers that he still puts his trust in Judith whom she regards as a mad deceiver. Outside the soldiers are heard running to arms. Chabris enters, warning Ozias of a hubbub by the city gates. He is pushed aside by Judith whose re-entry has the grandeur and self-assurance of Brünnhilde in the last scene of *Götterdämmerung*. She is in full command of the situation: the noise of soldiers was her doing, and what she has done requires praise to the Lord. Holofernes has been slain by her own hand. The strings support her as she narrates her experiences since leaving Bethulia. She went to the enemy camp, was conducted to Holofernes (undulating violins) who received her kindly, though she found his face devoid of pity, and invited her to supper with him. Wine flowed freely; one by one his followers retired and finally she was left alone with her intoxicated host. (Bold enterprise, interjects Amital, who is instantly put in her place by Judith's 'All enterprises are easy when the heart is inspired', matched by the loud-soft dynamics of the strings.) Half-way through the night (a beautiful descending string phrase) Judith observed her insensible foe and arose (vigorous but subdued ascending string arpeggios), prayed for divine assistance (a telling melody in E minor, full of courageous leaps), and then drew the sword hanging above his bed (the string melody dramatically continues), and with two blows decapitated him—two ascending scales for violins. Here, she announces, is his terrible head divided from its shoulders (a bloody shudder by violins)—but she is not yet ready to remove it from the bag into which her servant placed it. The strings again respond melodiously as she relates how, the deed accomplished, she gave thanks to God. The company reacts incredulously. Judith now exhibits her trophy as proof. Achior recognizes it instantly, and falls to the ground unconscious —which Judith regards as a promising omen for his future spiritual development. She explains her brutal comment in **No. 12**, her D major **Aria** with oboes, horns and strings, *Prigioner che fa ritorno*:

> (*Adagio*) The prisoner just released from gaol cannot bear to look at the light and has to hide his eyes. (*Andante*) But soon he recovers, and enjoys the sunshine.

This is again a shortened *da capo* aria whose main section is thoroughly extended. The main tune is a galant tag, familiar to us from many other Mozart works, but in its day borrowed from earlier examples now forgotten.

3

I have written out the thematic appoggiaturas which later occur in quantity (the New Mozart Edition, usually scrupulous in this respect, is careless here). The first group of ideas is carefully worked out, with beautiful string textures, the second only introduced in the solo exposition (at bar 30). The vocal line is agile, and may suggest Donna Elvira, but once again includes no rapid divisions—implying that Mozart may have been catering not for an unaccomplished mezzo but for someone like Manzuoli (see *Ascanio*) who would supply the missing graces. The *andante* middle section is more gentle and pastoral in feeling. There is a new return to the first section.

Achior recovers from his faint, totally converted to the worship of the God of Abraham. He expresses this transformation in **No. 13**, the *andante* F major **Aria** *Te solo adoro*.

> I adore you alone, infinite mind, fountain of truth.

It is a short, minuet-like and rather Handelian aria with string accompaniment, expressive and carefully elaborated, especially admirable for its confidently moving bass line.

Ozias praises Judith's beneficial effect on Achior, and Amital entreats God's forgiveness for her sinful cowardice—all this would go well as part of a Quintet.

Amital expatiates in **No. 14**. Dramatically her **Aria**, in E major with strings only, is quite dispensable, and the *cognoscenti* would doubtless complain of her musical sighs—so *cliché* for them: but *Con troppo rea viltà* is warmly expressive, pleasantly varied in mood with its fresh pastoral *andante* opening and more reflective *adagio* contrasting group.

> My spirit offended you with wicked baseness when I despaired of your help.
> Have mercy, O Lord, for my repentant heart has measured its own error with its remorse.

The tempi alternate vividly, and the string writing is always attractive. Are the vocal leaps rather automatic here? Mozart seems less than engaged in the significance of the piece, though ready to parade through the necessary motions.

Chabris and Charmis offer praise to Jehovah. Charmis tells the tale of the Assyrians' flight and slaughter and tells Ozias to listen to the sounds of gloom outside.

He describes them in **No. 15**, his F minor **Aria**, *Quei moti che senti*, a simple but strongly imagined *allegro*, full of dramatic feeling, scored with oboes, bassoons, horns and strings. Several arias ago we may have thought it was time to make an end, but here is one aria which must not be omitted. It is superbly scored with striking wind chords, exciting scrubbed strings, nice harmonic excursions, and powerful accents.

> The sounds you hear in the night are the moans of our conquered enemies.
> Fear has made our swords redundant.

They all congratulate Judith until, with imperious finality, she turns their praises to the Lord who alone is praiseworthy.

The inhabitants of Bethulia begin the final **Chorus** of praise to the Almighty for the destruction of the enemy, **No. 16**, *Lodi al gran Dio*, surprisingly accompanied only by oboes, horns and strings (we had surely expected the whole orchestra at this point). The ritornello theme is big and solid in the galant manner, extremely noble. The choral writing cultivates block harmony so as to support the violins' rapid motion. E minor is a key seldom found in Mozart, here perhaps required by use of the old plainchant *In exitu Israel* as the thematic foundation (later it was to occur in the *Te Decet* of his *Requiem*). At *Venne l'assirio* Judith has a solo in heroic contrast. The alternations between *tutti* and *solo* become more and more elaborate and ecstatic until the fourth chorus moves to D major for a closing *allegro*, rhythmically propelled with great gusto.

5

Some readers may wonder why I have troubled to include a chapter on *La Betulia liberata* which is not an opera but an oratorio. In four words, because it is musicdrama. The music as well as the text presupposes stage presentation, at least as much as in Handel's oratorios: Mozart set Metastasio's text with the technique and imagination of an opera composer, however young. It developed his creative sensibility as a musical dramatist in particular ways, and has bearing on later works which he composed for the theatre. In one respect it is unique as Mozart's only heroine-opera. But this was implicit in the story which had been used for oratorio by earlier composers. The heroine-opera, as a concept, was impossible until the age of the castrato was over.

Let us consider it as the immediate successor of *Mitridate*. Mozart's sense of key, particularly of tonal equilibrium, is still fallible; the structure of arias is less diversified, less carefully considered; the accompanied recitatives, especially for Judith, are much more imaginative though in the secco recitatives there are moments of more interest, such as grew increasingly numerous in later works, starting with *Ascanio in Alba*. Illustrative and expressive touches are more numerous in *La Betulia* than before. The orchestral writing, though scrupulously elaborated from time to time, is seldom striking and never positively brilliant as it was here and there in *Mitridate*. The vocal writing likewise makes no excessive demands, unless on Ozias; but it is often effective by simple expressiveness. All this is explained by the presumable fact that Mozart was composing *La Betulia liberata* in the dark, without certain knowledge who could perform it or how accomplished any of them would be. His *prima donna*, Judith, is a female Manzuoli who must portray youth and beauty yet has a mezzo-soprano range which is scrupulously catered for. She is a competent vocalist, but Mozart writes no florid divisions for her. Ozias is a tenor of the Ettore type (see *Mitridate*), but the other roles have no virtuoso demands made on them, apart from some leaps; what a contrast with *Mitridate* where Mozart had to rewrite many arias several times! The choral music is simple, the orchestral writing, especially for horns and trumpets, could be managed by decent hacks without strain. All this contradicts Mozart's normal practice, yet the music is often expressively deep and sometimes bold. The deducible conclusion is that he designed the piece for unknown provincial musicians who would include one forceful vocal personality. Because of this he knew that his music must make some effect however poor the performers: so he was obliged to seek un-virtuoso effects, not only for slow cantabile arias, like some in earlier operas, but in arias ranging through every mood. He had to rely on his own invention, not on interpretative skill, and this expanded his creative range. The best numbers in *La Betulia liberata* are those for chorus, Nos. 4 and 9, the overture (a significant exercise in thematic integration), and the accompanied recitatives, though the arias are not without some splendours. This feat of musical self-assertion worked well for Mozart's expanding genius, just because he was not tailoring the music for specific performers. More than the other operas which surround it *La Betulia* will impress an audience in modern performance, especially on stage. It must have been a daunting task but the result on the whole pleases well—though we may wish nowadays to make some wholesale cuts, especially towards the end. Liberated from rigid convention Mozart, however hard pressed, was learning how he would compose his great operas. That they did not eventuate during his boyhood will surprise nobody.

7 ASCANIO IN ALBA

ASCANIO IN ALBA

Festa teatrale in due atti

Text by

ABBATE GIUSEPPE PARINI

K. 111

VENUS	SOPRANO
ASCANIO (Ascanius), her grandson fathered by Aeneas	MALE SOPRANO
SILVIA, a nymph descended from Hercules	SOPRANO
ACESTE (Acestes), priest of Venus	TENOR
FAUNO (Faunus), shepherd	MALE SOPRANO
Geniuses ⎫	
Shepherds ⎬	CHORUS
Shepherdesses ⎭	

First performance: 17 October 1771, Teatro Regio Ducal, Milan

As a result of *Mitridate* Wolfgang Mozart received three further commissions. For the Teatro Regio Ducal in Milan he was to write the first opera for the 1773 carnival season; this was *Lucio Silla*. For Padua he was to compose 'at leisure' an *azione sacra* or oratorio, *La Betulia liberata*. In the nearer future there was the forthcoming wedding in Milan of the Archduke Ferdinand, third son of the Emperor Franz I and the Empress Maria Theresa, with the Princess Maria Ricciarda Beatrice d'Este, only daughter of the Prince of Modena. For this event operas were commissioned from J. A. Hasse and Mozart, Count Firmian (see p. 75) acting as the Empress's agent. Hasse, as the senior composer, was assigned the *opera seria*, while the *festa teatrale* went to Mozart. This latter, also described as *serenata*, was conventionally placed between the acts of a serious opera, as an intermezzo (Pergolesi's *La serva padrona* is the most familiar example). But for this particularly grand occasion a full-scale work was projected. It was to be an allegorical idealized representation of this royal marriage, designed to disguise the fact that it had been arranged for political ends, and that the bride was no beauty.

Mozart's literary collaborator was the Abbé Giuseppe Parini, professor of rhetoric in Milan and highly eminent among the poets of his day; he had translated Racine's *Mithridate*, the literary source of Mozart's previous opera. Parini devised his libretto during the summer of 1771, perhaps borrowing his theme, which deals with the fictitious marriage of Ascanius and a nymph named Silvia, from Dr Claudio Nicolo Stampa (1700–80). The text had to be approved by the Emperor in Vienna, and it was not delivered to Mozart until 29 August, by which time Wolfgang and his father had already spent eight days in Milan on their return there from Salzburg. Mozart promptly composed the overture and the first two musical numbers. At this stage he could complete all the choruses, the ballets, the recitatives, but could not compose the arias until he had met the principal soloists and decided with them how their vocal accomplishments would best be displayed in this context. Parini, however, had second thoughts about what he had written and requested the return of the libretto which Mozart sent back on 5 September. It is probable that by then Mozart had already written much of the recitative, since there are numerous divergences between the text in the autograph score and that in the printed libretto —which suggests that when Parini sent back the revised text Mozart never bothered to alter the texts in his score. On 7 September, having sent the libretto away, he was busy writing the ballet music: of the eight movements only the bass part survives. The ballet music was complete and in rehearsal by 13 September, by which time all the recitatives were done, as well as (said Leopold Mozart) eight choruses of which five involved dancing. As will be shown later, only three choruses included ballet in the finished opera, and several of the choruses have identical music.

By now the solo singers must have arrived, since Mozart himself said on 21 September that he only had two more arias to compose, and two days later all the music was finished and the first rehearsal of recitatives was held. The singers were not a celebrated collection, with the exception of Giovanni Manzuoli, the Florentine male soprano whom Mozart had met in London in 1764. Manzuoli then gave him some free singing lessons, and was cited by Daines Barrington as the model Mozart should take for the impromptu vocal improvisation about which Barrington reported (see p. 9). Mozart and Manzuoli had met again in Florence in April 1770 (see p. 75). Burney wrote that Manzuoli was 'the most powerful and voluminous soprano that had been heard on our stage since time of the Farinelli, and his manner of singing was grand and full of taste and dignity'.

Chorus rehearsals began on 27 September, full rehearsals on the next day—there were five in all (it is interesting to compare such information with rehearsal details of modern operas). The royal wedding took place on the 15th, and was followed by a concert and a banquet with music. On the 16th Hasse's *Ruggiero* was performed —it was his last opera and had a text by Metastasio. *Ascanio in Alba* had its première on the 17th in the evening, at the Teatro Regio Ducal (burned down in 1825 and replaced by La Scala). It was repeated on four later evenings (19, 24, 27 and 28 October—these last two dates are not perfectly authenticated—a performance on the 29th was certainly cancelled due to the illness of Signora Girelli). Leopold Mozart gleefully noted that *Ascanio* had put Hasse's *Ruggiero* in the shade. He professed sorrow at this verdict, but not very convincingly. Parini, not an un-prejudiced reporter, chronicles that 'this second production met the gratitude of princes and public by its noble and varied simplicity'. The scenery was particularly admired.

Mozart and his father remained in Milan until early December. They were entertained by Count Firmian and by old Hasse (who wrote about Wolfgang, 'I do love him infinitely; he is certainly marvellous for his age'), and were received by the seventeen-year-old Archduke who would have liked to appoint Wolfgang Mozart to his musical staff; Maria Theresa would not hear of it. Leopold noted that the bridal couple seemed happy: Beatrice had such a sweet nature and good heart that everybody loved her, and even her husband was reconciled to her plainness.

2

The provenance of Parini's text is summarized in a note which prefaces the original libretto.

'It is known that Ascanius, famous son of Aeneas, went for reasons of state to dwell in a delectable part of old Latium; built a city there to which he gave the name Alba; took a wife there, governed a people and originated the Albanians.

'It is likewise known that Hercules travelled and lived for some time in that vicinity.

'The similarity of these historical and poetic data gave rise to the allegorical fable of the following work.'

Ascanius is known to have built Alba Longa in 1152 B.C., and transferred the seat of his kingdom thither from Lavinium. Whether he married there, and whom, is less certain; he is only credited with one son Iulus, born of an anonymous mother in Lavinium.

There is a story that Hercules, while returning to Mycenae with Geryon's cattle, passed Mount Albanus near modern Rome and, collecting the inhabitants of the district, settled them in the country now called Albania. Hercules is also believed to have killed King Faunus of Latium and fathered Latinus on Faunus's widow (here is doubtless the source of the name of Parini's shepherd, just as the priest Acestes derives his name from the Sicilian king who helped Aeneas to bury old Anchises). It is presumably in this sense that Parini claims Silvia as *ninfa del sangue d'Ercole*, a Latin descended from Latinus; her name would link her with Rhea Silvia, mother of Romulus and Remus, perhaps also with Silvius who was Ascanius's step-brother by Aeneas's marriage with Lavinia, and who succeeded Ascanius as king of Alba. It was important that Silvia should descend from Hercules since the Princess Maria Beatrice's father was Duke Hercules (Ercole) III of Modena, just as Venus, grandmother of Ascanius, would be seen as an allegorical parallel to the Empress Maria Theresa.

3

The prominence of the chorus in *Ascanio* is made clear from the start. Mozart begins the *serenata* with an Italian overture in three sections, *allegro-andante-allegro*, makes the second of these a dance, and firmly involves the chorus in the third section.* Mozart himself drew attention to this structural scheme, though in the score only the first of the three sections is labelled Overture. Marked *allegro assai*, and set for flutes, oboes, horns, trumpets, timpani (two of each) and strings, this **Overture** is in D major. It comprises three groups of subjects—the second and coda groups being in the dominant—a very short new idea leading back to D major, and then a reprise in the tonic. The music is conventionally cheerful in the galant manner: the coaxing and tiptoeing second group, with its nice touches of wind colour, is particularly pleasant, and the mood is sustained through the beginning of the third group.

The scene represents an idyllic rural landscape of rolling meadows, lofty oaks, and distant blue hills—all described at rapturous length by Parini. In the centre of the stage stands a rustic altar on which is sculpted a huge white sow (giving suck to thirty young ones according to tradition)—Parini merely refers to 'l'animal prodigioso' 'the prodigious animal from which it is said the city of Alba took its name' (*alba* means 'white').

At the moment this Arcadian spot is occupied by the Graces (eleven of them according to Leopold Mozart, though Wolfgang mentions 'only a few'—so as to leave room on stage for the chorus in the concluding section of his *sinfonia*) who are dancing **No. 1**, *andante grazioso* in G major, a gentle minuettish piece whose cool melody for violins is nicely coloured by flutes and oboes. Its even course is broken only by a precipitous swoop for first violins, of a kind that Mozart later used to explore deeper passions.

---

* Jommelli's *Fetonte* (1768) had even more drastically brought singers into the overture, beginning in the *andante*, a solo with chorus; Gluck's *Alceste* (1769) ends the overture with a short chorus.

1

[Andante grazioso]

The goddess Venus is now seen descending, with her son Ascanius by her side, in a chariot from heaven. The graces resume their ballet in the **Chorus No. 2**, *allegro* in D major (the closing section of the *sinfonia*)★ which Wolfgang Mozart described as a *contredanse* or country dance; they are joined on stage by a chorus of Spirits (*Geni*) who sing Venus's praises (*Di te più amabile*) in block-harmonized support to the rapid dance-tune. The middle section of this number brings out in turn the female and male halves of the chorus. The orchestration of this movement is as full as in the overture's first section. Venus and Ascanius alight from the chariot which disappears upwards in a cloud.

Venus steps forward and, in secco recitative, dismisses her Graces, Geniuses, and Cupids (these last have not been mentioned before—they may be the female choristers). She lights the sacred altar, recalls happy days here in the company of her son Aeneas, and tells Ascanius that she has destined him to be the elected ruler of the local inhabitants. This, the fourth day of autumn, is the appointed time. It is also the cue for her first solo.

No. 3, *L'ombra de rami tuoi*, Venus's **Aria** in G major, *allegro*, with oboes, horns and strings, is addressed to Ascanius, comparing him fancifully to a giant tree which will shelter this land.

> The friendly ground awaits the shade of your branches. Live, my chosen tree; you will be worthy of me.
>
> My heart already perceives your role henceforth, and can hear praise for your diligent achievements to come.

The music in *a-b-a* (varied) form is decisive and energetic, as the *coup d'archet* first theme† makes clear.

2

Allegro

The young composer may seem in too much of a hurry to expose too many contrasted ideas—three within the first eleven bars. The two ideas in the second group are both repeated, and the second of these is delicately coloured for oboes doubling *divisi* violas. Before this group arrives in the solo exposition Venus has introduced new material and, heralded by a *fermata*, some sort of cadenza. She has a dignified and not unbrilliant run in triplet quavers towards the end of her exposition. The *b* section, moving from D through C back to G, is characterized by a serenade-like cantabile for both violins in octaves. In the reprise Venus's florid

★ Mozart simultaneously composed a purely orchestral *presto* movement (K. 111a) to replace this chorus when his *sinfonia* was performed in the concert hall. It is lighter and more frenchified; the trumpets here are specified as *trombe lunghe*, Mozart's name for *clarini*.
† Cf. incipit of C major piano sonata K. 330, G major violin concerto K. 216.

melisma is rather more elaborate; before the second subject she will have sung a more exciting flourish than at first. Notwithstanding these opportunities the aria gives the violins more to do than the soprano.

Ascanius asks, in recitative, when he will see his promised bride, descendant of Hercules, much praised, much longed for by himself and the whole world. Venus promises that this paragon will be his before sunset. Already she loves him, since she had seen him in a dream when Cupid assumed his likeness. Ascanius must now seek her out, recognize her loveliness and the gorgeousness of her attire but, for the present, must on no account reveal his identity. Venus herself has to go elsewhere, her services being required by everybody. Ascanius promises to obey her will, cruelly as it constrains his ardour. (From this, we assume, the Archduke was supposed to recognize the kindly wisdom which forbade him to meet Maria Beatrice until their wedding.)

As Venus departs (the chariot is not mentioned) the graces and spirits repeat *Di te più amabile* in an abbreviated version which counts as **No. 4**.

Ascanius is left alone to lament the hardness of his grandmother's edict (some of his sentiments here are set to music in the score, but were diplomatically censored in the official printed text), and to hanker after Silvia who must be a perfect specimen of womanhood, he is convinced. He expresses himself in accompanied recitative (strings only), powerfully diversified in tempo and mood, full of ardent lyrical phrases that come and go spontaneously, with strongly moving bass-lines and the richness of divided violas (always indicative of Mozart's emotional involvement). The accompaniment is scrupulously and vividly elaborated. The passage where Ascanius imagines the appearance of his unknown beloved may look simple but in performance sounds perfectly ravishing. This is its second, more ornate appearance.

The whole recitative is extremely fine and suggests Mozart's warm admiration for his erstwhile singing teacher Manzuoli,* more perhaps than his response to the ardent clichés of Parini's text at this point. This admiration is underlined in the first **Aria** that Mozart writes for Ascanius-Manzuoli.

> Though you are far away, my dear, your virtue has inflamed me. I have learned to sigh at your lovely name. In vain you hide: your rare quality shines the more brightly within your modesty.

* Rossini attributed Mozart's superiority as a composer of vocal music to his work in Italy during the days 'when singing was still good'—i.e. when *castrati* set the standard that collapsed with the rise of tenors and sopranos as stars in their place, and the resultant coarseness of nineteenth-century romantic vocal writing.

Cara, lontano ancora, **No. 5**, marked *allegro*, in B flat major, with accompaniment for oboes, horns and strings, is full of imagination. Distinction is lent to its mechanically heroic mood by the prominence of the oboes in the orchestral exposition, by the tough swagger of the lively second subject, the premature and very dramatic entry of the singer at the end of the orchestral exposition, singing one of those *mese di voce* (swelling and dying away on one sustained note) for which Manzuoli was famous, for the imaginative orchestral writing at this and its later parallel spot, for the intense harmony in the middle section ('In van ti celi, o cara'), and the unconventional but thematically relevant closing bars. At one point (after bar 82) Mozart loses control of his modulations, and we note with surprise that he does little to exploit Manzuoli's famous contralto register—B flat is the *terminus ab quo* of this aria. Ascanius, unconventionally, remains on stage after his solo, as the stage directions make clear. He sees the Albanian shepherdesses approaching and remains to seek Silvia among them.

The shepherds enter singing **No. 6**, the **Chorus** *Venga, venga de sommi Eroi,* in which they entreat Venus's grandson to appear among them where love will keep him captive (Venus had instructed her priest Acestes of her intentions). This is a charming pastoral piece in G major: the flutes convey an effect of rustic piping, and the doubling below the tune by oboes, bassoons and celli in unison (horns and double basses have separate parts) creates a suitably nasal sound of rusticity. The shepherds here are tenors and basses only, and their mellifluous duetting in triple time looks forward to the lovers' *al fresco* serenade, *Secondate aurette, amiche* in *Così fan tutte,* especially with this instrumental accompaniment for woodwind and lower strings (no clarinets, no violins or violas as we would later expect of Mozart).

It is now that Ascanius leaves the stage, wondering what this chorus betokens. He has not been seen by the young shepherd Faunus (a second male soprano) who steps forward to call his mates to worship. He tells them that Acestes, who is on his way, looked very happy, though thoughtful, when last seen: perhaps this means that Venus, their tutelary goddess, will fulfil her promise to appear among them.

As **No. 7** the shepherds repeat their chorus *Venga, venga.*

Ascanius presents himself as a tourist attracted by the pleasing local scenery, whose unusual fertility he much admires. Faunus explains that this natural bounty is the work of a goddess, daughter of Jove, whom they worship and who does everything for them.

Faunus enlarges on his statement in an **Aria, No. 8**, *Tempo grazioso* in A major, *Se il labbro più non dice.*

> We know how lucky we are to live here but we can't explain why. When, stranger, you return home you can tell your compatriots that you have seen the Age of Gold.

The scoring, for strings alone, is compact and melodically eventful, the orchestral introduction cast in irregular phrase-lengths (mixed threes and fours). This is a less ambitious aria than some—only one group of subjects, for instance, before Faunus enters—and therefore less tempting to prolixity or hurried juxtaposition of disparate ideas (this is not necessarily an artistic virtue, but makes it easier to avoid glaring miscalculations in a context of creative inventiveness). Adamo Solzi evidently had a remarkable florid technique, as we shall discover later and as the running-scale divisions in this aria show; few modern singers could manipulate them with the ease and musicianly moulding that justifies them—or rather justifies the singer's attempt at them. The modulations in the middle section ('Quando agli amici tuoi') move towards C sharp minor and form a high-spot of interest, though the reprise has new felicities and was doubtless further elaborated. Faunus also remains on stage when his aria is over. He has to tell Ascanius (who is delighted to hear such praise for his grandmother) that graceful, lovely Silvia, so high-minded and equanimous, is now approaching with the priest Acestes. Strangers will not be welcome in this company and Ascanius had better conceal himself among the crowd.

Again the choristers and dancers re-enter, singing and miming praises of Silvia, likening her to Diana and Athene, lauding her taste in the arts but granting that her modesty is unique. **No. 9**, their **Chorus**, begins with an F major *allegro comodo*, rather stiff though pastoral, using oboes and horns to add strength to the string music, and ending unconclusively on C major.

The *Ballo* which now begins in the same key is equally stiff in expression, but well contrasted with the chorus's even less flexible exclamations, *Hai di Diana il core*. Soon the choral writing thaws a little and in the middle section (*I vaghi studi*), Mozart treats his choral voices more liberally and independently. The first choral section is repeated.

Now the priest Acestes steps forward and tells his devotees that Aeneas's son, their future sovereign, will be with them before nightfall. In **No. 10** the chorus repeats its No. 6. Acestes goes on to prophesy that a splendid new city will arise in this glorious unspoiled place (in the twentieth century this would be unwelcome news), a refuge for the miserable and a fortress against marauders.

The chorus yet again repeats *Venga, venga* as **No. 11**.

Now Silvia joins the company and is informed in recitative that today she will be Ascanius's bride.

It is Acestes who has spoken and who must therefore sing the next aria—not Silvia as modern drama would expect. Acestes's **No. 12**, *allegro aperto* in B flat major, *Per la gioja in questo seno*, is a big, spacious **Aria**, with oboes, horns and strings, heroic in tone, expressive of Acestes's joy.

> O God, I feel my spirit leap for the joy in my breast. It cannot resist the abundance of gladness.
> Dear Silvia, and friends of mine, if you are happy like me, then come and share the pleasure in my heart.

There is a typical secretive tiptoe second subject whose later penchant for big leaps may remind us that the whole aria is quite close to the parody of such solos in Fiordiligi's *Come scoglio* in the same key. The middle section begins interestingly in C minor (dominant of the dominant) and ends with a touch of melancholy (though the text is about 'the pleasure within me') for oboes. The reprise is somewhat varied and leaves room for what should be a grand cadenza. Mozart did not temper his vocal invention to an ageing singer who must still have had a lot of vocal technique.

Now for the first time Silvia begins to sing, in recitative: she is miserable and doesn't know what to do. Acestes tells her about Venus's appearance in a vision. Silvia explains that she is already in love, but insists that she will nevertheless surrender herself to the bridegroom whom already she respects and honours for his prestige and noble lineage. Mozart's secco recitative, mostly negative in this work, achieves a moment of emotional reaction at Silvia's admission of love, *Sono amante*, which leaps sensationally from A minor to a tortured B minor, relaxing into G major for Acestes's sigh of relief (a touch of *Don Giovanni* here).

Silvia now has her first solo, **No. 13**, a **Cavatina**, slowish in tempo, scored for oboes, horns and strings, *Si, ma d'un altro amore*.

> Yes, but another love burns in my breast and I cannot control this innocent affection.

This is a brief but most attractive introduction to the opera's heroine, balmy, sensuously flowing E flat music already characteristic of its composer, not least in the anxious hints at F minor and G minor before the reprise. The accompanying figures are especially worth a Mozart devotee's attention (e.g. with the *Figaro* Letter Duet at the back of the mind).

Acestes sensibly asks for fuller details and Silvia recalls her erotic dream ('What admirable candour,' comments her father-confessor). When she reiterates her loyalty to the unknown Ascanius, Acestes assures her that the vision came from Venus and is a good omen. Silvia now sings another, faster **Aria**, like the cabaletta to a nineteenth-century slow cavatina, **No. 14**, *allegro* in C major, *Come è felice stato*.

> How happy is the faithful soul where innocence dwells and love does not condemn.
> That soul is ever content with its blessings, the heart beats on in gentle tranquillity.

This is a big aria with double exposition and trumpets restored to the score. The phraseology is lively in invention and closely detailed, vocally brilliant and expressive; once again the obligatory rapid divisions are individually characterized, and the vocal writing as a whole bears the mark of youthful enthusiasm.

Acestes answers this formidable demonstration of amorous idealism with the information that, since the sun has passed its meridian, all concerned should go and pray before receiving Venus in the style to which she is accustomed. The shepherds once again sing *Venga, venga*, now labelled **No. 15**, and all retire save Ascanius.

Left alone the young hero expresses his astonished, overwhelmed feelings at the sight of Silvia, his well-nigh intolerable pain at being forced to remain silent in her presence. How, Venus, could you handicap me so? Venus promptly reappears with her chorus of Genii, in time to be addressed in Ascanius's next **Aria, No. 16** in D major, *adagio—allegro—andante grazioso—adagio—allegro*, with oboes, horns, trumpets and strings.

How much I want to talk about such a noble character. If you seek to know all her qualities, then ask my heart.

Leave me but a moment's calm, O goddess, and then I will be able to tell you her many excellences.

Once again Mozart responded in *Ah di sì nobil alma* to Manzuoli's expressive powers, with music of unusually diversified mood and pace, though the musical invention is, by contextual standards, no more than acceptable. The aria lays the ground for a powerfully expressive statement at these contrasted tempi. If Mozart wrote a simple, undecorated vocal part it was because he left the expressive vocal detail entirely to Manzuoli—here it is obvious that, in any modern revival of *Ascanio*, the name-part must be given to a superb vocal artist with a good low register who will decorate the music to bring out her/his outstanding technical and expressive accomplishments—the orchestral music presupposes a considerable degree of vocal dexterity.

Ascanius again remains on stage after the aria is finished. Venus assures him that soon this landscape will be thronged with noble architectural exhibits, the first buildings of Alba Longa, his new kingdom. For the moment Ascanius must keep his silence, watch the crowd reassemble, and observe the astonishment of his future subjects as they see the miraculous apparition of their future home, the emblem of love's triumph.

Her noble sentiments are elaborated in her next **Aria, No. 12**, *Al chiaror di que' bei rai*, an A major *allegro* movement accompanied by strings alone.

If love stirs your wings at the brightness of her fair eyes, it will exalt your heart to love all mankind.

Then you will be famed by the gods and by your illustrious children, and so you will be divine like me.

This is a short *a-b-a*, invigorating piece, characterized by brilliant, fluttering string figures ('If love stirs your wings'), touches of imitation, dashing dotted rhythms, and vocal divisions that portray the ideas of flying and divinity in the text.

The chorus, in **No. 18**, repeats the shortened version of its earlier *Di te più amabile*. And the first half of the entertainment closes with a sequence of eight ballet numbers in which the assembled company collects garlands of flowers and watches astonished while miraculously the city of Alba Longa rises in front of them. But the dance music exists only in its bass-line, and stage directors detest the idea of scenic transformation. So you are unlikely to see this splendid spectacle in our day.

4

The second part of the *serenata* begins with Silvia attended by a chorus of shepherdesses. She stands starry-eyed as she contemplates the divinely ordained architecture before her, the prospect of her groom and Venus, divine presences which she already senses, and the marvellous sunset in the sky.

Her **Aria, No. 19**, *Spiega il desio le piume* is a big *allegro* movement in G major, heroically accompanied by an orchestra including four horns (probably the trumpets doubling, though Mozart had used four horns, as well as trumpets, in *Mitridate*).

> Longing unfurls its wings, my heart soars and coos, and only hope returns it to my breast.
> Come at last, O my longing, with my fair god. Say to me just once, O god: 'Here is your beloved.'

The music actively involves chiefly the violins, adds some oboe shading, and uses the horn choir mostly for strengthening cadences and instrumental ritornelli—rather tame considering the pretension. Silvia is more vivaciously characterized than Venus, but her music is unadventurous—an augmented triad sounds positively revolutionary, and in the *andante grazioso* middle section, basically in C major, a turn via a German sixth towards B major seems quite hair-raising.

A female **Chorus** of shepherdesses, in **No. 20**, *Già l'ore sen volano* tells Silvia that her lover is on his way. The light-hearted, faintly smug C major music looks forward to the wedding duet in *Figaro* and arguably suggests two soprano solo voices. The scoring is for strings, *un poco allegro*.

Now we hear Ascanius who is looking in vain for Silvia. Suddenly he catches sight of her and his recitative acquires orchestral accompaniment for added intensity (oboes, bassoons, horns, and strings with predictably divided violas). It is Silvia who responds first and to whom the panting, sensuous orchestral music refers: he is the boy that she saw in her dream. Ascanius longs to introduce himself but does not dare. He is agonized. The music switches violently between slow and fast and the instrumentation is accordingly vivid. She recognizes her destined bridegroom but he recoils, so she seeks guidance, if not from Venus, then from Acestes.

We expect an aria here, but perplexingly the recitative returns to *secco* as Faunus returns to announce the imminent presence of Venus as consultant architect of the city they see already arising in their midst. Faunus treats Ascanius quite casually, much to the distress of Silvia who, almost certain that the young stranger is her destined husband, wonders if she has been misled by her dream, particularly since Faunus instructs him to remain concealed until Venus's arrival. Silvia collapses among her female chorister friends, Ascanius stands nonplussed, and Faunus announces his intention of returning post-haste to report to Acestes.

But first he has to sing a big **Aria**, the longest in the whole opera (the middle section and *da capo* were omitted at the first performance). We may well wonder what a young totally unknown *comprimario* male soprano had done to merit two whole arias, the second of such imposing dimensions. The vocal music of **No. 21** supplies one answer. *Dal tuo gentil sembiante* is *allegro moderato* in B flat major, accompanied by oboes, horns and strings.

> A great soul shines from your kindly face; its expansive brightness almost makes me worship you.
> If ever you fall in love, the damsel will be happy who is ignited by so fair a flame.

The orchestral introduction exposes two groups of subjects notable, after the gentle opening phrase, for their cheerful, almost saucy swagger, as for example—

The words of the aria refer to Ascanius but the music paints a vivid portrait of the shepherd, viz. young Adamo Solzi. The vocal writing tells us even more cogently about his musical ability. Florid runs were more or less expected in every aria, one or two usually. But Faunus here has a two-bar flourish of semiquavers at the end of his first sentence, rising from middle B flat to the octave above (the top of the average male soprano's compass). When the second subject (Ex. 4a above) arrives in F major he sings another, four-bar division full of cascading semiquaver scales, again rising to top B flat for the start of the last one and six bars later another division which jubilantly soars to top C and top D before cadencing in the dominant. The quasi-development section has a more passionate excursion into C minor but soon returns to the tonic for a recapitulation which again consists largely of rapid runs, the last of which includes the following *gorgia*.

After delivering this item of vocal space-fiction Adamo Solzi must have been taxed to supply a more exciting cadenza four bars later, unless he had a top F to fetch out. Small wonder that he omitted the remainder of the aria. This comprises a short *andante ma adagio* in E flat with a beautiful passage in C minor moving to G minor in which the violin figuration, above glowing viola chords, eloquently suggests the sweet torments of love; and then a formal *da capo* in which Solzi would have had to repeat his conjuring tricks with new elaborations.*

* The exceptional length and formidable difficulties of No. 21 presuppose a singer of either supreme importance or unique accomplishment. Riccardo Broschi did not include a top E in the aria *Qual guerrier* which he composed for his brother Farinelli; but Farinelli was celebrated everywhere for (among other things) his top notes. His compass in his prime (like other high male sopranos) extended only to a top D. We would therefore expect Adamo Solzi to have achieved at least some fame. But he did not: was he a disappointment to Mozart when it came

[*footnote continued overleaf*

At whatever point Faunus ends this aria he leaves the stage. Ascanius, in recitative, voices his distress at the sight of Silvia reclining unconscious among her shepherdess friends. He realizes that he is the cause of her collapse: virtue and love are in conflict within his heart. He could end her misery if it were not for his promise to Venus. He decides to conceal himself in her vicinity, observe her more closely and hear what she says when she recovers. Before suiting action to word he has an aria to sing, in which Mozart must have been hard pressed to avoid anticlimax after the fireworks and large dimensions of No. 21. Manzuoli, after all, was the *primo uomo*, the most eminent singer in the cast, a musician whom Mozart admired and to whom he was indebted.

His solution was an **Aria, No. 22**, *Al mio ben mi veggio avanti* of unusual expressive diversity, low-lying in tessitura to display Manzuoli's best register, and captivating for the plainness of the writing (no written-out divisions at all), calculated as a complete contrast which the singer could *ad libitum* soften by the addition of his own ornamentation. After virtuosity only expressiveness can stir more profoundly. Ascanius's aria, in E major accompanied by strings alone, begins *un poco adagio* with a melody which might later have occurred in one of Mozart's horn concertos:

6

—though what follows is essentially galant in character, spiky triplets, fizzing *gruppetti*, sudden alternations of forte and piano.

> Here I stand before my darling. I feel the anguish in her heart, yet an order restrains me. (*Allegro*) Let the cruel noose be broken. The heart has suffered enough. (*Adagio*) Fair goddess, if your breast be moved to pity living souls, do not continue to trouble them with such tests.

The music moves swiftly to the dominant of B and, after an unwritten vocal flourish, an *allegro* section in B, rather tonic-bound, ensues as Ascanius longs to be released from his pledge. Again the tempo slows to *adagio* for a new section in C sharp minor, with doleful violin octaves to which Ascanius begs Venus to test these lovers no further; the spiky triplets of the first *adagio* are resumed and the tonality shifts more restlessly. The *allegro* returns to E major to close the aria.

Ascanius leaves the stage to hide near Silvia. But she has recovered and runs towards him, begging him to remain. Strings heighten her recitative as she

to rehearsal? Is that why this aria was shortened, or was this done so as not to steal Manzuoli's thunder? I suspect that Solzi was proud of his top notes and agility, boasted of them to Mozart who enthusiastically responded with a grand vehicle that misfired when Solzi appeared on stage (castrati lost their top notes quite soon) and that the composer then shortened this aria and perhaps even told the singer to lower the compass of the vocal writing. This is a supposition. Manzuoli may have put his foot down. But why did neither Mozart mention in his letters what must have been either a triumph or a catastrophe? Vocally it is the most remarkable of all Mozart's arias until *Entführung* and *Zauberflöte*.

remembers her divine dignity and modesty, her public spirit which compels her to marry the unknown man chosen for her. Again the tempo is much varied, each time with a striking thematic orchestral phrase prodigally thrown away by young creative genius. She decides to seek Acestes's advice. In her **Aria, No. 23** Mozart again underlines the emotional conflict with abrupt changes of tempo. This E flat major aria, *Infelici affetti miei*, is grand and noble in feeling, suave and tender in vocal style, strongly characteristic of Mozart's heroines—Ilia and Fiordiligi come most immediately to mind.

> Unhappy feelings of mind, I sigh and suffer through you alone. My heart is innocent; do not come to torment me.
> Everlasting gods, restore to me my soul as it was. Do not upset me again with that alluring vision.

Plangent oboes in thirds, tender and sincere, dark and dependable bassoons, warm enriching horns, support the fluent, amorous string accompaniment (two violas of course) to Silvia's liquescent cantabile lamentation. From *un poco adagio* the orchestra breaks into an *allegro* for a still noble but more weighty middle section ('Ah quest' alma') that moves into the heroic-tragic climate of C minor but rather too quickly turns back to the dominant of E flat for a reprise of the first section with varied, subdominantly inclined harmony. The coda is full of expressive vocal sighs. Abert condemned them as facile and modish but today's listeners must think them moving, and so perhaps did the Milan audience. This is surely the emotional highlight of the score and the most thoroughly, precociously Mozartian number.

In a short recitative Ascanius runs impetuously to Silvia who capriciously now repulses him and departs to consult Acestes.

The shepherdesses softly murmur their surprise at Silvia's behaviour, and their intention of catching her up at once, in a little **Chorus, No. 24** in B flat, *Che strano evento*, accompanied by strings. The texture is quasi-imitative, like earlier canzonets, though it tends to relax into block triadic chords or parallel thirds which are not inappropriate.

Ascanius is alone on stage, recognizing his good fortune in being granted such a bride. His F major *andante grazioso* **Aria, No. 25**, *Torna mia bene*, is a concise, pretty, slightly formal pastoral with elaborate scoring for flutes, bassoons, horns and two serpents in F (notated in the treble clef and therefore equivalent to *cors anglais* rather than double-bassoons) as well as strings.

> Come back and listen, beloved: I am your true love. Only love me, my dear— no, Cupid does not deceive you.
> That rare virtue within in your breast must prepare to contend with your innocent heart.

The middle section is more chromatic and intense in manner.

Ascanius departs. The shepherds return singing, as **No. 26,** their prayer *Venga, venga* (originally No. 6). With them is Acestes, holding Silvia's hand and exhorting her to behave with her usual composure, undisturbed by the curious events which she has narrated to him. These trials are sent by heaven. Happiness will shortly be hers, he promises Silvia in his **Aria, No. 27**, *Sento che il cor mi dice*, a bland, demure *allegro* piece in A major with string accompaniment.

> My heart tells that you must not be afraid; but you may not pierce behind the hidden veil.
> You know that you are innocent, dependent on Heaven. Await with joy the fate that Heaven has marked out for you.

The music is cheerful but harmonically unadventurous; Tibaldi's agile runs ascend to a C sharp in *altissimo*, a high note for an old man but Mozart expressly wrote it for him.

Silvia promises to do her duty. Acestes tells the shepherds to begin the rites for Venus and duly they sing the **Chorus, No. 28**, *Scendi celeste Venere*, entreating the goddess to descend and give them a token of her love. This C major (probably *andante*) movement, with oboes, horns and strings, is nicely invocatory in mood, inventively resourceful and chorally less primitive than some numbers in the work: the fragmented syllables of 'sospiramo' ('we sigh') were unoriginal but effective.

Silvia complains that Ascanius (she calls him 'that dangerous object', which is hardly polite) is following her. She is told to go to the altar and await the imminent arrival of Venus through the smoke which can be seen rising to heaven. As **No. 29** the chorus repeats its previous prayer to new words, *No, non possiamo vivere* in which they reiterate their desire for a love-pledge from Venus.

Acestes draws attention to the light shining through the smoke. Venus is among them. The shepherds again sing *Scendi celeste Venere* as **No. 30**.

Silvia, on Acestes's instructions, begs Venus to bring her bridegroom and make her happy for ever. The clouds promptly divide to reveal Venus once more descending in her chariot, while her Graces and Spirits pour in from the wings. Ascanius runs forward and Venus bestows him on Silvia who has not, until this moment, dared to look at the man beside her. Now she asks him why he maintained that painful incognito. You shall know all, he replies.

There follows the first and only vocal **Trio, No. 31**, *Ah caro sposo*, in B flat major, *andante*, with oboes, horns and strings. We might expect it, coming from the master of operatic ensemble at the moment of climactic tension in a not-too-tense drama, to knock us all over. But Mozart was not yet ready for such a challenge and the trio is dry and static, if not indeed lethargic. It begins *andante* in B flat with conventional interchanges for the embracing lovers and Acestes over a plodding bass line and beneath minimally redeeming oboes. Interest revives a little after the *allegro* in bar 30. Silvia's B flat interjection 'Numi' bursts dramatically out of the preceding G minor and subsequently intensity increases and the texture thaws (bar 65) when a simultaneous duet begins. After a declamatory passage with pause the three voices actually sing together, rather unadventurously, to the effect that this is the sweetest love, the most sacred knot on earth (important moment for Ferdinand and Beatrice!). The texture gains interest and intensity with some florid passages in trio but the characters remain mouthpieces, not human beings.

Venus (alone, according to the arcane stage direction) tells Silvia and Ascanius that they must be happy now; they were kept apart so that Ascanius might realize how good and virtuous Silvia is. But they must always think about the happiness of others (hint to the royal pair). Ascanius must rule benevolently, create his own satisfaction by caring for the satisfaction of his subjects, and so deserve the divinity which will one day be his.

As **No. 32** the lovers and Acestes repeat part of their foregoing trio.

Venus bids the company farewell and prepares to return to heaven. Acestes informs Ascanius that from now on he must be his grandmother's substitute, the buttress of his people. In time Ascanius's numerous descendants will be heroes, demigods, and will occupy the world.

The chorus, *molto allegro* with oboes, horns, trumpets, drums and strings concludes the entertainment with **No. 33**, a short, cheerful D major item, *Alma dea, tutto il mondo* which unites genii, graces, shepherds and nymphs in a paean of jubilation.

5

The task of composing *Ascanio in Alba* was, comments Alfred Einstein, 'wholly suited to [Mozart's] age and talent'. It may be true that for such an occasion he was not required to reveal great originality or depth of feeling, and we may grant the boy our admiration for the warmth and invention which he unleashed on the best numbers (e.g. Nos. 21–23). But the achievement of these throws into contrast the great stretches of conventionality which may be condoned under the circumstances, but show, by comparison, how much more eloquently he was already able to rise to operatic character and situation. Mozart's distinctive personality as composer is to be discovered here and there, as Friedrich Blume has pointed out, but only intermittently. The irregular format of the overture suggests a penchant for textural flexibility, and the choral reprises remind us that he had absorbed this French device for musical unity even as a boy, and liked the effect of repetition, as modern audiences do. The trio shows (like the duet in *Mitridate*) that Mozart the ensemble composer *par excellence* had not yet arrived. But he had begun to draw curtains on the exit aria and the formal *da capo* aria. He confirmed his pleasure in recitatives accompanied by more than strings. Perhaps his greatest achievement, in *Ascanio in Alba*, is that he keeps us interested in the progress of a non-drama, yet writes music that needs to be appreciated by an audience which sees the characters and scenery in front of them. Maybe this is a toy theatre. But it is theatre, and real music.

8   IL SOGNO DI SCIPIONE

IL SOGNO DI SCIPIONE

(SCIPIO'S DREAM)

Dramatic Serenade

Text by

PIETRO METASTASIO

K. 126

SCIPIONE (Scipio)	TENOR
LA CONSTANZA (Constancy)	SOPRANO
LA FORTUNA (Fortune)	SOPRANO
PUBLIO (Publius), Scipio's adopted father	TENOR
EMILIO (Æmilius), Scipio's own father	TENOR
SOLOIST in closing Licenza	SOPRANO
Heroes	CHORUS

The action takes place in Africa in Massinissa's kingdom,
Numidia, in 149 B.C.

Mozart and his father left Milan, after the performances of *Ascanio in Alba*, on 5 December 1771 and arrived home in Salzburg on 15 December. One day later their master Archbishop Schrattenbach died. He was succeeded by Hieronymus, Count Colloredo, who was elected on 14 March and made his solemn entry into Salzburg as Prince-Archbishop on 29 April. Mozart, who had passed his sixteenth birthday on 27 January, was commissioned to compose the dramatic serenade for these celebrations. He was given another drama text by Metastasio, *Il sogno di Scipione*, originally written in 1735 for the birthday of Charles VI whom Metastasio commiserates, in his text (recitative before No. 9), on recent, crushing military defeats in Italy; the music was then provided by Angelo Predieri.★

Mozart's setting was performed in early May 1772, perhaps (as Loewenberg decided) on 1 May, the date of the later *Figaro* première. Details are unforthcoming about this performance and its cast—a Salzburg one, perhaps including several of the *Finta semplice* principals. The work was given in the archiepiscopal palace (presumably indoors, not in the courtyard where modern festival opera performances sometimes occur). It is not dramatically eventful: the producer's problem is to make *Il sogno di Scipione* visually interesting. Mozart concentrated on musical interest: extended, showy arias, and pleasant orchestral writing for an orchestra whose best capabilities were well known to him. Since it was a Salzburg work we have no Mozart family letters, or even diary entries, to tell us how much rehearsal or how many performances it had. In 1776 or 1777 Mozart rewrote one of the arias (No. 11), possibly for a revival—unless for a concert—but nothing further is known of this.

The source of Metastasio's libretto is Cicero's *Somnium Scipionis* together with the story reported in Book XV of Silius Italicus's *Punica* that Scipio was told to choose whether his life would be ruled by Virtus (Courage or Virtue) or Voluptas (Pleasure). Metastasio changed these visitants to *Costanza* (Faithfulness) and *Fortuna* (Good Luck). The Scipio in question is Cicero's ideal Roman, Scipio Africanus the younger, son of the first Africanus's cousin Lucius Aemilius Paulus: he was adopted by Publius Scipio, son of the first Africanus. Both of these figure in *Scipio's Dream* but not the first Africanus who is Cicero's chief interlocutor. The young Scipio's real name was Aemilianus. Massinissa (245–149 B.C.) was a king of Numidia in Africa who, touched by the elder Scipio's generosity to his captured son, seconded all his country's troops to Scipio's army and made himself Rome's firmest ally. At his death aged ninety-six he bequeathed his kingdom to Scipio Aemilianus (hero of this opera) who divided it equably between Massinissa's fifty-four sons.

★ Mozart set the bits about unlucky wars even though they made no sense in the new context. Some authorities declare that the original was written for the birthday of Empress Elisabeth on 1 October 1735, but the military allusions speak against such an ascription. Metastasio's text had also been set to music in 1743 by Giovanni Porta for the nameday of Francis I.

Much of Metastasio's libretto comes directly from Cicero: for example the passages about the music of the spheres and about the inhabitants of the Nile who cannot hear its torrent.

2

The **Overture** begins *allegro moderato* in D major (flutes, oboes, horns, trumpets, all in pairs, timpani and strings), jubilant formal unisons alternating with secretive tripping thirds for violins. The second subject begins like an attractive bland tune but almost at once takes a Neapolitan switch into its own dominant for cadential noises, their conventionality silvered over by sustained wind harmonies, rather mysterious. No sooner has the exposition ended firmly in A than the orchestra plunges on to a loud F sharp dominant seventh chord with the third at the bottom. A new tune, with delicate harmonic colouring (flutes and violas much in evidence), is heading for B minor, and farther—since this melody, unlike the second subject, is allowed to go on flowering until, after hovering long on the brink of D, it slithers into the recapitulation. But only of the first subject. A diminished seventh interrupts and new music takes over, at first energetic, then becoming drowsy and chromatic, until a sustained A major chord.

There are hints here at a dramatic tone-painting of the warrior Scipio collapsing into sleep in Massinissa's palace. The smooth, gentle minuet which ensues—charmingly coloured by flutes and oboes—was firmly assumed by Abert to portray the start of Scipio's dream. Preliminary action-painting of this sort was not in Mozart's line, and he did subsequently turn these two movements into a short symphony, for a concert in Milan at the end of 1772, by adding a new finale (K. 141a). Here, however, just when we expect the third appearance of the minuet tune, the music turns even more spectral and harmonically mystifying.

This, no doubt, *is* a deliberate illustration since at once we find the two divine spirits of Constancy and Fortune hovering over the sleeping form of Scipio.* Each invites him to entrust his life to her tutelary guidance. Scipio is annoyed at this disturbance of his rest, and blinded by the unearthly light radiating from these ladies' faces. To his question they introduce themselves: Constancy as the hand-maiden of heroes, Fortune as the dispenser of universal happiness. He is to choose, once and for all, between them. When he hesitates they are both somewhat piqued. He protests that he has no idea where he is: he needs time to collect his wits.

Scipio explains this in his *andante* **Aria, No. 1**, *Risolver non osa* in F major, scored for oboes, horns and strings. It is typical of Salzburg taste at the time: audiences wanted vocal and instrumental brilliance and full scale *da capo* arias, for preference with outer sections in concertante sonata-form with double exposition. By now this extensive pattern had been somewhat contracted: the following concise yet fairly detailed summary of this aria may be taken as a criterion for other divergently shaped numbers in *Il sogno di Scipione*.

In the orchestral exposition, twenty-four bars long, three bland melodies are stated: running passage-work follows the second and third.

---

* The parallel with the opening of *Die Schuldigkeit des ersten Gebotes* will be obvious to those who have read the first chapter of this book, or seen that sacred music drama. But Metastasio had the idea first, and he claimed his treatment of a hero who dreams, then awakes, as an original stroke of fancy.

My confused mind does not dare to decide, oppressed as it is by such a shock.

Scipio expounds these sentiments to the three melodies above mentioned, adding a new, equally bland one; the violins end the solo exposition with a fresh outburst of energy. The music so far has scant connection with the words. The singer's statutory brilliant running passage occurs at the words 'da tanto stupor', sounding anything but shocked.

The link (doing duty for development) inverts the text so as to begin with 'confusa la mente'; the shifting tonality and chromatic lines—tune doubled by bass—may be thought more illustrative than the foregoing. Very soon the recapitulation arrives, beginning with the new theme from the solo exposition (the first and second subjects are thus omitted). This part ends with the vigorous orchestral coda from the first exposition.

The middle section of the aria begins in D minor and moves through F to A minor; evidently it goes faster, though the autograph (as so often in this opera) does not say so.

When the heartbeat fluctuates, every spirit raves incoherently.

Here the sentiments are more positively expressed by the repeated string chords with sudden dynamic contrasts and the panting vocal ejaculations.

The *andante* is resumed with a new bridge passage to the *da capo* which starts from the shifting link section, 'confusa la mente', restating the music thereafter unchanged.

Scipio's auto-analytical confession placates Constancy who offers to answer his questions. Fortune tells him to be brief: she never likes to stop too long anywhere.

She characterizes herself more exactly and fully in her **Aria, No. 2**, *allegro* in C major, *Lieve sono al par del vento* with oboes, horns, trumpets and strings. Luck is a vivacious quick-tempered lady as the long orchestral exposition makes clear. Second violins scurry along busily below a spacious, wide-ranging melody for first violins, and with humming, airy double-stops for violas. Wind and trumpets do not enter until the end of the first group whose skipping bridge-theme is much used, inverted and straight, for structural purposes. Oboes in thirds bring a touch of charm to the second subject.

> I am as capricious as the wind, changeable of aspect, fleet-footed, sometimes angry, sometimes calm.

Fortune's music presents her as forthright and aggressive, roving confidently through a compass of two octaves from middle C upwards.

'Serenar' must seem an unsuitable word for such a voluble division; the other runs in this aria are, more appropriately, on 'fugace'. After this double exposition the aria continues with a binary second half, taking the exposition material from the dominant through A minor back to C major. The middle section moves from F major to A minor, still keeps to the first subject but uses new text.

> I enjoy raising up ruined buildings, then suddenly I am pleased to knock them down again.

There is a shortened *da capo*, all in the tonic C major.

Scipio is still perplexed about his whereabouts. Surely this cannot be Africa? No, answers Constancy, they are in the temple of heaven. Didn't you guess as much, asks Fortune a touch peevishly, from the bright lights and colours and the music of the spheres? Scipio, unlike pre-Enlightenment scientists, has not learned about all this, so Constancy explains to him Pythagoras's law of the crystal spheres and their natural harmony, achieved by true proportion of motion. Scipio is surprised that this glorious sound is inaudible on earth, but Constancy assures him that it would be too much for the sensory perceptions of earthlings.

She gives him an analogy in her **Aria, No. 3** (presumably *andantino*) in A major, *Ciglio che al sol si gira*, scored for strings alone. Metastasio uses a favourite simile (there are two related examples in *La Betulia liberata*, No. 12 and the recitative before No. 10).

> The sun's brightness is too intense for our eyes to behold.

This starts like a sedate minuet but soon it breaks into running patterns which are taken up by the voice too. Neither the runs nor the Neapolitan leaps (at 'non vede') detract from the gently expressive musical characterization of Constancy—whose vocal range extends to top C sharp, incidentally. The aria is a binary structure (more concentrated than No. 2) whose second half is repeated after the vocally melodious middle section.

> The man who lives beside the rapids of the Nile doesn't notice the noise of the raging waters.

After these two arias, so contrasted in character and tone of voice, Scipio's choice should be easy, and Fortune impatiently orders him to make it instead of asking all these questions. Constancy is more forebearing: to his question she replies that this heavenly spot has many inhabitants—he can hear some of them approaching, adds Fortune.

The new arrivals are a chorus of heroes (presumably heroines as well, since it is a mixed chorus),* Publius and Aemilius among them. They burst at once into a **Chorus** of D major welcome to Scipio, **No. 4**, *Germe di cento eroi*, with oboes, horns, trumpets, timpani and strings—the tempo is deducibly *allegro maestoso*.

> Come, descendant of a hundred heroes, Rome's chief pride, so that your name may not be found in foreign heavens. You can find a thousand footprints of your ancestors on the brilliant path where you have set your foot.

The effect of this chorus is grandly Handelian with its block choral harmony against rushing upper strings, braying brass, and firmly striding bass line. Handelian too when a single vocal phrase is immediately repeated by the other choral voices in harmony:

---

* But see *Die Zauberflöte*, p. 619, for another instance of sexual confusion.

The rhythm of the first bar recalls Handel, and the repetition of 'No!' followed by a pause is vividly dramatic, though not unconventional in rococo sacred music. The word 'Vieni' is also much repeated. The ternary form of the number involves a short, harmonically bolder middle section that pays its respects to imitative part-writing. The first and last thirds end with orchestral bravura.

Scipio is astounded to recognize among this crowd his adoptive father Publius. Is not Publius dead? Publius steps forward and gives the young man a lecture on the immortality of the soul and the place assured in heaven for all dedicated benefactors of their fellow-men. In case Archbishop Colloredo had not taken this hint Publius expands on it in his **Aria, No. 5**, in B flat major (*un poco allegro*, perhaps), *Se vuoi che te raccolgano*, scored for oboes, horns and strings.

> Remember your ancestors and me, if you wish one day to reside here. Those like us who have died do not cease to live. But the man who lives for himself alone did not deserve to be born.

This is another binary, shortened *da capo* aria, with a brief middle section, a forthright piece with athletic violin writing, prominent horn parts, but generally careful scoring so that the tenor voice of Publius projects easily: the singer was perhaps an older man, though he still had a (probably *falsetto*) top C and could manage vigorous runs.

Fortune once again interrupts Scipio's reply to this piece of advice with a testy order to make his decision at once. Constancy, more tolerant, reminds her that what Scipio learns up here will help him to make his choice. So Scipio asks if his father Aemilius Paulus is not among those present. Here indeed is the old man standing before him and looking, Scipio notices, less enthusiastic than Scipio expected or himself feels. Aemilius explains that earthly attitudes of mind and human emotions are differently experienced in heaven. Let Scipio cast his eyes down through the clouds to the minute speck which is the terrestrial globe. He must see how puny and ineffectual are mortals, even the most worthy and beneficial among them.

Interest is impartially shared between Aemilius (another tenor) and orchestra (flutes, bassoons, strings) in his G major, *allegro moderato* **Aria, No. 6**, *Voi vollagiù ridete*. The orchestral ritornello is thoroughly agreeable—even if the second subject be thought dully formulated.

> Down there you smile at boys who weep; you know what causes their grief. Up here we smile at you; for when you are old and grey you become boys again.

When Aemilius begins to sing, an ineptitude may be sensed. This is music for a soubrette soprano, for Despina or Sandrina, not for the grave spectre of a noble Roman hero discoursing philosophy.

Mozart has perhaps concentrated on expressing 'ridete' and 'fanciullìn'. The mood is pastoral and jovial with flutes in thirds, and in octaves with bassoons. There is a nice vocal triplet for laughter, and a touching phrase for tears, when the opening sentence is first repeated.

And immediately after that quotation the music breaks into a new, rather giggling motif, typically feminine. The middle section, in C major, four instead of three time, specifically marked *allegretto* (faster in effect but slower in terms of note-values), is bland as well, galant in character. It is a charming number, perfectly irrelevant to the dramatic context. The *da capo* involves some new touches to accommodate the all-tonic scheme, and also to give variety.

Scipio's head is quite turned by these experiences and he longs to leave earth now and dwell in heaven with his nearest and dearest. The two goddesses and two solo heroes have to assure him that his place is still on earth where he has much work to do. He is not, says Publius, yet worthy of his ancestors. Disasters as well as victories must come his way and he must learn to accept them for their edifying effect on his character.

Mathematical scholars will have observed that by now everybody on stage has been given one aria. Publius (shortly to withdraw with the other heroes) is the first character to be given a second solo. His is a simile **Aria**, in a style beloved by Metastasio, **No. 7** in F major, *Quercia annosa*, gigue-like in character therefore probably an *allegro*, and accompanied by horns and strings. The orchestral introduction (not an exposition) is short and stormy; I quote it as immediately repeated with added voice-part.

As the old oak on the slope struggles against hostile winds it becomes all the more firm. When winter strips its foliage it digs its feet firmer into the soil. It may lose its beauty but it gains strength.

This is an aria full of character and atmosphere, apt for Publius and distinctive in its own right. The instrumentation in Nos. 5 and 6 may be more *recherché* but this one is more inventive musically. It makes its effect without florid divisions or voyages to top notes (and so strengthens the supposition that Mozart's Publius may have been an elderly singer, musical and well preserved but physically inclined to tire), yet gives the singer gratifying passages and involves plenty of dramatic gusto—in the jagged dynamic changes and fizzing tremolos which describe the 'contrasto de' venti', for example. The development and middle section are both short but striking, the *da capo* abbreviated, to the benefit of the aria's impact.

Scipio has understood Publius's meaning. When the two goddesses ask him now to select his tutelary guide through life, he declares himself ready though perhaps Publius could give him eleventh-hour advice? But Publius declares firmly that such a choice has no virtue unless it is made independently. Scipio asks Fortune why he should attach his career to her. She explains how influential she is in her **Aria, No. 8**, *A chi serena io giro*, which is in A major (maybe *andantino*) accompanied by strings only.

Already the opera has suggested that Fortune is a quick-tempered lady, more likely to threaten than to coax. The orchestral introduction to this, her second aria, may seem not to support this characterization: it exposes two subjects, each divisible by two; all four ideas are attractive but, if for that reason, not obviously suited to changeable Fortune or her bullying ways.

The phrasing of the first violin part is extremely exact, rather prim. The undulating, aqueous second violin and viola parts are characteristic of music in this period: if they have any emotional connotations these have to do with purling streams, not a capricious goddess. The second part of Ex. 7a and the first part of Ex. 7b both show the repeated attack which indicates wilfulness in late eighteenth-century music. Ex. 7a (second part) and 7b (second part) exemplify the triplets that regularly, throughout this aria, are contrasted with ordinary duple note-values. The twos and threes may well be Mozart's characterization of Fortune's caprice. At all events the string ritornello is eventful, and will be re-used when the singer enters.

> For those whom I favour, the night-sky turns bright and the frozen earth grows fertile. When my glances become dark and gloomy, the forest showers no leaves, the sea no waves.

Fortune's vocal line is more attractive than dictatorial; perhaps her triplet runs, ending with a (cadential?) pause, do suggest authority. The brusque *allegro* middle section in D major should give necessary contrast, and a powerful soprano might bring the whole aria into line with a consistent impersonation.

Scipio is much impressed by Fortune's advertising copy. How could anyone refuse such an offer? Constancy proposes herself as an alternative. Luck is not limitless, not beyond human regulation: it is Constancy which sets limits on the instability of dependence on chance and upholds government—Scipio's ancestors, and Rome itself, bear witness to the blessings of Constancy as guiding star. When Hannibal moved against Rome it was Constancy which drove him back, not Fortune who tired quickly (presumably a reference to the battle of Cannae).

Constancy describes her steadfast loyalty in a Metastasian analogy—**Aria, No. 9,** *Biancheggia in mar*, a powerful *allegro maestoso* (again the tempo must be deduced) in E flat major with oboes, horns and strings.

> The rock turns white in the sea which appears great and strong enough to batter and submerge it. Yet the rock proudly survives the conflict.

The first subject is very striking, characteristic of Mozart's E flat music: the broken chord traced by first violins in bars 3 and 4 recalls the opening of the Sinfonia Concertante K. 320d. The undulating accompaniment, derived from the up-beat figure in the first two bars, is often used for aqueous music, though best known maybe (in D major) from the finale of the Paris Symphony No. 31.

When this subject is repeated for the vocal exposition the voice adds a part, starting later. I quote the theme in this form:

Rushing patterns, of the kind quoted, occur in the third subject, employed to finish sections, and in Constancy's florid divisions, the first of which (never recapitulated in the same form) imaginatively derives one feat of bravura from the orchestral cadence-clincher used elsewhere in this aria.

9 *

(ma) ——

The tiny development section features a purposeful dropping diminished seventh figure. The recapitulation involves new working for purposes of tonal stability. The contrasted middle section (short as usual in this opera) adopts B flat major and triple time for the victory of the battered rock; but it goes at the same pace. The *da capo* is taken from the start of the development, all the more helpful because the middle section has ended in F major, two doors down the street from the aria's home-key of E flat.

This eloquent aria is more than enough to tilt the scales. Scipio gives his vote to Constancy. He will not refuse the aid of Fortune but he will not ask for it either. When Fortune advises him to observe her menacing eyes before he finally makes his choice, he boldly answers that he has already chosen.

He addresses Fortune in his last **Aria, No. 10**, *Di che sei l'arbitra*, an *allegro* in B flat major with a short declamatory slower introduction (*un poco adagio e maestoso*—Mozart remembered to indicate the speeds for this number) scored again for oboes, horns and strings.†

> You may say that you are the arbiter of the whole world. But do not therefore claim control of fearless souls and noble hearts. Let base folk worship you, tyrannical goddess, those who have nothing to boast of but the favours you bestow.

The *allegro* is thematically quite dull, interest concentrated on Scipio's strenuous runs (alternative versions are given for some of these, usually facilitatory but in one case more taxing) which leave their mark on the orchestral coda groups. The aria is given character, though, by the five slow bars at the beginning, brought back after the exposition. The initial motif is closely related to that of the *allegro*, and Scipio's part includes wide leaps on the words 'del mondo intero' ('of the whole world')—they are even more far-reaching at the repeat which moves the key from F major to G minor. The second *allegro* returns to F and adjusts the first subject-group so as to shift back into B flat almost immediately in time for the second subject (which was in the dominant originally). This section has elements of a sonata-form recapitulation, though in the larger context it partakes of binary form such as Mozart prefers in abbreviated *da capo* arias of this period. The central section of the aria ('Te vili adorino'—'Let base folk') is a staid F major minuet

* Cf. a similar example in Donna Anna's *Non mi dir*, from *Don Giovanni*.
† Mozart infrequently uses the same instrumentation for two consecutive arias.

featuring divided violas and violins in mellow thirds and sixths, and a couple of rough outbursts for the 'nume tiranno'. From its close, still in F major, the strings bump back to E flat major with some new *allegro* rushing music that swerves into F whereupon the *da capo* ensues, beginning with the repeat of the second subject in the tonic.

A modern audience may regard this aria as somewhat clumsily composed and musically uninspiring. Yet its style accurately reflects what we know of Salzburg taste at that time; preference was for extended arias in academic idiom and full of virtuosity. Mozart may have been writing exactly what his principal tenor vocalist had asked for.

Fortune declares her astonishment that any mortal being could decline her favours (though we are given to understand elsewhere that all the departed Scipios had chosen Constancy in preference). She promises that Scipio will instantly experience her hostility (accompanied recitative, *E ben, provami avversa*) and the full orchestra excepting flutes explodes into loud vengeful *allegro* music in D major, as she calls on disasters of all natures to quell this rash creature. Amid bristling tremolos and precipitous rapid scales Scipio is beset by lurid light, tempests, flashes of lightning in his hair. Yet he still cries defiance in the wake of the scorned harpy.

Then all is silent. The orchestra resumes serenely and with dignity (presumably *andante*) in E flat major. Scipio looks about him, observes that the vision and his divine visitants have disappeared, and that he is once again in Massinissa's palace. Was it a dream? The full orchestral *allegro* returns purposefully; perhaps that nightmare was imaginary. No, he decides: Constancy was real enough; she will remain with him. He accepts this dream as a divine omen.

The curtain may fall at this point. But there is still the epilogue or *Licenza* customary at the close of a gratulatory allegorical stage-piece. A soprano, representing the author, comes out to tell Girolamo (the Italian form of Hieronymus, first-name of the new Archbishop) that although the opera's subject has been Scipio, yet while she wrote her verses her thoughts were of the Archbishop.

She enlarges on this idea in an **Aria, No. 11**, *Ah perche cercar degg' io*. This exists in two versions, the second composed in the mid-1770s, as mentioned earlier. Both are for soprano, both orchestras include horns and strings, and they set the same text. Otherwise they differ completely. Both must be described so that readers about to attend a modern revival may recognize which of the two settings is being performed. The musical director embarking on a new production of *Scipione* will understand that he, like the opera's hero, has also to make his choice; some account of their respective merits may be helpful here too.

The text is appropriately fulsome.

Ah why should I scour historical relics for qualities that Heaven has given us in yourself? Anybody demanding proof of virtue may hear it in my opera, but can see it in you—and the ear is always less keen and less accurate than the eye.

The 1772 setting has two flutes in the orchestra, with horns and strings. It is a concise binary form aria—a relief after so many *da capo* numbers. The orchestral ritornello (something like *allegro aperto*) promises cheerfulness and enthusiasm, with its jolly first subject, strongly supported by independent accompaniment figures, and silvered over with high thirds for flutes—even if the bass line is sluggish.

The bridge passage and codetta are voluble, the second subject still in embryo and rather humdrum, though relieved by flute colouring. The singer, at her entry, gives a skeleton version of the tune in Ex. 10, adds to the bridge passage, enters late for the second subject but does complete it to its advantage and, after a burst of fioritura, produces a new third subject ('e l'orecchio ognor') which runs in sixths above the bass and clashes with an off-beat dominant pedal in the second violins—symbol perhaps of Metastasio's 'tardy ears'? After the D major cadence which ends the first half Ex. 10 is re-shaped for its dominant entry, as if it were a tonal answer in a fugue. There is a feint at A minor, then a return to G major for the reprise of second and third and codetta subjects, with new and pleasing bravura divisions.

Mozart's later setting (No. 11b) has oboes instead of flutes, and specifies *adagio* alternating with *allegro*. The opening is pensive, almost amorous with its pairs of oboes and violas echoing in languid thirds the violin's melody, also in thirds; the roles are reversed when the singer enters. It is a real melody, too, one that unfolds gradually and effortlessly, phrase after matching phrase.

The 1772 arias for *Scipione* have short themes and patterns, not melodies of this kind; where their basses move about very cautiously, in galant manner, the bass line of this aria has acquired animation and interest. The second strain of Ex. 11, doing duty for a separate second subject, uses canon very winningly, and its mixture of semiquavers and slower triplets towards the end sounds relaxed and ecstatic, not contrived as in Fortune's No. 8. Triplets are introduced gently and naturally into the vocal line as well. The melodic strands twine lovingly especially as the *adagio* reaches its final half-cadence (Mozart was asssuredly not thinking of Archbishop Colloredo when he set the text this second time).

The contrasting *allegro* (*Di virtù chi prove chiede*) begins in D major with a rustic cheerfulness more akin to No. 11a, though the phrases and the bass line are more vital. When the dominant arrives the string writing becomes more elaborate, decidedly enthusiastic in effect, though the overlying tone of voice is more aristocratic. At 'e l'orecchio' Mozart reworks the 'tardy ear' effect mentioned above, more intricately: the off-beat middle pedal is now on the seventh of dominant harmony; first and fifth degrees sway in another rhythmic pattern for violas, first violins and bass are in parallel tenths (much as in No. 11a) but the singer has an independent melodic part. The similarity is worth pointing out because the two settings are otherwise so different. The vocal part in this *allegro* presupposes an agile throat (Mozart's 'geläufiger Gurgel') for chains of broken thirds and, in the big division, a leap from top A down to middle C.

The glorious *adagio* is resumed in D major, beginning with the demonic second subject, reworking the music, effecting the illusion of a recapitulation, then pausing on an interrupted cadence, with a vocal flourish. The *allegro* now returns and works towards a partial recapitulation in the tonic, as beautifully scored and designed for soprano as before.

If a soprano today wished to include one of these two settings in a concert she would, it is plain, find the later version more gratifying to herself and her audience. It is a much finer and more expert piece of music. In a production of *Il sogno di Scipione* No. 11b is too strong for the rest of the score whose qualities have, wherever possible, been stressed in this chapter, though they have to be sensed in context. No. 11b is not part of that context and, to this extent, it is unjust to the opera if a performance includes this more advanced example of Mozart's art. The Scipionic choice is not only between two rival settings of the same text, but between Mozart's opera and one soprano's personal success. If she is an able singer she will shine in No. 11a as well.

The *Licenza* ends with a jubilant **Chorus, No. 12**, in praise of the Archbishop; an allusion is even made to the opera he has just witnessed.

> May such a happy day dawn a hundred times, illustrious prince. And may the inconstant goddess respect the mitre on your brow and the great soul in your breast.

The final chorus in an *opera seria* was usually sung by the soloists. This time a full chorus of mixed voices had already been prescribed for No. 4 and could be used again now. *Cento volte con lieto sembiante* is in D major, an energetic jig, if the string parts can be heard jigging through the massed block harmony of the chorus. The orchestra comprises oboes (no flutes), horns (high-pitched and jubilant), trumpets, drums and strings.

3

Il sogno di Scipione is not a large work. It was designed as a *pièce d'occasion* and, in the absence of further information, we may assume that no more than one festive performance was ever intended for it. The occasion was an important one for Wolfgang Mozart who had to persuade the new Archbishop that he should be retained as composer in the service of the Salzburg court. He wrote *Scipione* quite carefully, though quickly, to suit Salzburg taste and the abilities of given singers and orchestra. It needed minimal staging: lighting effects are required, and room for a chorus as well as soloists, but no curtain and nothing much in the way of scenery.

Mozart had to convey to his new prospective employer how well travelled and *au fait* he was in matters musical. He included Frenchified flutes in thirds and lilting dance-rhythms, Neapolitan vocal leaps, a certain amount of skilful academic writing, one strongly diversified *recitativo accompagnato*, two choruses (one in the contrapuntal Baroque manner, or nearly), a variety of formal structures amply deployed. He showed off the abilities of six singers, those impersonating the two goddesses with striking versatility. And he made the most of his Salzburg orchestra, its flutes, oboes, horns, and string section, bringing in trumpets and drums for lively additional effect. He also showed his skill in musical portraiture, not only in the characterization of Constanza and Fortuna, but in the mysterious atmosphere at the end of the overture, the throng of heroes in their chorus, the spectacular revenge of rejected Fortune, the solemn awakening of Scipio (a foretaste of Constanze in *Entführung*), and in many other momentary illustrative touches mentioned already.

He was not to know, at this stage, that Archbishop Colloredo, although fond of music, preferred short compositions and must have enjoyed the *Licenza* better than the opera, musically as well as for its flattering literary content.

For a modern audience *Il sogno di Scipione* is a historical exercise. Mozart was writing music-drama only by chance or through the inevitability of creative percipience.

If you gear your receptivity to the conventional climate of courtly opera in the 1770s in an enlightened Austrian town, the virtues of *Scipione* and its real shortcomings will be obvious. There are two superb arias, Publius's *Quercia annosa* and Constanza's *Biancheggia in mar* (I do not count the 1777 *Licenza* aria); and several other stretches of decent young Mozart. A just comparison, in terms of Mozart's musical development, must be with *Ascanio in Alba* and *Lucio Silla*. By this standard *Scipione* has little to offer. The challenge of Italy brought out Mozart's lyricism and his dramatic flair, both of them constrained in provincial Salzburg. In Italy he could goad his singers into blazing activity, could spur his own imagination. The pleasant or stimulating moments of *Il sogno di Scipione* happen seldom, under constraint, within the bounds of local (almost family) etiquette. The genius was half-scared to blow his nose or raise his voice in his home town, particularly with the new employer looking on. Under less restricting circumstances he would have burst into accompanied recitative for Constancy's explanation of spherical harmony, or Aemilius's glance at the world through the diminishing lens of the telescope. He would have sharpened the idiosyncrasy of all the arias, and varied more firmly the instrumentation and form of the musical numbers.

His music for *Scipione*, even at this age, is less tedious and conventional than that of relevant contemporaries (this is not self-evident: some Telemann compares well with Handel, early Beethoven poorly with the best Dušek or Clementi), and so, particularly since the composer was Wolfgang Amadé Mozart, it will always be revived. It means nothing at all except in terms of 1772 and Salzburg taste and a teenage genius. Comparisons even with *Lucio Silla*, let alone *Idomeneo*, are irrelevant, still less with Mozart's last operas. E. J. Dent dismissed *Il sogno di Scipione* in a sentence. He was judging by eternal and untypically unhistorical standards. We should not do so.

9 LUCIO SILLA

LUCIO SILLA

Opera seria in three acts

Text by

GIOVANNI DE GAMERRA

K. 135

LUCIO SILLA (Sulla), dictator	TENOR
GIUNIA (Junia), daughter of Gaius Marius and betrothed of	SOPRANO
CECILIO (Cecilius), proscribed senator	MALE SOPRANO
LUCIO CINNA (Lucius Cinna), Roman patrician, friend of Cecilius and secret enemy of Sulla	SOPRANO
CELIA, sister of Sulla	SOPRANO
AUFIDIO (Aufidius), tribune and friend of Sulla	TENOR
Guards	
Senators	
Nobles	
Soldiers	CHORUS
Populace	
Maidens	

The action occurs in Sulla's palace and the vicinity

Mitridate, rè di Ponto was sufficiently successful to encourage Count Firmian to commission another opera from Mozart for the Milan carnival season of 1772–3. Mozart would be given furnished lodgings and a fee of 130 gigliati for the composition of *Lucio Silla* to a libretto by Giovanni de Gamerra (1743–1803), a native of Leghorn who had been both priest and soldier, was now Governor-General of Lombardy, and was to attempt the foundation of a national theatre in Naples, (besides translating *Die Zauberflöte* into Italian, a version known to all London opera-goers during the nineteenth century—when G. B. Shaw referred to *Qui sdegno* and a character called Astrafiammante he was referring to Gamerra's version). Mozart would deliver the recitatives by October 1772, then arrive in November at Milan to compose the arias and assist at rehearsals. In the meanwhile Milan called on his services yet again for *Ascanio in Alba*.

Wolfgang Mozart, now well into his seventeenth year, left Salzburg with his father on 24 (or 26) October 1772 en route for Milan. He had sent off the recitatives for *Lucio Silla*. During the journey he passed the time by composing a string quartet, perhaps K. 134a (K. 155) in D major. There were choruses and an overture for *Lucio Silla* to be written; arias had to wait until he met the soloists. Father and son arrived in Milan on 4 November, only to discover that the librettist Gamerra had asked Metastasio to approve his text, and that the great man had made several alterations, removing one scene and adding a new one. Mozart had at once to revise his recitatives, then compose the three choral numbers and the overture, having heard the orchestra in its present state.

Leopold Mozart's letters home to Salzburg give a good idea of how the eighteenth-century opera composer had to work. Wolfgang's first customer was the soprano Felicità Suardi who had the breeches-part of Lucio Cinna (a male soprano part could, in those days, be given almost impartially to a castrato or a female singer, whoever was available and suitable, just as a castrato often took the part of a woman). By 14 November, Mozart had met Giuseppe Onofrio, the tenor who was to sing Aufidio. The castrato star, Venanzio Rauzzini, did not arrive until 20 November; he was cast as Cecilius, and was twenty-six years old.* Leopold Mozart reported home that Rauzzini sang Cecilius's first aria, which was 'superlatively beautiful, like an angel'.

On 4 December the *prima donna* arrived. She was Anna de Amicis Buonsolazzi, another of Italy's greatest singers, an outstanding actress as well as vocalist, whom

---

* Rauzzini (1746–1810) settled in England in 1774, made a career in London as singer, pianist and prolific composer, and spent his last years in Bath of which he became an eminent citizen. Haydn visited him there and Michael Kelly. His pupils included Nancy Storace, Mrs Billington and John Braham. He wrote an admired set of vocal exercises with some important advice about ornamentation. His voice was beautiful but not very large. It may be mentioned that he made his debut in a female (travesty) role and that, a few weeks after the première of *Lucio Silla*, Mozart wrote for him the superb solo motet *Exultate, Jubilate*. He deserves this brief biographical note for his importance in Mozartian lore as much as British musical history.

Mozart had met ten years earlier in Mainz. She had the part of Junia, and for her Mozart wrote the arias which, in later years, he most prized in this opera—he had them sung by other sopranos in concerts of his own.

The *primo tenore* and sustainer of the name-part, Cordoni, had still not appeared in Milan. On 5 December word arrived that he was ill and must be replaced. The title-role required a handsome personage, good actor, and—well, a principal tenor singer for whom Mozart could write music that would appeal to the audience. An official of the Milan theatre went off to Turin to find such a paragon. Mozart, we gather, still had fourteen musical numbers to compose. Daniella Mienci, the Celia, must have arrived by this time; she evidently needed to display her ability in *staccato* music, and her gift for comedy. Mozart had enough work to keep him busy (orchestral rehearsals started on 12 December) until the arrival of the substitute Lucio Silla on 17 December. This was Bassano Morgnoni, a church tenor from Lodi, a feeble actor who had only been on stage twice in his life. Presumably he looked well and could sing accurately though evidently not with brilliance. Four arias were allotted to Silla but Mozart only set two; doubtless there was no time for Morgnoni to learn any more, even if Mozart had composed music for them all.

There were orchestral rehearsals on the 20th and 22nd, parties at Court Firmian's residence on 21, 22, and 23 December, at each of which Mozart had to play. The dress rehearsal was also on the 23rd. Then the première on the day after Christmas 1772. It was due to begin at 5 p.m. ('one hour after the Angelus,' writes Leopold) but had to be delayed while the Archduke—he for whose wedding *Ascanio* had been composed—finished lunch and then wrote formal letters of New Year greeting to the Emperor, Empress and other important people. Since he was a slow writer the musicians and audience were kept waiting until 8 p.m., crammed into the overheated theatre, many of them obliged to remain standing. The performance included not only *Lucio Silla* but also three ballets, one after each act of the opera; the first of these, *Le gelosie del seraglio*, had music by Mozart who had found time to compose its thirty-two movements since his arrival in Milan. Only the composition sketch of this is extant, the full score having doubtless been burned in the fire which destroyed the Teatro Regio Ducal in 1775, and led to the construction of the present so-called Teatro alla Scala. No wonder, then, that the performance was not over before 2 a.m.

There were other difficulties. All the singers were nervous. Rauzzini had warned the Archduchess of this, and she therefore applauded noisily at his first entrance, much to the annoyance of de Amicis, the *prima donna*. Furthermore the tenor Morgnoni over-acted absurdly in his scenes with de Amicis, and the resultant laughter in the audience took her aback and prevented her from singing her best. Leopold Mozart noted in her favour that she was an 'angelic' singer and actress, and exceptionally kind to Wolfgang. Later performances went well, with full houses and many encores; *Lucio Silla* was given as many as 26 times before the Mozarts left Milan on 4 March 1773, but not thereafter in Mozart's setting until 14 December 1929 when it was given in Prague in a German translation. Gamerra's libretto, more or less revised, was set by other composers including J. C. Bach—Mozart read and admired Bach's setting during his visit to Mannheim in November 1777.

2

The Lucio Silla of Gamerra's libretto is better known to English-speaking readers as Sulla or Lucius Cornelius Sylla (138–78 B.C.) the scheming, vainglorious, exhibitionistic and bloodthirsty tyrant* who rose from poverty to great wealth acquired by seduction or extortion, conquered Greece, concluded a treaty with Mithridates of Pontus, made friends with Parthia, patronized the arts and sciences, himself completing twenty-two volumes of his memoirs, reformed the political and legal systems of Rome and having, after the slaughter of thousands of Roman noblemen, achieved the omnipotence of a dictator suddenly abrogated his power and restored government by public elections. Sulla's character was well blackened by his contemporaries, and modern biographers have questioned some of the lurid detail in, for example, Plutarch's account of him. Gamerra, when contriving his libretto, seems to have drawn largely on Plutarch. His purpose was immediately to present Sulla, as a lover who happens to be a dictator, in various situations and moods; ultimately to extol the monarch's magnanimity for the benefit of the Milanese and their Archduke; yet he was able to find these (if not deliberate avoidance of all violent action) in his classical source-material. Gamerra, in his preface, remarks of Sulla that 'in his heart the light of reason and virtuous impulse was not wholly extinguished'. Gamerra alludes, in his text, to Sulla's foxiness ('L'arte di Silla per trionfar del di lei fido amore'), his 'perverso amore' in fixing his heart upon the daughter of his great (and equally ruthless) enemy Caius Marius, herself the wife of a proscribed senator; Sulla's hot temper and cruelty matched against indefatigable amorousness ('given to rapine and prodigality' is Plutarch's censorious verdict, backed up by many an example). Aufidius in Act I, Scene iv reminds the audience that Sulla is 'the proud terror of Asia, the conqueror of Pontus, the arbiter in the Senate, he who saw a Mithridates crouch at his great feet'. And Junia, addressing the ghost of her father Marius, recalls his enmity with Sulla. Plutarch provided Gamerra also with his fictitious as well as historical characters. Lucius Cinna was by no means Sulla's secret enemy but the fellow-conspirator of Caius Marius in the *coup* which took over Rome while Sulla was fighting overseas against Mithridates. After Marius died, Cinna was in fact plotting a campaign against Sulla when he was assassinated by one of his own officers. Aufidius is named by Plutarch as 'one of Sulla's fawning companions'. Junia is an invention, though Marius had a wife named Julia (of the Caesar family). Cecilius may be Quintus Cecilius Metellus called Numidicus, an accomplice and then victim of Marius. Sulla was married to Cecilia Metella of the same illustrious family. Another of his numerous wives was called Clelia, who perhaps suggested to Gamerra the name of Lucio Silla's imaginary sister Celia.

3

Mozart again reverted to the conventional Italian form of operatic *sinfonia* in three separate movements, fast–slow–fast. As noted above he wrote it after discovering the potentiality of the Milan orchestra (their horns and trumpets were

---

* 'He is half-lion, half-fox,' said his adversary Carbo, 'and it is the fox in his breast which troubles me most.'

evidently reliable, their violas capable of taking independent *divisi* parts), but before the rest of the opera—for reasons of time-saving. Thereafter he always left the composition of the overture until the rest of the score was complete, so that it might have some bearing on what followed.

The **Overture** to *Lucio Silla* has no such special relevance, except conceivably at one point. It uses pairs of oboes, horns, trumpets, timpani and a string section. The first movement, in D major *molto allegro*, has a jerky, drum-like opening subject (though the timpani never play the tune, and Mozart does not ask the player to attempt anything faster than a crotchet/quarter-note) that develops nicely, at its first repetition, with trumpet fanfares, a bouncing bass, and the tune on oboes and horns supported an octave lower by violas. The second subject establishes A major in the accompaniment, then causes mild surprise by starting its melody right outside that key (on the dominant chord of the supertonic, B minor). In between and afterwards there is plenty of mechanical atmosphere-making, running scales and cadence-figures. The development section, so-called, consists of a new tune, even prettier when repeated by oboes. In the recapitulation the first subject group is abbreviated.

The middle movement is a balmy A major *andante*, for oboes and strings, notable for strong dynamic contrasts and for the unusually extended second phrase in its main tune. The second group is delicately diversified in content, with a charming access of melodic triplets that survive into the central section. Here is the only indication that Mozart had thoughts about the libretto. With a loud wail from the oboes the music plunges into E minor and a quickly subdued mood of evanescent mystery; we may wonder (Hermann Abert was convinced) if he was already pondering the mausoleum scene.

The overture's finale is another *molto allegro* in rushing triple time, gay and voluble.

Act I begins on the banks of the River Tiber in a lonely grove. Decayed ruins can here and there be seen, further away the Quirinal Mountain topped by a small temple. Cecilius, a proscribed senator, has secretly returned to Rome and is waiting here for his friend Cinna. With every moment his doubts and fears increase. Cinna arrives, delighted to see his exiled friend again. Cecilius's first inquiries are for his beloved wife, Junia, left behind in Rome. To his dismay he learns that she is mourning his death, following a rumour put about by the dictator Sulla in order to secure Junia's love. Cecilius proposes at once to go and undeceive her but Cinna advises caution: as a proscribed person he is under sentence of death if spotted in Rome. Sulla moreover has abducted Junia to his own palace. Cecilius dare not risk entering it. Cinna advises him to hide in the mausoleum of dead heroes just outside the palace grounds. Junia and her handmaidens are accustomed every day to visit her father's tomb there. Cecilius can surprise her during her next visit and they can be safely re-united. Cinna will meanwhile stand guard at the spot together with a number of Cecilius's most trusty friends who are all working to liberate Rome.

Cinna preaches optimism in his *allegro* **Aria, No. 1**, *Vieni ov'amor t'invita*, in B flat major accompanied by oboes, horns doubled by trumpets (most unusual), and strings. This is a fully extended *da capo* aria with double exposition, the longest in the opera (though Cinna is a subsidiary character). The thematic material of the first, orchestral exposition is plentiful but purposefully concentrated into two subject-groups, each containing ideas to be used (as from a third group) for coda sections or linking ritornelli. The elaborate scoring and textural lay-out were not at all typical of Italian opera but were becoming a necessary part of Mozart's operatic technique.

Thus the first subject-group comprises a vigorous, rather heroic principal idea, similar to that of *Una bella serenata* in *Così*, and firmly wedded to a loud fanfare pattern for second violins. The bass is static, the oboe and bass parts quasi-independent.

The continuation of this, repeated notes and descending scale, suggests independent phrases later in the aria and always follows Ex. 1 in reprises. The third element in this group, a run with an echo (keyboard filling-in is obviously required here, and is everywhere else appropriate), recurs as codetta material. The second group similarly contains one subsidiary main theme, laid out on three levels:

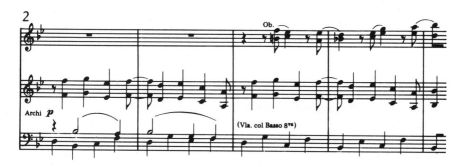

—and two cadential ideas for coda treatment. All this occurs in the aria's tonic, B flat.

> Come where love invites you. Already my breast senses omens of your approaching happiness.
>
> The sea is not always angry nor the sky overcast. Eventually they become serene and smiling.

The solo exposition repeats the first group's first two elements followed by the second group's third limb, then turns to the dominant F major and introduces a new idea, more like the conventional symphonic 'second subject' in its ingratiating melodiousness. This precipitates a florid division out of which Ex. 2, with an added vocal part, emerges and leads to the exposition's firm F major cadence and the orchestral linking ritornello as described above.

In classical concerto design there now follows the development section, re-manipulating exposed ideas and exploring other keys. Mozart, in his adaptation of this form for arias (sometimes in concertos as well), prefers to introduce new ideas which may pass through foreign keys but, at this period, scuttle back quickly to dominant or tonic. Here the new orchestral idea is dimly related, through the voice part, to Ex. 1, makes an overt reference to the second limb of that first group and edges into E flat major—but only so as to regain the dominant for a running passage that passes through C minor on the way to B flat as tonic. This is done smoothly and with two exquisite moments of chromatic harmony to point the journey. The recapitulation begins (as not infrequently in Mozart's extended arias of this period—see the account of No. 1 in *Il sogno di Scipione*) with the second group in the tonic, then makes quickly for the closing ritornello.

A formal sonata-movement would be complete by now—though it would have recapitulated the first group. In Mozart's extended aria forms of this period the foregoing is the outer cover of a sandwich whose filling is represented by a central contrasting section with new words, a new key, sometimes a new tempo and time-signature. Here the key is E flat, but the mood rather similar to the foregoing. The poetic contrast between the two new sentences of text prompts Mozart to make a pause after the first, then bump into F major for the second sentence where the orchestra has the main musical interest. A linking orchestral ritornello re-establishes B flat and leads to a complete restatement, not from the very beginning (*da capo*) but from the beginning of the vocal exposition, as baroque composers often did. Even this makes a longer aria than was usual for Mozart; he generally took his *da capo* from the start of the development or even from the recapitulation.[*] It has to be remembered (in modern performances is quite forgotten) that these massive repetitions were by no means mechanical. It was here that the singer showed special, personal musical ability by embellishing and varying all that had been heard before. Some less elaborate decoration had already occurred in the recapitulation.

Cinna goes off to organize his watch-party. Cecilius, left alone, breaks into orchestrally accompanied recitative, a texture that elsewhere Mozart uses sparingly, for moments of great emotional intensity, though *Lucio Silla* is particularly rich in *recitativo stromentato*. This was certainly an appropriate moment, the loving heart's delighted anticipation of reunion with the beloved, tenderness mingling with ecstasy, impatience, and visions of the still mournful Junia. The accompanied recitative allowed each of these emotions to be established, even if nutshell-fashion, by orchestral commentary more detailed than was possible in dry recitative notated by a bass-line alone.

---

[*] This has no doubt encouraged modern editors further to reduce the length of these arias, with effects not merely surgical but mutilatory. Perhaps this is why one reads that *Lucio Silla* contains no *da capo* arias!

Cecilius's first sentence ('Dunque sperar poss' io') against sustained string chords is remarkably similar to Susanna's *Giunse alfin* in the last act of *Figaro*, showing that Mozart's musical responses remained consistent, even if he had no need to remember how he had treated such a moment in a youthful opera long since forgotten. Similarly the end of the recitative ('Ah forse adesso') will recall Countess Almaviva in the third act of the same opera: she laments that she must rely on a servant's co-operation to reunite her with her renegade husband; Cecilius imagines his wife in tears and alone. In both passages Mozart introduces a touch of tearful melancholy. In the context of Cecilius's joy the dive into warm E flat major, immediately after a burst of frenzied impatience, is all the more moving, as is the plaintive harmony and drooping vocal line for 'Lagrime . . . lagrime'.

The ensuing **Aria, No. 2**, is not pathetic at all but exceptionally jubilant, touched here and there with galant expressions of amorous warmth in keeping with its verbal content.

Already my heart can depict the tender moment, reward of such great love.
What will be my extent of happiness by her side when already the thought of my pleasure so excites me?

Il tenero momento is an *allegro aperto* in F major with oboes, horns and strings. What was written above about the exposition's ingredients applies again, given the different emotional circumstances. The form is slightly different in that the central section, which begins in B flat and ends on the verge of D minor, is very closely related, like a variation, to the ideas and contours of the first group. The motives of the orchestral exposition are even more subtly interwoven in the subsequent design. The spring-heeled-Jack Neapolitan vocal leaps beloved of virtuoso sopranos (e.g. Fiordiligi, but male sopranos and tenors too, not to forget the solo pianist, Mozart, in several of his piano concertos) are included copiously, and worked thematically into the orchestral exposition. Castrati loved to enter on a *mesa di voce*, a sustained tone beginning softly, swelling out, then diminishing: Mozart gave Rauzzini just such an entry, and prepared for it by dovetailing the end of the orchestral exposition into this entry as he was to do in K. 320d, the Sinfonia Concertante with violin and viola. The orchestral ritornello leading to the cadenza at the end of the outer cover is new, but it returns to end the central section, and of course reappears in the *da capo*.

The vocal part proudly displays the singer's agility and expressive qualities through two octaves from low A to high A. Oboes and horns are felicitously exploited on their own, thematically as well as for supporting colour.

The scene changes to the apartments in Sulla's palace which he has set aside for Junia (we can in any case add a pinch of salt to Cinna's earlier remark that Sulla had already 'dragged Junia into his own bed'). It is appropriately decorated with statues of Rome's most celebrated heroines. Sulla, attended by his sycophant Aufidius and guards, is entrusting his sister Celia with the task of softening Junia's heart to his amorous advantage. She promises to do her best. Aufidius advises him to employ force for the sake of his dictatorial prestige. Sulla is inclined to agree, but Celia disapproves on moral and diplomatic grounds. Violence is never as effective as gentleness and persuasion. He must woo her affections. Sulla promises to exercise kindness yet again (he is not Plutarch's Sulla evidently). Celia adds that his task should be easy. Junia's husband is dead, and no dead lover can be a difficult rival for a living one.

Celia summarizes her advice in her **Aria, No. 3**, *Se lusinghiera speme* which is *grazioso* in C major, accompanied only by strings.

> Lovers who cannot feed on flattering hopes must find their fidelity weakening, however constant they may be. This same faithful, tender heart, at present so obstinate, will give in.

Celia is a minor character and her first aria is therefore a much abbreviated variant of the *da capo* form examined above. It also hides its symphonic tracks under cover of a sweet, maidenly lyricism and a dance-orientated lilt. With an initial bass line like the following, there is less occasion for the bass line to scrub away on tonic or dominant unchanged for bars and bars and bars. And though two subject groups can be heard in either exposition, they sound like two strains of a single melody.

4

[Grazioso]

Se lu—sin—ghie—ra spe—me pa——scer, pa—scer

non sa gli a—man—ti, an————che frà i più co—

-stan—ti lan—gui—sce fe——del—tà—.

I have cited the first group as it appears in the vocal exposition, so as to show the noble low-lying second half of the first melodic sentence, a variant of the group as first heard—the original version is used for linking purposes. Evidently Daniella Mienci specialized in high staccato fioritura for all her divisions are of this pointillist nature (see Ex. 12). The quasi-development features an imitative point for upper strings, and a brief collapse into slow waltz rhythm. The recapitulation is foreshortened and partly rewritten for key stability, as is the drastically abbreviated apology for a *da capo*. The central section goes faster (*allegretto*), starts quite boldly, in F major ('Quel cor si fido'), turns chromatically to A minor, with a stab on 'pieghera' and ends in E minor. An orchestral bridge leads back to the second subject in C and a closely selective reprise of exposition and recapitulation material.★

When Celia has left, Aufidius protests that Sulla should so demean himself as to

★ In the only available (1971) recording the form is obscured by the removal of central section and *da capo*, as well as another cut earlier. The new BASF version is complete.

put up with the stubborn rudeness of Junia, a mere woman, he who has all Asia at his feet. Sulla answers that the magnanimous heart cannot be debased by love. He promises that Junia shall this very day become his bride. Aufidius tells him that Junia is approaching, hatred and grief written on her features. Sulla orders him to leave them alone together.

Sulla asks Junia when her tears (for once the nondescript harpsichord accompaniment dwells on the emotional implications of a word) will dry and she turn a smiling face to him. At first she does not reply and he begs her to explain her sorrow. But the more kindly his tones, the more she abuses him: her hatred for Sulla is as all-consuming as her love for Cecilius. Sulla tries to pretend that his conduct towards her, and her late father too, has been blameless; but she reminds him that he was the enemy of her father, and has exiled her husband to pine away and die in a foreign land. How should she love the man who did all this? Even if Cecilius is dead, she vows she will love him for ever, for his own sake and as her father's chosen son-in-law. If that is her intention, answers Sulla, he will leave her time to mend her ways: either she abandons her proud hatred, or she must prepare for death. Junia despises him the more for even imagining that the threat of death would weaken the fortitude of a Roman heart, of Caius Marius's daughter. She will obey her father's teaching: to abhor Sulla, adore her husband, then die.

Her **Aria, No. 4** in E flat major, *Dalla sponda tenebrosa*, grandly scored for oboes, horns, trumpets (separate parts this time, of course) and strings, falls into three parts, a prayer to her father and husband (*andante ma adagio*), alternating with scorn for Sulla (*allegro*), and a faster *allegro* coda in which she contrasts her future happiness away from him with the pangs of conscience he will experience.

> Come from the gloomy shore, father and beloved husband, to receive my last breath.
>
> Cruel man, you may rage at my disdain, but this is not your greatest punishment.
>
> I shall be satisfied not to have you near me, while you will remain with the remorse in your heart.

The form is quite simple but creative. The *adagio* (the apparently contradictory instruction *andante ma adagio* means 'slow but not stagnant', or one might say that the melody should have great breadth while the semiquaver accompaniment moves gently along) consists of two expositions with a single subject group whose first limb is eloquently solemn, its continuation a rocked dotted-rhythm figure much developed. In the vocal exposition a new episode ('d'una figlia') continues the melody so as to modulate towards the dominant and propose a *gruppetto* accompaniment figure. The words 'l'estremo fiato' are pictorially set:

5

[Andante ma Adagio]

l'es-tre ——— mo fia——to...

The pause over the quaver/quarter-note rest betokens a moment's silence, not a vocal flourish but a symbol of death.

The *gruppetto* comes into its own in the *allegro*. The voice's two unaccompanied initial entries, interspersed with energetic orchestral gestures (the trumpets, silent in the *adagio*, make their effect here), always suggest impatience in Mozart, and are a regular feature of *allegro* after a slower section. They recur later in this *allegro*, after a telling episode ('la pena tua maggior') of soft staccato strings, tiptoe footsteps as it were, interrupted repeatedly by a surprise loud full chord, like the unexpected blows of stealthy vengeance. The singer's rapid division, at the end of this section, involves a strenuous fanfare effect testifying to the agile gullet of Mad. de Amicis.

The *adagio* is now recapitulated in B flat major, almost rhythm for rhythm and texture for texture, but in melodically varied form so that it has been composed afresh. Likewise with the second *allegro*, now in E flat major (the fanfare divisions are even more hair-raising this time). The quicker coda (*allegro* should surely read *più allegro*) is hectic and emotionally inspired with characteristic brass punctuations of Do–mi–sol, and a thrilling vocal leap of a major seventh (really a diminished octave). Mozart had made good arrangements for Mad. de Amicis's applause.

Junia leaves the stage. Sulla, in dry recitative, still questions his almost limitless tolerance; it is only because he fancies her ('e pur mi piace'). The idea drives him into accompanied recitative (strings alone, *allegretto*, C major). The relevant orchestral theme is much too bland for the circumstances and it is quickly dropped in favour of a dramatic tremolo with a motif of decision in the bass. Sulla decides to strangle his infatuation and kill this proud woman. If she will not love him let her fear him (as the Romans said, 'oderint dum metuant'); she detests him so let him play the tyrant. The situation is exactly that of Bassa Selim with Constanze in *Die Entführung*. How regrettable that Mozart did not let Selim sing!

Sulla's solo **Aria, No. 5,** has been long postponed for maximum effect. Now it floods forth heroically in D major (some sort of *allegro maestoso*), with oboes, horns, trumpets and drums as well as strings, *Il desio di vendetta*. It is essentially an eighteenth-century Establishment D major, the key appropriate to God and the monarch; Mozart's music is geared to this mentality, at least in its first subject-group, though the second-group tune and intimate string writing have strayed out of a serenade or *Nachtmusik*.

A crescendo restores the governing instinct and an eminently dictatorial leap on first violins, from low G sharp to top D and back to low A, introduces the codetta flourishes.

The lust for vengeance and death so inflames me that all tender feelings have been transformed into anger, now that I have been scorned.

Perhaps at the last moment you will beg for life, but your weeping will be useless.

It will be seen that Ex. 7 refers to 'ogni debole affetto' ('all tender feelings') and the loud scrubbing at the top of the crescendo to Sulla's wrath ('furor'). The dictatorial leap features among the ritornello material but, surprisingly perhaps, there is nothing like it in the vocal part which is fairly simple, without any florid divisions or room for a cadenza. The singer has to create an impression by the intensity of his vocal delivery and his ability to express 'furor'.

The aria is again of the design discussed in No. 1 but truncated both in recapitulation and *da capo*. The first group of the solo exposition includes a new idea; the development takes an inflammatory turn into E minor; what appears to be the start of the recapitulation is new material in the subdominant G major, the return to exposition material in the tonic occurring immediately afterwards, from the third limb of the first group. The central section ('Forse nel punto estremo') moves from G to B minor, and sounds relentlessly cheerful as it chugs along, except where the change to B minor is made via a loudly wailing diminished seventh.

The scene changes during an *andante* orchestral passage (oboes and strings, *divisi* violas) that begins in B flat but at once moves slowly, in a mood of solemnity and veneration, towards A major—sostenuto oboes floating above pulsating strings. By what sounds like a miracle, all the more because the step is child's play, A major becomes A minor. Oboes and violas, in thirds, wail downwards and the stage reveals the entrance to the catacomb of Roman heroes, a dark and magnificent vestibule.

Cecilius enters and this orchestral music, enriched by the addition of bassoons, horns and trumpets, continues without pause as the introduction to an accompanied recitative (*Morte, morte fatal*). We are now embarked on the finest music Mozart had yet composed, music that sends constant shivers down the spine because the composer's imagination is completely engaged in a dramatic situation worthy of it, and so this imagination works at least one jump ahead of anybody listening to it. The introduction is heavy with destiny and reverence. The pungent brass instruments, newly added to the texture, are playing sustained weighty chords. The bass rocks momentously to and fro, balanced and strengthened by contrary motion in the oboes. First violins are intoning on their lowest string; seconds play regular patterns of broken chords that aerate this heavy sound, like the slowly flapping wings of a gigantic bird, the bird of death. Presently the strings are left by themselves with a doleful melody (Phrygian or Neapolitan seconds to the fore). Cecilius's cue is a loud harmonic progression from the dominant of A minor to shadowy, tragic C minor. He reflects eloquently on the presence of death in these vaults.

Morte fatal della tua mano
ecco le prove in queste gelide tombe.
Eroi, duci, regnanti,
che devastar la terra,

Fateful death, your hand
is proven here in these icy tombs.
Heroes, leaders, monarchs
who laid waste the earth,

angusto marmo or qui ricopre,	are now covered by narrow marble
e serra. Gia in cento bocche	and enclosed. Once on a hundred mouths,
e cento dei lor fatti	and a hundred more, their deeds
eccheggio stupido il mondo,	re-echoed through an astonished world.
e or qui gl'avvolge un muto orror profondo.	Now, dumb, deep awe envelops them here.

The destiny-laden orchestral music, now imperious, now hushed, intersperses his sentences. Oboes and bassoons have deeply expressive comments and the harmony quakes with plangent chromaticism. A dynamic burst of *allegro assai* signals his disturbance as he sees a crowd approaching. It is Junia (tender, dignified melodious *andante* in E flat) and she is accompanied by others (*presto*). Cecilius's heart pounds wildly (shuddering violins). He decides to hide behind the funeral urn of Junia's father Marius.

A steadily progressing C major figuration for strings suggests the approaching procession. Tension rises when C major becomes C minor again. Solemn trumpet calls divert the music to E flat for **No. 6**, a **Chorus** (probably *andante mosso*, though tempo is not indicated) of Junia's companions, her handmaidens and a group of Roman noblemen. The stage directions mention their 'lugubre canto'. Mozart sets this in dignified E flat major with orchestration as before (horns and trumpets are now doubled for weight-giving purposes), with violent dynamic contrasts to load the music's pulse, and with plentiful chromatic interest to stress the implicit grief. Yet the words are positive and inflammatory.

Emerge from these doleful urns, souls that we honour, and indignantly avenge Rome's freedom.

Accordingly Mozart's music for this chorus is eventful, dramatic, unwilling to remain in simple block harmony, powerfully and boldly scored, in fact grandly beautiful and rather animated, not really 'lugubre'. The coda of this chorus brings forward the individual instruments in pairs (still loud and soft on alternate beats—violins first, then horns and trumpets, oboes, violas, lastly muted violins); Mozart may have imagined the 'donzelle 'and 'nobili' stepping forward, two by two, to place tributes beside Marius's tomb. The organization is formal but each instrumental entry is turned by Mozart's imagination into a musical event. The muted violins creep downward into G minor for Junia's *molto adagio* prayer to her father's ashes. The horns and trumpets are silent here, the bassoons attain independence, and the oboes; the violas prick the elaborate string texture with their *pizzicati*, like lutes in a baroque orchestra. And Junia's voice is uplifted in a grief-laden Mozartian G minor which may unpatronizingly be set beside Pamina, Constanze and Ilia in the same key, a smooth and flowing lament, exquisitely coloured yet profoundly classical in tone, indefatigably momentous.

Dear shade of my father, if you are hovering around me, let my tears and sighs move you to pity.

The chorus resumes *allegro* in E flat, calling imprecations on Rome's tyrant. This is a more conventional section, structurally necessary (it is a construction which we may connect, like the key-scheme, with Gluck though choruses with a central solo were a feature of French opera); there are thematic links with the earlier chorus.

Junia, still accompanied by a warm haze of strings to emphasize the solemnity of the moment (a harmonic progresssion when she speaks of supplication makes this evident), appeals to her father's shade—then to her dead husband. The strings vanish and she confesses in monochrome, as it were, the dreariness of a widow's existence.

Cecilius steps from behind the urn and reveals his presence. The shock to Junia (*tremolando*) restores the string accompaniment. At first she supposes him a spectre, then the violins begin to move positively. Cecilius firmly admits that he is her living husband.

Junia launches the **Duet, No. 7**, *andante*, in A major (significant Mozart key), *D'Eliso in sen m'attendi*, in the belief that he is still dead and awaits her there. This is more stilted, more *opera seria*, in manner than the foregoing. Wife and husband begin with the conventional *mesa di voce*—an emotional effect for those days. The orchestration is reduced to oboes, chattering in thirds, horns giving basic punctuation, and strings. The serious aspect of A major is disclosed in the low-lying violin melodies and the emotional leaps in Junia's first solo. Cecilius persuades her that he is truly alive; the music gains expressiveness, though the tone of musical voice remains, by later Mozart standards, formal. Once she has been convinced the violins begin a rushing figure, and husband and wife duet together in thirds and sixths, harking back briefly to their earlier 'dolor'. They move into a joyous *molto allegro* with two lots of running divisions, a strong moment of heightened orchestral tension and further contrasts of dynamic. With their duet the first act ends.

4

Act II begins in an 'archway adorned with military trophies'—out of doors and in character with Sulla's position. Baroque stage directions are usually as sensible as this, ignored to the disadvantage of the opera. Aufidius is doing his best to arouse Sulla's pride and lordliness towards the scornful Junia. It would be unwise to kill her, because she has too many supporters. Best to wed her in public; she will not resist.

Aufidius is now given an **Aria, No. 8**, *Guerrier che d'un acciaro* in C major (perhaps *allegro maestoso*), with oboes, horns doubling trumpets, and strings. Mozart shows no signs of being inspired either by the artistic personality of the singer or by the contrast implicit in the words.

> The warrior who turns pale at the flash of steel should not expose his cowardice on the battlefield.
> If he gives way to base fear, and then to hope, this is unsteadfast.

Mozart evokes the martial character at once, but in stiff conventional ideas and monotonous scoring. There are two or three effective modulations, a quantity of running divisions, and a *mesa di voce* on the word 'acciaro' ('steel') at the singer's first entry. Felicities are not otherwise in evidence (no illustration of 'timor' or 'speranza') and the shortened *da capo* form seems all too lengthy. One could hardly blame the London production of 1968 for excising this aria, and with it the entire role of Aufidius.

Celia comes to commiserate with her brother on his lack of success with Junia. He is not disheartened: this day she will be his bride, he will not tell Celia by what inducement (he mutters aside that women can never keep secrets), though he does add that she too will marry Cinna this day—the news delights her, and she runs off to tell him the news and reveal her love for him (this is the first we have heard of it). Sulla too hurries off to the Capitol to carry out his plan.

A moment later Cecilius runs in, pursuing Sulla with a drawn sword, Cinna trying to restrain him. It is not, he urges, only Cecilius's life that is in danger if he attacks the tyrant. Rome's freedom demands that the plot must not misfire. What has caused Cecilius's sudden bloodlust? No sooner had he left Junia, her husband replies, than he fell asleep and dreamed that Marius's tomb was open and that the dead man's skull addressed him saying (here Cecilius is accompanied by sustained string chords): "Do not delay to kill Sulla or you will lose your bride and I my daughter.' Cecilius awoke (dry recitative is resumed), seized his sword and set out. Cinna begs him to consider that on his life Junia's own depends also. This thought checks his impetuous rage. But only for a moment. The strings break into a passionate D minor theme (*allegro assai*) emphasizing the falling third—it is developed consistently in this accompanied recitative *Ah corri, vola*. Conflicting emotions rage in Cecilius's heart and they are ardently reflected in the music. After a moment's thought (slow rising figure, C–E–G) he resolves (same figure in quick tempo, based on the tonic triad, no longer doubtful but determined) to save Junia or perish at her side.

This same figure opens Cecilius's **Aria, No. 9**, *Quest' improvviso tremito* in D major, *allegro assai* scored for oboes, horns, trumpets, drums and strings.

> This sudden trembling that rises in my breast may be hope or may be anger.
> But whichever it may be it shall terrify that traitor.

Mozart is here at his most impassioned and dramatic. For once he abandons the *da capo* concept, and the double exposition. Stormy basses, copious tremolo figures, violent dynamic contrasts, and perpetually developing themes are typical of the music. There is no development section as such. The recapitulation is signalled by the recurrence of the orchestra's initial motif, but the writing is new and the words too are those of the second verse. The number is noble in design, but unconventionally so. We may be reminded of Donna Anna's *Or sai chi l'onore*, but even that great aria is more rigidly put together. In analytical terms this one must be described as a binary structure disguised: when the first half ends with an orchestral ritornello, cunningly and gradually evolved from an ascending half-scale bass near the start, the music plunges into F sharp (as dominant of B minor) for a new version of the pit-a-pat theme connected with 'speranza' (hope'), makes a pause, then bursts again into D major for the pseudo-recapitulation. The 'speranza' theme is given two new, equally striking variants.

Cinna, left alone, remarks that Sulla's crimes are likely to be as wicked as Tarquin's if he is not struck down soon. Now Celia comes to tell him about their wedding and her love. But she is so embarrassed that she cannot get an intelligible sentence out. Finally she asks him to look into her eyes and read her meaning.

She says this again in the **Aria, No. 10**, *tempo grazioso* in G major, *Se il labbro timido*, with flutes and strings. The music is fresh and feather-light, inventively compact, a binary structure like No. 9 but without that aria's capacity for thematic self-renewal: the tunes remain the same, even when the details are varied—there are similar binary arias in *Scipione* and *Rè pastore*. The ideas and texture remain firmly galant, enchanting.

> If my shy lips dare not reveal my hidden flame, let my eyes speak for them, and unveil all my heart to you.

Cinna has cleverly understood Celia's message. He tells himself that, although he has never yet been in love, when he does succumb it will not be to a tyrant's sister. Junia, careworn and thoughtful, approaches: she alone can execute his plan.

She asks him why Sulla has commanded her to appear before the Senate and populace, and begs him to watch over her husband and conceal him from the tyrant. He promises to do this and warns her that Sulla will ask the Senate's approval of his marriage to her. Junia replies that she will never agree. Cinna suggests she should marry him, then kill him in bed and please the gods who love to see criminals punished. Junia refuses: even a plebeian life is sacred to her, how much more a man put in command of Rome, though he be unjust? He mentions Junius Brutus who saved Rome by killing one of the hated Tarquin family. Junia reminds him that Brutus killed in open battle. It is for heaven and heaven alone to remove Sulla.

She breaks into accompanied recitative (strings, *allegro* in B flat major, urgent).

> Go, take charge of my husband and hide him before he acts impetuously. If he loves me, he must trust me.

This is another vividly illustrated soliloquy. At its end Junia confides Cecilius to Cinna, and the orchestra (oboes, horns, trumpets and strings) initiates her **Aria, No. 11** *Ah se il crudel periglio* in B flat major, *allegro*. This is grandly scored and designed as a sonata movement with double exposition, but without venturing into *da capo* territory. The orchestral exposition is full-length, with three subject-groups. The first summons to attention is not only the principal subject but is also used as bridge material either with or without third group ideas. The rich scoring and independent touches for oboes and horns will be remarked. Junia's solo exposition abounds in virtuoso runs of unusual difficulty and length, as well as new melodic passages. The text is illustrated generally but aptly—Abert missed an expression of helplessness in the music. But Junia is a proud Roman heroine.

> Ah, when I think of my dear one's danger I am terrified and turned to ice.
>   If his friend does not guard that precious life, from whom can I expect help or compassion?

There being no central contrast section the second paragraph of text is set in the development section which is longer than in the foregoing arias. The recapitulation involves much new writing whenever an old theme returns in a different key.

A curious *non sequitur* ensues. Junia has departed. Cinna is alone. The strings leap straight from B flat to D major, *vivace* at a canter, and Cinna without commenting on the topics of Junia's aria announces: Yes, it is time to shake off the yoke of servitude. If Junia will not kill Sulla, another (viz. Cinna) will go forward and do the deed. And in the middle of this accompanied recitative there is one bar supported only by continuo—it sounds most peculiar. We may suspect that Junia's aria No. 11 was spatchcocked into the score at a late moment to accommodate the *prima donna*.

Cinna's recitative is to introduce his **Aria, No. 12,** *molto allegro* in F major, *Nel fortunato istante*, accompanied by strings alone. The three-bar introduction promises urgency and determination.

> In the moment of fortune that he now vows to expedite, I will cause him to expire at my feet and avenge the community.
> Another hand shall deal the happy blow and it is not far from him.

This is a vigorous but expressively superficial aria, contributing little to dramatic characterization. The ideas are pleasing and conventional; there is little bravura vocal writing. Nor is the music harmonically bold. But the form is decidedly unusual and this, by its animation, good balance, and freedom from stilt make the aria attractive.

The exposition is quite lucid. The first group consists of the three introductory bars and the singer's first phrase both used for sign-posting purposes, as well as a gleeful instrumental pendant:

This group also includes a rapid-scale vocal melisma, one bar only, a rising orchestral scale (Mannheim mini-rocket), a five-finger exercise, down and up, theme, and a big vocal leap that never recurs. The music arrives in C major.

The second group is a good tune backed by a symphonic idea for first violins, canonically imitated by violas.

This section in the dominant gets to its structural cadence with a further burst of Ex. 8a. The orchestra, instead of finishing the section with more C major, introduces a relevant, more angular idea that immediately moves away from C into other keys, eventually the dominant of D minor.

Is this meant to indicate the demise of the tyrant?

To a sonata-form mentality it proposes a development section. In Mozartian operatic aria this usually means new tunes. But what follows is rhythmically and thematically close to the first group, Ex. 8. And the continuation unashamedly returns to C major. Ex. 8a confirms this but twists its own tail in the direction of G minor, a key accepted by the singer with a confirmatory upward scale (from the first group). Quickly, however, C major restores us to F major for a return of Ex. 9, as if for a shortened recapitulation which the corollaries confirm, though with some corrections for the different key. When the orchestra adds a coda ramming F major home, the aria appears to be over. Not at all.

The scale from the first group returns, in D minor as at first, and a new development section begins, to the words of the second verse, thematically referring to that scale, then to Ex. 10 starting from A minor, after which Ex. 8 reappears in the tonic for a second recapitulation telescoped from available material but quite regular.

It seemed worth describing this aria at length in order to analyse how an invigorating piece can be contrived, by a creative virtuoso, out of commonplace materials.★

★ The only recording of *Lucio Silla* available at the time of writing does not reproduce this aria's design because it is carelessly and unmusically abbreviated—as are most of the opera's other arias. It is my experience that when an unfamiliar baroque or galant opera (including those by young Mozart) fails in effect the reason, granted competent singers, is usually that their music has been unbalanced by abbreviation.

The scene changes to Hanging Gardens (not in Babylon, nor yet those of Nymphaeum which we met in *Mitridate*—such a venue was meat and drink to the scenic designer of a baroque opera and I am sure that if Hasse had composed *Giulio Cesare in Britannia* his librettist would have fixed a scene in the 'orti pensili' of London). Aufidius tells Sulla that the Senate awaits him. Sulla knows that the execution of his plan requires the co-operation of his friend Cinna, but he thinks constantly of Junia. Aufidius assures him that he will persuade her if he uses his prestige and power. Sulla promises that Rome's streets will run with the blood of its citizens if he does not get his way. Then he sees Junia and all his faculties for cruelty are melted by her face.

Junia sees him and tries unsuccessfully to withdraw. Sulla appeals to her affections, pleads his virtuousness and sensibility. Junia prefers to die rather than love him. Die then, answers the tyrant, but not alone.

Before his meaning can be explained (he knows nothing yet of Cecilius's return—does he mean the whole of Rome, as in his earlier recitative?) he dives into an angry **Aria, No. 13** in C major, *allegro assai* with oboes, horns, prominent trumpets and drums plus strings, *D'ogni pietà mi spoglio*. It has three stanzas of text, the second more introspective.

> Rash, treacherous woman, I have given up all pity. Even if you die gladly I shall see your pride suddenly quail. (*Aside*) My pounding heart! ... Lose my beloved? Cruelly slay my sweetheart? Can I be so vile? This disdain maddens me. You call me cruel, so I will be cruel.

This is quite short, a ternary structure whose second verse is set in C minor and collapses miserably into emotionally broken recitative before reviving spirit for the third verse which has new music somewhat similar to that of the first verse— the tremolo passage at 'crudel sarò' echoes that properly designed for 'tremar vedrò' just before the half-way dominant cadence, and the opening phrases of both outer verses use the same theme. The music is inventive in detail, for example the shivering figure in second violins at 'tremar vedrò' the first time, and the pathetic turn into C minor with oboes and violas in thirds. The aria certainly broadens our view of Sulla's character, even though Mozart had to reckon on a mediocre vocalist.

Junia is left reflecting on Sulla's curious threat. Whom besides her does he intend to kill? She sees her husband at the moment when we all think of him in this connection; the basso continuo of the recitative takes a heart-sinking turn. She reproaches him for appearing in this palace where he may be recognized and killed. Cecilius answers that her danger is the greatest of all. Sulla is about to drag her, by force and with public consent, to his bed; Cecilius must and will prevent this with his sword. She must put away fear, an emotion vile to Roman hearts. Junia answers that he must escape public attention and trust in her love and fidelity which make such a marriage impossible. Heaven will watch over her. If he stays here, she is sure to die. He hesitates at this, and her tears of anxiety for him induce him to promise that he will remain in abeyance. She pours numerous endearments, promises, hopes, upon him as she bids him farewell.

Cecilius counters with an accompanied recitative and aria. The recitative, *Chi sa, che non sia questa*, is poignantly accompanied by string harmonies as he muses that he may never see her again. Junia (rare for a second character to join in an accompanied recitative) tells him not to fear, but to love her and vanish. Here the music quickens to *allegro*. After her final words, 'e spera' ('and hope'), we expect a cadence but get none, simply the E flat major loud *adagio* introduction to **No. 14**, which is not her **Aria**—as must be expected—but Cecilius's *Ah se a morir* in E flat major with oboes, horns and strings. Here is another curious *non sequitur*; conductors will surely feel obliged to intersperse one harpsichord B flat chord if not the cadential dominant-tonic.

The aria is unproblematic though structurally different again from preceding ones. It is a prototype of the classical ternary form aria, somewhat swollen at the front. The main section is *adagio*; brief introduction, varied repetition with voice, transition, second group, codetta, development (mostly new), and minimally varied recapitulation ending in tonic E flat. There is a short C minor *andante* central section ('vorrei mostrar costanza'), then a varied reprise of the initial *adagio*, creatively reworked. The aria as a whole is a reformation of the Handelian *da capo*, rather than the concertante mutant that Mozart inherited. It suits admirably the compact mood of affectionate warmth and intimacy that Mozart rightly found (as he did not always just then) in the text.

> Ah if cruel destiny calls me to death, I shall always be beside you as a faithful ghost.
>
> I would like to show my constancy as I say goodbye to you, my dear; but my footstep falters as I leave you.

This aria is famous for the extravagant vocal leaps tailored to Rauzzini's artistry; the most celebrated example spans nearly two octaves (though we have had some in *Mitridate*):

11

There are several others almost as dashing and all are consistently worked into the total context. The striking feature of the aria is bound to be its richness of texture and invention consistent with Mozart's response to the key of E flat major—and this includes the contrast section in that key's relative minor. The scoring for oboes and horns is typically mellow and individual, likewise the elaborate part-writing for second violin and viola. Galant snaps figure in the vocal divisions, hard to execute these days but evidently a polished weapon in Rauzzini's armoury.

Junia feels her heart pounding, her tears flowing, as her husband leaves her (she said goodbye to him a whole aria and accompanied recitative ago). Celia comes bouncing up to her, full of joy and tactlessness. She tells Junia to give up this boring tearfulness: after all Cecilius is dead by now and Rome's ruler will be an excellent husband. Cheerfulness is all. Celia wants others to share her own enthusiasm at the prospect of wedding the man she had been languishing so long for.

Mozart evidently enjoyed composing Celia's music, of which the **Aria No. 15** in A major, *Quando sugl'arsi campi*, is the next delectable example. It jogs cheerfully along, a true *allegro*, at great but not excessive length, sustained by the light effervescent accompaniment for strings alone, and the rich fertility of invention. Both these qualities are evident in the orchestral exposition, two subject-groups of three limbs each: 1a and 2a are melodious, the others specifically Celian in their feathery agility and volubility.

> When summer rain falls on dry fields, the flowers and leaves revive, forest and lawn turn green again.
> Just so my loving soul begins to breathe again after its long torment.

The solo exposition repeats the first group and adds a new section that breaks into Celia's florid speciality of staccato high notes, best exemplified in the development variant:

12

The second group is re-exposed in the dominant: a new melodious idea follows 2b, includes more pop-gun fioritura, and leaves 2c for codetta material. The development reshapes the four first-group limbs in or on the dominant, including the division as cited above. The second group only is recapitulated in the tonic. The central section has new material and inhabits D major, moving to F sharp minor when the 2c idea returns and leads back to A major for a full recapitulation of the solo exposition material in the tonic. Thus 1a, b and c are as in that solo exposition; 1d, Ex. 12, and the second group as in the development and first recapitulation.

As soon as Celia has made her formal exit, high tragedy invades the music once more, D minor tragedy of an unexpectedly intense variety.

13

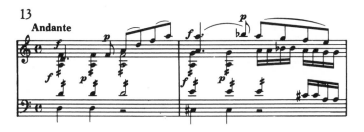

Junia reflects on a sudden access of fear that her husband may have already been arrested and condemned (*molto allegro*, G minor). She begins to quake with horror (a grandly arching bass line under palpitating A minor). She must go at once to the

Senate and implore them to pardon Cecilius. If not, then Heaven grant that she die with him:

She breaks impetuously, unpreluded, into her **Aria, No. 16**, *Parto, m'affretto* in C major, *allegro assai*, with strings alone.

> I am in a hurry to go. My heart is breaking, I cannot breathe, I feel near death but I cannot die. If only death would claim me in my grief for my beloved, death would be kind.

Junia's urgency is reflected in her broken phrases (some individual words are broken up by rests) and in the violin theme (*cf.* the equivalent in *Aprite un pò* from *Figaro*) which dominates the greater part of this binary structure.

There is a second subject, smoother in tone, but Ex. 14 returns after it. Hysteria impels Junia to throw off four fiery and strenuous bravura divisions in the first half, and three in the second. Mozart renews the dramatic impact after the first half by pausing after the G major cadence, then plunging straight into E flat major. The blend of tearfulness and determination is powerfully sustained by the music. Junia is visibly standing on the stage, *not* hurrying to the Senate. But the aria creates the illusion that she is voicing these emotions even as she runs from the hanging gardens through Rome's streets until she reaches the Capitol.

When her aria is ended the scene at once changes to her destination, the Capitol where senators, soldiers and populace are greeting the arrival of Sulla in a (deducibly *allegro con brio*) **Chorus No. 17**, in F major, *Se gloria il crin ti cinse*, accompanied by oboes, horns and strings.

> Just as glory crowned your brow in battle, now let love crown it. May you soon embrace your beloved, and may myrtles enhance the warrior's laurel wreath.

Sulla has not yet made his application for consent to wed. Perhaps Aufidius has made the secret public.

The music is characterized by a pompous opening phrase, energetic runs for the violins (signifying a jubilant hubbub) and solid block choral writing. Between the two full choral bursts there is a middle verse for female voices followed by male voices. During the closing bars Junia appears among the senators.

Sulla formally announces to the assembly that, having fought and laboured for Rome, he now seeks his reward, the hand of Junia which will for ever delete the old strife between Marius and himself; this will totally compensate for his years of hard work on Rome's behalf. Junia, aside, notes with horror the silence of the Senate. Sulla takes this for approval, like the festive cries he hears coming from outside the Capitol. Let them all go, then, to the matrimonial altar.

At this Junia protests that no Roman should connive at a dictator's violence in this manner. Sulla tries to silence her. She produces a dagger with which to stab herself; Sulla orders it to be taken from her so that she may obey his will.

On the instant Cecilius, also with a drawn sword, hurries forward. Junia is appalled. Sulla can hardly believe his eyes—has an exile returned to attempt his murder? The traitor shall die at sunrise. Now Cinna, also armed, runs in, to Sulla's further amazement. Fear leads Cinna to pretend that, realizing Cecilius's murderous intent, he had hurried to defend Sulla. The excuse convinces nobody and Sulla tells him to go away, which he does. Sulla orders Cecilius to give up his sword, and Junia seconds this wish, to Cecilius's amazement, as proof of his affection for her. Action must come from heaven, not from human violence. Furious Cecilius obeys and is condemned to rest in Sulla's darkest dungeon for the brief space graciously permitted him to live, likewise his wife.

Before Junia and Cecilius are led away they join with Sulla in the **Trio, No. 18**, which concludes Act II. This is an *allegro* in B flat major, *Quell'orgoglioso sdegno*, scored for oboes, horns and trumpets (doubled again) and strings. Each of the three participants is musically characterized. Sulla's inaugural exclamation, that he will humble this proud disdain, is portrayed with a choppy accompaniment to peremptory wind and violin chords. Cecilius expresses defiance to compact chords and fiery, contrasted dynamics. Junia enters third, promising her husband to die by his side, with loving mellifluous phrases, again switching rapidly between *piano* and *forte*. After another threat from Sulla, husband and wife duet in harmony. The tension is sustained along these lines. Violins launch a bold B flat figure and all three singers unite, Junia and Cecilius vowing constancy, Sulla infuriated to see it. They engage in contrapuntal imitative entries, then husband and wife in florid runs (with this Sulla could not compete), and the act ends very solidly.

5

The third act begins in a forecourt of the dungeons. Cinna is visiting Cecilius who is fettered, telling him that he spoiled the enterprise; not far behind him was a posse of their friends ready to unite in killing Sulla. Cinna, in pursuit of Cecilius, had to leave the fellow-conspirators behind, and when faced with a hostile mob he lost his nerve. Not that this excuses the cowardly lies he told Sulla. Cecilius is resigned to death, fearful only for his wife. But Cinna is resolved, he says, to save them both. Celia has joined them and promises that her brother will listen sincerely to Junia, since he wishes to remove her scorn for him—a hopeless task, Cecilius is sure. Cinna tells Celia to use her influence on her brother by persuading him that, hated as he is by all Rome and the gods as well, he cannot escape death unless he forswears his hopeless infatuation. If Celia is successful Cinna is willing to marry her (he is either a cynic or totally selfless, in either case a most unsuitable husband).

She is delighted and diplomatically inspired at the prospect of saving her brother from assassination and securing the bridegroom she pines for.

In Celia's **Aria, No. 19**, *Strider sento la procella*, Gamerra gave the singer an opportunity to express more varied, darker emotions than heretofore.

> I hear the storm howl. No friendly star shines. But even when I am enveloped in such horror, hope and love stand firm in my heart.

They would have made the role more interesting. Mozart set the text quite cheerfully, ignoring its stormy implications perhaps because his singer was not able to do them justice. It is an *allegro* in B flat major, with oboes, horns doubled by trumpets (powerful stuff for such a character), and strings. The main interest is centred, not for the first time, on the string-writing, particularly the violins as dual interlocutors after the Italian baroque manner: we hear this in the first subject, the second part of the second subject, in the codetta of the solo exposition (a derivative of the first subject) and in the second new idea of the development section—since this is a straightforward sonata-form structure, without any *da capo* pretensions, this occurrence of new ideas could truthfully be described as a central section—where cheerfulness is momentarily overcast by 'tanto orrore'. Celia has a little florid singing to do, not greatly taxing.

Cecilius asks Cinna if he truly believes that Celia can soften her brother's bloodthirsty heart. He himself has given up hope, and recommends Junia to Cinna's protection. Let Cecilius's death be swiftly avenged so that his soul may rest in peace. Cinna is, however, quite sure that Cecilius will not be executed: Sulla must be aware that it would bring ruin upon him.

Cinna formalizes his meaning in his **Aria, No. 20**, an *allegro* in D major, *De più superbi il core*, with oboes, horns, trumpets and strings. Architecturally this is peculiar. To the casual ear it sounds like a straightforward *da capo* aria with double exposition. Examination shows several idiosyncrasies. The orchestral introduction exposes a principal subject, to which the voice will add significantly, some running passages, another subject which turns out to be codetta material and a concluding Mannheim rocket, also for linking purposes. The solo exposition includes four new ideas in the dominant, but none of them is ever recapitulated. After a development section, consisting of new ideas, ascending scales lead to a fanfare and a recapitulation most of whose ideas are new including running divisions and a cadenza. When the succeeding central contrast section in G major is done the ascending scales and fanfare lead to the *da capo* which is actually a recapitulation of what earlier had posed as a recapitulation.

The music is proud and dogged and galant, hardly at all illustrative of the text's implied contrasts.

> When Jupiter flashes angry lightning, even the proudest hearts are full of fear; only the shepherd under a laurel tree is not terrified. Tyrants may be afraid of chains and slaughter. Only the innocent heart can smile in face of death.

Still, if one does not think too much about the text, it is a pleasant and fairly showy aria, though not strongly typical of Mozart.

Cecilius, alone, admits he has no fear of death, only shame to be in fetters. Junia enters. Sulla's purpose will not be changed. He desires either Junia's hand or

Cecilius's death, and since she will not yield he had sent her to take her last farewell of her husband. She has resolved to die beside him, as a faithful wife and obedient daughter.

Aufidius, with guards, enters ordering Cecilius to follow him. He will not tell Junia their destination: 'Always I obey and am silent,' he says. Cecilius takes a fond leave of her; it is her tears, not the prospect of a cruel death, that moves him.

His farewell is the beautiful and once celebrated **Aria, No. 21**, *Pupille amate* in A major, *tempo di menuetto* with strings only.

English does not do justice to these exquisitely turned verses. Did Gamerra steal them or Metastasio contribute them?

Pupille amate,	Beloved eyes,
non lagrimate,	do not weep,
morir mi fate	you make me die
pria di morir.	before my death.
Quest'alma fida	This soul faithful
a voi d'intorno	to you inwardly
fara ritorno	will return
sciolta in sospir.	melted into sighs.

For once in this opera the aria is not in sonata form or any variant of the *da capo* epic structure, but a simple rondo or Lied-form with two episodes and three appearances (four counting the orchestral introduction) of the simple yet beguiling melody.

15

A special effect of this tune is the sensitive repositioning of the harmony at bar 10 when the melody of bar 6 is repeated, making the *Liebestod* even more bitter-sweet.* The string-writing is transparent, warmly expressive, the vocal line calculated with miraculous suavity and tenderness—we can only guess at the effect a Rauzzini must have made on the audience with his singing of *Pupille amate*. The aria is too pure and delicate to bear romantic treatment. To a post-romantic ear the first episode may seem flippant, almost Dorabella-like, and the NGA *forte* indication for the opening bars a Philistinism. But Mozart carefully marked *piano* only at bar 13; and the first episode is meticulously notated.

There is not much else to remark except that the aria unites galant style, the young Mozart, and touching love-poetry, to perfection; and that this aria was again particularly admired when J. C. Bach set it, in the same key and metre but quite differently, for his own *Lucio Silla*.

Cecilius leaves with the guards and Aufidius. Junia is left a prey to loneliness and apprehension. Her strong, mingled emotions are too much for dry recitative. Mozart heightens them by adding flutes (which he always reserved for special effect) and trumpets to the strings which accompany her.

Her recitative (*Sposo, mia vita*) begins distractedly, then becomes nervously animated as she longs to hurry after Cecilius. Premonitions of horror prevent her (the text says nothing, Mozart's music explains all, and unusually he figures the bars so that the harmony will not be distorted). There is a baffling moment of bland yet agitated G major, usually a cloudless key, when she fears that Heaven has let her down. She imagines her husband already dead, mutilated, bleeding; the strings break into a passionate lament in C minor, *andante*, with violas in thirds for emphasized intensity. She seems to embark on an anguished aria in F minor (*Ah pria ch'ei mora*), but it peters out quickly because her mood becomes urgent again. A voice seems to call from the distance to her: it is solemn *adagio* music in E flat major, tremolando violins in the bass, flutes in thirds doubled by violas, an eerie effect and for Mozart profoundly significant as he makes every listener realize this is holy dread. Junia resolves (*presto*) to find his corpse and fall where he fell.

Her last **Aria, No. 22**, is her finest, *Fra i pensier* in C minor. It retains flutes and divided violas, adds oboes and bassoons to the foregoing. Alfred Einstein declared it 'so deeply felt that it would do honour to the role of Donna Anna'. With respect to that great Mozartian it wouldn't do anything of the kind. The key, the expression, and the manner are quite unlike any character in Mozart's late operas. They are nearer to the world of *Idomeneo*, still closer to the French operas of Gluck. The short *andante* instrumental introduction has a special character with its subtle shifting of rhythm, its trailing thirds for oboes and violas (the one instrument wailing, the other quietly sobbing), its silvery sustained top part for flutes, and dully resigned bassoon bass.

This is an introduction, not an orchestral exposition. Junia enters with a quite different though obviously relevant tune, suavely melancholy. Connoisseurs of Mozart's piano concertos may think of minor-key slow movements. This one is not like them: its nearest equivalent is the F major slow movement of the K. 467 concerto in C major, and that only because of the slowly rocking triplet

* Death was a standard symbol for erotic orgasm in the sixteenth-century madrigal.

16

accompaniment by muted strings with plucked bass, perhaps also because of the eloquent wind interjections; the slow movements of K. 271 and K. 456 which are in minor keys, are quite different. Mozart's task was to set the following words for a highly accomplished singer.

> My thoughts are of gloomiest death: I see my bloodless husband stretch out his icy hand. He asks me, why do you hesitate to die? I hesitate, faint, and my beloved encourages me to follow him.

He begins smoothly, pathetically, keeping the triplets going over a purposeful bass. Soft but striking woodwind chords reinforce the fearful atmosphere. The music edges to the borders of E flat. In this key a chivalrous *allegro*, airily but firmly poised, ensues ('Gia vacillo'). It soon ventures back towards C minor, its destined key, the key of Junia's real emotions, with plenty of tremolo and plenty of flutes. As far as concerns Junia's character this aria is not found wanting.

The scene changes to a hall in the palace. Sulla is discussing his ideals with Celia and Cinna. Senators and populace are in attendance. He wants crimes to be judged publicly: he admits that, as dictator, he has to be rid of opponents; but his heart is bewildered by so many contradictory feelings. Junia appears and tells the Senate to grant her pity and compensation for her dead husband.

Sulla tells her not to be so hasty. For here, to everybody's astonishment, is Cecilius. Sulla introduces him as the man who tried publicly to assassinate Rome's dictator. Sulla had tried to obtain Cecilius's wife as his own consort. Now Sulla restores Cecilius to Junia as man and wife, and releases all political prisoners at present in custody. Aufidius is appalled by this and foresees his own ruin. Sulla, in his delight, seeks to embrace his friend Cinna. But Cinna feels bound to confess his plots against Sulla; Celia sees her marriage shot down in flames; nevertheless Sulla gives her to Cinna as his bride. All acclaim Sulla's nobility. Even Aufidius repents of his obsequiousness, and is pardoned (a sickly moment). Sulla now removes his kingly crown and abdicates. He does not actually declare free elections but is content to utter pious generalities about innocence and virtue.

So all on stage join in a mixed final **Chorus, No. 23** in D major, *Il gran Silla*, with oboes (no flutes), horns, trumpets (no drums), and strings. It has an ebullient triple-time lilt and inevitably sent the audience home in the right frame of mind. The touches of independent choral writing enliven the music, like the firm cadence ('oggi si fà') in octaves. For special pleasure a vaudeville element is introduced.

Junia and Cecilius engage in a short duet (*Sol per lui*), then Cinna and Celia, then after a burst of chorus these four in vocal quartet, to which Sulla adds an epilogue daring any triumph to equal his own victory over his heart's infatuation.

6

The important points to consider about Mozart's *Lucio Silla* are not the ones that first spring to mind. History says that Gamerra's libretto is illogically constructed and poetically uninspiring. Apart from a couple of wild moments in Act II, when the action moves backwards instead of forwards, it goes moderately well. The diction has its downs and ups. We know that Mestastasio wrote one scene; but there is more than one good scene, so Gamerra cannot have been a totally incompetent librettist. We have, furthermore, to judge *Lucio Silla* by the lights of 1772, as a dramatic medium *sui generis*.

If you have read this book chapter by chapter (even though I try to make each chapter self-sufficient) you will gather that by now Mozart was paying great attention to orchestral scoring, and formulating the structure of each aria with real diversity and imagination. Delineation of individual characters, such as nowadays we look for, did not mean much to him in *Lucio Silla*: he was working according to the conventions of baroque *opera seria* which meant diversity of mood and expression, not detailed description of inward thoughts or even musical illustration of the text—though there are some examples.

Scoring, structure, character: *Lucio Silla* stands out for its abundance of accompanied recitatives, very varied, often vivid, more often a mere heightening of atmosphere than a great deepening of feeling though there are profound emotional statements in some of these recitatives, as described above. We can observe the moments that chiefly inspired Mozart from the instrumentation, when he adds to the regular string complement; the addition of flutes, seldom used in this opera, is especially thrilling. It is easy to write an accompanied recitative where each new verbal idea has its musical equivalent. In these recitatives we are specially gripped by those in which themes are consistently, revelatorily employed. These accompanied recitatives are chiefly important for their prognostication of Mozart's later dramatic techniques. He had discovered their dramatic effect: just now he was using the special effect too lavishly maybe, though nobody will object.

Structurally Mozart was bound, at this stage, to the *da capo* aria on which principal singers insisted. We may often wish that these arias were shorter, but Mozart varied their structure with real skill and expertise; they are seldom twice the same. A modern commentator or student is particularly gripped when an aria, in such a context, breaks formally free from the norm. It is tempting to regard *Pupille amate* as the highlight of the whole score, because it is exceptionally expressive and employs a simple unpretentious form. Yet we must respect the eighteenth-century taste for which Mozart was writing. For his listeners the singer's technique, diversity of expression and staying power was of first importance (as, for us, is the brilliance of a pianist in a big piano concerto) and we should not dismiss these big *da capo* arias as great bores: Mozart was careful to make them as interesting as possible. For him and his audiences the shorter, for us more expressive, arias were sweetmeats while the big arias could be likened to main dishes. We should revive this standard of appreciation if we are to judge the virtues of Mozart's *Lucio Silla*.

The composer's portrayal of individual character means everything to a modern operatic spectator. When *Lucio Silla* is performed today we expect that Sulla will be a real baddy, violent, irate, demanding and rapacious towards Junia. But Gamerra was at pains to emphasize his good qualities and, throughout, to stress the all-importance of non-violent action. Sulla therefore becomes a less positive character; when he condemns somebody to death nobody believes him. Mozart was further hamstrung by the church-chorister impersonator of this role. Sulla became a subsidiary part, deprived even of his clinching solo in the last scene which is feeble by *opera seria* standards.

Cecilius is much more impressive because of his music, written expressly, tailor-made, for a great singer who could thoroughly convey affection, determination, rage, resignation. Celia's charm must throughout be felt. Junia is the most complicated character of all, the most completely portrayed in music; it is for her that Mozart breaks the bonds of *opera seria* convention, again and again.

It is sometimes written that her No. 22 aria is the only minor-key number in *Lucio Silla*. Perusal of this chapter will show that this is by no means so. *Lucio Silla* is a big but in every way well balanced opera. Its style is particular, perhaps more difficult to appreciate than Handel's baroque or Meyerbeer's heavy romantic opera. The good music to which attention has firmly been drawn will please anybody ready to accept the young Mozart as a personality, the composer already fascinated by *opera seria*, soon to fledge his wings in *Idomeneo*.

LA FINTA GIARDINIERA

Opera buffa in three acts

Libretto attributed to

RANIERO DE CALZABIGI

revised by MARCO COLTELLINI

K. 196

DON ANCHISES, Podestà of Lagonero, in love with Sandrina	TENOR
MARCHIONESS VIOLANTE ONESTI, in love with Count Belfiore, believed dead but disguised as a garden girl under the name of Sandrina	SOPRANO
COUNT (CONTINO) BELFIORE, earlier in love with Violante, now with Arminda	TENOR
ARMINDA, lady from Milan, niece of the Podestà, earlier in love with the knight Ramiro, now promised bride of Contino Belfiore	SOPRANO
CAVALIER RAMIRO, Arminda's rejected suitor	MALE SOPRANO
SERPETTA, Chambermaid to the Podestà, in love with him	SOPRANO
ROBERTO, Violante's servant, now her pretended cousin named Nardo, disguised as a gardener, in love unsuccessfully with Serpetta	BASS

The action takes place in the land of Lagonero

I

Mozart was never to return to Italy again. On the other hand he was wretched in Salzburg, working for a Lord Archbishop who regarded him as an unextraordinary boy musician. Leopold tried to find appointments for his son outside Salzburg, but nothing turned up. Wolfgang Mozart composed industriously: numerous symphonies, the Concertone for two violins, church music, string quartets (during an abortive search for employment in Vienna), the first attempt at Gebler's *König Thamos*, the three symphonies which we regard as Mozart's first superior achievement (Nos. 25, 28, and 29), the glorious two-piano sonata, the bassoon concerto, several party entertainments, and numerous piano sonatas.

While he was composing some of these he was commissioned to write a comic opera for the Munich Carnival season 1774–5 (starting after Christmas and ending on Shrove Tuesday). The beneficiary was the Elector Max Josef, his agent the Controller of Opera Count Joseph von Seeau. The libretto was to be *La finta giardiniera* (The Fake Garden-girl), supposedly written by Gluck's poet Raniero de Calzabigi, set to music a year earlier by Anfossi for the Rome carnival where the opera had been well liked. (It was produced in many other cities and various languages.) Composition of the libretto, revised by Marco Coltellini, was begun by Mozart while still in Salzburg, i.e. the parts which did not require the participating presence of the chief singers. On 6 December Mozart and his father travelled from Salzburg to Munich where Wolfgang completed his work. He was kept busy during this time with other performances and parties. When the opera came to its first rehearsal it was acknowledged so good, by all the musicians, that extra time was granted for careful preparation and the first performance was therefore postponed. The singers were not great celebrities. Rosa Manservisi, the *prima donna*, was adjudged a 'wretched singer' by Leopold Mozart. She sang Sandrina, while her sister Teresina took the part of the *buffo* maid Serpetta. The principal (castrato) male singer was Tommaso Consoli who accompanied the Mozarts back to Salzburg. Contemporary records name other singers (Rossi, Petroni, Valesi, Pario, Sutor) but do not say which roles they sang. The dress rehearsal was ready by 12 January and the première took place on the 13th, having twice been postponed, in the Redoutensaal in Prannergasse. Already Mozart had been asked to compose a serious opera for the following season: it was to be *Idomeneo*.

Then as now the Munich Opera worked on a repertory basis: Leopold Mozart noted that after a couple of performances *La finta giardiniera* would have to be dropped for other works. Mozart's sister Nannerl managed to see it, but not Archbishop Colloredo who was embarrassed by the compliments shed on his protégé by the Elector and all his family and courtiers. Colloredo bowed his head and shrugged his shoulders, but could not bring himself to answer verbally. He did not talk to the Mozarts at all. This curious behaviour is perhaps explicable if we recognize Colloredo as a master who required obedient servants and by no means appreciated a young, much flattered genius who was sure to plan his career in terms much bigger than the provincial court of Salzburg's archbishop. Colloredo was not a musical fanatic, though not inimical to music. A musical servant likely to rank as more important, in the world's eyes, than his master was a millstone for the Archbishop, not an ornament of his establishment. Hence the subsequent troubles between Colloredo and Mozart. Granted a self-respecting, authoritarian Archbishop they were inevitable.

At the first performance of *La finta giardiniera* the theatre was full. Many were turned away. Curtain calls, in which royalty joined enthusiastically, were numerous, even during the intervals. 'Bravo!' and 'Viva il maestro!' were much exclaimed. The subsequent ballet was much enjoyed as well. The second performance was abbreviated because of the indisposition of the 'wretched female singer', according to Mozart. There were in fact only three performances of *La finta giardiniera*. Mozart foresaw that his work would suffer if he left Munich where, he said, 'very strange things happen'.

He need not have feared that *La finta giardiniera* would be dropped for ever. Before May 1780 it was being performed in German translations (the work of the older Stierle or alternatively Andreas Schachtner, the Mozarts' Salzburg friend who must have made his German version at the time of the opera's composition since Mozart underlaid it below the Italian in his manuscript) as *Die Gärtnerin aus Liebe*, by several travelling companies. As such it remained popular until at least 1797. At some time Mozart's Italian setting of Act I with sung recitatives was lost. We are left with the last two acts as set, but only the airs and ensembles of Act I to German words, not Mozart's recitatives—spoken dialogue was used in these performances. The Italian libretto survives and some have tried to supply the missing Italian recitatives, so far unconvincingly because only Mozart could write Mozart's music, though in our style-conscious age some inventive scholar must soon succeed.

2

As in *La finta semplice* the overture to *La finta giardiniera* is a three-movement Italian sinfonia whose finale is effectively the opening chorus—though Mozart supplied a new finale, probably K. 121 = K. 207a, when he performed this sinfonia at a concert in Salzburg. The scoring is for oboes, horns and strings, the standard orchestra, though not the full instrumental force as used in the opera.

The first movement is an *allegro molto* in D major, using a short sonata form. Its principal subject has strong rhythmical distinction and will instantly recall the opening trio *La mia Dorabella* in *Così fan tutte*.

In the bridge passage a figure involving trills strikes the attention. It takes the music into A major: so when the orchestra returns in this key to Ex. 1 it might be supposed that this is a Haydnesque second subject, i.e. not a new melody at all. However, there is a new second group theme, soft and stealthy, much dependent on the trills from the bridge passage. In the recapitulation this, but not the re-reprise of Ex. 1, is transferred formally to D major and we must assume that the re-reprise was transitional, not part of the second group (though it is unusual to find any recapitulation material outside the tonic in early Mozart). The exposition ends with a third statement of Ex. 1, still in the dominant (but recapitulated in the tonic, of course). The tiny development section is occupied with a new chromatic sighing figure, then with gently tripping scales, quite fizzy, that lead back easily to D major for the recapitulation. This time the second subject is placed low and mysterious on the violins, with a low-lying pedal point for horns. This section ends on solid unisons.

The overture's central movement is an *andantino grazioso* in A major for strings only, with a warmly ingratiating theme whose first two bars seem connected with bow and curtsey.

This returns three times after lightly fluttering episodes. Since the whole movement is quite short the form is not so much rondo as song—refrains with verses. It is basically unsuitable to repeat the first *allegro* as conclusion to the overture: it must finish, in stage performance, with the first chorus.

D major and the oboes with horns are restored when Act I begins with *Che lieto giorno*, the **Introduction, No. 1**, *allegro moderato*. I said it was effectively the overture's finale. But it is too long and too closely involved with the stage characters, to be suitable for transcription into an orchestral symphony—hence the need for a different, purely orchestral finale, when Mozart turned the overture into an independent symphony. No. 1's purpose in the opera is to introduce five of the principal characters and their several predicaments.

The scene is set in the garden of Don Anchises's palace. Sandrina and Nardo are carrying out their duties, observed by their employer Don Anchises, the Podestà, who is accompanied by his guest Ramiro and attended by his servant Serpetta.

The orchestra proposes a portly theme with a lighter-footed corollary, then a secretive, rather giggly contrasting idea, and a codetta passage with a positive and prominent bass; these do sum up the five characters on stage. They are repeated while the five characters announce in more or less block harmony (oddly like the first chorus of Bach's *Christmas Oratorio*) what a happy day it is and how contented they all are. They do this at some length while the exposed ideas are repeated, modulating to the dominant then instantly returning to the tonic as if other possibilities were out of the question.

As soon as this quintet-chorus has reached its cadence the music makes straight for B minor so that Ramiro can explain, to developments of the principal theme, how he is beset by hidden sorrows; the string-writing here, with undulating second violin accompaniment to broken first violin phrases, is touching. This modulates to A minor for the next solo. The Podestà—administrative head of the local community, a sort of Don Pasquale elderly comic figure—has the next solo, mostly in G major, telling how he adores Sandrina, his garden-tender. She, in turn, expresses her unhappiness, in E minor and F sharp minor with plaintive sustained oboes and a repeated off-beat phrase apt for the German word 'hart' though the Italian text gives 'da'—hint that Mozart was here concentrating on the German version. Now Nardo, supposedly her cousin and fellow gardener, reveals his soul—he loves Serpetta who will not respond. His solo is rather stiff. Nardo's real name is Roberto, just as Sandrina is really the Countess Violante Onesti, and he is her servant who has accompanied her in search of a lover who deserted her. Serpetta does not love Nardo but the Podestà, and is furious because he apparently fancies Sandrina. Serpetta's solo is more melancholy with affecting repeated *coulés* on the German 'betrügen' (Italian 'stuzzica'). The characters again sing solos, shorter and less inventive this time, with thematic accompaniment expressing the same sentiments. Their opening ensemble is repeated, but now the joyful sentiments are heard to be totally untruthful and ironical.

At the end of the introduction the characters move into secco recitative, when the opera is sung in Italian, spoken dialogue when the language is German. In order to connect the set numbers in this account I have used the recitatives set by Anfossi, though they are by Calzabigi, not Coltellini.★

The Podestà congratulates Sandrina on her diligent work and her prettiness. Serpetta is jealous of his attention. Ramiro voices his perturbation. But the Podestà assures him that they will all soon be happy. Though Ramiro was unsuccessful with Don Anchises's niece Arminda who is expected to arrive that day in order to be betrothed to Count Belfiore, Ramiro may be sure of finding a woman who will suit him.

Ramiro answers to the effect that the burned child dreads the fire, but explains himself more fully in a solo, the **Aria, No. 2.**

Ramiro uses the simile of a bird escaping capture for the heart's longing to remain fancy-free. *Se l'augellin sen fugge* is an *allegro* in F major, accompanied by strings only.

> If one day the bird escapes from its cage, it will not so cheerfully return to its captor.
>
> Just so have I escaped from Cupid's net, and the thought of another entanglement makes me tremble.

The music is full of ornithological illustration. We can remark it in the first bar's grace-notes (surely short, not long) and in the flutters which prolong the end of this phrase:

—then in the contrasts of loud and soft which also suggest fluttering and in the hopping figure of the next idea, exchanged between first and second violins:

★ They are printed in Anheisser's edition of Mozart's opera (published in 1934), where Act I is restored to its Italian text.

The same illustrative idea is extended in the off-beat patterns which end the exposition. They give charm and vivacity to what might otherwise be an ordinary formal aria for a castrato. The middle section is warmly intimate and sonorous, still imitative, with dropping sevenths in the vocal part and quivering strings at the lead-back to the reprise. Ramiro has some florid divisions but no cadenza. His vocal compass is extended only up to G.

Ramiro has made his conventional exit. The Podestà tells Serpetta, Sandrina and Nardo to have the house and garden neat and tidy for the arrival of the bridegroom. Privately he informs Sandrina of his love for her—the difference in their station does not affect his wish to marry her. Serpetta, jealous of Sandrina, takes every opportunity to interrupt him with domestic questions, so upsetting him that he becomes quite confused as he now tells us. He embarks on one of those musical numbers, concerned with orchestras (usually with orchestral rehearsals), that became popular in the next century—Lortzing's *Opernprobe* and Dvořák's *Jakobin* give two familiar examples. In this case the Podestà is not conducting but imagining the instruments and their stimulating effect on his imagination. His **Aria, No. 3**, is in D major, *Dentro il mio petto,*★ accompanied by flute, oboes, horns and strings in its main *allegro maestoso*, to which bassoons, trumpets and drums are added, for further descriptive purposes, in the concluding *presto*.

> I hear within me the lovely sounds of the flute and oboe. They fill me with delight and contentment. Then frightening dark harmony (*from the viola players, declares the German, not the Italian text*).
>
> (*Presto*) Now a mighty noise by drums and trumpets, basses and bassoons which almost drives me mad.

Nothing is said about the horns who have quite prominent music, or the hardworked violins!

Mozart seems content to illustrate the text without lavishing much musical invention. The aria begins pompously, like the Podestà, shows off the violins, adds the flute (positively, as usual with Mozart) and oboes and divided violas, introduces a touch of plaintive D minor for the sadness expressed, then concludes the lengthy introduction jubilantly. All this is cheery and fairly non-committal, as when it is repeated with singer. (The German words are clumsily set.) The development section again brings out the flute. There is a recapitulation in the home-key, then the harmony moves into B flat for the violas' divided euphony in D with minor-key tendencies. Now the triumph of the D major *presto* with the extra instruments, especially drums, but still very straightforward music, illustrative more than comically significant.

Sandrina explains to the audience that she already has a lover whom she longs to

★ From Mozart's letters we learn that Emanuel Schikaneder asked for a copy of this aria, and sang it with great success.

see again even though they quarrelled a year ago and she left home with her servant Roberto, giving it out that he is her brother Nardo, and finding employment as gardeners. However, the Podestà's behaviour towards her is so nauseating that she is inclined to leave the job at once. She tells us so in **No. 4**, her B flat major **Aria**, *Noi donne poverine* (once familiar in English as 'A maiden's is an evil plight'), *grazioso* with an *allegro* conclusion, accompanied by strings only (a lot of divided viola-writing). The tune of this is delightfully cheerful, carefully and subtly phrased, as if to show that although Sandrina is singing the part of a country bumpkin (*vide* repeated notes in folksong style), she isn't really one.

> We girls are badly treated and unhappy because men force themselves upon us faithlessly day and night. But if we pay them back, they make sure we're done for.

This plea for female emancipation is in rondo-form. The first episode injects more energy into the music and produces a new melody in its second half (a characteristic and pleasing device), as well as melodramatic vocal leaps for the word 'Vergehen' (in the Italian 'tormentar'). There are several pauses for flourishes, and a touch of pathos when Sandrina mentions paying-back. After a written-out flourish the coda supplies a rapid new section in hunting-style (favourite Mozart device). Though by no means mature Mozart, aimed indeed at mimicry of street-song, the whole aria has the distinction and sparkle which encourage one to regard this none too pretentious opera as a significant forward step in Mozart's development.

Nardo, for his part, complains that his lot is the worst of all. He is determined to conquer Serpetta. But the man who tries to tame a woman has a harder job even than a sculptor with his hammer and chisel. **No. 5**, his **Aria** on behalf of frustrated manhood, *A forza di martelli*, is another pleb-orientated piece, *allegro* in G major, the strings augmented ominously (though quite discreetly) by the horns.

> Iron is tamed by the hammer, marble moulded by the chisel, but when was female egoism ever conquered by these or even by the fire of love? What fools we are to run after women, deuce take them!

The orchestral introduction, *à la gigue,* suggests horse-riding, and after this the high violin *acciaccature* recall the peasant dancing in the first act finale of *Don Giovanni*.

The text shows that this, on the contrary, is not music for dancing but forging (Wagner's *Siegfried* Act I finale comes to mind) and sculpting music, as is made clear when Nardo sings along with these themes, though it must not sound heavy. When he turns the subject to women the hammering gigue-theme turns into a quick waltz with dummy accompaniment. Gradually the forging noises retreat in favour of definite human dancing; there is an expressive moment of pathos, marked *ad libitum* and more sparely notated so that the singer may draw it out a shade to emphasize his question. All this is repeated binary fashion, emphasizing the home-key. The strong element of good-humoured non-involvement vanishes in the *allegro* coda with its curt string chords and angry declamation (we may think forwards, not too seriously, to the cross men in *Figaro* and *Così*) and taut rising chromatic scales and stiff-reined dotted rhythms. Nardo is emerging as something more robust and dangerous than a commedia dell'arte clown.

The Podestà returns with Arminda who complains that her bridegroom is late and thereby shows discourtesy to her. She snaps at Serpetta who is making her last minute preparations. Serpetta announces the arrival of a carriage occupied by Contino Belfiore. He enters very grandly, *andante maestoso* in E flat major, to string and wind (oboes and horns) antiphony, aristocratic dotted rhythms and proud descending scales in thirds, horn-calls and genteel grace-notes—all descriptive of the smart nobleman and hero. His **No. 6**, *Che beltà, che leggiadria*, is a Portrait **Aria** such as Tamino will sing in *Die Zauberflöte*, rather given to declamation that emphasizes his formality though this is relieved by more lyrical, amorous phrases. In this case, of course, he is addressing not only the likeness of Arminda, but her present self as well.

What charm, beauty and splendour in this portrait, radiant and striking as the sun! I can hardly believe my eyes.

This is a shapely binary aria, affectionately scored, with two rushes of *fioritura* triplets that are not just virtuoso but touched with human feeling. Later Belfiore will be shown in a less heroic light: for the moment Mozart allows him to make a starry impression.

In recitative Belfiore at once declares his love to Arminda. She warns him to woo less precipitately (*cf.* Rosina in *La finta semplice*, p. 44), for she admits herself capricious and quick-tempered. If he should show the merest sign of inconstancy she will punish him.

Her **Aria No. 7**, *Se promette facilmente*, in cloudless A major is scored for strings only, *allegro*. It is sensuous, ingratiating, high-spirited though not without dignity and a galant pride, as the string introduction promises.

Men in love automatically promise to be faithful, and delude girls with flattery into believing them. I am not so easily misled. You are the love of my life: but if you betray me I'll be revenged with my own hands.

The beginning is euphonious and suave and graceful. When Arminda admits her individuality a new strong will enters the music, briefly but impactively.

And when she professes her love for Belfiore, the string quartet texture assumes a real though still aristocratic warmth.

This sounds even more impressive in its recapitulation setting, a fourth higher. For her threat of vengeance Arminda returns to the conspiratorial stabbing quavers of Ex. 8. The middle section (this is a short sonata form) includes a mono-tone vocal passage, like a patter song, essentially *buffo* in character. Nobody in this comic opera is permitted to be entirely serious whatever the cast list pretends. There are two pauses in this aria which suggest vocal flourishes but, surprisingly, no rapid running divisions such as Mozart would automatically have included in his earlier operas.

Belfiore remains enraptured by her. She must surely be a goddess. But he too is well connected. His recital of famous ancestors and relatives has an alienatory effect, in modern terms, though from the eighteenth-century comic-opera viewpoint it merely shows that he is a *parte caratteristica*, not wholly *seria*. The joke is postponed by a brief, stiff and courtly orchestral introduction, two bars of fanfare suggestive of immense dignity, before he starts singing. His **No. 8 Aria**, *Da Sirocco a tramontana*, is *allegro maestoso* (with a further *allegro* coda) in C major, scored for oboes, horns, trumpets and strings.

> My noble lineage has long been famous in all points of the compass. I own property of all kinds, and among my relatives innumerable royalty, nobility, warriors, Roman consuls and the like. Why the hell are you laughing? My next of kin includes Numa, Scipio, Marcus Aurelius, Muzio Scevola, Cato, Tiberius and Caracalla. You should be bowing reverently to them through me.

Belfiore begins with gigantic confidence in diatonic C major, then seems to turn momentarily sly in a chromatic passage.

10

[Andante maestoso]

è   pa——le—se in–tor—no, in–tor–no   la mia an–ti–ca no-bil–tà,

Oboes genuflect in respectful thirds. When Belfiore, on the fringe of G major, goes on to enumerate his claims to fame he does so in the manner of a patter song, with scurrying and wriggling violin accompaniment. His protests at the others' mirth are declamatory with taut dotted rhythms. The tempo quickens to *allegro* for the recital of his famous ancestors, with scurrying violin scales (*cf.* a famous moment in Figaro's *Non più andrai*). Again the orchestral genuflection, more fully scored and much repeated until the orchestra finishes this section in G major, then moves quickly into D minor. For a development section? No, it is a refashioning of all the foregoing *andante* and *allegro*, at first so as to get back to C major, then so as to stay in that key. This is a sparkling piece which significantly enlarges our knowledge of the Contino. It should certainly not be given, as some suggest, to the Podestà who has no such aristocratic claims, for all his pretensions; nor should it be omitted.

Don Anchises expresses his delight at this promising introduction and goes on his way, leaving Nardo once again pursuing Serpetta. She regards herself as too young to be thrown away on an old man like him. The **Arietta, No. 9** *Un marito, o dio*, exists in two nearly identical versions, *grazioso* in F major with string accompaniment, one for Serpetta, the other for Nardo. The distinctions are in the texts, and in the octave at which the vocal part is sung. Serpetta is due to sing No. 10, so that if choice be obligatory, No. 9 must go to Nardo. However, the Arietta is very short and may effectively be sung twice, once by each of them. This, as Mozart told his father in a letter of 24 December 1783, 'is a practice which is quite out of date and is hardly ever made use of. It can only be tolerated in the case of a soubrette and her *amant*, that is, in the *ultime parti*.' So it may be done here.

> I / You would like to taste married bliss soon. But an old / young man is unsuitable for me / you.

This has a charming, lilting tune of the kind familiar from Despina's *Una donna a quindici anni* in *Così fan tutte*.

The rising sixth for 'amoroso' (second time) is particularly fetching, as is the unaccompanied emphatic repetition of 'un pò vecchietto' (or 'giovinetto') later. The number ends with the same F major chord played four times, as in the duet *Bei Männern* from *Zauberflöte*, also concerned with marital companionship for which these compact, cosy chords seem an apt symbol.

Serpetta is in no doubt that she could make a handsomer match than this weather-beaten old gardener. She explains her mantrap technique in her **Aria No. 10**, *Appena mi vedon* in A major, *allegro-andante*, with strings only. Three brisk A major chords are sufficient introduction to her no-nonsense exposition.

> As soon as they see me they're caught. They come running to win my heart. They all admire my eyes, colouring, demeanour, and expect me to touch them if they gaze at me.
> But I modestly lower my head and keep silence, and let them go their way.

Serpetta begins conversationally in patter-fashion, with octave-confirming phrases by strings to underline her self-confidence. Her philosophy becomes more tuneful when the second subject-group arrives ('mirate che occhiette'); this is delicate and buoyant, yet quite plebeian, in the character of a street song.

At the end of the first section the no-nonsense chords return in E major and Serpetta repeats the text to a reformed, somewhat expanded version of the first half, getting back to the tonic and staying there. The second group now appears even more melodious.

The surprise in this aria is its coda, not faster as was often customary, but slower, more intricate, more ornamental, more voluptuous. (There will be another example later in the opera.) The monotone opening of this *andante* ('Io tutta modestia') is comically demure, the mellifluous semiquavers just afterwards ('neppur gli respondo') exquisitely expressive like the subsequent ripples of *fioritura* ('li lascio passar') The aria is an interesting experiment in design and expression. Elisabeth Schumann would have made it eternally popular.

Sandrina now reappears and laments her loneliness in a simile **Aria, No. 11,** as though she were an *opera seria* heroine. The text seems ripe for pathos, too.

Far from its nest the gentle turtledove longs for peace and coos out its grief.

Sandrina, nevertheless, is not such a heroine and Mozart accordingly sets *Geme la tortorella* in a bland C major, *andantino*, with a smoothly flowing melody for muted first violins over a muted dummy accompaniment (strings only) in triplets with plucked bass.

Sandrina's vocal line, when she enters, is a heterophonic counterpoint to a refracted version of the above. The first two phrases of Ex. 13 may suggest the turtledove: when Sandrina speaks of longing, the music touches on C minor with sustained thirds for violas. Towards the end of the exposition she floats off into delicately florid divisions. The dominant-clinching cadence introduces some more obviously pictorial cooing and chromatic turns, very attractive, moving into G minor and F minor.

But this is only the way back to C major for the recapitulation which involves a few graceful alterations; the new divisions are even more delicious than before. It has beautiful moments and almost persuades us that the brilliant boy has turned already into the mature Mozart.

Sandrina, in recitative, explains that she is the turtledove. Arminda, entering, finds her in tears and, while ostensibly comforting Sandrina, lets slip the news of her approaching marriage to Belfiore. The name upsets Sandrina to such an extent that she faints. Arminda goes to fetch her smelling-salts, meanwhile calling to her betrothed to watch over the unconscious servant. Belfiore at once recognizes Sandrina as his ex-fiancée, whom he had assumed to be dead. The shock pushes him into **No. 12**, the first Act **Finale**, which will eventually expand, as the title heading promises, into a **Septet**. It begins with accompanied recitative. Oboes and horns have enjoyed a long break but are now returned to the orchestra pit. Strings play a questioning scale-phrase as Belfiore voices his astonishment to see Violante alive.

His heart beats strangely and here the orchestra accompanies him offbeat with strong dynamic contrasts and disturbed chromatic harmonies. Sandrina has not seen him and, in an affecting, Pamina-like arioso *andantino* (E minor moving to G major) interspersed with recitative, she calls for her absent lover to watch her die of love. Belfiore is puzzled not only to see her at all but in this rustic plebeian attire. Even so he is convinced of her identity.

At this moment she sees and recognizes the Count and promptly faints again. Arminda and Ramiro are passing by and lend assistance with smelling-salts of (the German text specifies) *Balsam sulphuris* (*allegro*). The finale now gets going with a taglike theme that Mozart prolongs resourcefully into a concerted quartet of perplexity and embarrassment. Each of the characters voices, in tiptoe monotone solo, his or her dismay; Sandrina's and Arminda's turn pathetic, Belfiore's is frankly *buffo* like his No. 8 aria. They end this section with another concerted passage involving the familiar hesitation effect for dumbstruck surprise. The scoring, with sustained oboes over oom-cha strings, is especially pleasing, but so is the whole passage.

E minor modulates, with syncopated rhythms, to E flat major, *adagio ma non molto* for the entrance of the Podestà ('Che silenzio') who is himself perplexed by the dumbfounded expressions on all their faces and demands an explanation. Mozart points the moment by producing, after long restraint, a real tune, even if it is more like the refrain of a popular song.

15

The others, however, remain uncommunicative apart from complaining, together with the Podestà, of incomprehension and heart-pounding (pitapat figures for strings in C minor, going to G minor thence to D major).

The Podestà explodes, to a cheerful patter six-eight, *allegro* in D major, at their lack of respect for him (and here, we may deduce, Sandrina and Belfiore walk away into the garden). Serpetta is the first to explain their general surprise: the Count, Arminda's betrothed, and the Podestà's pretty garden-girl can be seen, if he will use his eyes, kissing and cuddling in the garden. Nardo assures them that Serpetta is telling an untruth; the two bicker waspishly (buzzing tremolos and chromatic harmony) while the Podestà laments this double disaster to his plans (a momentary *maestoso* unison passage in G major). The three of them end this scene with another dance-like 6/8 concerted passage. Arminda and Ramiro have been left out of this latest episode altogether, though there is no indication that they have left the stage.

The concerted passage announced that the Podestà, Serpetta and Nardo would go and find out the truth about the Count and Sandrina. The truth now comes in their direction. Presumably the eavesdroppers hide while Sandrina and Belfiore enter in lively conversation (*allegro* in G major, 4/4; oboes and horns return to the score, marking a new turn in the action). She begs him not to torment her with his advances, he who is betrothed to Arminda. Belfiore replies that Violante was his love before Arminda, and here beside him is Violante, to which Sandrina replies that he is gravely mistaken. Their dialogue is carried on to familiar and expressive *opera buffa* melodious phrases, notably these two:

16*a*
[Allegro]

Ma voi, che pre—ten—de—te,

b

Ar—min—da non son i——o il vostro dolce a—mor—

Ex. 16*a* will suggest pride and protest (*cf.* the Countess in *Figaro*, Act II) though it is used more generally here. Ex. 16*b* is a blander cadence idea expressing conviction. The music naturally becomes more animated when the eavesdroppers exchange shocked asides. Arminda has enraged tremolos, Ramiro off-beat *fortepiano* jerks. Only Nardo is sympathetic and he is concerned to help Sandrina out of her predicament. So many contrasts of expressive material tend to break up the musical line but the revival of Ex. 16*a*, now in C minor, when Sandrina assures the Count that Violante is dead, keeps continuity going through several minutes of resourceful ensemble and dialogue. In the meanwhile there is a striking tiptoe unison spread across four vocal entries ('Gebt mir Antwort'—in the Italian 'Rispondete'), a supple E minor melody for oboe when the spectators comment on the blameless innocence of this *tête à tête* (several of them find it helps their amorous designs) and a telling antiphony of rage and sadness ending with all seven voices together. It is not made clear at what point the eavesdroppers reveal their presence to Sandrina and the Count. I incline to the sarcastic E minor passage as motivating the subsequent duet of remorse for Sandrina and Belfiore, and then the septet involving all the characters.

Violins, with a sequential figure, lead through to the final section, *allegro*, beginning in D major with angry cries of recrimination by the spectators, wretchedness by Sandrina, and amused indecision by Belfiore—'How happy could I be with either,' is his sentiment. Then all unite in a fiery A major concerted ensemble expressive of their common perplexity, with some *sostenuto* collective harmony.

3

In a musicdrama, even an *opera buffa*, it must be expected that the first act will end with some sort of confused situation, setting off an ensemble of perplexity. This has to advance the intrigue to a definite point where we can say that the relationship of characters, and the dramatic journey from square A to the ultimate square Z, has advanced significantly since the curtain originally rose. In *La finta giardiniera* it has not truly done so. Granted it is now clear that Belfiore and Sandrina have re-encountered one another again, and have recognized one another, that Belfiore is almost certain of Sandrina's identity though she, for psychological reasons of her own, refuses to admit that she is his old love Violante whom he believed dead. Serpetta believes her to be a rival for the Podestà's affections, Arminda thinks she is getting away with her betrothed Belfiore; Ramiro hopes that this may be so. Nardo has chiefly been concerned to extricate his employer Sandrina from a socially perilous contretemps. If he wants Serpetta to marry him, then he must want Sandrina to marry the Podestà—or should her consort be Belfiore? The libretto does not make this clear; it treats all the characters as if they were chambers in a gun playing Russian roulette. The promising intrigue of the first act has been bungled, and when the curtain descended on Act I nobody was much the wiser about anybody on stage. Coltellini as librettist will now attempt to create enlightenment. From here onward his Italian text as well as the German is extant, and Mozart's recitatives too.

Ramiro finds Arminda in a hall in the Podestà's palace, and begs her to stop and listen to him. He upbraids her for inconstancy. She does not appreciate his moral claims on her; the Contino is so pretty. He promises revenge on Belfiore and departs. Arminda pities him but intends to go through with marriage to the Count, whether out of seriousness or caprice.

Belfiore enters, does not see Arminda and voices his mental perturbation since his re-encounter with Sandrina with whom he needs to speak further. He sights Arminda and greets her courteously. She asks who it is that he wishes to seek out. He pretends that it was she, but she has heard him mention Sandrina by name and, repeating his words to him, Arminda upbraids him for betraying her on what should have been their wedding day.

For the **Aria, No. 13**, which emphasizes Arminda's frame of mind, Mozart selected his favourite emotional key of G minor, and buttressed the strings with bassoons as well as oboes, and four horns who have dull supporting parts, seldom heard all at once. *Vorrei punirti indegno* is an aria of anger and tearfulness, *allegro agitato* in a simple ternary form.

> Worthless man, I would like to punish you, to tear out your heart.
> My bosom burns with scorn but love still restrains me.
> Is this the reward you grant to my love? O God, I am torn between
>   anger and compassion.

The stormy opening, with its offbeat reiterated notes and choppy dynamics, recalls the G minor symphony No. 25 of a year earlier, just as the expression looks forward to Electra in *Idomeneo* (Ex. 17).

The bass line may be rather static but this is offset by rich orchestral texture. The offbeat violin figure continues into the transition in B flat where 'amore che sospirar mi fa' finds Mozart responding with appoggiatura sighs and a hint of B flat minor. The second subject-group includes impetuous contrary-motion five-finger exercises (nicely doubled by oboe and bassoon—a feature of the closing ritornello too), *fortepiano* scrubbing on strings for 'ardo nel sen' and, for the repeat of 'amore', galant snaps. The codetta group is equally eventful. The middle section stresses Arminda's questions with emotional pauses, and the mood is even more intense than before or afterwards. There is a powerful lead back to the recapitulation. It is a big and expressively mature aria in its context, typical of the *seria* element being imported into a *buffo* intrigue.

Arminda flounces away in her best *seria* manner, while the Contino comments that she is more demon or fury than lady. His spirited reflections are cut short by

17

Allegro agitato

the entry of Serpetta who has observed Arminda's vessel of wrath imitation and advises Belfiore to follow her and apologize. He is in no mood to do so, curses all women and the requirements of good manners, and himself flounces away, less heroically than Arminda.

Serpetta sympathizes with him in his unexpected entanglement with the 'foreign lady' as she calls Sandrina. She has other problems, however, for Nardo enters demanding to know how to make her love him as he loves her. Shall he kill himself? He produces a knife and offers to persuade her by *felo de sè*, but when she tells him to proceed since she will not be moved at all, he admits that he has not the courage. She decides to herself that she will render him crazy (Calzabigi evidently believed in the curative properties of madness), so she promises to love him if he will sing her a rustic love song with all the required gesticulations. Her pretty face induces him to obey and he does so in **No. 14**, his **Aria** in A major, *andantino grazioso*, scored for strings alone and entitled *Con un vezzo all'Italiana*, a novelty number of special agreeability.

He decides to woo her polyglot-fashion with amorous phrases in numerous languages, a device that Mozart loved dearly (since he had travelled widely in his boyhood and had to pick up basic phrases of human communication, there are several examples in his occasional canons, and many more in his letters). Mozart understood, nevertheless, that, if the aria were not to fall apart musically, the polyglot virtuosity must be integrated, which he did thematically. For him at this stage A major was only a key of friendliness, without deeper emotional undertones. The strings propose a cheerful, robust, rather popular type of melody.

18

Andantino grazioso

Nardo takes up this tune to explain how an Italian would express his feelings.

> In Italian I would tell you: your face has set my heart on fire (*Serpetta is unmoved*). If that doesn't please you, let me try it in French: your servant, Madame, with all my heart. You don't like that either? Then let's see what it's like in English. Ah, my life, pray you say yes. Your cursed indifference makes me lose patience: none of these languages helps. Truly I'm lost with the moods of you foreign women.

The German version of this aria is linguistically more amusing than the Italian. Here at last is an aria through-composed in the manner of Mozart's mature operas. The tune, as quoted above, is quite attractive, and the vocal writing exploits the top of Nardo's bass register. The French lesson sends him, typically, into French 3/4 and a quantity of trills; the attempt at English is pushed into an *andante*, though the first tune remains. Violas are playing here in thirds. The true recapitulation happens at Nardo's 'Your cursed indifference'. There are several pauses for flourishes; one of them is filled in by Mozart with a rising scale. Evidently Nardo leaves the stage, like an *opera seria* character, after this aria. Serpetta stays only long enough to voice her growing love for Nardo and annoyance that he is Sandrina's cousin.

Sandrina enters, amazed to have rediscovered her lover and afraid she may yet have lost him, since he thought her dead and is now betrothed to Arminda.

Intuition tells her that it is too early for her to throw off her disguise, but at least she must try to postpone the wedding of Arminda and Belfiore. And here he is, still more convinced, as he looks at her again, that she is his Violante. She calls him a faithless villain and reminds him how he made her miserable, stabbed her and then abandoned her. This was, she hastily adds, what the wretched Violante told her as she lay dying. She orders him to go away before Arminda finds them together. The thought intimidates him but he still has difficulty in removing himself from the sight of her lovely face, the face of his Violante.

The **Aria, No. 15** which follows, is unusual in that it involves stage action. By now predictably it presents Belfiore as a comic character as well as a romantic lover. *Care pupille* begins *andante* in F major. The elaborate instrumentation calls for two flutes, much exploited on one of their rare contributions to the score, two horns in a dull supporting role, and strings of which the violas are frequently *divisi*, often doubling the flutes at the octave below.

The opening ritornello is quite extended, introducing two subject-groups, blandly amorous in character and galant in style.

> Dear eyes, turn your gaze upon me and make me insane. (*Sandrina motions him to depart*) I am going. How cruelly stern you are.

These words serve Belfiore for a solo exposition, where 'Parto' coincides with the start of the second group; a brief middle section, and a recapitulation as far as the second group. There is a pause and Belfiore moves to new words and new music, though still *andante*.

> But before I go, my dear, please allow me to kiss your hand as a mark of my love. What a tender hand it is! I am turned to ashes, my sweetest Venus.

The tender hand does not, however, belong to Sandrina but to the Podestà who has sidled up to Sandrina and taken her place beside the Count—a situation to be closely paralleled in the fourth act of *Figaro* where the mistaken kiss was placed not by Mozart's librettist but already by Beaumarchais. In this earlier manifestation of the joke Mozart relishes the humour with music full of tenderness. The texture at 'oh che manina tenera' is especially beautiful: independent flutes at the top, flowing arpeggios for violins and violas in sixths and thirds, plucked chords for second violins.

Belfiore realizes his mistake when the music reaches a silent pause. Quickly he changes his tune again to an *allegro*.

> Your servant, estimable sir! Cursed fate, it had to happen to me.

This brings the aria to a jovial, not particularly eventful close. Belfiore angrily walks away.

The Podestà is just as angry. How could they so behave to a man of his station, the man who loves Sandrina—he turns to her. She protests her innocence and her wretchedness. The Podestà attempts to console her with endearments but she will have none of them and berates him for behaving so insultingly to her. A moment later she is apologizing for her abruptness. Her unhappy heart was to blame. It must move him to compassion.

So she wheedles him in the **Aria, No. 16**, *Una voce sento al core*, a rondo structure, *grazioso* in A major with one *allegro* episode and an independent coda. The scoring is for strings alone, the violas being often divided.

> A voice within my heart tells me softly: 'Your master is full of goodness. His eyes may appear scornful but you can see pity there.'
>
> (*Allegro*) Alas, he runs away and will not listen. He has turned tyrant and I am wounded by his rage.
>
> (*Coda*) Maidens, when you hear me, if you feel pity for an unfortunate girl, come and console her.

The rondo theme is an ingratiating one, melodically well formed; we may observe that Sandrina expresses herself in the musical idiom of the streets, i.e. in disguise (Ex. 19).

This is music in which Blondchen, from *Die Entführung*, might have voiced her opinions, German rather than Italian in tone of voice (it does not sound quite like Despina or Susanna), as the continuation with its jaunty bass line confirms. The octave-leap cadential figure, on 'bontà' and later 'pietà', is more ambivalent, a

19

Grazioso

fingerprint that Mozart adopted for his own. The rondo's first episode begins at the second paragraph of text above. The second episode, as there noted, is *allegro*, and in common time and A minor with distraught *coulés* for violins, and rushing scale figures and passionate scrubbing, thoroughly eventful and so an ideal contrast to the demure rondo theme which returns after it. A brief bridge-passage hints again at A minor and the Podestà's flight. Then the coda in 3/8, but still A major marked *grazioso*, and thus more easily paced, to the last paragraph of text above, with new material, elegant and strong in invention though still proletarian in tone. Towards the end Sandrina bursts three times into florid divisions. Although this aria begins mildly it ends as a vital piece of music. *Exit* Sandrina. *Manet* the Podestà cursing himself for his weakness, but convinced that he should go after her and comfort her. At this moment Arminda enters telling her uncle that she wishes now to marry Belfiore. On her heels comes Ramiro with a warrant for the arrest of Belfiore as murderer of Violante Onesti. The Podestà is determined to quash this charge; but he is also unwilling that his niece should be joined in matrimony to a homicidal criminal.

His outrage is expressed in **No. 17**, the Podestà's **Aria** in G major (deducibly *allegro*) for oboe, horns and strings, *Una damina, una nipote*. This is not a situation for an orchestral ritornello. After three loud chords the Podestà speaks his mind.

> Am I going to ruin a lady, my niece, noble, attractive and possessed of a goodly dowry? The marriage will not occur. I would be despised in Germany, France, Spain, the whole world, if such a thing should happen to a celebrity, a cavalier, a litterateur, a Podestà. Think no more about it. So it will be.

It is a patter-song in binary form. The beginning is almost like an accelerated recitative, with its crude jerk from G to F major and the defiant German sixth at 'affogarlo'. After a pause for breath, a lilting tune begins to emerge.

20

[Allegro]

Il matri—mo—ni—o sia per non fat—to,

Though it does not progress far it does arrive as a breath of fresh air; it also looks forward to later Despina-like arias, carefree and swaggering. There are suitable orchestral whiplashes at 'sarei tacciato' where the Podestà imagines his world-wide humiliation, and a dramatic end to this episode on a broken diminished seventh figure ('d'un Podestà'). The concluding section of this half is exceptionally lively in the Despina manner again ('non ci pensate'). At the dominant cadence the orchestra breaks in with a swelling ritornello; the second half rephrases the musical setting of the start, still in recitative fashion, looks at B minor, dodges back to G and completes its binary restatement in that key. We are left perplexed by music surely meant for a soprano, sung by a character who should be a comic bass but whom Mozart cast as a comic tenor.

The Podestà's conventional exit leaves Arminda and Ramiro alone. He approaches her lovingly, but she cuts his every phrase dead with syllables of scorn and hatred and soon follows the Podestà off stage. Poor Ramiro! Yet he is not disconsolate; he has hope to sustain him, as he reminds himself in the **Aria, No. 18**, in B flat major, *Dolce d'amor compagna speranza*, supposedly *larghetto* and accompanied by strings with two bassoons who are there to bestow a rich, dark, yet translucent glow on the texture. The introductory ritornello, fairly short, emphasizes this with its heavy harmonic colouring over a strong bass, and its doubling of first violin with first bassoon an octave lower, an effect movingly characteristic of the whole aria (a simple ternary form with brief middle section). Later the texture is enriched by violas in two parts. This is a moment of seriousness, deep expression as the musical invention underlines. The special orchestral colouring is only appropriate when the singer is a soprano (properly a male soprano singing gently like a clarinet, not loudly like a trumpet); to recast Ramiro as a tenor would be to ruin this aria because the orchestra would no longer set off the quality of the voice. Ramiro's vocal music here is more like that of, shall we say, Tamino than Pamina—though in an essentially Italianate not German vein except at one point just before the reprise—and it must sound ardently masculine, not like a lady, let alone a white-voiced soprano, yet accurately in the soprano pitch. Ramiro's sentiments are as follows:

Wheedling hope, sweet companion of love, my soul has faith in you and lays everything in your charge.
   You sustain my life, you guide me to harbour, lovable consolation of my sincere faith.

The vocal part of Ramiro is essentially dignified and poetic, especially in its leaps at the beginning of phrases, even in the delicately moulded triplets of the bravura runs. The spirit of the music generally is much influenced by the copious, often imitated or off-geared trills. This is not a spectacular highlight of the opera but one of the most expressively substantial musical numbers.

The stage is now empty, everybody having sung an aria and made an exit. Back comes the Podestà with Arminda and Serpetta. He is determined to sort everything out. At first he is perplexed and asks his niece for advice. She, and Serpetta, assure him that he must take positive action. His problem is Ramiro. Now fortunately it is Belfiore who enters, makes loving advances to Arminda, but is told by the Podestà to restrain his enthusiasm. The Podestà wishes further information about him: for example, does he know Marchioness Onesti? Arminda persuades Belfiore to deny all knowledge of her. Further pressed whether he assassinated the Marchioness, he begins to incriminate himself, and is told to defend his case. In this moment of deep embarrassment Sandrina enters and defends Belfiore by admitting that she is Violante, was wounded by the Count but still lives, and pardons him. The others are suitably stupefied. Belfiore seconds her admission.

The Podestà, who counted on Sandrina's love, departs enraged. Arminda likewise goes to meditate revenge. Serpetta leaves because she finds the whole affair so comic. Belfiore, discovering himself alone with Sandrina/Violante, is overjoyed. But she scornfully instructs him to go and console his official betrothed, Arminda. And she leaves as well. Belfiore, in an accompanied **Recitative, No. 19**, with oboes, horns and strings, *Ah non partir*, attempts to restrain her.

> (*Andante*) Ah, do not go, listen to me; alas she spurns me and departs.
> (*Allegro*) The ground quakes, a dark cloud revolves within me. Is it a whirlwind, a storm, is it night or day?

It has already been noted that Mozart always approached accompanied recitative as a special occasion. This example is typically eventful. When Belfiore realizes that his pleas have been ignored, the violas divide in thirds, plaintively doubling violins in their gesture of supplication. There is a moment of agitated frustration at 'rispinge'; then the pace becomes *allegro*, oboes and horns are added, sustaining high chords, the bass line moves purposefully, off-beat violins convey anxiety and hallucination. The whirlwind is dynamically described, night and day considered in terms of utmost loveliness. A separate German setting of this recitative is extant; the ideas are differently ordered though the given continuo bass-line remains the same, and we may wonder, tentatively, if musical imagery follows the German rather than the Italian libretto at this point.

Plucked strings under sustained wind, *andante* in B flat major, appear to launch an aria, *Arminda, Violante*, since the mood becomes more lyrical. But not for long; recitative declamation quickly resumes. There is a doleful violin figure as Belfiore questions the value of the ladies' tears, and up-thrusting scales as he longs for the thunder and lightning to strike him. Again a sensation of solemn E flat major *adagio* and melancholy imitative figures as he longs tearfully for death. The music is moving towards **Aria**, and this arrives uninterruptedly in E flat, still *adagio*, with strong dynamic contrasts and rushing violin figures: *Già divento freddo freddo*.

> I turn cold, my feet tremble, my blood stops, my breath falters, my heart flags. What a situation! Icy sweat runs on my brow and nose. But soft, near by I hear a gentle breeze ('ciufoletto') as if from Elysium. The wind sighs softly, strokes the air. I see the sun, the daylight, do not doubt it.
> (*Tempo di minuetto*) What happiness! Still there are thoughts, ratiocinations; my heart can blaze jubilantly.

The short, unmelodious but highly dramatic introduction signifies palpitating excitement—not the coldness mentioned by Belfiore. There is a hint of pain at 'trema il piè' (in German, more logically for these sighs, 'und der Schmerz'); but the prevailing lyricism of orchestra and, by suggestion, the voice is more compelling. At 'gelido sudor' the music turns heatedly chromatic. The clipped, agile thirds, at 'Ma pian, piano,' bring Papageno to mind (until now Belfiore has adopted his ardent Tamino image). At 'giro l'occhi', the dialogue between oboes and *divisi* violas with violins is thoroughly illuminating. The 'ciufoletta' or breeze is expressed in a fluent violin run, swelling and receding. At 'zitto, zitto' the orchestra's running figures are mingled with sensuous woodwind thirds, and the lyrical yet disrupted vocal line suggests German, not Italian vocal writing. This most engaging section, through-composed not structurally formulated as in early Mozart, falls into a final minuet section, still in E flat, *Che allegrezza*, rather restrained in its joy. A passage of galant snaps and curt wind chords, at 'penso ancora', captures attention and seems more vividly geared to the German text's 'hüpfen und springen' (words connected with Osmin in *Entführung*!) There is one short pause soon after the singer launches into arpeggio divisions, the second of them perhaps graced so as not to sound repetitive. Apart from the Papageno moment this aria has done much to establish the Contino as a serious hero.

The stage is empty again. Nardo enters, worried because he cannot find Sandrina. Hearing voices he hides. Ramiro arrives, determined to prove whether Sandrina really is the Countess Violante; the Podestà, with him, is ready to wager as much from the open frankness of her conversation. Serpetta, much scared, tells the men that Sandrina has disappeared. The Podestà insists that they must find her at once, even though night is falling. He takes Ramiro with him to reconnoitre.

Serpetta now reveals that she knows Arminda, out of jealousy, has abducted Sandrina into a neighbouring wood full of wild beasts. Nardo at once makes a furtive escape to look for his mistress. Serpetta admits that whereas her cause would be helped if Sandrina were devoured by a ravening wolf yet, on the other hand, she would be sorry. However, in matters of the heart one must keep quiet.

This is the tenor of her **Aria, No. 20**, *andantino grazioso* in G major, *Chi vuol godere il mondo*, scored with strings alone.

The introduction is jovial, with a brief main tune and a bridge that rises quickly to a precipitate climax and descends for a cadence in time to let Serpetta begin.

> If you want to enjoy the world, then leave it as it is. Nobody worries me. A girl, I know, should be good-hearted, sincere; but that's all pointless with men of today.

Serpetta's diction is melodious in a conventional manner, gentle at first, then more breezy in her second subject, more like patter in the codetta followed by a bland ritornello. The short middle section hardly wanders in terms of key but remains tuneful. The recapitulation involves some tonal re-setting, profitably in the second group which emerges more maturely in its lower register.

At the end of the reprise a new *allegro* in 6/8 begins (*Bisogna essere accorta*), still in G major.

> You have to be curt, indifferent, feign shyness, invent excuses ('fare la gatta morta'), make him pine. When I was a girl my mother instructed me and I intend to follow her teaching.

This coda flows cheerfully along like a lulling patter-song. Serpetta becomes more melodious at 'la voglio seguitar' where her repeated rising phrase has a saucy charm.

The orchestra continues with the same music, comes to a cadence in G but then breaks away into highly dramatic, chromatic territory, landing in C minor with wailing oboe thirds that lead straight into the next scene.

This represents a rocky deserted spot with a dark cave prominent. Sandrina has just been deposited here by her abductors who have promptly run as far away as possible. She is in a great state of terror and is attempting, in her **Aria, No. 21**, to call them back. *Crudeli, fermate* is in C minor, *allegro agitato* for oboes, bassoons, horns and strings. It is dominated by the anxious motive played at once by first violins and repeated like an ostinato. Its off-beat string accompaniment enhances the tension, and the phrase's *crescendo* nature is underlined by the loud woodwind chord at the end of each bar so that the total effect is unmistakably of the waves of terror which assail Sandrina wherever she looks.

21
Allegro agitato

Cru—de—li   fer—ma—te

Stop, cruel people, stop for God's sake, you're leaving me alone here. Who will help me in my plight? Ye gods, I am lost, take pity on me.

Ex. 21, with Sandrina's breathless cries, continues until sustained chords turn towards B flat major (as dominant of the relative major) for a bridge passage ('misera chi m'ajuta') in which the violin pattern of the first subject is broken up and the oboes squeal high suspensions full of heartache. E flat major arrives for the second subject ('Ah Numi, son perduta') which is more melodious and takes the aria to its half-way cadence whereupon Ex. 21 returns, interrupted by a less agitated but searingly mournful descending phrase. After two such alternations there is a return to the music of the earlier bridge passage, now on the verge of C minor, and so the reprise continues. The abductors have gone beyond earshot so there is no dramatic point in repeating Sandrina's first group (the motif of Ex. 21 has been present until this moment). The natural design for music to these words is accordingly binary not ternary, Mozart must have concluded.

When the second half is finished, the orchestra returns to Ex. 21 and stops suddenly on a foreign chord (D major). Sandrina moves into accompanied recitative. Mozart is well into a long span of uninterrupted music which will eventually link with the start of the finale. We may indeed feel that the finale began musically at the start of modest little No. 20, even though there has been a scene-change in the middle. This grand musical span consists of 864 bars, only slightly less long than the second act finale of *Figaro* (937 bars), world famous for its length.

Sandrina, still accompanied by Ex. 21, now in G minor, wonders where she is, whether she must die here alone—a plaintive *andante* F minor derivative of Ex. 21, slower but still swelling and diminishing. Ex. 21 reappears for the last time when she realizes that she can find no path through the rocks about her. The music slows down, through a tearful F minor—oboes, violins, violas, all in pairs and independent, richly affecting, to a muted string cadence in A minor as Sandrina gives way to grief.

Nevertheless she does not stop singing. At once, without orchestral ritornello, she attacks *Ah dal pianto*, her **Cavatina, No. 22** in A minor, *allegro agitato*, with solo oboe and bassoon as well as muted strings.

> I can scarcely breathe for weeping and sobbing. I have no voice nor vigour, my spirit wilts within me.

This again is a binary structure, though so close knit that no real seam is audible, so insistent is the rhythmic drive. As in No. 21 the vocal line is laid, even more fragmentarily to illustrate Sandrina's tears and sighs, over a steady accompaniment and against another fragmentary line of melody for first violins consisting of shivery trills and hesitantly tiptoe steps, a beautiful and subtle texture enhanced when the two woodwind soloists join in. It is the voice part, fragmented though it be, which holds all the music together. Oboe and bassoon induce a powerful turn into F major ('non ho voce'), and the oboe dominates the second subject a moment later. At 'l'alma in sen mancando va' Sandrina is inappropriately pushed into gay virtuoso feats—Mozart was to set these words more eloquently in the later concert aria *Ch'io mi scordi di te*. After the halfway cadence the oboe and bassoon guide the music through F major, G minor, even B minor, before returning to the tonic A minor for a concluding reprise of second-group material. The tone of the music is curiously lightweight, its eloquent sweep thoroughly Mozartian.

The ending runs, as in No. 21, straight into another accompanied recitative strongly diversified in tempo.

Sandrina's loneliness becomes more intense, her footsteps stumble (unsynchronized strings, alternately loud and soft). She imagines noises (a precipitate downward figure), perhaps a poisonous snake horribly hissing (*presto*). She longs to hide, and now (kindlier strings, surely *andante*) perceives the near-by cave into which she cautiously tiptoes while the strings do likewise, moving from C major to the margin of E flat major.

In this key **No. 23**, the **Septet-Finale** begins, *andante sostenuto*, with flutes, horns and (now unmuted) strings. Remote and inaccessible as is this rocky fastness all the other characters are quickly finding their way to it, as if they were taking part in a romantic operetta. First comes Belfiore led by Nardo: the phrases to which they enter look like Mozartian furtive music, but structurally the old complete edition may be right in marking them at a firm *forte*. In either case the E flat music is solemn, pregnant with *dénouement* as Belfiore wonders at this desolate spot ('Fra quest' ombre'—the German text makes a good librettist's point by having each character enter to more or less the same words; Mozart brings in his flutes, vehicles of musical illumination). Nardo is terrified, as scrubbing strings attest. Sandrina from her cave is all the more scared to hear these voices. Another is added, that of Arminda who has followed the Count here, hoping to trap him with his illicit sweetheart (Arminda has had Sandrina abandoned here). Together all four join in a block harmony ensemble, each cautioning himself/herself to listen carefully (it sounds like one of the moralizing ensemblettes in *Zauberflöte*, though the music of this scene is more Italianate than German). In G minor the Podestà arrives, perturbed by the ruggedness of the countryside; behind him comes Serpetta. A further moment of concerted surprise and anxiety.

In the darkness they mistake one another's identity: the Podestà approaches Arminda: he thinks her to be Sandrina, she assumes he must be the Count. Belfiore takes Serpetta for Sandrina, she him for the Podestà. Only Nardo and Sandrina truly recognize one another: they all express joy at supposedly rediscovering one another. They end in B flat. Now enter Ramiro, *allegretto* in G major (rushing figures), counselling his fellow conspirators to keep quiet and watch. A further ensemble, doggedly old-fashioned, expresses their joint tension, while the orchestra remains remorselessly jovial. By now the listener may expect this finale to proceed in terms of individual dialogue summed up, every so often, by short block ensembles. At present only Nardo and Sandrina are upset, but the next sextet passage somehow expresses corporate fear. Ramiro promises general self-confidence, since he has brought with him a number of servants carrying torches (flutes and high horns to illuminate the music). By this light they are astonished to find themselves all wrongly paired; so they again join in a brief choral refrain of surprise and chagrin, and the ladies delightfully point out the men's mistakes (the whole of this passage has been strongly German in character, for example in the unclassical square phrasing and repeated-note melody, belonging to street music, not *bel canto*). Arminda is the first to turn haughty and *seria* as she rebukes Belfiore. The Podestà vents his rage on Sandrina who is near to collapse by this time. Nardo and Serpetta seem more amused than angry with one another, but Arminda pours hatred on Ramiro as well as the Count (again rushing scales accompany her outburst).

Sandrina and Belfiore, in plaintive C minor, share their stupefaction in a duet on the verge of delirium. The others express anger in energetic C major. After a pause G major emerges, *andantino*, and Sandrina proves to have really lost her reason, for she is serenading the shepherd Thyrsis in pastoral mood (oboes *vice* flutes). He likewise calls to her as Cloris, promising that Orpheus's lyre will move forests and animals. These two are united in their euphonious delusions. The Podestà and Ramiro each challenge Belfiore to a duel, though Arminda, Serpetta and Nardo all run forward to restrain them. Sandrina and Belfiore are miles away by now, she believing herself to be Medusa, he the intrepid Alcides (Hercules). Gradually the others realize what has happened. Tension mounts as the deluded lovers duet ecstatically. At first the sane and insane are antiphonally alternated. Finally they all briefly unite in a closing ensemble which ends the act in a vigorous C major.

4

Sandrina and Belfiore were evidently conducted back to the Podestà's villa in whose courtyard Act III begins. Nardo is supposedly courting Serpetta still, for her first words are that, frankly, she never fancied him though there is no reason why he should not go on hoping. He finds her obstinacy infuriating: would it cost her so much to give him a kind word? But Serpetta cannot bring herself to say either yes or no. She leaves him.

Nardo is about to follow her when Belfiore stops him, addressing him in terms of passionate love and announcing that Nardo is Venus while he, Belfiore, is Mercury. He has left his serpent-entwined wand in heaven. Nardo, much embarrassed by all this, offers to fetch it for him but on his way out he is stopped by Sandrina who declares that she is Herminea, his faithful lover, and she intends to marry him at once. Nardo resorts to the old subterfuge for escape and points at the sky, instructing Belfiore, in his **Aria**, the first part of **No. 24**, *Mirate che contrasto* (no orchestral introduction), to

observe the difference between sun and moon.

Likewise he tells Sandrina to

watch the amorous stars as they collide and embrace.

The aria, *allegro* in E flat major (oboes, horns and strings), begins on tiptoe, as Nardo supposedly is, for best persuasive effect. There is some violin activity for the sun and moon. A blatant modulation to B flat introduces the second subject ('vedete ad una') where he turns to Sandrina and tunefully draws her attention to the stars. His asides about longing to run away (so like Leporello in the second act sextet of *Don Giovanni*) have oboes answered by violins, very pleasing. The coda section ('sono incantati'), in which he notes with relief that the two lunatics are completely absorbed in their stargazing, is in suave thirds repeated like a refrain after a more frenetic passage about the activity of the stars.

Nardo manages to escape and the music continues in the same key and tempo as a **Duet** for Belfiore and Sandrina (it is unusual to find a structure of this kind anywhere but in a finale in operatic Mozart). The active star-frenzy texture is resumed as they gaze with mounting terror at imagined catastrophes in the sky. There is a dynamic touch of diminished sevenths, hot and percussive on one another's heels, when Belfiore declares that the moon is tumbling down (or, if you prefer the German, that the sun is burning up). The two singers join together in C minor anxiety, then the music plunges back into E flat major for a *più presto* coda, 'Che turbine si desta'.

What whirlwinds, thunders, tempests! Help, have pity!

Their plunging runs in tenths, the turbulent, strongly accented string figures, and the pompous oboe and horn fanfares all give this coda distinction. We are near to the world of *Don Giovanni*, particularly the duetting of Anna and Ottavio and the first act finale: the musical drive is stiffer here, but it remains a purposeful moment. Amid a whirling orchestral conclusion the maniacs leave together.

The Podestà is congratulating himself on his jurisprudential acumen in solving all the problems of the moment: he will have Belfiore removed from the house on the grounds of insanity. Arminda's visit will have been fruitless but he, the Podestà, will then be free to give his hand to Sandrina. Serpetta, who has heard the strategy, objects that he once promised to make *her* his bride, and she, after all, loves him. The Podestà calls her an impudent chatterbox and she runs away. He is now faced simultaneously with Ramiro who wants to marry Arminda at once, especially since Belfiore has lost his wits; and Arminda who is equally insistent on marrying Belfiore. They argue tooth and nail until the Podestà is quite distraught. When they ask him to arbitrate, his judgment, given in **No. 25**, his **Aria** in C major *Mio padrone, io dir volevo*, is more or less gibberish, since he turns from one to the other without ever finishing a sentence, except to remark that his brain is bursting. This is in a putatively *allegro* first section. In the *presto* coda he tells Arminda to marry her Count, and Ramiro to wed his niece; they may do what they please so long as they leave him in peace.

The immediate attraction of this aria is its feathery, lilting texture: staccato strings with an animated bass line; horns rhythmically marking in the second and third of each bar's four beats, so as to accentuate the dance character of the music; oboes pushing each bar-end on to the next beat (there are trumpets too, but cautiously used). The mood is of a country dance, but on tiptoe. The closest familiar equivalent is the music of Monostatos in *Zauberflöte*. We might think of Leporello or perhaps Masetto in *Don Giovanni* if the Podestà's music (orchestral as well as vocal) were not essentially that of a buffo tenor. Yet this is German more than Italian music—a distinction unusually difficult to draw in *La finta giardiniera*, because Mozart set it simultaneously in Italian and German; I shall return to this idea later. A sign of dawning maturity is in the firm excursions of the middle section to A minor and D minor; usually young Mozart had touched on foreign keys then scampered home at once. The *presto* coda has immense impulsiveness. The whole aria adds distinctly to the dramatic point of the Podestà's dithering part in the play. It is both comical and supremely musical.

So the Podestà goes off to find some serenity. Arminda assures Ramiro that he has no hope of securing her love; he had better go away and forget her. He promises her that she will soon repent but she has departed.

What a cruel faithless monster she is, he reflects. And he plunges, after a short but violent orchestral introduction (oboes, bassoons, four horns, and strings) into an angry C minor **Aria, No. 26**, *Va pure ad altri in braccio*, which is supposedly *allegro agitato*. C minor for Mozart was a key that inspired chromatic intervals, and we get them full measure in the opening bars which look forward to the piano concerto, K. 491.

22

Go to the arms of another man, you faithless lady. I shall always be yours.
Even now I am wretched; far from your gaze I shall die.

Here, after a surprisingly long absence, is a sonata-form aria in Mozart's formal
manner (though with only one exposition and no *da capo* convolutions). The
introduction, quoted above, returns only in the orchestral coda. The vocal exposition is dynamic and eventful (plenty of prominent work for oboes, bassoons and
horns); it reaches E flat major quite quickly and stays there until the middle section
which wanders through A minor and G minor (very effective horn-parts here). As
the textual resumé above indicates, the middle section ('Già misero mi vuoi') is
more pathetic in tone, the outer sections full of angry reproach. In the recapitulation the E flat material appears in C minor, even more eloquently.

The scene changes to a garden where Sandrina and Belfiore are lying asleep at a
discreet distance from one another. They awake from delusions to the sound of
oboes, horns and muted strings with plucked basses, *adagio* in E flat major, the
introduction to their accompanied **Recitative, No. 27,** *Dove mai son!* (Mozart left
a separate setting of the voice parts to suit the German translation). It is exceptionally
sweet music with one of those chugging leisurely accompaniments (usually in
triplets though not here) that so often herald Mozartian magic. The first melody is
curiously shaped; the entry of oboes and horns, answered by violins, strengthens
the spell. And because these motifs persist right through the recitative there is all
the more reason to quote this introduction.

The above suggests an aria or duet rather than a recitative, and the first phrases
(*con stupore*) for Sandrina and the Contino sustain this illusion as they wonder
where they are. Thereafter they express their wonderment in recitative, their
remarks separated by excerpts from Ex. 23. Suddenly the strings break the dream
with a loud switch from one dominant seventh chord to another. It is a shock: they
have at last seen one another. But for both it is enchantment, so Ex. 23 continues to
comment on their mutual rediscovery. There is an odd discrepancy (not the first)

between the Italian and German texts: when Sandrina asks Belfiore whom he is seeking, he comments aside 'Worse, worse' in Italian, but 'Much better' in German! When he asks if she is Violante she admits her identity and the orchestra replies with a loud perfect cadence, the first so far. Violante/Sandrina insists that Belfiore must feel obligations to his formally betrothed Arminda, and she protests that she herself is unworthy of his love, adding that she is supposed to be wedded to the Podestà. As she attempts to go the strings remove their mutes (though Ex. 23 is resumed). Belfiore refuses to let her depart. Either she remains his or he must die.

After a formal orchestral gesture, *adagio* in B flat major (the scoring remains the same), Belfiore entreats her to recognize his true love, in the duet *Tu mi lasci?* In his first two phrases we can recognize already Mozart's appreciation of the musical need, in a highly charged context, to make a gradual change from recitative to melodious aria—here through gracefully phrased declamation. We shall notice the development of this in later operas: Richard Strauss wrote much about the territory between musical speech and song, but every expert dramatic composer has recognized and exploited this near-arioso field, at least since Monteverdi.

It may be helpful if I quote the first five bars of this duet: the orchestral lead-in, Belfiore's intermediary phrases, the orchestra's encouragement, and then the start of Belfiore's ease into expressive melody:

Because the drama is reaching its emotional climax, with the reconciliation of hero and heroine, Mozart's music unfolds at its most voluptuous.

BELFIORE   Can you leave me? Sweetheart, you do not know how my heart falters at the thought.

SANDRINA	Yes, I must leave you, though I love you; your heart does not belong to me.
BOTH	Then I will go. But what restrains me?
BELFIORE	At least let me kiss your hand.
SANDRINA	Do not flatter me, go far away.
BOTH	Be brave: perhaps we shall meet one day.

This is all in the young Mozart's most elevated and affecting vein. At the hand-kissing moment the strings attempt courtly French graces but sensuousness creeps back. There are hints of F minor and C minor, and further courtly trills when they pretend to talk lightly of some future meeting.

The duet appears to end firmly in E flat but continues *andantino* in C minor with plaintive oboe thirds, interrupted by pauses and recitative, as they try to restrain one another's departure. First violins turn into an elegant chain of galant snaps: the thin ice of formality certain to crack. Their defences snap in a B flat major *allegro*, where they duet together: 'Alme belle, innamorate', realizing that their love is real and inspiring. The flood of melodious invention, imitative, antiphonal, conjunct, is no longer stately but warm, almost plebeian rather than aristocratic in the cut of the tunes and phrases (Zerlina and Masetto, for instance, rather than Anna and Ottavio), though they duly burst into florid runs. Yet the orchestra ends somewhat stiffly however exultantly.

They leave the stage together. At once the Podestà returns with Arminda, protesting that he cannot possibly further her marriage to a maniac. Nardo, however, informs them that Belfiore and Sandrina have both regained their wits and are married. The Podestà and Arminda are thunderstruck, Ramiro and Serpetta hugely relieved by this news. Belfiore and Sandrina return, announcing their marriage: Sandrina explains Nardo's real status as her servant Roberto, and her disguise as a ruse to score off her suitor. Arminda apologizes for her cruel practical joke on Sandrina, is forgiven, and offers to marry Ramiro. Serpetta is willing to take Nardo; she has evidently abandoned hope of catching the Podestà who assures them all that he will only wed when he finds another Sandrina. Always let the Podestà's kindness and goodheartedness be remembered, concludes Sandrina, through his behaviour in the case of the 'finta Giardiniera per amore', the lady who worked as a gardener in the cause of love.

The **Finale, No. 28**, *Viva pur la Giardiniera*, is entitled *Coro* but, as other chapters in this book indicate, this merely means that the seven principal characters line up at the footlights and sing a short ensemble, almost entirely in block harmony, to conclude the entertainment. The key is D major, the opera's home tonic; the scoring is for oboes, two horns and strings, the tempo *molto allegro*.

Long live the garden-girl whose heart remained faithful. Long live the Count, and love which makes all people happy.

This is a dance-like number in 3/4, full of dotted rhythms, with a few short interpolations for violins, one nice though quite straightforward harmonic slide, but nothing else to recommend it unless its indubitable conclusiveness.

5

La finta giardiniera is without doubt the most fascinating opera that Mozart had yet written. The libretto is feeble, stereotyped, often downright incompetent in matters of dramatic consistency and clarity (for instance Sandrina's wavering about revealing her identity). The situations are shamelessly borrowed from other plays, and familiar nowadays from well known works (e.g. the abducting of Sandrina from *La finta semplice*, the kiss mistakenly given from *Les noces de Figaro*, the disguise of the heroine, the comic man's escape by making his interlocutors look at the sky, the amorous old man, ambitious serving maid, lovers who go mad, from many sources). One can hardly believe that the great Calzabigi, who had already worked with Gluck on the reform of opera, or Coltellini, a respected dramatic poet, could have had a hand in such epigonic nonsense. Yet Mozart seems to have derived positive inspiration from the gallimaufry, from its absurd as well as solemn moments.

This was only Mozart's second comic opera, but already a miraculous improvement on *La finta semplice*. The characters are still basically *commedia dell' arte* puppets, but most of them have turned into recognizable, empathetic persons. The easiest was no doubt Serpetta, the traditional soubrette of Neapolitan comic opera, strong-willed and ambitious, committed to a laissez-faire policy in love as in work, downright in her prejudices yet liable to change opinions without warning. Ramiro, a conventional lover, the rejected noble suitor who eventually regains his beloved, may have presented no problems to the opera's first audiences, and only does now because male sopranos, with their special vocal timbre, are unknown today—even then uncommon heroes in comic operas. Nardo ought to be a faithful *buffo* bass servant; but his part is not so *buffo*, and Mozart made it unusually sympathetic, unusually forceful, and unusually high in compass (we must remember that in Mozart's day the distinctions between various kinds of bass and baritone were not acknowledged). Arminda is a typical *opera seria* soprano, and from her music sounds more prima-donnaish than any of the other ladies, though Mozart catches her off as well as on her dignity. Sandrina, however, has to portray both the noble lady and the supposed peasant. Mozart gave her music of both types, asked her to play Fiordiligi and Despina within the space of a few minutes. Dramatically she changes hardly at all, but she has to produce two voices and two vocal styles, and convince an audience that the character is still one. Belfiore is a nobleman with natural manners, though his pompousness is supposed to appear ludicrous: he is the most ambivalent of the characters. Sandrina adopts a disguise, Belfiore simply drops his mask of gentility from time to time. The Podestà is most surprising of all. His part seems destined for a *basso buffo*, a Leporello or Don Pasquale, but he is cast as a tenor, not a comprimario but a real comic tenor with some vocal and personal substance. His name is Don Anchises (to show that he is old, like Aeneas's aged father who had that name), and he has to be able to sing fluently and musically as well as comically. Julius Patzak would have given us a splendid Podestà a few years before the time of writing, and in 1976 Hugues Cuénod would interpret the part exquisitely. At the end of the opera, when Don Anchises promises not to wed until he has found another Sandrina, we should not regret his loneliness (as we do that of Sullivan's Bunthorne) but warm to his new equanimity—he is surely not the paragon of benevolence invoked by Sandrina.

No character is quite what he/she appears to be in *La finta giardiniera*. This is partly because Mozart wrote music exploiting a mixture of comic and serious parts: and the serious roles were liable to fall into absurd situations. The mixture of comic and serious was to become essential to the mature Mozart's music whose invention is so ambivalent that often the listener wants to smile and weep at the same moment. Theatre from the earliest times had countered tragedy with comedy on a similar theme: it was a familiar feature of Neapolitan opera. Mozart was later to present this ambivalence in truly subtle terms. Here he has just perceived the possibilities, in Arminda's first aria (No. 7), in Belfiore's No. 8, in the proletarian music of the heroine Sandrina (e.g. No. 4), perhaps in No. 27 where Sandrina and Belfiore recover their senses, and the music is delectably expressive, though *opera buffa* is not far away, nor is the stiffness of *opera seria* in which he had served a precociously long apprenticeship.

The unpredictable, yet very human, juxtaposition of comic and serious elements in arias for principal singers is a special quality of *La finta giardiniera*. Its other speciality is the mixture of Italian and German music. To travel deep into Mozart's vocal music is to discover that, from his youth onwards, he cultivated special styles for music set to Italian and to German words. I have tried to identify these during this chapter, using as a basis the known character of say, *Don Giovanni* and *Die Zauberflöte*. In *La finta giardiniera* the distinction breaks down: this number may sound perfectly Italian, that one absolutely German, several others a mixture of the two. It has been suggested that Mozart used either style discriminatingly, and that sometimes he set his music to the German, not the Italian text. Several numbers bear this distinction out, as has been retailed above. The dilemma for young Mozart was a purely practical one: to please the singers and the audience, and to write new music as interestingly and entertainingly as he knew how. In the first act he managed ably, more so in the finale. He got into his stride in Act II which ends with a finale as strong, musically, as those in the great operas. Act III seems to belong, sensitively and creatively, to the very best Mozart; it gets away from standard models and gives us good music all the time. Because the beginning is less personal the opera is unlikely to join *Idomeneo* in the new canon of Mozart's great operas, though from No. 20 onwards it deserves to do so. When its music seems to fall below the quality of, say *Figaro*, the reason is not entirely Mozart's boyhood. Rather it is because he was writing another sort of comic opera, unfashionable, indeed hardly known today in the world's opera houses.

A first-rate production of *La finta giardiniera* would result in the immediate acclaim of the second half, perhaps of Act II as well as Act III—Nardo's No. 14 needs a revised text to incorporate the polyglot sentences into the Italian. And the recitatives of Act I need to be set impeccably in Mozart's style. There would still remain, maybe, a certain indifference to the early musical numbers, until other Italian comic operas of the period are revived. The rescue operation (as an *opera buffa* in whatever language, not as a *Singspiel*) is possible and desirable.

II   IL RÈ PASTORE

IL RÈ PASTORE
(The Shepherd King)

DRAMMA PER MUSICA

Text by

PIETRO METASTASIO

revised by

GIANBATTISTA VARESCO

K. 208

ALEXANDER, King of Macedonia (Alessandro)   TENOR

AMINTAS, shepherd, in love with Elisa but, unknown to
himself, revealed as Abdalonimus, only legitimate heir to the
kingdom of Sidon (Aminta)   MALE SOPRANO

ELISA, noble Phoenician girl, descended from Cadmus, in love
with Amintas   SOPRANO

TAMYRIS, refugee princess disguised as a shepherdess,
daughter of the deceased dictator Strato, in love with Agenor
(Tamiri)   SOPRANO

AGENOR, Sidonian nobleman, Alexander's friend, in love
with Tamyris   TENOR

*Scene: countryside near the Macedonian camp,
within sight of Sidon*

The Mozarts, father, son and daughter, returned home from Munich on 7 March 1775, disheartened maybe that no offer of more permanent employment had been forthcoming from the Bavarian court. Back in Salzburg Wolfgang began to compose the series of violin concertos (starting with K. 207) which he hoped would establish him as a leading virtuoso fiddler. He added a finale to the *Finta giardiniera* overture, thus converting it into a symphony. A bigger commitment was the Archbishop's call for music to entertain the Archduke Max, Maria Theresa's youngest son, who was to visit the Salzburg court in April. Wolfgang Mozart was required to compose a new opera for the occasion. Evidently a new libretto was reckoned unnecessary for this formal princely entertainment and, not for the first or last time in history, recourse was had to the well thumbed volumes of Metastasio which the good Count Firmian had presented to Mozart.

Choice fell upon Metastasio's *festa teatrale* entitled *Il rè pastore* which deals with Alexander the Great's conquest of Sidon and installation of King Abdalonimus upon the throne there. It had been written by Metastasio in 1751 to be performed in the theatre at Schönbrunn Palace on Maria Theresa's birthday, by her five children; the part of Alexander was then played by the future Emperor Joseph II, fourteen years old. For some twenty years Metastasio had been required to compose plays for these birthday festivities. The conventions were circumscribed. The content should glorify monarchy, inculcate the performers with helpful ethical and diplomatic education, and above all be scrupulously decorous. Thus no villain could be portrayed, since this would reflect discredit on the royal impersonator. It was even considered shameful for the child-actors to show their legs, so that the characters had to be taken from countries and periods where ankle-length robes were worn—history does not relate how the costumier fitted these restrictions to the shepherd Amintas and the soldier Alexander.

The music for the first presentation was composed by Giuseppe Bonno (1710–88) who collaborated at other times with Metastasio in lyric dramas for *giovani distinti donne e cavalieri*, and who subsequently became court conductor (*Hofkapellmeister*) in Vienna (Mozart had visited him in 1773). Metastasio's libretto was set many times by composers, such as Sarti (1753), Hasse (1755), Gluck (1756), Jommelli (1764, when an English version with music by George Rush was given at Drury Lane Theatre in London), Piccinni and also Giardini (1765—this last version was seen in London at the King's, Haymarket, by Mozart and his father).

Although Mozart was saddled with an already familiar, rather old-fashioned text, he was admittedly allowed to have it adapted for modern taste. The new poet is supposed to have been the Archbishop's chaplain, Abbé Varesco,* who reduced the last two acts into one, abbreviated the lengthy dialogue and some arias, and inserted material of his own, including words for the new vaudeville finale which

* See *Idomeneo*, p. 253.

replaced Metastasio's concluding chorus (or rather block-harmony ensemble for all the soloists, no chorus being used in *Il rè pastore*).

Information about the first performance on 23 April is even sparser than usual. Of the cast we know only that Amintas was taken by Tommaso Consoli, an admired male soprano from Munich who had sung Ramiro in *La finta giardiniera*, the other roles going to resident singers of the Salzburg court chapel. The Archduke's travel diary refers to the new work as a cantata and to the evening's entertainment as a *musique-concert*, but does not comment further. Nor does Baron von Schiedenhofen whose Salzburg diaries are usually informative sources on Mozart; Schiedenhofen refers to *Il rè pastore* as a Serenade. We might deduce that the opera was very simply staged. Elsewhere it is entitled *Dramma per musica* or *componimento drammatico*; historians class it as an *opera seria*. Subsequently Mozart thought sufficiently well of *Il rè pastore* to convert the overture into a symphony by transcribing Amintas's first aria as an orchestral slow movement and adding a new finale (K. 213c). He also gave four of the soprano arias to his sweetheart Aloysia Weber (who sang them in public), and sent a copy of the complete score to his admired friend and fellow-composer Josef Mysliveček. One aria, Amintas's *L'amerò* with violin obbligato, achieved independent and lasting popularity; it was separately published, perhaps as early as 1795, certainly by 1820. The whole opera was not revived until 1906, the 150th anniversary of Mozart's birth, when there were productions in Salzburg and Munich.

2

Metastasio based his play on *Aminta* (1581) by Torquato Tasso, adding that the story of the shepherd king Abdolonimus (Metastasio regarded it as a hypochondriacal name for a hero) was related by the classical historians Justinus (Book XI, Chapter 10) and Curtius (IV, 3 ff); he might have added Diodorus (Chapter 17). They, however, make Abdolonimus not a shepherd but a gardener (*il finto giardiniero*, indeed). The story does not figure in Plutarch. Amintas, Tamyris and Agenor are all names familiar in ancient history: one Amintas was Alexander the Great's grandfather, and an Agenor was King of Phoenicia, the capital of which was Sidon where the action of *Il rè pastore* takes place. Elisa may have been suggested by Elissa, the alternative name of Dido, Queen of Tyre next to Sidon, and later of Carthage (*cf.* Purcell, Berlioz, etc.).

We are to understand that Alexander, King of Macedonia (356–323 B.C.), in the course of subduing the Middle East, has conquered Sidon whose dictator Strato, a lackey of the Persian king Darius, refused to surrender, preferring suicide. Strato's daughter Tamyris thereupon fled from Sidon disguised as a shepherdess, leaving behind her faithful lover the nobleman Agenor, Alexander's friend and adviser. The royal family of Sidon had dispersed during Strato's rule and the legitimate heir could not be found. He was in fact working as a shepherd, unaware of his true identity, known to all as Amintas and deeply enamoured of Elisa, a noble Phoenician girl of the family of King Cadmus, the dragon-slayer. Alexander and his army are encamped in the countryside on the outskirts of Sidon.

3

The **Overture**, *molto allegro* in C major (oboes, horns, trumpets, strings), is a vigorous galant piece, conventionally sluggish in harmonic activity, shaped in sonata form with a short development and a recapitulation reordered as 2–3–1 in the manner we have met earlier. Mannheim influence can be heard in the first subject's gradual crescendo from furtive *piano* to determined *forte*, and in the regular dialoguing alternation of *forte* and *piano* thereafter. Antiphonal semiquaver runs for violins in the bridge-group make a welcome contrast; they figure in the development. The second subject is more winning (especially when recapitulated low down on the violins), with galant snaps and nice oboe scoring. The furtive first subject returns instead of a codetta group. After the reprise of the first subject a new theme, bland and expectant for horn and violins followed in canon by two flutes (their first entry) all on a dominant pedal, leads directly into **No. 1, Aria**, for the shepherd-boy Amintas: *andantino*, C major, *Intendo, amico rio* with flutes, horns, strings.

> I hear your low murmuring, river my friend. You are asking where our dear one is.

The pastoral scene is charmingly set with cool flutes in sixths and thirds, heaving alternations of loud and soft, a murmurous accompaniment directly illustrative of the singer's words 'quel basso mormorio'—illustration too at the word 'intendo' ('I am listening') towards the end of the aria where the music stops while Amintas listens. The last vocal phrase runs impetuously into *secco* recitative as Elisa arrives in person. Amintas is anxious for her safety so close to the Macedonian encampment. But she professes no fear when love draws her on. She has heard that Alexander is looking for the legitimate heir to Sidon's throne, a man himself unaware of his royal position. Amintas reminds her of her own royal blood and suggests that he, a humble shepherd, is unworthy of her. But she loves Amintas for himself, loves even his sheep and his poverty since they are part of him. She must run back to her dear mother and then will return quickly to him. She is a prefiguration of Barbarina in *Figaro*, completely happy, bubbling with energy and voluble enthusiasm, scarcely able to finish a sentence before a new idea strikes her. Metastasio has characterized her deliciously and the singer should race through Mozart's recitative for her, so as to bring out her chatterbox impulsiveness.

She has, however, to restrain her behaviour to fulfil the conventions of her exit **Aria, No. 2**, *Alla selva*, G major, *allegro* (oboes, horns, strings) which begins with an extended orchestral exposition. Formality is established with a conventional opening tag to be subsequently used as introduction to new sections or new ideas. This first time it is balanced by the soft initial theme which Elisa will sing.

1

To the wood, the meadow, the spring I go with my beloved flock, and my sweetheart will come with me.

In that rough narrow cottage which gives us shelter, joy and delight and innocence will find their lodging.

The bouncing woodwind echo is also treated thematically and seems part of Elisa's musical characterization, as is the compulsive semiquaver movement that explodes sporadically. The second main idea in this exposition suggests Elisa's softer side though it lasts no longer than this quotation.

2

Elisa's part lies high and runs along freshly and gracefully with a good measure of brilliance; this is the first of several arias in *Il rè pastore* to remind us that Mozart was busy writing concertos and discovering the medium's possibilities. The aria is rich in charming, resourceful ideas. Metastasio's opening words, 'Alla selva, al prato, al fonte' give rise to a winning repetitive idea:

3

e al—la sel—va al fon—te al pra———

The fountain itself murmurs softly the second time it is mentioned. One might expect it to have inspired florid runs but Mozart deliberately inverts the line so that the first florid vocal passage is on 'prato' (a practical decision for easier vocalization). Just before the end of the vocal exposition Elisa turns into sensuous chromatic intervals at the thought that 'l'idol mio con me verrà' ('my beloved will come with me'):

4

l'i—dol— mi—o——————— con me ver—rà

—the passage is even more intense in the reprise when it appears a fourth higher.

This stirs the orchestra to a bridge passage agog with running semiquavers. The middle section introduces new ideas or rather new metamorphoses of exposition ideas, as though this were a thematic symphonic development; harmonically it sticks to D major either in its own right or as the dominant of G, comes to a pause (implying a vocal flourish) on the edge of D, then has to expand Ex. 1 in order to bring the music back to G, in time for Elisa's re-entry and the formal yet still vigorous recapitulation. A splendid aria for this delightful heroine.

As she scampers away, the violins pacing her on her way, Amintas thanks the gods for giving him the brightest of all guiding stars, the most complete happiness known on earth. It occurs to him that in his blissful state he has forgotten to feed his flock. At this moment Alexander and Agenor approach him with questions about his name, parentage, and way of life. Alexander, who has been assured by

Agenor that this young man is Sidon's hereditary monarch, asks if, in his discomfort and poverty, he has no longing for a more prestigious, easy life. Amintas prefers the safety and calm of his present existence—a confession that touches Alexander's heart. He invites Amintas to accompany him to his tent; but the boy demurs: his life and Alexander's are totally different, and neither can profit from the other's conversation. In any case it is feeding-time for his sheep; it is for shepherding that heaven has destined him.

He reflects on his happiness (it is not clear whether or not Alexander and Agenor remain on stage at this point, since Amintas addresses his remarks only to imaginary shepherds and painted forests) and on the fire of Elisa's love which makes him constantly reborn like a phoenix.

As Amintas's thoughts become increasingly possessed by his love for Elisa, so Mozart switches the accompaniment to his recitative from *secco* (harpsichord and cello) to *stromentato*—as usual, strings, but quite rich in texture (plenty of double stops) and intense in feeling, with yearning phrases and arching instrumental sighs purposefully nuanced.

5

This material is deployed consistently through the recitative whose vocal line is elegant and expressive if not inspired. There is a burst of movement to describe the 'ruscello garrulo' ('busy noise') which links surrounding nature with the talkative shepherdess.

Amintas's recitative verbally repeats what he has told us already about a shepherd's happy life, and his own love for Elisa. The music closes in B flat, to introduce Amintas's next **Aria, No. 3**, *Aer tranquillo* (formerly as popular as *L'amerò*), *allegro aperto* in B flat major, accompanied by oboes and horns with strings.

> Calm air and untroubled days, fresh springs and green meadows, these are the lucky destinies of the shepherd and his flock.
>
> If the fates were pleased to change my duties, the gods would have taken care to change my heart and mind.

The opening of the orchestral introduction immediately recalls those of the G major (K. 216) and B flat major (K. 207) violin concertos of the same period.

6a

7

Allegro aperto

When the main subsidiary idea arrives it too is reminiscent, this time of the *Alleluja* from the soprano motet *Exultate jubilate* (K. 158a, 1773)

8

Al—le—lu—ja, al—le—lu--ja,—   al—le—lu—ja, al—le—lu——ja,

9

When the opera's run was over, Mozart had no qualms about giving *Aer tranquillo* to a female soprano to sing. But with Elisa's No. 2 aria still in our heads we are aware that Amintas is singing a different sort of vocal music, more affirmative, demanding a more brazen attack and strong sustaining power, in fact the music of a human trumpet that people likened to the voice of a castrato soprano. The vocal part here lies quite high, as does Elisa's in No. 2, but the phrases are more intense and demand full note-values (pretty Viennese pecking by travesty Amintases will never do here). Two examples occur side by side; first the chromatic cadential phrase, twice repeated, sensuously insinuating, then the plaintive D minor phrase that looks forward to Donna Anna; but in both of these the slurs are short and give a more dogged, forceful effect—the male soprano voice, even when emasculated, sounded male.

10

del—la   greg—gia e del pas—tor,   so—no i vo—ti   for—tu—

—na—ti,   for—tu——na——————

The falling chain of thirds in his codetta section is especially attractive.

11

The first half of Ex. 10 leads to a dominant conclusion by the orchestra, and to a contrasted middle section, *grazioso* in F major and minuet style, featuring oboes in thirds and dignified suavity in general, vocally mellifluous and later florid, quite short. The formal reprise ensues, after a cautious key-change, without orchestral introduction; it includes some heady leaps of a seventh and an octave for a singer, in the best Neapolitan style. The nice proportions, inventiveness, and fanciful structure of this aria must suggest that *Il rè pastore* promises unusually well at this point.

Alexander and Amintas engage in further conversation (this section of recitative is excluded from the old complete Mozart edition). Alexander is now convinced that Amintas is the sought-for king of Sidon, not only by Agenor's researches, but by Amintas's noble soul and forthright opinions (the Hapsburg children had to learn their monarchical duties). Here is virtue to be crowned, a happy outcome to the destruction and violence of war, and the happiest of all duties known to beneficent Alexander.

Accordingly he, or rather the orchestra (oboes, horns, trumpets, and strings), launches into Alexander's **No. 4, Aria**, in D major, *allegro, Si spande il sole*.

A cloud in front of the sun often bursts and lightning threatens the parched ground.
But after many elements are joined in this fashion, they all dissolve in rain which nourishes the soil.

There was only one sort of music to write for this moment. Mozart, experienced in the genre, knew his duty and paraded the glittering imperious heroics, but put them in 3/4 metre thus suggesting, rather than a four-square robot despot, a splendid and essentially likeable man of action.

The introduction abounds in impressive gestures: the rapid upward string scales, later explained by reference to lightning ('folgora'); the downward chromatic droop ('nube talor'); the horn and trumpet repeated-note rhythm which anticipates the new melody on its heels; the energetic semiquaver runs. The oboes are prominently deployed, as echo to Alexander's obligatory fioritura and as expressive colouring in the tender middle section. The form of the aria is a miniature concerto first movement with two expositions. In the recapitulation the running vocal divisions are somewhat altered, and there is a further burst, powerfully harmonized, of the repeated-note rhythmic idea just before the cadenza. The aria is spacious yet quite compact. Mozart had tired of Salzburg's taste for lengthy movements. He had been experimenting with new forms, but here felt obliged to work on a large canvas though he managed to make it less long-winded than the old style *da capo* aria.

The second leading lady, more high-powered than Elisa, now makes her entry. She is the princess Tamyris, in disguise as a shepherdess like Elisa with whom she has been staying. At first Agenor does not recognize his sweetheart for whom he has been searching ever since her father Strato was overthrown by Alexander. He is overjoyed to be reunited with her; she, on the other hand, adopts a reserved manner towards him. He after all is the crony of Alexander, the man she regards as her father's murderer. She as Strato's daughter wants only to quit the country: to remain would be to endure scorn and insults from the usurper. Alexander is not a bit like that, Agenor reassures her; he had no part in Strato's suicide and will be delighted to show friendship to Tamyris. She regards such talk as treasonable; can

Agenor still love her? Her beautiful eyes, he answers, should be able to see the quantity of his adoration. He addresses those 'stars of love' in his **Aria, No. 5**, *grazioso* in G major, *Per me rispondete*, accompanied by strings alone.

Answer for me, fair stars of love: if you do not know, who will?
You have learned all the ways of my heart since you robbed me of my freedom.

The aria begins as a demure minuet, chiefly notable for a persistent triplet figure, and for the unusual marking *calando* (rather than *diminuendo*) every time the melody moves towards its half-cadence. In the second new melodic sentence the triplets pervade the inner accompaniment with delectable effect (compare the *andante* of the C major K. 467 piano concerto):

Thereafter triplets are rarely absent from this number which accordingly throbs tenderly with affection. Agenor appears here as a proto-Ferrando.

Tamyris is left alone on stage admitting that, though her fate has greatly altered, the gods have at least left her a faithful lover. The restorative effect of finding Agenor is discussed in a grand and regal **Aria, No. 6**, *allegro aperto* in E flat major, *Di tante sue procelle* (oboes, horns and strings).

My soul has already forgotten all its tempests. I have found calm again on the face of my beloved.
At the anger of the stars my heart palpitated with terror, but now it beats contentedly in my bosom.

The key itself has noble connotations in Mozart, and already in the orchestral ritornello we notice the big sound, strong harmonies buttressed by horns, enriched with string double-stops, enhanced by incisive two-part oboes (second subject), and enlivened by rapid polyphony for first and second violins (this last a recurrent feature after the solo exposition and in the ultimate coda). Tamyris's music is high-mettled, nervous in phrasing. When she mentions spiritual calm an oboe solicitously echoes her phrase; almost immediately the same word 'calma' causes her to embark on a hectic run, and the orchestration becomes gloriously rich. When the middle section begins, the orchestra is busy with running semiquavers, but eventually it dutifully pants in sympathy, and before long the reprise is reached. It involves some new working, including a dignified, low-pitched transposition of the initial second subject. Again this is a short aria that suggests grandiose size.

Tamyris departs. Elisa knocks on Amintas's door vainly, then remembers that he must be watering his sheep, but is met by him. Out of breath as he is, she urges him equally breathlessly to seek her father's willing benediction on their immediate marriage. Their departure is halted by Agenor who comes to tender homage to Amintas as king. The shepherd boy shrugs off this obsequiousness but, helped by Elisa, Agenor assures them that Amintas is truly Abdolonimus, only heir to the kingdom of Sidon, brought up from babyhood by Agenor after the former king was exiled by Strato. Agenor knows his identity and the proofs of his right to succession which he kept entirely to himself until Abdolonimus could claim the throne as is now Alexander's wish. Elisa is highly delighted that her lover is also her king, and Agenor points to the royal guard which will conduct the new monarch to his coronation by Alexander.

Agenor evidently goes on ahead. Amintas, having established that Elisa approves of this new turn, asks her to accompany him to her father. But she insists that he must first assume the throne which awaits him: it is his immediate responsibility.

Amintas is surprised, and string orchestra with him. Love is his first duty. The strings quickly etch his naïvely ecstatic, wholly Elisa-centred feelings.

13

Andante

He then changes his mind (*allegro*) and decides that, for her sake and her father's, he must quickly get the succession ceremony over so that he himself can declare his rank to his father-in-law before rumour gets there first.

The strings become pensive and harmonically sensuous ('Ah! se sapessi') as he reflects how wretched every moment is for him when he is not with her. Elisa caps his fears, and the wounded violin theme acquires a wider gap and bewildered harmonic implication, bursts into jubilation as she expresses her joy for him, turns laconic as she represses her fears for herself. She need have none if her lover is not made king—the strings here offer a theme for Kingship, recognizably similar to other royal themes in these operas:

14

Maybe Alexander has changed his mind, she hopes. Amintas assures her that her anxiety is too high a price to pay for a throne.

They end the first act with a **Duet, No. 7**, *andante* in A major (a special key for Mozart, at this stage indicative only of outward pleasure, though in later years more introspectively concerned), *Vanne a regnar* (oboes, horns and strings). The generously affectionate opening idea, descending from the fifth to the tonic, twice, is like an embrace, and typical of Mozart in A major, as it is typical of Elisa's nature.

15

It was sensitive and magical to drop the strings to a lower register in Elisa's first sentence ('Go and rule, but be faithful to me, if you can') so as to let her voice ring out radiantly; typical too, after that, to introduce a soft oboe upper E as anchor for a rapturous violin theme that is quickly followed by another characteristic A major Mozart idea even more intimately concerned with love.

16

Amintas enters ('Even on the throne I shall still be your faithful shepherd') to a variant of Elisa's opening phrase, but now the string accompaniment has begun to fizz with vivacity (like Dorabella's first entry in *Così*, though that is in E major) as he promises to remain her faithful shepherd, though obliged to assume a royal throne. The themes of Ex. 16 accompany Amintas's music also. They indulge in a brief spell of antiphonal duetting, elaborately accompanied, then proceed to an *allegro* ('Protect our innocent love, ye gods') involving more conjunct sensuous thirds, though also some antiphonal divisions in triplets, decidedly exhilarating. The *andante* music returns, re-notated for this quicker tempo, then a reprise of the *allegro* that works up forcefully to a big cadence reinforced by a presumable duet-cadenza before the invigorating instrumental coda.

4

Amintas has gone off to become king. Elisa, after giving him time to do his duty, has followed him and, as the curtain rises on Act II, is attempting to enter the largest of the Greek tents where she assumes her royal beloved to be holding sway. She is prevented by Agenor who informs her that the tent is out of bounds, and that the new king has too much royal business to come and meet her. No need for her to wait here. Agenor will shortly bring Amintas to her; meanwhile he will tell Alexander about her—he tried earlier but was interrupted. Elisa continually breaks in on his official communications but is always halted before she gets into her accustomed stride. Finally she gives up the struggle with this cruel man, as she calls him, and takes her leave in a big, emotionally diversified appeal to his sense of compassion. **No. 8, Aria**, *Barbaro, oh Dio!*, in B flat major, *andante–allegro* alternating (oboes, low-lying horns, and strings).

Cruel man, you see me parted from my beloved, and will you not allow me even to ask after him?

How can you not take pity on my great love? Surely you have a heart and a soul in your breast.

The insinuating thirds at the beginning may suggest a cosier atmosphere than is revealed—and they may encourage a slower tempo than the lilt of the subsequent

17

crotchets makes advisable: the right tempo must accommodate those crotchets and Elisa's difficult high-lying semiquaver runs, and indeed all the detail in this passage leading to them, where nothing is subsidiary.

The *andante* music, it will be seen, is quite intense and expressively grand, nothing for a little soubrette. If Mozart did not miscalculate in his characterization of Elisa, he was writing for a soprano of real potentiality and versatility. The *allegro* (*Come di tanto affetto*) is fiery in F major, with urgent offbeat wind chords, an emotional oboe duet unaccompanied, and close imitative string writing; Elisa herself has to sing in a blazing passionate style, such as we may associate with Donna Elvira:

18

She ends the *allegro* with a well known, always striking, breathless effect—

19

—and the strings take the music on tiptoe to C minor for the *andante* reprise which accordingly begins two bars late when it reaches the home-key of B flat. The digression, though touching, is conceivably too short to make a worth-while point, though the idea of injecting freshness into a restatement is furthered in the altered vocal part at 'Barbaro! e non concedi' for purposes of staying in the tonic. The florid passage, newly embellished, lies a fourth higher this time, taking Elisa to top C. She has an optional flourish, and the *allegro* is then resumed, also with variants to accommodate the home-key, and prolongation for another flourish and a coda—there has been no running division in the *allegro*. Perhaps it is in line with Elisa's volubility that this fine aria leaves room for few pauses for rest and no extended orchestral ritornelli.

Agenor is not at all swayed by this cry from the heart. When Elisa leaves, he only comments that he hopes Alexander will favour the cause of Tamyris. And when Amintas comes in search of Elisa, Agenor answers his questions laconically to the effect that Elisa has left and Amintas cannot follow her; royal decorum does not permit it—he makes a fawning apology for speaking so bluntly and imperiously to his own king. Amintas admits that he prefers plain speaking, yet Elisa must be consoled. This is no opportune moment, however, for the council of war is over and Alexander is approaching.

Alexander is disturbed to see Amintas still dressed as a shepherd; the boy has not yet been officially instated by Alexander. The two rulers exchange noble sentiments and compliments about the qualities of a good monarch. Alexander tells the boy to trust in God and change his clothes. Amintas leaves—though not, it turns out, to find Elisa as might be expected.

Alexander informs Agenor of his intention to leave Sidon now that the city has an ideal king and, in Agenor, a sound regal counsellor. His sole remaining concern is Tamyris whose happiness he wishes to secure. He therefore requires her presence —easily achieved, says Agenor: she is waiting to meet him. In that case Alexander can make her instantly happy by wedding her to Sidon's new king. This will content all political parties, strengthen Amintas's position and restore honour to Tamyris. Agenor is naturally horrified, but too servile to put Alexander in possession of the existing facts. The Macedonian conqueror has blundered tactically by confusing love with war, but also through Agenor's negligence to tell him about Elisa, Tamyris and their bespoken affections. The confusion shortly to be witnessed is caused by Agenor's character, that of an Establishment-happy nincompoop, a bad adviser to royalty since he will never get his priorities right.

Alexander is all smiles: the effort of battle is rewarded by his conviction that he leaves Sidon without an enemy, since he has made everybody happy. These noble, erroneous sentiments are expressed in his **Aria, No. 9**, *Se vincendo* in F major, *allegro moderato* (flutes, oboes, horns, strings).

> If my victory brings you all happiness, if on my departure I leave no enmity behind, what a wonderful day it will be for me. I ask no greater reward for the sweat I shed in battle.

Structurally this is almost a sonatina form, yet another protest against Salzburg *langer Geschmack*: it has two expositions and a recapitulation but no middle section to speak of, only a brief orchestral bridge modulating from C back to F. Inventively, however, it is strong. Alexander's talk of military prowess brings out galant snaps and flutes in thirds and sixths, as if they were fifes, and sets the first flute in duet with the singer in his heroic long divisions. The exposition material is very rich in short, flexible ideas, and there is plenty of polyphonic writing to bejewel and magnify the atmosphere. Alexander himself has to display agility and power over two octaves from bottom C (he will go lower in his next aria) to as near top C as he cares to take his obligatory cadenza. The total effect is not at all stiff but does suggest the hero with a warm heart that Metastasio portrays in the text. Edward Dent regarded this as the finest musical number in the opera; for wealth of instrumental colour and textural incident it certainly stands out.

The libretto suggests that, at the conclusion of this aria, Agenor and Alexander leave the stage, and Amintas returns, unconvinced that he was born to be king. He assures the returning Agenor that his duty is clear, he must perform what Alexander requires of Sidon's king. When Agenor hints that Elisa and the throne do not go together automatically, the new king misconstrues him. Only a hero's daughter is worthy of such a throne, he replies. Amintas refers to Elisa's ancestor Cadmus. But Agenor thinks only of Strato's child Tamyris, destined by Alexander for Amintas. Lucky king, love her, advises the bitter Agenor. How should I not love her, answers King Abdolonymus-Amintas; there would be no point in being king otherwise.

He now sings the **Rondo-Aria, No. 10**, *L'amerò* in E flat major, *andantino*, curiously scored with cors anglais* and obbligato violin, as well as flutes, bassoons, horns and muted strings.

> I shall love her, I shall be constant: faithful husband and faithful lover. I shall sigh only for her. In such a dear, sweet person I shall find my joy, my delight and my peace.

This can be interpreted as a song of deepest devotion, or as an expression of royal duty buttressed by ideal love. The music is not without a melancholy undertone—the flutes doubling the opening phrase of melody, accompanied by sustained, plangent English horns. The key, and its setting, has in Mozart often a sombre, dedicated connotation (as in the first *allegro* of the 39th symphony, or much of *Die Zauberflöte*). The high-lying solo violin is surely a vision of the adorable absent Elisa, the king's *ferne Geliebte*; the voice yearns characteristically while the violin chirrups above:

20

Amintas's music lies idealistically high and includes a touching excursion into C minor (as if he sensed the problems to come). After the formal final cadenza the theme and the voice reappear in the orchestral coda to reaffirm Amintas's unshakeable love—which may remind us that Agenor has meekly accepted Tamyris's destiny as the bride of a boy who to him must seem to have switched sweethearts with extraordinary versatility. The music of *L'amerò* can be taken in two ways, from Amintas's or Agenor's point of view. From either aspect the aria works perfectly, because Mozart's subconscious appreciation of the drama was nudging his conscious, Amintas-orientated creative faculty.

A pause is really needed while the idyll of *L'amerò* sinks in. But drama has to move forward. So Amintas walks off in a dream. Agenor bids a stupefied farewell to cherished hopes of Tamyris, then finds himself once again confronted by the irrepressible Elisa. What, she asks, are these absurd rumours about Amintas and Tamyris? Not absurd at all, stiffly replies Agenor; Amintas has just told me himself—Agenor wishes to share his own pain as hurtfully as possible. Fate is the decider, he adds philosophically; what can you do about it? Elisa is no fatalist: she will go to Alexander, tell all, learn from Amintas's own mouth that he has betrayed her, and then go mad and die in his presence. True to herself she dashes away, without so much as an exit aria.

* See *La finta semplice*, p. 44, for an earlier use of these and a possible explanation.

Agenor has the decency to admit compassion for her plight, if only because it is his own; adding that he had better be off before he meets Tamyris. She promptly turns up, glacially demanding an explanation. He blames the kingdom whose subjects have to pay for it, salutes her as queen and takes his leave. No, says the proclaimed Queen, I order you to stay and witness my marriage. I obey, cruel creature, Agenor answers.

This is the situation in which later Donna Anna will protest against Ottavio's accusation of cruelty. Tamyris responds likewise, not in accompanied recitative, but in her **Aria, No. 11**, *Se tu di me fai dono* in A major, *andantino grazioso*, very closely scored for strings alone.

> You have given me away to another, so why am I to blame?
> Copy my gentleness: I have been forsaken but I do not insult you or call you faithless.

The why, 'Perchè', is much repeated, as the libretto surely intended (*cf.* 'Barbaro' in No. 8). Judged by Mozart's music Tamyris is adopting a calculated coolness, demure formality (like Cherubino's in *Voi che sapete*); she might be a rustic mother bluntly counselling her daughter to keep the boys at bay.

21

This is another rondo, with pauses (needing flourishes) before reprises. There is plenty of musical invention, in the teasing passages, in the access of accompanying rich texture (double-stops for violas), in the tonal excursions before the third reprise, right to the final flourish for violins. Such an aria was probably apt for Tamyris by baroque conventions (she must display her skill in flowing leggiero music somewhere), but surely wrong dramatically. It sounds as if Mozart either could not be bothered to respond as the situation demanded or was told by the singer what sort of music to compose—whereupon he put as much interesting work as he could into a genteel drawing-room song.

After this, Tamyris has to flounce off leaving Agenor even more sorry for himself—the worst is yet to be. And so he delivers the opera's only minor-key number, **Aria, No. 12**, *Sol può dir*, a surprisingly daemonic *allegro* in C minor, accompanied by oboes, bassoons, four horns and strings.

> How a lover feels in my situation can only be explained by another hapless lover who has experienced the same as I.
> I feel a torture more cruel than any other, desperate and unbearable.

This is an impetuous, angry C minor piece with harsh woodwind scoring, bare unisons, furious string scrubbing, stammered vocal phrases, horror-struck pauses (not for vocal flourishes, surely). It should pass like an ill wind and therefore not be examined too closely, though the beheading of the reprise may be remarked as increasing dramatic tension.

The final scene discovers Alexander alone, praying to the gods of victory in his **Aria**, *Voi che fausti*, **No. 13**, *allegretto* in C major, with oboes, horns, trumpets, and strings.

> You who always favour me with new shoots for my laurels, gods my friends, look kindly too on the motives of my heart.

It begins softly and serenely with strings alone, gathering speed until the entry of military rhythms appropriate to a soldier emperor; this seems expressive of the textural dichotomy between gentle love and dynamic war—rapid semiquaver movement is a feature of this aria and Alexander's solos generally. The setting of 'Secondate, amici Dei' is noticeably more ingratiating, though the return of rattling runs for military laurels spills over into the second half of the text, involving a long difficult florid passage on 'Secondate' involving low B for the singer. Instead of a middle section there is a short appealing sentence modulating back from dominant to tonic, closely written for strings round voice.

Alexander summons his court, and calls for the King and Tamyris. She answers from Alexander's feet where she is pleading for him to appreciate Agenor's patriotism in giving up his promised sweetheart, Tamyris herself, out of loyalty to Alexander and Amintas. The Emperor is greatly touched, but is interrupted by Elisa who comes to complain that *she* has been robbed by Alexander of her lifelong beloved, Amintas. The drawback, Alexander explains, is that King Abdolonimus cannot marry a commoner. Amintas promptly enters and announces his solution: to abdicate so that he will be free to marry Elisa.

Alexander accepts the workings of fate and declares that the lovers shall not be parted. Amintas and Elisa shall reign in Sidon. Agenor and Tamyris will be given a kingdom as soon as Alexander can conquer a new one. It will be just reward for Agenor's virtuousness. The lovers thank him in four-part harmony, a striking effect.

After two bars of orchestral fanfare (oboes, horns, strings—no trumpets!) the five singers burst into the **Finale, No. 14**, *Viva l'invitto duce* in D major, *molto allegro*, singing in block harmony as if they were a chorus. Although they are saluting the 'unconquered leader', Alexander has to sing too since he is in charge of the bass line, there being no basses in the cast. The violins race away in exuberant semiquavers or triplet quavers above the voices; wind sustain harmonies. The finale atmosphere is evident in this passage, heard three times:

Also finale-ish is a passage just afterwards, with the melody in the middle and a dominant pedal-point in the two upper voices.

After a repeat of the fanfare phrases the violins introduce Elisa and Amintas in the first episode of this rondo-structure, a duet still in D major, mostly in amorous thirds and sixths though with a breath of part-writing in the middle: the word 'rida' ('love *laughs* more happily') is set to an explosive idea first played by violins, then to a repeated phrase with an appoggiatura that is presumably short for illustrative effect.

The quintet is resumed from half-way through and ends by dropping into G major for the second episode, initiated by Elisa alone, the other voices entering gradually and severally. Amintas's entry is distinguished by poignant oboe suspensions on 'cara' ('my dear') which further clash with the two-part violin writing. This elaborate and beautiful texture is worth quoting.

The violins chase an imitative point above the two tenors whereupon Amintas launches another imitative entry, *a cappella*, for the four lovers, and the completion of this sentence, with sustained oboes hovering above block harmony on 'resistere' repeated, even incredulously stammered, marks the high-point of the movement, a foretaste of the maturest Mozart.

25

Bland duets for each loving pair lead to a reprise of the glorious section quoted in Exs. 24 and 25. The opening of the finale is now recapitulated in full and brings the opera to an end. It is a grandly scaled, inventive and charming conclusion to an opera full of good things

5

Nobody will pretend that *Il rè pastore* is great drama, even first-rate baroque drama. It is a simple play about royal benevolence and the course of true love, written for a royal nursery. It chanced to fall into Mozart's lap when he was nineteen and on the threshold of *Idomeneo*, and fortunately he made something of it.

He responded to the love duet No. 7 and the quintet-finale No. 14, inevitably because he was stimulated by the vocal ensemble as a dramatic and human concept. He gave his orchestra plenty of expressive and atmospheric and musically prominent opportunities—the flutes in No. 9, the solo violin and cors anglais in No. 10, the skittering runs for violins again and again—such as were to distinguish his mature operas. He poured charm into the pastoral music, affection into the love music, and minor-key dynamism into No. 12. He contrived to convey grandeur and spaciousness while cutting down the conventional length of arias. He heightened dramatic moments by dropping into orchestrally accompanied recitative. E. J. Dent was surely mistaken in believing that Mozart set the text 'without much interest'.

His job was principally to provide five singers with the requisite number of contrasted arias—three each for Alexander and Amintas, two for the others. In doing so, and to some extent in the recitatives (which are less dreary than Abert supposed), he strengthened Metastasio's already neatly etched characters: voluble Elisa, haughty Tamyris, easy-going Amintas, egotistical and officious Agenor, heroic yet warm-hearted Alexander. Mozart's characterizations are not quite consistent (e.g. Tamyris's No. 11, and you may think that such a nasty bit of work as Agenor does not deserve the tragic grandeur of his second aria, No. 12). But in stage performance by intelligent singers—quite simple staging with minimal scenery and costumes would do—and even on gramophone records (there is a skilfully presented version in the catalogues at the time of writing) the characters, and therefore the drama, come to life, more so than we may expect in an *opera seria* by a young composer. Mozart, however, was soon to show, in *Idomeneo*, that *opera seria* was still a living, viable theatrical form.

WAITING FOR IDOMENEO

Five years intervened between the completion of *Il rè pastore* and the commission for Mozart's next opera, *Idomeneo*. They were vital years for his development as composer and as man. He had learned by experience the various manners of Italian *opera seria* and *opera buffa*. He had collected, on his travels, other dialects of music, and he had grown weary of the long-winded old-fashioned Salzburg taste. His adolescence was not as precocious physically as spiritually; only now and again in *Il rè pastore* and *La finta giardiniera*, more rarely in his earlier operas, had he shown the intensification of human expression through music which marks the emergence of an adult master from a *Wunderkind*.

Mozart remained in Salzburg, increasingly discontented with service under an unsympathetic, superficially music-minded employer, for two years after *Il rè pastore*. He composed his most famous violin concertos, some of his best party music, some masses and epistle sonatas, as well as his first masterly piano concerto, K. 271 in E flat major.

During the late summer of 1777 Leopold Mozart begged leave of absence from the Archbishop of Salzburg so that he and his son could travel elsewhere. The Archbishop consented on condition that father and son considered themselves dismissed from the service of the Salzburg court. Leopold preferred to remain. Wolfgang departed with his mother on 23 September 1777. Their first stop was Munich. Here they renewed acquaintance with Tommaso Consoli (Aminta in *Il rè pastore*) and with Mysliweček, now incurably sick in hospital but still working and determined to obtain a commission for Mozart to write a new opera for Naples. Nothing came of this. Mozart had an interview with the Bavarian Elector Max Joseph, begged to write a new opera for Munich but was told there was no vacancy. He had a wild scheme that several rich patrons might each contribute a regular sum so that he might stay there and write operas; this did not work either. He attended some German *Singspiele* which gave him an uncontrollable urge to write one; it was suggested that he should write an *opera seria* for Munich to a German libretto; but no text was forthcoming. Original German libretti were not being written. The operas seen by Mozart were Piccinni's *Le pescatrice* (also set by Haydn) and Sacchini's *La contadina in corte*, both rendered into German. Creatively frustrated, even after giving some concerts, Mozart and his mother travelled to Augsburg, Leopold's native city. Here too he gave concerts, became acquainted with the fortepianos of Johann Andreas Stein which henceforth remained his favourites, and met his cousin or *Bäsle*, Anna Maria Mozart, with whom he flirted and joked and maintained a cloacally comic correspondence (similar to that between his mother and father).

The next stop for Mozart and his mother was Mannheim, and it was vital to his development, especially to the genesis of *Idomeneo*. Mozart renewed acquaintance with the Elector Palatine Karl Theodor who had seen *La finta giardiniera* and was interested to commission a German opera from Mozart; he made friends again with Count Seeau, Intendant of the Mannheim Court Opera, a somewhat haughty courtier. He heard the famous Mannheim Orchestra, its marvellous strings almost all trained by the principal violinist Christian Cannabich (himself a composer and conductor of note), its superb woodwind soloists. These included Johann Baptist Wendling, the first flute; Friedrich Ramm, first oboe and, appropriately for his name, a noted amorist; J. W. Stich called Punto, first horn; and the musical director Ignaz Holzbauer whose new German opera *Günther von Schwarzburg* Mozart lauded to the skies though he despised the text.

Mozart and his mother spent much time with Cannabich and his two daughters, and with Wendling at whose house Mozart actually conducted rehearsals of Anton Schweitzer's opera *Rosamunde*. For Wendling's daughter Gustl (ex-mistress of the Elector) Mozart wrote two charming French ariettes. Wendling's wife Dorothea was to be his Ilia, and her sister-in-law Elisabeth the Elettra, in *Idomeneo*—Elisabeth's husband was a leading Mannheim violinist. At Leopold's urgent request they made friends with the now elderly and failing but still celebrated tenor Anton Raaff who was to sing the name part in *Idomeneo*.

Rosa Cannabich made a conquest of Mozart's heart and he wrote for her the piano sonata in C major K. 284b which Leopold Mozart found curious in style —Wolfgang was adopting the Frenchified taste popular in Mannheim and presently to contribute momentously to *Idomeneo*. By 17 January 1778, however, Mozart had made friends with Fridolin Weber, a bass singer, copyist and prompter at the opera—he was the uncle of Carl Maria von Weber. Among Fridolin Weber's six children were three daughters: Josepha (later Hofer), a good cook and soprano (Mozart's first Queen of Night); Aloysia (later Lange), a splendid soprano especially skilled in *portamento*, with whom Mozart fell violently in love; and the still childish and plain Constanze whom eventually Mozart married.

Mozart found occasion to compose music expressly for most of the above named musicians. He found a certain amount of work in Mannheim, took Aloysia on a brief concert tour, and grew a beard. Opera was always in the front of his mind. Vienna held out hopes—realized later in *Die Entführung*; Mannheim too— but not until *Idomeneo*. He told his father: 'Do not forget how much I desire to write operas . . . but Italian, not German, seriosa not buffa.' Much has been made of this. He may have been buoyed up by Mysliweček's promises about Naples, by ambitions for Aloysia Weber—he was reminded that she had never appeared in the theatre nor received training as an actress. He was doubtless disappointed by the poor response to his confessed interest in composing German operas. But this counter-confession did have a major result: *Idomeneo*.

It was not yet to be. In March 1778 Leopold Mozart, prompted by a letter from his wife, told Wolfgang to leave Mannheim and Aloysia, and proceed to Paris where work was to be found. The Mannheim court had already moved to Munich in January, after the death of the Bavarian Elector and the accession of Karl Theodor to the joint electorates of the Palatinate and Bavaria—this led to the war of the Bavarian Succession. The Mannheim orchestra went to Munich too; but several of Mozart's friends also travelled to Paris, among them Raaff and the four leading Mannheim wind soloists—Wendling, Ramm, Punto and Ritter, for whom Mozart wrote his Sinfonia Concertante K. 297b, nowadays only known in an inauthentic transcription, the original having been (perhaps deliberately) mislaid.

There was plenty of work in Paris for Mozart, including the ballet *Les petits riens*. He studied French *opéra comique* and had every opportunity to attend performances of operas by Gluck, Grétry, Piccinni and other prominent composers—maddeningly his letters do not specify which ones he saw or was impressed by.* He fancied, of course, writing an opera for France—*Démophon* and *Alexandre et Roxane* were mooted but came to nothing. He detested the French language musically† and despised French singing, but was mightily impressed by the use of chorus in French operas. One minor by-product of his French stay was a set of keyboard variations on Beaumarchais's own tune for 'Je suis Lindor' in *Le barbier de Séville*.

The Paris visit had not been a real success. In the middle of it Mozart's mother declined in health and died. Mozart was reasonably but profoundly shocked; he had never witnessed death before. There was some consolation in the arrival of his musical idol J. C. Bach who had come to write *Amadis des Gaules* for Paris, bringing with him the male soprano Tenducci for whom Mozart promptly composed an extended concert aria, K. 315b (now lost, though possibly still extant in England).

Mozart had no wish to remain in Paris. His first longing was to return to Aloysia Weber; his last desire was to resume service with the unappreciative Archbishop Colloredo in Salzburg where there were no facilities for opera, the genre in which he knew he could achieve most. Fate was against him. Leopold wrote that Wolfgang had been offered a post of Court and Cathedral organist in Salzburg at three times his previous salary, and that Leopold's own post depended on his son's acceptance. In September Wolfgang began to travel back home. He called at Nancy and Mannheim, where he saw Schweitzer's *Alceste*, a German *Singspiel* which he had already appreciated in score, as well as Benda's melologues *Ariadne auf Naxos* and *Medea*—music accompanying spoken dialogue—a genre

---

* Operatic premières given in Paris during Mozart's stay include Grétry's *Le jugement de Midas*, Anfossi's *Il curioso indiscreto* (for which Mozart was to compose two additional arias in 1783) and his *Le tuteur avare* (at Versailles), Paisiello's *La frascatana* and Piccinni's *Le finte gemelle*.
Piccinni's *Roland*, Monsigny's *Félix* and Gluck's *Armide* may still have been in repertory by the time of Mozart's arrival; they had been introduced to Paris earlier in the same season. Gluck's *Iphigénie en Aulide* and *Alceste* were still performed from time to time.
† Influenced perhaps by Rousseau's opinions, though Rousseau had by now changed them.

231

which fired him to compose a *Semiramis* in the same manner (K. 315e, either abandoned or lost). He contemplated another opera called *Cora*★ to a German text but asked too high a fee; the libretto was never set.

The Webers had gone to Munich where Mozart next halted. But Aloysia was no longer in love with him. Mozart had written the superb concert aria *Popoli di Tessaglia* from Calzabigi's *Alceste* for her, and she sang it with much success. But Mozart was in tearful mood throughout his stay: no mother, no sweetheart, and only the prospect of a dull, unappreciated post in Salzburg where his father would nag him. He invited his *Bäsle* to travel back with him and stay with the family in Salzburg. This lessened his despair a little.

★ Perhaps based on Marmontel's novel *Les Incas* as was Naumann's *Cora* of 1779.

ZAIDE

(Das Serail)

Deutsches Singspiel

Text by

JOHANN ANDREAS SCHACHTNER

K. 336b

ZAIDE	SOPRANO
GOMATZ	TENOR
ALLAZIM	BASS
SULTAN SOLIMAN	TENOR
OSMIN	BASS
ZARAM, Captain of the Guard	SPEAKING ROLE
FOUR SLAVES	TENORS

and Incidental Music to

Thamos, König in Ägypten, K. 336a

Mozart returned from his travels in France and Germany to Salzburg on 15 January 1779. He spent that year and most of 1780 living at home, fulfilling his courtly duties to his employer Archbishop Colloredo, and generally grumbling at the lack of opportunity in Salzburg for the development of his superior gifts.

During 1779 the travelling theatrical company of Johann Böhm gave a lengthy season in Salzburg. The Mozarts were old friends of Böhm and during this visit Wolfgang revised and expanded some incidental music for Tobias Gebler's heroic drama *Thamos, King of Egypt* which was in Böhm's repertory. At the same time he began work on the *Singspiel* nowadays known as *Zaide*. This may also have been for Böhm's company, or perhaps that of Emanuel Schikaneder, another family friend whose troupe visited Salzburg. The Mozart family letters tell us almost nothing about *Zaide*—not surprisingly since Wolfgang was composing it at home where his father and sister also were. From Munich where he wrote *Idomeneo* at the end of 1780 he asked his father for the *Schachtner-operette*. Leopold replied that it was pointless to proceed with the Schachtner drama 'since the music was not quite finished' and the Vienna theatres were closed due to the death of the Empress Maria Theresa. Mozart wanted the score in Munich for a private run-through at the house of the composer Christian Cannabich who had come to Munich as leader of the Mannheim Court Orchestra. When Mozart went to Vienna in 1781 he took *Zaide* with him, showed it to Stephanie and in return got the libretto of *Die Entführung* which treats a similar subject. Reporting this to his father Mozart remarked that the Schachtner operetta was 'no use ['*ist es nichts*'] for the special reason I often mentioned. . . . I only said that, apart from the long dialogues which are easily altered, the piece is very good, but not for Vienna where they prefer comic pieces.' Böhm and/or Schikaneder had commissioned *Zaide* for a subsequent season in the Austrian capital. Mozart accordingly put his *Schachtner-operette* into a cupboard, untitled and apparently without the libretto; there it stayed until 1799 when his widow unearthed it and sold it to the publishers J. Anton André. Eventually a new text was made by Carl Gollmick and as *Zaide*, the name of the heroine, the fragment was given a stage première at Frankfurt on the 110th anniversary of Mozart's birth, 27 January 1866. The score had been published in 1838.

Johann Andreas Schachtner (1731–95) was Court Trumpeter to the Archbishop of Salzburg and a close friend of the Mozart family with whom he spent many convivial occasions. He was an enthusiastic poet and composer; he translated *La finta giardiniera* and *Idomeneo* into German, wrote recitatives for *Bastien und Bastienne*, provided Mozart with words for an extra chorus in *King Thamos*, and wrote the above-mentioned *operette* or drama text which we may, however, uncertainly, identify with *Zaide*. All that we possess of this is the text of fifteen vocal numbers with short cues for most of them; they probably constitute two out of three acts. How the plot was elaborated in detail can only be guessed, but aids to guesswork exist. For the Seraglio adventure play was a staple favourite among European theatre audiences of the middle and late eighteenth century. Gluck's *La rencontre imprévue* (1764) and Haydn's *L'incontro improviso* (1777) are still famous. Mozart's heroine perhaps got her name from Voltaire's *Zaïre* (1732— Leopold Mozart saw a performance in Salzburg in 1777) though there were other French Zaide plays, and her Sultan captor is recalled by Perez's *Solimanno* (1757). Other examples are mentioned in connection with *Die Entführung*. Much more relevant is the textbook of *Das Serail, oder die unvermutete Zusammenkunft in der Sklaverey zwischen Vater, Tochter und Sohn*, music by Johann von Friebert, which was performed by Felix Berner (1738–87) and his company.

This textbook, whoever its author, gives us the cast of Mozart's *Zaide*: the Sultan; the Renegade (i.e. Christian turned Mohammedan) named as Allazim in Schachtner-Mozart; Gomatz; Zaide; Osman, a slave-trader, and others including a female slave (an Austrian dialect low comedy part). The plot of *Das Serail* tells us that Allazim is the father of Gomatz and Zaide, and that all three are saved from execution when the Sultan discovers that his life was saved twenty years earlier by Allazim—if indeed Schachtner did not make his own new plot. There are close similarities between the two texts at the beginning, in action and even wording: Schachtner's Nos. 3, 4, 5 and 6 are particularly close to equivalent pieces in *Das Serail*. But thereafter there are no such similarities and Schachtner's plot clearly goes off on its own tack. It may even have ended tragically, inasmuch as Mozart found it too serious for Viennese audiences, though his reservations may simply mean that Osmin is the only singing character not entirely serious.

The survival of *Das Serail* in libretto form does not, therefore, make Mozart's *Zaide* any less fragmentary. We can only investigate the music as it remains and draw general conclusions from such an investigation.

2

Mozart's autograph contains no overture. Alfred Einstein decided that the Symphony No. 32 in G major, K. 318, must be Mozart's intended overture to *Zaide*: it was composed in April 1779, it ends with Turkish noises, and its 'thematic dualism' suggested Zaide and the Sultan to Einstein. But the orchestra is larger than that of *Zaide*, and the date of composition earlier than scholars ascribe to the *Singspiel*. Furthermore there is no attempt at Turkish music in what remains of *Zaide*.

Act I begins with a group of slaves breaking stones. Their folksong-like ditty, **No. 1, Coro**, *Brüder, lasst uns lustig sein*, with strings, is unusually bucolic for Mozart, even in a *Singspiel*. The D major *allegro* is square, full of unisons; it reminded Abert of the folky music in Adam Hiller's *Die verwandelten Weiber*, a German version of Coffey's *The Devil to Pay* (1766). One tenor slave, described as *Vorsinger*, proclaims the verse, three others join him in the chorus. The strings supply a vigorous prelude and coda.

Among them is the slave Gomatz who slowly ceases work and steps forward to lament his hard fate. Here Mozart ventured into unconventional territory. On his way home from Paris in November 1778 he had seen in Mannheim two performances of Georg Benda's melodrama *Medea*: 'There is no singing in it, only recitation to which the music is like a sort of obbligato accompaniment to a recitative.' Mozart's plan to set a drama about Semiramis, daughter of the air, to music in this manner was reported in fashionable almanacks during 1779, but it came to nothing. In *Zaide*, however, he included two melodrama numbers.★

The first of these is Gomatz's **No. 2,** *Unerforschliche Fügung*, scored for two oboes, two bassoons and strings. It begins *adagio* with a pathetically expressive phrase, much repeated, to which Gomatz wrings his hands (compare it with the descending sevenths in K. 482/II):

The tempo varies with Gomatz's moods, becoming *allegro* when he wishes that his heart was stony like those of the convicts with whom he works, turning to a melancholy chromatic *allegretto* when he contrasts their cheerfulness with his own despair. Musical ideas pour out freely though not without being further used. There is an exquisite one for oboe solo when Gomatz attempts to lie down and sleep:

—and a murmurous, leisurely cadence, delicately scored, when at length slumber masters him. This is an exceptionally fine and unusual piece.

Zaide, the Sultan's favourite, approaches the tree under which Gomatz is asleep. In *Das Serail* (which begins here) she admires his European good looks and lays on his lap a purse with jewels, money, a portrait of herself (she walks abroad wearing a veil) and a letter inviting him to a *tête à tête* in that same spot. She then invokes the sleeper in her G major **Aria, No. 3**, *Ruhe sanft, mein holdes Leben*, charmingly scored for oboe and bassoon soli, muted violins, divided violas *pizzicati* and a shapely string bass line. *Tempo di menuetto grazioso*, writes Mozart over the main section which is based on this beguiling melody:

★ See also pp. 248–9 for a near-melodrama in *König Thamos*.

Sleep softly, dear one, till happiness awakes for you. I will give you my portrait; see how friendly it smiles at you.

Sweet tears of mine, lull him and grant his wish to bring his ambitions to mature reality.

The mood is Frenchified; at bar 5 the melodic line and harmony may recall Gluck, and the dance lilt in this minuet, as well as the C major 2/4 *andante moderato* middle section, has been attributed to Grétry's influence. The minuet reprise is more agile and florid in movement. It was from French style, and from Austrian street song in certain situations, that Mozart derived his German operatic style, from *Bastien* to *Zauberflöte*. His Italian operatic characters sing a different dialect of music. We may observe too that, from this music, Zaide is in characterization closer to Blondchen than to Constanze; this peculiarity will be mentioned again. Meanwhile it may be interesting to compare the lyrics of this aria with those of the corresponding one in *Das Serail*.

Zaide	*Das Serail*
Ruhe sanft, mein holdes Leben,	Schlafe ruhig, liebstes Leben!
schlafe, bis dein Glück erwacht;	Schlafe fort, dein Glücke wacht:
da, mein Bild will ich dir geben,	dieses Bildnis will dir geben,
schau, wie freundlich es dir lacht.	das viel andre hat verlacht.

The similarity is too close to count as coincidence, though Schachtner's subsequent lines have no connection with those of *Das Serail*.

In the other extant textbook Zaide hides behind a flowerbed as Gomatz stirs. He finds the purse, reads the letter, gazes fervently at the portrait (Zaide, aside, approves his evident nobility of birth) and dedicates his life to the portrait's original in his **Aria, No. 4**, *Rase, Schicksal*, a straightforward *allegro assai* in B flat major (oboes, horns, strings) in which Mozart contrasts Gomatz's bold defiance of adversity and destiny with the inspiring power of the lovely features on the painting.

Go on raging, destiny. This picture defies your anger. I have never feared your blows and this portrait will make everything well.

These lovely eyelids, this crimson mouth will restore everything tenfold to me even if your madness strangle me to death.

Here again the text owes much to the equivalent in *Das Serail*. No doubt in the music that Gomatz is of noble blood: we have the dotted figuration on a broken chord in bar 1, another at bar 15, the aristocratic fanfare for oboes and violas at bar 28, and other melodic or harmonic features which recall the noble heroes and heroines of his earlier and later operas—not specifically German operas. This might as well be Fiordiligi or Idomeneo or Sulla singing *Rabbia il cielo al mio destino*; Mozart in this opera was not perfectly in command of his musical style. All the same the aria—textually at least a foretaste of Tamino's *Bildnisarie* in *Die Zauberflöte*—contains some strong music, e.g. the turn into G minor at bar 15 with plangent oboes in its train, and the gentle, more German, music from 'Dieses Bild macht alles gut' where Gomatz considers the portrait, again where these words recur in the reprise, to different music (bar 94). The florid divisions near the end are nicely touching.

Following the *Serail* libretto, not necessarily *au pied de la lettre* (Zaide rushes from her flowerbed pretending to be angry with the slave who stole her purse, before declaring her affection for him, due to his noble spirit), we may assume that Zaide and Gomatz plan to escape together. At the thought of this their spirits are uplifted. Again the **Duetto, No. 5** in E flat major, *Meine Seele hüpft vor Freuden* (two flutes, bassoons, horns, muted strings), *allegretto ma moderato*, is textually close to the *Aria in zweien* from *Das Serail* which begins 'Ach, ich sterbe fast vor Freuden'. The vocal lines curve fluently and the lilt looks forward to the *Bei Männern* duet in *Die Zauberflöte*, likewise the comforting feminine phrases of which this is among the most ingratiating:

4

Charming music, German in feel, strongly supported from below by the orchestra (and above by the two flutes which Mozart always used for special effect in his dramatic music), but by no means heroic in tone—the concept of a 'hopping soul' is hardly a lofty one. There is one access of aspiration, after a lulling protracted half-cadence with pause, when the two lovers (as they appear to be) express their newfound bliss in a moment of canonic imitation—not as learned as it sounds, since the harmony is simply tonic and dominant. The quietly flowing end is most beautiful.

Zaide leaves, and Gomatz is joined by Allazim, the Renegade as *Das Serail* describes him, and overseer of the Sultan's slaves. He has heard their duet with horror. He has the authority to punish attempted escape by instant execution. But he is impressed by Gomatz's evident nobility of breeding, and promises to aid Zaide and Gomatz, once he has spoken to Zaide and tested her loyalty.

Gomatz thanks Allazim in his **Aria, No. 6** *Herr und Freund, wie dank ich dir!*

> Master and friend, thank you. Let me clasp your knees though I must leave you at once since I am burning with curiosity. Let me kiss you and embrace you. Alas in the transport of delight I don't know what I am doing because the force of my love robs my soul of repose.

This is *allegretto* in C major, accompanied by strings with oboes and horns giving discreet, charming support. Emotionally the aria depends on the alternation of two moods, respectful and enthusiastic. The former is polite and unassuming—

5

—perfectly acceptable from a hero. Gomatz becomes more voluble, breaking into semi-recitative quavers, at 'doch ich muss dich schnell verlassen', and his contrasting mood turns altogether out of character, though highly attractive at this point: this is amiable, unheroic with its neat orchestral accompaniment. There is a pleasant dramatic touch when, having apparently completed his aria, Gomatz leaves the stage only to return for a last burst of gratitude whose *calando* ending is shy and touching.

6

Laß dich küs—sen, laß dich drücken, laß dich küs—sen,

Here the libretto of *Das Serail* ceases to help us. The cue for Allazim's **Aria, No. 7**, *Nur mutig, mein Herze*, suggests that, after an interview with Zaide, she and Gomatz both depart, while Allazim decides that he will escape at the same time. This aria in F major is marked *allegretto maestoso* and is fairly extended. Two oboes, bassoons, horns, and strings are involved.

> Be bold, my heart, and try your luck. Create a better destiny for yourself. One must not hold back; by boldness a weak man can often prevail over a stronger one.

The beginning is quite stiff, concerned with Allazim's official position, as the running semiquavers and dotted rhythms suggest—he is almost a miniature sultan. But when he begins to sing, the strings accompany him confidently and the entry of bassoons with an Alberti figure and oboes with a defiant motive establish the less official mood of the text. Allazim's heart has to guide him to a luckier destiny. This involves some big leaps and daring passages of florid singing which justify the length of the aria; Allazim is a Don Giovanni role with a strong top register and a florid technique. He must make an impression here.

From *Das Serail* we may assume that Gomatz and Zaide, disguised as Musselmans, hunt for one another and then meet, being joined by Allazim (*Das Serail* is no use at this point). The three continue in a **Trio, No. 8**, *O selige Wonne*, set in E major, *andantino*, strongly characterized by cool flutes, divided violas, discreet horns, and bassoons doubling the lower strings. It is a delectable musical point that the instrumental introduction begins on the first beat of the bar, whereas the voices add their own up-beat. Zaide, who begins, and Gomatz, who follows her, both have rising scales as aspiring florid passages in their first entries. Allazim touches a darker note and Zaide deepens it with a vision of storms, thunder and comets in the sky, emphasized in busily scrubbing strings and dynamic contrasts. The two men divert her to kindlier weather and stress the personal tensions in imitative passages. After a half-close an *allegro* in the same key takes over, rather square and demurely lilting, as the harmonious vocal trio entry, 'Möchten doch einst Ruh und Friede' suggests.

7

Möch———ten doch einst Rüh'—— und Frie—de

The bourgeois jollity and aristocratic good form are carefully balanced here, especially when the voices turn to polyphony, at 'O mein Gomatz! O Zaide!', against high-spirited and independent string texture much dependent on a repeated-note theme; and at the start of the middle section launched by a cadence in the dominant. There is a full *da capo* of the *allegro* material, making this an extensive movement, perhaps designedly since Act I ends with it.

3

Act II begins with the entry of the Sultan Soliman, enraged by the escape of his favourite Zaide. In *Das Serail* he is told of this by the Renegade after a scene in which he has expressed his great joy. But Mozart's score includes no cue for Soliman's **Melodrama and Aria, No. 9**, so we must assume that the act begins immediately with music. This second melodrama, *allegro con brio*, is accompanied pompously by trumpets and drums as well as oboes, horns and strings and it begins with several archetypes of Mozart's music for ruling classes.

Here I have marked the initial phrase for its rhythm, the second for its 'Jupiter'-scrunch, the third and fourth for the proud imitation (*cf.* K. 503 piano concerto in C), the fifth and sixth for other pompous rhythms. These, together with a running scale figure, accompany the Sultan's furious outbursts—spoken of course, and for the moment only when the orchestra is not playing. Zaram, Captain of the Guard, enters to inform the Sultan of Allazim's deceit. Soliman bitterly curses the melting, deluding power of love, and here he does speak over music (Mozart noted that this was a special effect of melodrama, particularly potent). He concludes with further promises of cruel death for the three criminals, interspersed as before by fragments of the example above. The last of these lands the music back in D major for the start of his *allegro maestoso* D major aria *Der stolze Löw' lässt sich zwar zähmen.*

> The proud lion lets himself be tamed, be wheedled into fetters. But if he is degraded like a slave, his anger mounts to tyranny.
> He roars with terrible voice and in grim fury reduces his chains to ruins on the ground, and slaughters anything that stands in his path.

Mozart begins with an orchestral ritornello that rises from low-pitched gentle suavity (and oboes high above in tender thirds) to thumping fanfares exchanged between wind and strings (timpani here side with strings, not their usual partner the trumpet). When the voice enters and we discover that Mozart cast the Sultan as a tenor, this contrast is further developed, for example in the frivolous lightness of the strings, at 'er nimmt vom Schmeichler', to portray the tamer wheedling the king of beasts into accepting a collar and chain. And then at 'Doch will man sklavisch ihn beschämen,' with the agitated string chords and piercing support of woodwind, and soaring, plunging vocal part, we are suddenly projected into—can it be?—the world of Beethoven's Pizarro.

After a cadence on the dominant of the dominant the music quickens to *presto*, strings and wind exchange attempts at lion-roaring, the strings revert (in triple imitation) to Ex. 8/2, the Jupiter-scrunch, and the singer indulges his fury in what may be called Fiordiligi jumps:

All this is prolonged eventfully and in high passion. Both sections are recapitulated, the *presto* with a choppy coda (broken chords in contrary motion at top and bottom) and a proud orchestral postlude.

The next musical number, **No. 10**, is an **Aria**, *Wer hungrig bei der Tafel sitzt* for Osmin, *allegro assai* with strings alone. This is not Soliman's harem-master as in *Die Entführung* but, so we discover from *Das Serail*, a slave-trafficker who has brought more concubines for the Sultan. The libretto does not, however, provide an equivalent for this aria, though we may deduce (since Allazim has already absquatulated) that Osmin is brought in with a selection of voluptuous wives, and consoles the Sultan with the advice not to mope for escaped Zaide, but to compensate by enjoying the odalisques now being offered to him.

> The man who seeks anxiously for what he already possesses is as much a fool ['er ist fürwahr ein ganzer Narr'—the refrain of this ditty] as the man who sits hungry at a loaded dinner-table or he who complains of the cold when a fire is blazing near by.

This is a cheerful *allegro assai* laughing song in F major with a 6/8 lilt, thoroughly plebeian in tone, French rather than Italian in manner, typical of German comic opera as Mozart conceived it. Its refrain, for instance:

11

Er ist für—wahr, er ist für—wahr ein gan—zer Narr

—not far from the language of Mozart's comic *Lieder*; the laughing sections are typical of comic opera everywhere. But the touches of poignant harmony, e.g. in the verse about the cold weather, or the ironical music for 'Wer soll nicht drüber lachen?' at bar 114, are typical of Mozart's *buffo* music. Osmin's only musical contribution to *Zaide* is quite lengthy, very pleasing, and deservedly popular as a recital item.

Next comes a vengeance **Aria** for Soliman, **No. 11**, *Ich bin so bös als gut* in E flat major, *allegro moderato*, accompanied by flutes, oboes, bassoons, horns and strings. The cue for this is 'vor deinen Augen gezüchtiget werden' ('they will be chastised before your very eyes'). The libretto of *Das Serail* has a parallel moment which permits us to deduce that the captured Allazim is grovelling at Soliman's feet; Gomatz and Zaide are being conducted back to the palace, having also been apprehended; and the Sultan has told Allazim that he is to die a fearful death but not before he has witnessed the equally painful and protracted execution of the other two whose escape he abetted. This is another big aria with orchestral ritornello 28 bars long and in character akin to the opening ritornello of a concerto. Its incident is inspired by the text:

> I am as wicked as I am good, rewarding faithful service generously but, when roused to anger, ready to use my instruments of punishment which draw blood.

So Mozart starts with four bars of loud octaves careering up and down the chord of E flat and involving the Jupiter-scrunch (Ex. 8/2), for authoritative ('bös') purposes—and because they are part of his E flat concept (see the chapter on key-character). Then Mannheim-fashion, and also in the spirit of Soliman's previous aria, he builds up a melodious paragraph ('gut') from *piano*, strongly based on the tonic in the galant manner. When the bass begins to move at bar 8, we have a dapper tune on first violins high above skittering second violins—just as in the finale of the Paris Symphony (K. 300a). There is a momentous approach to the dominant with rushing basses, then (concerto-fashion) a relapse into the tonic for the second subject, gracious and in thirds, full of *forte-piano*. A firm, slightly unaristocratic idea (bar 24) and a typical open-ended *coda* figure complete this ritornello—plenty of material to work on. The autocratic rhythm of the last tonic chord is echoed softly by wind, enhancing the depth of musical perspective, before the Sultan undertakes the solo exposition, the Jupiter-scrunch being imitated twice this time. The mild tune is for rewarding the faithful, the open-ended coda introduces the idea of wrath, and the rushing basses, together with some loud dotted rhythm octaves, represent the blood-letting. A feature of Mozart's German operatic style is the declamatory element in the two passages quoted below, very typical.

12*a*

so hab ich auch wohl Waffen, das Laster zu be-strafen, das Laster zu be-strafen,

b

doch reizt man mei—ne   Wut,   doch reizt man mei—ne   Wut,

The aria's form is binary; after the dominant cadence the music makes for F minor and other keys, appears to be in a development section but returns to E flat and a sense of recapitulation almost at once. The Sultan's part is mildly florid but not virtuoso, though distinctively dramatic. The aria, musically well worth while, still inhabits a no-man's-land between the old formal sonata-form or *da capo* and the newer, shorter, Gluck-derived forms which were to typify the arias in Mozart's mature operas.

We must now presume a change of scene to some dungeon in which Zaide is discovered incarcerated; there is no such scene in *Das Serail*, though the juxtaposition of two vividly contrasted arias for the heroine is paralleled in Act II of *Die Entführung* where the moods, first tearful then defiant, are as here. Her *andantino* **Aria, No. 12**, *Trostlos schluchzet Philomele*, accompanied by strings alone (violas often divided), is a Frenchified *andantino* descriptive piece, a simple rondo. The key, A major, is already used in characteristic Mozartian fashion.

> The nightingale sobs inconsolably, confined in its cage, and with agile throat bewails the loss of its freedom. Day and night it cannot sleep, but hops in search of somewhere to escape. Who could punish it if it finds what it is seeking?

The vocal line is exquisitely melodious, at one point recognizably typical:

13

daß— man   ih——re   Frei——heit   kränkt, daß—   man—

ih————re   Frei————————————heit kränkt,

It is the string writing, miraculously light in touch and articulation, that makes this exquisite aria. It is young Mozart, but in the sense that *Das Veilchen* (a late work) is still young Mozart.

Zaide now looks forward to death with Gomatz as a martyr's sacrifice on the altar of true love, and Mozart moves from A major into his other favourite expressive key of G minor for **No. 13**, her **Aria**, *Tiger! Wetze nur die Klauen*, which adds two oboes, bassoons and horns (in high B flat and G respectively) to the strings.

> Just sharpen your claws, tiger, look forward to the prey you snatched. Punish my foolish trust in your pretended kindness. Only come quickly and kill us both, suck the innocents' warm blood, tear the heart from the entrails, and satiate your fury!
>
> Ah, my Gomatz, fate has no mercy on us poor creatures. Only death will end our bitter distress.

This is not the G minor of Konstanze's *Traurigkeit* or Pamina's *Ach ich fühl's*, but the hectic, violent G minor of the Symphony 25, K. 173dB, or No. 13 of *La finta giardiniera*, or the finale of the K. 550 symphony. It begins *allegro assai*; the high-pitched wind writing is as striking as the agitated strings and the copious changes of dynamic. Mozart makes a lot of the first word, hurtling it at the audience in the middle of a boil-up for orchestra (and it is to be thrown at us ultimately together with the last chord). At 'verstellte Zärtlichkeit' the strings go on tiptoe and the singer should take notice, especially as *fortissimo* breaks in just afterwards and precipitates heroic exclamations. Zaide now thinks of Gomatz in his neighbouring cell, likewise condemned to a cruel death. She calls to him, *larghetto* in E flat major (muted upper strings), and this is some of Mozart's most touching pre-Pamina music; it moves quickly into the key of *Ach ich fühl's*, Mozart's own G minor:

14

Then the *Tiger* music returns, and the changes of dynamic are even more violent, like lunging claws. On the very last chord Zaide calls the word 'Tiger' with terrific effect.

In Allazim's **Aria, No. 14**, *Ihr Mächtigen seht ungerührt*, accompanied by oboes, horns and strings, we are to understand that Allazim is pleading for the lives of Gomatz and Zaide.

> You masters look down on your slaves, and being blessed with lucky allure, you don't recognize that they are your brothers. The sufferings of others are only understood by the man who learned compassion before he became important.

In the first *un poco adagio* section, very short, the subtle chamber-musical string writing and deliberate harmonic movement, with plentiful trills at the top, suggest the singer's nobility; the texture is eloquently rich. The succeeding *allegretto* is more straightforward—rather like Blondchen's *Durch Zärtlichkeit* in *Die Entführung* though the sexes are changed. The tempo alters to *moderato* in F ('Nur der kennt Mitleid'), bland and unpretentious, dipping into Allazim's low register, and growing more agitated—the authorities are undisturbed but Allazim is very upset. Then *allegretto* resumes and he sings in a more persuasive tone of voice. His vocal part lies high but delves also into a low register that most baritones find ineffective. We may sense Gluck's influence here. The aria establishes Allazim as the chief heroic character in the opera.

The last extant number of this operatic torso, **No. 15**, the **Quartet** for Zaide, Gomatz, Soliman and Allazim, is throughout marked *allegro assai*. But *Freundin, stille deine Tränen* cannot, because of note-values, go very fast. The cue shows that Gomatz and Zaide are resigned to death together. It begins with woodwind alone, flutes, oboes, bassoons and horns, very serenade-like, closely compact, the oboes in thirds, all very suave and comforting since Gomatz is telling Zaide not to weep since their love will be crowned by death together. As he starts to sing, the strings take over accompaniment (bassoons doubling low strings). Allazim expresses compassion, Soliman (violins break into angry scales) insists that tears are valueless, Zaide claims guilt entirely for herself, in a touching solo, but Soliman insists on their two deaths, to more determined music. Allazim laments in F minor, Soliman counters him and a polyphonic texture in F major builds up, turning back to B flat. All this is elaborated with real skill and invention, and the orchestra is magisterially used—Mozart's most skilful scoring to date, especially in terms of contrasted moods between characters (the ensemble of perplexity was known only in Italian *opera buffa* and there only for two-part contradiction—here we have three different frames of mind). After a pause Gomatz and Zaide beg, in thirds (really tenths) for death alone, though the lively violin figuration above speaks of more cheerful topics. The three prisoners are now set against the implacable Sultan, even at the formal recapitulation. The orchestra heightens the intensity in terms of activity while the voices suggest increasing breathlessness (even Soliman); the number ends softly.

4

This is all we possess of the *Singspiel* known nowadays as *Zaide*. Was there a third act? Or merely a *dénouement* involving maybe one or two extra numbers before the Sultan's discovery that Allazim had saved his life twenty years earlier for which reason he pardoned the victims who were identified as father, son and daughter? Or were the relationships otherwise in Schachtner's libretto? Since Mozart said the text was too serious for Viennese taste, did Schachtner give his drama a tragic end? There must have been an ensemble finale.

No use to speculate. *Zaide* is a fragment, tantalizing (surely Schachtner's text must exist somewhere in Salzburg), musically fascinating. Not, it will be realized, as tantalizing as would be Acts I and II of *Die Entführung*, if the libretto and third act had vanished. At the time of *Zaide* Mozart was not yet sure how to characterize principal personages so as to communicate human identity; he was still half tied to the conventions of *opera seria* and *opera buffa* and their dehumanized types, though *Zaide* already pointed the way forward. And he was still uncertain how German opera, in which he believed, was to be distinguished from the Italian, or French, product. *Zaide* is important for its promise, for the subtleties of instrumentation or harmony, for the range of mood—Allazim's aria No. 14 is, in this respect, as effective as either of the big, highly inventive arias for Soliman. The ensembles, especially the Trio No. 8 and the Quartet No. 15, indicate on what a big scale and how multifariously he was able to deploy character and situation. Soliman's arias mark a step forward in his creative evolution (they must have been intended for a musicianly tenor of strong personality who worked for Böhm's company). But one cannot isolate the numbers for Gomatz or Zaide (including the ensembles) and distinguish in their sum a consistent musical portrayal of an individual, as one can in *Die Entführung* or the later Mozart operas. In *Zaide*, as in his earlier *opere serie*, Mozart was writing music to be sung, not creating characters that we implicitly believe in. It is a matter for regret that Mozart never persevered further with the melodrama. Beethoven in *Fidelio*, Schumann, Liszt and Richard Strauss, then Schoenberg and many modern composers, have followed Mozart in combining the spoken word with music. If only Mozart had gone on, he could have eliminated the stilted recipe of *recitativo secco* and invented an intermediary between spoken dialogue and aria that would have revolutionized music-drama. He did not persevere: he never heard *Zaide* performed and in his subsequent works he scrupulously avoided the melodrama. Perhaps conditions of rehearsal made it too difficult to get right and improve upon these pioneer efforts; in his mature comic operas either speech or recitative worked well for him. He was not an innovator by nature.

Attempts to turn this fragment into a viable theatrical musical experience cannot succeed. We can try to fill the gaps between existing numbers. But No. 15 is so far from the end that no gap-filling can complete what Mozart left incomplete. To stuff this final gap with other existing pieces by Mozart will satisfy nobody. The music of *Zaide* is of powerful interest to all Mozart students and the best use to be made of it is either by gramophone records or concert performance, recognizing always that this is a regrettably incomplete torso whose extant limbs are admirable in themselves and for what they, and they alone, can tell us about the genius who created them.

5

Mention was made, at the beginning of this chapter, of Mozart's expanded incidental music for *Thamos, König in Ägypten*, a heroic drama by Tobias Philipp, Baron von Gebler, a well known and admired dramatist of the day. Gebler at first commissioned incidental music from Johann Tobias Sattler whose work was touched up by no less a composer than Gluck. Gebler, however, was not satisfied with it and asked Mozart to write a new set of music; Mozart's was performed at the Kärntnertor Theatre, Vienna, in April 1774. It certainly consisted of two choruses for the first and fifth acts of the play; the autographs of these have survived. Some authorities suggest that Mozart's orchestral interludes were also written at this time or at any rate by 3 January 1776 when *Thamos* was performed in Salzburg. But early versions of these movements are not known, and our authority for this

Salzburg performance, Baron Schiedenhofen, was a friend of the Mozart family whose diary always mentions any event connected with Mozart: if Wolfgang's music had been performed it is unthinkable that Schiedenhofen would not have said so. My own belief is that in 1774 Mozart's two choruses were performed and that the rest of the music was by Sattler. He died on 19 December 1774. Mozart had no time to write new music until 1779 when he did it for Johann Böhm's company, as stated earlier in this chapter. For this he wrote the interludes that we possess, elaborated his two earlier choruses, wrote a new instrumental conclusion, No. 7a, then decided to suppress it in favour of a choral finale whose text had been written by Andreas Schachtner, and probably set to music also by Schachtner (himself a professional composer) for the 1776 performance. No. 4 of the incidental music, an entracte, has verbal cues written into the score by Leopold Mozart. They look like a melodrama and have therefore been taken for a Benda-influenced composition. But Mozart's music for this number includes no pauses and there is, in any case, too much music for the cues to be met by even a very slow speaker. I believe that Mozart intended No. 4 as a musical description of the scene just to come, and that Leopold Mozart wrote the references into Wolfgang's score as guides. Mozart's Nos. 2–5 might have been written earlier than 1779 but the evidence of the manuscript paper (so I understand) makes this seem unlikely.

Böhm not only used the 1779 revision of Mozart's music but employed some of the choruses for his production of Karl Martin Plümicke's *Lanassa* which was still in his repertory during the Frankfurt coronation festivities of 1790 when Mozart himself saw it. Another idea that the revision was made for Schikaneder does not hold water because the play was not in his repertory during 1779–80. Mozart noted that *König Thamos* was a flop in France, and that by 1783 it had fallen out of the dramatic repertory. The choruses Nos. 1, 6, and 7 were given wider publicity by their provision for Latin or German texts for church use. No. 1 was so performed in 1796 in Leipzig during one of Constanze Mozart's benefit concerts.

Being a matter of static choruses with a few unimportant solos (that for the high priest in No. 7 is more significant than others), this music hardly falls under the review of a book about Mozart's dramatic music. The *König Thamos* music is, nevertheless, interesting as a foretaste of *Die Zauberflöte* and perhaps for some of its particular compositional features. The **Chorus, No. 1**, *Schon weichet dir, Sonne,* includes pale, starry flutes in its 1779 version, and clarini too (what we call Bach trumpets). The beginning of this C major *maestoso* movement depends much on solemn dotted rhythms—elsewhere noted as symbols of aristocracy. At the entry of the chorus the violins' syncopations suggest Gluck (e.g., 'Divinités du Styx' from *Iphigénie en Tauride*). The duets for male and later female voices (extant in the 1773 version) are strongly characterized instrumentally—duller in the first version. Chromatic harmony, expressively used, makes certain that C major is not here at all a bland key.

The **Entracte, No. 2**, represents the plotting of two villains to replace Thamos on the Egyptian throne. The opening chords in C minor inevitably suggest those at the start of *Die Zauberflöte*, even though they are in the relative minor. Freemasons are much moved by these three chords, and Gebler was a Freemason, as Mozart was to become. I guess that the playwright asked Mozart to preface this entracte with three chords in a key of three flats and Mozart obliged without understanding why.* An *allegro* follows, full of chromatic writing, most expressive, especially in the placing of oboes high above the strings. The sustained woodwind chords at bar 119 are especially characteristic and appealing.

No. 3, Entracte, was designed to indicate the contrast between Thamos's magnanimity, expressed in a small oboe solo, and Pheron's treachery portrayed by bumpy alterations of *forte* and *piano*; the two opposites are presented concurrently after the dominant cadence, and in the coda. But musically the gem of this interlude is the dignified, melodious E flat major opening which suggests the K. 543 E flat symphony as much as anything in *Die Zauberflöte*.

No. 4 is the musical representation of Sais's monologue (not, I am sure, a melodrama accompaniment). The themes are themselves very dramatic, though not of archetypal interest to the thesis of this book. **No. 5** in D minor depicts dramatic conflict, confusion even. Mozart conveys this most potently when predictable implications of melody are harmonized unexpectedly on diminished seventh harmony.

No. 6 is another **Chorus** with duets for solo voices, as in No. 1. The trumpet is fetched out to match a reference in the text; but the high flute is just as compelling. The concept of falling at bar 29 finds a thoroughly vivid musical description. The whole movement is long (284 bars—only 105 in the original).

No. 7, the **Chorus** which replaced the conventionally D minor No. 7a, broods anxiously during the High Priest's solo, then moves into almost Schubertian cantilena. The fast D major coda is invigorating. As the coda looms, oboes in a pair float nostalgically above the orchestra (bar 113), and we know, as in *Figaro*, that the end is near.

Mozart's music for *König Thamos* is nowadays a practical possibility only in concert performance. It may have thrown Mozart's natural sense of style when he came to write *Zaide*. He had the joy of writing for a big orchestra, but his music in *Thamos* is symphonic rather than dramatically articulate. He needed to invent, but had not the best facilities for doing so.

* Jacques Chailley discusses these chords, from a Masonic point of view, and those in *Die Zauberflöte* in his *La flûte enchantée* (see Bibliography).

13　IDOMENEO

IDOMENEO ossia ILIA ED IDAMANTE

Dramma per musica in three acts

Libretto by

GIANBATTISTA VARESCO

K. 366

IDOMENEO (Idomeneus), King of Crete	TENOR
IDAMANTE (Idamantes), his son	MALE SOPRANO
ILIA, daughter of King Priam of Troy	SOPRANO
ELETTRA (Electra), daughter of King Agamemnon of Argos	SOPRANO
ARBACE (Arbaces), Idomeneo's confidant	TENOR
High Priest of Neptune	TENOR
Voice of Neptune (La Voce)	BASS
Women and Men of Crete	
Retinue of Idomeneus and Idamantes	
Trojan prisoners	CHORUS
Sailors from Argos	
Priests	

The action takes place at Cydonia (now Canea) in Crete, some ten years after the conclusion of the Trojan War

The Elector of Mannheim had promised Mozart that it would be easy to get him a commission for an opera. This did not occur while Mozart was in Mannheim or Munich to which the Elector had moved his court (see p. 231 above). But early in 1780 such an opera was commissioned: it was to be a serious opera for the 1780–1 carnival season in Munich. Unfortunately for Mozart, who wanted to write a serious opera in German, this one had to be in Italian. The language was, of course, perfectly familiar to him, and the style was the one in which he was (momentarily at least) most interested and with which, the score of *Idomeneo* proves, he knew he could work most purposefully after the six years of listening and study, and brooding on the nature of Italian and other opera, since *Il rè pastore* was completed. The opera was commissioned by the Elector not as a high-handed command but also by the expressed desires of the singers whom Mozart had befriended in Mannheim and who were now working in Munich (Mmes Wendling, Raaff, etc.), and of the orchestra too. Archbishop Colloredo of course made as many difficulties as possible, but he had to capitulate to the Elector of Bavaria.

The subject chosen was the legendary one of King Idomeneus of Crete. This had previously been used in 1712 as a five-act French libretto by Antoine Danchet for André Campra. For Mozart's purposes it was reworked in three acts of sub-Metastasian Italian and given a happy *dénouement* by the Salzburg chaplain Gianbattista Varesco: Count Seeau assured Mozart that there were no decent Italian librettists in Munich, and that it would be more convenient for him to work with a poet in Salzburg for speedy intercommunication. In the event most of Mozart's composition of *Idomeneo* was done in Munich and he had to communicate through his father with Varesco. Inconvenient as this was—he required many textual changes—the correspondence does give posterity much valuable information about Mozart's working methods, and about the genesis of one of his most important operas.

Varesco seems to have been unskilled as a dramatic poet, verbose and with little natural flair for drama though his principal characters are intelligently projected and diversified. He accepted Mozart's proposal that they should construct their opera after the French manner, with plenty of ensembles and dynamic choral set-pieces, and without conventional exit-arias except where dramatic logic recommended an exit. He bequeathed us some problems inasmuch as he expected frequent scene-changes—not difficult in the eighteenth century, but not desired by Mozart whose desire was to keep the drama moving forward during the music.

Varesco having completed the libretto, Mozart began work early in October 1780 at home in Salzburg. Before travelling to Munich he could complete the recitatives, the choruses and, theoretically, the solos and ensembles for those singers with whom he was already familiar, though his letters home from Munich make it clear that he left much of the composition until he got there.

He left Salzburg on 5 November, arriving at Munich next day at lunchtime,* after a very uncomfortable journey. He had leave of absence until 18 December, though in the event he stayed on in Munich until 12 March 1781. In his first letter home he already asks for some alterations by Varesco: for example an aside will not do in a sung aria because the words have to be repeated. He also notes that the recitatives will have to be abbreviated though Varesco's text will be printed in full.† Later we learn that some of the cuts in recitatives were due to the poor acting of the cast: Raaff, Mozart comments, acts just like a statue (Metastasio in 1749 had found him a 'freddissimo' actor), and 'mio molto amato castrato Del Prato' (Wolfgang's sarcastic joke) was no genius, though Mozart was wrongly informed that he had never before appeared on a stage. Del Prato had experience in Italy and Germany and went on singing successfully in Munich until 1805 when he was pensioned.

Mozart must have written the first scene of the opera, Ilia's accompanied recitative and aria, before setting out, since it won Dorothea Wendling's approval at their first re-encounter in Munich: she confessed herself 'arcicontentissima' ('most completely content') and asked Mozart to play it to her three times in succession. He presumably composed Electra's and Idomeneus's arias in Salzburg, since on 15 November he mentions that Lisl Wendling is as pleased as her sister with her arias, but that *Fuor del mar* is too difficult for Raaff at sixty-six—he eventually made an easier version of it which Raaff quite fell in love with and, out of respect for the dear old gentleman, added a new aria, *Torna la pace* in Act III. This last cost Varesco much trouble: he had to write it three times before Raaff was happy, and intimated that he should be paid extra for so much re-writing. The Abbé was evidently a tiresome moneygrubber: 'Varesco me ha seccato i coglioni' was Leopold's indelicate comment on the financial wrangling. Wolfgang Mozart wrote back that Varesco deserved no extra pay: the alterations were required for the good of the libretto as much as for the music. The composer too had his troubles: Vincenzo Del Prato who was twenty-four, like Mozart, was not only an unskilled actor but an ill-trained singer and poor musician who had to be taught every note of his part by the composer himself—'he hasn't a pennyworth of technique', wrote Mozart ('er hat um keinen Kreuzer Methode'). And for the first two weeks in Munich Mozart found himself unable to compose. Still, they were all very friendly, the Elector, the Intendant Count Seeau who had lost his former super-cilious manner, the producer and ballet-master Pierre le Grand, the scenic designer Lorenzo Quaglio, Christian Cannabich the conductor (Mozart the composer was, by Electoral protocol, not permitted to conduct his own work) and all the singers. Constanze Mozart subsequently recalled that these months in Munich were the happiest time of Mozart's life. The Webers had by then moved to Vienna, father Fridolin had died and Aloysia married the actor Josef Lange who painted the finest of all portraits of Mozart (even if it is unfinished). So Constanze must have been passing on what Mozart told her of the *Idomeneo* period. We have already seen that

* Information from O. E. Deutsch: Documentary Biography. This seems to conflict with Mozart's information that on 20 December he will have been away from Salzburg for six weeks, but he is thinking of his arrival in Munich not his departure from home.

† The Italian libretto was published together with a German translation by J. A. Schachtner (see *Zaide*, p. 235). A second libretto, in Italian only, was also published at the time, and this corresponds more closely with the score.

Mozart added an aria out of friendship for Raaff and, although Arbaces was a subsidiary character who merited no more than two arias, and Domenico de' Panzacchi the tenor who took the part was past his best, yet he was such a 'worthy old fellow' and such a good singing-actor that Mozart persuaded Varesco to enlarge his recitatives (whereas those for Idomeneus and Idamantes had to be shortened for want of this ability). Mozart also decided to omit a duet for Ilia and Idamantes, *Deh soffre in pace, o cara*, just before the subterranean voice of Neptune is heard. He decided to shorten Varesco's text for *Placido è il mar* (No. 15) leaving an *a-b-a* form. An aria for Idomeneus, at the height of the storm in Act II, was dramatically impossible to Mozart who refused to set it.

By 29 November Mozart was worrying about the length of Neptune's off-stage narration; he composed it several times, shorter each time, arguing that, 'If the speech of the Ghost in *Hamlet* were not so long, it would be far more effective' (Mozart had probably seen Shakespeare's play a month earlier when Schikaneder's company performed it in Salzburg—Schikaneder, for all his immortal reputation as the creator of Papageno, was a renowned tragic actor, and a famous Hamlet in particular). In the same letter Mozart asks his father to send mutes for horns and trumpets, unprocurable in Munich. This intelligence, added to the earlier decision that Schachtner in Salzburg should write the German translation of *Idomeneo*, because Mozart was assured by Count Seeau of the incompetence of translators in Munich, sheds curious light on the sophistication of provincial Salzburg compared with metropolitan Munich!

The voice of Neptune occurs very late in the third act of *Idomeneo*. But we may not assume that Mozart composed Varesco's text in order, since on 19 December he told his father that he still had to write three arias, the final chorus, the overture and the ballet music. By then two orchestral rehearsals had taken place: all were delighted, including the Elector who declared that he had never been so moved by any music, and the orchestra (the oboeist Ramm was especially enthusiastic), and the conductor Cannabich although he found the score difficult—he was dripping with sweat, Mozart wrote. After the first rehearsal on 1 December the number of orchestral violins was doubled to twelve. On 29 November the Empress Maria Theresa had died, and Leopold feared that *Idomeneo* would suffer (as *Così fan tutte* was to suffer when Joseph II died). However, the court mourning in Munich lasted only six weeks and did not involve closure of the theatres anyway. The Empress's death did mean that Leopold and Nannerl had to postpone their travel to Munich until Archbishop Colloredo had left Salzburg for Vienna; they reached Munich on 26 January. But fortunately the première of *Idomeneo*, due to its complexity, was postponed from 20 to 29 January.

Meanwhile Schachtner's German version was finished and sent off, together with all Varesco's revisions, on 22 December (comprehensive details of all the alterations are given in the preface to the NMA *Idomeneo*). On 3 January Mozart announced that he was so busy on the composition of Act III that he was turning into a third act himself. This act was rehearsed on 13 January, the entire score by 18 January. Already by Christmas, news of the general admiration for *Idomeneo* had spread from Munich to Salzburg, not only through Leopold Mozart; many Salzburgers, because of the absence of the Archbishop, travelled to Munich for the first performance in the Residenz (now Cuvilliés) Theatre. The dress rehearsal took place on 27 January, Mozart's twenty-fifth birthday, one day after the arrival of his father and sister. There had been cuts and scenic compromises, the letters suggest. Raaff, who for all his good qualities was musically a reactionary, tried to get the sublime quartet *Andrò ramingo* suppressed in favour of an aria because he could not imagine that an ensemble would sufficiently captivate the public at this moment of climax. Fortunately he changed his mind after rehearsals and apologized for his little faith. Mozart did, however, drop a hint that this title role would have been stronger if he had composed it for Giovanni Battista Zonca, a leading basso at the Munich opera. Later in the year he planned to rewrite the part for Ludwig Fischer—see *Entführung*, p. 293—in a new German version, with Bernasconi and Adamberger as Ilia and Idamantes. But he never effected the adaptation which would have made the opera more French in style: it would have set a precedent since bass roles in serious operas were, at the time, never of first importance. In Munich Act III was given without change of scene, and several last-minute cuts were made including Idamantes's *No, la morte*, Idomeneus's *Torna la pace* (after all that trouble), and, most surprising of all, Electra's *D'Oreste, d'Ajace*, a highlight of the whole opera, replaced by a short recitative to avoid the exit of everyone else and, after the solo, their sudden return.

But we have no reports from Mozart of the first performance because his nearest and dearest were with him by them. It was repeated numerous times until 3 March and greatly admired, the scenery as much as the music. Mozart stayed in Munich till 7 March when he, his father and sister visited Augsburg. They returned to Munich and on 12 March Mozart, at Archbishop Colloredo's command, went to Vienna where his employer, who was visiting his sick father the Imperial Vice Chancellor, required his Kapellmeister to preside at concerts. Leopold and Nannerl returned to Salzburg.

2

Idomeneo was not immediately taken up by other opera houses. This may appear odd since it is patently the greatest *opera seria* ever written. But *opera seria* had become unfashionable, and a specimen such as this which combined German orchestral prominence with freer French forms was too bold to appeal to conservative opera-goers who still liked the old Italian form. On 13 March 1786 the opera was given a performance in Vienna at Prince Auersperg's palace, with Giuseppe Bridi in the name-part. For this the recitatives were drastically cut, the roles of Ilia (Anna von Pufendorf) and Electra (Countess Hatzfeld whose husband led the orchestra) shortened. Mozart added the duet, *Spiegarti non poss'io*, K. 489, for Ilia and Idamantes, replacing their No. 20 in Act III; and a soprano scena with the rondo *Non temer, amato bene* which has a splendid violin obbligato. This performance by well born amateurs included a tenor Idamantes. Mozart must have had to alter the ensembles so as not to upset the part-writing. His alterations have not all survived, but in Nos. 16 and 21 a light high tenor can sing some of these ensemble passages an octave higher when Idamantes lies lower than Idomeneo, *viz*. at written pitch. Idamantes's solos probably had to be transposed, if sung by a tenor. In modern performances Idamantes is usually given to a tenor, occasionally to a female soprano. Neither compromise is really satisfactory, either in the arias or the ensembles; we need the robust, brilliant colour of a male soprano voice or, in post-*coltello* days, of a male counter-tenor with a radiant, masculine tone-colour and a strong upper register extending to top A. Such singers can physically exist, and will surely arise if the present popularity of eighteenth-century *opera seria* continues. (The upper notes do not survive long, but as an amateur counter-tenor I retained a loud, unforced even if unlovely, top C until the age of forty or so.) Standard conservative Viennese taste found *Idomeneo* 'too much filled up with accompaniments', in fact not Italian enough. Leopold Mozart had already observed in 1780 that Wolfgang's scoring far surpassed the norm for Italian *opera seria* just because the orchestration was scrupulously devised. On Mozart's very first day in Munich, having heard the Mannheim Orchestra, he decided to set Ilia's *Se il padre perdei* with four obbligato woodwinds, so as to give credit to his brilliant friends in the orchestra; and this is one of the miracles of the score; it was one of Mozart's favourite pieces. But throughout *Idomeneo* the imaginative orchestral scoring must be remarked.

Idomeneo was not forgotten after this Vienna performance. After Mozart's death some of its music was included in memorial concerts. It was given in Budapest in 1803 and in numerous German opera houses thereafter, likewise in the 1840s (Loewenberg's *Annals of Opera* show how frequently); by this time its antiquated features may have been compensated by its novel features.

From 1879 onwards *Idomeneo* was often presented in romantic editions of greater or lesser artistic brutality; the progressive music had to be matched by even more progressive dramaturgy, and even musical reconstruction. There was a famous version made by Richard Strauss and Lothar Wallerstein in 1931 which substituted the determinedly racialistic Cretan Priestess Ismene for Electra, and added other music by Mozart. Strauss contributed new music of his own, and re-wrote the recitatives so as to enhance the supposedly leitmotivic element in Mozart's original.* A later, overtly more scholarly, version by Bernhard Paumgartner was given at Salzburg and published: but here too there were wilful cuts and alterations, even though the twentieth century had by then renounced the doctrine of progressive musical evolution.

The only justifiable basis for study or performance of *Idomeneo* is the score as Mozart wrote it in 1781 and as the Mozart Complete Edition printed it, with its appendices, in 1881 (it has been reprinted since in miniature photostat score by Kalmus of New York), and the relevant volume of the New Mozart Edition published by Bärenreiter in 1973. If cuts or alterations must be made (as Mozart did on the first night, rather out of panic) the musical director must be able to take personal responsibility for them, from knowledge of the complete work. It was on this basis that Fritz Busch conducted the 1951 Glyndebourne production which has arguably led to the re-establishment of *Idomeneo* everywhere as part of the Mozart operatic canon, though in 1971 Paumgartner's version was still being used in Vienna.

3

The story of Idomeneus, King of Crete, was well known to classical antiquity. He was the son of Deucalion (not surely the survivor, with his wife Pyrra, of the great flood). As a youth he was famous for his good looks, and when Helen of

* A lucid comparison of Strauss's version with Mozart's original is given in Norman Del Mar's *Richard Strauss*, Volume II, pp. 381–4.

Sparta grew to womanhood Idomeneus was one of her many suitors, though unsuccessful. He married Meda. At the outset of the Trojan War Idomeneus promised to lead a hundred ships to Troy if Agamemnon would match this number. Thus Crete joined Greece in the war against Troy: Leopold Mozart must have thought of this when he advised Wolfgang that Varesco had now and then spoken of the Greek troops as Argives, whereas Leopold told his son to alter this epithet, in certain places, to Achaeans so as to include Idomeneus and his fleet.

Producers of Mozart's *Idomeneo*, and their scenic designers, may be glad to know that, according to myth,[*] Idomeneus wore a helmet ornamented with boars' tusks, and a long shield, protecting him from chin to toe, decorated with the figure of a cock, to show his descent from the sun god Helios. Mr Graves suggests that this must be a cock-partridge since the domestic hen was not known in Greece until several centuries after the Trojan War. Idomeneus distinguished himself by his valour during the war. At its conclusion he, and the other Greek leaders, set sail for home. We are to understand, in Mozart's opera, that Idomeneus had sent on ahead a convoy of Trojan prisoners including Priam's daughter Ilia (not identified in the books though her name simply indicates that she was a female Trojan—Priam's children were reputedly most numerous). Some prisoners reached Crete safely. Ilia's ship was wrecked and she was saved by Idomeneus's son Idamantes (again a name not to be found in history books) who brought her back to Crete. Already there for some time was Agamemnon's daughter Electra—presumably she had been evacuated from Mycenae and, in this version of the story, underwent none of the sufferings retailed by Sophocles (not to mention Hofmannsthal). Electra fell in love with Idamantes but he preferred the Trojan princess Ilia, much to Electra's fury.

According to mythology Idomeneus's wife Meda took a lover, Leucus, during the ten years of the Trojan war and the further ten years before the Greek leaders returned home. Leucus killed her; of this Varesco says nothing. During the homeward voyage Idomeneus, like Menelaus, was caught in a violent sea-storm, while already in sight of home. In despair Idomeneus promised Poseidon the sea-god (Neptune in Latin nomenclature) that, if he returned home safely, he would sacrifice to Poseidon the first human being he met after landing. The fated person was his son (later anti-matriarchal historians changed this into a daughter). Some myths tell that Idomeneus fulfilled his promise and sacrificed his child whereupon the people of Crete, encouraged by Leucus, were so appalled that they banished Idomeneus who sailed away to Italy and founded Salentum in Calabria. But most writers agree that, just as Idomeneus was about to perform the sacrifice, he was interrupted by heavenly action, a pestilence which showed that heaven no longer approved of human sacrifice. Similar celestial interruptions figure in the story of Abraham and Isaac, Jephthah and his daughter, and indeed Agamemnon and Iphigenia (sister to Electra). In another myth Maeander made a similar vow, and had to kill his son after which the guilty father drowned himself in the nearest river, whence the geographical name for a bend in a stream.

The remaining character named in *Idomeneo* is Arbaces who, mythologically, was the Mede who founded Media on the ruins of Assyria. This is interesting inasmuch as Idomeneus's wife was called Meda, and in one story Idomeneus was judge in a beauty contest where Medea (of Jason and the Argonauts) lost to

---

[*] As synthesized in Robert Graves, *Greek Myths* (Cassell, 1958).

Thetis. All this cannot be coincidental. Robert Graves suggests that Idomeneus must have made his vow to Aphrodite, because every parallel story involves a female tutelary deity (even Jephthah's is imputed to Anatha rather than Jehovah). But Graves had surely not heard Mozart's sea-storm music. Varesco had written a stage direction showing the appearance of Poseidon at the height of the storm when Idomeneus is shipwrecked. Mozart struck it out from his score, but I have seen it effectively staged by Colin Graham in the Aldeburgh Festival production which was conducted by Benjamin Britten.

4

Mozart had already learned from experience that it was preferable to write an opera's overture when the whole of the opera had been set to music: only so could the overture prepare the audience for what was to come.

The overture for *Idomeneo* at once demonstrates not only Mozart's newly acquired maturity (compare it with the overtures to *Mitridate* and *Lucio Silla*, which are also dynamic in content and *seria* by nature) but his awareness of the overture's relevance to the drama's contents. He knew that he was writing for the best orchestra in Europe, that his violin section had been doubled for the occasion, and that for the first time he had clarinets in the theatre pit—though in the overture their part is not prominent. Most important of all he had completely composed the opera by this time, and knew what it was about. The overture to *Idomeneo* is, so to speak, a symphonic poem about the drama, as is the overture to *Die Zauberflöte* to a lesser degree, that to *Die Entführung* more obviously and superficially, those to *Don Giovanni* and *Così fan tutte* more casually, as Beethoven's second and third *Leonore* overtures supremely, even pleonastically, are. Of all the Mozart operatic overtures that to *Idomeneo* seems the most closely linked with the total contents of the opera. One can believe this without accepting that Mozart deliberately used material already planted in the score of the opera.

The opera is in D major, therefore this is the key of the **Overture** which is marked *allegro* and uses pairs of flutes, oboes, clarinets, bassoons, horns, trumpets and drums, as well as strings.

It beings with conventional signals of pomp. No sooner are they completed than the strings plunge into fateful chromaticism *crescendo*, answered by inexorable woodwind.

This quickly leads to G minor, the key of Ilia's first aria out of which an anguished D minor phrase for first violins appears aloft, confirming the melancholy serious-ness of the contents, especially against sustained wind and agitated second violin scurrying. Mozart recollects himself and turns back to D major pomp. On the way formally to the dominant A major there is another awe-inspiring phrase that draws attention to an unbridgeable gap, surely between the gods and humanity.

It hints at A minor, and that sure enough is the key of the second subject, distraught even with its galant snaps.

There is a magical transition from doleful A minor to sunny C major and back, whereupon A major at last arrives, confirming Ex. 2 and bringing back Ex. 1. Almost at once D major is resumed and the reprise is here; this is virtually a binary-form overture. The second subject has to stick to the major home key and is therefore adjusted to match the musical background. But the D major tonic cadence is postponed by a dominant pedal over which G minor is momentarily and expressively re-introduced—rapacious string answers to the inviting woodwind interplay. When the tonic does return the rapacity, referring back to the unbridgeable gap, is set against this interplay. The descending phrases for flute then oboe, shadowed by violins still over a tonic pedal, look forward to the expectant close of the *Don Giovanni* overture, first light visible through the darkness. The overture closes chromatically, still suggesting G minor.

The responsibility of a firm close is evaded though the music ends with three D major chords. They are not final, feel almost dominant rather than tonic because the end of the overture is, as in *Don Giovanni*, not a dead end but a door into the first act.

There is a minim's pause. We see the apartments of Ilia in Idomeneus's palace, a gallery in the background. Ilia is there and begins without introductory chord for harpsichord, her cue being the orchestra's last chord in the overture. This is less drastic than the jump into *Notte e giorno faticar* in *Don Giovanni*, but in an *opera seria*, with unaccompanied voice entering cold, more startling even. If the audience is granted an opportunity to applaud the overture, the spell is broken.

Ilia asks when her troubles will end. The harpsichord does support the middle of her first sentence. But the strings, *andantino*, enter as she gets to the question mark. This is an accompanied recitative, right at the beginning of the opera, a sign that new techniques were being applied to the decrepit formulae of *opera seria*. The accompanying figures are highly expressive. There is for example the violin phrase when Ilia mentions her unhappiness.

5

Some have even regarded this, like Ex. 4 above, as a recurring *Leitmotiv*. The music turns to *allegro* as she admits that the gods have revenged Troy for its sack. The Grecian fleet has sunk in a storm, with Idomeneus on board (this is where Leopold Mozart told his son to alter Varesco's 'Argiva' to 'Achiva', since the former word only refers to Argos, not the whole of Greece and Crete; but the change was never made). This section is dominated by a descending scale figure. Ilia confesses that, even if Idomeneus has perished, his son has enchained her heart. The paradox of emotions brings out an *agitato* jumping figure for first violins which is sufficiently unusual to deserve quotation.

6

Ilia feels loyalty to her father, gratitude to the captor who brought her here, love for his son. For her life is unfortunate, death would be sweet. Strings confirm her feelings in a wonderful consolatory phrase in E flat major, close to the world of Sarastro's priests in *Die Zauberflöte*.

7

Ilia is interrupted by thoughts that Idamantes's love has a more acceptable claimant in the Greek princess Electra, her rival. She and the strings become jealously inflamed by this notion. They end *adagio* on the verge of C minor. The strings edge towards G minor. Bassoons cut in to support their cadence. This is Ilia's **Aria, No. 1**, *Padre, germani, addio*, a miraculous portrait, because so typical of this heroine, for *opera seria*. The tempo is *andante con moto*, the key G minor, a G minor worthy of the 40th symphony K. 550, for its nobility, flexibility, gentle melancholy and warmth of feeling. Such an emotional aria at the beginning of the first act was at odds with the tradition of *opera seria*, in any case, because it set a tone of unsettled discontent, not the usual radiant optimism.

Oboes, bassoons and two horns (differently crooked, in C and B flat respectively, for convenience—they have little to play) join the strings for this aria which is marked *andante con moto*.

> Farewell, you who were my father and brothers; you are lost to me. Greece, you are the cause; how can I love a Greek? I would be disloyal to my own blood. Yet I cannot hate Idamantes's features.

There is no orchestral ritornello here or anywhere in the aria; there are no big formal cadences either. The music is designed to move forward purposefully all the time, making its points strongly, without need for structural emphasis. Ilia's turbulent emotions are conveyed at once in the offbeat violin accompaniment—it returns for the second subject, *D'ingrata al sangue mio*—in the powerful, sinuous bass line, and in Ilia's broken, tearful phrases, notably the poignant falling seventh on the second *Voi foste*.

With her cry of 'Grecia!', pre-echoed by second horn with oboes and bassoons, the music switches abruptly to B flat major. Ilia repeats this cry almost at once, a tone higher and more pained; in the second half of the aria she will reverse the pitch of these cries for new impact. At the moment Mozart is establishing the relative major (B flat) by shoving up the peripheries of its dominant, with choppy violin figures and longheld wind notes, until an outraged German sixth ('how can I love a Greek?') drives the music on to that dominant for the second subject. Here again the bass line, a phrase similar to one in the overture, is determined and strong-featured, as if a parental reproach which moves her to admit the disloyalty. And yet, and yet—she cannot help loving her enemy: 'ma quel sembiante' is set to an anguished high-lying phrase, sparsely accompanied for emphasis by contrast. The inventive detail is typical of *Idomeneo*.

9

ma quel sem—bian-te,oh Dei!   o—dia————re an-cor—   non so.

This second group is repeated, with extra sustained wind chords, and extended with a short, fluent roulade in triplets. At the cadence, which marks the end of the first half, Mozart instantly jerks onward and upward, reaching G minor and Ex. 8 in three tense bars during which Ilia has already begun to sing *Padre, germani*. The bridge passage involves a new bar to retain the same tonality for the music of Ex. 9, all the more poignant in its revised G minor form. The florid extension is more richly textured and more doleful. At the cadence Mozart again rushes onward, into C minor for a secco recitative which ensues without pause.

Ilia sees Idamantes with his attendants coming towards her; she prays that her inner torment may be still for a moment. The prince orders his followers to assemble the Trojan prisoners and prepare the court for celebration. He tells Ilia that festivities are due because the fleet of Idomeneus has been sighted not far away. Ilia agrees that this is the work of Minerva, protectress of the Greeks; only the Trojans are unloved by the gods. Idamantes intends to alleviate their sorrows by freeing Ilia and all the Trojan prisoners—adding that he alone will remain enslaved, by her beauty, knowing that she can never love him. Impressed as she is by his bold words, allying his plight with the murder of Agamemnon, and Idomeneus's misfortunes at sea, as part of Venus's revenge on the Greeks for their victory in Troy, Ilia asks Idamantes to remember, when he talks of love, who his father is and who hers was.

This cannot be described as a humdrum or unresponsive recitative. The supporting harmonies move quite boldly and with the changing moods of the conversation (e.g., Ilia's references to the devastation of Troy). Towards the end the bass line begins to move jerkily, signifying Idamantes's ardent unrest, then in grave broken chords when Ilia tells him to ponder their parentage.

Idamantes answers her in a big, elaborate **Aria, No. 2,** *Non ho colpa* in B flat major which adds clarinets to the oboes, bassoons, horns and strings. This consists of an *adagio maestoso* introduction followed by a ternary *allegro con spirito*. As befits a prince and a *castrato* the music is rather formal and heroic, though an insensitive conductor could make it sound flippant and ignoble. But such orchestral ritornelli as there are were kept short. The clarinets give warmth to the aura of pomp. The *allegro* is softened by a number of larghetto cadences which suggest opportunity for expressive vocal flourishes; and the slow introduction is richly scored, especially in its chromatic string writing and contrary motion between oboes and first violins.

> I am not to blame, yet you condemn me for loving you, my beloved.
>
> You, tyrannical gods, are to blame. I am dying in torment for a fault that is not mine.
>
> If you command me, I will slit my breast open. I read it in your eyes, but you must say it with your mouth. I ask for nothing more.

The first sentence above belongs to the *adagio*, the second to the start of the *allegro*, the third to the second group, though strictly 'Se tu il brami' is still part of the transition since it is based on the dominant's dominant, and F major is not openly heard until 'ma me'l dica il labbro', the broad tune with the *larghetto* cadences. But the proportions of the aria assign a second subject group status to 'Se tu il brami'. Remembering Mozart's strong reservations about Del Prato's musical capabilities, we may be surprised that he assigned such testing chromatic music to the young singer as the following from the coda group.

When the end of the exposition is reached the orchestra adds four bars of ritornello whereupon we may expect a return to the *adagio* especially as the text returns to the first sentence translated above. However, Mozart decides to retain the *allegro* tempo so he sets up a pedal note F and plants contemplative figures above it, once broken by an aggressive reference to B flat major whereafter the F regains its original dominant function. The B flat minor references ('Idol mio perchè t'adoro') touch the heart with their warm orchestration and vocal appoggiaturas. Turning as they do, with a rapid vocal flourish, into the brightly sunlit B flat major of the reprise, this intermezzo between dominant and tonic has a rapt, first-light effect, one that Mozart loved to evoke (as in the overture here, though especially at moments of dramatic resolution before a jubilant finale). In the reprise the coda group is further extended, with heroic orchestral exclamations to introduce a vocal cadenza and a short closing ritornello. This brings the first musical pause since the start of the overture.

Idamantes does not, however, make a formal exit. The Trojan prisoners are brought on and he commands them to be freed from their chains. Helen of Troy, he remarks, sent Greece and Asia to war. Now let them be united by bonds of friendship, inspired by another princess, still fairer and more lovable—Ilia, of course.

The peoples of Troy and Crete welcome his announcement in a **Chorus, No. 3**, *Godiam la pace* in G major, *allegro con brio*, with oboes, bassoons, horns and strings (some divided violas) to accompany the SATB chorus which includes two Cretan female and two Trojan male soloists.

> Let us enjoy peace, let love triumph and all hearts rejoice.
>
> CRETANS Give thanks to him who extinguished the torch of war. Now the earth can take its rest.
>
> TROJANS We owe freedom to you, kindly gods, and your lovely eyes, princess.

Choral movements of this kind were an importation from France. French too is the character of the music with its fizzing orchestral trills and busy string writing, as well as its solo episodes separated by choral refrains.

While they are all basking in this delightful atmosphere of international amity, in storms the jealous and angry princess Electra, as unwelcome as Carabosse at Aurora's christening, and as determined to put a spoke in the wheel of jubilation. Idamantes firmly waves away her complaint that his kindness to the Trojans is upsetting his and her compatriots. The party is effectively broken up, not by Electra but by Arbaces who enters to announce that Idomeneus, so close to harbour, has been shipwrecked and drowned. Idamantes at once instructs everyone to hurry to the shore. Are not his sufferings, he asks Ilia, equal to hers at last? Ilia admits that she cannot remain unmoved by the fate of the heroic Cretan monarch, and she follows the others.

Idamantes's appeal to Ilia induced the start of an orchestrally accompanied recitative (strings alone) that began with agitated string scales, turned more pathetic then, after Ilia's exit, settles on a brooding melancholy figure as Electra, left alone, contemplates the implications of Idomeneus's demise. She regards it as the death knell for all her hopes since Idamantes, once installed as king, will certainly give his hand and crown to the hated Trojan woman whom Electra, like a typical chauvinist, regards as no better than a slave. Ilia's preference would bring shame on Argos and its royal line (it is easy to see how Wallerstein was able to use this as a cue for theories of racial purism). Electra's self-pity finds expression in pathetic sequential string phrases that creep chromatically through C minor, B minor, and A minor, ultimately exploding in the D minor of her **Aria, No. 4**, *Tutte nel cor vi sento*, for which Mozart brings out four horns and a flute to enhance the regular orchestra of oboes, bassoons and strings; the violas are much divided.

I feel you all in my heart, furies of harsh hell. From such great torment love, mercy, pity are far removed. She who stole his heart, he who betrayed my own, shall know my rage, revenge and cruelty.

Electra's recitative cadenced on a bare orchestral A, thus starting the aria expectantly on the dominant. Above the popping bassoons the violins shiver furtively and the icy flute describes broken chords, *allegro assai*, avoiding direct reference to D minor until the voice enters. As the furies boil up in Electra's heart so does the orchestral storm. She addresses the furies in wild vocal leaps slashed by full orchestral chords to which flute and horns contribute a white-hot strength. When these chords cease, the second violins are left scrubbing away below, like the bubbling of a deep volcanic abyss. 'Lunge a si gran tormento' seems almost too lachrymose, with its Phrygian seconds, for such unconstrained anger but it prepares for the explosive dynamism of 'Chi mi rubò quel core', its spiky violin rockets answered by flute, and its chugging middle strings. Electra's shouts about 'furore', against disjunct motion strings, and 'crudeltà' sound the note of Donna Elvira, but Electra is presented as a much more dangerous vessel of wrath (ironically enough her jealousy gets her nowhere). We are now into F major and the second group but the musical momentum is such that there is no feeling of architectural thematic groups, only perhaps a change of key-temperature (from bad-tempered

D minor to its bad-tempered relative major) and, when 'provin' dal mio furore' is repeated, of more tempestuous orchestration and a voice growing breathless with venom. The blustering central ritornello soon comes dramatically to a stop on a diminished seventh (a later composer would have required a drumroll here but Mozart is saving his trumpets and drums for public demonstrations). Whereupon the reprise apparently begins in the wildly foreign key of C minor (relevant, however, to the next chorus) which, having caused a shock, is quickly replaced by the true home key of D minor. Some creative variants keep the reprise in this key. At the end Electra leaves the stage; the orchestral postlude, still stormy and now involving two flutes, systematically wipes away D minor to substitute an approach to C minor for the next scene which represents the shore of the tempestuous sea. Fragments of wrecked ships have been flung ashore by the savage tide. The people of Crete are watching appalled. Out at sea their cries for heaven's compassion are answered by those of the shipwrecked sailors who are swimming for their lives. Without musical interruption Mozart has moved into this double **Chorus, No. 5,** *Pietà, numi, pietà,* retaining the same tempo and scoring as before, having only changed the key with the scenery and with just the same promptness (eighteenth-century sets could be changed simply by pulling a lever).

ALL   Have pity, gods, help, turn your eyes towards us.
SAILORS   Sky, sea, wind, all fill us with terror.
TOWNSFOLK Cruel destiny drives them to a harsh death.

The music strides inexorably forward in C minor while the two male choruses, on and off stage, answer one another dramatically. A block-chord passage for the sailors is accompanied by drooping woodwind counterpoints on a figure which Richard Strauss regarded as leimotivic, and which we may warily agree does recur throughout the opera, if only because Mozart was writing in long spans suitable for quasi-symphonic integration.

The sailors' cries of 'Pietà' grow fainter. The chorus on stage scatters. The orchestral figures derived from Ex. 11 turn towards E flat, then A flat. Idomeneus and his (obligatory though nowadays omitted) attendants scramble out of the sea, thankful to be saved. The music, still for the same full orchestra, pursues its flowing figurations into gradual serenity and E flat major. There is a hint of the drooping motiv from Ex. 1. Idomeneus, in secco recitative, asks his followers to leave him here alone for a while so that he may pray to the gods. A short and solemn *andante* string passage composes his thoughts for communion with Neptune. He remembers the fearful vow he made during the storm: that, if he came safely to land, he would sacrifice on the sea god's altar the first human being he met. He now entreats the gods to save him from the consequences of this brutal and rash oath. Again, as in Idamantes's recitative before No. 2, the bass line asserts itself in convulsive jerks.

Mozart subsequently scored these last bars as a string-accompanied recitative, involving a sizable cut of Idomeneus's soliloquy.

In his first **Aria, No. 6**, Idomeneus imagines himself haunted for the rest of his life by the ghost of the unfortunate mortal whom he must sacrifice. *Vedrommi intorno* is in C major, *andantino sostenuto* followed by *allegro di molto*. The orchestra consists of flutes, oboes, clarinets, bassoons, horns and strings.

> I shall see the doleful ghost that, night and day, will indicate its innocence to me. Stabbed in the chest its bloodless body will point out my crime.
> What fear, what grief! How many times my tortured heart will die!

If one inspects the *andantino* for evidences of Idomeneus's musical characterization —reasonable since this is his first cantabile music—it may well seem curiously noncommittal and unilluminating. The text, however, will show that Idomeneus's music is portraying not him but the spectre evoked by his already guilty conscience. So at least I would explain the static bass at the beginning, the sense of wonder in the first woodwind chords, the rising arpeggios for first violins, elucidated in the singer's phrase 'l'ombra dolente', and its echo by clarinets and horns. These all derive from Idomeneus's initial entry, as follows:

The developmental process continues when the music turns into C minor (suitably spectral key), and the same thematic germ returns during the dominant G major second group of ideas. This group, it must be said, would more convincingly express Don Ottavio's courtly love for Donna Anna than the ghost's dumb accusation of the guilty king. Nevertheless it is beautifully invented and scored, especially for woodwind: the doubling of flute, clarinet and bassoon in octaves towards the end of the *andante* is affecting and characteristic Mozart.

The *allegro di molto* second half of the aria has more to say about Idomeneus himself and the terror with which he faces the murderous task he has sworn to carry out as thanksgiving to Neptune. The *andante* having cadenced in G major, the *allegro* at once moves in shudders towards C minor which is achieved by 'Di tormento'—popping strings answered by woodwind, then a dynamic swerve on to the dominant of C major. This whole passage, from the advent of C minor, is repeated, sometimes with fuller scoring and with a new extended conclusion involving Idomeneus in a mild running division (kindness to the veteran Raaff). A short orchestral coda breaks away from C major to A minor for secco recitative, as Idomeneus sees a man approaching, Neptune's chosen sacrificial victim. Once again Idomeneus recoils in horror at his destined deed. But instead of admitting his own rashness and impiety in having sworn the oath he accuses the gods of injustice. His behaviour, we may begin to fancy, is not that of a hero and sovereign.

Idamantes enters, grieving for the death of his father. Seeing among the ship-wreck's jetsam a solitary surviving warrior the prince seeks to comfort him and asks what favours he ca: ' estow on the castaway. It is twenty years since he set eyes on his father, and neither recognizes the other. The king answers that he should reward the young man for rescuing him. During the course of a long dialogue full of asides by both characters (Mozart cut it heavily because Raaff and Del Prato made a hash of it), Idamantes reveals that he is sorrowing for Idomeneus who is his father. At once the orchestra (flutes, oboes, bassoons, horns, strings) enters *presto* in D major; Idomeneus, horror-struck, addresses the young man as his son. Idamantes is overjoyed. The orchestra's comment on his *trasporto* may or may not be derived consciously from Ex. 4 in the overture; Mozart does make use of it later in the opera, and Strauss in his edition of *Idomeneo* treated it as a *Leitmotiv* of the father–son element in the drama.

Much to Idamantes's astonishment his father at once rushes away, refusing the filial embrace and declaring darkly that it would have been better they had not seen one another, and that Idamantes must take good care to avoid his father's company. Idamantes is perplexed and scared by this behaviour: how has he offended Idomeneus? A hysterical repeated woodwind figure accompanies his soliloquy; it must represent the father's rather than the son's fear.

When Idamantes expresses his urge to follow the King and find out what is wrong, the strings again quote Ex. 13, cadence in D minor and at once scurry away in F major, *allegro*. This is **No. 7**, Idamantes's **Aria**, *Il padre adorato*, scored for flute, oboe and bassoon (one of each), two horns and strings. Again there is virtually no orchestral introduction; as soon as tempo and rhythm have been established Idamantes begins to sing.

> I have found my adored father again and lost him; he flees from me outraged and horror-struck. I thought I would die of joy and love. Now, cruel gods, I am killed by grief.

Idamantes was characterized in No. 2 as Prince; now we meet him as devoted and sensitive son. The musical character of No. 7 is determined and insistent as though sparked off by Idamantes's 'vo seguirlo e veder' a moment ago. So much we sense from the rushing first violin semiquavers, the dogged bass line and the strong initial vocal phrases, interrupted as the young man ruefully reflects 'e lo perdo'. But off he goes again into his determined music. After a firm first-group cadence in F the wind propose D minor for 'Morire credei', a bridge passage that moves to the dominant. However, what plainly stands as the second subject-group begins unequivocally in the dominant minor, as in the overture. Ex. 15 shows this and the very late admission of C major, just before the return to the tonic for the binary reprise.

The cadence in C major is curiously bland, even more so at its varied reprise in F major where the music could well have come from the proletarian heart of Susanna or even Blondchen. On the other hand the first tune of Ex. 15 sounds even more affecting when it is recapitulated in F minor with flute and bassoon in octaves. The aria ends with a nice, perhaps rather too placid dying fall. The pause here is virtually the first since the recitative following No. 3—another long span, like the start of the opera.

The Cretan army, such of it as has survived the storm, now disembarks and is welcomed home with jubilation and dancing by the local womenfolk. Mozart accompanies this with a D major **March, No. 8** in which trumpets and timpani are added to the orchestra already in use. This constitutes the beginning of the first act finale, since the march leads into the concluding chorus *Nettuno s'onori!*

The march is conventionally brilliant and pompous, constructed out of familiar rococo tags and wriggling French trills; the delectable woodwind scoring of the second theme should not escape notice even so, less still at its D major reprise with added horns.

The final **Chorus, No. 9**, is subtitled *Ciaccona*. Although this is the Italian for Chaconne or Chacony, it does not here signify a ground-bass movement but merely a triple-time dance, common in French operatic finales, pervaded by the rhythm of the chorus's first entry: ∪ / – – ∪ / – –. The choral writing is simple, block-chordal. As in No. 3 there are solo episodes for two women, then two men, then for the full quartet of choral soloists. After the choral reprise the orchestra moves to G major for another female duet, now in G major, 2/4, *allegretto* (it may recall the bridal scene in *Figaro*) with delicate accompaniment, each newly added pair of instruments creating a strong effect. The return to the opening music is clumsily made. The *coda* builds gradually, freshly and vigorously to its and the act's conclusion. Daniel Heartz, in the NMA, argues that this and the preceding movement probably involved ballet as the Intermezzo after Act I which ended with Idamantes's No. 7.

5

Act II begins in Idomeneus's regal apartments. The King is confiding his problem to the trusty Arbaces who is described as his confidant and who probably instructed him in the principles of monarchy before he ascended the Cretan throne—a sort of Mazarin to Idomeneus's Louis XIV.*

Idomeneus recalls, in recitative, the anger of Neptune at the Achaean victory in Troy, and the revenge taken by the sea god with the aid of Aeolus and Jove when the victorious armies set sail for home. He relates the circumstances of his oath at sea and reveals that the victim must be Idamantes—unless Arbaces can devise some way to save the young prince from sacrifice. Arbaces proposes that Idamantes shall leave the country at once or rather, since Neptune would certainly pursue him at sea, conceal himself from the Cretan populace until Neptune has been conciliated (presumably by some other poor victim) and the cause of Idamantes been championed by other gods. Idomeneus, who sees Ilia approaching, proposes that Idamantes shall take Electra back to Argos. This is obviously an unwise plan since it involves a sea voyage. However, Arbaces is instructed to make preparations and advise Idamantes, always keeping the king's oath a secret.

Before departing to carry out these orders Arbaces sings his stipulatory **Aria, No. 10**, *Se il tuo duol*, an *allegro* in C major with oboes, horns and strings. Perhaps because Arbaces is an elder statesman, and because Panzacchi was a singer of the older generation, Mozart gives him an old-style sonata-form aria of exactly the kind he was getting away from in *Idomeneo*, the kind that he had been obliged to write for Salzburg taste and which he had contrived to shorten until it turned into a concise binary instead of sprawling ternary movement. He may have been minded to return to the old structure because Varesco's text for this aria is so stilted and elaborate. Mazarin, in fact, is telling Louis that monarchy is responsible and perilous.

> If my desire could banish your troubles they would vanish quickly, so ready am I to obey you.
> These are the hazards of kingship. Whoever covets it must look and learn. Avoid it or do not complain if you only find it a penance.

The tone of the aria is set by its fairly long orchestral introduction which exposes a bland yet dignified first group including contrapuntal violins, and a coda group also polyphonic and imitative. Worthy old Panzacchi was evidently not too

---

* In Mozart's Vienna performance on 13 March 1786 Act II began with a recitative for Ilia and Idamantes followed by Idamantes's aria *Non temer* mentioned above (p. 256). This was described by Mozart as 'for Bar. Pulini and Count Hatzfeld'. The latter played the violin obbligato in the aria. If it were not for the duet K. 489, where Idamantes's part is carefully written in the tenor clef, we might suppose that Pulini was a Baroness and a soprano for it is in this clef, as in the original score, that K. 490 is written. In December of 1786 Mozart set the same aria text and Idamantes's part in the preceding recitative *Ch'io mi scordi di te?* as a concert aria for Nancy Storace with piano obbligato for Mozart himself.

Even if we assume that Baron Pulini transposed soprano into tenor clef (as in the 1781 portions of the score he would have to) the problems of K. 490 do not disappear. Ilia does not declare her love for Idamantes until Act III. Yet here she is addressing him as 'mia vita', and he talks of going off to face death. Granted that she urges him to go off with Electra ('your love is well known') and forget her. But the journey to Argos with Electra is not suggested until later in Act II. The German translation of this recitative is even less intelligible. Several of Ilia's sentences must be intended for Idamantes, others make no sense in any *Idomeneo* context. The aria is elegant and beautiful but not to be considered as part of the opera, any more than the magnificent version 'for Mad. Storace and me'.

decrepit to take over one of these agile polyphonic voices in his first group and he must still have had a strong top A, approached from D an octave and a half below, for the end of the reprise. Mozart made a feature of these wide leaps, and also implied that Panzacchi had a good legato technique; his staying power must have been robust too since the vocal part is active and the aria long, even though there are orchestral ritornellos to rest the voice. Nevertheless we do notice that the orchestral music is strongly characterized and inventive, full of interest, so that the audience would enjoy the aria even if the singer were not up to scratch. We also observe that, compared with the big sonata-form arias in, say, *Lucio Silla*, this one is structurally much more compact even though, in the context of *Idomeneo*, it seems long and mannered. As such the aria is often omitted in modern performance. If the Arbaces is a skilful artist this a a pity; and doubly so because Mozart clearly intended a different style of music at this point. Arbaces makes a conventional exit after his aria.

Ilia has come to find Idomeneus. She congratulates him on his return to his subjects. He assures her that she will find happiness after all her sufferings. She replies that he and his son have already showered her with kindness; she expected hostility but her troubles have borne sweet fruit. She explains herself in the **Aria, No. 11**, *Se il padre perdei* in E flat major, *andante ma sostenuto*. Mozart here paid tribute to his good friends the principal wind players of the Munich orchestra, reviving the old practice of the aria with multiple instrumental obbligato, in this case for flute, oboe, bassoon and horn.

> I have lost my father, my country and my peace, but you are a father to me. Crete is a lovely place to stay and I no longer remember my troubles. Heaven has given me joy and contentment.

The fourteen bars of orchestral introduction are most eventful. Besides supplying an opening theme for Ilia and a curtain-raiser for the wind quartet's dual entry as an ensemble and as soloists, it includes a useful coda-group. And it evokes a strong, cogent atmosphere: two, indeed, since the intensity of the low-lying first phrase (to be sung by Ilia an octave higher with a quite different effect of cool ecstasy) and its *Bildnisarie* corollary—see Ex. 12 in *Die Zauberflöte*—here rendered the more intense by the pulsating middle pedal on second violins, is contrasted with the gentle sparkle of the flute's descending scale, repeated a moment later by bassoon, and of the confidential coda group. This is not only Ilia but Wolfgang saying 'Thank you' for a happy stay: 'soggiorno amoroso è München per me'. Indeed that very sentence (Crete being substituted for Munich) is introduced by another woodwind divertimento-like theme, the opening idea of the second group. Its second leg, 'or gioja e contento', has a horn counterpoint made out of a dominant pedal (the dominant of B flat major, that is); the idea is at once repeated (standard procedure in *Idomeneo*), Ilia's tune now shared with oboe and bassoon to even more rapturous effect. The final leg is devoted to scales and repeated notes, classroom stuff that attains the leisurely everlasting bliss of heaven (Ex. 16).

The coda-group idea mentioned above is now, as central ritornello, reassigned to strings. Four notes from 'gioja e contento' are picked out and slowed down by wind quartet; strings add a cadence clinching the return to E flat, and Ilia joins them for the recapitulation. 'Soggiorno amoroso' now begins in the subdominant so as

16

to keep on the right side of the tonic. But 'Or più non rammento' is re-set in E flat major with heartfelt descending sevenths for the singer; and the wind repeat of 'gioja e contento' is enhanced by an Alberti accompaniment for the horn. Ex. 16's scales are now extended. There is a new coda idea and the middle ritornello recurs, now in E flat entirely. There is no more sheerly beautiful or perfectly self-expressive number than this in any of Mozart's operas.

No wonder that, as Ilia walks away, Idomeneus's recitative should be accompanied by string reminiscences of themes from No. 11, first 'soggiorno amoroso', then the coda group. Idomeneus is wondering, as we may have wondered, how Ilia can claim to be happy, her sorrows forgotten, when she had been speaking about them most committedly only a few minutes earlier. Can the cause be love, and for Idamantes, and must it not be reciprocated? The strings comment now with a new idea, roughly in D major, and so evocative of woodwind scoring that I wonder whether Mozart had planned to include it in *Se il padre perdei*.

17

The king now has his second **Aria, No. 12**, *Fuor del mar* in D major, *allegro maestoso*, scored for flutes, oboes, bassoons, horns, trumpets, drums and strings.

> No longer at sea I still feel an ocean in my breast, not less deadly than the real one, nor less menaced by Neptune.
>
> Proud deity, at least tell me if my heart is as close to shipwreck as when fate saved my body from destruction at sea.

The aria exists in two versions: the *Gesamtausgabe* prints Mozart's less taxing version as an appendix. This omits several long and arduous florid divisions, a rhythmically difficult passage, and the final unwritten-out cadenza. Nowadays such tenors as attempt the role of Idomeneus gladly accept this shorter version, even when their voices are not yet on the decline as Raaff's was. In the 1951 Glyndebourne production Richard Lewis, then in his early prime, sang an abbreviation of the second version but included the cadenza from the first version. Peter Pears, at fifty-nine an exceptionally impressive Idomeneus vocally and histrionically, preferred to omit the aria altogether. In the recording conducted by Colin Davis the Idomeneus is George Shirley who sings the first version and shows it to be both feasible and dramatically preferable. On stage we may find a middle-aged Idomeneus most credible: he has an adult son and manifests a pious fear associated with the old rather than the young. But he has got to sing like a monarch. Modern singers have been trained to declaim lustily and perhaps imperiously; but florid singing is seldom part of an incipient Tristan's technical armoury, and Idomeneus is a role for a tenor of Tristan quality. Do not expect in the opera house to hear the long first version sung. Merely be grateful when you do hear Idomeneus declaim such a passage as the following:

The orchestral introduction is spacious and imposing, representative of Idomeneus's regal personality and, secondarily but equally relevant, his anxiety. Thus in Ex. 19 the conventional fanfares are followed by the tremulous semiquaver theme, taken up in imitation; and in (b) the pompous flute tune, already proposed as a coda subject, acquires an off-beat, disquieted countertheme and an accompaniment of slippery descending scales.

The bass line is uncreatively static, but Mozart must have associated tonic and dominant pedal basses with the royal personages of his early *opere serie* when he was still dutifully aping admired galant models. Emotional involvement begins with the singer's falling sevenths at 'che del primo', and is pursued in the first violin phrase accompanying his long notes for 'funesto'. The orchestra is busy all the time, often imitatively (did Mozart here, and in Arbaces's music, instinctively call on the old musical techniques which were home ground to elderly singers?),

19a

Allegro maestoso

and always inventively. There is, for instance, an appropriate boil-up on diminished seventh harmony, with thematic imitation between bass and wind, at 'mai non cessa minacciar' just before the division quoted as Ex. 18. As elsewhere in *Idomeneo* the dominant beginning of the second subject group is enigmatically obfuscated: we know when A major is there but Mozart refrains from telling us directly so as not to interrupt the forward movement of the music.

The central orchestral ritornello confirms A major then turns away towards the mediant F major for 'Fiero Nume!' and more imitative counterpoint. A feature of the vocal part here is pauses (for improvised flourishes perhaps?) that lead directly into the next musical sentence. A short imitative orchestral interlude leads the way from F sharp minor back to D for the recapitulation which is still newly eventful.

In the original version of the opera the music comes to a halt at the end of this aria. But Idomeneus remains on stage, observing the approach of a radiantly happy Electra. She thanks him for his kindness in giving her Idamantes as companion on her homeward journey, adding a characteristically sour reference to the decline of certain proud and rebellious persons (Ilia is presumably meant). Mozart also set this more briefly in accompanied recitative growing out of the aria, and left a version in which the close of *Fuor del mar* leads directly into accompanied recitative, in C major, where Electra alone on the stage, Idomeneus having made a formal exit, congratulates herself on her good fortune, and expresses her optimistic hopes of winning Idamantes once they are at sea and rid of Ilia's tiresome company.

We now see Electra at her happiest and most attractive; but Varesco takes care to remind us, even here, of her bitchier side. This accompanied recitative, orchestrally very charming, cadences in D and the same string orchestra, with *divisi* violas, launches her **Aria, No. 13**, *Idol mio*, in G major, *andante* and tenderly lyrical.

> My beloved, if another lover gives you unwillingly to me, I shall not be hurt by your severity, rather gladdened by your cool love.
>   Warmth near at hand will banish distant warmth from your breast. My heart beside you will inspire your hands to love.

The text of this aria is curious; E. J. Dent decided that 'Varesco has surpassed himself in obscurity'. I am inclined to congratulate the turbulent priest on the psychological awareness of his characterization at this moment when the virago Electra is to be presented in a gentle, affectionate light. Believing that now at last she has her chosen lover to herself, and that he will of course succumb to her charms on the voyage, Electra is sexually afraid, as domineering women often are. So she voices the hope that he will not attack her too ardently but just sit and hold hands until she is ready to be wooed. Mozart's music gives no indication that he appreciated these undertones (any more than did Schachtner in making his German version); it is simply a demure lyrical binary movement, harmonically uncomplicated but elegant and warm in texture, with plenty of parallel thirds for violas. The vocal line does lie rather high and may aptly suggest a certain nervous strain in Electra's personality.

As Electra reaches her last cadence, flutes, a bassoon, horns, trumpets and drums are heard playing **No. 14**, a **March**, very softly as if in the distance; Electra recognizes it as the signal for embarkation and hurries off to the harbour. The march is in C major but Electra's aria ended in G. Mozart therefore starts in the middle, as it were, just after the double bar, so as to get back to C major and then plays the whole march several times gradually growing louder (he repeated this effect in *Figaro* Act III and there are similar transformation effects in *Silla*) until we arrive, with Electra, at the harbour where the band is playing. To start with, the orchestra is muted and it was for this purpose that Mozart required brass mutes to be sent from Salzburg.

The scene changes during this march to show the harbour of Cydon with its fortifications. Electra, attended by Greek soldiers, Cretan townsfolk and sailors, addresses the Cydonian shores where she has been so unhappy but which she now salutes joyfully and in friendship as she leaves them. After she has delivered this backhanded greeting the assembled crowd goes straight into the **Chorus, No. 15**, *Placido è il mar* in E major, *andantino* with flutes, clarinets, horns and strings.

ALL The sea is calm; let us go. Everything is reassuring, fortune is favourable, let us leave now.

ELECTRA Gentle zephyrs, blow alone and calm the anger of the cold north wind. Let peaceful breezes waft kindly for love of us all.

ALL The sea is calm, *etc.*

This lilting Siciliano is an idyllic point of repose at the centre of strong drama, literally the calm before the storm. The chorus, which frames Electra's solo verse on both sides (a device that Mozart had from Gluck), is strongly shaped. The contour and rhythm of the first three notes are developed at 'tutto, tutto', emerging as the even downward scale that is taken up in imitation at 'sù, sù! partiamo or, or' and 'felice avrem'; the harmonic pointing hereafter is particularly winning (e.g. the loud seventh chord on the leading-note for woodwind, held for a full bar) and the melodic line strains gratefully up to G sharp, its top note, the second time with a gentle elaboration for violins. The woodwind colouring too is applied with miraculous sensibility, flutes for airiness, clarinets for warmth; notice, for instance, the exquisite effect of the held flute octaves in Electra's first line, at 'Zeffiri', drawing the ship in imagination across the placidly rocking water along with Electra's rapturous cantabile line; then the horn pedal note as her solo moves towards B major and becomes more florid, sailing up to top B; then the flute's bridge, imitated from the violin accompaniment figure, back to the choral reprise.

On the last chord of the chorus, the strings burst into an energetic *allegro* phrase. Idomeneus bustles an unwilling Idamantes on to the boat with exhortations to good deeds. Idomeneus, we must remember, is uneasy about being seen with his son at all, and anxious to get him away as quickly as possible before Neptune catches up with them. They nevertheless say goodbye in an extended **Terzetto, No. 16**, *Pria di partir*, which emerges from the preceding recitative moving into its F major tonality obliquely from forlorn D minor. Oboes and horns support the strings. The trio begins *andante* as Idamantes begs his father for a farewell kiss, and Electra gives grateful thanks to her gracious host, the 'degno sovran'. The pain of parting is in both their addresses to him. He answers more formally, and, with them, prays heaven to grant their entreaties, by which time the music has arrived in C major. The figuration, as Electra begins the next section 'Quanto sperar mi lice!', looks back to her solo in No. 15. Idamantes laments privately that he leaves his heart behind. They say goodbye, and contrary motion and wailing oboes tauten and sadden the textures; there is a hint of F minor in Electra's cadential 'Che sara?', and a hint too of *Don Giovanni*, carried further in the F major *allegro con brio* which follows stormily—a tempest of the heart presaging what is to come. The close part-writing in this section particularly asks for a soprano Idamantes whose voice will blend with Electra's rather than Idomeneus's, for example in the running thirds at 'porgerà'.

They are asking heaven's blessing. As they embark a sudden storm arises at sea and the orchestra, by now with flutes, oboes, bassoons, four horns, as well as strings, bursts into F minor, *più allegro* with demoniacal rushes for violins and heavily pulsating background chords. Softly shuddering violins introduce a new **Chorus, No. 17**, *Qual nuovo terrore* which continues the ferocious storm music, now in C minor and with a piccolo added to the orchestra. Wide dynamic contrasts and grandiose full chords as well as rushing scales characterize this section. At the height of the thunderstorm a formidable monster rises at sea, to a burst of imposing B flat minor, and is recognized as Neptune's emissary. Who, the chorus cries, is the guilty party? Three times they ask and loud woodwind chords echo them. The fourth time Idomeneus answers, admitting (to heaven but not to the people) his guilt in a powerful accompanied recitative, and begging heaven to punish him alone and not the innocent victim (a poignant passage for woodwind alone) of his oath. He appeals, *adagio*, and with a phrase of moving intensity on a rising sixth, to Neptune not to make unjust demands. His defiance is heroic, and also hubristic. Varesco intended an aria here but Mozart refused to stop his tempest for any singer. The storm continues, *allegro assai*, in D minor, with full orchestra except clarinets, in **No. 18**, the last **Chorus** of this act, *Corriamo, fuggiamo*. Wrathful Neptune can be heard striding purposefully towards the proud rash king, as the chorus lament this disaster and scatter in terror. The woodwind writing here is particularly marvellous, and indeed the choral phrase, applied contrapuntally, which suggests the succession of huge rolling breakers crashing on to the quay.

20

[Allegro assai]

The storm seems to fade out of earshot as the crowd disperses. D minor turns to
its major, the texture thins out to almost nothing. The monster is still about and
the thunder and lightning may still remain active. Mozart has used music, as it
were, cinematically, removing the audience from a scene as theatre in his day could
not. The act ends in an uncomfortable serenity.

6

Act III begins in the gardens of Idomeneus's palace. Ilia is alone here, telling the
flowers and breezes how much it pains her to conceal her love from its object,
Idamantes. She says so in recitative. To a modern audience it often appears strange
to begin an operatic act with anything so dull and uncaptivating as a recitative. So
opera companies either begin these acts with a short orchestral piece in an appropriate key (and preferably from about the same period in the composer's creative
life) or cut the recitative, as would be feasible here, and start with the aria that
follows. To an eighteenth-century audience it was perfectly sensible to begin with
a recitative. There was no curtain to raise; it ascended at the start of the first act and
would not be lowered until the very end of the opera. Scenery was quickly
changed in view of the spectators. When they returned to their seats (if they had
left them for an interval, by no means *de rigueur*) a character walked on sta~
though nobody bothered to attend until the first aria beg~
the opera had begun again and who was on stage. If o·
was being sung one looked at the printed libretto·
lowered.

Those who do listen to Ilia's initial recitative may hear that it has string accompaniment and that it includes a conceivable forward reference in D major to the opening theme of the **Aria, No. 19**, *Zeffiretti lusinghieri* in E major, which she sings after the recitative. This, the third of Ilia's three consummately beautiful arias and the most sensuously beguiling of them, is marked *grazioso* and scored for flutes, clarinets, bassoons, horns and strings.

> Kind breezes, fly to my beloved and tell him that I adore him and that he should keep his heart faithful to me.
> And you trees and flowers, watered by my bitter tears, tell him that such uncommon love as mine has never been seen under the heavens.

The key of E major had strong associations of calm and consolation for Mozart, as for earlier and later composers (see Interchapter, p. 22). He used it rarely but for special effect. The garden setting, and the loving contentment that has settled here upon a charming heroine, must have made it an obvious choice for the sentiments of Varesco's text. Clearly too he needed flutes, clarinets and horns for their associations with such a mood. The orchestral introduction, quite long, establishes Ilia's mood in the first phrase, then proceeds to garden topics; the lightly floating semiquaver scales of the second idea, the hovering triplets in thirds, repeated against a balmy wind chord—ideas we associate with Mozart's divertimento *andantes*.

21a

When Ilia reaches Ex. 21b she expands it unhurriedly; the flutes' thirds above enhance the atmosphere. The transition ('e gli dite') has a bucolic doubling of clarinet and bassoon whose rising sixths are carried over into the second group ('Zeffiretti' again) for violin and voice, later flute as well, with bassoon. This time 'e gli dite' is gently pleading, echoed by flute and clarinet. The enriched chromatic harmony of 'che mi serbi' here, at its immediate repeat, rightly drew the attention of Dent ('no Italian composer would ever have thought of so delicate and so poetical an effect; or if anyone had vaguely imagined the feeling which it expresses, he would have interpreted it by a melodic variation of the vocal line, not by a change of accompanying harmony'—this is a Mozartian characteristic, typical of German, not Italian or French, music of the time). The repeat is also heightened by the addition of flutes. Here Ex. 21c joins the vocal exposition with a magical harmonic switch to the supertonic minor of B major. The second subject's first idea returns as central ritornello. Ilia begins again in E minor ('E voi piante') with a brief middle section based on Ex. 21b, turning with poignant harmonies to G major and new expressive ideas involving vocal swoops, always eloquent in Mozart, to a cadence on the dominant of E, with pause and probably flourish before the reprise arrives. The changes here are small but captivating. The final ritornello turns aside from E major to its subdominant for orchestral recitative, as Ilia sees her as yet unconfessed lover approaching. How can she retain composure in his presence? The strings intensify the dilemma with yet another reference to the recurrent theme of lovers, cited above as Ex. 4.

Idamantes's entry inaugurates a dialogue in formal secco recitative. He does not hope for his love to be requited but, because he loves her, has come to say farewell before going off to kill the monster, which has been devouring Cretans and destroying the land, or else be slain by it. His father shuns him but will not explain why: Idamantes assumes that his love for Ilia has roused Neptune's wrath. Ilia implores Idamantes not to risk his life: he is heir to an important throne and—she must now confess that she whole-heartedly returns his love. So of course Mozart brings the orchestral strings back to underline this revelation. They are in melancholy B minor for Idamantes's 'grand' ardore' and incredulity. Ilia regrets that family sorrows prevented her from declaring her love earlier. Now she has admitted it (a touching *larghetto* starting in F sharp minor, the key in which Idomeneus earlier suspected their mutual attraction) and, if he goes off to die, grief will certainly kill her too.

The music has reached the borders of A major in time for their **Duet, No. 20** with oboes, bassoons and horns, *S'io non moro a questi accenti*. This begins *un poco più andante*.

Idamantes expects to die of love and delight. Ilia assures him of her constancy. They pledge loving vows.

The pace quickens to *allegretto* as they sing together of the joy that banishes sorrow, of their invincible passion. It is a mellifluous but, in context, curiously stiff and unloving piece of music, though there is one redeeming touch where A minor is hinted at.

When Mozart found himself with a tenor Idamantes in Vienna he replaced this duet by a new one, *Spiegarti non poss'io*, specifically devised for soprano and tenor. This, entirely *larghetto*, scored for oboes, horns and strings, is emotionally more involved and eloquent, with telling oboe coloration, some affecting harmony and a heady contrapuntal passage, at 'non sa piacer', for the two voices and strings, after which Mozart brings back the strings' opening music as he had not done in the earlier version though the bars were there already. There is a gratifying florid run for soprano, promptly repeated for the tenor's benefit. Where a tenor is cast as Idamantes it is obviously sensible to perform this shorter but more inspired duet (as Glyndebourne did in the 1950s).

As the last chord sounds, Idomeneus and Electra interrupt the lovers, the king perturbed by awe, the Argive princess by angry jealousy. Idamantes firmly but submissively asks the king to say why he is angry with his son ('I could tell you,' mutters Electra). Idomeneus hints at Neptune's wrath which all a son's affection only aggravates. Idamantes still assumes that his love for Ilia is the cause. Electra longs to be the instrument of revenge. Idomeneus's solution is to send Idamantes far from Crete to make a home elsewhere. Ilia in despair tactlessly entreats Electra to console her; this is considered a crowning insult. Ilia offers to depart and die at her lover's side; strings have entered in melancholy accompaniment. But Idamantes tells her to remain behind.

I shall roam and seek death elsewhere until I find it.

Andrò ramingo e solo begins **No. 21**, a vocal **Quartet** in E flat major which has attained historic importance not only for its high musical quality and touching effect, but because it expresses separately and concertedly the contrasted sentiments of four characters, the regal bravery with which Idamantes faces his destiny, Electra's zeal for violent revenge, Ilia's sadness, Idomeneus's pious terror. Opera previously had used vocal ensemble as a substitute for the chorus, at the start or finish of a work, or as a substitute for the commentary of a classical Greek chorus, a composite reaction which the French called a *tableau*. The trio in Act II of *Idomeneo* did, rather stiffly, convey the emotions of three characters. *Andrò ramingo e solo* carries this development farther than any composer had yet done; it led to similar ensembles in later Mozart operas, to the canonic quartet in *Fidelio* which retains one tune but still manages to convey four predicaments, some marvellously expressive ensembles in Rossini and Donizetti and Verdi, and so on. E. J. Dent named this sort of ensemble the 'ensemble of perplexity', thinking perhaps of *Freddo ed immobile* in *Il barbiere di Siviglia* or *Questo è un nodo* in *La Cenerentola*. It describes this type of vocal concerted movement exactly. No doubt some other composer can be shown to have written such an ensemble before Mozart in *Idomeneo*—no great composer has ever made a complete innovation but has always borrowed another's experiment and perfected it for artistic viability.

No. 21 is scored for two flutes, two clarinets, bassoons, horns and strings, an orchestra calculated for human expressiveness in Mozartian terms. They launch the quartet, *allegro*, with a striking theme that plunges down the arpeggio of E flat major and continues onward, as Idamantes must, expectantly, doggedly.

The agogic rise to the tonic instantly conveys determination. Perhaps the pause of the melodic line does not strike home until Idamantes sings it while bassoon and low strings continue downwards—and he ends his phrase with an optimistic rise of a tone, before extending his statement for longer than the introduction led us to expect; he has far to go. Ilia breaks in, vowing to travel with him or else (desperate B flat minor) die with him. The harmony has moved impetuously forward to the dominant of the dominant, a step too far for classical procedure, and Idomeneus has broken its cadence by crying for Neptune's mercy and for his own death. He is joined by Electra's call for revenge. Ilia and Idamantes now sing together, asking Idomeneus's favour, and gradually all four voices are blended in an expectant, tense passage, poised as if on needles, about such suffering being worse than death. It climaxes in a powerfully chromatic cadence on the edge of B flat. Idamantes returns to his first assertion, tonally indeterminate; as he continues, Ilia breaks in sooner and more protestingly. Idomeneus and Electra are now set in stronger emotional contrast. Again the voices combine, three in empathy, but then all four in counterpoint ('soffrir più non si può'), with moments unaccompanied or heightened by bold wind chords. The curt string phrases ('Peggio di morte') now seem like peremptory demands by destiny, and full orchestra stresses this intensity as does anguished chromatic harmony until all stop on a dominant seventh. The first theme returns, as bare and desolate as before. Idamantes reiterates his willingness to go away alone. He leaves the orchestra to finish his statement, in broken phrases expressing the unhappiness in which he leaves the other three, even Electra—though the number does end with the classical repose of six tonic chords.

Arbaces now enters to announce that the assembled populace demands colloquy with the king. They are being encouraged in their insistence by the priest of Neptune. Idomeneus, well aware of the cause, goes off to parley. Electra and Ilia follow him. Arbaces is left behind so that Panzacchi could display his dramatic singing, which Mozart admired, in an orchestral recitative of remarkable musical quality but otherwise quite unjustified, and in a second aria.

Arbaces foresees the horrors to which Crete is doomed; the strings in G minor and D minor support him to the hilt. He does, however, hope that among all the gods one may take up the cause of Cydonia—a more optimistic rising seventh figure expresses his superstitious expectation. Then, with an *allegro* menaced by terrifying scale-figures, he sinks into pessimism, imagining the worst that the situation promises.

In his **Aria, No. 22**, an *andante* in A major, *Se colà ne' fati è scritto*, scored for strings alone, he nevertheless hopes that fate will favour Crete.

> If fate decides, o gods, that Crete must fall, let it pay the price but save the prince and the king.
> Be satisfied with one victim's blood; let it be mine, but have mercy on our people.

Again Mozart writes a full-scale ternary aria for Arbaces, amiably invented with plenty of thematic imitation, eventful string writing, some ingenious syncopations and a little fioritura as well as long vocal trills. An able comprimario tenor can do plenty with it, but it does not characterize Arbaces at all, not even as a shifty diplomat. And the whole episode holds up the drama at a moment when it has to move forward. Poor Arbaces! His arias are quite dispensable, but in the age of the gramophone he can record them separately and allow us to enjoy them at home away from the opera.

Arbaces's message has to be delivered, and the music has to move logically from the E flat major of the Quartet to the C major of **No. 23**, the **Maestoso**, which opens the next scene. This is musically feasible, if we accept some pitch-transposition in the recitative. It should end on the verge of C major.

Now the scene changes, according to Varesco—on the Munich first night Act III included no scene-shifting—to a great square in front of Idomeneus's palace. Idomeneus is accompanied by Arbaces and his retinue as well as the High Priest of Neptune and the populace. There is plenty of time for scene-changing during No. 23, the *maestoso* orchestral introduction for oboes, horns, trumpets and one drum with strings. The C major fanfares are followed by a *largo*, more thoughtful, A flat major passage, delicately scored in a low register with oboes above and flutes to mark a pause on a dominant seventh. There ensues an *allegro* beginning excitedly in B flat and moving to the dominant of C major. All this must convey something dramatic. Arguably the A flat bass indicates the entrance of a pensive Idomeneus, the C major opening the procession, the B flat *allegro* the populace's excitement. The High Priest first addresses Idomeneus, drawing his attention to the ravages of the predatory monster and instructing him, as sovereign, to end this plunder by going to the temple and ordering the necessary sacrifice. The dynamic orchestral music here is quite riveting, based on a short, hardly significant phrase that by repetition attains unexpected importance. The calm when the Priest calls for an answer is equally imposing. The orchestra at once identifies the victim with a variant of the father–son theme followed by another:

22

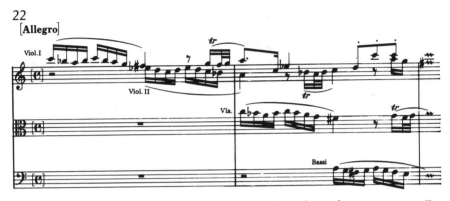

Idomeneus now confesses that Idamantes must die—the orchestra reverts to Ex. 4, reminding us of the consequences to Ilia. The father must slay the son. Having said this Idomeneus departs. The assembled people express their horror at this intelligence in **No. 24**, the **Chorus** in C minor, *O voto tremendo*, powerfully scored for full orchestra, *adagio*, without clarinets but with muted trumpets and drums. The orchestral approach to C minor, woodwind straining upwards by semitones, is mightily impressive, the horror emphasized by a rhythm for trumpets and drums. The harmony tightens its grasp with a Phrygian mode D flat, then attacks physically with a choral unison orchestrally backed up with a taut anguish we may rather associate with Verdi, especially when first violins cling to a top C and stab away at it ('palanca crudel'). The entreaties are passed to woodwind, made the more forlorn with sopranos alone, dolefully counterpointed. The harmony again heaves itself upwards until all return to the beginning, 'O voto tremendo', its horrified shock renewed by rich and detailed orchestral accompaniment. The chorus leaves the stage deeply depressed as the music ends, in a C major not bland but signifying a divine intention with which mortals cannot ever find contact. The C major cadence swerves towards F for the next scene which is set during **No. 25**, a **March** in F major for oboes and strings. In the Munich première no changes of scene took place. But Varesco prescribed them and the drama demands them. We must now view Neptune's temple, seen from outside, its visible altar being prepared for the necessary sacrifice. During this solemn, unpompous, Sarastro-like march (except that the flutes are missed), Idomeneus and the priest enter together with their respective retinues. Flutes, clarinets, bassoons and horns join the orchestra for the *adagio ma non troppo* **No. 26** in F major, which follows. It is a solemn **Duet** for Idomeneus and the **Chorus** of Priests, *Accogli, o rè del mar*, with an aqueous, quite unflippant plucked string accompaniment. They beg the god to accept his victim and restore calm to the ocean. Flutes and oboes, often used for charm by Mozart, now sound positively hieratic. The victim, Idamantes, had been sent away, we all know, and the god was certain to remain unpacified. They still pray, as eloquently as Mozart, with the mantle of Gluck close upon him, knew how to suggest prayer.

Proud fanfares from trumpets and drums break into the solemn rites. An offstage chorus announces victory and glory. Arbaces enters the temple to tell the king that Idamantes has slain the voracious dragon and returned safe and sound. But this, Idomeneus knows, will make Neptune all the more enraged. The crisis has been not alleviated but aggravated.

Idamantes appears, garlanded with floral trophies, surrounded by jubilant townsfolk as well as soldiers and priests. Idamantes, however, has learned the nature of his father's vow and is gladly ready to give his life on the altar for the good of the Cretan people. The string accompaniment makes copious reference to Mozart's father–son motif, more expressively than ever before. To Idomeneus's paternal objections his son insists that the sacrifice will benefit all Cretans by securing the favour of the gods. He only asks that Idomeneus will cherish Ilia as a daughter. This accompanied recitative is extended and full of eventful music, for voices as well as strings, a sublime *entente* between French and Italian styles. Since Idamantes proposes to be slaughtered at once upon the altar he has to sing another **Aria** before he dies. It is **No. 27**, *No, la morte* in D major for oboes, horns and strings.

> No, I do not fear death, if you, O gods, will give peace and love to my father and compatriots afterwards.
> I shall go contentedly to Elysium if my death brings calm to my beloved.

This is a vigorous and heroic aria, *allegro* with a *larghetto* middle section. The musical invention has its attractions, especially orchestral, and some briefly melodious. The slow section and fizzing *cabaletta* are most inspiriting but the whole suggests that Mozart was wilting under the incompetence of his castrato hero. In the event he removed that aria before the first performance, wisely. Idamantes goes straight into recitative, telling his father to obey Neptune without delay. They embrace a last time in *largo* D flat major, superb music. Idamantes thinks sadly of Ilia. But here she is, running to the altar and begging to die in her lover's place. The High Priest is appalled by this interruption and Electra cannot help remarking how differently she herself would have behaved. Ilia uses logic as her defence: Idamantes is innocent, furthermore the legitimate heir; the gods are not unjust, they merely want a victim, and Priam's daughter, fond as she is of Crete and its ruler-designate, will do quite well. All react diversely and consistently. The priest begs the King to make up his mind, which he will not since Ilia is not the chosen victim. Idamantes pleads with Ilia in a fine and fully scored G minor passage. She determines to die alone in his stead, and presents herself at Neptune's altar.

There is a terrific clap of thunder. Neptune's statue moves (did the High Priest press a button?). Below the stage **No. 28** begins: three trombones (nowhere else used in the opera and perhaps replaced by woodwind in the first production—trombones were only for church music or divine utterances in opera) and two horns intone solemn chords and Neptune's voice is heard announcing that Idomeneus must abdicate and Idamantes reign over Crete with Ilia as his consort. Mozart, concerned that the god's announcement should not be too long, set three different versions, increasingly brief. The longest is harmonically impressive and we may not want to do without it. But theatrical common sense supports Mozart: the supernatural is most impressive when it is most curtly manifested. Trombones give way to soft woodwind; the king, his son, Ilia and Arbaces give thanks. Only Electra is furious. Mozart indicated that the assembly should instantly leave her alone for her last outburst, a superb accompanied recitative which voices her frustration and intention to follow her brother Orestes to hell for ever and ever.

At the first performance Mozart, fearful that the opera would go on too long, took Electra off the stage here, writing a new accompanied recitative for her. He had, however, composed an exit **Aria** for her, the indispensable **No. 29**, *D'Oreste, d'Ajace*, grandly scored for full orchestra (no clarinets but four horns) and moving *allegro assai* from F minor to C minor.

> My breast feels the tortures that Orestes and Ajax knew; I am killed by Alecto's burning torch. Snakes, tear out my heart or else I will stab myself.

We can hardly imagine this aria omitted. It is the crowning impersonation of Electra and also a great piece of dramatic music by Mozart. The opening violin phrases and their corollary trills speak of eternal flagellation. Domineering Electra has abandoned herself to an eternity of frustrated physical torture (which she probably longed for, despite her prayers in *Idol mio*), and here she is, in imagination, being lashed venomously. At 'Squarciatemi il core' the blows give way to grief, as a woodwind phrase suggests and as more sustained harmony confirms. Then she returns to her martyrdom, and though the slower torment is also re-envisaged, the whips end this last demonstration of her internal self-destructive rage. The closing orchestral phrase, according to Dent, is a 'passionate distortion' of Ex. 4—an inspired deduction even if one finds it far-fetched.

Dent is surely correct, however, in noting a thematic link in the *adagio* string introduction to **No. 30**, the last scene, where Idomeneus returns to the stage accompanied by his loyal subjects. This is an accompanied recitative in gracious E flat major, richly textured, especially by clarinets and horns. He announces the end to Neptune's anger and to his reign; both give him contentment as he presents Idamantes and Ilia, Crete's new king and queen. Before 'I suoi comandi' there is another reference to Ex. 4. Mozart reset the closing bars more briefly.

Idomeneus summarizes his reign, and his role, in his last **Aria, No. 31**, *Torna la pace* which cost Varesco and Mozart so much trouble and which eventually the composer cut from the first performance. It begins *adagio*.

> Peace returns to my heart, and old age revives my tired enthusiasm.
> Just so an old tree may flower in springtime, feeling new vigour.

For the first time Idomeneus is associated with gracious, regal, heroic music with a spring in its step.

This is not the proud Mithridates nor the imperious, lusty Sulla but a monarch made wise by suffering and blessed by relief from responsibility. At 'torna, la spento ardore' we physically hear the revival of his tired spirits when the bassoons and clarinets dialogue volubly against jumping violins, and this reborn vitality is even more vividly conveyed in a subsequent elaboration of the texture.

A similar athleticism is suggested in the second subject, again with woodwind dialogue, first clarinet and bassoon in counterpoint answered by their partners likewise. The coda group is appropriately more relaxed, mostly with strings, once delightfully echoed by wind. But the middle ritornello is very active, based on Ex. 23b. It cadences in F major and a central *allegretto* section, to the second sentence of text cited above, moves the pace forward with neat, fluent string writing to halo Idomeneus's gracious phrases. Animated wind dialogues resume as G minor returns to B flat, while Idomeneus has already returned to the first sentence of text but to new music. The pause on his high F at the end of the *allegretto* implies a cadenza. The *adagio* reprise also implies discreet decorative variation by the singer. There are two quite hairy florid passages for Mr Raaff towards the end and an opening for a full-scale cadenza.

There follows **No. 32**, *Scenda Amor*, the final **Chorus** in D major, the opera's home tonality. The orchestra is complete but for clarinets and the two extra horns (they probably doubled on trumpets which do play here). The tempo is *allegro vivace* and the violin writing is agile as usual in a final chorus. Likewise we expect a deal of block choral harmony, perhaps a touch of choral imitative counterpoint, only just admitted. There is a dramatic stroke, orchestral two-note phrases followed by rests that suggest questions unanswered. And the orchestral texture becomes richer towards the end.

The chorus is praying that the new royal couple will be blessed by Cupid, Hymen and Juno and granted peace everlasting. Their harmonies are cloudless and direct, the melody elegant and attractive of its kind. A binary orchestral intermezzo, probably for ballet, and scored for wind and brass alone, is followed by a reprise of the chorus and this by three concluding orchestral bars fully scored.

7

Idomeneo is obviously Mozart's supreme achievement in *opera seria*, the goal towards which he had been moving ever since *Mitridate* or, before that, *Die Schuldigkeit* and *Apollo*—both subscribe to *serio* conventions and the very first musical number of *Apollo* prefigures the Temple Scene in *Idomeneo*. That Mozart did not suddenly produce a masterpiece out of his hat, with the score of *Idomeneo*, is clear from the letters he wrote to his father during its composition. Then there were the frustrating years after the completion of *Il rè pastore* during which Mozart self-confessedly hankered to write a serious opera: he was evidently putting in some quiet thought about the nature of opera, and he was seeing many operas. This important period of his operatic career has been summarized in my Inter-chapter called 'Waiting for *Idomeneo*'. The great achievement of *Idomeneo* stems nevertheless from the experience that Mozart derived from his earlier serious operas. I wrote the earlier chapters of this book partly to help anyone going for the first time to an unfamiliar Mozart opera, but also to show how such miracles as *Idomeneo* and *Figaro* have their origins in his less glorious prentice work. Even a genius has to learn his trade. Mozart learned his the best way, by writing music and subsequently understanding how he might have done it more perfectly.

Earlier in this chapter I called *Idomeneo* the greatest *opera seria* ever written. For modern audiences this is so, even for those acquainted with a number of Handel's serious operas. Our approval depends on our point of vantage in the late twentieth century. We may know quite a few *opere serie* but when we see *Idomeneo* we applaud its abandonment of the stiff old conventions essential to *opera seria* and its espousal of French ideas and German seriousness, in fact the foundation of the apparatus which we call musicdrama. The true connoisseur of Italian *opera seria* would not regard *Idomeneo* as a candidate for serious consideration: it contains too many choruses and ensembles, too much accompanied recitative, the arias are not drastically contrasted, the instrumentation contains far too much pictorial detail, there are scanty opportunities for applause or regular and extended opportunities in which an aristocratic audience can gossip and visit neighbours and generally enjoy itself without missing the opera's highlights. *Idomeneo* consists of too many highlights: even the recitatives are worth attending to.

It must be admitted that the apparently new features in *Idomeneo* were not really as innovatory as superficial historians try to claim. *Idomeneo* is full of marvellous choruses, some purely dynamic and theatrical, some gravely solemn with solo and duet episodes. These are attributed to Gluck's influence. But Mozart had included choruses of this kind in *Apollo et Hyacinthus* (its first number is a chorus with solo episode), in *Ascanio in Alba* and in *Lucio Silla*, all powerfully effective. There were choruses in *Il sogno di Scipione* and *La Betulia liberata*. The choruses in *Idomeneo* are not to be underrated, and they owe their frequency to French opera, but Mozart had been writing them assiduously into his operas before he was aware of Gluck or French operatic style. Their superiority does not mean that Mozart copied them from *Alceste*.

The ensembles, particularly the quartet *Andrò ramingo e solo*, are a glorious feature of *Idomeneo*. These had languished in serious Italian opera since the time of Alessandro Scarlatti. Singers persuaded composers that they were more taxing, in terms of rehearsal, than gratifying to public or singers. But Hasse had reinstated the vocal concerted number as a dramatic climax which he borrowed back from Italian comic opera. Mozart had composed something like an ensemble of perplexity in *La finta giardiniera*, and there is a trio in *Apollo et Hyacinthus*. They do not prepare us for the intensity and emotional diversity of the *Idomeneo* quartet, but the groundwork is there.

One great strength of *Idomeneo* is Mozart's highly theatrical joining of several musical numbers together without intervening pauses for exits, applause, change of scene or whatever. These are tremendously impressive yet we will find something of the kind in *Lucio Silla* and in *La finta giardiniera* if we look or listen.

The orchestration of *Idomeneo* is certainly superb, especially the carefully economical contribution of flutes (we have noticed this in *Lucio Silla*) and the grand use of four horns (already employed in *Mitridate* and *Ascanio*). Clarinets, on the other hand, appear for the first time in a Mozart opera, and the composer scrupulously saves them for moments where they will contribute most distinctively. His use of strings is quite consistent with his earlier practice, including his reservation of divided violas for special effects. We may remark how, in *Idomeneo*, Mozart avoids orchestral introductions to arias where it is dramatically important that the singer's sentiments should be voiced as soon as possible, but there are eloquent and parallel examples in *Mitridate*, his first *opera seria*. What is new in *Idomeneo* is the prevalence of binary rather than ternary form arias; Mozart had been moving in this direction ever since he became bored with the old-fashioned insistence on the *da capo* aria. In *Idomeneo* he exercised his preference with masterly determination, though we notice that he gave old-fashioned arias to his elderly singers, Raaff and Panzacchi.

All the way through *Idomeneo* the orchestral recitatives are quite wonderful, full of emotional point and expressive colouring. Even here we can find good precedents in Mozart's earlier operas; many in *Lucio Silla*, some in *Mitridate*, a fine example as early as the death of Hyacinth in *Apollo et Hyacinthus*. Where *Idomeneo* gains is in the scrupulously expressive quality of its dry recitatives. They are not for boring narrative alone. Does a new character interrupt in passionate soliloquy? Convention prescribes *recitativo secco*, but the emotional tension is preserved, by tonality or bass movement. Mozart was still to learn how to write totally involved dry recitative, in his da Ponte Italian comic operas; it is the greatest shame that he did not do so, for posterity's benefit, in his last serious opera, *La clemenza di Tito*.

People who have studied Mozart's operas, in detail and comprehensively, are driven to the decision that he had his own musical styles for French, German and Italian texts. In *La finta giardiniera* he puzzles us every now and then; I think, and have said so in the relevant chapter, that he was setting the German not the Italian text at these moments. The confusion is just as great in *Idomeneo*. Mostly the music is Italian Mozart quite firmly. The orchestral detail, which so enchants posterity (most of all in *Se il padre perdei*) is purely German. Mozart tried deliberately to borrow procedures from French opera, which he knew well. All this does create a linguistic confusion in the musical vocabulary of *Idomeneo*. Its musical style is not consistent, even if we must admit that every bar is essential Mozart; he was a cosmopolitan musician, not a small-town Salzburger, and he wanted to combine all that was operatically most eloquent in all the music he knew. If he had written *Idomeneo* entirely in his acquired Italian musical language he would never have contemplated revising the score for a German version, as he did. He knew that the music of *Idomeneo* was as much German as Italian or French: he had a German translation to spur him though fortunately not until he had single-mindedly set Varesco's Italian, otherwise there would have been more stylistic problems.

One real achievement in *Idomeneo* is its powerful treatment of characters, something that never occurred to earlier *opera seria* composers (because they worked to a different brief). Mozart had always been saddled with an impossibly benevolent monarch as hero. This time he had a shifty, guilt-laden, elderly king trying to evade a bad bargain involving his nearest and dearest. It did not much matter that Idomeneus was to be sung by an elderly tenor of reactionary taste and failing voice. The words and the music would convey this anti-hero's character, so different from the lifeless goody-goodies of Mozart's earlier serious operas; and Raaff could certainly sing, even if he was a poor actor—until the last scene Idomeneus is dramatically obliged to behave as if he were ashamed of himself.

Then Mozart had the shrew Electra, excellent material for a composer, and the sweet yet sometimes jealous Ilia, the two of them splendidly contrasted. Idamantes would not be much fun, and in Del Prato's person clearly wasn't; but he must have been able to sing, for all Mozart's complaints—the evidence is in the music.

With this drama and these, not perfect, singers Mozart was able to write music that carries, more or less, complete conviction when other singers take their place, and before audiences which know more about Mozart than about *opera seria*.

Mozart was going to have his great success, for posterity, with his later operas which are overtly comic but fundamentally serious. *Idomeneo* is not comic, and is not a true Italian *opera seria*. Almost all of its music, and an extraordinary amount of its drama, hits an audience hard in a right-minded performance, so that we experience *Idomeneo* as the upbeat to *Fidelio* and the *Ring*, to look no further. Some think that *Idomeneo* killed *opera seria*, if that form wasn't dead already. Some believe that the time for the re-union of comic and serious opera, as in *Don Giovanni*, was due, and that Mozart recognized and accomplished it. Myself I believe that Mozart helped *opera buffa* because he enjoyed doing so, and that he longed to write a new and really good serious opera. *Titus* never filled the bill and, if he had been spared, he would have given posterity the serious opera to whose splendour *Idomeneo* points the way, the setting of *Faust* which Goethe wanted him to make. The thought of Mozart's *Faust* is too awesome to contemplate.

14 DIE ENTFÜHRUNG AUS DEM SERAIL

DIE ENTFÜHRUNG AUS DEM SERAIL

(The abduction from the Harem)

Komisches Singspiel in three acts

Text by
CHRISTOPH FRIEDRICH BRETZNER
revised by GOTTLIEB STEPHANIE JR.

K. 384

PASHA (*Bassa*) SELIM, has captured and is wooing   SPOKEN ROLE
CONSTANZE, noble Spanish lady   SOPRANO
BLONDCHEN, her English personal maid, assigned by   SOPRANO
    the Pasha to
OSMIN, Custodian of the Pasha's country house   BASS
BELMONTE, Constanze's lover   TENOR
PEDRILLO, his servant, now custodian of the Pasha's   TENOR
    garden
KLAAS, a sailor ⎫
A mute servant ⎬   ACTING ROLES
Guards ⎭
Janissaries   CHORUS

Scene: The pasha's country estate in Turkey

Mozart's first important German opera was brought into being partly by the success of *Idomeneo* in Munich and partly by the determined efforts of the Austrian Emperor Joseph II to establish a German opera in Vienna. Already in 1776 the Emperor had abandoned the practice whereby the Court Theatre was regularly leased to visiting impresarios: instead he created a national theatrical company with a resident troupe. Two years later he formed a *National Singspiel* on similar lines for opera and ballet, opening with the musical director Ignaz Umlauf's one-act comic opera *Die Bergknappen*, specially written for the occasion.* The Emperor was encouraged in his plan by the success in England of *The Beggar's Opera*, and in Paris of the French-language *opéra comique*. There were two drawbacks to the Emperor's policy: the operatic company consisted of more actors than singers, which meant that musical and vocal standards never rose very high; and since German-language opera had never been popular in Germany there was a shortage of German-language operas, which meant that the company had to rely on translations of Italian operas. For although *opera seria* had steadily lost popularity since the early 1750s, which saw the rise of *opera buffa*, Italy remained faithful to the older style, and Vienna followed Italy in matters of taste—when the great singers, upon whose art *opera seria* devolves, were available. The nature of Mozart's music, with its considerable demands on several of the singers, in *Die Entführung aus dem Serail* shows that he did not have to accept mediocre standards. Indeed his principal singers were properly trained in the Italian manner, as we shall see.

In March 1781 Mozart was recalled, after the success of *Idomeneo*, from Munich to Vienna where his employer the Archbishop of Salzburg was in residence. Mozart had carefully followed the fortunes of this Imperial German Opera in Vienna and knew the sort of standards that had obtained there. Unconfirmed legend suggests that at this time Mozart was approached by the director of the Court Theatre, Count Rosenberg, with a request for an opera. He had *Zaide* on the stocks, but he was becoming disillusioned by the piece: the text was too feeble, the drama (he suspected) too serious for Vienna, the whole quite useless—'but Stephanie will give me a new, and (so he says) a good one'.

Gottlieb Stephanie, known as 'the younger' to distinguish him from his elder brother, also a playwright, was an actor and functioned as inspector of the National Singspiel in Vienna. He had the reputation of an unpleasant character, but Mozart seems to have got on well with him, and he was later to provide Mozart with the libretto of *Der Schauspieldirektor*. Stephanie gave Mozart the promised libretto at

---

* Ignaz Umlauf (1746–96) had begun his career as a court violinist. He was made Kapellmeister of the German Opera in Vienna on its foundation and, as such, composed the opera for the first night. It was followed by others equally successful (though Mozart, as we shall see, found them child's play). *Die Bergknappen* is published in Vol. XVIII of *Denkmäler Tonkünstler Österreichs*. Umlauf's son Michael (1781–1842), also a musician, acted as co-conductor in several of Beethoven's concerts after the composer's hearing had given way.

the end of July 1781. The completed work was intended for performance in mid-September during the visit to Vienna of the Grand Duke Paul Petrovich, later Paul I of Russia—though eventually the première was postponed. This was a decisive summer for Mozart. On 8 June he had left the Archbishop's service after his resignation had been received with angry, insulting words and a final kick of dismissal. Mozart was now, most unconventionally, a freelance composer (and, of course, virtuoso keyboard player) determined to make a living in Vienna. At first he found lodgings with the Weber family, friends from Mannheim of whom his father disapproved. In September he moved to the Graben, one of Vienna's best known streets. But by this time he had fallen in love with Constanze Weber, and after much difficulty he succeeded in marrying her on 4 August 1782, one day before his father's consent arrived and almost three weeks after the first performance of *Die Entführung*.

The oriental harem was a popular subject for drama in the mid-eighteenth century. Stephanie's libretto, *Bellmont und Konstanze oder die Entführung aus dem Serail*, was no original production. It derived immediately from a libretto of the same name written in 1780 by Christoph Friedrich Bretzner (1748–1807), a Leipzig merchant who was later to write an opera based on Hogarth's cycle of paintings *The Rake's Progress* (1787). Bretzner protested bitterly against Mozart's pilfering of his work. But Bretzner himself had drawn considerably on earlier dramas, notably *La schiava liberata*, whose setting by Schuster he had seen at Leipzig in 1777, and the English libretto *The Sultan or A Peep into the Seraglio* by Isaac Bickerstaffe (1769) which Bretzner also knew. It is to this English work that we owe the idea of Blondchen as a high-spirited and independent English servant enslaved in a Turkish harem. But plays (and comic operas) about Turks and harems and foreigners enslaved and rescuers were rife in Europe at the time of the Turkish wars. The Tamburlaine–Bajazet drama is familiar from Marlowe's play and indeed from Handel's opera *Tamerlano*. Features in Mozart's *Entführung* have been traced back to Hiller's *Grab des Mufti* (1777), Holly's *Bassa von Tunis*, Vogler's *Kaufmann von Smyrna* (1771), Gluck's *La rencontre imprévue* (1764). Bretzner himself noted that his *Bellmont und Konstanze* was similar to *Adelheit von Veltheim*, written by Grossmann and set by Beethoven's teacher Neefe at about the same time as his own piece. Neefe's opera was thought much superior to Bretzner's libretto, which had been set in the first place by the Viennese publisher Johann André, who was known as a witty composer. We may smile at some of Stephanie's phraseology and indeed at some of the changes that Mozart made; they exchange sophistication for just the sort of popular naïvety which Viennese audiences have always loved. And we suppose that Mozart was familiar with at least some of the Turkish harem rescue operas, since he asked Stephanie for details, and wrote others into his music, that he knew had already pleased audiences in existing operas on similar subjects.

This is the opera about which (possibly excepting *Idomeneo*) Mozart has left most information on his principles of composition. He still tailored his arias to fit the vocal specialities of his chosen singers. Writing to his father on 1 August 1781 he names the principal singers—Catarina Cavalieri (Constanze), Therese Teiber (Blonde), Valentin Joseph Adamberger (Belmonte), Johann Ernst Dauer (Pedrillo), Karl Ludwig Fischer (Osmin), and for Pasha Selim a certain Herr

Walter, though this last role eventually fell to an actor and was taken by Domenik Jautz. Cavalieri (1760–1801), despite her name, was an Austrian soprano from Währing near Vienna. She had studied under Salieri and at the age of fifteen joined the Italian Opera in Vienna. She was one of the founder members of the Emperor's German Opera. An anonymous Leipzig gossip-column in 1781 speaks of her vocal quality as strong but 'peculiar', and remarks that she is ugly, one-eyed, and a pitiable actress. But Mozart, who wrote the roles of Constanze and Mme Silberklang (in *Der Schauspieldirektor*) for her, evidently thought better, at least of her vocal agility, for which he admitted making allowances in *Ach, ich liebte*, and which is amply catered for in *Martern aller Arten* and in Mme Silberklang's music; Constanze's other aria *Traurigkeit* would, one imagines, have been appropriated by Silberklang's rival Mme Herz, but Mozart also wrote it expressly for Cavalieri, like Donna Elvira's *Mi tradì*, and therefore presumably respected her expressive powers. Mozart's last extant letter refers to a performance of *Die Zauberflöte* at which Cavalieri and her old teacher Salieri were guests in his box.

The *seconda donna* Therese Teiber (1765–1830) was reputed a good actress and must also have been a fluent vocalist to judge from the brilliant scale-passages up to top E in *Durch Zärtlichkeit*. Adamberger (1743–1804) came from Munich, and had won success in Italy (under the name Adamonti) and in London before settling in Vienna in 1780. Adamberger was admired for his vocal schooling and his tone-quality, though his high notes were thought unpleasantly nasal; the Leipzig columnist declared his singing 'soulless', and in *Die Entführung* Count Zinzendorf wrote that he acted like a statue. But Mozart approved of Adamberger, wrote other music for him, (including the tiny part of Buff in *Schauspieldirektor*), and remained friendly with him. Johann Ernst Dauer (1746–1812) was reputed a fine tenor and excellent actor. Karl Ludwig Fischer (1745–1825) was the greatest German bass of his day, pre-eminently popular with the Viennese public, having a vocal compass from bottom C to baritone high A (Archbishop Colloredo complained to Mozart that Fischer sang too low for a bass) and a florid technique that was unexcelled. Mozart and Stephanie enlarged the role of Osmin, comparatively insignificant in Bretzner's libretto, to display Fischer's talents; and Mozart at one time intended to rewrite the namepart in *Idomeneo* for a bass so that Fischer might sing it. The Fischer who sang Count Almaviva and Don Giovanni in London in 1812 was not our Osmin but his son. Fischer senior was, however, the composer of the favourite *basso* party-piece 'In cellar cool' (*Im tiefen Keller*) which showed off the wide leaps characteristic of his Bolognese vocal schooling. At some later performances during the first run of *Entführung* Constanze was sung by Aloysia Lange, elder sister of Constanze Mozart and one of Wolfgang's major earlier flames; Belmonte by Friedrich Karl Lippert who was to translate *Don Giovanni* into German for Vienna; and Pedrillo by Gottfried Heinrich Schmidt who subsequently produced the opera in Prague and Salzburg (Leopold Mozart attended the latter production which was thought superior to the Vienna première). All these parts, though designed for particular singers, were able to be satisfactorily taken over by others; except significantly that of Osmin, a role so satisfying that, in time, it brought into being a German *basso buffo* of a particular type.

Mozart had been given the libretto by Stephanie at the end of July, and by

1 August he had composed three musical numbers: Belmonte's *O wie ängstlich*, Constanze's *Ach, ich liebte*, and the final Trio of Act I, *Marsch, marsch, marsch!* Osmin's first song, *Wer ein Liebchen*, was completed soon after, and by 7 August Mozart was able to play much of Act I to Countess Thun. By 22 August the whole act was complete. Mozart had already persuaded Stephanie to add Belmonte's first solo, *Hier soll ich dich denn sehen*, and the duet which grows out of Osmin's *Wer ein Liebchen*, as well as Osmin's *Solche hergelaufne Laffen*; and he importuned Stephanie to add another aria for Fischer in Act II—Osmin finished up with two duets in Act II and an aria in Act III for which the music was sketched before the text—so as to make a prominent role out of Bretzner's unimportant one. If it is true (as Henry Pleasants reports in *The Great Singers*) that Mozart at one time planned Osmin as a *castrato* part, thinking of eunuchs in charge of harems, it is amusing that this eventually became a role for a deep bass.

By 26 September 1781* Mozart had decided that Stephanie's libretto would need other changes. He felt that the vocal quartet† then placed at the start of Act III should be transferred to the end of Act II—which meant adding new material to fill up the last act. This same letter includes some elucidatory comments by Mozart on the expressive contents of what he had already composed. The letter is very famous but it needs to be quoted again here, because it is according to these lights that I have ventured elsewhere in this book to touch on the dramatic and expressive implications of Mozart's music.

> *Drum beim Barte des Propheten* is actually in the foregoing tempo, but with rapid note-values, and as [Osmin's] rage goes on increasing, therefore by the time one thinks the Aria must be coming to an end, the *Allegro assai* in another tempo and another key must surely make its best effect. For a man in such a towering rage exceeds all control, moderation and purpose; he does not know what he's doing—and just so, the music mustn't know either. But since the passions, whether violent or not, must never be expressed disgustingly, and music, even in the most terrible context, must never insult the ear, but even there must give pleasure, i.e. must always remain music, I have therefore chosen, not a key foreign to F major [the aria's tonic key], but one related to it, and not the nearest, D minor, but A minor, the next further away. Now Belmonte's Aria in A major, *O wie ängstlich, o wie feurig*: d'you know how it's expressed? Even the beating amorous heart is indicated, by two violins in octaves. One sees the trembling, reeling, one sees how the heaving bosom expands, which is expressed by a crescendo, one hears the murmurs and sighs which are expressed by muted first violins and flute in unison.

Stephanie took some time to complete the alterations desired by Mozart, but the National Opera was able to wait while three of Gluck's major works were produced, as well as a new one by Umlauf (which Mozart sight-read faultlessly in the composer's presence and much to his chagrin), whose première had been postponed because of his illness. In May 1782 he played the second and third acts to Countess Thun on the piano (on the 7th and 30th respectively, which suggests that Act III was composed between these two dates). The opera went into rehearsal

---

* Letter to his father.   † Mozart calls it a Quintet or Finale.

on 3 June. Its preparation was attended as usual by much intrigue, including protests that the roles were unsingable—though Cavalieri, Adamberger, and Fischer had all personally approved of the arias written for them—and machinations, thwarted by the intervention of the Emperor, to prevent the première which at last took place on 16 July 1782 in the Burgtheater. Mozart's report to his father on the first performance is alas lost, but it seems to have been noisily received, with some encores and much inimical whistling, likewise the second performance. The libretto was condemned as unpoetical and immoral, and the Emperor, even after intervening on the opera's behalf, told the composer after the première, 'Too beautiful for our ears, my dear Mozart, and monstrous many notes!' To which the composer replied, 'Exactly as many as are necessary, Your Majesty.' But thereafter it was played repeatedly in and out of Vienna; during Mozart's lifetime it remained his most popular opera. Gluck had a performance given at his special request on 6 August, and afterwards invited the composer to supper. During the autumn it was most successfully staged in Prague (shortly to become the centre of the Mozart cult during his lifetime). And Goethe declared, after trying to write a *Singspiel* for Weimar, that after *Die Entführung* everything was an anticlimax ('es schlug alles nieder'). The reputation of *Die Entführung* began to wane during the nineteenth century, it being thought too childish for the admiration of cultured adult audiences though Covent Garden gave the English première in 1827. German nationalists tried, none too convincingly, to claim it as a monument of German Opera. It has only found its proper place in the repertory during the present century when each work of art is judged by its own standards, we hope.

2

Mozart was an experienced hand at the Turkish musical style which he adopted for the **Overture** and several other numbers in *Die Entführung*. Apart from the unTurkish trial-run of *Zaide*, he had explored this fashionable manner in the finale of the A major violin concerto K. 219, and in the *Rondo alla turca* finale of the piano sonata K. 331, doubtless also in keyboard extemporizations which were never written out. He told his father that the *Vivat Bacchus* duet (No. 14 in *Entführung*) was based on his Turkish Tattoo—though this original, if it ever existed on paper, is now lost.* The Turkish style involved noisy use of triangle, cymbals and bass drum, excitably fluttering piccolo and primitive repeated chord cadences, as in the opening phrases of the *Entführung* overture which is *presto*, in C major, for piccolo (more likely a piccolo, but later a flute), oboes, clarinets, bassoons, horns, trumpets, timpani, triangle, cymbals, bass drum and strings:

1 **Presto**

* Mozart only began cataloguing his compositions in 1784, starting with the E flat piano concerto K. 449, and there must be many lost compositions of his that were not mentioned in writing.

Similarly in the *Rondo alla turca*:

These repeated notes are characteristic of peasant or popular music in general. Sophisticated music of the period would have applied the law of the appoggiatura to render bars 1–4 as follows:

Repeated notes, performed as written, are inimical to the sophisticated artistic style of this period.★ The *andante* of *Eine kleine Nachtmusik*, unless designed as an expression of comfortable bourgeois sociability, must surely be interpreted:

Mozart himself did not regard Ex. 1 as Turkish music, or rather, by Turkish music he meant the loud passage, with piccolo and percussion, from bar 9 onwards. He described the overture as follows:

'It is quite short, constantly alternates between *piano* and *forte*, and at the fortes the Turkish music breaks in every time, and so it goes on modulating through the keys, and I believe nobody will be able to sleep through it, even if one hadn't slept at all the night before.'

Nevertheless Ex. 1 may recall the Turkish music of Monostatos's pianissimo *Alles fühlt der Liebe Freuden* in *Die Zauberflöte* (p. 626) which has the same type of chordal repetition. The structure of these opening phrases is irregular: the first soft + loud sentence consists of 4 + 4 + 6 bars (i.e., two bars short of normal), the second of 4 + 4 + 10 (i.e., still four bars short though four bars longer than before). The loud, specifically Turkish music (Ex. 5a) is re-presented as the second quick subject of the overture (Ex. 5b), in the manner of Haydn's later symphonies —though at this time Mozart was less familiar with Joseph Haydn's music than with his brother Michael's.

★ See also the remarks below on Belmonte's No. 15.

The movement is planned as an Italian overture (*cf.* the overture to *La finta semplice*), two quick sections separated by a slow movement. But it is unusual in that the third section recapitulates the initial material of the opening (though not its quasi-second subject which is firmly forgotten); and that the *andante* middle section in C minor (ordinary flute, no brass or percussion) looks forward to the melody of No. 1, pauses and all—and is very short, no more than an aperitif for what is to come. The reason for this brevity, and the non-recapitulation of Ex. 5, is that the overture stops short on the verges of C minor, then tiptoes into the music of **No. 1** for the rise of the curtain and Belmonte's **Aria**, *Hier soll ich dich denn sehen*, C major, *andante* with clarinets, bassoons, horns and strings.

> Here I shall see you, Constanze, my delight. Heaven grant it and the return of my peace of mind.
> O Love, I have endured suffering in abundance. Now in exchange give me joys and bring me to my destination.

Belmonte has found his way from his home in Spain to the grounds of a country estate belonging to the Pasha Selim who has evidently taken Belmonte's beloved Constanze captive and brought her to the palace, in the square before which Belmonte now stands. The libretto tells us that it is on the shores of the sea, and later Constanze and the Pasha can effectively make their first entry from a boat on the water. We also gather that the palace square includes some fig trees, from the stage directions for Osmin's entrance. We may deduce, by collating the directions for all three acts, that Belmonte, as he stands facing the conductor, and with his back to the palace, is looking at Osmin's dwelling and the palace gardens behind it. The sea is to one side of him (whether stage left or right is never specified).

In the overture the *andante* melody in C minor expressed, we may suppose, Belmonte's sadness at being parted from Constanze, since now he sings the same tune in C major in eager expectation of seeing her again at last.

The dynamics and staccati are quoted as they appear in the orchestral introduction, where they already suggest Belmonte's furtive approach, startled by any sudden noise. The tiptoe first phrase has affinities with Ex. 31 (p. 401), *Susanna? Signore.* The fourth phrase of the introduction expresses Belmonte's yearning, with its built-in *fermata* on the top note, and the subsequent dotted semiquaver rest, like a missed heart-beat:

7

—though before the aria is over we may regard the *fermata* rather as a composer's indulgence towards a tenor's top notes. Especially attractive is Mozart's use of the pause on top G as preparation for the triplet cadence that topples from the A a tone above.

8

und brin———————————————————ge mich ans— Ziel,

The aria makes a feature of clarinets in the middle section ('Ich duldete der Leiden') where their gently dragging phrases are echoed by violins and violas inside a three-octave dominant pedal-point; and later for jubilant fanfares which accompany Belmonte's plea that he may reach his goal ('und bringe mich ans Ziel').

The music having ceased, Belmonte realizes that he has been melodiously yet fruitlessly enumerating chickens—or rather, a single delectable fowl—yet to be hatched from the eggshell of the Pasha's harem. His further deliberations are interrupted by the appearance of a formidable interlocutor who carries a ladder, sets it against a fig-tree and, climbing up, picks some figs. He is Osmin, the over-seer of the Pasha's estate, described by Mozart as a rude fellow.

But since Belmonte has as yet no notion that this is not the pleasantest fellow in the world, Osmin is introduced by a gently melancholy string instrumental strain in G minor, the refrain of his entrance Song (it is called *Lied* rather than, as in No. 1, *Arie*), *Wer ein Liebchen hat gefunden*, **No. 2, Lied und Duett**, *andante* at first.

> When you find a serious, faithful sweetheart, reward her with thousands of kisses, sweeten her life, be her comforter and friend.
>
> To keep her loyal, be sure to imprison her other lovers; those loose fellows will hustle your butterfly and be far too keen to sip foreign wine.
>
> When the moon shines she's especially aware of her friends. Often a young fellow is listening there, tempts the little fool and then—goodbye faithfulness.

This was one of Mozart's additions to the libretto originally given him by Stephanie, and we know that he had thought of the music before asking for the words. He was not yet making a musical point of Osmin's nationality: no Turkish percussion or piccolo; the song, and the duet springing from it, use flute, oboes, bassoons, horns and strings. Mozart does hint at popular music, with repeated notes and a momentary uncertainty about the diatonically sharpened or modally (peasant) flattened seventh in G minor. He at once made a feature of the Bolognese wide melodic leaps which were Fischer's *forte*:

9

Sei ihr Trö—ster, sei ihr Freund, sei ihr Freund. Tralla—le —ra

Osmin's ditty is strophic. At the end of each verse Belmonte interrupts with spoken dialogue, attempting to establish contact. But Osmin pays no attention until he has sung three such verses, differently accompanied and scored—the harmonizations of 'Trallalera' are marvellously varied. The third of these verses has a particularly expressive flowing countersubject for woodwind in three octaves; and at the third line it breaks briefly into *allegro* tempo—Osmin is just beginning to be needled by the stranger's persistent questions—though he finishes the strophe in his original *andante* tempo, whereupon Belmonte bursts into song, *allegro*, alluding briefly to the refrain before moving into common time. Osmin's angry riposte ('Was Henker lässt Ihr Euch gelüsten') involves a typical orchestral figure signifying impatience:

10

Belmonte now ventures to ask the most pertinent questions about the house and Osmin's status within, and for these Mozart brings out another version of the tiptoe motif:*

11

Exs. 10 and 11 continue to punctuate their irritable dialogue. Then Belmonte broaches the first question relevant to his search, a request to speak with his ex-servant Pedrillo, now the Pasha's chief gardener. But Osmin detests Pedrillo (for reasons shortly to be discovered) and regards any friend of this villain as a gallows-bird ('Galgenschwengel'). Belmonte protests Pedrillo's admirable qualities, giving scope for an argumentative duet, quite stormy and German Mozart in feeling. Belmonte returns to Ex. 11 with a further request that he does not even specify before Osmin has diagnosed him as a woman-stealer, and ordered him to be off—the shooing-away motive is distinctive here:

12

If Belmonte supposes Osmin is thinking of Constanze, he is wrong; the *Mädchen* in Osmin's mind is Blondchen, Constanze's maid and Pedrillo's sweetheart who has been given by the Pasha to Osmin. In fact Belmonte's protests are merely general, and encourage Osmin to break into the final section, *presto* in D major, full of brusque *fortepiano* accents and none-too-strict suggestions of canon. It spins the number gaily to a close.

Belmonte gives up the struggle and goes in search elsewhere. Osmin gives vent to some characteristic sadistic threats directed against Pedrillo who has evidently

* Abert connects it with J. C. Bach. Mozartians may compare it with Ex. 53 (p. 637), or with the Prague Symphony second movement, from bar 9.

wheedled his way into the Pasha's favour. While he is in full spate Pedrillo comes, quite unsuspecting, to greet him and is welcomed with promises of slow, painful and violent extermination. Osmin explains his intolerance in an explosive **Aria**, added for Fischer's benefit, **No. 3**, *Solche hergelaufne Laffen*, in F major, accompanied by oboes, horns and strings (the standard eighteenth century small orchestra). The many repeated Fs at the beginning are typical of his music (the blunt endings of 'uns auf den Dienst zu passen' and 'Eure Tücken' are eminently plebeian) as is the repetition of a whole passage (the second 'Ich hab auch Verstand') an octave lower—both times with sarcastic comments from the oboe. The section 'Eure Tücken, eure Ränke' brings out a Decision motif common in Mozart (e.g., *Nozze di Figaro* No. 9, 'Schioppo in spalla') and indeed composers of many ages.

13

The aria appears to come to an end with a low F for Osmin, only to start again (after the expected applause) at 'Drum beim Barte' with the first of two codas to which Mozart refers in the letter quoted on p. 294. Though the music is quasi-Turkish in its musical repetitiousness and harmonic simplicity, the Turkish percussion is still held in reserve. And though the rate of note-values is stepped up, the tempo is still only *allegro*, as Mozart observed—and for good reasons. This section too comes to an end after a pause that, knowing Fischer's gifts as a florid singer,[*] obviously implies an extremely brilliant cadenza. But Osmin's garrulous instinct is not yet satisfied. One remark of injured innocence from Pedrillo and the old fellow resumes, *allegro assai* in A minor, with *Erst geköpft, dann gehangen*, his sadistic nursery patter-song, the second coda of this aria. Mozart could not, of course, tell his father that the oboe and bassoon scrunches looked forward to the wedding march in *Figaro*, though he might have remarked that now at last he had fetched out his piccolo, cymbals and bass drum for Turkish local colour.

The rushing figures for piccolo and strings depict the violent fury in which Osmin storms away inside the palace. Pedrillo's good-natured comment, that he would have a real party digging a grave for this misanthrope, is interrupted by the reappearance of Belmonte who is delighted to learn that Constanze is alive and faithful to him. Pedrillo tells him and us that their ship was captured by pirates (we never learn where Constanze was travelling to, or why Pedrillo as well as Blonde was with her), and that they were all bought as slaves by Pasha Selim, a renegade Muslim who insists that every woman in his harem shall love him. Pedrillo has no fears for Constanze's virtue, but many for his poor Blondchen since Osmin has no such sophisticated scruples, and is moreover the Pasha's favourite and chief spy. Fortunately Pedrillo has also won the Pasha's favour and has access to these two ladies during their walks with the Pasha in the garden, where even Osmin has to keep his distance—whence Osmin's jealousy. Belmonte outlines his plot for their escape. He has a ship moored a little way from the harbour. If only they can collect the girls and get aboard, they can be homeward bound. But first they must outwit 'the old watchdog' Osmin, and set the Pasha's mind at ease. Pedrillo sees the Pasha's boat returning from a pleasure cruise on the water and, telling Belmonte to keep out of the way, goes to meet his temporary

[*] He was castigated for over-decorating the music of Sarastro in *Die Zauberflöte*.

employer with a view to introducing Belmonte as a skilled architect—gardening and architecture being the Pasha's hobbies. At the prospect of seeing Constanze, Belmonte bursts into song.

No. 4, Recitative, *Konstanze, Konstanze!*, and *andante* **Aria**, *O wie ängstlich*, A major.

> Constanze, to see you again! How anxiously, how ardently my loving heart beats; and the tears of reunion make up for the fearful pain of separation. Already I am trembling and shaking, my bosom heaves and swells. Is that her whisper? I am so on edge. Was that her sigh? My cheeks burn. Does love deceive me with a dream?

The accompanied recitative is only four bars long, scored for strings *sotto voce* (a bassoon adds incisiveness to the opening sustained chords); an oboe tenderly echoes Belmonte's ecstatic murmurs of his beloved's name. 'To see you again— you!' He repeats 'dich' enrapt, and after a pause (doubtless though not indispensably a cadenza was intended here) moves straight into his aria which Mozart composed on first receipt of the libretto and which he elucidated in the letter quoted on p. 294. Mozart mentions the crescendo at 'es hebt sich die schwellende Brust', but not the Italianate contrast of *piano* for 'ängstlich' and *forte* for 'feurig', which reappears later in the aria ('schon zittr' ich und wanke') as though thematically, and which is the more striking because the whole aria otherwise takes place at *piano* and *pianissimo* levels. The orchestral music (flute, oboe, bassoon, two horns and strings) is very rich in characteristic figuration. As well as the pit-a-pat violin octaves remarked by Mozart (bar 5, 'klopft mein liebevolles Herz' and later, at 'schon zittr' ich' and off-beat after 'Es wird mir so bange', and again in the formal reprise and the coda) there is the affecting veer towards A minor at 'lohnt der Trennung bangen Schmerz', the violins' throbbing figure in the crescendo for 'es hebt sich die schwellende Brust', the gently purling flute and violin demisemiquaver passage before 'Ist das ihr Lispeln?', and its reflection in the coda, on woodwind in three octaves. The vocal line includes some blunt phrase-ends which require appoggiaturas, especially in the reprise ('Lispeln', 'Seufzen', etc.) where the tune should certainly be varied with discreet gracing; a cadenza is implied by the pause before the reprise.

The orchestral prelude ends *pianissimo* whereupon Pedrillo runs back telling Belmonte to get out of sight, as the Pasha is coming.

No. 5, Janissaries' Chorus, *Singt dem grossen Bassa Lieder*, C major, *allegro*, full orchestra (one piccolo, no flutes). Pasha Selim is escorted by his bodyguard of Turkish infantry who enter to a splendid Turkish ritornello with a curious A minorish tune in C major, rendered the more curious by the ties across the first two bar-lines and the extension of the second four-bar phrase by one extra bar; this recurs at both its repetitions. The main melody of the chorus is firm C major with a penchant for the sharpened fourth degree (*musica ficta* rather than Lydian mode); again the phrase lengths are irregular, 7 + 4 + 7 + 7 + 2.

14
[Allegro]

Singt dem gro—ssen Bas-sa Lie-der, dem grossen Bassa Lie-der,

The tune has been traced* to the kingdom of Moldavia, and was ascribed to Dimitri Cantemir who was a composer as well as the governor of that kingdom. It had been brought to Vienna and published in 1781, in a *History of Transalpine Dacia*, by Joseph Sulzer, an Austrian who had seen service in Wallachia. It has since been shown† that Cantemir had spent some years in Constantinople, and was a scholar of Turkish music. The tune of Ex. 14 is in Turkish style, even though it, and others like it written by Cantemir, became widely known in Moldavia and Wallachia and influenced traditional music there.‡ The middle section for solo voices is contrapuntal in texture, to start with, by contrast with the relentless block chordal writing of the rest of the chorus.

Constanze and the Pasha are left alone. They have to converse in spoken dialogue since Mozart had decided on second thoughts to make Pasha Selim a non-singing role. It is odd, though, that he did not take this opportunity to indulge in the melodrama style which had captured his enthusiasm and which he had featured in *Zaide* (see pp. 236 ff.). It is odd too that he did not transfer any of the *Zaide* music to the *Entführung* opera which replaced it and which has so similar a plot—to mention but one number, how can he have resisted bringing the quartet *O selige Wonne* to its proper place in the theatre?

The Pasha attempts to console the weeping Constanze, to draw her affections towards him, to discover the cause of her grief and her coyness, promising on no account to be angry with her. She praises his magnanimity (thus letting us know at once that Selim is no villain), asks his forgiveness, and launches into **No. 6, Aria**, *Ach ich liebte*, B flat major, with oboes, clarinets, bassoons, horns and strings. The *adagio* opening is magical: an oboe strikes and softly sustains the fifth degree, Constanze outlines a melody in short, hesitant phrases, and soft strings soon add a formal accompaniment. Her melodic line, throughout the aria, is full of blunt phrase-endings which demand appoggiaturas, above all in music expressing grief and tenderness. They should at first be interpreted as shown (though at the reprise with longer note-values in the *allegro* they may be elaborated):

15

Adagio

Ach ich lieb—te,   war so   glücklich, kannte nicht   der Liebe Schmerz,

Once I was in love, so happy, did not know the pains of love, vowed loyally to my beloved and gave my heart to him.

My joy faded quickly. Separation was my sad fate and now tears swim in my eyes, and misery reposes in my lap.

Very soon Mozart quickens the pace to *allegro* for an *aria di bravura*. He admitted that he had 'sacrificed a bit to Mme Cavalieri's agile throat', and he was not exaggerating: for the *allegro* coincides with Constanze's lament for her vanished joy and enforced separation from her lover. These poignant sentiments are set to bland B flat major music full of brilliant running passages taking the singer up to repeated top D's—suitable for the Queen of Night's wrath, but not for Constanze's

---

* By Erich Schenk—see Bibliography.   † By George Breazul—see Bibliography.
‡ Information from Zeno Vancea—see Bibliography.

'Kummer ruht in meinem Schoss' (an oddly phrased remark, as Mozart pointed out). The music only twice touches on melancholy, the first time when it turns for a moment into F minor, only to slide into F major for the second subject of the aria, scored for woodwind in three octaves, giving a hurdy-gurdy or even merry-go-round effect. The reversion to the *adagio* music ('Ach ich liebte') in *allegro* tempo is delightfully managed with the intrusion of a dominant seventh on the clear skies of F major, soon to drift towards B flat minor (but here the singer is contrariwise singing about her old happiness!). The bold rapid scales and divisions are contrasted, at the end, with lucent leaning phrases capped by chromatic woodwind. The aria ends with triumphant orchestral music.

Constanze's confession has roused Selim's spirit of determination and he threatens her with coercion, though later after her tearful departure (note that the exit-aria convention did not apply here, even after a heroic formal solo showpiece) Selim confesses to himself that he could never use force against such a heart. Pedrillo interrupts his thoughts to introduce Belmonte as an architect from Italy; Selim likes the look of the stranger, offers him hospitality and makes an appointment for the following day, then departs. Pedrillo and Belmonte congratulate one another on this first lucky success, and start to enter the palace. But Osmin is standing in the doorway, altogether unimpressed by Belmonte's rank or reception by the Pasha; he orders them both away from the palace in **No. 7, Trio**, *Marsch, marsch, marsch!*, C minor–major (scoring as for No. 6 plus trumpets and drums). The *allegro* in C minor begins bluffly, 'and because the words lend themselves to it, I have made it a fairly respectable piece of three-part writing' (Mozart to his father). Respectable means contrapuntal imitative texture, in the orchestra as well as the solo voices. The rushing downward patterns, the smooth woodwind harmonies, and the curt broom-sweeping motif, all give pace and substance to an absurd piece of punch-and-judy farce. The three singers and orchestra pause on a dominant seventh, and then *allegro assai* in C major supervenes, with tauter, less elaborate music designed, Mozart admitted, for brevity, noise and immediate effect. The weakness of this number (to be felt chiefly by the producer and the three actors on stage—by the spectators only if the others have not solved the problem) is that the words imply vigorous physical action which is contradicted by much verbal repetition. During the final orchestral bars Belmonte and Pedrillo slip past Osmin into the palace, and this act is over.

3

Act II takes place in the gardens of Pasha Selim's palace, outside Osmin's dwelling. Osmin has just been ordering Blonde to satisfy his carnal desires, and she is now explaining to him that, even though she has been presented to him as a chattel, she is not a Turkish slave who trembles with fear at his commands. She is a European and has to be wooed very differently. She explains the technique in **No. 8, Aria**, *Durch Zärtlichkeit und Schmeicheln*, A major (strings only).

> By tenderness and flattery, amiability and jokes, the hearts of good girls are easily won over. But cross imperiousness and stupid insistence and annoyance cause love and loyalty to disappear in a day or two.

The desirable qualities are abundantly represented in the initial melody, *andante grazioso*, played by first violins and violas an octave apart, and ingratiatingly doubled at the third below. The second half of the text deals with the contrary method which Osmin has favoured, crosspatch hectoring and quarrelsome nagging; Mozart sets this also to good-natured musical banter, though it might be interpreted in a stiff authoritarian manner.

16

And the phrase in which she declares that bad temper soon puts an end to faithful love is radiant with charm and bonhomie.

17

Blonde is very much her mistress's maid, and is expected to possess a *Gurgel* as *geläufig* as Constanze's: the vocal line of this aria includes several imposing octave jumps of the kind shown in Ex. 17, and three brilliant scalic divisions (in the Mannheim rocket manner) culminating in repeated top notes (like those in No. 6), the last of them sailing up to top E. The material of the aria's first half is recapitulated entirely in A major, after Blonde's first burst of fireworks, and some of it is presented differently—Exs. 16 and 17, for example, are not heard again. After the third rocket there is a gently wheedling coda. The aria was slightly longer originally: Mozart cut two short passages. Blondchen is a prototype of the Viennese soubrette role (Mozart's Susanna, Zerlina and Despina are a shade less brilliant) which persisted throughout the nineteenth century and later in several of Richard Strauss's operas (e.g., Sophie, Zerbinetta, Fiakermilli). Constanze's music, though similarly agile and high-flying, is that of a more serious, noble woman, and should be cast accordingly. In this act, particularly, where the two sopranos are heard in alternation and finally together in the big quartet No. 16, a marked contrast of timbres is needed if the listener's ears are to be kept alert. Unfortunately the twentieth century breeds more Blondes than Constanzes, and the heroine's part is often assigned to a singer who would be more successful as the maid.

Osmin is not convinced by her sermon, and he resumes his bullying. Blondchen may be 'an English girl born to freedom', but she is his slave and he orders her to love him. They bicker at length, and Blonde predictably gets the best of it, threatening him with bastinado if he doesn't go away at once.

No. 9, Duet, *Ich gehe, doch rate ich dir*, E flat major (oboes, bassoons, horns, strings). In shape this is like an Italian overture—in fact like the overture to this opera, with two quick sections in the major enveloping a slower interlude in a minor key. In the first *allegro* (in E flat major) Osmin agrees to go away on condition Blonde keeps away from Pedrillo, which of course she refuses to do. Osmin's broken-chord phrases in 6/8 lend themselves to orchestral imitation that pushes the music zestfully along, and the contrapuntal frame of mind persists in Blonde's reply and in their ensemble. The idea of a duet for high soprano and low bass is humorous in itself, and Mozart caps the joke at 'bis du zu gehorchen mir schwörst' where Osmin descends chromatically to low E flat, far out of Blonde's reach, then swings pugnaciously up the arpeggio (his excavations have led to B flat major) to his top F. Blonde is not at all daunted: she contrives a rapid switch back to E flat major and mimics his feat, grovelling down to her low A flat, then triumphantly soaring up to top B flat three times with the utmost glee. Osmin now ruefully licks his sores, *andante* in C minor, to further arpeggio figures (what fools those Englishmen are to give their wives such freedom) which act neatly as a bass for Blonde's (previously the oboe's) ambling countersubject. This is definitely a mock-tragic C minor, almost a sarcastic comment on the usual associations of the key which were noble and classical music for heroic tragedy.

18

After this the E flat major fanfare tunes return even more exuberantly, *allegro assai*, with spicy woodwind accents and plentiful imitation. We are close to the world of Mozart's horn concerto finales.

Osmin departs and in the same moment Blonde sees her mistress walking sadly across the garden towards her. As Constanze approaches she gives vent to her grief in a solo that, unlike No. 5, really does express her loneliness and misery. It is **No. 10, Recitative**, *Welcher Wechsel* herrscht . . .*, adagio, E flat major—**Aria**, *Traurigkeit ward mir zum Loose*, with flutes, oboes, basset-horns, bassoons, horns strings, *andante con moto*, G minor. The recitative is scored for strings only and begins with a glorious introduction, instantaneous in its evocation of atmosphere and moment: sinuous lines and sighs in thirds, bitter-sweet harmonic tension, nagging appoggiaturas, a steady, tolling tonic bass. The sighs intersperse Constanze's recitation of sorrow, which ends on the dominant of G minor. By contrast the woodwind alone briefly introduce the aria, pre-echoing Constanze's first phrase; they are strongly to the fore in this aria, often contrasted. antiphonally with strings.

> Sadness was my destiny because I was snatched from you. Like the worm-devoured rose, like grass in winter moss, my wretched life is fading. I cannot even tell the bitter pain of my soul to the breezes since they will, unwittingly, broadcast all my heart's lamentation.

Mozart had already apologized for playing down the lachrymose implications of Constanze's first aria. It was obviously wise at that point to make the most of Mme Cavalieri's vocal agility and *Silberklang* characteristics, knowing that she would have further opportunity now to play Madame Herz. So Constanze

* Some texts give *Kummer*.

305

gives expression to her sorrows in G minor, for Mozart the tonality of tears *par excellence*.

The harmony of the woodwind's opening is like a cry of pain, but it is typical of Mozart's G minor music, from his boyhood days when G minor was just a key in which one from time to time wrote a prescribed sort of music (e.g., the little andante for clavier K. 15r written at the age of eight and astonishingly mature in emotion simply because little Wolfgang was imitating the G minor music of other, older composers) until Pamina's *Ach ich fühl's* in 1791. Mozart makes an affecting point of the Neapolitan second (A flat in the key of G minor) in the third vocal phrase; but this too was a device he had known from his boyhood—there is a bold example in the D minor largo, No. 11 of the *Galimathias musicum*, K. 32, written in 1766. Most stirring of all in *Traurigkeit* is the repeated high phrase:

19

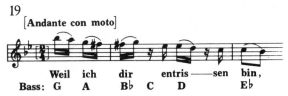

Similar in effect is the treatment of the line 'wieder in mein armes Herz', particularly when the first of each four semiquavers becomes a rest, like a missed heartbeat; and the poignant response of the woodwind to 'meiner Seele bitter'n Schmerz'—a heady foretaste of the 40th symphony:

20

The effect of the flutes' major second when Constanze sings of the 'wurmzernagte Rose', Blake's sick rose destroyed by the invisible worm, is not lessened when Mozart repeats the whole phrase for the next line of text which is less relevantly about grass in winter moss. The return to the opening is marvellously contrived; so too are the woodwind counterpoints to the violin semiquavers in the aria's postlude. None of these is an original discovery: the essence of Viennese classicism, as we understand it in Mozart's music, is that the small change of baroque and galant and rococo musical conversation is given freshness and depth by being used imaginatively.

Blonde exchanges encouraging words with her downcast mistress, telling her to go on hoping for Belmonte's arrival. Now here is the Pasha and Blonde prudently disappears; but her advice must have gone home, for Constanze's grief has been replaced by defiance when Selim commands her to return his love or else to suffer—not death but 'torture in all varieties', 'Martern aller Arten'. Constanze is not cowed by his threats, as she makes clear in **No. 11, Aria**, *Martern aller Arten*, C major, allegro. This is a display number in the old manner, even more glamorous than most since it boasts obbligati for four solo instruments—flute, oboe, violin and cello—the two woodwind voices being otherwise absent from the ripieno orchestra of clarinets, bassoons, horns, trumpets, drums and strings.

Tortures of all sorts may await me; I laugh at misery and pain. Nothing will shake me except the possibility of being unfaithful; that would make me tremble.

Be moved! Forgive me and heaven's blessing will reward you.

But you are determined and I willingly prefer every pain and distress. Command, ordain, shout, rage, demonstrate; death will eventually set me free.

Mozart had this and Blonde's No. 12 inserted in place of a duet for the two ladies, *Hoffnung, Trösterin im Leiden* ('Hope, comfortress in suffering') to whose sentiments their dialogue still leads up. We could have done with a two-soprano duet, and Mozart has been castigated for imposing two difficult arias, one after the other, on the *prima donna*: E. J. Dent even ranked *Martern* 'out of place in any opera on any subject'. This is surely too harsh. The diametrical contrast of emotion in these adjacent arias is most effective, and was presumably approved by Mme Cavalieri and the German operatic public of the time. The aria was originally somewhat longer, but was abbreviated by Mozart who thought the full-length version ill proportioned to the rest of the opera though suitable for separate concert performance.* Mozart still left a long orchestral prelude as a thorn in the flesh of modern opera producers who are ashamed to let Constanze and Selim stand quite so still for sixty bars of *allegro* music. It is possible, though they have, or should have, nothing to do with torture, to fill these bars with mimed altercation and animated gesture and movement (one production I remember made Constanze spend a period running up and down a flight of steps, an effort not calculated to prepare her best for the delivery of this diabolically strenuous music); the music, both ripieno and concertante, is very strongly characterized, and can readily be translated into appropriate sentences of defiance, courage, menace, pleading, and the like, though some brilliant dialogue in semiquavers between the four instrumental soloists would tax the casting powers of even Boris Goldovsky, the American opera producer who specializes in this method of actor-training. I have no doubt that Mozart wrote these sixty bars in full knowledge that his *prima donna* would pass the time quite acceptably indulging in a spit and adjustment of her costume, some *plastik* gesturing, advancing to the footlights, composing herself and fixing the spectators with a beady, imperious eye. The introduction, which has the dimensions and tonal stability of a concerto first movement exposition, is designed to give the whole opera a central point of opera-seria-like weight and magnificence. For this is the point: *Die Entführung* is not a comic opera as Naples, or Paris, or London, or even Vienna had understood the genre. It is the first of Mozart's operas, even including *La finta giardiniera*, to balance different genres and idioms, hitherto kept strictly apart, within a single frame that posterity must regard—more than the operas of deliberate reformers—as true and complete musicdrama.

Constanze, as soloist in this vocal concerto, cannot sing chords like the obbligato quartet, but she can throw off divisions as rapidly as they, and she does so almost at once to illustrate her derision of pain and suffering ('ich verlache Qual und

---

* The abbreviated passages, which should be included in concert performances, are printed in the Gesamtausgabe as an appendix.

Pein'). She introduces a more pathetic, minorish mood by way of transition to the aria's second subject-group (the *concertante* consolatory four-part harmony) whose musical content is explained by her promise that heaven will bless the Pasha if he spares her—is it just coincidence that the solo cello's bouncing octave dominant pedal-point suggests Mozart's Turkish style? Perhaps so, for to the same words she is off immediately in a dazzling stratospheric division that deflates gradually against beautiful harmonic suspensions, while the solo instruments spring into activity, until Constanze leaps from low B to G above the stave and thence to renewed bravura before a trilled cadence in the dominant, marking the central point of the aria. After an orchestral burst of animation the aria sags a little on the dominant, waiting for new revelations. These soon occur at a quickened tempo, curt and staccato with violent changes of dynamic to represent the Pasha's hard heart ('Doch du bist entschlossen'). This central section comes to a close with cadences strongly looking forward to *Die Zauberflöte*.

21

The original tempo is then resumed with the harmonious obbligato second subject. Constanze is given many high notes sustained over several bars: these were certainly designed as material for *mese di voce* and should be sung *crescendo-diminuendo*. The *allegro assai* occurs again, determinedly and dully (unless it is brilliantly decorated this time), but the aria closes with a tremendous eruption of running scales, ending with a commanding interrupted cadence on a held top A flat—crowned presumably by a cadenza—before the concluding rush.

After such an aria Constanze has to exit, in *opera seria* fashion. Selim soon follows her, after remarking (like Monostatos) that if force won't succeed he must employ cunning—which he never does.

Blonde now returns, surprised to find nobody about, and inclined to despise Constanze's eponymous firmness; she herself, if Pedrillo were not there, would be almost willing to adopt the attitude of female Muslims. But Pedrillo is here, with two jars of wine which he requires for his stratagem (as well as a sleeping draught which Blonde must dispense to Osmin), and with news that must be rewarded with a kiss: the arrival of Belmonte and his acceptance by Pasha Selim as a potential employee. Blonde greets this delightful news with **No. 12, Aria**, *Welche Wonne, welche Lust*, G major, *allegro*, with flutes, bassoons, horns and strings.

> What bliss, what delight has taken my heart over. Unasked I will jump and bring her the news at once and foretell gladness and joy to her weak, cowardly heart.

Mozart usually found it less strenuous to write a new tune rather than to adapt an old one, but here he borrowed the finale rondo theme from his D major flute concerto (itself a transcription of the C major oboe concerto of 1778).

22

It is a pleasing melody characteristic of a high-spirited young lady. A feature of the accompaniment is the prevalence of jumps in the violin part (at 'Ohne Aufschub will ich springen'), sometimes octave jumps that recall the voice of the quail as portrayed by Beethoven and Berlioz (or the transparent domain of Wolf's *O wär dein Haus*):

The rondo form allows for cadenzas and decorated repeats as well as appoggiaturas, though repeated notes, we have seen, are not uncharacteristic of peasant music. But Blonde would be far from pleased to be equated with a peasant.

Blonde runs off to bring the good news to Constanze, and Pedrillo realizes that this happy outcome of which his sweetheart has been confidently singing will only be possible if he steels himself to boldness, and combats his natural timidity.

No. 13, Aria, *Frisch zum Kampfe*, D major, *allegro con spirito* (oboes, horns, trumpets, drums and strings): Pedrillo tries to bolster his spirits.

> Off to battle, off to war! Only a cowardly chap would decline. Shall I quake, shall I quiver, not bravely venture my life? No, I shall be daring!

Mozart puts this into human perspective by interspersing heroic military fanfares with confidential tiptoe music for Stephanie's contrasting phrases. At 'Sollt' ich zittern', for instance, the second violins carry on a sturdy pattern of dotted crotchets and quavers while first violins tremble in triplets, lower strings pluck a descending bass, and semi-confident horn fanfares are even more uncertainly echoed note for note by oboes.

Pedrillo banishes these auguries of danger and failure and returns manfully to tonic and dominant attitudinizing, though the conventionality and repetitiousness of the results sound hollow and absurd. When 'sollt' ich zittern' returns, the oboes are wailing unashamedly in thirds, and though the subsequent call of valour takes Pedrillo splendidly up to top B the cadence with a trill on an ineffective middle

A lets the pose down. The aria ends with a helter-skelter of descending scales, which may be formal but can equally well be interpreted less gloriously.

Osmin has heard Pedrillo's cheerful concluding remarks and asks, as he enters, what is their cause. Pedrillo indicates his bottles, remarking how sad it is that Mohammed forbade alcohol to his followers. Gradually he overcomes Osmin's scruples and soon they are both sitting on the floor, each with a bottle, singing the praises of the god of wine in **No. 14, Duet**, *Vivat Bacchus*, C major, *allegro* (full orchestra without horns, but including three flutes). Mozart told his father that this 'consists entirely of my Turkish Tattoo', and that he had included it 'per i signori vienesi'. It opens irresistibly with a scampering, *sotto voce*, tune for three flutes and violins, the third flute contributing descants and imitations that heighten the pace. This, inferably, is the relic of the lost Tattoo, perhaps a piano piece that Mozart played at parties and never bothered to write down. It is possible that another section of the Tattoo is to be found in the repeated phrase which accompanies the second and third statements of 'Es leben die Mädchen'. But the vocal line here very strongly suggests popular melody of the German student-song type, and I think it is more likely that this was another sort of sop to the 'signori vienesi', with an appropriate (not so obviously Turkish) obbligato accompaniment. But it is curious that 'Es leben die Mädchen' is sung the first time to a quite different musical idea. The duet is constructed in rondo fashion and involves several recitative-like or semi-cadential phrases with written-in pauses and implied rubato of the kind that Mozart used in other rondos to delay the expected return of the tune, and that allow in this case for vocal flourishes. At 'Ob's wohl Allah sehen kann?', the pause on 'Allah' invites Osmin to raise a bonus laugh by inserting an oriental-style muezzin cantillation. It would not be out of character.

The trumpets and Turkish percussion are kept in reserve until the first return of the rondo theme after which their gay clatter remains uninterrupted until the end of the duet.

Osmin is now mellower and more amiably inclined to Ped..llo, indeed he is growing increasingly sleepy. Stephanie (or is it the cautious Mozart?) adds a remark to the actor of Osmin that the remainder of this scene must not be played exaggeratedly—he 'must simply go on remaining half dreaming and drunk with sleep', though contrariwise he is almost at once told to nod his head sleepily as he remarks on the cheering effect of wine, and reach out 'in a laughable manner' for the second bottle which Pedrillo gives him before leading him solicitously off to bed.

The fellow conspirators have been in punctual liaison. As Pedrillo emerges from the cottage of the now deeply slumbering Osmin, Belmonte comes to meet him, and, a moment later, Blonde is walking down the path with Constanze. The moment of reunion has been so long awaited and much discussed—it is, after all, the first dramatic climax of the work—that one would expect Mozart to insist that it should be set to music. He and Stephanie decided otherwise: modern producers should think more than twice before they, reasonably to be sure, cut the dialogue and Belmonte's No. 15 which postpone the great emotional release of the vocal quartet. As we know, Mozart had already persuaded Stephanie to move this forward from Act III. If he had wanted the quartet now he would have placed it here, but instead he has insisted on a second aria for Belmonte (not in

Bretzner) before Constanze starts to sing. Adamberger's needs as *primo tenore* had to be considered; but his aria could have been placed earlier or later, and I can only assume that this is the build-up which Mozart thought most effective, even though he subsequently shortened it.

In the score as we have it, at any rate, they fall into one another's arms, while Pedrillo mimes to Blonde what has happened and been planned for later that night—Pedrillo has just told us that it wants three hours to midnight.

Constanze's immediate reaction to reunion with Belmonte is that she wants to lean on his chest and cry for joy. This seems quite parodistic in character, fated to draw laughter from the most reverential modern audience. But it is designed, however crudely, as a cue for Belmonte's **No. 15, Aria**, *Wenn der Freude Tränen fliessen*, B flat major, *adagio-allegro* with oboes, clarinets, bassoons, horns and strings.

> When tears of joy are flowing, love smiles kindly on the lover; to kiss them from her cheeks is love's fairest, greatest reward. Ah Constanze, to see you, to press you ecstatically to my faithful heart is worth more than all Croesus's riches.
>
> If we had never met again, we would not have realized the pain caused by separation.

This is a consolatory piece, and the first strain may seem to be marked too slow at *adagio*, since the melody is of the serenade *andante* type, closely related even, by its initial repeated notes, to the second movement of *Eine kleine Nachtmusik*, and indeed the *andante* of the E flat string quartet K. 614.

In the mouth of a patrician operatic character the second of these three initial D's should, I am convinced, be interpreted as a C sharp if the effect is not to be cosily bourgeois. It should, however, be tender and delicate, oil poured on troubled waters, as witness the gentle contour of the first phrase, even at its forte repeat by woodwind, and the ensuing *dolce* for the sensuous string phrases in sixths and tenths just afterwards ('ist der Liebe grösster Sold') and the prolongation by repeat of the last instrumental phrase in the introduction, initially for charming effect though later to make a seamless transition into the next section, the more animated heart-fluttering 'Ach Constanze! dich zu sehen' whose undulating violin semiquavers held the tempo back at the beginning. At 'lohnt fürwahr' we hear the

Decision motiv mentioned earlier in connection with No. 3, and there is an opulent leap of a twelfth, perhaps inspired by the thought of Croesus's splendour (some texts give 'Kron und Pracht'), just before the first F major cadence and pause. At this point Mozart had originally included an extra return of the main tune and further setting of lines 5 to 8; when he revised the opera he removed them, perhaps wisely for operatic purposes, though the boldly ranging vocal line and harmonic dips from E flat to C minor, G minor and ultimately a cadence in D minor, are musically to be missed—on gramophone records or in concert performances of this aria by itself the aria might well be restored to its original state. In the revised version a return of the initial melody leads to cajoling thirds and sixths, an exquisitely heartfelt touch of ♭VII harmony ('voll Entzücken' it certainly is), and a dash of running semiquaver divisions linked by that leap of a twelfth, to emphasize Croesus's wealth.

The coda of the aria moves into 3/4 and *allegretto*. A woodwind sextet steps forward as if to serenade Constanze (the rhythmic structure looks forward to Figaro's *Se vuol ballare*), retreating in favour of strings when Belmonte repeats the melody. There is a suggestion of reunion and separation ('dass wir uns niemals wiederfinden') in the contrary motion of voice and bass line around the dominant pedal-point, and a stab of pain, though not more, at the thought of 'welchen Schmerz die Trennung macht'. This coda originally included thirty-two more bars, mostly florid and at one point decidedly exacting.

A notable aria indeed. The sudden jump from its B flat major to the D major of No. 16 sounds decidedly peculiar in performance, but the solution is surely not to postpone No. 15 to the third act where its sentiments would be unmotivated. Much better to invent some new dialogue that will soften the key switch.

No. 16, Quartet, D major, initially *allegro* (full orchestra without clarinets or Turkish percussion). Mozart particularly wanted this quartet to end Act II, and he made Stephanie rewrite it as an expression of joy at loving reunion contrasted with male anxieties about the fidelity of the ladies in the immediate past, where Bretzner's quartet was concerned with the conspiracy of abduction and its chances of success. Mozart wanted a quantity of voices to end the act, which was sensible; but, as Abert wisely points out, this is a highly unconventional end to an *opera buffa* act, since its drama is introvert, not animated by busy situation (as for example it was at the end of Act I). The animation and quantity of activity is left to music.

Mozart begins blamelessly enough with a well tried opening theme that may nowadays recall largely the second half of Leporello's *Madamina*. With its persistent repeated tonic bass it looks back to the galant sons of Bach. Recognizable Mozart begins to occur with the rising sixths from 'Ist es möglich' onwards, and then unmistakably at 'dass es doch' with six moving parts, Belmonte and Constanze counterpointing sequentially against pairs of contrary-motion oboes and bassoons in thirds. This complex takes the music into A major as dominant. Belmonte and Constanze having had the first subject group to themselves, it is for Pedrillo and Blonde to step forward in the second group which is firmly characterized —a frisson of giggles (flute and first violin) for her, a slower rising scale pattern for him, not unlike Figaro's *Menta il ceffo, io non mento* in the second act finale,

27
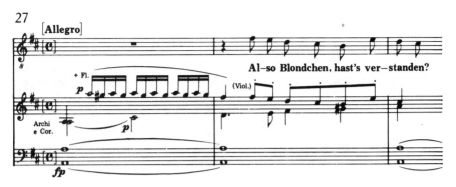

and for the two of them as vocalists a more animated dialogue in quavers than that of their cantabile employers, this section at least concerned with the conspiracy as in Bretzner. When the first theme returns the two couples combine as a quartet: at 'Voll Entzücken' a new version of the giggling motiv, in tenths, arrives, and its similarity to a phrase in the second movement of the Haffner Symphony (composed immediately after *Die Entführung*) cannot be coincidental.

28

29

The full loud cadence in the tonic D major paves the way for a more cloudy *andante* in G minor. Once again a pedal note, to convey emotional tension, but this time a dominant pedal on horns and first violins above a hesitant theme, since Belmonte hardly likes to voice the doubts in his mind. Constanze begs him, on the verge of B flat minor, to be frank but he still hesitates—the oboe wordlessly completes his sentence, as it does when Pedrillo attempts to sound Blonde on her relations with Osmin. The two men conquer their embarrassment in an E flat major *andante* duet delicately sustained by smooth woodwind chords and helped along by the strings' dummy accompaniment.

The effort was hardly worth making. Constanze is deeply hurt by the suggestion, Blonde slaps Pedrillo's face and the two men have to beg for forgiveness, *allegro assai* in B flat minor, while the ladies exchange expressions of outrage to a comical clucking violin duologue. The next section is to be in distant A major and the clucking *allegro* now moves purposefully and with tonally blurring effect through D minor, C minor, B flat major, G minor, to a block harmony *adagio* close on the dominant of A minor which is duly resolved in A major at the start of a short *andantino* in siciliana style with glee-type block harmony that Mozart was to feature in *Die Zauberflöte*.

This middle section of the quartet has rather fallen apart into short rhapsodic sections at different tempi and in different keys, more like an extempore fantasia than an operatic finale. Mozart now begins to acknowledge the needs of structure in a more extended A major *allegretto* whose charming rococo melody ('Liebstes Blondchen! ach verzeihe') is adorned by the 12/8 triplet counterpoint sung above it by Blonde. The men are still asking forgiveness. Charity asserts itself with a chain of ravishing upward arpeggios for woodwind. Pardon is granted in prim imitative minims that reach back to D major, the movement's home tonic. A little burst of concerted relief and contentment, and the final *allegro* is upon us ('Es lebe die Liebe') with rushing scales, canonic entries and plenty of four-part block harmony to bring down the curtain satisfactorily.

4

Act III begins in the palace square as for Act I except that it is viewed from another angle: the palace which was facing us is now to one side; straight ahead is the sea; on the other hand (Stephanie does not specify which) is the front of Osmin's house which we saw from the back in Act II.

It is midnight, the time appointed for the abduction. Pedrillo has been put in touch with Klaas, one of the sailors on Belmonte's ship (is it a Dutch barge, or why such an un-Spanish name?), and Klaas is now helping Pedrillo to carry in and hide the two ladders by which the ladies will soon be rescued from their sleeping-quarters. This done, Klaas is sent back on board to lift anchor and hoist full sail so that they can leave as soon as the harem snatch has been effected.

Belmonte comes to find out if all is ready. Pedrillo wants to make a final inspection of the palace to ensure that they will not be disturbed. Meanwhile he advises Belmonte to divert suspicion by singing a serenade, a practice the palace guards have grown accustomed to during Pedrillo's stay here. This obviously unsubtle cue for music gives Belmonte the excuse for **No. 17, Aria**, *Ich baue ganz auf deine Stärke*, E flat major, *andante* (flutes, clarinets, bassoons, horns, strings).

> I build entirely on your strength, O Love; I trust in your power. How many achievements have been accomplished through you! What all the world thinks impossible can still come to fruition through Love.

Again, as in No. 15, the woodwind is deployed prominently as if it were a serenade wind-band, but the atmosphere is wholly cheerful in this hymn to the power of love. The thematic material of this short sonata-form movement is conventional but attractive and affectionately detailed; we might suspect, if we did not know, that Mozart was busy writing woodwind music before and immediately after *Die Entführung* (the serenades KK. 370a, 375, 384a, for example). For all the interest of the woodwind writing this was primarily a virtuoso vehicle for Adamberger and it contains florid divisions that demand such agility and flexibility and breath control that tenors usually shy away from *Ich baue ganz* or attempt it and are defeated by, for example, the fluent arpeggios written first for clarinet and then repeated by the singer.

30

[Andante]

doch —————— ver — eint ——————

Pedrillo returns, satisfied that all is as quiet as on the day after the Deluge. And now you would think that the abduction could (and should) quickly be carried out. But first Pedrillo has another solo to sing, his signal for the ladies to make ready. It replaced a duet for the two men, K. 384A, *Welch ängstliches Beben*, E flat major—another number that is to be missed.

No. 18, Romanze, *In Mohrenland gefangen war ein Mädel* (plucked strings only, imitating the mandolin on which Pedrillo supposedly accompanies himself).

A pretty girl was captured in Moorish lands. She was pink and white with black hair, sighed and wept all day and night and longed to be rescued.

From a foreign land arrived a young knight. The girl longed for him. I'll risk my head and my honour, he cried, to rescue her.

I come to you at dead of night; sweetheart, let me in. I'm not afraid of locks or guards. Listen: at midnight you'll be rescued.

Good as his word at 12 o'clock the bold knight stood there. Gently she gave him her soft hand. At dawn the cell was found empty, she was off and away!

No tempo indication is given but the siciliana character of the music suggests an *andantino*. Nor can I specify the tonality since it veers between B minor, D major and F sharp major, with switches into A major, C major and G major. The melody inclines to a Phrygian mode on B which explains the choice of ♭II and ♭VII harmonies and postulates the other keys as dominants. The word-setting includes numerous misaccentuations and was doubtless intended to resemble a ditty in an exotic folk-like style hurriedly improvised by an amateur serenader. Was Pedrillo supposed to be cultivating a Spanish or Moorish style? The effect is certainly novel and rather pretty.

After two verses Belmonte orders Pedrillo to cease, but the ladies have not shown any response so he sings two further verses, and by this time Constanze is opening her window, so the song finishes and Pedrillo holds the ladder while Belmonte climbs into Constanze's room and escapes with her through the main palace door. This done Pedrillo puts the second ladder (why were two needed?) under Blonde's window and likewise climbs into Osmin's house.

No sooner has Pedrillo disappeared inside than Osmin staggers, still half-asleep and intoxicated as well as drugged, out of the house. He has been woken by his black servant, a mute, who has heard noises. The mute now draws attention to the ladder and is sent to fetch the guards while Osmin, after an outburst of fuddled alarm and fury, sits on the ladder and dozes. As Pedrillo begins to descend the ladder backwards, Blonde at the window catches sight of Osmin and draws her lover back inside. Osmin hears their voices and begins to climb after them. They quickly leave by the main door and are away before Osmin can totter after them.

The guards bar his way and are at first suspicious of him, not recognizing him. But now Blonde and Pedrillo are led back by other guards, and a further detachment soon arrives with Constanze and Belmonte. Blackmail and bribery do not for a moment divert Osmin from his long-held ambition to see them dangling on the gallows. The four escapers are led into the Pasha's palace to Osmin's unbounded delight, voiced in **No. 19, Aria**, *O wie will ich triumphieren*, D major, *allegro vivace*, with piccolo, oboes, clarinets, bassoons, horns, strings.

> O how triumphant I shall be when they lead you to the gallows and string you up by the necks. I will skip, laugh, jump and sing a hymn of joy, because I shall be rid of you.
>
> Nicely and quietly you may crawl, cursèd harem mice, but our ears detect you, and before you can slip away you're in our clutches and you'll get your reward.

Another vehicle for Fischer, and a crowning explosion of Osmin's childish sadism (e.g. the gleeful repetitions of 'und die Hälse schnüren zu'). Fischer's low notes are exploited (as in No. 3 and No. 9) by descending phrases repeated an octave lower, long-held low notes, comic octave jumps that inevitably involve facial grimaces which the singer may not notice but will delight the audience (we know that Mozart calculated for this effect in *Così fan tutte*), and a measure of florid divisions spanning two octaves, as well as the usual scope for ornamentation and cadenza that would allow Fischer to introduce his lowest and highest notes.

The aria is also an ace in a strong suit of Turkish trump-cards. The Turkish percussion are not required in so quick and light-footed a number: piccolo and Turkish musical phraseology are sufficient for Mozart's needs. The opening phrase is a Turkish version of the finale subject in Mozart's forthcoming Haffner Symphony (to link the opening theme of the symphony's first movement with the octave leaps at Osmin's 'Schleicht nur säuberlich und leise' is tempting but perhaps far-fetched—it is enough to indicate that *Entführung* was still spinning in Mozart's head when he came to write the Haffner Symphony). The 'Schleicht nur' section is especially full of captivating detail: the taut conspiratorial suspensions accompanying the leaps, the scampering of the 'Haremsmäuse' on violins *fp* immediately after, and the hint at capture in the accompaniment of 'entrinnen', and 'Schlingen'—the cat pouncing on the mice—then the nice addition of contrapuntal imitations before the repeat of 'Schleicht nur säuberlich'. It is worth pointing also to the dance-tune provided for Osmin's hopping and jumping when 'Hüpfen will ich' returns: a country dance, as much German as Turkish.

31

[Allegro vivace]

Picc. Fag. 15ᵛᵃ

And to the 'Freudenliedchen' which now emerges as a wordless florid melisma full of triplets. Altogether a highly inventive as well as brilliant end to the scene.

For although some productions find it practical to play the entire third act in the palace square, Stephanie here indicates a change of scene to the Pasha's room.

Pasha Selim has been woken by the noise, and has hardly demanded an investigation when Osmin rolls somnolently into the presence of his master bringing news that treason has been going on and that the criminals, favourites of Selim among them, have been apprehended.

Constanze pleads to die for Belmonte: he promises that they will both be ransomed at any price by his family of Lostados. This is a name familiar to the Pasha. It emerges that Belmonte's father, the commandant of Oran, once treated Selim mòst cruelly, depriving him of home, sweetheart, possessions, prestige, everything and forced him to settle here, far from his native land (Spain was a Moorish territory for many centuries). To have his hated enemy's son in his power, Belmonte admits, can mean only a miserable fate for him. Selim and Osmin go to prepare the torture chamber for Belmonte and his bride who are left alone with their guards.

No. 20, Recitative, *Welch ein Geschick* (strings), F major; and **Duet,** *Meinetwegen sollst du sterben,* B flat major (flutes, clarinets, horns, strings). Very considerately the serious climax of the opera's music follows immediately upon the comic climax.

The *adagio* recitative opens with direct, deeply expressive falling phrases, literally and metaphorically downcast; it follows, from what was written earlier, that since these concern the two noble lovers apparently *in extremis* the phrase-ends cannot conceivably be left blunt as written, but must be softened with appoggiaturas. Belmonte's opening sentences are desperate, but his close in D minor is turned firmly into confident B flat as Constanze consoles him. What, she asks, is death, after all? 'Ein Übergang zur Ruh'—'a transition to repose', beautiful, illuminating phrase: the romantic reader, thinking perhaps of Mozart's letter to his father on the subject of death, will automatically ascribe the authorship to Mozart though if any of the libretto is likely to be his it is the less sublime text of No. 19.

The duet begins *andante* with an orchestral figure of determination, in its context a little more than a call to attention. Belmonte opens with a certain agitation in his string accompaniment. Constanze's positive attitude is gently underlined by the first entry of woodwind (flutes and first clarinet), but the strings' semiquaver agitated repeated notes persist since, for all her calmness, she sees death before her in clear F minor, though her courage turns this minor into F major at 'Wonne ist mir dies Gebot'; her heroism is at this point indubitable and superb. It infects Belmonte as the marvellously varied subsequent third and sixth doublings indicate—they are of one mind in their confidence, though Constanze's determined 'Wonne ist mir die Gebot' in E flat with woodwind accompaniment only shows her to be the leader of, so to say, the suicide squad. Their B flat *allegro* resolution, its ecstatic duetting melismata on 'O welche Seligkeit' (the bliss signifying slow and excruciating death), and particularly the soft high gruppetto for violins, all suggest self-abandonment of a Tristanesque order, emphasized by the thirds and sixths, symbolic of complete union, though with this square text we may more quickly think of *Die Zauberflöte*. The ending is solemn yet decidedly excited. Death together will be equivalent to a superterrestrial eternal physical union, in fact a Wagnerian *Liebestod;* for any very musical citizen of Vienna in 1782 this duet must have seemed as wild and exhilarating a death-wish as that presented by Wagner in Munich eighty-seven years later, though not a submission but a bold self-sacrifice.

Italian-trained opera singers, even in an *opera buffa*, would automatically leave the stage here. And the next scene, short as it is, concerns only the *confidanti*. Pedrillo has discovered that he is to be boiled in oil, then roasted on a spit. Blonde, less inquisitive, knows only that death comes to all, none more agreeable than another, a stiff-upper-lip British point of view that astounds her self-confessedly Spanish-orientated lover.

The Pasha returns, and they all expect the worst. But this renegade Muslim, versed in cruelty, has also his pride and he has determined that an eye does not merit an eye in return. All four prisoners are to be set free and allowed to sail home. Contemptuously he tells Belmonte that if his action persuades the young man to behave more humanely than his father did, then this deed will be well rewarded. Stephanie had altered this dénouement from Bretzner's where the hero turns out to be the Pasha's son. Clement tyrants were already old hat, but Vienna still favoured such dramatic conventions. Osmin of course explodes with his favourite oath, 'Gift und Dolch!' ('Poison and dagger') at the thought of losing his sparring partner Blonde. But the Pasha assures him that what cannot be won by kindness is better got rid of.

And so the cast lines up for a formalized finale, a French-type vaudeville where each character sings subjectively appropriate words to the same tune, all joining in a refrain.

No. 21, Vaudeville, *Nie werd ich deine Huld verkennen*, begins *andante* in F major with flutes, oboes, bassoons, horns and strings. Belmonte leads off mellifluously with string accompaniment; the refrain is signalled by a more active bass. Constanze's verse introduces a bassoon doubling, Pedrillo is matched by an oboe, Blonde by a flute—her refrain is not directed at the Pasha's goodness but at Osmin's intractability and, humanly enough, in place of the so far communal refrain, Osmin bursts in, at slower tempo, hungering for the deaths that have slipped past him, modulating from F major to A minor, *allegro assai*, for a surprising and rewarding reprise of his coda to No. 3, 'Erst geköpft, dann gehangen'—which brings back, most welcome, the full Turkish percussion, as well as Osmin's most violent mood in which he leaves the stage. The four remaining soloists, *andante sostenuto*, join in one of these quasi-moralizing block harmony vocal quartets (this one begins in A minor and moves back to F) which look forward to *Die Zauberflöte*—notice the biting of woodwind on the word 'hässlich'. And then Constanze brings back the F major refrain which they all take up once more.

Immediately the opera closes, *allegro vivace* in C major, with a chorus of Janissaries, or rather of female and male employees in the Pasha's service, based on the ritornello of No. 5 but newly set to the same texture, touching on C minor but ending firmly in the opera's major tonic.

5

Carl Maria von Weber called *Die Entführung* 'Mozart's youthful *unicum*'. If he meant that it was the one outstanding masterpiece of Mozart's pre-maturity, he must be refuted, for can *Entführung* be thought to surpass *Idomeneo* or the E flat Sinfonia Concertante K. 320d, or the B flat wind serenade K. 370a? From the retrospective standpoint of *Figaro* we may concede that *Entführung* is the best and most fully developed of Mozart's comic operas up to that point, the only one in which Mozart works out a clear and thorough contrast of relationships between the various groups of characters. It is the great stepping-stone from *La finta giardiniera* to the complete human comedy of *Figaro* and its successors, and in this sense it is the opera in which Mozart first became an adult.

But emotionally he had already shown maturity, though in a style that did not offer his genius full scope, with *Idomeneo*. Mozart was at pains, as we have seen, to get the libretto of *Entführung* fashioned to his satisfaction. Yet when it was completed (and we should grant credit to Stephanie for reshaping the end of Act II and the first scene of Act III so that, with Mozart's sovereign assistance, they do not much betray his process of marking time) Stephanie's work did not, could not give airborne power to the wings of adult genius. Its sublimities collapse all too often into banality or absurdity, its comedy into exaggeration or mere tomfoolery. In No. 15, for example, the allusion to 'Crösus Pracht' sounds false and unpoetical in context, as in No. 11 the change of mood between 'Lass dich bewegen' and the very next words 'Verschone mich' does not survive intelligent listening (Mozart almost ignores it). The naïve diction of No. 6 has been noticed in Mozart's own words. It would be unkind to continue picking holes in Stephanie's libretto: it is hack work with moments of poetic illumination (such as 'Was ist der Tod? Ein Übergang zur Ruh'). More seriously, though, Stephanie's stilted diction prevented Mozart from bringing his hero and heroine to life, sing as angelically as they may. Pedrillo and Blonde, the Arlecchino and Smeraldina of this piece, have more blood in their veins, and Osmin alone is a vital character, though still allied to the nursery bogeydom of Colas in *Bastien und Bastienne*. Where these characters are pitted against one another, as in No. 9, the conflict is at an entirely superficial level; or its intensity, in No. 20, is musical but not personally vivid—it is a duet for generalized male and female, not for two recognizable people. We need only look forward to the duets in Act IV of *Figaro* to recognize what great strides Mozart's dramatic language had taken (and to appreciate how much they were helped by da Ponte's words).

This is not to say that *Die Entführung aus dem Serail* does not succeed on stage. Almost always it does, because the music is successful. The solos are beautifully contrasted, the ensembles full of musical activity; they are even bigger than the characters to which they are assigned—Belmonte's last two arias, for example, comprise superlative music which does not, in either case, add to our deeper acquaintance with the hero, but reduces him to an animated singing-machine. Mozart's great comic operas are chiefly fascinating for their emotional ambivalence, the charmed life that they lead on the tightrope above laughter and tears. We are sometimes drawn on to this tightrope in *Die Entführung*, in the second act quartet, Pedrillo's serenade perhaps, even maybe in Osmin's *Wer ein Liebchen*; but not where we would expect it, in the big arias for Belmonte and Constanze.

We should perhaps be content to enjoy and admire this opera from another point of view, as a jolly rescue opera, deliberately calculated for success with a naïve eighteenth-century audience for whom the formalities of Mozart's music, and the blunt contrasts between the personages, were more appreciable, because connected with the familiar traditions of *opera seria*, than any emotional or dramatic subtlety would have been. The orchestration, to which attention has often been drawn, is full of subtleties. But it gave the Emperor cause for complaint about 'monstrous many notes', and this reaction as well as the others noted earlier in this chapter show how very remote we are from the *Entführung* that Mozart wrote, and how impossible it is to judge it nowadays by his standards.

15 L'OCA DEL CAIRO

L'OCA DEL CAIRO

(The Cairo Goose)

Dramma giocoso per musica

Libretto by

GIOVANNI BATTISTA VARESCO

K. 422

DON PIPPO, Marquess of Ripasecca, in love with Lavina	BASS
DONNA PANTEA, his wife, believed dead, known as Sandra, living across the bay	?SOPRANO
CELIDORA, their only daughter, intended by her father to marry Count Lionetto of Casavuota, but really in love with:	SOPRANO
BIONDELLO, a rich gentleman of Ripasecca	TENOR
CALANDRINO, Donna Pantea's nephew, friend of Biondello and requited lover of	TENOR
LAVINA, Celidora's companion	SOPRANO
CHICHIBIO, Don Pippo's majordomo, lover of	BASS
AURETTA, Donna Pantea's chambermaid	SOPRANO

Wigmakers, Tailor, Shoemaker, Sailors and Dockers, Barrowboys,
Populace, Courtiers, Servants of Biondello and Calandrino,
Soldiers guarding the rock

Scene: Ripasecca, maritime city and capital of a marquisate

After *Die Entführung* it might have seemed that Mozart was made as an opera composer, and that commissions for new operas, whether in German or Italian, would keep him permanently busy. But four years were to elapse before his next full-length opera appeared.

Nineteen days after the première of *Die Entführung* Mozart married his Constanze, having prudently told his father too late to obtain anything but a *post facto* blessing: not that he had lost contact with Salzburg—he wrote his second Haffner Serenade during July, the one now only known in its abbreviated form as the Haffner Symphony (the finale recalls Osmin and his Triumph Song) and, fortunately for us, maintained his newsy correspondence with his father. In December 1782 Wolfgang and Constanze moved into lodgings with Baron Raimund Wetzlar von Plankenstern, a Jew who was to introduce his family friend Lorenzo da Ponte to Mozart. Wolfgang was finding employment playing the piano in the homes of the Viennese nobility. His thoughts were constantly with operatic subjects. Despite the appearance of disastrous German operas in Vienna, such as Umlauf's *Welche ist die beste Nation?*, the libretto of which Mozart had turned down, he told his father on 5 February 1783:

> I do not believe that the Italian opera will keep going for long, and besides, I hold with the Germans. I prefer German opera, even though it means more trouble for me. Every nation has its own opera and why not Germany? Is not German as singable as French and English? Is it not more so than Russian? Very well then! I am now writing a German opera for myself. I have chosen Goldoni's comedy *Il servitore di due padroni*, and the whole of the first act has now been translated. Baron Binder is the translator. But we are keeping it a secret until it is quite finished.★

This plan came to nothing though two surviving concert arias may have been intended for *Der Diener zweier Herren: Müsst ich auch durch tausend Drachen* (K. 435) for tenor; and *Männer suchen stets zu naschen* (K. 433) for bass—nowadays often sung by sopranos under the title *Warnung*.

Mozart had, notwithstanding his lack of faith in Italian opera, been examining Italian libretti. He had been asked, pending the arrival in Vienna of several Italian guest singers, to write an Italian opera; the invitation came from Count Orsini-Rosenberg, the general director of spectacle in Vienna. Mozart sent to Italy, even to Salzburg, for every usable text. After looking, he told his father on 7 May, at more than a hundred libretti, he concluded that it would be best to compose a brand new libretto, and by now his heart was set on an Italian comic opera, doubtless because he had met da Ponte who showed interest in working with him, and who promised to write a new text for him as soon as an existing commission for Salieri was completed, which would be in July. Mozart was fired with

★ Translation by Emily Anderson, Vol. II, p. 839.

eagerness but sceptical of the promises, so he asked Leopold whether Varesco, after the quarrels over *Idomeneo*, might still be willing to devise for Mozart 'a new libretto for seven characters . . . two equally good female parts, one of these to be *seria*, the other *mezzo carattere*, but both parts equal in importance and excellence. The third female character, however, may be entirely *buffa*, and so may all the male ones if necessary.'*

2

The predictably unpromising return to collaboration with Varesco was caused not only by da Ponte's involvement with Salieri but also by Mozart's intention to bring his wife for a stay in Salzburg where his family could at last make Constanze's acquaintance and learn to love her. This would be an opportunity for Wolfgang to work on the opera with Varesco. The subject of *L'oca del Cairo* was suggested and approved. On 21 June Mozart wrote to his father:

> I must now talk to Count Rosenberg at once to ensure the poet's remuneration. But that Mr Varesco has doubts about the opera's success I find very insulting to me. I can assure him that his libretto will not be liked if the music is not good. The music is the chief thing in every opera. So if it is going to be liked (so that he may hope for payment), then he must alter things for me and revise as much and as often as I wish, and not follow his instinct which has not the smallest practicality or knowledge of theatre.†

The Mozarts were besought by their friends not to go to Salzburg where Wolfgang could well be arrested by the Archbishop from whose service he had not yet been officially dismissed in writing. He himself was in no hurry to work with Varesco since in early July he was in possession of a new libretto by 'a foreign poet'—evidently da Ponte's *Lo sposo deluso*, of which more later—though he was not yet sure how much he would like it or whether the poet would be willing to trim it to suit him. However, husband and wife did make the journey at the end of July and stayed in Salzburg until the end of October; Abbé Varesco is known to have spent at least one afternoon (22 August) with the Mozarts. They had left their infant son Raimund in Vienna with a fostermother; he died of intestinal cramp while they were away.

Mozart may or may not have begun composition of *L'oca del Cairo* while in Salzburg; his letters suggest that his father had seen none of the music. Varesco is assumed to have completed the text of the first act during this period. The young Mozarts returned to Vienna, after a visit to Count Thun at Linz, at the end of November. By 6 December Mozart had completed all but three arias in the first act, having 'worked quite speedily within the short time'. We shall see that this included seven numbers incompletely scored, a little recitative, and sketches for another aria: not so much that Mozart, who had written the Linz Symphony during four days in November, could not have written it 'at speed' since his

---

* Translation by Emily Anderson, Vol. II, p. 848. The recipe may interestingly be compared with those for *La finta giardiniera* and *Così fan tutte*, which adopt this pattern, and for *Le nozze di Figaro* and *Don Giovanni* which deviate slightly in the male characterizations.
 † My translation.

return from Linz where he had certainly been pondering the weaknesses of the scenario—the goose-disguise, and the appearance on stage of the two leading ladies only in the third act. Between early December and early February he made numerous suggestions for alterations in the plot, and mentioned that some more text had arrived. He begged Leopold to spur Varesco, then contrariwise blamed the poet for writing in too much haste, saying that the opera could wait. By 10 February he had enough paid work to want to put L'oca del Cairo aside. He never returned to it.

L'oca del Cairo remains a tantalizing fragment. Its remains were published in 1855 in vocal score, performed in concert at Frankfurt in 1860, and subsequently elsewhere. In 1867 a stage version was produced in Paris. T. C. Constantin supplemented the extant numbers with parts of Lo sposo deluso and some Mozart concert pieces, and fitted them to a new French text in two acts. This version was also performed in German, Danish, and Italian (in London, with recitatives by Bottesini—better known as a double-bass virtuoso). In 1936 Virgilio Mortari made a new stage version for a fringe event at the Salzburg Festival. Dr Hans Redlich reduced the plot to one act, using only Mozart's seven numbers which he scored more fully, for performance at Sadler's Wells by an *ad hoc* company in 1940.* This was revived in 1955, again in London with additional recitatives by Jan van Loewen. The music of L'oca del Cairo was used, by the Swiss musician Hans Erismann, together with that of Lo sposo deluso and other contemporary works by Mozart, for a three-act opera to a new text, entitled Don Pedros Heimkehr; it won some brief acclaim in the early 1950s, but is not to be recommended as an unknown Mozart opera.

3

Varesco's complete libretto for the first act tells only part of the story as retailed in his three-act scenario. Ripasecca is a maritime fortified town, governed by a despotic Marquess. The present ruler, Don Pippo, has exiled his wife Pantea and gives himself out as a widower. He has promised their only child, a daughter Celidora, to a certain Count Lionetto di Casavuota ('empty house'), and has decided himself to marry her companion Lavina. Since they both have swains, he has shut them up in the fortress, which is evidently not uncomfortable and gives on to a garden surrounded by fortified walls and guarded by sentries. He is so sure of his omnipotence that he has promised Biondello, Celidora's lover, permission to wed her if, within a year, he manages to penetrate the fortress. Lavina's beloved, Calandrino, has kept in touch with his aunt Pantea who is alive and well and living across the bay under the pseudonym of Sandra. He has constructed a huge mechanical toy, shaped like a goose (mechanical props were favoured by audiences of the period). Pantea will disguise herself as a Moorish lady, bring it to Ripasecca, insert Biondello inside it, and persuade Don Pippo to show it to the girls in the tower. Whereupon Biondello will have won his bet and be able to marry Celidora; Calandrino, for his share in the plan, is promised Lavina's hand, whatever Don Pippo may say.

All this has taken place before the opera begins. Some of it is narrated, as will be shown, in the first act recitative. But with only one extant act, and that

* Loewenberg, p. 509.

fragmentary, of Mozart's opera, intelligence may be helped by knowledge of the foregoing.

4

Mozart wrote no overture to *L'oca del Cairo*. It was now his custom to compose it last. Nor did he set the first chorus, very likely because he intended, as with earlier comic operas, to set its verses as the third movement of an Italian operatic *sinfonia*, maybe (not necessarily) bringing back the material of the first quick section—as he was again to do in *Lo sposo deluso*.

The opera begins in the servants' quarters of Don Pippo's palace, a large room strewn with uniforms and less official clothes, as well as signs that here the staff eat and take their leisure. At present they are being bewigged by hairdressers, all costumed in the height of fashion.

In the chorus the assembled staff look forward to a day of feasting and jubilation; a semichorus explains that this is to be the wedding day of the dear old man who will be the bridegroom and source of their festivity. The general paean is renewed. This would have been an *a–b–a* chorus. When it ends, everybody has been coiffured except Auretta, who remains with her hairdresser alone; her lover Chichibio, the majordomo, eavesdrops on them. She offers the barber money, but he wants only her love. She responds with a kiss, perhaps some token even more harmless—though Chichibio is incensed—and the barber departs highly contented.

So it is when the shoemaker and tailor come to fit her with new apparel for this great day. She pays them with compliments or tokens of love to come, and they are delighted, while Chichibio's jealousy rises. Auretta is no polyandrist: she uses her charms to save money, having no intention of taking her flirtations further, as she admits in the opening sentences of **No. 1,** in A major, a **Duet,** probably *allegro*, for which Mozart only indicated string accompaniment, though he left empty staves in case woodwind were needed (yes, they would be apt, on the analogy of the first duet in *Figaro*). The duet, *Così, si fa*, occurs because Chichibio emerges from his hiding-place and accuses Auretta of inconstancy. They argue and eventually make up. The situation looks forward to *Batti, batti* in *Don Giovanni*. Some phrases suggest Figaro with Susanna, perhaps Count Almaviva—

1

or ben si ve–de ch'è un bacca–là, or ben si ve–de —— ch'è un bacca–là.

or even Leporello. The Almaviva reference is inappropriate: this is music for servants, as the following passage from the concluding *allegro assai* should make plain (Ex. 2).

The violin tune is one of Mozart's few indications of orchestral accompaniment, apart from the bass line. The high violin epilogue, blissfully serene, is superb mature Mozart that must make every musician want to fill in the gaps.

They are joined by Calandrino, a member of the family but an aristocrat who seems out of place below the stairs. He has only come to learn whether his hated

rival Don Pippo is awake, to promise him a drubbing (like sheep-shearers who come home shorn themselves), and to send Chichibio to wake Don Pippo, whereupon Calandrino at once makes up to Auretta. She is afraid, especially when Calandrino sings an aria, *Per esempio, s'io dicessi*, explaining his amorous but harmless intentions. Mozart did not set this: its feeble text was surely one of those which he told Leopold would have to be improved before he put it to music.

Auretta sees Chichibio returning; Calandrino tells her to remain motionless. So, while Chichibio again eavesdrops, she soliloquizes in public, as it were, about his jealousy and the harmlessness, even absurdity, of this situation.

No. 2, Aria, Auretta, *Se fosse qui nascoso*, in F major, for strings alone (woodwind perhaps to be added), *andante*, begins almost heroically, like a foretaste of Donna Anna's *Or sai chi l'onore*:

The heroism is a mockery, designed for Chichibio's ears, insincere therefore sung in noble *pastiche*. The fragmentary orchestral ideas look promising, and it was a nice stroke to interrupt the end of the aria with Chichibio's arrival, echoing Auretta's self-deprecating amusement, and leading into recitative.

Chichibio explains how angry Don Pippo was when roused from sleep, how the master threw a pot at him, and how Auretta had better go and calm the old fellow with her famous charm. Calandrino decides to follow in search of a path to his sequestered beloved.

Chichibio now goes, via a recitative in which he summarizes the tale of the ladies' imprisonment and Biondello's wager, into one of those popular *opera buffa* tirades against female coquetry, further examples of which we shall find in Figaro's *Aprite un pò quegli occhi*, and Guglielmo's *Donne miei, le fate a tante*. This **Aria**, **No. 3** is marked *presto*, is in C major, 6/8, scored for oboes, horns, trumpets, and strings (though only for the first nine bars, the rest left unscored), and begins *Ogni momento dicon le donne*.

> Ladies swear they are pillars of fidelity, but show them a scented male wig and they will collapse.

The aria is quite brief, a patter song, strongly invented. It ends this first scene with a potent bid for applause.

The scene now changes, at Mozart's insistence, to the interior of the fortress where Celidora and Lavina are working at their embroidery, and longing for their lovers. It begins with a cavatina for Celidora, about lovers' sadness, and ends with one for Lavina about lovers' happiness, the ladies having meanwhile decided to look in the garden for some means of getting to their lovers. Varesco wrote both aria-texts to the same verse-scheme, and suggested to Mozart that the same music should be used for both. Mozart protested that the contexts were quite different and that, in any case, this sort of musical repetition was appallingly old hat, only possible in special circumstances, such as he had used in *La finta giardiniera* (see p. 185). So he set neither aria. The sentry-bell rings, and the girls decide to go separately into the garden.

A new scene-change shows the apartments of Don Pippo who, in *déshabille*, to a recitative actually set by Mozart, is glorying in his forthcoming triumph over Biondello. When Auretta enters, he complains that Chichibio disturbed a particularly ravishing dream of wedded bliss—he describes this with much flowery mythological allusion of a kind that librettists, some more celebrated than Varesco, loved dearly and that da Ponte lampooned, I suspect, in the last scene of *Figaro* (see p. 437, *Tutto è tranquillo e placido*) for the amusement of regular opera-goers. Auretta protests Chichibio's benevolent intentions. Don Pippo forgives him as he enters and orders them both to carry out his orders for the nuptial day.

No. 4, Don Pippo's **Aria**, *Siamo pronte alle gran nozze*, which turns into a trio when his two servants join in, explains what a spectacular event he intends: 136 coaches, for instance, drawn by hippogriffs. The manuscript shows only part of it, in short score, voice and bass line; but a copy of the complete aria, fully scored for oboes, bassoons, horns and strings, was found in Bergamo, as part of Simon Mayr's bequest, in the 1960s. Mayr is known to have visited Mozart's widow and may have copied out the aria, either as he found it, more likely in its extant short score which he subsequently completed as a musical exercise. The concluding trio does not exist in Mozart's autograph. But Mayr's copy, with its able writing yet poverty-stricken primitive harmony, does not tempt one to regard it as authentic, especially since nothing else in Mozart's score is anywhere near so comprehensively instrumented.

This trio ends the scene. A second duet for Auretta and Chichibio by Mozart does exist. If it belongs in Act I, it can only occur here (it concerns Biondello's vow which had not been mentioned before No. 3). The text is not in Varesco's libretto. It must belong in Act II, especially as Mozart was careful to give his singers no more music in each act than they claimed by right, for fear of complaints from others. Curiously, no particular vocalists are named.

The scene now changes to the exterior of the fortress. Varesco's stage indications are lengthy and detailed. We see the high wall of Ripasecca. In front, the wall hides a garden, and the wall is broken down at one point, and has been disguised with leafy branches—though a moat stands between this aperture and Biondello who is waiting on stage for a view of Celidora. To our right (stage left) the fortress and tower are seen.

Biondello, convinced that this evening, after sundown, will see him re-united for ever with Celidora, triumphant over his absurd rival, sings an **Aria** which Mozart only sketched, *Che parli, che dica*. One of the few instrumental indications shows that a clarinet was required, as nowhere else in this act. The first part of the aria, probably *andante con moto*, declares that love is on Biondello's side and will ensure his triumph. The concluding section, *allegro assai*, explains how he will laugh when Don Pippo has been outwitted. The vocal writing is graceful and elegant: it seems reconstructible.

Biondello sees some movement in the foliage round the escape-hole. He hides as the orchestra begins **No. 5**, a vocal **Quartet** in E flat major, scored potentially for oboes, horns and strings. The orchestral introduction, minimally scored as it is, and without tempo marking though presumably *allegro*, sounds excitable but not momentous. Celidora jumps first through the gap, leaping an octave plus a minor sixth as she does so. Biondello emerges and greets her (they are separated by a wall still, as Mozart complained vainly). Lavina follows her, the music having switched to the dominant, calling for her own lover who duly arrives, promising immediate escape. The girls duet in thirds, the men in canon. There are two ways open (the goose is not yet mentioned): either a boat across the moat, Charon's bark to Hell, or the bridge of Cocytus (*cf*. Horatius in Macaulay's *Lays*). The girls beg for a bridge and their lovers scatter.

Mozart cut some text here. He wanted to move straight to the first act finale. Here would have been the place for tales of Pantea and the goose, and the storm. But already the bridge, the second path of escape, had been mooted. Varesco's scenario had been argued out of dramatic credibility, since we know that the second act begins with Pantea, accompanied by her goose, arriving in the market-place, much to the delight of the barrow-boys. Keen as Mozart was to get his leading ladies on stage, he forgot to tell his audience, during Act I, why the opera was called *The Cairo Goose*.

The **Finale, No. 6**, begins in B flat, with oboes, horns and strings, as Calandrino and Biondello return with carpenters and bridge-building material to scale the moat and the wall, and extricate the imprisoned ladies. The men exhort their workers. The ladies emerge to watch. They all sneer at Don Pippo and Lionetto. The vocal parts and bass show how telling this section would have been, if completed. Even more the *adagio*, full of poetic violin figuration, in which they fear the arrival of Don Pippo during their escape.

Sure enough (D minor) Auretta and Chichibio enter, lamenting that (although his clothes should have been removed and hidden, according to Varesco's scenario), he has left the palace. They will go and spy after him.

But at once he is seen in the distance, questioning all this activity—the lovers complain about the number of carpenters and their slowness in building the bridge. Don Pippo calls up his sentries. A crowd collects. The girls wail excuses: they have come to look for songbirds in the garden. A bustling ensemble crowns the act, vocal septet with chorus. At the end, according to the stage directions, they all escape while Don Pippo and his sentries run after them.

5

Mozart was too disheartened to attempt any more. Who could believe in a libretto where such an important suitor as Lionetto is not ever destined to arrive (he might be even more attractive than Biondello or Calandrino), and where Pantea, the *dea cum machina anserale*, has not yet made an appearance, or been mentioned?

Act II was to take place in the market, with the arrival of Pantea and her curious exhibit which excites much interest among the stall-holders. Chichibio persuades Don Pippo to receive the black lady (Pantea in disguise) and allow her to take it into the fortress garden where its voice may recover after grazing in the herb-garden. Biondello starts a fight which Don Pippo has to quell while Biondello escapes and inserts himself into the model goose's skin.

In Act III Calandrino announces the departure of Biondello. Lionetto sends an apology and calls off his part in the wedding. Don Pippo mounts to the tower but there finds his own wife, whom he is obliged to acknowledge, and Biondello who climbs out of the goose's feathers to claim his bride.

The story is sillier than any Mozart had accepted for a comic opera, and poorly put together. More disheartening, on the musical evidence, is the ordinariness of his creative response to the first act. We can see omens of *Figaro*, etc., and we must admit that he did not complete any number (except, just possibly, No. 4, which I doubt). But the score, as we have it, shows no advance on *La finta giardiniera*, indeed a backward step after *Die Entführung*.

His heart was not in the task, though he tried to pretend to his father that the music so far was good.

16 LO SPOSO DELUSO

LO SPOSO DELUSO

ossia

La Rivalità di tre donne per un solo amante

Opera buffa in two acts

K. 430 (424a)

BOCCONIO PAPPARELLI, a stupid rich man, promised in marriage to:	BASS
EUGENIA, young, capricious noble lady of Rome, faithful lover of:	SOPRANO
DON ASDRUBALE, Tuscan officer, very brave, loved by:	TENOR
BETTINA, Bocconio's niece, a vain girl	SOPRANO
PULCHERIO, a misogynist, friend of Bocconio	TENOR
GERVASIO, Eugenia's tutor, in love with:	BASS
METILDE, virtuoso singer and dancer in love with Asdrubale, supposed friend of Bettina	SOPRANO
Servants, etc.	

The scene is set near Leghorn in a country villa and on the seashore

We have seen in the previous chapter how Mozart made the acquaintance of Lorenzo da Ponte and was promised a new opera libretto by him. We also know that in early July 1783 a 'foreign poet' ('wälscher Poet') gave Mozart a libretto which the composer contemplated setting, instead of the not yet extant *Cairo Goose* by Varesco.

At this time Mozart sketched a vocal trio for an opera about the Amazons, but did not get far with it. This libretto has been identified with one by Giuseppe Petrosellini set by Agostino Accorimboni and performed as *Il regno degli Amazoni* at Parma in 1783. This would surely therefore be one of the many new Italian libretti which Mozart read and considered (see above, p. 323). We may conclude that the rival to Varesco's *Goose* was *Lo sposo deluso*. Alfred Einstein was convinced that its author could only have been da Ponte. There is no evidence for this, admittedly possible, guess (da Ponte's Memoirs do not mention it), nor for the generally accepted time of composition as the summer of 1783 during Mozart's visit to Salzburg. Einstein believed that Mozart was still considering *Lo sposo deluso* in 1784, because of the cast which he projected and wrote down for this opera. *Lo sposo deluso* is a mystery worth examining tentatively, when we have perused its contents. One day, no doubt, science will be able to establish its exact date of composition and the authorship of the text. It exists complete, though Mozart only composed an overture and four musical numbers, some scored in bare outline.

Lo sposo deluso is fundamentally a characteristic *commedia dell' arte* farce about a rich old man who, desirous of matrimonial comfort, contracts a marriage with a young lady who has bestowed her heart elsewhere. His intentions are foiled by a conspiracy between the other characters. The resemblance to Donizetti's *Don Pasquale* among familiar comic operas, and to Ben Johnson's *Epicœne* in English spoken drama, will be plain; but the story is ages old. It figured regularly in comedies about Pantalone, Colombina, Arlecchino and Spavento (see *opera buffa*, pp. 355 ff) and in Roman comedy. There are some unusual twists to the plot in *Lo sposo deluso*, and these doubtless drew Mozart, in despair for an opera libretto, to it.

The opera begins with preparations for the wedding and Mozart, accordingly, made the **Overture** a festive affair in D major, beginning *allegro* with a fanfare for trumpets and drums, repeated by full wind (flutes, oboes, bassoons, horns as well as trumpets and drums) against skirling violins and a viola dominant pedal-point. Another pompous idea ensues but it is the third idea of this group which needs first to be quoted as a signpost (Ex. 1).

The spacious arpeggio mood is resumed and leads to a half-close on the dominant of the dominant, via a chattering, gossipy running passage for strings. The instrumentation is not fully completed, but can be filled out from hints in the score,

and from reprises to come. The second group's main idea is rather quizzical and galant, expanded at the reprise. There follows a transition in which the dominant A is much leaned on by B flat, as if that key or D minor at least were expected. What emerges is an *andante* in D major again, in 3/8 time, gentle and pastoral, quite elaborate. It leads back to D major, *allegro*, the initial fanfares (putatively—Mozart left these bars blank) rather abbreviated and the rise of the curtain on Ex. 1.

The stage shows Bocconio's* dressing room, leading to his living-rooms. He is being dressed by servants and powdered, perfumed, et cetera, for his forth-coming nuptials. With him is his old friend Pulcherio, a misogynist who ridicules Bocconio's tardy longing for wedlock and is making no secret of his opinion. At a table in the room Bocconio's niece Bettina is playing cards with her idol the army officer Don Asdrubale.

The overture has been integrated by Mozart with the opening ensemble, as he had done much earlier in his *opere buffe*, *La finta semplice* and *La finta giardiniera*, as well as in the German *Entführung*. This had become well acknowledged *buffo* practice through Italian composers (see pp. 355 ff) before Mozart who adopted it deliberately for stronger construction. How his creative inspiration must have deflated, we may assume, when he reached this point and realized that he had set just this scene twice before in the two *Finta* opening numbers. Well, he may have concluded that he was now better equipped to introduce the stock characters effectively (after all, the instrumental characters in a piano concerto or symphony remain the same, and the forms—it is the new material which changes them and keeps them distinctive and vital). So this opening ensemble, unlike the earlier ones, reverts to the material of the overture's first section and reworks it in terms of voices and situation.

Bar 2 of Ex. 1 becomes a motif for laughter: the woodwind chords accompany Pulcherio's 'Ha-ha' as he ridicules his friend Bocconio for deciding to get married. Pulcherio, quite susceptible to feminine charm, prefers to court freely without venturing the matrimonial altar. Motif (b) of Ex. 1 is now heard as the complaint of Bocconio for his heart-wounds dealt by Cupid's darts ('Le freccie amabili'—slippery and curious they sound when sung). The second idea of the overture's first group is brought back for Pulcherio's lament over the dear young lady who will

---

* Mozart's score names him so, though in the libretto he is Sempronio. Mozart renamed several of the characters and I use his preferred nomenclature here. The libretto referred to Eugenia as Giulia, Don Asdrubale as Annibale, Bettina as Laurina, Pulcherio as Fernando, Gervasio as Geronimo. The libretto used by Mozart was inaccurately copied, to judge from the reprint in the *Revisionsbericht* of the old *Gesamtausgabe*. Abert thought that the libretto was old and that Mozart had restored the original names but he may have preferred them himself as more striking.

find herself married to an old buffer. Bocconio is too vain to object, but Bettina and Asdrubale look up from their cards to observe that the old man must be unprecedentedly thick; at which all four voices and the orchestra begin to develop Ex. 1 until a recapitulation involving extra guffaws by Pulcherio. The quizzical second subject (not heard since the overture) is now in the tonic, allied to Bocconio's splendid watch and ring, reckoned precious—in both senses—by Pulcherio, this illuminating the foppish element of the music. Bocconio's irritated comments, verbally primitive, acquire life from the music. A servant advises Pulcherio that the bride has arrived (all the servants in this opera are mute, a strange device due for comment later). Bocconio calls distractedly for his diamonds and sword, and curses everybody. Asdrubale, Pulcherio and Bettina urge him to get moving, she to press her eagerness for marriage at once (she fears she will lose her uncle's money if he weds). The music gains speed and brings back the initial fanfares and the subsequent overture *allegro* themes as all four repeat their earlier expressed sentiments.

Only Bettina and Pulcherio leave the stage. Bocconio admires himself in the mirror and assures Don Asdrubale that he is handsome and by no means old. When Asdrubale suggests that Bettina should be allowed to marry, so as not to share the house with another woman, Bocconio calls him a fool, whereupon Asdrubale (in his traditional role of Spavento) demands satisfaction in a duel, but as usual is frustrated.

Bocconio fusses helplessly about his appearance, as Eugenia enters with her tutor Gervasio and sings Mozart's **No. 2**, an **Aria** in E flat, *Nacqui all'aura*, a diatribe against the incivility of the bridegroom who has not come to receive her on her arrival. She is a haughty Roman lady, proud of her ancestry. Mozart only wrote out her vocal line and the orchestral bass, with an indication of the strings' introduction, pompous Mozartian E flat major, most promising (and room left on the paper for woodwind—oboes, clarinets, bassoons and horns, one guesses from key and context).

> I was born in the triumphal aura of the Capitol in Rome and do I find nobody on the steps to meet me?
> Ah, I am like a demented fury. I will not tolerate this insult but go at once to the Tarpeian rock.

Eugenia is given wide leaps to demonstrate her patriotic pride—her vocal compass goes from low A to top B flat. Mozart was writing for Nancy Storace, a superb vocal technician and sensitive artist, to whom he was personally attached but who might have found this part rather heavy. She would have responded to Eugenia's high-flying histrionics and *allegro* triplet divisions ('I shall go at once to the Tarpeian rock'), so powerfully looking forward to the equally put-on demonstrations of Fiordiligi in *Come scoglio*. Though unscored by Mozart, this would have been a brilliant solo vehicle. Eugenia, now faced with the strutting, fawning, heavily courteous person of Bocconio, refuses to believe that he is the bridegroom chosen for her by her tutor. She still thinks passionately of her old fiancé Don Asdrubale, presumed killed in battle (*cf. Finta giardiniera*), and is only prevented from returning home when she sees Pulcherio who, alas, admits that he is not her contracted husband, indeed an incorrigible bachelor.

Pulcherio does try to mediate for his old friend and haughty bride-to-be, in Mozart's **No. 3, Aria**, *Dove mai trovar quel ciglio?*, which is in G major and has few indications of scoring (for strings, though room is left for wind).

(*To Bocconio*) Where will you find such a forehead, such lips?
              No such face exists on earth.
(*To Eugenia*) What a groom, a face, a shape, a model husband!
              The Adonis of this era! No audience anywhere in Pettitmetri or Paris
              has applauded such a beauty.
(*To himself*)   I can foresee trouble ahead.

The aria is lively, beautifully written for tenor voice (the admirable Francesco Bussani, but see p. 340) and full of dramatic possibilities since the mood and tone of voice change so frequently. Any devoted Mozartian would like to complete the scoring of this aria which is beautifully designed. At the end Pulcherio withdraws, then returns secretly to deliver his *coda* (*più allegro*) in which he gives thanks for his bachelor freedom—the orchestral conclusion looks forward aptly to Guglielmo's *Donne miei* in *Così*.

2

Pulcherio leaves—this libretto is designed with conventional exits after arias, in the *seria* manner.

Bocconio pays court to Eugenia, using plentiful references to Roman tradition. He leaves, then she, then her tutor after a possible aria (badly versified).★

The next scene takes place in Bocconio's garden. Bettina complains to Pulcherio that her uncle's marriage will make her a slave in the house, but she has faith in her brother who lives in Spain, and who will surely come to her rescue, dispatch Eugenia back to Rome, and leave Asdrubale free to marry Bettina who adores him. (Typically extravagant female reasoning, comments Pulcherio.) All you men, she continues, have hearts made of jasper. Pulcherio resents the equation of himself and that fool Don Asdrubale. The gallant soldier happens to be passing by, hears the insult and promptly demands satisfaction from Pulcherio. Before they can come to blows Bettina steps between them and begs them both to assist her in outwitting her uncle's marriage to the Roman lady who would make her existence in the house unbearable, as she describes vividly in an aria caricaturing Eugenia's behaviour and mode of speech; Mozart did not set it. Bettina makes her conventional exit, followed by Don Asdrubale who agrees to help her and then fight Pulcherio.

The last remaining character to be introduced is Metilda, a singer and dancer who has made friends with Bettina in order to get near to Don Asdrubale for whom she also nourishes a passion. She enters now in conversation with the old tutor Gervasio who is already in love with her. She opines that Gervasio has made a suitable marriage between Eugenia and Bocconio—it will encourage Don

★ Da Ponte's poetry had been praised for its elegant versification ever since his student days, though he admitted that his command of Italian grammar was faulty—he had been brought up on Hebrew, Latin, and Venetian dialect, not *lingua toscana*.

Asdrubale to follow suit, and she can surely conquer his heart with her musical bravura. The scene includes a possible duet followed by a solo for Metilda, both referring to techniques of *bel canto*.

The setting changes to Eugenia's room where Bocconio is trying to court her favour with a display of jewellery. Don Asdrubale enters to pay his respects. Eugenia is astounded to see the lover she believed dead in battle. She faints. Bocconio hurries out to find smelling-salts, smouldering parchment ('carta bruciata', presumably a remedy akin to burnt feathers for the vapours) or hot broth. Eugenia recovers but now it is Asdrubale's turn to feel faint at the discovery that his love is to marry another, just as he was returning to Rome to wed her.

Bocconio returns with *acqua vulneraria* (is this brandy or something absurdly inept for the vapours like *liquor hamamelis*, witch hazel?) and is amazed to see the altered situation. Tremolando strings launch the only other number set by Mozart, **No. 4, Trio**, *Che accidenti!*, in E flat major, *andantino*, fairly elaborated in orchestration for oboes, clarinets, bassoons, horns and strings. A unison motif of intrigue or tension—

sets the tone promisingly and to it each character responds individually, all in some confusion. Eugenia and Asdrubale are the first to sing together with dramatic supporting harmony.

337

The woodwind scoring here is pungent, the orchestral interest strong through-out, indeed. The trio is simply but vitally constructed in ternary form, Ex. 3 sustaining the main burden of the musical argument though one other theme, also unharmonized, proves helpful: I quote it in a later more diversified context from the central section.

This is no *pièce d'action* but a static ensemble in the old Scarlatti tradition, justified to a sophisticated musical dramatist by the thunderstruck surprise of all on stage. The maturity of the textures, part-writing and invention indicate the Mozart of the great comic operas. Here are the closing bars, based on Ex. 3.

With this splendid trio Mozart gave his last to *Lo sposo deluso*. On the strength of it we may wish that he had persevered. Since he did not, and the work cannot therefore be staged, this résumé of the action had better be completed.

Bocconio asks what has happened. Eugenia then accuses Asdrubale of faithless-ness since he sent her no word of his love or even existence; she therefore consents to Bocconio's proposal of marriage.

The ensuing scene ten finds the extant libretto in total confusion. The written indication is that Metilda joins the three characters originally on stage, delivers her congratulations to Eugenia* and refers to herself as a long-standing servant and friend ('serva e amica') of him for whom 'she' is already dead. This must apply, not to Bocconio (with whom Metilda had no connection) but to Asdrubale (whom she loves and believes to have no interest in Eugenia). Then, in the libretto as printed, Metilda says no more. But Bettina has more to say, and Pulcherio has two gratuitous speeches which make no sense. I suggest that it is Bettina, not Metilda, who enters, congratulates the betrothed couple, and expresses her interest in Don Asdrubale who replies 'Heaven forbid' ('non voglia il cielo'). Bocconio

---

* In the printed libretto, for those who care to verify my contentions, all the names are those of the librettist, not those preferred by Mozart and this synopsis.

(not Pulcherio) replies that Eugenia has agreed to the marriage and that he is at that lady's disposal (Eugenia's not Bettina's). Lauretta then retorts angrily, insulting Eugenia (not Pulcherio!) who leaves in a huff. Asdrubale protests that Lauretta is unjust to the Roman lady. Citizens of Rome had special qualities which even a *Livornese* may admire. These he characterizes in a jovial complimentary aria. Bettina finds it exaggerated but determines to ask Eugenia what caused the fuss.

The first act ends with a scene in a dark room facing Bocconio's garden, at present concealed by drawn blinds. Bocconio, lamp in hand, is searching everywhere for Eugenia whom, he was told, he would find here.

This was part of Pulcherio's plan. As soon as Bocconio moves to another room Pulcherio and Asdrubale enter and conceal themselves. On Bocconio's return they blow out his lamp and announce in duet that they are ghosts from Elysium and have brought the spirit of Eugenia to parley with him. Bocconio quakes with terror, the blinds are raised and, outside in the garden, Eugenia appears costumed like a wraith telling him that she belongs to Pluto and Cerberus now. Bocconio, contrary to theatrical convention, recognizes that she is flesh and not ghost and decides to hide and watch. Eugenia at once is reunited with Asdrubale, Bocconio emerges angrily. So do the other characters. Bettina accuses Asdrubale of double-dating, likewise Metilda who threatens him with a dagger. Gervasio scolds his ward and her lover. Eugenia now accuses Asdrubale of making advances to Metilda and Bettina.

Pulcherio admits to Bocconio that the masquerade was a joke to entertain Eugenia. He instantly assumes that his marriage is on again. In the final ensemble, musically promising, they all turn upon Bocconio, one at a time, shattering his confidence completely. The structure of this finale does accord with da Ponte's written formula though the episodes are unskilfully fragmentary. It is hard also to believe that da Ponte wrote such a couplet as:

EUGENIA Va della mia nemica. . . .
DON A. Tu sei la fiamma antica.

In Act II Metilda accuses Asdrubale of promising to marry her; he denies it. Alone she vows to conquer him by her virtuosity.

Pulcherio tries to dissuade Bettina from chasing Asdrubale. She suspects that he fancies her himself and, against his will, he admits half as much.

Bocconio decides to sue Eugenia for breach of promise. Pulcherio begs him to be less noisy; all the neighbours are listening avidly outside to his tirades. Bettina tells them *she* will sue Asdrubale for breach of promise.

Pulcherio persuades Asdrubale and Bocconio to confer about their intentions, so as to avoid jealousy. The libretto seems confused here also: it must be Bocconio who sings the aria describing how he will sway the verdict by proclaiming his distinguished ancestry (a chestnut *lazzo*, already set by Mozart in *La finta giardiniera*). Pulcherio promises Asdrubale another stratagem to put Bocconio in his place. Metilda tells Gervasio that she also is suing Asdrubale for breach of promise. He offers himself as a loving suitor for her hand.

Asdrubale is determined to convince Eugenia of his fidelity. Bettina eavesdrops and swears revenge. She writes Asdrubale a passionate letter of requited love and tells her manservant to give it to Asdrubale in Eugenia's presence.* This takes place and Eugenia, who was ready to believe Asdrubale constant, now changes her mind and is determined never to see him again. Pulcherio has formed his new plan. A Spanish warship has docked near by, a friend of his in command. Asdrubale and Eugenia must go there and dress as Spaniards, then do as he says.

Now Gervasio asks Metilda how her lawsuit fared. She explains that her skill in song and dance so enchanted the judge that he proposed to her himself. Gervasio offers his hand to Metilda. She refuses. He sings an anti-feminist aria to the audience.

The scene changes to the seashore at the end of Bocconio's garden. A Spanish boat is sighted. Bettina is sure that her brother Don Quasco has arrived to help her. The occupants are led by Don Ercole, a fire-eating Spanish Cavalier, with his bride Donna Fausta, Eugenia's sister. They have come to approve or forbid her wedding with Bocconio. Once again they are recognized by all as Don Asdrubale and Eugenia, except by Bocconio who is threatened with murder by Don Ercole and whose marriage contract is angrily torn up by Donna Fausta. Bocconio is ordered to find Eugenia. Bettina has determined to put on her own fancy dress show. She disguises herself as a gypsy fortune-teller and, reading Asdrubale's hand, urges him to give up Eugenia and take Bettina. He recognizes her. She threatens that, if he refuses her, she will reveal all to her easily fooled uncle. Asdrubale and Eugenia persuade Pulcherio to wed Bettina so that she will not endanger their marriage. Most reluctantly he agrees.

In the final scene Pulcherio and Bettina enter, as *promessi sposi*, followed by Gervasio and Metilda who break the good news to Asdrubale and Eugenia. Bocconio, having failed to locate Eugenia, returns in fear of violence by the Spanish invasion. Bettina explains Pulcherio's ruse. His instinctive rage is questioned (as usual in mask comedy) and he tells the audience that old men must give up aspirations to wedlock. The final ensemble includes copious references (traditional) to the musical instruments which will perform at this triple wedding.

3

It has long been assumed that the text of *Lo sposo deluso* was by da Ponte, that Mozart composed the four extant numbers between July and October 1783 while he and his wife were on holiday at Salzburg, and that he abandoned it because, not having been commissioned, *Lo sposo deluso* had almost no chance of being accepted for the Vienna Court Opera. Nobody seems to have noticed that in 1783 Mozart was commissioned, by the not excessively friendly Count Orsini-Rosenberg, controller of the Vienna Theatre, to write a new Italian comic opera in anticipation of the arrival there of several Italian guest singers. Mozart must surely have been apprised of their names. Two who arrived in 1784 were Francesco Bussani and Stefano Mandini. Bussani was to be Mozart's first Dr Bartolo and Antonio, Commendatore and Masetto, and Don Alfonso—all bass roles. Mandini sang Count Almaviva in the first *Figaro*, a baritone part. But in *Lo sposo deluso* Mozart cast both singers in tenor roles, Pulcherio and Asdrubale respectively. There was a tenor Paolo Mandini (see p. 346 n.); but the Bussani role is a mystery. Mozart names Mme Fischer as Eugenia. She was Nancy Storace, the English singer who arrived in

---

* The printed libretto confuses *soglio* = throne with *foglio* = sheet of paper!

Vienna in 1783 and became one of Mozart's favourite sopranos; he wrote Susanna for her and, even more revealing of his emotions, the concert aria with pianoforte obbligato *Ch'io mi scordi di te*. It was only in 1784 that Nancy Storace met, and married in Vienna, the violinist John Abraham Fischer. He treated her badly and they soon separated, whereupon she resumed her maiden name. The cast list must therefore have been made early in 1784 but it is not impossible that Mozart intended *Lo sposo deluso* for the Christmas carnival season of 1784 when these singers were all available. It is perhaps worth adding that Mozart wrote the other roles with the following singers in mind: Francesco Benucci (his first Figaro) as Bocconio; Caterina Cavalieri as Bettina (she had been Mozart's first Constanze in *Entführung*); a Signore Pugnetti as Gervasio; and Therese Teyber (an old Viennese family friend of the Mozarts, and the first Blonde in *Entführung*) as Metilda. A marvellous cast!

The libretto does not read like da Ponte's work. Characterization is almost non-existent; the personages remain stock types throughout. The situations are forcedly but weakly contrived. The language includes a juicy phrase or two but much to shame a literary schoolboy by its poverty of diction or poetic imagination. Mozart may have found a spur in a stock *commedia* plot which yet contains no scheming servants, and in which the standard, only, female (Columbine) is multiplied by three, each slightly different—though not as distinctive as might be wished. Metilda is an ungrateful part for a composer, no more than a canary—and what composer will thank the librettist for arias about trills and appoggiaturas? Bettina would contrast better with Eugenia if she were more charming, less haughty. Abert asked us to compare Pulcherio with Shakespeare's Benedick in *Much Ado about Nothing*; if we do so we find Pulcherio an unfulfilled promise, a misogynist or *sprezzatore di donne* without fire in his belly, and a contriver of plots that consistently misfire—perhaps this failure is to his credit as a personality. In favour of the ascription to da Ponte it should be noted that several situations, or aria structures, recall particular ones in other da Ponte operas: the other characters turn on Bocconio in the first act finale much as the masquers turn on Don Giovanni in the first finale of that opera—one can almost hear Mozart's music for the repeated 'Taci' cries, and the similarly worded individual solos which follow. Now and then in a comic aria we may read pre-echoes of Zerlina or Despina, perhaps Dorabella. But careful study shows line after line which would certainly have been thrown out by a composer as sensitive to words as Mozart. In 1783 da Ponte was an inexperienced poet; even later he was willing to make alterations for Mozart who noted that he grumbled. The text, even the scenario, of *Lo sposo deluso* needed major, basic readjustments and much rewriting for the purposes of Mozart in 1783 and 1784. But if da Ponte was the author, why did Mozart not tell his father the poet's name? Da Ponte was famous in 1783, and Mozart had mentioned him already in a letter to his father. A 'wälscher Poet' was by July 1783 likely to be someone quite unknown to Leopold Mozart—which da Ponte was not. It is conceivable that da Ponte tried to keep Mozart happy with one of his early Goldoni imitations, and that Mozart, having tried out the feel of the libretto in several contrasted set pieces, realized the worst and asked for something more original and peopled with credible human characters. I am also inclined to believe that in 1783 da Ponte, still with a name to make in Vienna, would not have put his name to *Lo sposo deluso*, even heavily revised—not least because he had already discovered the advantages of adapting a good extant play (he provided Martín and Gazzaniga with two effective and characterful rehashes of this kind in 1783). Quite apart from anything else, Mozart would not have suggested *Figaro* to a librettist who had given him *Lo sposo deluso* in such a jumbled ungrammatical state as the libretto presents. Why, finally, should da Ponte choose to give Mozart a copy of the text not written out by himself?

Subsequent attempts were made to bring this music by Mozart before the public, usually together with that for *L'oca del Cairo* and separate numbers (added to operas by others) of proven authenticity. They have not attracted favour because the context of the music, the dramatic motivation which prompted its creation, had to be changed—new words, other characters, different dramatic situations, quite apart from new recitatives or, least harmful, additional woodwind parts.

The extant music for *Lo sposo deluso* shows the masterly Mozart on the threshold of his destined kingdom. It is worth hearing but can only be heard with help from scholarly creative musicians of our time, and alas! only in concert performance, as the bare but lengthy synopsis above will have made clear—unless television is willing to show us, for example, the trio No. 4 as an item in a programme.

17 DER SCHAUSPIELDIREKTOR

DER SCHAUSPIELDIREKTOR

K. 486

Comedy with music, in one act

Text by
GOTTLIEB STEPHANIE, JR.

FRANK, an Impresario		SPEAKING ROLE
EILER, a Banker		SPEAKING ROLE
BUFF HERZ	} Actors	SPEAKING ROLES
Mme PFEIL Mme KRONE Mme VOGELSANG	} Actresses	SPEAKING ROLES
VOGELSANG, a singer		TENOR
Mme HERZ, a singer		SOPRANO
Mme SILBERKLANG, a singer		SOPRANO

Scene: a room

In January 1786 Mozart was still deep at work on *Le nozze di Figaro* (see pp. 363 ff); but, when the Emperor Joseph II commanded him to provide music for an Imperial entertainment, his Court Composer could not decline the order. The Emperor was to entertain his well loved sister the Archduchess Christine Marie and her husband Duke Albrecht Kasimir of Sachsen-Teschen★ who were the joint Governors-General of the Austrian Netherlands. A year earlier he had successfully held a 'Spring Festival on a Winter's Day' in the Orangery at the palace of Schönbrunn. Now he decided to repeat this spectacular event: one special attraction was that the Orangery could be adequately heated. The Imperial intention was to show off the quality of his new Italian opera company and his German theatrical troupe (remnants of the National *Singspiel* for which *Die Entführung aus dem Serail* had been written).

So on Tuesday 7 February 'forty-one Cavaliers and an equal number of ladies', together with the royal party, set off from the Hofburg at 3 p.m., arrived at Schönbrunn at 4 p.m. and there, in the Orangery, sat down to a banquet of eighty-two covers, during which the royal wind band played selections from Salieri's recent opera *Il grotto di Trofonio* (*cf. Così fan tutte*, p. 522). A stage existed at either end of the Orangery; the banqueting table amid the orange trees occupied the space in between. When lunch was finished the party took coffee at one end while the table was removed and chairs drawn up facing the stage at the other end. This done, the company took their seats and watched the German company perform *Der Schauspieldirektor* for which Mozart had composed the music. Then they moved back to the second stage where members of the Italian opera company gave another newly commissioned work, Salieri's *Prima la musica e poi le parole*. 'After which, about 9 o'clock, the company rode back to the city in the order in which they came, in barouches and carriages, each preceded by two outriders with lanterns.'†

The double bill was publicly performed (for Joseph II was unusually liberal-minded as eighteenth-century Emperors went) in Vienna at the Kärntnertor Theatre on 11, 18 and 25 February, 'with extraordinary success and attendance', according to a Berlin report.‡

Curiously, in a royal entertainment, both works treated a far from noble backstage theatrical topic: Mozart's comedy with music caricatures the foibles of actors and singers, and the trials of the impresario who forms a travelling company; Salieri's miniature *opera buffa* deals with the collaboration of composer and librettist in the writing of an operatic duet suddenly required in a hurry by the nobleman who is their patron. The duet is to be for the *prima donna*, who is the nobleman's

★ Later King August III of Poland.
† *Protocollum aulicum in ceremonialibus*, 1786. Vienna National Archives. Quoted in *Doc. Biog.*
‡ Christopher Raeburn has shown that the performance on 11 February was *not* cancelled, as authorities long maintained.

lover, and a male soprano. The poet's inspiration is cooled by the idea of love music involving a *castrato*, but the composer quickly sketches a situation, writes some suitable lines, and then composes his music while the poet, now encouraged, completes the text. The duet is then rehearsed by the *prima donna* with a serving maid. The librettist of *Prima la musica* was Giovanni Battista Casti, professional rival in Vienna of Lorenzo da Ponte whose mannerisms are burlesqued in Casti's part of the librettist.* As the prima donna Nancy Storace took the opportunity to mimic the singing of her castrato rival Luigi Marchesi in Sarti's *Giulio Sabino*, well known to Viennese opera-goers from performances some few months earlier. The other singers in Salieri's work were Celesta Coltellini and Francesco Benucci.† After this brief run, *Prima la musica* was forgotten until 1934 when Stefan Zweig read the libretto in the British Museum and sowed the first seed of Richard Strauss's last opera *Capriccio*.‡ *Der Schauspieldirektor*, on the other hand, has continually held a minor place in the Mozart repertory, though revamped dialogue has introduced the music almost invariably.

2

As librettist for the German contribution to this festal occasion the Emperor had selected Gottlieb Stephanie, junior (see p. 291), his Inspector of the Imperial German Theatre and already the librettist of *Die Entführung*. According to the *Wiener Realzeitung*§ 'the author had both the plot and the number and names of the actors engaged in it prescribed for him'. But Stephanie, who had been in the theatre in Vienna since 1769, and an actor for eight years before that had, on Mozart's admission, a keen sense of what pleases an audience, and could draw abundantly on his own experiences. Nobody nowadays may wish to sit through the spoken original text of *Der Schauspieldirektor*, but to read it is to know that every scene is drawn from life.

Mozart had the text by 18 January on which day he set the trio, No. 3. The whole opera was completed on 3 February. It was no skimped job, even though *Figaro* was on the stocks at the time. The overture is elaborate and extended for its purpose, the two arias very carefully characterized and invented and scored, like the trio; the Vaudeville-Finale might have been more quickly written down. Mozart's singers for *Der Schauspieldirektor* were Aloysia Lange as Mme Herz, Catarina Cavalieri as Mme Silberklang, Valentine Joseph Adamberger as Herr Vogelsang, and Joseph Weidmann as Buff.¶

* In 1826 Michael Kelly recalled, in his *Memoirs*, how he delighted the Emperor, his audience, and even da Ponte with his imitation of that poet. This was not, however, in *Prima la musica* but in an opera by Vicenzo Righini with text by da Ponte, as Kelly clearly explains; the opera was probably *Demorgogone ossia lo Filosofoso confuso* given in Vienna in July 1786. The role of the poet in *Prima la musica* was taken by Paolo Mandini, the tenor and younger brother of Mozart's first Almaviva, the baritone Stefano.

† Coltellini's father wrote the libretto of *La finta semplice*. Benucci was Mozart's first *Figaro*, Storace the first Susanna, Kelly the first Don Curzio and Basilio. Mozart had friends on both stages that night in the Orangery.

‡ Cf. William Mann, *Richard Strauss*, pp. 359 ff.

§ 21 February 1786, quoted in *Doc. Biog.*

¶ Aloysia Lange (née Weber) had been Mozart's sweetheart in Mannheim (see p. 230); he married her sister Constanze when she accepted the widowed heroic actor Joseph Lange who painted the last, unfinished and reputedly most vivid portrait of Mozart. He wrote numerous

The wholly speaking roles were led by Stephanie, the author, as the impresario Frank. Johann Brockmann, a famous Shakespearian and tragic actor, played Eiler. Aloysia Lange's husband, Joseph, was Herz. Maria Anna Stephanie, an actress of some range, played Mme Pfeil; Johanna Sacco, a noted tragic actress, was Mme Krone, and Anna Marie Adamberger, much admired in ingénue parts, Mme Vogelsang. Thus husbands and wives played husbands and wives.★

The interpolated scenes from existing plays (more of these later) were presumably chosen from those which the actors in question had recently played successfully in Vienna, and which the Emperor (or Stephanie) wished the Archduchess and her husband to applaud themselves. Mozart's score was being marketed in Vienna by 4 March, in manuscript copies. He was paid 50 ducats by the Emperor for his work, plus a personal gratuity.

Mozart provided *Der Schauspieldirektor* with an extremely grand overture, *presto* in pace (originally he marked it *allegro assai*) but spacious in design and ample in scoring—pairs of flutes (who are silent in the other musical numbers), oboes, clarinets, bassoons, horns, trumpets and timpani, as well as strings. For a short playlet about the absurd conceits and rivalries of small-time provincial actors and singers it must appear overblown: Hermann Abert decided that Mozart's intentions were parodistical, but the music is surely too real to be comic, let alone burlesque. We may hear conspiracy in the soft consequents of the loud opening:

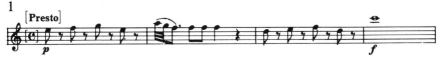

and good humoured, perhaps slightly bourgeois comedy in the third subject with its bassoon doubling two octaves below the oboe.

But the total impression left by the overture is of splendour and festivity—which makes sense if Mozart planned this simply as the overture to the evening's entertainment at a grand imperial occasion. If so the first group may be expressive of the Emperor's majesty and the expectancy of his guests as they travel to the *Lustfest*. The second group, lyrical and lightly imitative, could refer to his sister

---

arias expressly for her—including the glorious *Vorrei, spiegarvi, o Dio*—but no other complete operatic role, though she was his first Donna Anna in Vienna. Cavalieri has been discussed in *Entführung*, see p. 293, like Adamberger. Weidmann was a very popular comic actor who appeared in comic operas though he could hardly sing.

★ I have adopted the casting suggested, with cogent arguments, by Christopher Raeburn in 'An Evening at Schönbrunn', *Music Review*, May 1955. This article, based on much original research, includes biographical notes on the cast and is illustrated with a contemporary engraving of a *Lustfest* in the Schönbrunn Orangery. It clears up many long sanctified errors and only, I think, goes wrong in confusing the tenor Mandini with his baritone brother. It was Mr Raeburn, however, who later resolved for me this confusion by reference to salary lists that clearly distinguished between Mandini and wife and Mandini junior.

and guest more convincingly as a vocal ensemble without words in general praise of the monarch, and the third subject as a reference to the theatrical programme in store. Yet this convenient topical descriptive programme does not fit the strokes of pathos and drama (e.g., at the G minor beginning and German sixth end of the development section) which also leave an impression on the listener to this overture. It was meant not only to reflect existing emotions in its audience, but to inspire new, larger feelings, too complex to be categorized in words, certainly too complex for a farcical play and a noble audience gathered for pleasure, but not beyond the understanding of those who knew the language of Viennese music in the Vienna of 1786. Twentieth-century listeners can only hope and endeavour to attend in some appropriate and similar frame of mind, remembering that Mozart's creative faculties were strongly engaged on the robust yet infinitely sensitive comic battle of *Figaro* and that, during this time, he also wrote the great piano concertos K. 488 in A major and K. 491 in C minor, both expressively relevant to *Der Schauspieldirektor* as to *Figaro*. It is no accident that the overture to *Der Schauspieldirektor* has become a favourite concert piece.

4

The overture finishes and the scene reveals a room where Herr Frank is waiting to receive applicants for membership of his theatrical company. At the rise of the curtain one of his engaged actors, Herr Buff, announces that permission has been granted for this company to play—in Salzburg.* For Frank, Salzburg is a cultural slum, 'the home of Hanswurst' (our British Mr Punch, Italy's Pulcinella), a source of improvised comic stage brawls, a place totally inimical to serious theatre. Frank hopes to create something artistically distinguished, but Buff assures him that his company's season must comprise only comedy, ballet and opera. The least praised of the genres, too, because they fetch most money: culture fills the head but not the pocket.

Buff's text is the Latin *Mundus vult decipi ergo decipiatur.* If an actor declaims badly, he is to be advertised as a supreme intellectual of the stage; poor singers may be publicized as revelatory intellectuals of the opera; incompetent dancers must be understood as renovators of the true classic style. Frank can rely on the press to support him: on arrival in Salzburg he must offer free tickets to four or five chosen hacks, give them lunch with one of his company, and free supper. Then his cast will be acclaimed as the equivalents of Roscius, Clairon and Garrick.

In the battle for superior theatrical standards Frank has lost. He can only ask where the money will come from. Easy, answers Buff: he has the permit to play in Salzburg; he need only advertise it for subscribers to flock.

Promptly enters a banker, Herr Eiler, who offers to lend Frank as much money as he requires if Frank will employ Eiler's fiancée Mme Pfeil, a fine actress. Frank thinks she may prove too expensive for so small a company; but Buff advises him to engage her, and leave the rest to less noted, cheaper actors. Eiler offers to pay his future wife's wages out of his own pocket, if only to be rid of the duty of rehearsing scenes with her continually. Mme Pfeil duly appears and offers her services as leading lady in all roles, for twelve thalers a week. She chooses to play,

---

* Will this have been Mozart's contribution to the libretto?

for her audition, a scene from *The Provoked Husband* by Vanbrugh and Cibber in which Mr Eiler will read the part of the title. They do so, and Eiler has to work himself into a state of fiendish jealousy in order to inspire Mme Pfeil to sufficient eloquence in this scene of passionate dispute, tears and reconciliation. She responds beautifully—but rage is her forte, rather than amorous charm, as Buff ironically comments.

Now enters Mme Krone, a specialist in classic tragic heroines—far too old-fashioned, Buff advises, for a modern Salzburg audience. She offers a duologue from F. J. Jünger's *Bianca Cappello* (adapted from A. G. Meissner's *Hallo Dialog, Hallo Erzählung*), introduces her partner Herr Hertz, and they act it together at great length, a boring scene of marital jealousy and heroic fidelity, full of sentimental platitudes. Buff warns Frank that the audience will laugh at such corny acting, not cry at all. But Frank has made up his mind and offers these two actors fourteen thalers a week.

Buff, being a comedian, is more glad to see the entry of Mme Vogelsang. He suggests that their audition should consist of a scene from the comedy *Die galante Bäuerin*, which they have frequently played together. This may have been Stephanie's elaboration of Rautenstrauch's *Der Jurist und der Bauer*.★ They act it out; it is no hit for a modern audience, but Frank is happy. He accepts her offer of eighteen thalers a week. Buff warns Frank that the company will disband if wages are not equalized (Mozart got half Salieri's wage for his work, though it was less demanding), but Frank is content. Mme Krone of course is enraged. Herz and Mme Vogelsang offer to fetch their talented husbands. Mme Krone leaves angrily for her own purposes as will be seen, not for ever.

Now Herz introduces his wife who displays her great accomplishment in her **Ariette, No.** 1, *Da schlägt des Abschieds Stunde*. At last a Mozart aria! Mme Herz is an exponent of great expression as we should understand from the dark, translucent, contrapuntal nature of the woodwind introduction to her solo, and its chromatic harmony, as well as its typically Mozart key of G minor.†

> The hour of vespers strikes, and parts us cruelly. How shall I live without you, Damon? I will accompany you, hover like a ghost beside you, though perhaps you forget me for ever. But no! Surely you cannot be faithless to me. (*Allegro*). A heart so hurt by parting knows no mutability; whatever Fate encourages, the firm band will not be split.

The text of this aria is based on a poem by Johann Joachim Eschenburg itself indebted to Metastasio's oft-composed *Ecco quel fiero istante*; some of its lines recall a poem later set by Mozart as *Lied der Trennung* (K. 519). The first, G minor half, however, comes very close to the mood of Pamina in the same key.

3
[Larghetto]

ach nein,   ach nein,   du kannst ge—wiß   nicht treulos sein,

★ See Christopher Raeburn: 'Die textliche Quellen des Schauspieldirektors', in *OMZ* 1958.
† The introduction, obviously authentic, was omitted from the manuscript score.

The *allegro* second part goes on encouraging the woodwind and draws Mme Herz into brilliant runs extending up to top D and involving a nice musical representation of the firm bond between lovers.

Frank is sufficiently bowled over by Mme Herz to accept her for his *prima donna* at a weekly wage of sixteen talers, her husband gladly remaining at his old price of fourteen talers. Buff notes that Frank's prices are still rising, a bad omen.

She is at once followed by Mme Silberklang, another virtuoso soprano of stellar pretension who has heard of this mooted company and, though sure of her renown everywhere, is willing to give Frank an audition. Her selected vehicle is the **Rondo, No. 2**, *Bester Jüngling* in E flat major, scored for clarinets, bassoons, horns and strings. Stephanie's poem for this is derived from J. M. Miller's *Der Liebesbund* (1779). Here again the orchestral introduction, simply a playthrough of the theme, is omitted from Mozart's catalogue and the manuscript; and again its scoring is sufficiently sensitive, unobvious, to oblige us to claim it as genuine Mozart.

> (*Andante*) Best of boys, I accept your love with delight since I see my fortune in your eyes. But, alas, if our love must be pursued by gloomy suffering, will it be rewarded by the joys of love?
> (*Allegretto*) Nothing is so precious to me as your heart and hand. So I, in pure and ardent love, give you my heart as pledge.

This is not a true rondo. The cheerful theme is followed by a more melancholy episode. The theme returns and is succeeded by an *allegretto* (non-thematic) which persists until the end. Abert correctly noted that the theme is a French gavotte. Its two phrases are completed by a third one which obligingly takes Mme Silberklang up to a top B flat (she is not asked to travel farther, unless in her cadenza). The episode derives its melancholy from the minor ninth in the bassoon part and other chromaticisms, later its brilliance from Mme Silberklang's cadenza which occurs just before the return of the rondo theme: an able singer will obviously decorate this delightfully. A bubbling *allegretto* ensues at once, with much obbligato woodwind, a buoyant vocal line and, quite soon, a florid passage of scales (rather like Donna Anna's *Non mi dir* which Cavalieri was later to sing). This aria is intended more mercurially than Mme Herz's, though parts of it are as carefully worked.

Frank offers her sixteen thalers per week, the same as Mme Herz. Buff warns him that Silberklang is often prone to cancel because of catarrh. Mme Silberklang is herself content to know that her weekly payment is the same as Mme Herz gets. She only insists that she is billed as *prima donna*. Mme Herz protests and so they embark on the **Trio, No. 3,** *Ich bin die erste Sängerin*, surely the highspot of this score. It is marked *allegro assai* in B flat major, with oboes, clarinets, bassoons, horns and strings. The dotted rhythm of the introductory figure suggests pride and determination, and Mme Silberklang's words are set *quasi parlando*; melody does not emerge until Mme Herz's tart reply.

MME S.	I am the prima donna.
MME H. (*mocking*)	I am sure—to your own way of thinking.
MME S.	You must not dispute that.
MME H.	I will not.
VOGELSANG	Explain yourself.
MME S.	No one is my equal, everybody will agree.
MME H. (*mocking*)	Certainly, I have neither seen nor heard your like.
HERR V.	Why wear yourself out with empty boasting? Each of you has special virtues.
MME H. + S.	Everyone praises me that hears me.
MME H.	Adagio.
MME S.	Allegro, allegrissimo.
HERR V.	Piano, pianissimo! No artist must fault another; it demeans art.

When Vogelsang enters in his mediatory role the trio texture becomes delightfully smooth and airy and diversified, especially with the violins in antiphony and the faster-moving violas. The movement arrives at dominant F major and Silberklang's boasts ('Ich bin von keiner zu erreichen') are matched by violins with a descending arpeggio figure, three times repeated, which may evoke Cavalieri's 'geläufige Gurgel', as Mozart called it. Vogelsang's *credo* ('Ein jedes hat besondern Wert') induces a note of melodramatic *tremolo* in the orchestra, and a further bout of polyphony. The orchestra settles into serenity, lulling triplets, and the two ladies compete openly, leading one another up to top C, Vogelsang still attempting a more legato conciliation that leads to G minor and a pause. Then Mme Herz proposes her 'Adagio' cadenza, soaring up to E flat. Silberklang answers with 'Allegro, allegrissimo', even more florid but not so high. Vogelsang's reply suggests possible flourishes too, not written out. *Andante* and calmly he states his maxim about dog not eating dog (mellow wind writing here, as throughout this trio). The ladies fall in with him, superficially and suavely ('Art cannot be further ennobled') as they glorify their own accomplishments in florid imitative duet—Mme Herz soars to a top F. Vogelsang goes on preaching modesty while the ladies whisper aside their convictions ('I am the first') as interruptions to their loud moral assertions. The *allegro assai* is resumed for a blatant recapitulation; neither lady will yield an inch, though Vogelsang insists that the trio shall end *mancando, calando, pianissimo*, a delicious close.

In comes Mme Pfeil followed by Mme Krone, who obviously left the room to seek out her rival and kindly acquaint her of the unjust, discriminating wages being offered to their colleagues. Mme Pfeil demands a higher salary since she is an all-purpose actress (as indeed we know Mme Stephanie had proved herself). Eiler hurriedly whispers to Frank that he will be responsible for this rise and Frank promises Mme Pfeil a separate contract. This she finds acceptable. The other ladies have only heard her last words and demand an explanation. Frank quickly recovers his diplomacy and announces that he will give up his new company unless its members cease to squabble and impede him. One by one the ladies agree to stand by their fees, sacrificing to art or to applause. Buff congratulates Frank, fearing only that the impresario has assembled a company without any supporting actors—they are all stars.

Mme Silberklang introduces the final Vaudeville, **No. 4, Schlussgesang**, *Jeder Künstler strebt nach Ehre*. It is *allegro* in C major, with oboes, clarinets, bassoons, horns, trumpets, timpani and strings (the big orchestra of the overture but without flutes). Her verse, introduced by orchestra, is typical *Singspiel* material, jolly and slightly shapeless but harmonically square.

> Every artist strives for recognition, wants to be unique; if there were not this compulsion, Art would be small beer.

6

She ends with a florid run up to top C and the three principals sing the refrain of this *vaudeville*.

> Artists must work to be worthy of their calling, but selfish ambition demeans even the greatest artist.

This is even more primitive musically, with a hint of the *Entführung* harem and Monostatos's slaves in the Lydian scale at the end.

7

Herr Vogelsang adds his own verse in G major, to his own tune (with Lydian hints in the middle and a back-reference to Ex. 6). He preaches *Einigkeit*, unanimity or perhaps single-mindedness; the integral effect is important, not the contribution of individuals. The refrain (Ex. 7) is repeated. Mme Herz follows, starting in F major and returning to C with a display of vocal fireworks at the end, up to top F and back. Another refrain. Now Buff gets his only musical outing, in C minor, not vocally too simple. He explains that he is, as his name shows, the company's first *buffo*, even though he is not much of a singer.* A final refrain ends the work.

5

At the time *Der Schauspieldirektor* was described as a *pièce d'occasion* ('Gelegen-heitsstück'). This was accurate. We of today may go into raptures about the mature splendours of Mozart's music for it, the expressive textures and harmony, the brilliance, the surprising grandeurs. Then, upon reading Stephanie's text, we are likely to complain that six long scenes go by—thirty-six half-columns of text—between the end of the overture and the start of the next musical number. In another seven half-columns the whole comedy is finished including Mozart's four vocal numbers. Bad proportions, surely? Particularly, we may add, since Stephanie's spoken dialogue is poor stuff while Mozart's music is excellent even by his own standards.

Those who attended the performances in February 1786 reacted quite differently. The noble Viennese diarist Count Zinzendorf, a cultured, honest, and tireless chronicler of his times, found *Der Schauspieldirektor* 'very mediocre', and *Figaro* 'boring', but other works by Mozart attractive or admirable. Zinzendorf was better entertained by *Prima la musica*. The *Wiener Realzeitung* spent much space on the dialogue scenes and choice of excerpts from other plays, then cursorily mentioned that 'the music by Herr Mozart also distinguished itself by some especial beauties', and went on to discuss the Salieri. The *Allgemeiner Wiener Bücher-Nachrichten* reported the evening sentimentally, in terms of the Emperor and his dear sister; but did go on to comment that 'the German piece infinitely surpassed the Italian one in intrinsic value'. This judgment falls into perspective when the writer singles out Adamberger as superior to Coltellini—these singers had the least significant roles in their operas—rather than Frau Lange and Nancy Storace.

Der Schauspieldirektor was an occasional piece, for the display of the German theatrical company in Vienna. The audience wanted to see its national actors suitably cast, and in favourite scenes from recent productions. Stephanie, who knew the company and its work as thoroughly as anybody in Vienna, provided just this. He threw in some music as well, partly for entertainment, partly because he and Mozart had written a German *Singspiel* for the same company a few years earlier—and perhaps to show that good singing in German was still to be heard in Vienna. Kaiser Joseph II has come down in musical history as the monarch who told Mozart that there were 'too many notes' in *Entführung*; but contemporary reports agree that he was very musical, and that he enjoyed Mozart's music, often sending for the manuscript of *Figaro* just when copyists were trying to get parts written out for rehearsals. I dare say he enjoyed the cheerful euphonious overture more than the complicated music of the trio or the subtlety of the two soprano roles.

For all the guests the music of *Der Schauspieldirektor* was comparatively insignificant. Mozart was not a generally revered composer as Salieri was; and so

---

* In one early copy this last reservation is removed, leaving repetition of the previous words.

his music was no special attraction for this grand social occasion. Descriptions of this Imperial *Lustfest* remind me of the Christmas party put on annually, at the time of writing, by the Royal Opera House in London for Friends of Covent Garden. Ballet dancers sing opera, the opera company dances, absurd miscasting takes place for humorous effect. If a young, reasonably admired composer provided a new score for such an entertainment, few of the Friends would pay exceptional attention to it—even in the 1970s now that new music attracts more notice than in Mozart's day when all music was newly composed.

Stephanie's libretto for *Der Schauspieldirektor* was designed, no doubt with many topical allusions that mean nothing today, for the occasion. If we want to rediscover *Der Schauspieldirektor* we may do so by finding such an occasion and writing a new topical libretto to introduce Mozart's still fresh and effective music. I saw just such a production at Bath Festival in 1968. Robert Morley wrote new dialogue, referring to local personalities and topics, and he designed speaking roles for the Festival's artistic director Yehudi Menuhin, who conducted the music, and for Mrs Menuhin, formerly a well known ballet dancer and still a lively comedienne. There have been many less openly frivolous texts made for *Der Schauspieldirektor*. In some of these Frank sings the music of Herr Vogelsang, or Buff's part is tele- scoped with that of Eiler who becomes the protector of Mme Silberklang. The latter recourse will tempt the new librettist to write new words for Buff's little solo in No. 4, a dangerous experiment where the meaning of Mozart's music is concerned (Vogelsang's moral observations can well be sung by Frank without alteration). A tasteful and intelligent treatment along these lines was made by Hans Hammelmann and Michael Rose for production at Glyndebourne Festival Opera in July 1957. The two *prima donna* roles were assigned to Rita Streich and Joan Sutherland, sensible choices—it is essential that Mme Herz and Mme Silberklang shall be heard to be worthy successors of Aloysia Lange and Catarina Cavalieri—though in the end Miss Streich was ill and had to be replaced by a less experienced singer. The effect was thereby given that Mme Silberklang was only the 'erste Sängerin' by virtue of her protector's moneybags; reasonable, and yet the point of the comedy, on reflection, would have snapped instantly.

Another version along these lines, in English, was made by Eric Blom in 1933 and performed several times. It preserved the eighteenth-century flavour of the Stephanie text, and was praised for its wit[*] yet seems, as the Glyndebourne version seemed, faintly lacking in the atmosphere of urgency and excitement which the music exudes, the sense of occasion. Vulpius's adaptation (Weimar, 1797) in connection with Cimarosa's *L'impresario in angustie* (a similar theme also premiered in 1786) would doubtless now seem unequal in quality; and Schneider's long- popular *Mozart und Schikaneder* (1845) which puts the composer and his contem- poraries into the boots of Frank, Buff et cetera, was even then considered too sentimental by some commentators.

There remains the possibility of reviving *Der Schauspieldirektor* as Stephanie and Mozart wrote it (perhaps with some abbreviation of the dialogue scenes). This was done in Vienna in 1916 and in London in 1952. It explains and motivates the sung numbers and their context; it also has the virtue of telling us something about attitudes to the drama in the Vienna of 1786. To please a modern audience it would

---

[*] It is printed complete in Blom's *Mozart: Master Musicians* (Dent, 1935).

need actors as well as singers of known brilliance and fame—in fact a lavish festival cast. But *Der Schauspieldirektor* is not a curtain-raiser for everyday repertory.

ITALIAN COMIC OPERA

The operatic genre which Mozart was now to favour with three of his and its most durable masterpieces had largely supplanted, in popular favour, the Italian *opera seria* with which it had grown up. *Opera seria* and *opera buffa* had both sprung from deep roots. The Florentine *Camerata* had intended to revive the glories of classical Greek tragedy, but instead invented opera. Just as the ancient festival of Dionysus followed a serious dramatic trilogy with a comic postlude or satire, so Shakespeare in England, Calderón in Spain, and Tasso in Italy often interlarded serious scenes with purely comic proletarian ones. And accordingly the first Italian operas, from Peri's *Euridice* (1601) onward, were interleaved in performance by comic *intermezzi* which dealt with quite separate situations and characters. Monteverdi's *Orfeo*, the first opera nowadays in repertory, contains none of these. But his very last operas, still performed, do include comic scenes, e.g. those for Irus in *Il ritorno d'Ulisse*, and for Arnalta the nurse, and the flirtation between the valet and serving maid (*Valetto* and *Damigella* are descriptions, not names) in *L'incoronazione di Poppea*. Such scenes were typical in seventeenth-century Italian opera, though material of the kind was not always so precisely integrated into the serious work.

The comic scenes in early Italian operas, whether integrated or, as intermezzi, distinct, could trace their ancestry back to the Roman comedies of Terence and Plautus with their libidinous, vainglorious soldiers and scheming servants, flirtatious daughters and pompous, anxious fathers.* Such characters, with the situations arising from their interaction, had remained in favour with later audiences. French puppet shows, English mummer-plays, the *jongleurs* or tumblers and jugglers and pratfall comedians everywhere merged with the stock characters of Terence into the improvised clowning of the Italian *commedia dell'arte* which was firmly established throughout Italy by the end of the sixteenth century—the time when Italian opera, as we know it, began. The stock characters of the *commedia dell'arte* and the *lazzi*, stylized virtuoso scenes of mimicry or situation farce, were to be the backbone of Italian *opera buffa*, and can be found, hardly disguised, in three outstanding joint creations of da Ponte and Mozart. Another immediate source of Italian *opera buffa*, equally linked with the *commedia dell'arte* though probably non-visually, were the madrigal comedies from Rome, such as Orazio Vecchi's *L'anfiparnaso* (1597) and Adriano Banchieri's *La saviezza giovanile* (1598) in which comic dramas were set to music for unaccompanied vocal ensemble; the music,

---

* The modern reader may be unacquainted with Terence, though in English-speaking countries he may remember the Terence-inspired *A Funny Thing Happened on the Way to the Forum* or *Up Pompeii*; somewhat similar are the brilliant French strip cartoons by Goscinny and Uderzo about Astérix the Gaul.

strongly dramatic, does not match individual characters with soloists but with groups of voices, high for females, low for males. These unstaged music dramas descend from the descriptive choral pieces of Clément Jannequin (*La bataille de Marignano*, *La chasse*, and *Le chant des oiseaux*, for example, all published in 1529).

When we remember the Neapolitan *Farsa Cavaiola* and the Florentine carnival comedies, both established before the coming of opera, the inevitability of *opera buffa* in Italy is assured. Its birthplace, like Homer's, is disputed. In Naples it was particularly cherished: when an opera from elsewhere was to be produced, if it contained no comic *intermezzi* these were added on the spot by local composer and librettist, existing *intermezzi* often being transferred from one *opera seria* to others. But the first Neapolitan comic opera seems to be Faggioli's *La Cilla* produced in 1706.*

Florence claimed to have started *opera buffa* with *Chi soffre, speri* by Mazzocchi and Marazzoli, produced in 1639. Rome, however, had staged Cornacchidi's *Diana schernita* in 1629, and Rome gave us Giulio Respigliosi, librettist of *Chi soffre, speri* and of Landi's earlier, partly comic *San Alessio* (1632), as well as of *Dal male il bene* (1653), another claimant as the first comic opera. Respigliosi had been Papal Nuncio in Spain and learned, from Calderón, the value of temperamental *chiaroscuro*, tragedy highlit by comedy, in drama. In 1667 he became Pope Clement IX and encouraged opera enthusiastically, some opined at the sacrifice of his papal duties. Venice, the first Italian city to open public opera houses, is said (by Donald Grout following H. C. Wolff) to have been the home of a school of comic and satirical opera since 1650; but according to Loewenberg's *Annals* the first comic opera produced there was Ruggier's *Elisa* in 1711. The conflicting claims arise perhaps because it is difficult to decide what is comic and what serious when operas customarily included scenes of both types, until the Arcadian reform of Zeno and Metastasio banished comedy from élite music drama. Comic librettos were much extemporised too, often performed by touring companies who travelled and played in awkward circumstances, regularly subject to loss of property through hasty escape, negligence or Act of God, furthermore denigrated, even by their authors, even by Goldoni, as inferior to the formula-ridden *opera serie* of their hack contemporaries. Evidence still shows that the *buffo* element in opera was established and appreciated during the seventeenth century.

In the context of this book it is interesting to note that in 1674 Draghi's *La lanterna di Diogene* was produced in Vienna, an operatic satire about European royalty, though so inoffensive that the Emperor Franz I composed the music for one aria.

A comic opera about nobility was a contradiction in terms. The essence of *opera buffa*, once it had been separated from *opera seria*, was its proletarian content. The characters were servants or tradesmen, or members of professional classes. Noble characters did not sing with them in the same scene or number until after 1770. This is why comic scenes were separated as intermezzi, then retained for a cheerful concluding ensemble (to hold the audience, who were waiting for it,

* According to Claudio Sartori, 'Gli Scarlatti a Napoli', in *Rivista musicale italiana*, Sept.– Oct. 1942). Loewenberg dates it 1707.

in their seats), ultimately banished from the new *opera seria* into an independent existence where the nobility, as contrast, were replaced by *parvenus* and *mezzo carattere* personages of good education but not actually noble birth.

Initially too the *opera buffa* had a text in local dialect, like *commedia dell'arte*. This amused the courtly audiences to whom the first *opere buffe* were played, and led to popular favour when public houses began to proliferate. The first complete season of *opera buffa* was not given until 1709, in Naples, where *cummedéja in museca* was particularly loved. The dialects of Naples and Venice are especially savoury, and arcane to foreigners, those of Tuscany and Rome less obtrusive; so the dialect *opera buffa* flourished where local language fertilized it. It was nurtured by local speech and by popular music of the district, dance-rhythms, melodious speech-inflections. More generally the *opera buffa* reflected the Italian's inborn delight in the absurdities of everyday human life: gesticulation and mimicry, animated motion whether dance or the athletics of the juggler and conjurer, the acrobat; mockery of the pretentious and the physically or mentally eccentric; pleasure in the finding and putting together of unusual, extravagant but always expressive words and phrases apt to the moment.

Long before Mozart came on the scene Italian *opera buffa* was revelling in stock comic situations, many of them amusing because regularly employed in serious drama. Goldoni made a speciality of ridiculing the affectations of aristocrats or would-be fashionable society; some of these traits were noted in connection with Mozart's *La finta semplice* and *La finta giardiniera*, and we shall observe them in the extravagant moods of the ladies in *Così fan tutte*, less obviously in Donna Anna and Don Ottavio, quite openly in the plot of *Le nozze di Figaro* though expressed with some diplomacy. Disguise and, in particular, travesty were standard dramatic practice: *opera buffa* thrived on these, either to mock *opera seria* (as in the Albanian disguises of *Così*) or to make genuine comic points (as in Despina's disguises in that opera). The English pantomime dame (played by a man, the more robust the better) has her origin in the veto, by Pope Innocent, of any woman to appear on stage: so *castrati* took female roles, and other male singers impersonated, *falsetto*, the old hags who rebuked their young charges and longed for a robust lover.★

Opera buffa regularly parodied or caricatured the conventions of *opera seria*. At first the same sort of music sufficed for serious and comic subjects. Then *opera buffa* moved away from polyphonic music, imitative writing, canonic treatment, anything florid or elaborate, as being too intellectual for a plebeian audience and a popular entertainment. Instead these trappings of *opera seria* reappeared as

★ This old, once necessary, recourse was resurrected at Glyndebourne during the 1960s when the special talent for female impersonation of the tenor Hugues Cuénod was imaginatively utilized by Raymond Leppard, in his performing editions of seventeenth-century Italian operas, so that several old-lady roles were assumed by Cuénod and elsewhere, following his example, by other histrionically gifted tenors. Male lovers would dress as women to come near the beloved (as in Rossini's *Comte Ory*), or for other juvenile designs, as Cherubino twice in *Figaro*—note that Beaumarchais required Cherubino to be played by a pretty young lady. These pages must not be played by adult men—their sexual potency has to be presumed dormant, not only Verdi's Oscar but even, to the outside world though not the audience, Strauss's Octavian. The young female soprano in a puerile breeches part was imaginatively extended into a bisexual hermaphrodite in Carl Johann Almquist's *Drottningens Juwelmyke* (1816), used as operatic material by Wehrle in 1973 (*Tintomara*). The girl dressed as a boy obviously had relevance to the phenomenon of the male *castrato* who sang heroic soprano roles in *opera seria*: in the down-to-earth realistic world of *opera buffa* he found no place.

357

caricature: the elaborate simile aria, imitations of birdsong, echo-effects, magical transformations. All were frequently introduced for caricature purposes. Gluck's *Das Bächlein*, a favourite soprano item in Lieder recitals, reverentially performed and applauded, is really a comic parody of the pretentious artist describing, in extravagant and inane detail, his latest *trompe l'oeil* painting; it comes from the comic opera *Le cadi dupé* and should be sung in French. Leonardo Leo had already parodied simile arias, and Mozart did likewise, very prettily in *La finta giardiniera*, most absurdly and grandiosely in Fiordiligi's *Come scoglio*.

Some other special features of *opera seria* were the Tomb scene—parodied in Mozart's *Don Giovanni*; the Letter scene revived, not humorously, in the *Figaro* duet *Canzonetta sull'aria*, and Leporello's Catalogue aria (but this was a standard stylized number, apt for patter, of great antiquity); the Echo scene, most familiar now through adoption by J. S. Bach for ecclesiastical purposes though *buffo* composers must have parodied it gratefully; and the magical transformation— sent up in Haydn's *Mondo della luna* (previously set by Galuppi) and in Mozart's *Così fan tutte*, as well as in Casti's libretto *I dormienti* (1793), whose characters sleep for hundreds of years after the Crusades and awake in another century— like Janáček's Mr Brouček but in the opposite direction.

As a plebeian entertainment the Italian *opera buffa* naturally traded in violence by word or deed.* Threats and insults promised lively vocabulary: Mozart set them to music in Masetto's *Ho capito* ('Briccondraccia, malandrina', etc.). The same opera gives a Mozartian exhibition of the beating-up scene which was always a feature of *opera buffa*. Duels are borrowed from *opera seria* (one in *Don Giovanni*), but sometimes parodied by making one duellist a coward, as in Strauss's *Der Rosenkavalier* and Mozart's *Finta giardiniera*. Plebeians turn out to be noblemen (like presidents, theoretically, of the United States) as with *Lo sposo burlato*. Foreigners, with their weird clothes and speech and habits, are fair game (the fake lovers in *Così* obviously, but also the polyglot aria of Nardo in *La finta giardiniera*, and indeed the harem inhabitants of *Die Entführung*). Old people have always been comic. *Opera buffa* dwelt much, for musical as well as hilarious effect, on old ladies who longed for love and old gentlemen who felt likewise, and on both exhorting their young charges to behave decently. Goldoni was fond of such scenes, in *Lo speziale* (eventually set by Haydn). We find them in Paisiello's *Barbiere di Siviglia* and Pergolesi's *La serva padrona*. We meet old ladies addressing the audience about their disapproval of modern habits (Mozart set just such a scene in his non-operatic song *Die Alte*). This age-old harangue *ad spectatores* has powerful Mozartian operatic equivalents in Figaro's *Aprite un pò* and Guglielmo's *Donne mie*, indeed Papageno's *Der Vogelfänger bin ich ja*.

Some of the other favourite characters in *opera buffa* were doctors, especially with surgical instruments and weird remedies; soldiers whether licentious or drunken or hot-tempered or cowardly; scholars and lawyers and pedantic tutors and fake magicians; bluestockings, pretentiously intellectual young ladies; deaf, dumb, stammering, sneezing or yawning people, usually servants but sometimes masters, or one of the categories mentioned above. Most derive from the characters of the *commedia dell'arte*. There was Pantalone, a rich, miserly old merchant from

* It has been pertinently observed that the Renaissance working man's relaxations were drink, sex and wife-beating.

Venice, sometimes called Cassandro or Il Barone, always being robbed or cuck-olded; Graziano, the Doctor from Bologna, an old pedant full of bogus learning; Spavento, the Venetian selfstyled *capitano*, a braggart and bully but a coward at heart; Arlecchino from Bergamo (hence the Bergamasque), Pantalone's valet, athletic and graceful, a ladykiller though a pander too, cynical, claiming noble birth, addicted to transvestism, darkskinned; Brighella, also from Bergamo, another servant, more quick-witted than Arlecchino, an able musician, much in demand for acts of violence and other dirty work—he is also known as Scapino and, from the name of a French actor famed for his comic shaving routine, as Mezzetin. There was the stammering cleric Tartaglia from Naples; the gross gluttonous Truffaldino with his string of sausages; Pulcinella from Naples (or Benevento, some said) with his hunchback and paunch—indeed he is our Mr Punch, also called Cucurucu and Hanswurst. Pagliaccio, in French Pierrot, in Russian Petrushka, is the moonfaced, simple fall-guy, servant to Graziano. Colombina, the pretty young girl loved by all, though feared for her sharp tongue, is the only woman in the standard traditional team of Masks—and as a woman she wore no mask. Other characters popular from time to time were Cavicchio, a hayseed rustic; the wily Scaramuccio (sometimes identified with Spavento, though this seems implausible); the gardener Pasquariello; the servants Coviello, Burattino and Stentorello; the rich, handsome, young but dull and foppish, suitor called Lelio or Leandro or Octavio; and his female counterpart Isabella, pretty, rich, and snobbish. Indeed the only character regularly involved in *opera buffa* who does not figure in the cast-list of the *commedia dell'arte* is the old hag, whether nursemaid–confidante or rapacious spinster; and she was a stock-character in classical Roman comedy, as were the cowardly soldier, the scheming servant, and the miserly or generation-gap-conscious rich old father.

A little thought will show that these stock characters, however much refined by Molière in France, Goldoni and Gozzi in Italy, survived into Beaumarchais's *Figaro* dramas and into the three comic operas which da Ponte wrote for Mozart. Figaro himself is Brighella in his Mezzetin guise; Count Almaviva is Spavento, Antonio obviously Pasquariello, Dr Bartolo in *Le Barbier* was Pantalone, and Don Basilio perhaps Graziano; Don Curzio is clearly derived from Tartaglia. We can trace the *commedia* characters in many later comic operas.

It has been mentioned that Italian *opera buffa* did not require the *castrato* voice. It did however bring back the bass voice, neglected in serious opera after Monteverdi and Cavalli, for ripe, comic, musical use, especially in the role of Pantalone. This foundation for a musical solo texture encouraged the development of the vocal ensemble, foreign to *opera seria* which emphasized solo song, varied seldom by a duet, and with a final chorus sung by the assembled principals often, as in *Mitridate*, consisting only of sopranos and a tenor or so.★ Given at least one bass soloist *opera buffa* could elaborate concerted music to gratification: intellectual polyphony for voices, considered rather difficult for singers who were less musi-cally accomplished than their colleagues in *opera seria*, was not necessary even here, though by Mozart's time it began to reappear effectively. Such an ensemble was helpful to introduce the cast at the beginning of a comic opera (e.g., in *La finta semplice*, *La finta giardiniera* and *Lo sposo deluso*) where the rising curtain reveals a

★ The true chorus of mixed voices was reintroduced into comic opera by Goldoni.

359

number of characters assembled on stage busily occupied. In the course of the drama, ensembles at first tended to be static, and this may have fostered the popularity of the thunderstruck ensemble of immobility following some drastic *coup de théâtre*: a familiar and typical, though post-Mozart, example is *Fredda ed immobile* in the first act finale of Rossini's *Barbiere di Siviglia*. It was in the finale to an act that the ensemble found its happiest outlet and was most commonly used in *opera buffa*. We rightly regard the Act II finale of *Le nozze de Figaro* as one of the major glories of classical music, let alone of opera: it is a triumph of invention and musical construction, masterfully balanced in the finest Viennese classical style (artistically the most perfect yet known to music). But the construction of such a scene had already been described in writing by da Ponte about an earlier opera libretto of his; and the dramatically active finale-ensemble (such as this is), with several events and entrances and scenes, had been elaborated by Leonardo Leo and Leonardo Vinci, then by Piccinni (rondo-form), Galuppi (chain-form) and Logroscino (through-composed) for several decades. The lively inventive interest of the orchestral music in the *Figaro* concerted finales, quintessential Mozart as it is, was developed from the work of Paisiello who first made demands on the *opera buffa* orchestra, hitherto assumed to be lazy and incompetent.

Comic opera, as a popular entertainment of a relaxing nature, invited freer dramatic forms than the strictly organized *opera seria*. Bertati regularized a three-act structure, but Mozart's masterpieces were in two acts, except for *Figaro* which is in four—though the first and third acts end quite unpretentiously, as though no interval were envisaged. The great variety of forms employed in Mozart's arias for his comic operas will be remarked, much more diversified than those of *opera seria* where the hallowed *da capo* form of aria was much shortened or altered by Mozart but effectively remained traditional until *Idomeneo*. Dry recitative, when performed rapidly and with vivacity, accorded well with the spirit of Italian comedy though, for entertainment's sake, it was subordinated to the musical number, solo or concerted. Outside Italy these numbers were separated by spoken dialogue unaccompanied, which is why the first act of *La finta giardiniera*, which survives only in a German translation, lacks Mozart's linking recitatives. The accompanied recitativo, musically so effective in *opera seria* was a special effect, and parodied as such in *opera buffa* at moments of absurd pretension—though Mozart, appreciating a new atmosphere, used it in his comic operas for genuine feeling as well as for caricature.

Mozart inherited a *buffo* musical convention whereby song was less sustained, *bel canto*, than in serious opera, often eloquently disjointed, strongly accented. Leporello's *Madamina* is an example. The ideal had from the inception been ingratiating yet forthright, later became more sentimental. The change was marked in Goldoni's vain but glorious attempts to sophisticate the blatant crudity of *commedia dell'arte*, turning stock types into distinctive people (Jommelli as composer supported this venture), introducing more charm into his characters (Piccinni and Paisiello followed him here), writing attractive verses, sometimes of Metastasian eloquence, for his well born lovers and motivating the reactions of all his characters less crazily than before—our term 'zany' for wild farce derives from the term *commedia dei zanni*, where 'zanni' means 'servants'. His insistence on the proletarian nature of Italian comedy was hotly contested by the aristocratic Carlo Gozzi who introduced fantasy and magic into comic operas, the most famous offspring of which is Mozart's *Die Zauberflöte*. In Italy the regional *buffo* styles of Venice, Naples and Rome gradually fused, and added appropriate elements from more serious opera. Mozart, experienced in French and German adaptations of *buffo* music drama, and aware of what the musical styles of *opera seria* could contribute (as Leonardo da Vinci had been, fifty years earlier), concocted his own blends. He built on what he found. In these last comic operas he built durably and superbly.

LE NOZZE DI FIGARO
(Figaro's Wedding)

Commedia per musica* in four acts

Text by
LORENZO DA PONTE

K. 492

FIGARO, valet to Count Almaviva	BASS
SUSANNA, chambermaid to Countess Almaviva, niece of Antonio, orphan	SOPRANO
BARTOLO, physician in Seville	BASS
MARCELLINA, chatelaine to Almaviva, duenna to the Countess	SOPRANO
CHERUBINO, Count Almaviva's principal page	SOPRANO
COUNT ALMAVIVA	BASS
DON BASILIO, music master to the household	TENOR
COUNTESS ALMAVIVA	SOPRANO
ANTONIO, chief gardener at the Castle	BASS
DON CURZIO, counsellor-at-law	TENOR
BARBARINA, Antonio's daughter	SOPRANO

The action takes place in the castle and grounds of Aguasfrescas outside Seville

* *Opera buffa in Mozart's private catalogue.*

I

Literary history is littered with unpopular sequels to successful works of art. The temptation to squeeze some more out of a popular formula is both natural and challenging for a creative artist, especially when his admirers are not only applauding but shouting 'Encore'. Yet how often is a *Paradise Lost* followed by a *Paradise Regained*, an *Oedipus Rex* by an *Oedipus at Colonus*, a *Gargantua* by a *Pantagruel*, a *Winnie the Pooh* by a *House at Pooh Corner*?—the original a masterpiece, the sequel a disappointment. The pot of tea never, it seems, survives the topping-up process, however potent the initial brew, however boiling the new infusion of water. Or hardly ever. One author who capped a masterpiece with a sequel no less immortal was Pierre-Augustin Caron de Beaumarchais (1723–99, ennobled 1761) whose *La folle journée ou Le mariage de Figaro* (1784) was at once, and has continued to be, recognized as the equal if not superior of his *Le barbier de Séville* (1775)—though it must have seemed unpromising to bring back the characters of Figaro, Rosine, Count Almaviva, Dr Bartholo and Don Bazile and watch them *after* the marriage of Rosine and Almaviva with which *Le barbier* culminated. Beaumarchais, a sly and experienced student of human nature, knew that to retain interest in them he must show them developed and strengthened or transformed in personal characteristics by the passing of three years since the end of *Le barbier*, that he must introduce new characters at least as impressive and attractive, and that the contents of the new play must be even more unconventional and striking, in a word controversial.

Beaumarchais was born in Paris on 24 January 1723, during the regency between the death of Louis XIV and the accession of Louis XV. He was the son of a clockmaker and became expert in his father's trade, inventing an escapement mechanism in 1754 (characteristically he had to struggle for the rights in it) and becoming clockmaker to Louis XV. His first marriage was short-lived; his wife died in 1757, leaving him some property at Beaumarchais from which he later took his title. He became harp-teacher to the King's daughters, financier, secret agent, armaments manufacturer and army contractor, foreign agent of the Committee for Public Health, and dramatist, as well as founder of the French Authors' Society. He spent some time in Spain, where he bought the monopoly of Louisiana for France from Spain, and picked up local colour which can be observed in the Figaro plays. He was bankrupted, imprisoned, exiled to Hamburg, lost his civic rights, and endured total failure in the theatre. He married three times, and only just survived the French Revolution for which his work had sounded the Reveille. He returned to Paris in 1796 and died there three years later. It must be added that, as a sequel-writer, he pushed his luck too far. In 1792 he produced a third Almaviva play, *La mère coupable*: it was a total flop and deserved to be, since the action is heavily contrived, the sparkle missing. (Darius Milhaud derived an opera from it.) It did not prevent Odön von Horvath from writing *Figaro's Divorce*, which Giselher Klebe turned into an opera.

Le barbier de Séville had succeeded, despite initial disfavour, because it was fundamentally *commedia dell'arte* spiced with some topical epigrams. Paisiello's operatic version of it (dramatically more piquant than Rossini's of thirty-three years later) came to the stage at St Petersburg in 1782, to Vienna in 1783. *Le mariage de Figaro* was thought altogether more dangerous: the characters were more lifelike, the situations most unflattering to male aristocrats anywhere (females of the genre were allowed to suffer from the vapours but not to demonstrate about their wounded pride as every Almaviva did), the dialogue positively impudent, showing the servants bettering their master and giving eloquent justification for themselves too. Beaumarchais had completed *Le mariage de Figaro* in 1778. Louis XVI, by now King of France, declared, 'Celà est détestable, celà ne sera jamais joué'. Other monarchist countries followed suit, including Austria where the liberal-minded Emperor Joseph II declared that 'since the piece contains much that is objectionable, I therefore expect that the Censor shall either reject it altogether, or at any rate have such alterations made in it that he shall be responsible for the performance of this play and for the impression it may make'. The Austrian censor could take a hint. He banned *Der närrische Tag*, as the German version was entitled.

Beaumarchais did not accept the French King's verdict. He instigated a campaign of intrigue that Figaro would have been proud of,[*] against the French censors and with the assistance of the aristocrats on whose inquisitiveness, intellectual snobbery and love of scandal he played unceasingly—though they were the targets of the play. By September 1783 the King was willing to permit one of Beaumarchais's cronies, M. de Vaudreuil, to give a private performance in his own home at Genevilliers. Louis XVI supposed that his courtiers would find *La folle journée* more tedious than crazy. Three hundred of them attended this private performance, among them the King's brother, the Comte d'Artois (later Charles X), and Marie Antoinette's closest friend, Mme de Polignac. Their enthusiasm broke down the King's resistance and he authorized an official production (with a few cuts) by his Comédie française on 27 April 1784. The French public was no less delighted. *Le mariage de Figaro* ran initially for sixty-eight performances, broke box-office records, and brought about the death by suffocation of three women in the throng to gain admission. It remains a classic item in the repertory of the Comédie française and the Barber himself has given his name to a leading French newspaper.

2

Interest in *Le mariage de Figaro* quickly spread outside France. In London Thomas Holcroft quickly got wind of its success and made his own pirated English version, *The Follies of a Day*, which was produced on 14 December 1784[†] and much repeated in Ireland as well as England. A pirated edition brought out in Amsterdam may have been the source of other translations, including a German one by Johann Rautenstrauch which the Austrian censor allowed to be published

---

[*] Indeed it has been suggested that the name Figaro is a corruption of *fils Caron*. A Spaniard will automatically pronounce the name Figáro.
[†] Interesting details in R. B. Moberly, *Three Mozart Operas*, p. 37 ff.

but not performed. There were almost a dozen other German printed translations available in Germany by the time Mozart's opera was performed.

This was exactly the subject that Mozart had been searching for since Christmas 1782 when Count Orsini-Rosenberg had invited him to compose a new *opera buffa* for Vienna.* He had looked at dozens of opera libretti and found them all wanting, rehashes of *commedia dell'arte* characters and situations, ultimately uninspiring to a young composer with musico-dramatic aspirations. He had the friendly if not unduly enthusiastic ear of the Emperor, who made him Court Composer; and his commission had come from Rosenberg-Orsini whose taste was Italophile and anti-German. On the other hand Mozart had powerful rivals in Vienna: Salieri, Paisiello, Sarti, and the Italianized Spanish Martín y Soler were all more highly esteemed than the indigenous Mozart who, for all his operatic experience, was reckoned to have produced only one opera, *Die Entführung*, and that German. He had been given the key to this closed shop but he knew that, to qualify for entry, he must make a great effect. He had met Lorenzo da Ponte, one of the staff court poets, who had offered to collaborate with him. Perhaps Mozart knew that da Ponte had succeeded well with opera libretti based on French plays about real identifiable characters rather than *commedia dell'arte* masks. In August 1784 he attended the première in Vienna of Paisiello's *Rè Teodoro in Venezia*, just such a human drama with a text by the Abbé G. B. Casti. Then he laid hands on Beaumarchais's *Mariage de Figaro*. Here were the characters, situations, inflammatory ideals, which exactly matched his operatic longings. Paisiello's *Barbiere di Siviglia* had been applauded everywhere. *Le mariage de Figaro* promised even more: it was banned as a play, but much read and discussed everywhere. Figaro in the second scene of *Le barbier de Séville* had announced, 'Ce qui ne vaut pas la peine d'être dit, on le chante.' It was not permitted to act Beaumarchais's *Figaro* on the stage, but could it not be sung—especially in Italian as an *opera buffa*? The success of Paisiello's *Barbiere*, and the gossip about *Le mariage*, would ensure good attendance. Mozart knew himself to be experienced in all branches of opera, and in small ways (additional musical numbers for the operas of other composers, for example) he had made a mark in operatic Vienna. Even if da Ponte was not the author of the unpromising *Lo sposo deluso*, he had worked with this Italian poet on the cantata *Davidde penitente* (March 1785, music based on the C minor unfinished Mass, K. 417a) and in September 1785 on a (now lost) cantata celebrating the recovery from illness of Nancy Storace, Vienna's *prima donna* and a dear friend of Mozart (she had lost her voice for several months, perhaps a psychosomatic result of her disastrous marriage).

Could da Ponte, not too overworked at that moment, adapt Beaumarchais as an Italian comic opera for Vienna? Even da Ponte, who took the credit for everything possible by the time he wrote his *Memoirs* in 1826, admitted that Mozart suggested the Beaumarchais comedy as operatic material. It was a long and elaborate play, well known to all, not quite *sub rosa*. The fumbling author of *Lo sposo deluso* could not have turned it into the concise, pointed literary masterpiece da Ponte drew from it. Clearly da Ponte knew Beaumarchais's play: he translated long passages into Italian verse, *au pied de la lettre*. He abbreviated for musical effect and cut for diplomacy. It was a brilliant adaptation of a great play. Da Ponte was

* See *L'oca del Cairo*, p. 323, and *Lo sposo deluso*, p. 333.

to write two later libretti for Mozart, masterpieces both, and other admirable libretti for other composers. It may be interesting to summarize his curriculum vitae.

3

He was born Emmanuele Conegliano in Ceneda (now Vittorio Veneto) near Venice in 1749. He was a Jew who grew up speaking Hebrew and Venetian dialect. At school he learned Latin, but no pure Italian; he confessed to difficulty in writing pure grammatical Italian. In 1763 his widowed father proposed to a Gentile woman and was accepted. Twelve days before the marriage father Conegliano accepted the Christian faith and was baptized, together with his three sons, by the Bishop of Ceneda whose surname, da Ponte, they formally assumed. Emmanuele* was given the Bishop's Christian name as well, and thus became Lorenzo da Ponte. He studied for the Catholic priesthood and became an Abbé; this did not inhibit his attention to the delights of the flesh (his *Memoirs* are full of saucy romances) but did introduce him to Italian poetry of which he was a master acknowledged by all from his days at Treviso in 1774. His love affairs and political pamphleteering constantly obliged him to become a Scapino and take up residence elsewhere. During a stay at Gorizia in 1779 he became a member of the Accademia there and discovered his technique of adapting creatively from French drama. A bogus letter called him to a post in Dresden where its supposed author Caterino Mazzolà did his best to make the time profitable for da Ponte, taught him much, and gave him useful work as a literary ghost. When da Ponte left Dresden, Mazzolà gave him a letter of introduction to Salieri who had been Court Composer in Vienna since 1766.

Da Ponte was fortunate enough to arrive in Vienna early in 1782, in time to meet the great Pietro Metastasio who read part of a poem by da Ponte to an enthusiastic circle, then bade the author finish reciting his own work, thereby obtaining admirers and patrons for him. The letter to Salieri resulted in an opera *Il ricco d' un giorno* (1784) which flopped disastrously, causing Salieri to promise that he would never again work with da Ponte (though he later changed his mind). When G. B. Casti, an author from Italy, arrived in Vienna the intrigues grew, since Casti was already friendly with Count Rosenberg and worked well with Salieri. Then as now Viennese society (plebeian and aristocratic) lived for the opera, and for the intrigue and gossip surrounding it. Da Ponte regarded himself as the victim of intrigue since Rosenberg was determined that his friend Casti should succeed Metastasio as Imperial Poet (notwithstanding the Emperor's judicious verdict that 'as for myself I cannot use a poet; as for the opera we have da Ponte'). Da Ponte believed the worst of Casti who seems to have treated him always kindly and appreciatively; later they were good friends, when rivalry was not in question. As for the Theatre Director, da Ponte admitted that Rosenberg was 'gentle, humane and learned'; da Ponte did write libretti for Gazzaniga, Martín, Righini, and Mozart's pupil Stephen Storace (*Gli equivoci* after Shakespeare's *Comedy of Errors*) while in Vienna. He worked effectively there but after the death of Joseph II his fortunes began to decline and when he resigned his post as court poet he was told to leave Vienna. He repaired to Trieste, a well known 'refuge des

---

* Remember this name when we arrive at Act III of *Le nozze di Figaro*.

êtres disgraciés', where he met his future wife Nancy Grahl, a Jewish beauty twenty years his junior. The couple settled in London in 1793, then in 1805 followed Nancy's parents to New York, where Lorenzo published his racy and often inaccurate *Memoirs*, and died in 1838 revered as the father of Italian Studies in America.

4

Mozart was normally a dutiful letter writer to his father. In the late summer of 1785 he became dilatory: one letter on about 18 August, the next on 14 September, and then nothing until 2 November. These are all lost but Leopold retailed the gist of the last to his daughter Nännerl:

> He begs to be forgiven, as he is up to his eyes having to finish his opera *Le nozze di Figaro*. . . . He adds that in order to keep the morning free for composing, he is now postponing all his pupils until the afternoon, etc. I know the piece, it is a very laboured play and the translation from the French will certainly have to be freely altered if it is to be effective as an opera. God grant that the action may turn out well. I have no doubt about the music.

Leopold Mozart had heard rumours of a new opera from the editor of the *Salzburger Zeitung*, though Mozart and da Ponte agreed to keep their project a secret—presumably to minimize intrigue against them and their work on so controversial a theme. Da Ponte did tell Martín y Soler, who obligingly offered to take second place in the queue for new libretti until that for *Figaro* was finished— he was rewarded for his amiability since the libretto was *Una cosa rara*, the success of the season at the expense of *Figaro*. Mozart and da Ponte also sought the advice of Baron Wetzlar: how to circumvent the official ban on *Le mariage de Figaro*, how to get their *Nozze di Figaro* on to the Imperial stage against the powerful competition of Paisiello, Salieri, Righini and other composers preferred by Count Rosenberg and, despite his desire to rule justly, by the Emperor? Wetzlar magnanimously offered to commission both libretto and music and then, if *Le nozze di Figaro* could not be produced in Vienna, to promote it himself in Paris or London, where Beaumarchais's comedy was already much in demand. Da Ponte and Mozart both wanted a success in Vienna and they decided to work secretly and get their way by surprise.

Leopold Mozart, in the letter quoted above, foresaw 'a lot of running about and argument before [Wolfgang] gets the libretto adjusted just as he wishes it for his intentions'. Leopold knew how much extra work his son had demanded of librettists in the past. Da Ponte's *Memoirs* show his discouragement at the quantity of revision which Salieri required of him in his first opera libretto *Il ricco d'un giorno*:

> What did the 'little changes here and there' consist of? Shortening or lengthening most of the scenes; introducing new duets, trios, quartets; changing metres half-way through a song; introducing choruses to be sung by a German ballet; deleting almost all the recitatives, and therewith all the plot, all the dramatic quality of the action, if any there were. When the drama went on to the stage, I doubt whether there remained a hundred verses of my original.*

* *Memoirs*, p. 134.

Mozart will not have been less demanding than Salieri. But da Ponte this time mentions no such hang-ups. On the contrary: 'I set to work, accordingly, and as fast as I wrote the words, Mozart set them to music. In six weeks everything was in order.' If we assume that da Ponte was not inventing these idyllic circumstances of collaboration, then which were the six weeks?

From Wolfgang's letter we know that he was up to his ears in the composition of *Figaro* in early November 1785, arguably in mid-October (for the rumour to get from Vienna to Salzburg). In mid-October he finished his G minor piano quartet K. 478. In mid-September he must have composed his share of the Nancy Storace Recovery Cantata. During November he wrote two fine additional numbers for a production of Bianchi's *La Villanella rapita*, and several pieces of music for his Freemasons' Lodge; he had become a Mason in December 1784. During December he gave three subscription concerts in Vienna, including a piano concerto in each; only K. 482 in E flat major was brand-new.* In January 1786 he was ill with head and stomach pains, and wrote only the D major pianoforte rondo K. 485 (on a theme borrowed from J. C. Bach), but he must also have composed most of *Der Schauspieldirektor* which he completed at the beginning of February. In March he had to make additions and revisions for the amateur revival of *Idomeneo* in Vienna, besides composing KK. 488 and 491.

Mozart was a quick writer-down of music. He sketched seldom, or else destroyed all but a few of his initial experiments (*Deh vieni*, in *Figaro*, gives a rare example of Mozart at the drawing-board). He had the special gift of retaining in his head the music which he had worked out there while playing billiards or travelling, or whatever. He had composed the Linz Symphony, from start to finish, in three days. Even the concertos and piano quartet named above, superlative in quality as they are, could have been composed in less than a week.

Since Mozart's extant letters to his father do not mention his work on *Figaro*, we must guess. My own imaginative assumption is that he broached the subject to da Ponte in about August 1785. Mozart already knew Beaumarchais's play, inferably da Ponte as well since he at once agreed to the adaptation. Both spoke French and could work from the original text. Da Ponte was lazy and easily distracted but a hard worker when occasion demanded. He will have made a detailed scenario in two or three days and, after discussion, prepared to write the libretto before the end of August. Mozart, as was his custom, will have thought out an ideal available cast—obviously the lovely Nancy Storace as Susanna, and Benucci whom he had already seen and esteemed as a *basso buffo* as Figaro; perhaps Stefano Mandini who had arrived in 1783 in Vienna; maybe Bartolo was already designed for Bussani who had joined the company in 1784; surely Michael Kelly for Don Basilio, already a friend. Kelly was allowed to hear *Crudel, perchè finora* before anybody else, at Mozart's forte-piano (if we trust Kelly's memory).

In September 1785 I think that da Ponte wrote the libretto and 'as fast as I wrote the words, Mozart set them to music'. Not so fast, if we know Mozart. Granted (imaginatively) that during August they chose what to omit and how to turn Beaumarchais's five acts into da Ponte's four, and which lines must be trans-

---

* There is some doubt whether these concerts ever took place, since they are mentioned nowhere else. Mozart wrote two other superb piano concertos, K. 488 in A and K. 491 in C minor, before *Figaro* was produced; but they are dated March 1786.

lated straight into Italian, and which others turned into verse for set numbers, and then how many set ensembles must be provided (the ensembles are the special glory of *Figaro*; da Ponte is as much to be credited for them as Mozart who may have given a hand, being more experienced in music-theatre)—granted all this, if the quotation above is true, Mozart will still have come back to da Ponte all the time with second thoughts based on the music he had worked out in his head and could not accommodate (never could) to what his poet had written. Both lived in Vienna; they did not have to communicate, time-wastingly, by post; Mozart needed only to go round to da Ponte's house and explain what was wrong.

It is a pity that the Storace cantata is lost. Its music might have shed some light on, or been illuminated by, Mozart's *Figaro* as we know it. The G minor piano quartet suggests to me that Mozart wrote it in the middle of Act II of *Figaro* not because of key, though the G major finale may seem suggestive, not because of the highly florid B flat slow movement, but because the drama and characteristic invention of all three movements strongly recall the situations and characters of that act—the plot with Figaro, Cherubino's scene, his escape, the Count's anger, the litigation ensemble. The piano quartet is not *like* the music of Act II; it is a drama about a piano (Mozart himself) and three string players. But no other part of *Figaro* is so vividly reflected in K. 478 and I have an inkling that on about 10 October Mozart got stuck in the middle of Act II, asked da Ponte for alterations, and meanwhile occupied himself with this piano quartet.

By then he had more or less completed Act I, except for the overture, and some of Act II. And he was well advanced with the rest of the opera. Recent research on paper-watermarks and inks has shown that Mozart did not compose the whole opera in chronological order, but set arias of similar type one after another, then put himself in another frame of mind and pursued that one. He seems to have started composition with No. 2 and its preceding recitative, then demanded a text for No. 1 and set that, proceeded to the recitative after *Cosa sento* and the following chorus, then returned to Bartolo's *La vendetta*, jumped to Cherubino's *Non sò più*, and then to No. 14, *Susanna, or via sortite*, followed by the Act II finale up to its final scene. He next went back and completed the rest of Act I, before broaching No. 15, *Aprite presto aprite* which, for all its brevity, cost him much labour. He then completed Act II, working in reverse order from the close of the Finale back to *Porgi amor*. At what point he began work on Act III cannot be known until Soviet authorities publicly acknowledge the whereabouts of their autograph and allow scholars to examine it.★

Even Mozart could not have composed the whole four acts of *Le nozze di Figaro* during those six weeks in September and October, working in the mornings (some evenings conceivably). It is likely that he persisted with *Figaro* during later November and part of December (when he composed K. 482), harrying da Ponte the while. Since he had to write *Der Schauspieldirektor* in January he must, I think, have been far advanced with *Figaro*. Any remains will have been completed in February. Mozart was busy in March, and the first performance of *Le nozze di Figaro* was announced for 28 April—meaning that by then it should have been accepted, copied, learned, designed and rehearsed. The première was postponed until 1 May, and on 29 April Mozart wrote the overture, one of his most brilliant,

★ Cf. Karl-Heinz Köhler, 'Mozarts Kompositionsweise', in *Mozart-Jahrbuch 1967*, pp. 31–45.

and longer than the piece of music which we all know. The six weeks which da Ponte remembered were, I am sure, those in the autumn of 1785 when Mozart was writing, writing, playing his music to da Ponte perhaps, and explaining why the poor poet had to write some more for their opera—which both knew, by then, was going to be 'a new kind of spectacle to a public of so refined a taste and such just understanding'.* It had to be something remarkable and convincing if it was to succeed on the Vienna stage and make their promising reputation established and financially beneficial—both were hard up; Mozart had to appeal for funds to a publisher in November 1785.

In February 1786 Mozart obliged his Imperial Majesty and employer with *Der Schauspieldirektor*. It must have been before this that da Ponte went to Joseph II with the text of *Le Nozze di Figaro*. Later he retailed the story thus:

Emp. Don't you know that Mozart, though a wonder at instrumental music, has written only one opera,† and nothing remarkable at that?

Da P. Yes, Sire, but without Your Majesty's clemency I would have written but one drama for Vienna.

Emp. But this *Mariage de Figaro*—I have just forbidden the German company to use it.‡

Da P. Yes, Sire, but I was writing an opera, not a comedy. I had to omit many scenes and cut others considerably. I have omitted or cut anything that might offend good taste or public decency at a performance over which the Sovereign Majesty might preside. The music, I may add, as far as I may judge of it, seems to me marvellously beautiful.

Joseph II favoured da Ponte, and so gave his blessing on *Le nozze* and sent a messenger to Mozart who arrived with his score and played it to the Emperor who was much enchanted by the music, and ordered it to be copied, and the opera scheduled for immediate production.

Figaro was thus given official favour at the expense of Martín's *Una cosa rara*, and Righini's *Demogorgone* (where Kelly mimicked da Ponte). The Casti–Rosenberg faction did all they could to hinder the production, so Josepha Duschek and her musician husband Franz, then visiting Vienna, reported to Leopold Mozart. The singers were bribed, according to Franz Xaver Niemeček, to sing wrongly, until Mozart persuaded the Emperor to intervene and threaten them. The climate changed, according to Michael Kelly (the Irish tenor who doubled Don Basilio and Don Curzio) when Benucci rehearsed *Non più andrai* on stage and, by his vocal splendour and musicianly eloquence, won over the entire company and the orchestra.

The first performance was postponed until 1 May 1786 (appropriate day for such a left-wing opera). Storace as Susanna 'enchanted eye, ear and soul', according to one Hungarian spectator. She was the *prima donna* of the company and for many years Susanna's was generally considered a more important role than that of

---

* Da Ponte's Preface to *Le nozze di Figaro*.

† Therefore before the production, arguably before commissioning, of *Der Schauspieldirektor*.

‡ 2 February 1785.

Countess Almaviva—Susanna sings in many more musical numbers. Count Almaviva was sung by Stefano Mandini.

The Countess was sung by Luisa Laschi, later Mozart's Viennese Zerlina, by then Mad. Mombelli—we would be surprised at such a change of *Fach*, or vocal characterization. Mandini's wife Maria sang Marcellina and was evidently a soprano with a compass up to high B, not a contralto as often nowadays. The Cherubino was Dorothea Sardi-Bussani, good-looking rather than vocally or musically gifted, but the wife of Francesco Bussani, manager of the company, who (surely a last-minute decision necessitating a change of order in Act III) doubled Don Bartolo and Antonio and was, according to da Ponte, 'a jack of all trades save that of an honest man'. Mozart wrote Barbarina for a very young girl. By good fortune he found Nannina Gottlieb, who was just Beaumarchais's prescribed twelve years old; later she was his first Pamina.

The first performance seems not to have been particularly accomplished. But the house was full, Mozart was obliged to take numerous curtain calls, and if some hissing was heard from the top gallery (it was attributed to the rival faction's claque) there was much applause and so many encores given that the performance lasted almost twice as long as the opera. Leopold Mozart could not attend, but reported, after a letter from his son, that at the second and third performances respectively five and seven numbers had to be repeated; 'among them one little duet had to be sung three times'—this may have been *Canzonetta sull'aria* or more likely *Aprite presto*. On 3 May, the day of the second performance, the music was advertised for sale in handwritten copies. From 8 May onwards Mozart handed over the conducting to Joseph Weigl. On the following day the Emperor ordered that encores would not be given for musical numbers involving more than one voice. Later the Emperor told the singers, during a rehearsal, that he had hoped to spare them the fatigue of singing so much in a long opera. They thanked him meekly, except Kelly who said, 'Do not believe them, Sire, they all like to be encored; at least I am sure I always do.' The order was allowed to lapse during the autumn while *Figaro* was still in the Vienna repertory.

Le nozze di Figaro was performed nine times between May and December 1786 and was then withdrawn. It was considered less successful than Martín's *Una cosa rara* which had its first performance on 17 November. At about that time *Figaro* was produced in Prague by the Italian opera company of Pasquale Bondini, then resident there. Caterina Bondini, the manager's wife, sang Susanna; Felice Ponziani was Figaro; Luigi Bassi played the Count.

Here the opera was immensely successful, for its music as much as the social content of the action. Mozart and his wife travelled there in January: he went to the opera in what is now called the Tyl Theatre, conducted at least one performance of *Figaro,* and was agreeably surprised at a ball to find quadrilles and waltzes being danced to the music of his opera. 'For here they talk of nothing but *Figaro*. Nothing is played, sung or whistled but *Figaro*. No opera is drawing like *Figaro*. Nothing, nothing but *Figaro*.' Before he returned to Vienna Mozart agreed to write a new opera for Bondini's company. It was to be *Don Giovanni* and it was brought to Vienna before *Figaro* was revived there in August 1789. *Figaro* remained thereafter in the Vienna repertory until November; further performances followed in 1790 and early 1791. After Mozart's death it was not given until 1798.

For the 1789 revival in Vienna some roles had changed hands. Nancy Storace had gone home to London; Susanna was now taken by Adriana Ferraresi del Bene, da Ponte's new mistress. Mozart wrote two new arias for her, to be considered in context below. Countess Almaviva was sung by Catarina Cavalieri.* The immediate result of this successful revival was the commission, by the Emperor, of *Così fan tutte*.

5

Ever since *La finta giardiniera* Mozart had been in the habit of composing his operatic overtures after the rest of the score was completed: it enabled him to give the overture particular musical relevance to what follows. The D major *presto* (or, in Mozart's own catalogue, *allegro assai*) **Overture** to *Le nozze di Figaro* was written on 29 April (though sketched earlier), several weeks after the remainder of the score had been copied and the rehearsals had begun. For once, however, Mozart did not allude to the opera's music in this overture. A more appropriate introduction to *La folle journée* could hardly be conceived. Here is the perfect musical portrayal of stealth, conspiracy, tender assignations, festivity, aristocratic grandeur, and repression, a touch of pathos (bar 101), plebeian good cheer (bar 108) and ceaseless activity. The movement hardly pauses to take breath. Mozart does not attempt a symphonic development. He did, after the fashion of the *Entführung* overture, contemplate an *andante con moto* middle section, a siciliano in D minor (at bar 135):

1

To those who have revelled for years in the helter-skelter dash of the overture's *presto* it may seem unthinkable that Mozart even contemplated a slow intermezzo. He not only did so: he composed his *andante* straight through to the end, to judge from the final dominant seventh chord before the *presto* is resumed. Then he wrote *vi-* and *-de* in the appropriate bars, and tore the intervening page out. Constanze Mozart's second husband was in possession of a 'Fragment, arguably from an opera, with violin, viola, oboe, horns, clarinets, timpani, bassoon and bass. D minor. 64 bars. It is quite complete, lacking only what precedes it.' Sadly, the fragment has disappeared—for, though we may prefer the *Figaro* overture without it, there remains the curiosity to know how Mozart continued his siciliano melody. There remains the likelihood that the 64-bar fragment had nothing to do with the *Figaro* overture: only one page of the autograph is missing but 64 bars needed four pages. I believe that Nissen's fragment was in short score and that Mozart, in the act of scoring fully, realized that his siciliano must go, and removed the page before writing it in full score. It is still a loss to posterity.

Failing an answer for the moment we must ask why Mozart wanted this D minor

* See *Die Entführung*, p. 293.

siciliano in this overture; he did not have to continue the quick–slow–quick Italian comic pattern. It has been noticed that in later life Mozart always wrote his operatic overtures last and always gave them some connection with the dramatic body of the opera. *Figaro* is the only exception. Several arias for the opera are known to have been composed by Mozart, then deleted, or added to another production. None of the known texts or situations seems suitable for Mozart's one-bar siciliano; otherwise we could suppose that the siciliano referred to one of these.

What then was the relevance of this siciliano to *Le nozze di Figaro*? It can possibly be related to Barbarina's 6/8 F minor No. 24, *L'ho perduta*. But the relationship is not clear, not pertinent. The only other minor-mode number is No. 16, *Crudel perchè finora*, whose A minor becomes A major very quickly and significantly.

I will hazard, most tentatively, that Mozart, sitting down on 29 April to write this *presto* overture, possessed by the *folle journée*, wanted to include reference to Countess Almaviva, the odd-woman-out in this drama, the person who is trying to recover her gaiety and peace of mind. Her two arias are both in major keys, but perhaps Mozart wanted to allude musically to her suffering and therefore thought to interrupt his *presto* overture for a D minor *andante* expressive of Rosina's dominating influence. Yet chiefly this tiny 6/8 *incipit* recalls the F sharp minor *andante* of the A major piano concerto K. 488 which Mozart had very recently completed. This is a most melancholy movement indeed, and I have some-times thought that, if most of *Figaro* had not already been composed, Mozart would have brought on the Countess in F sharp minor, a key he used in K. 488 but nowhere else. Given the D minor fragment it is hard to believe that any of the principal *Figaro* singers would sound well beginning on F at the top of the stave, unless perhaps a tenor, not in this opera a likelihood though apt in *Don Giovanni* for Donna Anna's *Non mi dir*). So I conclude that the siciliano was non-thematic, a reference to the lovelorn content of the opera, but not direct— and therefore the more quickly abandoned. What nevertheless would anybody not give for a sight of Nissen's sixty-four bars?

With music of such pace as the *presto* overture Mozart can afford a leisurely rate of harmonic movement and plenty of pedal-note basses *à la* J. C. Bach. Having enucleated his elaborate middle section Mozart extends the overture with a big, atmospheric but not developmental coda. Scoring is for pairs of flutes, oboes, clarinets, bassoons, horns, trumpets and drums plus strings. Nissen's fragment omitted flutes and trumpets, as the one-bar fragment does.

It used to be said, in the days of coarse-groove records, that a playing of this overture on record provided the perfect egg-timer. The value of this advice depends on how soft one likes a boiled egg, and how clearly one wishes to hear Mozart's music. The commercial three-minute egg-timer adds up to a rushed account of the *Figaro* overture. A breezy but meaningfully articulated performance gives a breakfast egg with firmly coagulated protein (4 minutes 40 seconds), though a really fresh large egg, straight from the hen-coop, requires a *Figaro* overture of deliberate, Klempereresque proportions.

The curtain rises during the unusually extended introduction to **No. 1, Duettino**, *Cinque, dieci*, in G major, *allegro*, for Figaro and Susanna, with flutes, oboes, bassoons, horns and strings. The scene presents a room in the castle of

Aguasfrescas. Beaumarchais, and da Ponte after him, describe it as 'half-unfurnished'. It has been part of the master-apartments, grandly decorated and furnished. But now, though it separates the Count's suite from the Countess's, Count Almaviva has bestowed it on Figaro, the steward of the castle, who is about to marry Susanna, Countess Almaviva's personal maid. Surely the Count and Countess do not want to walk through their servants' quarters in order to talk to one another. Surely a newly married couple will hope for some privacy. The room, however, has not been chosen by accident. It is a symbol of the unspoken alienation which has taken place between Count Almaviva and the lovely Rosina since they were married, about three years earlier, at the end of *Le barbier de Séville*. Rosina was then very young, about fifteen or sixteen, Almaviva not much older. Upon marriage that gay young spark took her to his castle, some three miles outside Seville where he met and married her, and transformed himself, in a thoroughly Spanish fashion, into the stern, imperious Gran Corregidor de Andalucía, the major power of the region. An Andalusian, with his naturally friendly, jovial temperament, would have found this sudden establishment transmogrification unsympathetic and difficult. But Count Almaviva is a Castilian,* immensely proud, selfish for the prestige which he calls Honour, aware of his position. Quickly he changed his habits, asserted his authority. And within these three years he has been rewarded with the post of Spanish Ambassador to the Court of St James's in London.

When Count Almaviva set up his establishment at Aguasfrescas he took with him from Seville† not only Rosina, who had been the ward of the medico Dr Bartolo, and the Sevillian barber Figaro who had helped Almaviva to win Rosina despite the opposition of Bartolo (Figaro became the steward of the castle and Almaviva's personal valet), but also her old governess Marcellina, who had been Bartolo's housekeeper and, twenty-eight years earlier, something more besides (Marcellina became châtelaine of Aguasfrescas) though she did not take the stage in *Le barbier de Séville*; he also engaged Rosina's singing teacher, the priest Don Basilio, a reptile of calumny and intrigue, as his *maestro di cappella*. It was obviously unwise to employ these last two: they were Almaviva's opponents in the intrigue of *Le barbier de Séville*. He might as well have added Bartolo to his staff for, though he robbed the good Doctor of his intended bride, he gave him her dowry. It is, however, a convention of comedy that the first act characters must all turn up in the second act, no matter how far away its location; the same applies to sequels. And it is recognized by non-Spaniards as a historical fact that Spaniards, when pushed to a crisis, have always taken the least provident, most certainly disastrous decision. Almaviva seems at first to have acted wisely, since Basilio, Marcellina, and Dr Bartolo, who makes his predictable appearance, all join the Count in his intrigue against Figaro. By the end of *Le nozze di Figaro* these allies are fighting for, or at least temporarily supporting, the other side.

Figaro would have been a sounder ally perhaps. But Almaviva's present intrigue concerns Figaro's bride-to-be. There was an old feudal right, called the *droit de*

---

* *Cf. Mariage de Figaro*, I, scene 10.

† According to *Le barbier de Séville* Almaviva knew Figaro in Madrid, and had just met Rosina there. Bartolo and Marcellina must also have lived in Madrid at the time. They moved to Seville very recently. Heaven knows where Basilio came from: probably under some stone.

seigneur, whereby the lord of the manor was entitled to deflower every maiden in his service on her wedding night. Almaviva, in an access of romantic monogamous love for Rosina, renounced this right on his wedding-day. Another Spanish short-sighted decision: he soon reverted to his philandering nature, neglected his Countess and began to chase the pretty wenches on his estate. Among these were two in the cottage of his gardener Antonio: his daughter Barbarina (Fanchette in *Le mariage*) and his orphaned niece Susanna who waited on the Countess. But Susanna preferred the bachelor valet Figaro and in due course they became affianced. She was to be the first bride on this estate to go to her husband a maiden. Count Almaviva, however, does not intend to go without the pleasure of her company. He has promised her a dowry on certain conditions . . . and he has given her and her bridegroom this smart room as their bedsitter—though it is extremely accessible to all for private quarters, for the noble seducer as well as for the married couple. Figaro, nevertheless, is impressed by its importance as a status symbol and Beaumarchais (da Ponte too) found it convenient of access, since it is approached by three doors, a familiar feature of *château* architecture— the Count's room, the Countess's room, and a corridor with other rooms leading off it.

While we are still mentioning what happened before the rise of the curtain, there is one other question of loyalty: you would expect Almaviva to be grateful for Figaro's brilliant efforts in outwitting Dr Bartolo during *Le barbier de Séville*. But a nobleman of his stamp would not dream of being grateful to a servant. Almaviva simply intends to cuckold his benefactor, and not only on Figaro's wedding night; he has told Figaro to travel with him to London. The Countess will go with them, and Susanna. Almaviva has laid his plans. Mozart and da Ponte, following Beaumarchais, will show them in action.

6

The Follies of a Day, Figaro's wedding day, begin in his future living quarters; we should be made instantly aware that this is Spain, nowhere else, by bright light and stage design. I said that the room was 'half unfurnished' ('mezzo smobiliata'). Somebody has dumped a large invalid chair there, and Susanna has provided herself with a looking-glass. The master suite has lost its elegant furnishings but the paintwork is still smart. She and he are preparing for married life. The orchestral introduction shows them generally busying themselves with what is most important. The first subject-group is about Figaro (Ex. 2).

The dummy accompaniment in bar 1 seems unpretentious, but is quite rare in Mozart, though fairly common in *Figaro* which prefers musical numbers to begin without much delay. It tells of activity. The violin melody gradually extends its reach, with pauses in between. Figaro is measuring room space with a yard-rule: the Count has given him not only this room but, also not entirely unselfish, a bed for Figaro and his bride. Figaro is measuring the dimensions of the bed, and then perhaps various places in the room where it might go (Jean-Pierre Ponnelle makes him measure Susanna as well); the bass line in Ex. 2, sharpened by the incisive tone of Coleridge's 'loud bassoon', tells us that the calculation is putting a strain on his intellectual capacities, since the bass swears, by accented passing-notes, against the

2

tune. He has to measure, therefore, during this bit of introduction and then, singing the while, twice more before joining Susanna in her music, which is the duet's second group.

3

Susanna is in front of her mirror, adjusting her bridal bonnet on her head. Beaumarchais tells us that it is a wreath of orange-blossom. She says proudly that she made it herself. As a *cappellino* it may include a small white bridal veil.

Figaro's theme (not a leitmotif) is for strings mostly, Susanna's largely for woodwind, with telling rushes for strings which indicate her mercurial temperament and physical energy. Figaro, rather effortfully, measures again:

Five, ten, twenty, thirty, thirty-six, forty-three.

Susanna compliments herself on her bonnet-making. It is amusing, but not important, that one of her remarks in this connection looks forward to the first line of *Deh vieni*, No. 27; the staccato violin triplets are musically more relevant.

Figaro takes up her tune, Ex. 3, and they duet happily in thirds and sixths, spiritually at one. Their duet has some new and attractive invention in the coda.

In the subsequent recitative Figaro explains that this is their bed and this their room. Susanna objects violently to the location of their quarters, because she is sensible, she stubbornly avers, and Figaro not. Figaro endeavours to enlighten her in **No. 2, Duettino**, *Se a caso Madama*, in B flat major, *allegro* with flutes, oboes, bassoons, horns and strings. This is a second duet for the same characters and orchestra, but now some drama will animate their humdrum activity.

How convenient this room is, Figaro points out: if the Countess requires Susanna in the middle of the night, she has only to tinkle her bell (flutes and oboes, 'din-din') and Susanna is with her in a trice. Likewise when the Count needs Figaro: 'don-don (more masculine bassoons and horns) and there is Figaro with his employer. Now B flat shifts into G minor (a sad key for Mozart): Susanna suggests another use for this room. The Count can ring for Figaro (but Mozart musically uses a different, high-pitched bell, as if the Countess's) and send him on a mission three miles away, then 'don-don', his own low-pitched bell, sounds for Susanna to join him in his room. The horns tell a warning. Figaro is shocked by the idea that his benefactor Almaviva could behave so unscrupulously. Susanna, the better diplomat, presses her suspicion, recalling each probable step. Do stop, Figaro repeats, and lands on a pause mark—signifying a short vocal flourish, appropriate for emphasis. Susanna answers in recitative, a popular dramatic dodge in comic musical numbers. She will explain so long as he believes her faithful to him. He agrees, slightly dubious; his words are several times broken by anxious rests, most effective.

6

i dub—bi, i so—spet—ti ge-la——re mi fan.

They duet to the end. The circumstances have changed but Mozart, perhaps ironically, re-introduces the number's opening tune in the orchestra to remind us how gullible Figaro is. For the first time, it may be, we wonder whether Figaro is as brilliant in the head, as quick-witted, as ingenious, as in *Le barbier de Séville* he was, whether he has really retained his ancestral prestige as Arlecchino and Brighella and Scapino. He is, we suspect, a little slow in the uptake. He has become less political, rebellious, than in Beaumarchais, more pessimistic, less a clown and more a real human being with grievances but an undying sense of humour. He is now about thirty years old, an age when rebellion becomes interiorized and love of intrigue more slowly awakened. Yet he is a match for his master, as we shall see. He is the prototype of the middle classes then more or less unknown, though since the French Revolution the mainstay of French and indeed European society, both good and bad but surviving through merit, not through inheritance. Figaro is the first operatic hero with whom a modern audience can naturally identify. Yet he is not the hero truly. By the end of the opera we shall find that the protagonist hero is Susanna, as Brünnhilde is in Wagner's *Ring*. Susanna will soon show her quality.

7

Their duet turns into *secco* recitative. Susanna explains to Figaro that the Count is suffering from philanderer's itch and has fastened his lust on Susanna; hence his kindness to Figaro and his bride. Susanna is given singing lessons, like the Countess, by Don Basilio who continually begs her to accept the Count's love. She knows well that the *droit de seigneur*, though officially dead, is still alive under the counter and she is expected to be on the receiving end.

It has taken some time to put Figaro into the picture. As he brings his binoculars into focus the Countess rings her bell and Susanna has to go. 'Use your brains,' she exhorts him on her way to the adjoining room.

Use his brains he certainly will. Mozart cannot at present give the plebeian Figaro a *recitativo accompagnato* such as serious operatic characters enjoy at moments of emotional anxiety, though later he will get one.

At present the dramatic situation merely remains strong and Figaro's recitative has a vigorous and expressive instrumental bass line, very human when he thinks of Susanna. Conductors of the past sometimes used all low strings here, unstylish but appreciative. The music becomes *andante*, slow and smoother. Here Figaro understands at last the implications of Almaviva's appointment to London, and his desire that Figaro and Susanna shall accompany him. Figaro is roused to his old capacity for plotting: he does not have to intrigue for others; he must protect his own, and himself. The Count's evil plan must be miscarried by Figaro. Figaro explains his determination in his **No. 3, Cavatina**, *Se vuol ballare*, in F major, with oboes, bassoons, horns and strings.

If you are going to dance, my Lord Count, I shall be playing the guitar for you. If you come to my school I will teach you how to kick your heels. I know how to keep quiet, then let the cat out of the bag. I'll use all my skill, here a joke, there a thump, so as to upset the apple-cart.

The *allegretto* introduction, without orchestral prelude for greater dramatic urgency, sounds like a minuet, though it has the typical rhythm of the galliard.★ It does sound unsuitable music for an aristocratic dancer, with its repeated notes (*appoggiature* out of place here). This is the superior underdog (Abert's *Dritter Stand*) speaking, very firmly as we hear in his 'le suonerò, si!' with its determined top F, and in the subsequent 'Se vuol venire' section with wobbly violins and insistent horns, and the rising violin scales at 'Saprò . . .' But Figaro knows he must proceed carefully and quietly, 'piano, piano,' etc., on the verge of D minor. He releases his zeal in the *presto* conclusion, 'L'arte schermendo', a sort of *galop* dance, curiously close to Don Giovanni's *Fin ch'han dal vino* (the 'Champagne Aria'). Yet even here he is not quite self-confident; there is an intellectual worry in the soft violin counterpoint to his confident 'tutte le macchine rovescierò':

7

Then Figaro returns to his galliard and its *presto* consequent (still with the hang-up of Ex. 7).

The convention of leaving the stage after an aria no longer applied in *opera buffa*. But it was usually observed if only because dramatists and composers were accustomed to it. Tidily Figaro walks away—not pointlessly; he is going to collect other servants of Almaviva for a ceremony. The room is empty.

Through another door enter Marcellina with her ex-employer Dr Bartolo. She has fetched him from Seville to give her advice on a legal matter—though he is no lawyer. Some time ago Figaro borrowed two thousand piastres from her and for security gave her a written promise of marriage. Figaro is not rich, cannot repay her and would not bring wealth to Marcellina, but he is much younger and therefore a desirable husband for her, more suitable than Don Basilio who desires her hand (he would have to renounce his priesthood). As an ex-ally of Bartolo she would like to be revenged on Figaro: so would Dr Bartolo though he chides her for fetching him from Seville at this eleventh hour. Marcellina, who works in the castle, knows all the gossip and has elaborated a plan. Urge Susanna to accept Almaviva as lover. She will refuse. The Count will withdraw his promised dowry, and Figaro will have to marry Marcellina.   Q.E.D.

★ Cf. *Festschrift für Karl Geiringer*, p. 382.

Bartolo sees here a chance to pay back Figaro who robbed him of his lovely ward and expected bride. This would be a true revenge. He expatiates on the subject in **No. 4, Aria**, *La vendetta*, a big and typical *buffo* aria for bass in D major with flutes, oboes, bassoons, horns, trumpets and drums, and strings.

> Vengeance is the wise man's balm and pleasure. It is base and vile to forget shame and outrage. One can be astute, acute, judicious, critical and . . . the matter's grave, but, believe me, it can be done. I'll find a way if I have to turn the law upside down and read every index there is. All Seville knows Bartolo. That scoundrel Figaro will be downed.

Mozart composed this aria impeccably. It is full of musical detail and some subtlety—especially where Bartolo's confidence is psychologically undermined. The orchestration is suitably pompous and also vacuous. The patter follows good models. The weak ending is surely deliberate. But Bartolo remains the least real character in *Le nozze di Figaro*, physically but not personally substantial, and his aria also remains dull. Da Ponte has not thought this Pantalone into a human being. It is not surprising that this aria was omitted from the music on sale in Vienna on the day of the second performance, though I doubt whether that means that the aria was omitted since the manager of the company played Bartolo, and this is his only solo.

We should, nevertheless, at this point discover what Bartolo is like. Beaumarchais describes him through Figaro as 'handsome, fat, short, precociously elderly, his grey hairs lightened with pomade (does this mean he is not always bewigged?), clever, weatherbeaten, cynical, a gambler and maniac, grumbler and whiner, brutal, miserly, amorous and jealous to excess of his pupil (Rosina) who hates him to death'. He has not changed since *Le barbier de Séville*, except that he detests Figaro even more.

Having delivered his unconvincing speech for the prosecution, Bartolo leaves by exit convention. He should have remained, according to Beaumarchais, to witness the lovely female duel now in store. Marcellina remains in the room. Susanna returns from the Countess, carrying a dress which she throws over the invalid chair (Beaumarchais), a broad ribbon (see Cherubino, below) and a mobcap—but not the one destined to cover the page's hair in Act II. Marcellina no sooner claps eyes on her rival in matrimony than she inaugurates a campaign of bitchery, supposedly to herself but spoken aloud. At length both move towards the door, meet there, and with exaggerated formality offer one another precedence in *Via resti servita*, **No. 5, Duettino**, in A major, *allegro* for flutes, oboes, bassoons, horns and strings.

Marcellina and Susanna are evidently old enemies, even before Marcellina produced this marriage contract and became Susanna's rival for Figaro's hand. The principal violin motif perfectly suggests their mock formality:

Triplets are rattling underneath and from time to time they invade the melody on the strong beat, underlining the sarcastic curtseys of both ladies.

There they stand at the door, bowing and offering one another precedence in hypocritical and sarcastic compliments. Susanna is the bride, the Count's sweetheart, preferred by the aristocracy. Marcellina is the châtelaine, every Spaniard's lover, and so experienced with her years. The emphasis on age infuriates Marcellina, but because this is an operatic duet the music and words have to be repeated, and Marcellina, 'decrepit sibyl' as Susanna describes her, has to suffer twice before she sweeps out.

Curiously enough this excellent duet was not performed in the first performance, and its music not published by Lausch. In a performance of the opera, shortly afterwards, at Donaueschingen it was also omitted and replaced by a Cavatina for Marcellina, *Signora mia, garbata vuol* in C, *andante maestoso*. Alfred Einstein, a great Mozart scholar, at first thought this to be authentic Mozart but later decided otherwise. Modern audiences can hardly imagine *Le nozze de Figaro* without this duet which perfectly characterizes the *piquante et amère* nature of Marcellina.

Susanna lets Marcellina retreat, with some remarks about pedantry and arrogance. Then another visitor arrives. He is a young nobleman, León de Astorga by name though everybody calls him Cherubino ('little cherub'), a boy who has been sent to court to polish his education. It is an *éducation amoureuse*, so devoted is Cherubino to the pursuit of the opposite sex, even at the age of thirteen.★ He was accepted as Almaviva's chief page because the Countess is his godmother and a germane relative. He is madly in love with her, but also with Susanna, and indeed any woman in the castle, even Marcellina. The Count has caught him with the gardener's daughter Barbarina and would have expelled him from the court but for the intervention of the Countess. He envies Susanna for her constant attendance on the Countess, her duty to undress her every night. Then Cherubino sees the ribbon which Susanna brought from the Countess's room and appropriates it, in return offering a song of love which he has just written. It is *Voi che sapete* which he will sing later. He summarizes its content in another solo, less formal and even more beautiful. This is **No. 6, Aria**, *Non sò più* in E flat major, *allegro vivace* with clarinets and bassoons, horns and strings. Note that the previous duet was in A major, an augmented fourth away—unusual key-progression.

> I no longer know who I am or what I am doing. One moment I am on fire, the next I am freezing. I change colour and tremble at the sight of every woman. Even their names set my heart throbbing, and an indescribable longing forces me to talk of love all the time, awake or asleep, to the water,

★ It is said that Beaumarchais elaborated Cherubino from his own memories of early puberty.

mountains, flowers, even the air which carries away my dreams. When no one is there to listen, I even talk about love to myself.

Mozart most brilliantly conveys the boy's impetuous, blurted-out confession. The voice enters almost at once, above a storm-tossed dummy accompaniment on muted strings, the sentences tumbling out between gasps for breath, one might think. It has to be admitted that da Ponte's beautiful verses do themselves strongly prescribe the rapid anapaestic rhythms of the music—as if Mozart had postulated them to da Ponte when asking him to write this lyric. Equally vivid and impetuous is the end of the aria, *allegro* and stopping almost at once, or rather breaking into recitative without waiting for a *continuo* chord.

The erotic content of the verses obviously demanded an orchestra with clarinets, warm and voluptuous in flat keys, B flat for the first episode ('Solo ai nomi d'amor'), A flat and F minor in the second—rich sustained chords for clarinets, bassoons and horns in the transition to this episode. Especially sensuous are the chains of chromatic thirds for clarinets and bassoons after the first pause.

10

Sensuous too, after the hurried start, is the touch of expansiveness and grand curve of the melody at 'Ogni donna mi fa palpitar'—the top of the curve not at 'Ogni', as natural stress would imply but on 'donna', the adorable object herself.

11

Clarinets are left blissfully aloft while Cherubino dives below. Sensitive touches of the kind abound in this aria—for example the minor third in B flat major at 'un desio' (a longing) which suddenly brings the music out in a juvenile hot flush; or the exquisite nervous hesitancy of the *adagio* before the end.

12

(I have added the necessary appoggiaturas; Cherubino is an elegant person, above blunt ends).

The form of this aria is curious, though very satisfactory. When *Non sò più* returns after the B flat episode, we expect a rondo; then the orchestra moves into A flat major, and though the home-key is restored the *Non so più* theme is not again repeated (Mozart did contemplate another A flat episode inferably followed by a third reprise) though there is later a free variation of the second episode. It is Ex. 10 which dominates the last part of the aria. These various strands are psychologically true to life and dramatically effective.

Non sò più is said to have been omitted at the first performance (on the evidence of a libretto in Library of Congress) though its music is listed in Lausch's advertisement on 3 May. It is not in the 1788 Donaueschingen score. In the Florence production of the same year it was replaced by an aria for Susanna, *Senza speme ognor s'aggira*★, and at Monza in 1787 it was appropriated as an entrance aria by Count Almaviva. Reassignments of this sort were common practice especially when a particular number became a favourite.† Mozart subsequently transcribed the aria for concert performance with obbligato violin and keyboard accompaniment. Frederica von Stade has recorded it to admiration.

Cherubino, as mentioned above, completes his aria and goes straight into recitative, exclaiming, 'I am lost,' to which Susanna replies, 'What are you afraid of?' He, but not yet she, has seen Count Almaviva approaching her room. Cherubino dodges behind the invalid chair; he dare not, at this stage, be found again by the Count in another room alone with a woman. Almaviva, in hunting attire, strolls into the room, ignores Susanna's confusion, and sits down in the chair, taking her unwilling hand and seeking to reassure her with talk of the forthcoming journey to London, then of his love for her which Basilio has communicated and his desire to fix a rendez-vous in the garden at dusk, a favour for which he would pay her. . . . Almaviva is interrupted by the voice of Don Basilio from outside; he is looking for the Count and supposes him to be with the Countess. He will have to come through this room. At first Almaviva tells Susanna to go out and prevent Basilio from entering. She is not keen to leave the Count alone in the room with Cherubino. In any case it is too late. Almaviva decides to hide behind the chair. Susanna tries to bar his way, unsuccessfully, but meanwhile Cherubino manages to jump into the chair which Susanna quickly covers with the Countess's dress (what a fragrant shelter he will think it!).

Thank heaven nobody has been seen by any of the others. Basilio, full of hypo-crisy and malicious tittle-tattle, wants to warn the Count that Figaro, with his wedding chorus, is looking for their master. Susanna comments that the Count hates Figaro less only than Basilio does. The priest drops saucy hints about the pageboy who has been skulking near her door with his song (can Susanna tell him for what lady it was written?) and who must really not fawn so on the Countess during meals—the Count will notice. Susanna accuses him of disseminating lies. Basilio insists that he adds nothing to common knowledge.

This is too much for the Count who reveals his presence, much to Susanna's embarrassment and Basilio's delight, and precipitates **No. 7, Terzetto** in B flat major, *Cosa sento!* which begins *allegro assai* and is scored for oboes, clarinets, bassoons, horns and strings. It is a trio, not a vocal quartet, because Cherubino is out of sight, hidden under that dress in the chair. It is also the first moment of dynamic dramatic interplay in the opera. Mozart is going to show his fangs.

The terzetto begins with an explosion of rage by the orchestra, not the Count though the anger is his. He begins white, tight-lipped and *piano* by telling Basilio

★ Jack Westrup, in *Fanfare for Ernest Newman*, argued that Mozart may have set this aria to the melody he composed that summer for the opening of his G minor symphony 40, K. 550, because the two melodies have much in common and the new words fit the G minor tune quite well.

† For some choice specimens see Harry R. Beard, 'Figaro in England', in *Maske und Kothurn*, 1964 Heft 3/4.

to find Cherubino and turn him out; the music for this is conspiratorial, not imperious, because it refers to Basilio's task, not to the Count. Basilio excuses his presence with a typically slimy solo.

13

[Allegro assai]

In mal punto son qui giunto, per—do—na—te, o mio si—gnor.

Smooth wind chords, rushing second violins help perturbed Susanna into F minor; she *must* get these two men out of her room before they sit on Cherubino or something. Now the Count is raging in F minor to the introductory music while Basilio sings Ex. 13 in that key, and Susanna decides that she had better stage a faint—first violins slither helplessly in F minor to lend colour to her distress.

14

son op—pres—sa dal dolor son op—pressa dal do—lor

Almaviva and Basilio catch her as she droops, and fuss over her imitatively in an F major bridge passage that begins dully (though it proves useful later) but improves strongly when they start feeling for her heartbeat—even together they are not to be trusted with an unconscious woman.

15

The chromatic harmony here is almost pornographically physical. Basilio decides to rest her in the armchair. Instantly Susanna revives, upbraids the two men for their insolence and orders them out of her room. They calm her again with the imitative bridge passage, now a tone lower, even more tranquil in E flat major, almost churchly, though it rouses Susanna to active fury and takes the music back to B flat, the home-key, for a reprise of the beginning ('Parta, parta il damerino'—'Away with the womanizer!' orders the Count; he, of course, is an even more addicted *damerino*). Susanna and Basilio begin to pity the *damerino* and the trio proceeds by question marks. The Count slips into accompanied recitative to narrate how he visited Susanna's cousin Barbarina, found her door locked, was let in with some embarrassment (the strings are wriggling vividly) and therefore carried out a search of the cottage. The count drops into Basilio's Ex. 13 as he describes how he quietly removed the tablecloth and under the table discovered the page. To enliven his anecdote Almaviva has moved to the chair and, suiting action to word, removes the dress. Cold, dark woodwind underlines his fatal gesture (low bassoons in thirds, most sinister). There is Cherubino, as we knew. The Count is furious, Susanna aghast; Basilio breaks the spell with a peal of *schadenfreudig* laughter.

Another return to the stealthy opening of the *Terzetto*. 'Onestissima signora,' the Count sarcastically addressed Susanna—he has married her off, by a Freudian slip, before the event which he seeks to postpone. Strings begin to flow again in the direction of Basilio's cynical comment:

This is much repeated and has special interest because it recurs in the overture to the opera whose title Basilio names long before da Ponte or Mozart thought of it! The terzetto has now worked up a head of dramatic steam and can flow nicely along. Basilio delightedly repeats his earlier Ex. 13 about his unfounded suspicion of Cherubino, without diverting the forward surge of the music. Two perceptible new musical sentences are taken in this gorgeous diminuendo coda. *Cosa sento* is not to be underestimated. Mozart had never composed an operatic ensemble half so pointed and brilliantly inventive. It was for the makings of such a movement that he had been searching so diligently ever since *Entführung*, or rather since *Idomeneo*.

9

Back in *secco recitativo* Almaviva peremptorily orders Basilio to fetch Figaro who must see . . . 'and hear', adds capable Susanna. The Count's confidence is checked, especially when he realizes that Cherubino heard all his amorous pleading with rock-faithful Susanna. To add to his rage he sees Figaro enter with a deputation. Cherubino is still curled up in the armchair, rather, it may be admitted, like the 'little serpent' that the Count calls him.

The deputation has been drummed up by Figaro to thank Count Almaviva formally for abolishing the *droit de seigneur*—though, we may contemplate, that was all of three years ago; how time flashes past! Their hymn of gratitude is **No. 8, Chorus**, *Giovani lieti* in G major, *allegro* with flutes, bassoons, horns and strings. The choral music is dull, almost listless, not to say sullen, though the orchestral parts are busy and very cheerful, an example perhaps of Busoni's 'Together with the puzzle he gives us the solution.' The staff sprinkle flowers on the parquet. Figaro carries a white bridal veil in his hand and ceremoniously presents it to his master,* explaining that this is the first wedding on the estate since the Count abolished 'a privilege so unpleasant to true lovers' (Beaumarchais's Figaro speaks out more frankly). He asks the Count to perform the civil ceremony now in the presence of them all. Almaviva makes a short, stuffy and hypocritical speech

---

* In *Le Mariage* Fanchette (i.e. Barbarina) and the Countess also attend this ceremony.

about nature and duty, and promises to perform the ceremony later with richer pomp, adding aside that Marcellina must be found.* The Chorus is repeated and the staff departs.

Figaro is left with the cast of *Cosa sento*. He establishes the cause of Cherubino's non-participation in the loyal cheers and the Count is begged to pardon this innocent child—not so childish as all that, Almaviva suggests. When Cherubino swears secrecy the Count yields to his blackmail, rallies and appoints him an officer in his own regiment, on condition that Cherubino joins immediately, before the wedding. Beaumarchais tells us that the regiment is stationed in Catalonia, well out of harm's way. Cherubino has to accept the offer, kisses Susanna farewell and is offered by Figaro some fatherly advice about the new life before him. The Count, congratulating himself on his surprise one-upmanship gambit, departs with Basilio. Figaro, before bursting into song, whispers to Cherubino that he wants a private word with him. In Beaumarchais he tells Cherubino to ride away publicly, stall his horse, then creep back to the castle and hide. Figaro needs him for the plan against Almaviva, as Act II will show. In *Le nozze di Figaro* this private advice has to be understood. Da Ponte and Mozart end Act I firmly with Figaro's celebrated **Aria No. 9**, *Non più andrai*, a C major *vivace* with flutes, oboes, bassoons, horns, trumpets, drums and strings.

> Now you're an amorous butterfly no longer, flitting hither and thither day and night, disturbing pretty girls' rest, you Narcissus, you little Adonis of love. No more pretty feathers, gallant soft hats, falling locks of hair, airs and graces, or effeminate rosy complexion. You'll be among warriors now! Moustaches, a loaded pack, sabre at your side, chin up, eyes front, and a big helmet on your head, lots of honour and not much pay. Instead of the fandango, you'll step out to a march, over hill and dale, through snow and heatwave, fanfares, bombardments, cannons, thundering and whistling in your ears. Off to victory, to glorious war!

This is a nicely constructed rondo on a buoyant, dancing theme: Mozart gives us the keynote and Figaro at once exposes the rondo tune.

17

The learned allusions to self-loving Narcissus and Adonis beloved of Venus are paralleled by Figaro in the finale of Act IV (see p. 437). Note that Figaro addresses Cherubino in the second person singular, because he is still theoretically a child, though superior in station to Figaro (Susanna calls him 'voi', to keep him at arm's length, though he addresses her familiarly).

* From Beaumarchais we learn that she has gone into Seville with Bartolo to take expert legal advice.

The first episode moves firmly and busily into G major with wriggling flutes and violins, perhaps for Cherubino's fancy plumes ('questi bei pennacchini'), just as 'quella chioma' ('that coiffure') may have set off the fancy imitations for violins.

Soft, brilliant descending violin scales help Figaro to repeat the tally of the page's courtly habits, soon to be put away. They also lead to the first reprise of Ex. 17. Episode 2 is martial and explosive in C major ('Tra guerrieri'), strongly rhythmical, gradually moving away to E minor, the only excursion from tonic and dominant, its pathos inspired by 'poco contante' ('not much cash'). From here the music quickly gains the brave spirits of C major for a new march theme, at first *piano assai* on wind band alone with voice. This march is to dominate the last part of the aria though we have not done with the rondo theme. After one soft hearing of the march (Cherubino's future) the brilliant descending scales return mockingly to bring back the second reprise of Ex. 18 (Cherubino's present and past). Now a second hearing of the march, on a larger wind band, completed with trumpet triplet fanfares, finally a fully orchestrated further repeat of the march while they all leave the stage in mock-military style.

It was *Non più andrai* which first won the Viennese to *Le nozze di Figaro*, and *Non più andrai* which became an international success. Mozart quoted it in *Don Giovanni* (see p. 512) and arranged it as a *Kontretanz* (from English 'Country Dance'), K. 609, No. 1, in 1791 for a party in Vienna. It was quickly adopted as the official slow march of the English regiment of Coldstream Guards—regimental tradition claims since 1787.

An early copy of this aria exists in Florence, together with an accompanied introductory recitative beginning *Ehi, sor paggio* (it is reprinted in the 1947 edition of Köchel–Einstein, p. 1018). Benucci's name is signed in one corner. Alfred Einstein believed that Mozart and da Ponte wrote this recitative for concerts given by Benucci after the success of *Le nozze di Figaro*. Stylistically this is possible, though it seems unlikely that Mozart would have quoted from the march before its entry in the aria; the N.M.A. regards it as unauthentic.

10

Beaumarchais had introduced Countess Almaviva during the first act of *Le mariage de Figaro*. Da Ponte and Mozart, realizing the exceptional possibilities of the character, postponed her appearance until the rise of the curtain on **Act II**, and then introduced her, alone on stage, singing a serious and touching **Cavatina, No. 10,** *Porgi amor* (more likely *andante* than the usually assumed *larghetto*) in E flat major, accompanied by clarinets, bassoons, horns and strings. Its context and contents are da Ponte's own Prelude to Beaumarchais's second act.

The scene is now the Countess's own grandly appointed private room, with a large window overlooking the garden, an alcove for her bedroom, and three doors: one leading to her wardrobe, one to the antechamber where Figaro and Susanna will live, and a third formal entrance for all other visitors.

Rather unusually in Italian comic opera, the Countess is a *parte seria* who is neither a lay figure nor a caricature but a thoughtful, kindly, noble young lady who has attained magnanimity by suffering. Literary taste of the period was cultivating heroines of the kind and *opera buffa* had attempted to follow suit (Mozart's Sandrina was not really a character in focus, and Constanze is surely too self-centred to inspire affection in an audience). Some outstanding *Figaro* Countesses of the past have encouraged us to consider her as a mature *prima donna* heroine, almost a Tragedy Queen. This would be a mistake. Countess Almaviva was under age when she married; now, three years later, her age in *Le Mariage de Figaro* is about eighteen, maybe younger but hardly much older. Hers was the *seconda donna* role in early performances—though, as usual in Mozart, the *seconda donna* is well served; Mozart preferred a libretto that included three good female roles. As to the heroines, well, the Countess is noble and appealing, and in the finale of the last act a very great lady; but the heroine is demonstrably Susanna. All this is merely to emphasize that *Porgi amor* should not be taken as a sign of the Countess's every-day mood: she will reveal a sense of humour and ability to tease and, though da Ponte has removed the delight in plotting and the reciprocation of Cherubino's infatuation from Beaumarchais's portrayal of her, he has left opportunities for an actress to exploit both.

At present the Countess Rosina is feeling a little depressed, though not as suicidal as the words of her cavatina may lead the literal-minded to suppose. Dear loyal Susanna came into her mistress's room, soon after Figaro had finished singing *Non più andrai*, and told her all that the Count was planning. Not out of spite (she loves the Countess sincerely), nor out of goody-goody self-protection, let alone hope of remuneration, but simply because she is a practical, level-headed young woman. The Count is preparing an assault on the happiness of his wife, his valet, and her personal maid. He has Marcellina and Basilio working for him; Susanna must collect some allies too, and the best are those most closely implicated—her mistress and her intended bridegroom, she with authority, he with a nimble cunning. Figaro has already made some plans, Susanna has told the Countess, and will shortly wait on her to unfold them.

Rosina is all too aware that her husband leaves her alone most of the time, no doubt pleading civic duties. And with such toadying gossips about her as Marcellina and Basilio, she is likely to have suspected her husband of extramarital amours. Susanna's information, and request for help, wounded the Countess's *amour propre*—not for the first time ever, otherwise she would not recover spirit so quickly. But Susanna has left the room (perhaps been sent to collect something from next door while Rosina has a little cry in private) and the Countess feels even lonelier.

> Love, grant me some solace for my pain, for my sighs!
> Give me back the lover I treasure, or at least let me die.

Most of the musical numbers in *Le nozze di Figaro* arise out of the previous sentence so directly that the singers must begin singing almost at once. This time

Mozart permits himself an extended orchestral introduction, for good deducible reasons. This is the beginning of an act, and the audience must be settled before this new, important character begins to sing a far from *buffo* aria. The stage set is supposed to be *magnifica*, so the audience must have time to admire it, and then settle to hear Mme Laschi. The music is quite different from any in Act I, full of heartfelt sentiment; to accept this change requires more than a moment's attention. And it is slowish in E flat major with the orchestral instruments which for Mozart summarized the leisurely, introspective connotations of that key. He could have begun with the four tonic chords, firm and full, as in many other E flat major pieces of his (e.g. K. 364, K. 365, K. 482), completed bar 2 as it stands, and let the Countess begin. Instead he adopted a sort of piano concerto procedure and introduced some of the aria's themes on the orchestra, making much of his woodwind (as though they were virtuosi themselves) and fashioning a miniature concerto-exposition. So we may discover when the Countess begins and adds to the orchestral *donnée*, often but discreetly and with maximum illumination. The form of the aria is, however, much more concise: after her first pause, poignantly ascended to, the coda already begins, with a new, conceivably more agitated idea (voice and strings, with a bodyblow entry by bassoon at bar 38). The Countess's last phrase, though, is in purest Mozart concerto slow-movement style, a new idea which clinches everything and only needs to be rounded off by woodwind.

An aria for everyone's treasury. How fast or slow is this particular example? Sometimes the sweet melancholy is drawn out to romantic excess. Mozart has left us some guidelines, worth consideration. Here is the opening of the slow movement to an early string quartet, K. 175 in B flat major (1773, Milan):

19

The texture is elaborate, the style rococo, not romantic. Now here is the start of the *adagio* (same pace-mark) third movement in the E flat wind serenade, K. 375:

20

The texture is thinner, the mood closer to that of *Porgi amor*. Neither of these is 'all passion spent', though that is how some performers see the opening of the aria just discussed.

The clarinets and bassoons define a tempo with their quick passages but a young Countess will suggest an unlingering pace for them as well as her own vocal music, more telling and not impossibly difficult.

II

Susanna returns from wherever she went to. The Countess sits down and asks for the completion of the naughty story about the Count's efforts at seduction. O no, answers Susanna, with girls of my class a nobleman doesn't bother to woo—it is just a business proposition, quite unemotional, but financial. This is the beginning of a very long scene in *secco* recitative. Mozart wisely found opportunities to inject musical juice into the dryness. For a start Figaro comes along the corridor singing the end of *Se vuol ballare*, with string bass and harpsichord only as accompaniment, but with the appropriate bass which does move instead of remaining somnolent as recitative basses are usually constrained to appear. Figaro is in high spirits, not apparently jealous at all: why? the Count's desires are both natural (every man desires pretty girls) and feasible (if Susanna is acquiescent)—Figaro flashes the hyperbolistic superlatives ('naturalissima' and 'possibilissima') like false grins, for at heart he is both jealous and determined to protect his own by every imaginable trick. In *Le barbier de Séville* he told Count Almaviva, 'I force myself to laugh at everything for fear of being obliged to weep at it.'

Figaro explains to the Countess about the London plan and about Marcellina's place in the Count's emotional blackmail of Susanna. Figaro's counterplot has been to send a note, via Basilio, warning the Count that his wife has a rendezvous with a lover in the garden that evening during the court ball. With his jealous nature the Count will be so enraged and disturbed at the knowledge, so anxious to catch his wife at her tryst, that he will quite forget about his plan to frustrate Susanna's marriage. Their next step must be for Susanna to let the Count know she will grant him the twilight rendezvous in the garden; in her place they will send Cherubino, whom Figaro has persuaded to hang around the castle, dressed up in Susanna's clothes. The Countess can then catch the Count in a compromising situation and overrule his wishes for Marcellina, and even Susanna. Beaumarchais's Countess finds it a lovely plan, truly inspiring; da Ponte's Susanna is more cautious—is there time enough? Figaro is certain that the Count will not return from his hunting expedition (stalking birds and beasts on foot with guns, not foxes on horseback) for some hours; so Cherubino can have a dress rehearsal now. Figaro goes, with a reminder (fully orchestrated) of some bars from his No. 3.

The Countess is chiefly concerned about what Cherubino overheard: 'Ah, you don't know . . .' she murmurs enigmatically—and the *continuo* has a chance to finish her comment before she and Susanna turn to the canzonet which they will make Cherubino sing. In he comes—not yet in army uniform (he has not yet left the estate, and in any case his female disguise has got to look convincing), and indeed there is no reason why he should have visited the quartermaster's stores at any time during this opera, except that Beaumarchais prescribes uniform for him specifically in the last act. Stage designers like ladies in male military uniform, so they respond creatively when Susanna greets the page as 'Signor ufficiale'. The very reminder of his soldierly fate depresses Cherubino, especially in this room belonging to his godmother whom he must now leave in all her kindness and beauty. Susanna mimics his lovelorn intonations—it is sensible to let the Countess stroll over to the window, out of Cherubino's sight, before he walks in; he will not so expose his feelings for her in her presence before a witness whom he loves almost as much.

Susanna tells Cherubino to sing his canzonet to the Countess. Now she *does* come forward, takes the sheet of paper and asks slyly who wrote it. Cherubino blushes and confesses to almost speechless embarrassment but is delighted to sing it, with Susanna to play the guitar for him and Madame as appreciative audience. Beaumarchais derived this tableau, he said, from Vanloo's *Conversation espagnole*.★

The song is **No. 11, Canzona**, *Voi che sapete* in B flat major, traditionally *andante* with flute, oboe, clarinet and bassoon, soloists one apiece, two horns and strings. Da Ponte based his poem on lines from Dante's *Vita nuova*, Canto XIX (*Donne che avete intelletto d'amor*), so he admitted in 1825.

> Ladies, you who know what love is, see if I have it in my heart. What I am undergoing is so new to me that I do not understand it. I feel full of desire, sometimes pleasurable, sometimes agony. I freeze, then I burn, and in a moment I am freezing again. I search for some benison outside of myself; I don't know what or where it is. I sigh and groan involuntarily, quiver and tremble unwittingly. Night and day I am never at peace, and yet my longing gives me pleasure.

In Beaumarchais Chérubin sings eight verses of a *Romance* to the tune of 'Malbrouk s'en va-t'en guerre' which the English know as 'For he's a jolly good fellow'. Beaumarchais's new words refer specifically to the singer's passionate adoration for his godmother (*marraine*) and refusal to accept other offers, even on the recommendation of the King and Queen.

★ By Beauvarlet, says Michael Levey. Which is right?

Da Ponte was too cautious to dare anything so outspoken in his Italian version, so he wrote the neat formal couplets translated above. Their contents are very close to those of *Non sò più* whose verbal rhythms, however, are curiously reminiscent of those in Beaumarchais's 'Mon coursier hors d'haleine'. We may wonder idly whether Mozart, looking for an entry aria for Cherubino, begged da Ponte for some verses, similar in content to the completed No. 11 but more spontaneous, why not in the anapaestic, galloping rhythm of 'Mon coursier'?

que mon cœur, que mon cœur a de pei—ne!

As in No. 10, which happened ages ago, Mozart gives No. 11 a fairly lengthy orchestral introduction. Cherubino is allowed to settle himself for the audition of his composition, the solo woodwind are allowed to radiate artistry unmasked by any singer. The clarinet leads off this song of love (for many clarinet students it will have been the first solo by a genuine composer that they learned in their first tutor volume, ideally chosen), the others take over, then Cherubino begins.

Voi che sa—pe—te che co——sa è a—mor don—ne ve—de——te

s'io l'ho nel cor, don——ne ve—de——te s'io l'ho nel cor.

The nippy triplet punctuation by flute and oboe, after 'vedete', and 'cor', rapidly and completely betrays the incongruity of this stately set piece: the *primo uomo non castrato*, a man with a boy's voice, is either tripping over the carpet or just beginning to enjoy himself. Humanity has triumphed over the artist's would-be dignity. Cherubino's second verse ('Quello ch'io provo') moves demurely into F major and introduces some lovely woodwind counterpoints. At 'ch'ora è martir' the flattened third again induces a hot flush, as in *Non sò più*, but this time physically more uncomfortable. It also brings on a third verse in A flat major (the flat seventh of the home tonic, full of mystery in Viennese classicism) which includes a felicitous yet natural reversion to the last bars of Ex. 23, now a tone down but still acting like a reprise. The next verse ('Ricerco un bene') reverts to A flat so as to move away more pathetically and draw the solo woodwind more fancifully into the singer's emotional net—there is one harmonically outstanding passage for first horn, at 'ma pur mi piace', which goes unnoticed because it makes perfect sense. Then Ex. 23 returns as before, concluded by a couple of woodwind wriggles, embarrassed maybe but thoroughly content.

The Countess brims with adulation, and surprise that Cherubino is such an excellent singer (she has been studying for years!); but Susanna merely observes that he succeeds in everything he does—is she remembering his hiding places yesterday and today? He knows about the conspiracy in which he will have a drag part; how he will enjoy wearing the garments of the ladies he adores! Susanna observes that he is just the right height for any of her clothes. She removes his cloak; the Countess fears a strip act, so Susanna locks the door against intruders, then turns attention to his boyish curly hair (mentioned by Figaro in No. 9, visible in the 1785 French engravings—a formal masculine *perruque* is out of place). The Countess suggests covering his hair with a mobcap from her dressing-room.

Susanna goes to find one; meanwhile Cherubino seizes the moment to approach his adored godmother. Sticking out of his breast pocket is his military commission, given him by Basilio, and so hastily completed by the Count that it has not even been sealed, the Countess tells Susanna. Susanna produces the cap and rehearses Cherubino in his role during **No. 12** in G major, *Venite inginocchiatevi*, surprisingly her first solo **Aria** in this opera, though she has sung in all the ensembles and been on stage almost uninterruptedly since the beginning. It is *allegretto*, scored with flutes, oboes, bassoons, horns and strings.*

> Come and kneel down in front of me, and stay still. Now, turn round. Bravo, very good. Now turn your face to me, look at me, I say, straight in the face. My lady is not here [*though she may be sitting just behind Cherubino*]. Stay still, turn round, look at me. Very good. Your ruff a bit higher, your eyes lower, your hands below your bosom. Get on your feet and let's see you walk. [*To the Countess, quietly as he does so*] Look at the rascal, how pretty he is. What naughty eyes, what airs and graces! Can't you understand why girls all love him?

Its equivalent in *Le Mariage* is quite close.

SUSANNA (*sings with pins in her mouth*)
> Turn in this direction,
> Jean de Lyra, my sweetheart.
> (*Chérubin kneels. She does his hair.*)

Cherubino is mincing round the room like the girls he adores. The Countess is perhaps too frightened to enjoy Susanna's teasing; or is she jealous that another woman should admire Cherubino's good looks? At any rate she gives advice about the basis of the disguise. The boy's sleeves must be rolled up ... look! there is a ribbon on his arm, belonging to the Countess, stolen from Susanna. It covers a bleeding wound. Cherubino makes excuses. The Countess recognizes a witch's charm—the lover's blood, a garment worn by the beloved, will they act as a reciprocal love potion? Diplomatically the Countess takes the ribbon and tells Susanna to find some sticking plaster for Cherubino's arm. When the page protests, she pretends ignorance, binds his arm with the sticking plaster, and

---

* In 1789 Mozart replaced this delectable piece, with its flouncing gestures, delicately interwoven textures, and needlepoint charm, by a new aria, *Un moto di gioja*, specially written for Adriana Ferraresi del Bene who was da Ponte's mistress. It is musically uninteresting, dramatically and texturally a hindrance to the plot.

sends Susanna for a new ribbon and a dress.* Cherubino babbles wildly of a soldier's death and dying avowals of deathless love. He begs the Countess to take him seriously. She does, she is wiping the tears away.

Then she hears a knock at the door leading to Figaro's new quarters (not the main door through which Susanna has just walked out). Her inquiry is answered by the Count who, having received the note from Basilio, has not gone hunting but come to demand an explanation. A lover this evening is dreadful enough; but her room locked this noon is worse. She answers distractedly, picturing her husband's jealousy when he finds his juvenile philandering enemy half undressed (*mezzo smobiliato* like the setting of the first act) at her feet. Quickly she temporizes while Cherubino, without his cloak or floppy hat (both taken away by Susanna), locks himself into the wardrobe. The Countess secretes the outside key in her corsage, then unlocks the other door for the Count who remarks her perturbation, as unusual (she is level-tempered always, we may gather) as her locked door. She explains that she was trying new costumes, being dressed by Susanna who went to find something in her room. The Count demands an explanation of this anonymous incriminating letter he has received. As Rosina racks her brains for an explanation, a crash from the wardrobe is heard: Cherubino has, at the worst possible moment, inevitably knocked some furniture over. The Countess pretends to have heard nothing. It must be Susanna there. Nonsense, replies her husband, Susanna has gone to her own room, so you said. Who is there? Why were you so upset when I walked in? It is not I, she answers, who is upset about Susanna, but you (meaning 'Susanna has told me everything about London and the imperilled marriage and the dowry, and the rendezvous in the garden').

Count Almaviva ignores her taunt just as Susanna slips back discreetly through the other door and hides in the alcove (the traditional producer's screen is not authentic). He begins **No. 13, Terzetto**, *allegro spiritoso*, C major, *Susanna, or via sortite* with oboes, bassoons, horns and strings, by demanding that she leave the wardrobe. The Countess, equally determined, orders Susanna neither to talk nor to emerge. We can see and hear Susanna; for the Count and Countess she is invisible.

The ensemble begins loud and brusque like the Count's insistence; the phrase is at once repeated softly. When the Countess adds her contradictory order (and Susanna wonders what is going on, and if Cherubino managed to escape), the strings take up more sustained, smooth part-writing. Another brusque loud idea in unisons: who, asks the Count, dare forbid Susanna to obey his order? His wife answers with spirit that honesty must dare: Susanna is, after all, trying on her wedding dress—again *sostenuto* takes over, more chromatic this time, and with eloquent soft bassoon colouring of the strings. The trio begins in earnest, to the the same music, as the three characters sing in contrapuntal imitation to individual words—the Count declaring that a lover is obviously in the cupboard, the Countess lamenting the mischance, Susanna resolving to help:

---

* 'Vestito mio', wrote Mozart but not da Ponte or Beaumarchais. This was a Freudian slip. Cherubino is to be disguised as Susanna, not as the Countess! Rosina's head was full of Cherubino's passion for herself (and perhaps *vice versa*). Susanna, head screwed on, knows best. She leaves through the main door to walk to her old room, perhaps some way distant.

The music builds again from *piano*, with a more springy step this time—even when the voices move into sustained harmony the violins are weaving actively to promote energy up to the first climax, a glorious passage of taut harmony (anguished seventh chords for the Countess's feelings) enriched by the vocal part-writing, and released in the Countess's upward run:

(When heavier sopranos began to sing the Countess, her runs in this trio were taken over by Susanna; during the 1960s a new generation of young, vocally agile Countesses made it possible to restore Mozart's disposition of vocal lines.)

The second half of the ensemble begins stormily with much *fortepiano* accent over a pedal G which leads back to the first idea in the tonic. The Countess's counter-order breaks off on the dominant, and the Count turns calm in mysterious A flat major ('Consorte mia, giudizio'). Each in turn tells the other to be judicious, to avoid a scandal. The music returns to the dominant of C and the reprise of Exs. 24 and 25 set to these new words. The onward flow is powerfully interrupted while Count and Countess earnestly exchange this vital word 'giudizio' unaccompanied and slowly, with pause, as recitative. Then the trio hurtles again to the end. A marvellous presage it is of the extended finale to come.

Since his wife refuses to open the door, Almaviva threatens to have it broken down by servants. She persuades him that this would be dishonourable. Instead he takes her with him to fetch a crowbar for himself. He also locks Susanna's door—but of course the filly has already bolted—and, upon leaving, the main door too, remarking loudly that Susanna will stay there till they return.★

Instantly Susanna leaps from the alcove and runs to the wardrobe door while the strings alone, *allegro assai*, imitate her noiseless sprint in the opening bars of **No. 14, Duettino**, *Aprite presto, aprite*, G major.

26

She tells Cherubino to come out and escape at once. He is breathless and confused. They exchange hurried sentences, vainly try the available doors, merge into pelting thirds. Then Cherubino decides to jump out of the window. Susanna says it is too far from the ground but on inspection he decides it will be a soft fall even if he lands on one or two flowerpots.† For the sake of the Countess (a turn into G minor, very charming pathos) he will risk the jump, and does so, as the duettino ends loudly and suddenly.

For Susanna to shriek and subside an instant is human but no more authoritative than the traditional noise of breaking glass— inspired no doubt by Beaumarchais's mention of melons growing below the window; in cold countries they are cultivated in glass frames, but in Andalusia they grow uncovered in plots by the roadside.‡ According to da Ponte and Mozart Susanna simply exclaims on

★ In the Eulenberg miniature score (print 4446) this line is notated a third too low, as if in the old baritone clef.

† This is one of three short passages in the duettino often omitted though Mozart composed them and they all help the balance of this brilliant number. It is not known who warranted their removal. Abert's score for Eulenberg, and Erich Kleiber's gramophone recording, include them.

‡ In fact Beaumarchais (II, 21) makes Antonio enter asking the Count to have his beds covered over so that people will not fall on to them from above.

Cherubino's speed as he dashes across the garden, then hurries to take his place in the wardrobe and wait for that 'smargiasso' her Master.

He, with his lockpicking tools and his wretched wife, returns to find the room even emptier than before. The Countess, given the alternative of unlocking the wardrobe door herself or of watching him break it down, asks for a moment's audience. Timidly she begs him believe her incapable of faithlessness when he sees who is in the cupboard. She has been preparing a harmless charade. (The Count interrupts her continually, his anger rising the more she tries to pacify him.) The person in the wardrobe is above suspicion, a little boy . . . Cherubino.

This is too much for Almaviva—for the third time in two days he has entered a woman's bedroom and found Cherubino hiding there, even now when he is supposed to be in Seville with the troops. But, of course, nobody's faults are as heinous as those of people who behave like ourselves.

12

Shaking with rage Almaviva bellows through the wardrobe door to Cherubino. The orchestra (oboes, clarinets, bassoons, horns, strings) has entered with a loud chord of E flat major. This is the *allegro* beginning of the monumental **Finale, No. 15.**

Its dramatic coherence, both verbal and musical, has long been a byword: there is not a sag anywhere—even the moments of repose are tense—while the musical invention is so vivid with meanings, which Mozart draws out and illuminates in long stretches, that music examples are bound to be numerous. It is, nevertheless, designed in closed sections, carefully balanced. For lucidity's sake I shall discuss it sectionally.

(1) 'Come out now, you villainous, misbegotten boy,' Almaviva cries—*Esci, omai, garzon malnato, sciagurato, non tardar.* The orchestra assures us, even if we cannot see him, that he is trembling in his homicidal rage—hence the *fortepiano* on every strong beat, supported by woodwind chords.

27

The Countess still tries, hopelessly, to calm him, and she too is trembling with injured innocence and fear for her godson and her own future. Her music is more sustained and dignified, as in No. 13 (these two ensembles, and the first act terzetto No. 7, also involving the Count, are musically akin, but this time emotions are greatly intensified). Her chains of quavers at 'per lui fammi il cor tremar' must be felt as anxiety, not in any way frivolous.

Bassoons and low strings splutter with indignation as the Count rebukes her for daring to defend herself. Ex. 28 is repeated, now in the dominant, as she pleads for a further explanation, acidly granted. It is even more incriminating: the boy is innocent, even though half-undressed to be disguised as a girl. The Count is unimpressed by this excuse. He turns his wife's musical phrase to his own violent frame of mind:

This musical idea is vigorously extended against new ideas and illuminating orchestral commentary. The music returns to E flat. He demands her key, with peremptory orchestral unisons—but softly, even more sinister—while she bewails with woodwind Cherubino's innocence, moving towards A flat. The Count veers from this cosy key into harsh F minor, prefaced by a dramatic pause. Addressing her in the undignified second person singular ('tu' instead of 'voi'), as if she were a worthless pleb, he coldly orders her to leave him since she is faithless and wicked (but, through the F minor, inferably a sorrow to him). Ex. 28 returns in this key as she still exculpates herself. Finally she plays her highest card, the key, with the words 'I am not guilty'—'non son rea'—to which he roughly answers, in recitative with a pause (or flourish), 'I can read it in your face.' An octave drop in the orchestra curtly, and apparently permanently, drops the guillotine on her neck, or at any rate that of her concealed lover.

'He shall die,' vows Almaviva as the coda of this duet begins. The Countess trembles for his jealousy. His phrase is menacing enough but above it the clarinets and bassoons, in runs of liquid thirds, give his violence the lie. The conjunction is weird in the extreme.

Ah la cie-ca ge-lo—si—a,

Il C. Mo ——— ra, mora, Mo——— ra,

Chains of woodwind thirds in a major key always signify contentment. For Edward Dent often they sounded 'voluptuous and hypocritical', telling the listener to *chercher la femme*. Perhaps this passage may be explained according to Dent's reaction: Almaviva threatens but Mozart answers that two women have already got him in their power. The woodwind chains of thirds for 'Mora, mora' will persist. Unexpectedly but aptly he brings back Ex. 28 from the earlier half of this number, with nice effect, and his wife takes it up in duet. The orchestra consolidates this section heroically with view-halloos in E flat, as Almaviva draws his sword and unlocks the door. The same view-halloos continue downwards softly, out of E flat towards the dominant of B flat (i.e. as if the door had a double lock requiring two turns of the key: thinks—did they have double locks in 1785?).†

There on the threshold stands Susanna. Not Cherubino. The Almavivas are quite astounded, for different reasons, though both expected to see a boy shivering in shirtsleeves, his shirtbuttons unfastened.

(2) *Molto andante* (not *andante con moto*, a long-standing scribe's error, *moto* and *molto* being regularly confused now as then) in B flat major, the strings patter out a captivating rhythm.

Molto andante

Susanna sarcastically asks her master why he is so upset. Drawn sword and promises of slaughter? This is no misbegotten page but Susanna.

She has developed a pleasing but not flippant tune out of the initial rhythmic

* The music examples in this book have appoggiaturas written out. Here, exceptionally, the Count is given a blunt ending. The appoggiatura is a grace, like trills and florid cadenzas or runs, apt to well behaved and dignified persons. At this moment Almaviva is behaving with the blind senseless aggressiveness of a navvy returning to his wife after the hallowed drinking bout on pay night. Graces would be inappropriate; even the flourish, five bars earlier, will not be very dignified—though this interpretation is a personal guess.

† We can hear the 'double-lock' effect twice in the Act IV finale, and in some earlier operas by Mozart.

pattern; she treats the situation very seriously—she knows what is at stake and would not attempt feigned jollity or coquetry at this point. Bassoons and low strings sit down on a low B flat. First violins and first bassoon inaugurate a new descending figure like certainty deflated. The Almavivas mutter to themselves, Susanna also but in more active triplets, a fantastic texture of introspection and wonder. Susanna tells the Count to silence suspicion by assuring himself that she was in the wardrobe by herself.

(3) No sooner has the Count disappeared within than, *allegro*, in B flat still, a new idea hurries on to the scene.

The flutes, for brighter musical lighting, have returned to the orchestra and join the repeat of Ex. 32. The Countess, panting with surprise and terror, demands Susanna's explanation. She reassures her mistress that the boy has escaped—to a new, cheerful, non-aristocratic phrase for bassoon doubling violins.

Almaviva bursts, incredulous and already half-ashamed, out of the wardrobe wondering how he could have made such an unpardonable mistake—for he has, remember, told his wife never to darken his doors again. His theme, like another sudden trip over the carpet, is to recur.

He then takes up Ex. 33, asking the Countess's pardon. Odd that the Gran Corregidor and master of Aguasfrescas should ally himself with working-class music; but he has been hoodwinked by a servant, Susanna, and servant-class Mozart is delighted to stress the point.

Almaviva exerts his station ('ma far burla simile') with proud dotted rhythms and sustained chords to complain of this practical joke against him. The women answer gleefully in thirds that his stupidity deserves no pity (in Beaumarchais Almaviva protests, in true Castilian character, that an affair of personal honour cannot be described as stupidity; da Ponte discreetly left it out of earshot, if not out of mind). Ex. 33 again returns in connection with Almaviva's pleas for his wife's forgiveness; she throws his earlier insults back in his face ('mentite, son l'empia') most piquantly.★

So the Count turns to Susanna to intercede for him, again with Ex. 33, now mock-pathetic in G minor. Susanna refuses point-blank, supported by the indignant

★ In Beaumarchais the Countess announces that she would rather enter an Ursuline convent than so demean herself as to pardon her husband who has so offended her.

Countess in quasi-recitative. After a second appeal, Susanna pretends to implore her mistress. The Count addresses her as Rosina—most tactless when he has just renounced her. There is an embarrassed pause. The music jumps from C minor to A flat (a warm key for Mozart, remember) and a trio, based on Ex. 33, develops out of their mixed feelings, to heightened purpose: the Count has been punished enough, Susanna thinks he is truly penitent, the Countess alone is unwilling, she declares. Now Ex. 34 returns as he seeks explanation of the situation which he found so suspicious. They claim to have invented it all, including the hidden page and the love-assignation which Figaro wrote. The Count's vindictiveness revives but the women warn him that pardon deserves pardon all round.★

A new passage of reconciliation and repose stretches out, still based on Exs. 32 and 33, exquisitely prolonging this important part of the drama, carrying the music farther afield until Rosina at last accepts her husband's apologies, with a twinge of minor third (bar 303, most poignant), and they settle down to a moralistic trio,† low-pitched for the voices as if speaking in confidence below Ex. 33 and a background of time-stopped sostenuto wind chords, in which they vow to understand one another better (Susanna vows as well, for the good of the music). The finale comes now to an artistic pause in B flat major.

(4) The key changes abruptly to G major, the rhythm to rustically jolly 3/8 for Figaro's entrance, 'Signore, di fuori son già i sonatori'. Those who have always known this opera were surprised to find, when we first heard Mozart's third symphony K. 22, that its finale has exactly the same theme as here, though this is not important since the music never refers to it again. In any case J. C. Bach used the same tag in one of his clavier concertos.

Figaro bustles in to say that everything is ready for the wedding—the band, even the trumpets (none in the orchestra), the pipers (flute and bassoon), the singers and dancers, all have met to celebrate Figaro's great occasion (except clarinets who are given a long rest).‡ He takes Susanna by the arm to lead her to the nuptials. Not so fast, answers the Count. Now it is Figaro's turn to insist with orchestral unisons. But the Count drops his voice, the music also, to ask a few questions. A dummy accompaniment (i.e., nothing emotionally vital) dominates the music of the ensuing vocal quartet ('La cosa è scabrosa') in which the Count intends to gamble all, while the others wonder what is up his sleeve. This quartet is simply but generously conceived.

(5) *Andante* in C major, 'Conoscete Signor Figaro': was it deleted at the first performance perhaps because Mozart was afraid the opera would last too long and bore the audience? It must have been included in Lausch's published copies, otherwise the number would have been exorbitantly expensive. At least this section is

---

★ This scene (Act II, scene xix) in Beaumarchais is much more sensitively written; in particular the Countess's profound nobility of soul shines out and must have led da Ponte to his more consistent characterization of her throughout his opera libretto.

† Its texture and rhythms look forward to the moralizing ensembles of *Die Zauberflöte*, rather than recalling any Italian operatic music by Mozart. Mozart usually kept his musical styles apart unless he was setting a bilingual text, as in *La finta giardiniera*.

‡ In Beaumarchais his excuse for entering was a message that the Countess felt unwell—Figaro still maintained his skill as barber and surgeon, though now promoted to steward and personal valet.

dramatically needed because it ties up the plot neatly. The Count sees a possibility of getting the better of Figaro on a point of fact, if he plays his cards skilfully. Almaviva produces that warning of a love-assignation which Basilio gave him (and probably brought him back from the chase). He wants to know if Figaro had anything to do with it. The theme is deliberately plebeian, unsuited to aristocratic gracing: the Count is talking down to his servant in a dislikable, faintly sarcastic tone of voice.

35

The ladies have told him that it is a farce written by Figaro—bad tactical move though good for the manufacture of comedy—but Figaro insists that he knows nothing of it, with frilly, graceful music that indicates a woolly mind. Susanna and the Countess, in C major, try to cudgel his memory; didn't he write it, and give it to Basilio? Figaro persists in his ignorance. The Count, an unimaginative prosecutor, insists that Figaro's face betrays him. It's my face, not myself, that isn't truthful, answers Figaro. This phrase is taken up and subsequently extended, in proper Mozart fashion.

36

The Count persists but Figaro will admit to no knowledge of the document, even though the ladies mutter to him that they have blown the gaff. He merely reverts to Ex. 35 and reminds the Count that he came to ask for the execution of the theatrical happy ending by an act of marriage. He and the two ladies combine as a trio, to Ex. 36, repeating this request, while the Count makes it a euphonious quartet with his exasperated asides about the lateness of Marcellina's return from Seville.* The bassoon's running baritone line (doubling the Count and Figaro alternately) and the cool radiance of flutes and oboes doubling the upper line enhance this section memorably—how often in late Mozart operatic ensembles we

---

* In Beaumarchais he tells the others that he wishes to change into formal dress before presiding over the ceremony. It is a pity that da Ponte omitted this, if only for the sake of the Count's *amour propre*, essential to his character.

remember the total colour of the texture as much as tune and words, and how rarely the ensembles of later composers.

(6) There was a short passage in the previous section, when the women were prompting Figaro, that I should have quoted for a violin punctuating motif.

37

It passed almost unnoticed at the time. But as the quartet ends loudly and piously in C major, the new section begins *allegro molto* with drumming unison C's to indicate the noisy entry of a new character, then quietens for F major and a new theme, equally ephemeral but clearly derived from Ex. 37 (and perhaps from Ex. 34):

38

It indicates an irruption of farce into the solemn quartet, a moment of welcome respite for Almaviva who is down on points in the battle of wits. It also links section 5 of this finale to section 6, most helpfully since they are connected by the Count's bipartite inquisition on the contents of documents.

The intruder, it will be seen from Ex. 38, is the gardener Antonio, uncle of Susanna, father of Barbarina (we have heard her mentioned but will not see her until Act III). He is clutching a pot of carnations which Cherubino broke as he landed from his high jump.* Da Ponte says that he is *mezzo ubriaco*, half tipsy, Beaumarchais that he is *demi-gris*, but defends this state with Antonio's excellent asseveration that 'boire sans soif et faire l'amour en tout temps, madame, il n'y a que cela qui nous distingue des autres bêtes'.†

Antonio is complaining of insolence, but the others interrupt him so much and so noisily, with full chords that we have come to connect with Almaviva's authority, that he is hard pressed to remember his story. At last they listen, and the first violins settle into a busy triplet 4/4 rhythm which persists: Antonio explains that the castle's inhabitants often throw litter into his garden, but not until now an unwanted man. From the balcony, asks the incredulous Count? Antonio asks him to inspect these poor snapped carnations. The women (who know the culprit, Cherubino) beg Figaro to help. The triplets descend to the bass of the orchestra as Figaro and the ladies accuse Antonio of drunken hallucinations. But the Count, still suspicious of the lover vanished from the locked wardrobe, asks Antonio to

* Da Ponte made Cherubino observe that he might damage a flowerpot or so. Beaumarchais had him notice only the melons below. It would have been much funnier to make Antonio appear with a pair of squashed melons, but Beaumarchais evidently decided against visualizing such a lewd idea, and settled for carnations, though he could not resist mentioning the melons.

† 'Drinking when we ain't thirsty, making love in all seasons, ma'am, that's all that distinguishes us from the rest of animal creation.' Beaumarchais also mentions that in later acts he becomes increasingly sober.

say more (still those violin triplets, now in thirds). The man jumped and ran away rapidly. Figaro is warned by Susanna that the jumper was Cherubino but he saw the event, so he begins to guffaw noisily. The Count (loud chords, characteristic of him throughout) asks Antonio to continue. Did he see the person who jumped? No, answers Antonio. Figaro had prepared for this admission and now jocularly pretends that it was he. Ex. 38 reappears while all the others express surprise. Antonio reckons that the carnation-destroyer was less fat, more like Cherubino. Figaro replies that everyone who jumps hunches himself for the fall. If it was Cherubino, he was on horseback when he left the castle; so Antonio would have seen a horse as well. Antonio is sure that the jumper was not on horseback. The others force Almaviva into mistrusting Antonio's recollections. Figaro explains that he was in the Countess's room and hearing her husband outside in a rage, he jumped and hurt his leg—the triplets have stopped for a moment so that the music can match Figaro's story—limping and limp as well.

(7) *Andante* in B flat, 6/8. The triplets are resumed.

39

Antonio therefore brings out a document and asks Figaro if it belongs to him. The Count instantly appropriates it. Figaro fears the worst, as do the women if he does not win this round. The clarinets have returned to duty. The theme of Ex. 39 is fairly straightforward, and grown old in the service of comic opera, but still highly serviceable with its stealthy staccato steps in tenths and its hesitations for thought, and its ability to change pitch in any direction, and above all its innate capacity to sustain tension. What is this document, asks Almaviva? Ex. 39 keeps on pounding, like everybody's heart. Figaro has so many bits of paper on him, he must search for the missing one. Antonio asks if it is (malicious) a list of his creditors; Figaro suggests it comes from a tavern bill (Antonio's, because he is drunk, so what relevance to Figaro? Or Cherubino? Da Ponte did not use his *testa* here!) They are all waiting for Figaro to give the right answer, and Ex. 39 plods on, played by strings with diverse additional colouring of great charm and piquancy.

Antonio is persuaded to reel away but the inquisition continues. The Count opens the document. The Countess recognizes Cherubino's commission, tells this to Susanna, who whispers it to Figaro who (apologetic in G minor, still with Ex. 39), having racked his brains, decides it must be the page's commission given to him for some official reason. Why, asks the Count. It was lacking . . . improvises Figaro. The Countess supplies the information which she knew all the time (so E flat major returns); it has not been sealed. The message is secretly passed from ear to ear until Figaro can give it to the Count who angrily tears up the document while the fertile Ex. 39 is still further extended in another sustained vocal quartet which ends softly in B flat major.

(8) *Allegro assai* in E flat major (a semitone above the home-key of the opera at this half-time mark) with full orchestra, including trumpets and drums.

Marcellina has arrived at last and bursts most unceremoniously into her mistress's private apartment, followed by Don Basilio and Dr Bartolo, demanding an audience from the Count. This section too is built on the alternating initial ideas, loud then soft, as usual.

The Count is greatly relieved to see them, not so Figaro, Susanna or the Countess who smell trouble. Figaro openly refers to them as lunatics but the Count calls for silence while they testify. Marcellina says she has a promise of a marriage signed by Figaro; she asks in rapid patter for it to be ratified. Protests are silenced by the Gran Corregidor, Count Almaviva.

Bartolo adds that he is Marcellina's selected counsel for the defence (he gabbles in patter too, either for amusement or to show that the case is absurd—he should be for the prosecution). Again the Count silences opposition with Ex. 41, a tone higher (Mozart wrote his first two notes an octave lower, for Mandini's comfort, but a Count with a firm top G should use it, as in No. 17 discussed below). Basilio offers himself as an honest witness—who would honestly believe him? The Count promises to consider their case.

The tempo increases to *più allegro*, and a double chorus, as it were for the two factions, ensues, still on Ex. 40a, with infuriated rising scales for the Countess and Susanna. There is a splendid soft interlude, still antiphonal, and again German rather than Italian in tone of musical voice.

This persists to the end of the act, aided by three or four new and delightful melodic ideas, and by a final *prestissimo*, terminated at this top pace by orchestra alone.

The structure of this closing section perfectly demonstrates da Ponte's written recipe for an *opera buffa* finale:

> This finale, which must remain intimately connected with the opera as a whole, is nevertheless a sort of little comedy or operetta all by itself, and requires its own plot and an unusually high pitch of interest. The finale must chiefly glow with the genius of the conductor, the ability of the singers, and the grandeur of the dramatic effect. Recitative is banned from the finale: everybody sings, and every form of singing must be available—*adagio, andante, amabile, armonioso, strepitoso, arcì-strepitoso, strepitosissimo*. For the finale almost always closes in an uproar which in, musical jargon, is called the *chiusa* or rather *stretta*. . . . The finale must, through a dogma of the theatre, produce on the stage every singer of the cast, be there 300 of them, and whether by ones, by twos, by threes or by sixes, tens or sixties; and they must have solos, duets, trios, sextets, thirteenets, sixtyets. If the plot of the drama does not permit, the poet must find a way to make it permit.

As Edward Dent pointed out, da Ponte wrote his first comic opera libretto in 1783. He did well to fulfil his recipe as perfectly as in *Figaro* Act II within just over two years. But he did have Mozart to help him. Together, in this finale, they invented real music-drama, something that Peri, Monteverdi, Cavalli, and the rest, including Gluck and Piccinni (from whom Mozart learned much), had not achieved at this level. The characters and situations are credible as well as amusing, sometimes touching. The words are worth hearing and can be understood. The music goes on revealing new subtleties, new truth, the more frequently it is heard and studied. To play favourites is infantile where works of art are concerned. When people insist on playing it about music, the second act finale of *Figaro* claims a prior place on the list, to say no more.

13

Beaumarchais ended his second act with a 'dying fall', the Countess and Susanna further discussing their plans. Da Ponte wisely postponed the contents of this scene, ending Act II on an upbeat, so to say. It is dramatically correct to perform *Le nozze di Figaro* in two acts with one interval, like *Don Giovanni*, *Così fan tutte*, and *Die Zauberflöte*, and other less famous operas as well; though the theatre barmen will protest.

All the same it is curious that Mozart raises the curtain on our Act III to disclose Count Almaviva, alone on stage, singing *secco recitativo*; in 1786 the words would be drowned by audience noise, and the audience would rightly denigrate an opera whose second half started so apologetically. Every other principal character in *Le nozze di Figaro* has at least two arias. Why does Almaviva only get one? Where else could room be found for another? In Act II such an aria could replace *Esci omai*; the beginning of No. 15, more awkwardly the trio No. 13, *Susanna or via sortite*; in Act I it could have been inserted where *Cosa sento* stands. The Count dominates all of these, but the music, essentially ensemble, dominates even him, and also brings out his character gratifyingly for a lively singing-actor (which Steffano Mandini seems to have been). He might have been given a second aria in Act IV, but that poor wing is already weighed down with standby passengers. Mandini must have been an obliging person, light on personal vainglory, who recognized that his part was sufficiently meaty not to need a second aria. It is not impossible that Mozart and da Ponte intended to begin Act III with Almaviva's No. 17—the aria without its recitative—but then decided that it made better effect after a scene with Susanna, and then the overheard confidence which rouses Almaviva's anger. In any case they were inventing freely here on the data of Beaumarchais, whose Act III is largely devoted to Figaro's trial, which da Ponte omitted. Mahler, in his famous Austrian production of 1906, musically rehearsed by Lilli Lehmann,* reintroduced Beaumarchais's trial scene with recitative music of his own composition. Good devotees nowadays will read and enjoy the scene as written by Beaumarchais, but prefer the opera as da Ponte and Mozart designed it.

The Count is wandering back and forth in his formal reception room which is decorated for the forthcoming marriage—Figaro's trial notwithstanding. It is mid-afternoon. He tries to explain to himself (as in Beaumarchais, III, iv) what went wrong in the intrigue of the second act: everything was explained to him, but it all still appears otherwise. He believes that his wife is totally faithful and loyal to himself. But he has taken the precaution of sending Basilio into Seville to check that Cherubino has already arrived.

The Countess and Susanna enter furtively. She is urging her maid to make an appointment in the garden with the Count for that night. As in No. 13 the convention is adopted that Almaviva cannot hear what the women say: he goes on meditating in his own slow-witted fashion. The Countess and Susanna have decided to exchange clothes for their meetings in the garden (therefore the Count will hold a *rendezvous* with his own wife, *vice* Susanna). Susanna is afraid, especially of Figaro, but the Countess insists that this trick is for the ultimate good of them both. She hides or disappears.

Susanna approaches the Count who is vowing that, if the worst comes to less than the best, Figaro will marry Marcellina (he would suffer as employer no less than they, we may reflect), especially if Susanna has betrayed his secret passion for her.

Now Susanna asks the Count for his bottle of smelling salts, which the Countess needs after the hectic events of the midday. She promises to return them soon but he advises her to keep them. Even a servant, not accustomed to suffer from the vapours, may need them when she loses her bridegroom at the altar. Susanna is optimistic: the Count has promised her a dowry. O yes, but on certain conditions. Where Milord is concerned, she replies, my duty is my pleasure.

At last a musical number, **No. 16, Duetto**, *Crudel! perchè finora*, which is *andante* in A minor–major, accompanied by flutes, bassoons, horns and strings. It is the first minor-key number in the opera, and in a key that Mozart used seldom, usually with reference to loneliness but also in particular connection with Turkey (see p. 24), nowhere else in anything resembling the context of this duet. Another sort of A minor is heard later in the act. The key Mozart really used for this number was A major, his key of sensual warmth and contentment. He wanted to begin

* For details see *Music Review*, Vol. VII, 1946; Paul Hirsch, *The Salzburg Mozart Festival 1906*, p. 149.

with music of passionate protest and entreaty and therefore took the minor mode of A major for the first twenty-eight bars.

The orchestra preludes with one short gesture—the Count extends his arms in pained question, as it were. 'Cruel girl, why keep me on tenterhooks till now?' Flutes coo in low thirds, there is some plangent chromatism, and lithe violin arpeggios climb quietly and provocatively as he repeats his question. Susanna answers, demurely in C major, that ladies take time about these decisions. Back come the arpeggios in the cheerful key as they agree to meet in the garden, and she will not disappoint him (A minor again, with further bitter-sweet chromatics coolly highlit by flutes). Almaviva's delight floods over into A major.

43

Susanna murmurs aside to 'you who understand love' her apologies for fibbing, as a less sophisticated counterpoint to the above, her mood prompting a plebeian continuation of great charm, so long as we do not link it with the Count.

44

Eagerly the Count asks for reassurance. She'll be there? Yes. She won't stand him up?... No. Because we know her heart is not in the affair, for good comic effect he asks again and Susanna gives the wrong answer, correcting herself quickly. Such an error is delightful once, but the joke is instantly repeated and becomes less funny, even when yes and no change places. Almaviva returns ecstatically to Ex. 43 and Susanna duets in seeming rapture with him while the flutes shed their blessing from above in radiant sixths and thirds. Violins suggest the Count's overwhelming ardour in the springing postlude to the duet.

45

The Count keeps her chatting for a while, in recitative, about the cause of her distant behaviour that morning. He mentions the smelling salts but she did not truly need them; they were an excuse for this talk. Susanna escapes, hearing somebody approach. The Count is sure of her now. Susanna mutters a coarse insult as she goes—but she bumps into Figaro and cannot resist telling him that he's won his trial without a lawyer, thanks to her. She spoke too loudly. The Count overheard. 'Won the court case?' The orchestra from the previous duet, oboes, bassoons, horns and strings, joins him in this, the opera's first accompanied **Recitativo, No. 17,** *Hai già vinta la causa.*

What did I hear? Is this a trap? Scoundrels! I shall punish them with a sentence to my taste. But what if he pays the old woman? With what? And then there's Antonio who refuses to let his niece marry a Figaro of uncertain background. I'll flatter the old fool's pride and then ... everything is in my favour.

Da Ponte elaborated this from a short monologue in Beaumarchais's Act III, scene xi. The music begins *maestoso* in C major with pompous accompanying rhythms. Light has dawned: Susanna was not serious. This is the moment for Almaviva to use his authority. He is enraged (E major, *presto*, fiery orchestra for the punishment), then pulled up by the suspicion of a hazard (F sharp minor): supposing Figaro pays up (*andante*, whining oboes, moving towards D major, the tonal target of this recitative)? Figaro's penury revives Almaviva's confidence, in D major and *tempo I* according to the score, though this means *presto* not *maestoso*, the music suggests. Thoughts of Antonio's usefulness prompt a brooding string chord and a placid G major phrase that ends decisively. The plan takes shape and D major is established vigorously with subdominant support. The play of conflicting emotions and changing keys is really vivid, as if the mechanism of Almaviva's brain were on show.

The **Aria**, *Vedrò mentr'io sospiro* which follows, is accordingly in D major, begins *allegro maestoso* and is accompanied splendidly by flutes, oboes, bassoons, trumpets and drums, plus strings.

> Shall I see a servant of mine happy when I am in anguish? Shall he possess what I desire in vain? Shall I see a low creature married to the girl I burn for and cannot have? No, I will not let you go in peace! You were not born, bold fellow, to bring torment upon me and perhaps laugh at my distress. Already the prospect of revenge comforts my heart and makes me joyful.

How Almaviva has changed since *Il barbiere di Siviglia*, let alone *Le barbier de Séville*! Then Figaro was his friend and accomplice; now he is a mortal enemy, the object of Almaviva's most sadistic fantasies. The personality, as we read it here, is to be found in *Le mariage de Figaro;* da Ponte, invention mothered by necessity, has distilled Almaviva's hate into this aria and thereby clarified the new relationship between the Count and the ex-barber—the class war is a hot one, and has left traces on the Countess too, as will be seen in the recitative to her next aria.

The Count's aria begins with a downward sweep by the orchestra—*chez moi le déluge*—and a low seething string trill while the oboes wail above (they did this in the recitative too). The wailing suspensions continue as the Count begins to sing, not a melody but a dramatic piece of *arioso*.

46

(I have shown the subsequent repeat of the introduction music.) The idea of Susanna's union with Figaro drives the violins into furious trills (Beaumarchais's Count says he can bear them being friends or lovers, but married—never!) and then a recurrence of self-pitying A minor★ with lamenting woodwind. Energy revives in D minor, a more dynamic key for Mozart. When the sentence about Susanna's wedding recurs, the musical expression, still in D minor, is more angry (glassy flutes in sixths, almost baleful). Almaviva refuses to let it happen: the drums roll, strings and bassoon undulate tempestuously on the dominant.

Relief arrives, *allegro assai* in D major, at 'Ah no! Lasciarti in pace', the second half of the aria: no more stiff *da capo* forms for the Mozart of 1786, even in a thoroughly serious *furibondo* aria. This is a carefully and formally constructed number for a reactionary aristocrat, but the music is sensibly and imaginatively proportioned.

The strings move purposefully, the timpani (this is their field-day) beat a strong rhythm. 'Tu non nascesti, audace' is given a line of Promethean grandeur, worthy of the Bastille-stormers—

and followed by a tense build-up, with telling chromatic touches for 'tormento' and 'per ridere'. At 'Gia la speranza' the violins trill vigorously in duologue and the woodwind call pungently to each other. The beginning of the *allegro* is varied on repetition, though Ex. 47 reappears intact and its consequents. 'Giubilar' induces the Count to triplet decoration. With the hot-blooded orchestral coda this has become a monologue for a hero.†

After this splendid solo the Count may be expected to leave the stage. Published scores and librettos tell us that he remains and is met by Don Curzio and the parties involved in the trial which has just finished. In 1963 R. B. Moberly suspected that the order of scenes in Act III had been changed before the first performance. Christopher Raeburn suggested that this had been decided so as to give time for Francesco Bussani to change from Bartolo's costume into Antonio's, since he was doubling the roles. The published order is unsatisfactory, musically as well as dramatically. Their solution was cogently argued‡ and has since proved itself on stage and in a gramophone recording. I shall follow it now and assume that Count Almaviva has left the stage after No. 17 to preside over Figaro's trial, as in Beaumarchais, though for convenience I shall refer to the old musical numbering where necessary.

★ Here perhaps is a link with the poignant A minor Mozart of the piano sonata K. 310 and the Rondo K. 511, and one episode in the finale of the K. 488 piano concerta, all superb and all just a shade self-pitying, as the outcome of the K. 488 passage shows by blatant self-mockery.

† For the 1789 Vienna revival Mozart obliged his new Almaviva, Francesco Albertarelli, with a revised *allegro assai* of startling virtuosity, its tessitura around or above the baritone's top D, even more agile and heroic than before. Christopher Raeburn found this version in Florence; Dietrich Fischer-Dieskau has recorded it magnificently.

‡ *Music and Letters*, April 1965, and *Mozart Jahrbuch*, 1966.

14

Barbarina, Antonio's twelve-year-old daughter, runs into the room; how she got past the servants is a mystery, and with her she has Cherubino who is liable to be garotted if anybody finds him on the premises. They are here to tell us that Barbarina will dress Cherubino as a girl and bring him with her friends to present flowers to the Countess, as will shortly be seen. This recitative, not really necessary, was inserted to create a pause between the arias of the Count and Countess. There was some intention to put here a third solo, an *arietta*, for Cherubino, *Se così brami*; it would have been manifestly unfair since Cherubino is only *terza donna*, unless his first aria had been annexed by Susanna (see above, p. 385). If da Ponte and Mozart had not been upset in their plans by Bussani's double-casting they would certainly have put something else more worth while in this slot.

Cherubino and Barbarina run away. From another entrance here comes the Countess, anxious to know how Susanna fared with the Count when she accepted the rendezvous in the garden.* The Countess is singing an accompanied recitative (*andante*, strings only), the first part of **No. 19, Recitative and Aria**, *E Susanna non vien – Dove sono.*

> Susanna not here? I am anxious to know how the Count received her proposal. I think the plan is somewhat rash with a husband so mercurial and jealous. But what harm does it do to exchange clothes with Susanna when night is in our favour? O Heaven, to what humiliation I am reduced by a cruel husband who treats me with an unparalleled mixture of infidelity, jealousy and disdain. First loved, then insulted, at length betrayed, now I must look for help to one of my servants!

Here again, as in No. 17, the recitative looks deep into the singer's heart and mind. The first orchestral comment is merely reflective, the next ones quick and active, extended but essentially the same even at *allegretto*. A third *andante* motif is again reflective but more lively. Here are all three.

The thought of her cruel husband inspires a loud, proud dotted rhythmic gesture such as we already connect with the master of the household. The fatal word 'tradita' launches a poignant A minor cadence for strings (A minor again! Who is lonelier than Rosina—and does she not rather revel in her moments of sadness?)

---

* So this *must* be said before the sextet, *Riconosci*, where Susanna enters with a purse, just given her by the Countess.

fam-mi or cer-car da u —— na mia ser-va a-i —ta.

This phrase also brings class-distinction to the front of her mind. She has to depend on her chambermaid's help to get even with her husband; just as his aria was provoked by the suspicion that his own valet was being more successful with the ladies.

She slides into the C major **Aria,** *Dove sono,* accompanied by oboes, bassoons, horns and strings, very delicately scored (Mme Laschi was a young, new soprano, a *seconda donna* not a Victorian *hochdramatische* at all). The first half is marked *andante,* not too slow.

> Where are those lovely moments of sweetness and pleasure? What has become of the vows sworn by those lying lips? Why has it all changed to reproaches and sadness? The memory of that happiness will not move from my heart. (*Allegro*) Ah, if only my constancy, which makes me love him even while I languish, can bring me the hope of turning his ungrateful heart!

The Countess is dreaming wistfully of the weeks or months, three years ago, after she and her Lindoro exchanged rings and embarked on the jolly adventure of Aguasfrescas, when they were as close as Susanna and Figaro are now. How long ago it seems!★

Do—ve so—no i bei mo—men-ti di dol– cez–za, e di pia——cer——,

Oboes and bassoons trail behind her memories, like echoes, the oboe solo after 'piacer' even more desirably. The string accompaniment to her lovely melody is pitched low, like well matured clear wine. But her memories are not old vintage, any more than she is. She is still a teenager and, though she feels insecure, she has position and wealth, and a quantity of love all around her. So she will sing *Dove sono* naturally, not sentimentally, still less like a grandmother bidding farewell to distant girlhood. When she repeats the melody and extends it, the horns discreetly support the woodwind, perhaps hinting at the cuckoldry in the back of Rosina's mind ('Dove andaro i giuramenti')—Mozart was a young person too, with a taste for lewd jokes; given the right context he knew that two horns meant two horns.

★ Mozart's first audiences may not have found this passage as original as we do. He had used the initial phrase in the *Agnus Dei* of his C major Coronation Mass, K. 317, and something closely akin in the slow movement of his symphony in D, K. 75. All tunes were common property at the time: originality consisted in staking a creative claim to a cliché by turning it into something independent, therefore new.

Rosina finishes her dreamy C major tune. The woodwind proposes another in G major, no, on repetition it is G minor ('tutto si cangiò,' everything is changed). Or is it? Memory can turn G minor back into G major and find an even more beautiful melody for it.

51

la me—mo—ria di quel be — ne dal mio sen non tra-pas—sò—,

Woodwind gladly confirm this, and the aria moves to a pause on the verge of C major. She sings a short cadenza or, rather, slow bridge-passage and returns to Ex. 50 with some new, captivating refinements of orchestration (listen to the deep-throated horns and the sympathetic bassoons, not always jocular plebeian). The one repeat is enough to inspire Rosina with optimism. The second half of her aria is *allegro*. It almost at once mixes C minor with C major, and she is too level-headed to banish pessimism on the strength of a whim, but hope is hope, and most stimulating.

52

[**Allegro**]

Mozart lets us know that she will be brave even if she has to act alone at first.

53

mi por — tas — se u — na spe—ran—za

di can—giar ——————————————————— l'in—gra-to cor —,

The orchestra ends with an uplifting reprise of Ex. 52. The Countess makes her formal exit and goes to meet Susanna.

Meanwhile Figaro's trial has been taking place in another room. The Count was there, as chief magistrate of the district (there is a contemporary engraving of the scene, showing him in the seat of office). But a professional jurist was brought in as judge. Beaumarchais called him Brid'oison; da Ponte, thinking this a not very Spanish name, rechristened him Don Curzio.

Don Curzio now enters, together with the Count, Marcellina, Figaro, and Bartolo. Curzio has arrived at a judgment. Figaro must either p-p-pay Marcellina back or m-m-marry her.*

Brid'oison in *Le Mariage* had a written-in stammer. Mozart excluded it, but Michael Kelly, after some argument, was allowed to follow Beaumarchais with popular success which Mozart himself admitted a good dramatic stroke. All, the Count included, applaud Don Curzio's v-v-verdict, except Figaro who refuses

* Her full name, according to Beaumarchais, is Barbe-Agar-Raab-Madeleine-Nicole-Marcelline de Verte Allure. If you believe that, you will believe anything.

either to pay or to marry Marcellina. He is of noble birth and requires the consent of his parents. The others treat this as a joke but Figaro insists that he was stolen or abandoned as a baby. His birth is attested by the fine clothes he was dressed in, some gold and jewels in his cradle, and a strange birthmark upon his arm. He has been searching ten years for his parents (Beaumarchais tells us that he is now thirty years old).

The birthmark rouses a memory for Marcellina: it is not, by chance, a strawberry mark on the right arm?* Yes, answers Figaro, just that—who told her? Marcellina, much moved, addresses him as Rafaello,† and Bartolo, pointing to Marcellina, tells Figaro to acknowledge his mother—no, not his wetnurse, but his true mother. All, especially Don Curzio and Almaviva, but most especially Figaro, are stupefied. Behold, adds Marcellina, your father. And she points to Dr Bartolo.

This is quite ludicrous, an old comic gag dating back to the Roman comedy of Plautus and Terence. But it solves Figaro's immediate problem and motivates **No. 18, Sextet**, *Riconosci in questo amplesso*, an F major assumed *andante* with flutes, oboes, bassoons, horns and strings which Mozart, according to Michael Kelly as well as Constanze Mozart, loved best of all his compositions. He is said to have performed it with some friends while he was on his deathbed.

After digs into the opening notes of the accompaniment the strings float blandly and peacefully along while Marcellina hugs her longlost son in an expansive embrace; high above, first violins seem to be tittering with delight.

54

Figaro requests his father's embrace also, to save his son's further blushes (we can take this two ways); bassoons descend with him darkly in thirds—perhaps a memory of Bartolo's unwillingness in Beaumarchais—and catch an echo-reflection from flutes and oboes. Bartolo obliges politely ('Do not allow conscience to prevent your wish'), and the violins' giggle becomes even cheekier, though still from behind a handkerchief, so to say. Don Curzio and the Count express amazement severally, against a tiptoe bass and disquieted suspensions on the oboes, while the newly found parents and offspring brim with gratification (two minutes ago they

* A scene of this kind occurs in Piccinni's *Lo sposo burlato* (1772), itself a take-off of a similar episode in his *La buona figliuola*, based on Richardson's *Pamela*.

† In Beaumarchais the name is Emmanuel. But da Ponte, *olim* Emmanuele Conegliano, must have been too superstitious to use his own first name in a scene about illigitimate birth, for fear of mockery.

were bitter enemies—isn't kinship wonderful?) and the violins' accompanying figure burgeons spaciously. Almaviva decides to leave this distasteful reunion which has moved into C major. But Susanna runs gaily in, waving a purse of money given her as dowry by her mistress (Beaumarchais explains, but not da Ponte), and restrains the Count to a new equally cheerful violin figure. She has the two thousand piastres to pay Marcellina and set Figaro free (she could not have obtained them if this scene had preceded *Dove sono* when the Countess has still not talked to Susanna). The music has reverted to the tiptoe bass and piquant oboe suspensions, now enhanced by a radiant flute counterpoint. Bartolo inaugurates a further round of family reunion kissing, more generously scored, which Curzio and the Count maliciously invite Susanna to watch. They hope (for Curzio now reveals himself as no unprejudiced judge but Almaviva's lackey) that Susanna will react unfavourably. She does. The strings boil over into C minor, tremolos everywhere for Susanna's assumption that Figaro is reconciled to marrying Marcellina. Angry rising scales in C major (action not tears); she breaks with Figaro and walks away. He detains her. The bland string music resumes as he tries to pacify her—'Listen, listen, my dear.'

55

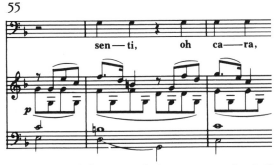

'Senti questo,' she responds (*sentire* means 'to feel' as well as 'to listen') and slaps his face. The bland music is not disturbed. Marcellina, Bartolo, and Figaro too, remark that her aggression is due to true love; only the Count disturbs the general aura of sympathy with expressions of fury reflected also, for other reasons, by Susanna, and by Don Curzio because he knows which side his bread is buttered (perhaps also, let us be charitable, he has travelled out from Seville to do a professional job and now finds his verdict reversed by the laws of nature and the

56

munificence of the lady whose husband pressed him to come all this way). Even at this crisis moment of climax in the ensemble Mozart lets us know, *via* the flutes (a weather gauge in Mozart) at bar 60, that the storm will subside. The climax is allowed its head, then flutes and strings exert a calming influence and bring the music back to F major. Marcellina overtly takes the initiative, telling Susanna to stop her temper and kiss Figaro's mother who will also be a mother to her (Ex. 56).

This is a recapitulation of Ex. 54, as we see from the violin giggle. But Marcellina's tune there has now passed to woodwind, and she is singing a new counterpoint weirdly, Freudianly, like what she sang to Susanna in the waspish No. 5 duet.★

Susanna is even more amazed than the others were. She has to ask all of them for confirmation of this news. They all admit its truth, and the violins trill with sniggering delight.

57

Figaro is the last to be asked and he points also to Bartolo, his father. So the charade begins again, with new, even more delectable scoring for woodwind. Figaro turns back to introduce his mother again, in case Susanna has forgotten, and they all combine in a *sotto voce* ensemble of the most marvellous suavity and discreet mastery.

★ This surprising coincidence is mentioned by R. B. Moberly.

At the end of this Almaviva and Curzio feel constrained to express their frustration in a *forte*. But the others continue, *piano* and blissful, Susanna most relieved and eloquent of all. Just before the end they all raise their voices in a *forte* which the orchestra takes up in the delighted closing bars (the violins allude to their opening giggle, now a peal of joy), while Don Curzio and Count Almaviva angrily leave the room.

Beaumarchais is most amusing about Bartolo's reluctance to marry Marcellina, and how he is forced to wed her because Antonio will not allow his niece Susanna to be united with a bastard. Da Ponte omits all this, the opera being lengthy already. Bartolo now quickly agrees to a double wedding this very day. Marcellina gives Figaro, as dowry, his promise of marriage. Susanna adds the Countess's 2,000 piastres, and Bartolo his own purse. Figaro, who never has enough money, is more than grateful for these offerings. They decide to go and tell all to the Countess and Antonio. Susanna declares herself the happiest person in the world. Figaro, Bartolo and Marcellina all in turn contradict her:* They tumble away in their glee, cocking an *a cappella* snook à 4 at the Count: who cares how furious the Count is?

59

Notice that Figaro's voice is reckoned lower than Bartolo's.

15

So long as Bartolo and Antonio are played by two singers, Antonio and the Count may now enter. Antonio insists, in recitative, that Cherubino is still in the castle grounds. Why, here is his hat! He is not in Seville; all Seville is at Antonio's house for the wedding. Cherubino has been dressed as a woman and has left his own clothes in Antonio's cottage.

They go, Susanna and the Countess arrive. Susanna relates how angry the Count was after the trial. The Countess tells her to make a written appointment with him in the garden. The Countess will dictate the note which Susanna will write. They will call it *Canzonetta sull'aria*—'a song born on the wind'. It is **No. 20, Duettino** in B flat major, *allegretto*, with oboe, bassoon (one player each), and strings. The message reads:

What a gentle breeze will blow this evening under the pine trees in the wood.

(Da Ponte has turned Beaumarchais's chestnut trees into pines.) The Countess knows that this is sufficient invitation for her husband.

* In some performances Bartolo is made to sing the final *Io* falsetto. I do not know how old this tradition is.

She dictates the letter in a long, much interrupted melodic line of great voluptuousness and spaciousness, played by oboe and bassoon when not sung by her. After it is dictated Susanna reads it back, so that the delectable melody is heard twice. Of all the ensembles in *Le nozze* this is the one most likely to have been encored twice. The Countess knows that such a note must be sealed. She finds a pin and makes Susanna add: 'Send back the seal.' Then Susanna has to hide her dictation, because people are approaching.

They are girls from the estate, led by Barbarina and including Cherubino dressed as one of them. All have brought a bunch of flowers for Milady. They sing **No. 21, Coro**, *grazioso*, in G major, with flute, two oboes, one bassoon, two horns and strings, *Ricevete, o padroncina*. With its seldom-moving bass and repetitive six-eight treble line in sixths and thirds it sounds rustic and primitive, very pretty.

Barbarina, in recitative, tells the Countess that she represents the girls on the Almaviva estate who are bringing flowers for their lady. The Countess, touched, asks who is the very shy one in their midst. Barbarina says it is her cousin—who is asked to present her bouquet in person. How she resembles someone they know! The shy relation is pushed forward.

At this moment Antonio and the Count re-enter and Antonio plonks Cherubino's hat on his none too well disguised head, to the amusement of the girls and the wrath of the Count (though he knew it was on the cards) who attacks first the Countess—she is as surprised as he—and then Cherubino. But the boy is saved by Barbarina who comes forward and tells the Count loudly that, whenever he had come to kiss and cuddle her, he always promised to give her whatever she fancied, if only she would love him. Now she wants Cherubino for a husband. If the Count will give him to her, she will love Almaviva as much as her pussy cat. Antonio congratulates her. The Countess marks her husband down a point. Almaviva admits that this is not his day. But he has to consent.

Figaro once again announces the arrival of the dancers for the wedding. The Count remembers his injured foot, but Figaro no longer feels it. Susanna and the Countess sense danger. Figaro brushes away all the Count's comments about Cherubino and the commission and the leap from the window. Figaro told no lie: what Cherubino claims to have done, he could also do, and *vice versa*. Looking the Count straight between the eyes Figaro asseverates that he for one never disputes what he does not know.*

In the distance the wedding march is heard. For Beaumarchais it was *Folies d'espagne*.

60   *Corelli*

*I have described this passage in accordance with the interpretation of Sir Geraint Evans, the outstanding Figaro of my life time. He turns this sentence into the crisis of the drama: the servant actually dares his master, so that we nowadays can understand how Napoleon could declare that *Le mariage de Figaro* was 'la révolution déjà en action'.

Mozart wrote his own march and, with real dramatic insight, brought it into earshot just half-way through; it begins in G major but its tonic is C major. Just now, at the half-way stage, it serves to dismiss the crowd which may have gathered, get the married couples ready for a *défilé*, and the Almavivas (she like an icicle, he planning revenge) ready to receive the bridal pairs, and allow the servants to make necessary adjustments to the furniture before the march, which opens **No. 22 Finale** in C major, with flutes, oboes, clarinets, bassoons, horns, trumpets, drums, and strings, finds it way back to its home key.

61

The march gathers impressiveness and scale during this interlude as the crowd, after retiring, returns in good order with everybody from the Aguasfrescas estate, huntsmen, peasants, footmen, everybody including the two couples to be married. Figaro conducts Marcellina, Bartolo Susanna (who passes her note quietly to the Count). The Count and Countess have to place the emblems of marriage upon their subjects' persons. The march rises to a magnificent climax and close.

There follows an epithalamion in C major, *allegretto* sung by two peasant girls, *Amanti costanti*; like No. 8 it praises Almaviva for renouncing the *droit de seigneur*, and is musically pleasing though lengthy, especially with the jubilant confirming chorus by the whole staff of Aguasfrescas. They are all liable to feel relieved when it is over and the dancing starts. At this moment the two married couples are claimed by their partners.

The dance is a fandango in A minor, much more demure than the one suggested by Marcello in Act IV of Puccini's *La bohème*, but authentic in its opening trill— so Abert shows—and indebted, for a phrase or so, to a fandango in Gluck's *Don Juan* ballet (1761) quoted in Abert's *Mozart*.

The Emperor had forbidden ballets in opera. Count Rosenberg insisted that this ballet should be omitted. Mozart and da Ponte, for the dress rehearsal, arranged that here the music would stop, but that Almaviva, Susanna and the Count would mime in silence—Joseph II was totally bemused by this spectacle but da Ponte stood at his shoulder and explained the plot. The Emperor at once instructed the ballet to be reinstated.

The key of Mozart's fandango was mentioned above in connection with the duet No. 16 and is further discussed elsewhere (p. 24). A minor may here stand for an exotic dance from a far country. It is florid and elaborately scored, flutes and bassoons, as usual in such a context, especially prominent and typical. While the dance is being performed by the imported flamenco company, Almaviva has a look at Susanna's note and pricks his finger on the pin. Figaro notices this mishap and tells Susanna that the pin must have been a loving seal from some lady, which the silly Narcissus is hunting for. The Count has dropped the pin and has to search for it—if Basilio were present he would be on the ground already looking, but he must still be in Seville since he is not mentioned (in Beaumarchais he makes a farcical entrance after all this, demanding Marcellina's hand which he releases upon learning that Figaro would be his stepson).

The fandango is completed, and the tempo becomes *maestoso*. In partly accompanied recitative the Count announces a programme of music, fireworks, a banquet and a ball: his guests will see how he treats those he holds dear. The bridal chorus is repeated to end the act.

Despite the smiles and ceremony, the proud statements and blazing C major, the wedding scene has been a tense one. Beaumarchais sums it up:

FIGARO (*jumping for joy*) In the end I shall have my wife.
COUNT (*aside*) And I my mistress.

We shall see whether he does, and how he treats those he holds dear.

16

The final act represents a garden, da Ponte writes, with two pavilions, to right and left respectively. It is night-time. Beaumarchais has included Fanchette's search and dialogue in the previous act; it is impossible that her journey from the Count to Susanna should take her out of doors. Some believe that the first four scenes of Mozart's opera, up to Marcellina's exit, should also be played indoors. But Barbarina's **Cavatina, No. 23**, *L'ho perduta*, is surely *al fresco* in musical character, as if Mozart were already imagining Beaumarchais's Fanchette in the *salle de marronniers* at the beginning of his fifth act.

Barbarina's *cavatina* is *andante* in F minor, with string accompaniment (the violins muted). It is the second and last minor-key number in the opera (excepting the fandango) and, like the missing *andante* of the overture, is in 6/8 metre. Voluptuous, balmy, night-scented, but not for indoors.

I have quoted the string orchestral prelude, quite long by *Figaro* standards and deliciously extended for two extra bars as shown.

Barbarina is searching on the ground for something. She has a paper lantern in one hand to light her quest. What is she looking for?

> I have lost it, naughty me! Who knows where it may be? I can't find it, I have lost it. My cousin, and the master, what will they say?

We are kept guessing—perhaps deliberately—by the authors who enjoyed mild lewdness and hoped we would guess something more *risqué*. There is all the world's grief in Barbarina's lamentation, in the drop from the higher F to B natural, and in the later, lesser drops when basses play *arco* and violins wriggle in anguish (like all small girls in trouble with their elders). There is a brief reprise of this wriggling. A new section promises to start when she thinks of Susanna and the Count; but she is cut short in her soliloquy by the arrival of Figaro and Marcellina and, after a brief flourish, ends on an imperfect cadence.

Figaro and Marcellina at last persuade her to tell. She has lost the pin which the Count told her to take to her cousin as the 'seal of the pine trees'. Figaro guesses half, is told the rest, borrows a pin from Marcellina, and dispatches Barbarina to Susanna.

Figaro turns despairingly to his mother: this news has killed him. Marcellina counsels patience but he, having discovered where his wife has agreed to make love with his master, is determined to fetch help and avenge all husbands. Marcellina decides that she had better warn Susanna: women, whether guilty or innocent, must stick together where ungrateful men are concerned.

This gives her the cue for her solo **Aria, No. 24**, *Il capro e la capretta* which is in G major and begins *tempo di minuetto*, again with strings alone.

This part of the opera is quite dull, dramatically, not to say incompetent. Can da Ponte, let alone the highly experienced Mozart, only now have realized how many singers had to be given a solo? Such a lapse would not have mattered in an old-fashioned, non-realistic comic opera; in *Le nozze di Figaro*, which is a quasi-realistic drama, it matters very much that vocal numbers should connect closely with the action. And, in an opera which has carefully spaced out solo arias between the newly fashionable and dramatically more effective ensembles, it seems careless suddenly to prescribe five solo arias one after another. One might blame last-minute panic in Vienna. But Mozart had the chance to order Act IV better with da Ponte before the Prague première, or at least before the 1789 revival in Vienna. The changes he made were not to the structure of the start of Act IV. One can only suppose that he was no longer worried about it, having new compositions on his workbench (composers are seldom interested in works they have already completed and brought before the public).

Marcellina's aria was, in any case, a duty: considering this, da Ponte and Mozart did generously by Maria Mandini. The text is indeed rather pleasing in its moralism and faintly absurd choice of imagery.*

---

* Did Mozart intend us to imagine these pairs of animals peacefully cavorting in a stately dance-measure? Abert regarded it as a deliberate joke and Gerard Hoffnung would have illustrated it to perfection.

The he-goat and she-goat are always good friends. The ewe and ram never fight. The most savage wild animals of forest and field leave their mates in peace and freedom. Only we poor women, who love these men so much, are always cruelly treated by these wicked fellows.

Beaumarchais's Marcelline merely wonders why human beings cannot live together peaceably. Da Ponte took the bestial comparison from Ariosto's *Orlando furioso*, and made a telling parallel for Figaro's anti-female No. 26.

Again a long introductory ritornello, this time because it is an old-fashioned aria for a member of the older generation: not, indeed, the full length da capo movement of an *opera seria* heroine, but the sort of bipartite ladylike yet cheerful dance aria that the boy Mozart might have given to Aunt Giacinta in *La finta semplice*. In the first strain, the music for Marcellina's opening line, violas and cellos are nicely intertwined, and the first phrase ends with a pre-echo of the later minuet in *Don Giovanni*; the second strain seems independent, but its trills and runs do have some connection with the *allegro* part of the aria. The wild animals rouse first violins to flourishes; there is a staid little subsidiary three-bar florid division of some intricacy, going up to top A and down again, for a formal reprise which closes on the verge of G minor. She has now reached 'Only we poor women' ('Sol noi povere femmine') and moves into a common time *allegro* jog-trot that would almost do for Zerlina.

63

It cannot go as fast as a conductor might expect, since Marcellina has some semi-quaver divisions which need time to negotiate. Two of them also rise to top B—one reason why the aria is often cut nowadays when the part is assigned to a mezzo-soprano unfairly supposed to be elderly. Unless you agree with 18th-century convention that a character means nothing unless granted a solo aria, this one is not indispensable to Marcellina's part. The two Marcellinas that I remember best were Rita Hunter and Pauline Tinsley, both young, both sopranos; both made this aria the high-point of their characterizations.

Marcellina goes to find Susanna and warn her of Figaro's plan. Barbarina has done her errand and (recitative) returns to meet Cherubino in the left hand pavilion; she managed to scrounge an orange, a pear, and a ring doughnut (*ciambella*)—this is Beaumarchais's Act V opening. She hears somebody approach and runs into the pavilion.

It is Figaro. He notices her, then turns to meet Basilio and Bartolo whom he has invited to witness the supposedly repealed *droit de seigneur* which their master will nevertheless perform upon Susanna, here tonight. They remark on Figaro's menacing expression: he tells them to hide, then rush out when he whistles. He leaves them. Basilio observes with amusement that the Count and Susanna have made their appointment without his mediation. As for Figaro he had better put up with a bad job where the aristocracy is involved: they always win, even if they give you a ninety per cent start.

Basilio makes his point to Dr Bartolo by telling a moral anecdote, his **Aria, No. 25**, *In quegli anni*, which is in B flat major, accompanied by flute, two clarinets, bassoons, horns and strings. It is quite a long aria for a secondary character, in three distinct sections.

(*Andante*) In years gone by, before I learned common sense, I used to be as hot-tempered as Figaro. I am not such a fool now. I came to terms with Madam Cool [*Donna Flemma, goddess of phlegmaticism*] who drove the nonsense from my head. One day she took me to a little cottage, removed an ass's hide from the wall, gave it to me and vanished.

(*Tempo di minuetto*) While I gazed silently at her gift, the sky clouded over, thunder, hail and rain came down. So I used the hide as a cloak. When the storm was over I set off: at once a ravening wild beast came to devour me. But the vile smell of my cloak so took away the animal's appetite that it scorned me and departed.

(*Allegro*) So fate taught me that with an ass's skin you can escape shame, danger, and death.

This excellent comic solo seems quite straightforward but is elaborated with a wealth of inventive detail, some of it really subtle. In the introduction we hear the clarinets and bassoons in warm thirds; they are prominent throughout this number, as is the *gruppetto* or scrunch motif in the first violins' tune which should sound dapper and conspiratorial and very knowing—Basilio's idealized self-portrait.

64

When this is repeated, at once with Basilio singing, the solitary flute adds sparkle to the light-footed downward scale. Mozart does not tone-paint the fiery Basilio for 'lo stesso foco'; he sets a gentle triplet accompaniment against the staccato tune and the glowing clarinets, and these reappear with bassoons as well, for 'donna Flemma' in F major. At the 'piccolo abituro' the violins scamper absurdly in opposite directions, and the donkey hide is most elaborately accompanied with violent loud–soft cadences and double-stopped violas and skittering violins. It does not seem to be pictorial, just excellent comic music, like the woodwind twiddle after 'o figlio caro,' though the downward scale of Ex. 64 may now refer to the fairy godmother's disappearance. This section comes to a full stop in F major.

The minuet returns to B flat and a wheedling tune—

65

which sounds even more Zerlina-like on the woodwind. The thunderstorm arises gradually in G minor and does without conventional drums, though the flute is useful. Considering that it is a thunderstorm-minuet it carries great conviction. Under his donkeyskin raincoat Basilio patters quietly along with rude and noisy comments by flute and strings. The ravening beast (still in minuet tempo!) roars fearsomely and chromatically in E flat, *forte* answered by woodwind *piano*; *vice versa* in B flat for Basilio's terrified impotence. When he mentions the saving stench he returns blandly and amusingly to Ex. 65, and the beast lopes back into the forest with a softly gliding arpeggio figure.

Basilio points the lesson in an *allegro* B flat major which enters without pause: a cheerful scrunchy tune, loud unison Fs for the fates avoided (how like aristocratic authority they sound!) and a typical street-song, buttressed by horns, for the redeeming ass's hide. I can quote them all together.

66

The orchestral coda makes Basilio sound even more heroic. But, as I said, this is his account of himself. We already know what he is really like, so Mozart can soft-pedal the musical caricature, like a good pupil of Donna Flemma (which he never truly learned to be—everyone speaks of his fiery temper).

Bartolo and Basilio leave the spot. They will be more interested to watch the fireworks than to assist Figaro in his above-station machinations. He returns to approve the scene he has set and wait for the actors to appear.

Now Mozart makes an amazing innovation: he gives Figaro a recitative with orchestral accompaniment. Opera, we have seen, was always rigorously class-conscious. It tried from time to time to create a theatrical *apartheid* so that the aristocracy and the lower orders did not have to act on the stage at the same time. Even when this broke down, and they actually sang the same music in an ensemble, it remained self-evident that their arias would be musically quite distinctive. The nobility would sing graceful, dignified solos with florid divisions and ambitious structure and scoring; the proletarians sang cheerful dance- or street-tunes, simply constructed without the princely trumpets and drums, often with just strings to accompany. Within this musical class-structure the *recitativo accompagnato* belonged very definitely to the gentry since this emotionally impressive recitative was reserved for moments of suddenly heightened or deepened feeling such as the working classes were assumed incapable of experiencing (even though the composer was usually a member of those classes, in the eyes of his noble employers). Mozart had automatically observed these rules in his operas, few enough of which had involved servant principal roles. *Le nozze di Figaro* was a different case: the class-structure is still there, but the drama is much more serious than usual in an *opera buffa*, and the music is almost unreservedly natural and human, such as each character would use for the expression of genuine emotional reactions. The only obvious *buffo* jocular number is Basilio's *In quegli anni*. For the rest we have gaiety and wit and charm, but always naturally, not artificially applied. And then the whole shocking aim of *Le mariage de Figaro* was to demonstrate that the man is not merely more cunning but also more admirable than his master, as an enlightened human being. Figaro is that new phenomenon, a working-class hero— truly 'la révolution déjà en action'. And so, though da Ponte felt obliged to remove the trial scene, where Figaro exposes the injustice of the French judiciary system, and to bowdlerize his monologue, at this moment in the last act, from a diatribe against class-privilege into one (only the beginning and end of that speech) against the fickleness of the female sex in general (a counterblast to Marcellina's less violent No. 24), Mozart was still able to strike a blow for the barber-hero and give him a 'heightened emotion' number in orchestral recitative such as Leporello and Papageno would never expect.

His **No. 26** is therefore a **Recitativo ed Aria**, *Tutto è disposto – Aprite un pò quegli occhi.* The recitative is accompanied only by strings and continuo.

> Everything is arranged and it must soon be time. I hear someone coming . . . it is she! No, nobody. The night is dark and I must begin to do the foolish job of being a husband. Faithless woman, in the moment of our wedding he read with pleasure and I, knowing nothing, watched and laughed, at my own expense. O Susanna, what pain you have cost me! With that ingenuous face, these innocent eyes, who would have believed it? Ah, to trust a woman is always stupidity.

This is no clowning Harlequin but a husband in distress, as the strings, having mimed the pitapat of the conspirator's heart, explain with their turn from F major towards G minor.

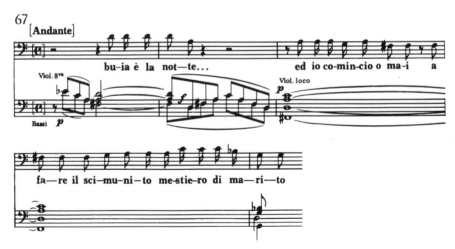

Conventional dramatic chords come next, but for Susanna's innocent features a more alluring, gentler figure is evoked. The end in B flat is quite strong.

Now the aria in E flat major, *moderato* with clarinets, bassoons, horns and strings.

> Open your eyes a little, careless and foolish men. Look at these women and see what they are like. Our senses are tricked into calling them goddesses, and we sacrifice our weak powers of reason as tribute to them. They are witches

who weave spells to pain us, sirens who sing to make us drown, coquettes who allure us and then pluck our feathers, comets that dazzle and blind us. They are thorny roses, charming vixens, kindly she-bears, cruel doves, mistresses of deceit, friends of trouble, who cheat, lie, feel no love, show no pity. I say no more, you all know the rest.

Mozart says *moderato* and the strings begin softly but the aria is stormy as may be gathered from the boat-rocking *fp* wind chords half-way through each bar, and the choppy violin *gruppetti* (compare them with the elegant ones in Basilio's aria).

68

'The clarinets in thirds, hypocritical and voluptuous,' raise their gentle voices above the word 'uomini' ('men'); but Edward Dent's memorable phrase (from the chapter on *Così fan tutte*) may appropriately be completed, for in this context too they 'tell us that the ladies are here'—in Figaro's mind and soon before our eyes. His first sentence ends with a brutal phrase for 'guardate cosa son':

69*a*

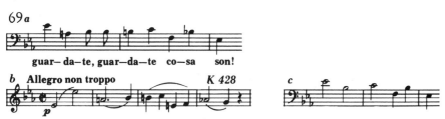

Hermann Abert correctly recalled the likeness to the first phrase in Mozart's E flat string quartet K. 428, equally striking; but the ungraced form shown as the third part of Ex. 69 may look more traditional, more apt to a valet in *opera buffa* (not sufficiently well bred to feel musical graces of this kind).

'Queste chiamate dee' ('these so-called goddesses') are given full imperial chordal and rhythmic honours which Mozart then reduces to size in the frenziedly wriggling violin trills and heart-searching seventh-chord progressions that follow. The trills are still present, more selectively, for the catalogue of vicious similes ('Son streghe', etc.); the flirts ('civette') are given a specially spell-like musical idea, and a big climax is built up on triplets until 'and show no pity'. At 'I say no more' Mozart brings out the horns for illustration of cuckoldry. This first half of the aria ends in the home key. The second half plunges back to the first line of text and makes the points again with musical variants, especially at the end with reference to the cuckold's horns.

Figaro retires to a near-by hiding-place: in the present context his could not be an exit-aria. Promptly enter the Countess and Susanna, each disguised as the other, escorted by Marcellina. Susanna is mentioning, rather too loudly, to the Countess that Marcellina says Figaro is hereabouts. For Susanna too the scene is now set. Marcellina, for ringside view, goes to join (little does she know) Barbarina in the left-hand pavilion.

The Countess declares, loud enough for Figaro to hear (though it is too dark for him to see), that it is a damp evening and she will go indoors. Susanna is given leave to promenade for half an hour or so in the deliciously cool night air here amid the shrubbery. The Countess discreetly hides near-by while Susanna decides to tease Figaro for doubting her constancy. She knows that he has recognized her voice; he does not know that, when he comes close to her, she will look like the Countess and, presumably, can mimic her voice.

Now in her own voice, for Figaro's audible but not visual benefit, Susanna begins her **No. 27, Recitativo ed Aria**, *Giunse al fin il momento – Deh vieni, non tardar*. Here too is a string-accompanied recitative for a non-aristocratic character, but for the different reason that Susanna is singing to and for Figaro, and for the amusement of her female accomplices watching. The C major music, *allegro vivace assai*, though cheerful and conspiratorial, seems more suited to the Countess's character. But, after all, Susanna is acting the part of an *alter ego*, the Count's promised plaything.

70

At last the moment draws near which I shall enjoy without shame in my lover's arms. Go, timid fears, from my heart, come not to disturb my delight. Oh how my fiery love is matched with the charms of this place, this earth, this sky. How well the night assists my plans!

There is little comment to make about this recitative except that it is radiantly beautiful, uses Ex. 70 three times, and ends in F major. Mozart sketched a longer version, with further entries of Ex. 70, so as to end in B flat for an alternative aria in E flat, *Non tardar, amato bene* which he never completed. It has been pointed out by several scholars that this *Non tardar* is too stiff in feeling for Susanna. It occurs to me, as a guess, that Mozart began composing it under the misapprehension that it was an air for the Countess; or he wanted Susanna really to mimic her mistress's voice. He then realized that Susanna must sing in her own voice, though with pretended ardour for her supposed clandestine lover, so had some words changed and wrote our *Deh vieni*. The vocal line of *Non tardar* strongly recalls that of Fiordiligi's *Per pietà* in *Così fan tutte*, written for Adriana Ferraresi.

Throughout this number, and Figaro's preceding it, I wonder if the singers adopt courtly appoggiaturas or stick to plebeian blunt endings. There are signs that Mozart wrote in the essential graces, but for the music's own sake surely not enough.

There follows the aria, also in F, *andante* with single woodwind, flute, oboe, bassoon, and strings plucked almost throughout. Susanna may sing as softly as she likes without being swamped by the orchestra. *Andante* does not mean 'slow', however.

> Come, lovely joy, do not delay. Come where love calls you to delight while stars are dimmed and darkness reigns and the world is silent. The stream murmurs here, and the wind plays softly, rejoicing the heart with its gentle whispers. Flowers smile, the grass smells fresh; everything quickens the pleasures of love. Come, my beloved, through these dark trees. I long to crown your brow with roses.

I could wish that my English version conveyed a tenth of the original's poetic quality. This is da Ponte at his finest. Because of its last sentence *Deh vieni* is commonly known, especially to German-speakers, as the Rose Aria. It has always been particularly loved by Mozart devotees, and evidently he took great trouble to proportion it to his satisfaction since he made numerous drafts to lengthen it, then cut them back to the length we know; there are sketches also that show the vocal line in an earlier, less polished state. When Adriana Ferraresi took Susanna in the 1789 Vienna revival Mozart wrote another aria, *Al desio*, for her to sing at this point. It is also in F, but much less expressive; Mozart did not share da Ponte's love for this lady (see *Così fan tutte*, p. 522), and may have been relieved when she spurned *Deh vieni* which he had composed expressly for dear Nancy Storace.

The allure of *Deh vieni*, for audiences in many successive generations and countries everywhere, hardly requires advocacy. The serenely loping 6/8, its leisurely diving and soaring vocal line, the delectable touches of delicate colour for solo woodwind, the lulling siciliano rhythm for 'qui ridono i fiorette' (for one bar the very notes of the overture's abandoned *siciliano*, but on the dominant, not tonic minor, so no help here), the calm emergence of *arco* violins before 'Vieni, ben mio', and the last three ascending vocal phrases—all these contribute to music of compelling, abandoned female sexuality at its most irresistible because seemingly so sincere. As a result posterity, including many careful and unsentimental scholars, have regularly decided that *Deh vieni* is Susanna's sincere declaration of love to Figaro, knowing that he is listening.

We may all agree that *Deh vieni* is every Susanna's acid test and, if she succeeds, supreme reward. But the sincerity of the musical expression is more questionable. Susanna has already declared her intention:

> *Il birbo è in sentinella.*
> *Divertiamoci anche noi.*
> *Diamogli la mercè de' dubbi suoi.*

(The rotter is standing sentry. Let's have some fun ourselves. Let's pay him back for his doubting.)

Susanna is not given to use of the royal first person plural: she means the Countess and Marcellina, who are both concealed near by, as well as herself. She will give them all a laugh. Therefore she will not sing a seriously sincere serenade to her lawful wedded husband.

There is some musical evidence too, necessarily inconclusive but worth contemplation.

Exhibit A is the end of the orchestral prelude, all leisurely charm and wooing until the semiquaver runs for woodwind, as shown.

They are not really amorous, though possibly provocative.

Susanna has only just sung her first, cool, lilting phrase when she ventures on a chromatic idea that contradicts that mood by its suggestion of passionate heavy breathing. It is out of (sincere) character.

vie—ni o-ve a—mo———re   per   go—der   t'ap—pel———la,

Three bars afterwards our girlish soprano wife and lover descends into the basement, into Almaviva's territory.

fin—chè non splende in ciel not—tur—na   fa—ce,

This is tiresome for a soprano to sing, and with its necessary resort to chest register will sound like fake passion, Mörike's *verstellter Pathos*. Mozart sent Adriana Ferraresi into these nether regions, in *Così fan tutte*, for private humorous effect (see p. 542).

After 'qui scherza l'aura' some cheerful comment is apt: the repeated woodwind chords can be made to sound like subtle zephyrs:

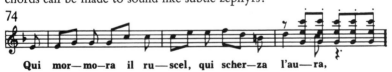

Qui   mor—mo—ra il ru—scel, qui scher—za   l'au—ra,

but, with the high bassoon G, are more likely to come out as a titter in three-part harmony (though not necessarily Rosina, Susanna and Marcellina). The siciliano rhythm, at 'qui ridono i fioretti', can sound entrancing; it could be sung in mock-passion—this is not real evidence.

If these details suggest that Mozart was not wholly in earnest about Susanna's ode to her lover, then I submit that Ex. 71 is coarsely comic, especially after it has been repeated variously four times and a bit during the aria, like the Australian phrase about 'a rat up a drainpipe' which it musically resembles. Rude words can be understood and censored: music can be much more obscene, but still sound blameless to non-musicians who do not understand the language and its imagery.

If Mozart was being serious, after all, then he was writing a love-song for Nancy Storace to sing to her beloved Mozart, a private and very tender joke between them—whence the replacement for another Susanna—rather less serious and more private than the glorious love duet *'für Mad Storace und mich'* which we know as the concert aria *Ch'io mi scordi di te?* Meanwhile:

Figaro, the wily barber of Seville, is in no doubt about her song, except to wonder whether he is awake or dreaming. No time to wonder. Cherubino's voice is heard approaching. Tiresomely Mozart did not write out the notes to which the boy sings *Lalalalalala lera*. Productions of *Le nozze* usually fix on *Voi che sapete* because it is famous. But he might (as a stroke through the words 'Voi che intendete' in the Prague textbook has persuaded Christopher Raeburn) be singing his newer masterpiece *Non sò più*. In fact the syllables printed in the 1786 libretto fit neither but do fit *Malbrouk s'en va t'en guerre*, the tune of Cherubino's *couplets* in Beaumarchais—and Beaumarchais brings the gallant captain into the chestnut walk, *en habit d'officier, en chantant gaiement la reprise de l'air de la romance:*

> *J'avais une marraine,*
> *que toujours adorai*

J'a——vais u—ne mar—rai——ne que tou—jours a—do—rai——.

the last two lines of 'For he's a jolly good fellow'. Mozart's Cherubino has shown no interest in this song, so he may as well quote from either of his existing solos by Mozart—though being proud of his new uniform he might try *Non più andrai* in B flat using his pseudo-male alto register.

Cherubino is about to join Barbarina in the pavilion (he will find it unromantically crowded) when he sees a woman standing outside. It is not the singer of *Deh vieni* but Countess Almaviva who has strayed into some visible moonbeam and, in her fancy dress, is mistaken for Susanna—but by the wrong person. The Countess is appalled: she is waiting for Susanna's dangerous lover, the Count.

Full of self-confidence Cherubino saunters towards her. This is the start of **No. 28, Finale**, *andante* in D major, with oboes, bassoons, horns and strings.

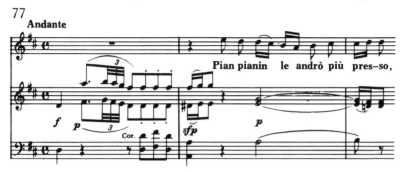

The horns have a couple of phrases to say about cuckoldry, but the music is chiefly concerned with the swaggering boy. The Countess's apprehension precipitates a tremolo in B flat major, neatly driven by a French sixth into A for new ideas connected with Cherubino's delight at the prospect of a flirtation, and perhaps a reference to Susanna who he assumes is standing there (the phrase rather recalls Ex. 3):

He takes the lady's hand and caresses it, but is surprised by the violent reaction—angry scales, sudden *fortes*, the hand angrily withdrawn, and a volley of abuse: 'Saucy, impudent boy, be off!' He persists, however, Susanna being always worth teasing, especially since Cherubino heard this appointment discussed while he was behind the chair.

Back comes Ex. 77 in A; the Count, strolling to keep the rendezvous, stops to watch Susanna (unrealistic—they can't see one another!). Susanna and Figaro, from their separate hiding-places, know him at once, the birdcatcher (*uccellatore*). How the Count's heart is pounding—Susanna's and Figaro's too, for another reason: Cherubino is likely to spoil their plans. The Countess continues to repulse him, threatening to call for help. Cherubino demands a kiss as the price of his departure. Their duet is carried on independently of the block commentary by the concealed others. At the mention of a kiss, the first violins execute an angry downward arpeggio of B flat to signify the Countess's horror. 'Temerario!' ('How foolhardy') they all observe, while the music veers towards D minor, then thinks better and builds back to D major for a tonic reprise of Ex. 77. Why won't Susanna grant him what the Count does all the time, Cherubino asks, and 'Temerario!' again they all cry.

They are growing weary of his interference. The other men decide on action, just as Cherubino dares to steal his kiss. The cheek that receives it is the Count's—he stepped in between the lovers. Enraged, he slaps the boy's face. But the boy has recognized him and dived into the pavilion where Barbarina is. The cheek that receives the slap is Figaro's—he having also come to separate them. The slap coincides with the access of B flat major again, followed by Ex. 77's return while the four characters remaining join in an ensemble. Three of them, in the darkness, assume that Cherubino got his just reward; only Figaro knows that he didn't—it was Figaro's reward for inquisitiveness. The ensemble takes a curious, not obviously motivated, turn to the sublime, perhaps to hint that more than farce is involved in the slapstick.

79

Figaro goes back to his hiding-place (Susanna has never moved from hers). The Count and his supposed Susanna are left, he supposes alone. The orchestra subsides into G major, moving a little faster than before (Ex. 80).

Earlier I mentioned a theme in this finale which looked back to the first scene of the opera. Here is another one. The first phrase of Ex. 80, in its rhythm and scoring, strongly recalls Ex. 5 in the duet No. 2, *Se a caso Madama*, when Figaro and Susanna were discussing their employer's nocturnal requirements of them. But the second phrase of Ex. 80, by its contour, harks back to Susanna's exit from the cupboard after Ex. 31. These are not quotations but something more than

80

'World of Figaro' family relations. The music of Ex. 80, its melodic character and rhythm, the Alberti accompaniment for second violins, is about Figaro and Susanna: it has no relevance to the characters in the centre of the stage, who are the Count and Countess Almaviva. He does believe her to be Susanna, but he does not talk down to the chambermaids he tries to seduce; a Spanish grandee is not Baron Ochs. We have heard Almaviva lead the real Susanna on, in No. 16, the music of which (though also involving bassoon doubling first violin) is quite different in character. Possibly Mozart was thinking that the real Susanna and Figaro are both eavesdropping in the darkness; òr he was still reflecting on that resounding smack in the face. The puzzle of Ex. 80 remains even though its melody does not literally return (it stays in the memory, though). More important to this scene is the three-note figure at the end of that example: almost at once it becomes a true Figaro theme. The Countess, adopting for the first time a persuasive Susanna voice (she had no need nor desire with Cherubino), has expressed her compliance with Almaviva's wishes. Flutes have just rejoined the orchestra. Compliant woman she certainly is, Figaro mutters from behind the bushes.

81

I let the example run on so as to show Almaviva courting in his own musical voice, unlike Ex. 80. Ex. 81's first theme dominates the rest of this scene since it is also apt to the scorn expressed by Susanna and the Countess at their lord's gullibility. Sometimes it recurs as the thematic germ of Ex. 77, to inaugurate new melodies. The scene continues as a vocal quartet, each voice in a different situation, united by fluent melody that seems to change colour and shape all the time. Something of the music's inventive resourcefulness may be seen if I quote the melodic line alone for several bars, with words where appropriate.

82

Towards the end of Ex. 81 Almaviva was presenting his dearest with a diamond ring and her promised dowry in token of his gratitude for services about to be rendered. What useful evidence for the Countess, though aloud she only murmurs Susanna's thanks. E minor at the end of Ex. 81 has now led to C major. The fake Susanna tells Almaviva (ruefully in A minor) she can see torches coming towards them. He finds this a good moment to draw her, his lovely Venus, into the empty pavilion (lucky he didn't choose the other one). The germ of Ex. 81 is fermenting potently. Susanna and the Countess both observe that their victims are now trapped, the two of them, since Figaro too reckons that, with such damning evidence, he can show himself. He comes out from the shadows, to a torrent of Ex. 81. Almaviva disguises his voice and calls, 'Who goes there?' 'People,' answers Figaro gruffly. The Countess, recognizing his voice, feigns fear and turns into the right-hand pavilion. The Count, preferring to bide his moment until the crowd disperses, lets her go and walks into the woods. The orchestra executes three turns with Ex. 81 (similar to the 'double lock' effect described on p. 401—another example is still to be heard)—perhaps one each for the Countess, the Count and Figaro, and finishes *larghetto* in E flat major. Clarinets return to complete the woodwind section—no, the oboes now have a rest until the next scene.

Figaro supposes himself alone: again the music sounds curiously inapposite, more like the Countess than the jovial barber, but most like a lover's serenade with melting woodwind and lulling strings. Figaro has turned philosophical. Almaviva drew his seducee towards the pavilion addressing her as Venus. Figaro knows his classical mythology★ (he gave us a taste in *Non più andrai*) and remembers what Vulcan did when he found his wife Venus in bed with Mars: he strung them up naked in a net which he had built to entrap them, and then called all the gods to see them. Figaro as *nuovo Vulcan del secolo* will fetch his fellow-conspirators to catch Susanna–Venus *en tête*, i.e. in the Pavilion, with *vago Marte*—Almaviva.† The slowly uplifted horn duet is doubly appropriate.

The real Susanna, dressed as her mistress, is concealed within earshot. She has no wish for Figaro to compromise her dear mistress, nor for him to make a public exhibition of himself, so she imitates the Countess's voice and tells him to keep quiet—*allegro molto*. There are two useful themes here, both short so I quote them together.

83*a*

The first of these represents urgency, the second determination (or it might be the conspirators and the Count). Figaro is taken in by Susanna's impersonation and tells her, as Countess, that she has arrived in time to catch his wife and her

★ Da Ponte's Figaro, that is: they both learned it from the priests who educated them. Beaumarchais's Figaro says nothing about mythological doings.

† The rest of the Vulcan story is less pleasant for Figaro to remember. After the exhibition of the adulterous lovers Venus left Vulcan and took up with other gods.

husband *in flagrante delicto*. She answers that she will stay here and be revenged; but Susanna forgets to alter her voice. Figaro recognizes her at once but decides to play her game for a little. He adopts grotesque attitudes of gallant courtship and, addressing her as 'Madama', pretends to woo her ardently. Notice the prominent horns, and Figaro's extravagant vocal line.

84

Susanna, for once taken in, longs to belabour this faithless fellow. Does he, then, love her? I respect you, is the answer, and I do not want to waste time. Give me your hand (Ex. 84 returns). She certainly does, on his face, not once but many times, and Ex. 83 is made to serve her fury. Figaro can bear blows good-humouredly: he continues, with sarcastic expression, to hymn his aggressor to the tune of Ex 84. They complete this exhibition of sado-masochism with Ex. 83b.

The tempo changes to *andante*, the key drops directly to B flat major. Figaro asks Susanna to calm down: he has recognized her voice from the beginning.

85

Susanna is much surprised: Milady got away with her mimicry, why not Susanna? The answer is in the music of Ex. 85 which they sing blissfully together until the Count is heard looking for Susanna to the same tune. Real Susanna is delighted: this means he never recognized his wife in Susanna's clothes. It is news to Figaro: he did not identify either. Susanna is concerned, however, for the Countess. She sees that the Count is about to enter the right-hand pavilion. So she tells Figaro to sidetrack this 'bizarre lover'. Figaro falls on one knee and, in a new context, pretends to woo the Countess as a nobleman might, though with absurd bassoon accompaniment.

86

The Count notices promptly and curses himself for walking abroad unarmed. The supposed Countess is as eager as the supposed Susanna was with Almaviva a few minutes ago. The Count explodes with fury and noisy string scales. Figaro and his lady agree, loudly in duet to Ex. 85, that they will be off and console one another for their sorrows (beautiful woodwind colours double the duet here).

They get to the left-hand, populous pavilion. The real Susanna scampers inside. Figaro is restrained by the Count, *allegro assai* in G major (oboes back, clarinets resting) who hollers for his staff. They come running—Figaro has posted them for something like this moment: Bartolo, Antonio, Basilio, Don Curzio and a posse of footmen with flambeaux (Mozart knew some roles would be doubled, so he composed vocal lines for Basilio and Antonio,★ not Bartolo and Curzio—we can still fetch these on as well and let them double up where desirable).

Figaro pretends terror—but not the music which remains formal and imperious. The Count declares that this culprit has deceived him with a person whom he will now show them. Figaro is overjoyed: he is the only person present who knows exactly how many people, and which, are in that pavilion. Where angels might fear to tread Count Almaviva plunges in, crying that Madama will receive her reward for virtue. It is not Madama. It is in turn Cherubino, then Barbarina, then Marcellina, finally a lady dressed in the Countess's clothes, holding a kerchief over her face (a veil would not have been inappropriate for this adventure—we may suppose the Countess possessed something of the kind). The Count has caught her. She begs forgiveness, in vain. All the onlookers ask him to pardon her. He is adamant.

87

No!   no,   no,   no,   no,   no!

The orchestra follows him with equal firmness, though the upper strings are *tremolando* for her sake. Did Mozart intend that 'No, no' should be sung to a *nono dominante*? He meant the Count to finish not on the root but on the inconclusive seventh. All is not over. A new character, dressed in Susanna's gown but clearly recognizable as Countess Almaviva,† has entered from the other pavilion—where the Count assumed his desirable Susanna was waiting to gratify him—and now steps into the centre asking the Count to grant her plea for the pardon he refuses to others.

The violins skitter helplessly on behalf of Basilio, Antonio and the Count who alone have voices to greet the generally dumbfounding arrival of the *dea ex machina* (for that is her function at this instant).

There is a long moment of silence and immobility, long enough for everybody, down to the newest scullion and gardener's boy, to draw in their breath for amazement when, still in silence, Count Almaviva, *Gran Corregidor de Andalucia*, falls on his knees before his wife, his chattel in the eyes of church and state, before all his servants, and begs her pardon.

★ Now sober, according to Beaumarchais.

† Romantic tradition, still prevalent, is quite wrong to bring the Countess back in a new, still more sumptuous gown. The last four scenes required her to be in the other pavilion, therefore still wearing Susanna's clothes. The apparel, in this case (as so often), does not proclaim the man or lady.

88

Con—tes-sa per-do -no! per—do - no! per-do—no!

He expresses himself in music quite lacking the master's usual formality. They are phrases such as we have only heard him use by himself or when making up to Susanna (real or disguised). Da Ponte forgot to mention that the Countess identifies herself by holding out the diamond ring which he gave her; but no Countess worth her salt will forget to do so. Nor will she forget to give the purse to Susanna—though she might retain the ring as a talisman, with Susanna's connivance.

Almaviva ended his plea with pauses, therefore expressive flourishes, over the last two notes. The Countess does not need to show ostentation. She has won, in the presence of all Aguasfrescas, and she can pardon him with simplicity and natural, undemonstrative grace.

89

Più do –ci—le io so—no, e di—co di sì, e di————co di sì.

As she ceases the violins catch the melodic line and lead it aloft to a divine benediction on this happy outcome which the entire company, surely including those poor, otherwise dumb, footmen, expresses in a repeat of Ex. 89 to general declaration of relief and delight. They sustain this moment of solemn, rapturous joy as long as possible (for they really love the Countess, their benefactress, and the Count too, up to a point—he provides the wages). Then in G major they cease and the orchestra modulates, by another, beautiful double lock mechanism, starry like the sky above, to the dominant of D major in which they all announce their intention of celebrating with all the festivity that has been promised to them. It is an active, eventful chorus (clarinets, trumpets and drums are added to the orchestra), and the ideas are as varied as the textures. One does not require to examine them in detail. They are gift-wrapping. We have already examined the present inside and only need to wrap it up again so as to reveal it afresh tomorrow, next week, for ever if possible.

17

Le nozze di Figaro needs from me no further hyperbolistic propaganda. It is inexhaustible, long and highly detailed, yet compact and (save for a moment in Act IV which can gladly be forgiven if Marcellina and Basilio are superior artists) as well balanced as a symphony. Its significance is protean, susceptible of numerous convincing interpretations. It is a merciless satire on the unenlightened *ancien régime*, yet it has remained topical ever since, in many different societies; a timeless comic masterpiece—always timely, unusually serious by intention, and by no means demonstrably superior to *Don Giovanni* and *Così fan tutte* where Mozart's masterpieces are concerned. Gerald Abraham summarized the contents as 'the re-education of Count Almaviva': that is inferably unconvincing and essentially irrelevant. Does anyone suppose that the randy lordling (who has admitted that after three years' marriage 'hymen becomes so respectable') will instantly turn into a model husband the moment his wife obliges him to apologize in public?

Brigid Brophy, in a book both thought-provoking and infuriating, describes Mozart's Aguasfrescas as 'an enchanted world'. She means that Mozart's music has bestowed enchantment on the *datum* of Beaumarchais's comedy; at first reading one's reaction may be that the 'world-in-itself' of Aguasfrescas (her description) could better be described as bedevilled, or bewitched, *The Nightmares of a Day* rather than *The Follies of a Day*.

Figaro is full of charm and wit (less than in Beaumarchais, however) and the situations are designedly amusing; the music is glorious, both inventive and mature (Mozart died young, we say, but he had been at the height of his, or any composer's, powers for several years). But the total effect of the opera, for a serious spectator-listener, is disturbing and unsettling. *Le nozze di Figaro* is not just about comic tussles between master and servant, or between men and women, but about the interplay of real human beings. If you can imagine a classless eighteenth century, da Ponte could have turned Beaumarchais's plot into an *opera seria* with contrasted solo arias for every character, such varied emotions do the main characters display. But they are moved through dynamic confrontation which alters feelings all the time and is most effectively communicated in vocal ensembles. By 1785 these were well established in *opera buffa* as was the possibility of letting serious and comic roles develop the plot together. What was not conventional was to let the comic characters appear as serious as the nobles, or to give the aristocrats plebeian music, as Mozart does in *Figaro* even though his musical styles were normally differentiated with unsleeping punctilio and sensibility. The importance of the opera is in its richness of character and situation, and the cogency with which text and music endow them. Almaviva is shown throughout as the victim of unthinking emotional responses which continually let him down (for all his fine music) in face of opposition from his servants who are helping his wife to rediscover some personal self-confidence if not marital contentment, and helping to better their own personal and working lives. Their machinations are for the general good, however temporary, not for the re-education of their employer; he is beyond permanent redemption. A more introspective Austrian Emperor would have found Mozart's Almaviva as unflattering as Beaumarchais's. Joseph II would have rejected da Ponte's libretto out of hand if Figaro had visibly triumphed over his master. It was possible to accept an opera in which the day is won by the grand lady through the clever scheming of her personal maid. For a male Emperor the idea was piquant, and absurd, but in such an opera Susanna was clearly the heroine, as she still is for an audience unswayed by sentimentality for a lovely Rosina. Figaro had to be made politically ineffective, however determined, a less astute clown than the barber created by Beaumarchais. The reality of *Le nozze* was hidden from a society which did not believe in real-life female heroines. But note that Susanna was the principal role in Mozart's *Figaro*, even before the French Revolution.

The exceptional seriousness of Mozart's *Figaro* music was commented on by Stendhal* in 1814, after the French Revolution, but before Mozart became a

_____
* *Lettre sur Mozart*: Monticello, le 29 août 1814.

cult. Stendhal adored Mozart and loved *Le nozze*, particularly the 'novel portrayal' of the Countess in her two arias and, in the ensembles, the grander stature of Mozart's Dr Bartolo. He observed that: '. . . the musician, by his sensibility, has turned into real passions the lightsome whims (*goûts*) which, in Beaumarchais, amuse the likeable inhabitants of Aguasfrescas Castle. There Count Almaviva desires Susanna, nothing more, and is far removed from the passion exhaled in the aria *Vedrò mentr'io sospiro* and in the duet *Crudel! perchè finora*.' He found Figaro's jealousy in the No. 2 duet and in *Se vuol ballare* too serious, lacking the French Figaro's lightness. Conversely he disliked the common streak in the melody of *Non più andrai* (did he not recognize that Figaro *is* a common person—that it is part of his appeal?). Stendhal concluded that 'Mozart has disfigured the piece as much as he could,' adding that 'as a masterpiece of pure tenderness and melancholy, absolutely exempt from any sudden blend of majesty or tragedy, nothing in the world can compare with *Le nozze di Figaro*'. Stendhal wrote much about music, very readably. He was no musician but because of that his independent, lively musical taste was unclouded by the established artistic fashions and prejudices of his age; his verdicts sometimes surprise or disgust a modern reader but he was a perceptive judge of Mozart, and it is interesting that he seized on the seriousness of Mozart's treatment, the real human passions breathed into Beaumarchais's characters. Mozart's characters do not think like Beaumarchais's, though da Ponte made them speak in almost direct translation from the French. It is not French music, nor yet true Italian *opera buffa* (compare any major number with an equivalent in, say, Cimarosa's *Il matrimonio segreto*), and yet it is not heavy German *Singspiel* either. Its emotional realism (not the same as sincerity) and instinctive neatness of structural proportions are hallmarks of Viennese classicism.

Da Ponte commented, in his Preface, on the length of the opera: this, and the unusual detail compacted within that length, have made the foregoing chapter much longer than I imagined before I began to write about *Figaro*. Almost all of the critical summary about style and character that, in other chapters, would find its place in this last section has already been placed where it is most relevant and, to me, illuminating—in a specific dramatic context. The final scene of Mozart's Act IV gives the impression that Countess Rosina is the heroine of the opera, as she is the *dea ex machina*; Mozart is to blame, for giving her two sublimely lovely phrases at a climactic moment. But earlier she has behaved regularly like a none too bright doll with a lovely voice and features to match. She did suggest that Susanna should write the *canzonetta sull'aria* (and Susanna was initially cautious about the wisdom of this); but elsewhere it is always Susanna who takes the initiative, not only with her mistress but with Figaro, the Count, Cherubino, and Marcellina.

Susanna is a match for them and for Basilio, probably Antonio as well. And, while we applaud the noble soul of Countess Rosina in 'Più docile sono', we may think back and realize that all the delectable and nervous intrigue of Act IV, leading to this grand public reconciliation, has been scripted, stage-managed, and invigilated by Susanna who now stands in the shadows but was on parade throughout, ever since the end of *Aprite un pò*. Susanna will not feel envious: she radiates love and loyalty, especially for Figaro and her mistress who, in terms of classical

proportion, balance her place in the drama, just as the Count is her chief interlocutor in the execution of her plans. She may appear indeed to balance all the
other characters, so much of this opera does she spend on stage; and she sings in
every ensemble number. I have tried in the foregoing pages to argue that Mozart
portrayed Susanna (perhaps for Nancy Storace's benefit) as the down-to-earth,
unidealized yet *nonpareil* heroine of the opera. In classical terms she is the weighing-
scales of the piece. Any production of *Le nozze di Figaro* has to cast Susanna first
and then choose the rest of the company to match her. She is not the mincing,
flouncing, self-fancying, cooing, moueing, pseudo-sophisticated café-waitress type
that does Despina very pleasantly and is therefore typecast for Zerlina and Blondchen, even Pamina sometimes, as well as Susanna. She is the most intelligent,
though self-educated, and probably the most admirable heroine Mozart created,
though credit is also due to Beaumarchais and da Ponte. It is also a part that
requires exceptional concentration by the singer: of all the roles that Elisabeth
Schumann sang, Susanna was the only one which she felt obliged to go through
before any performance.

The nice balance of *Le nozze di Figaro* may be forgotten in the length and
eventfulness of it all. Commentators regularly draw attention to its scrupulous
key-structure; much the same may be found in earlier, less celebrated operas by
Mozart, which also contain weird lapses from grace that crop up once or twice in
Figaro. The practised listener who knows *Figaro* well can aver that it is a beautifully poised large dramatic structure without making a detailed analysis. Anybody
who does attempt part of such an analysis will discover proof for this instinctive
recognition. In this chapter I have listed keys and tempi and scoring: the reader
can make a table to show how they connect and reflect and create an organic equi-
poise. The cast list shows how each character has an opposite number. Many
similar examinations in balance can be undertaken. As one example, *pour encourager
des autres*, I offer the following, concerned with the balance of musical numbers in
Le nozze di Figaro.

Overture	MATCHED BY	No. 28	Finale from bar 472
Nos. 1 and 2		No. 28	Action duets, part serious
No. 3		No. 26	Figaro in militant action
No. 4		No. 17	Male vengeance aria
No. 5		No. 14	Comic female duets
No. 6		No. 11	Same singer, same contents
No. 7		No. 13	Trios about concealment
No. 8		No. 21/22	Choruses about *droit de seigneur*
No. 9		No. 22	Marches
No. 10		No. 19	Countess Almaviva *sola*
No. 11		No. 6	See above
No. 12		No. 27	Susanna, contrasted aspects
No. 13		No. 7	See above
No. 14		No. 5	See above
No. 15		No. 28	Concerted finales (many indi-vidual reflections within, e.g. *Voi signor* and No. 18)

443

No. 16	MATCHED BY	No. 28	Almaviva love duets
No. 17		See above	
No. 18		See above	
No. 19		See above	
No. 20		No. 23	Garden music in 6/8
No. 21		See above	
No. 22		See above	
No. 23		See above	
No. 24		No. 25	Absurd imagery; minuets
Nos. 25–8		See above	

It had generally been assumed that *opera buffa* as an entertainment was more humorous if unstrictly constructed and that seriously felt music detracted from entertainment value. *Le nozze di Figaro* staked everything on a realistic therefore partly serious point of view. Mozart followed its achievement up in his later comic operas. It would be wrong to over-praise them romantically for what they are not. A new age, removed from earlier artistic fashions yet able to appreciate every one of them historically and seek aesthetic communication between them and us, can apply modern analysis and historical learning equally to *Figaro* so as to make the experience of Mozart–da Ponte–Beaumarchais infinitely more enlightening and inexhaustible. I have repeated the cant judgment that *Le nozze di Figaro* is inexhaustible. It is too. Even a poor performance may include a moment of first enlightenment about some small but vital point. The music may be appallingly played and sung, but somewhere a phrase will suddenly make perfect sense for the first time. It is not the greatest anything. It is *Le nozze di Figaro*.

19 DON GIOVANNI

Il dissoluto Punito
ossia

IL DON GIOVANNI

Dramma giocoso★ in two acts

Text by
LORENZO DA PONTE

K. 527

DON GIOVANNI, an extremely licentious young cavalier	BARITONE
DONNA ANNA, lady promised in marriage to:	SOPRANO
DON OTTAVIO	TENOR
COMMENDATORE, father of Donna Anna	BASS
DONNA ELVIRA, lady from Burgos, abandoned by Don Giovanni	SOPRANO
LEPORELLO, servant of Don Giovanni	BASS
MASETTO, lover of:	BASS
ZERLINA, country girl	SOPRANO
Country folk	CHORUS
Musicians	

Scene: a Spanish city [Seville]

★ Mozart entered it in his private catalogue as Opera buffa.

I

Mozart and his wife left Prague on or about 8 February 1787 to return to Vienna. He took home with him Pasquale Bondini's commission for a new opera to be composed expressly for that company and performed during the forthcoming season. The librettist would obviously have to be Lorenzo da Ponte again, after the excellent achievement of *Le nozze di Figaro*. But da Ponte was already busy. He had been commissioned officially to provide Vicente Martín y Soler with the libretto of an opera to celebrate the forthcoming marriage of the Emperor's niece, Archduchess Maria Theresia, with Prince Anton Clemens of Saxony (later Emperor Franz II). Da Ponte decided to write an original scenario for this occasion: he claims that he elaborated *L'arbore di Diana*, an allegory relevant to Joseph II's suppression of the monasteries, in half an hour when the composer visited and importuned him for a subject—da Ponte regarded this as the finest of all his libretti. *L'arbore di Diana* had its première in Vienna on 1 October 1787. Then Salieri forgot his old vow (see *Nozze di Figaro*, p. 368) never to set a word by da Ponte again and asked him to convert his French opera *Tarare* (another Beaumarchais libretto, this time written expressly for music) into an Italian opera. Now came Mozart with news of the Prague commission, an *opera buffa* which should build on the success of *Figaro* but not tax the strength of Bondini's company, three female and four male principals (though they required two extras for *Figaro*).

As Court Poet da Ponte was obliged to tell the Emperor his plans. Joseph II advised him against attempting three libretti at once, but the poet, who had decided to adapt an existing libretto on the Don Juan story for Mozart, insisted on trying: 'I shall write in the evenings for Mozart, imagining that I am reading the *Inferno*; mornings I shall work for Martín and pretend I am studying Petrarch; my afternoons will be for Salieri—he is my Tasso!' Da Ponte goes on to recall how he worked twelve hours a day every day, with a few interruptions, for two months on end. After sixty-three days *Don Giovanni* and *L'arbore di Diana* were complete, and two-thirds of *Tarare*, now renamed *Assur*. Da Ponte was fond of telling tall stories: this one becomes slightly more credible if we realize that his afternoons were spent translating French into Italian, his evenings in paraphrasing an existing Italian libretto (though he had some additions of his own to make, as will be seen later); it was only in the morning that he had to invent completely for himself. Credibility is somewhat strained by da Ponte's assertion that Salieri had produced *Tarare* in Paris before commissioning the Italian version. For *Tarare* had its first performance on 8 June 1787, and before that Salieri was staying with Beaumarchais in Paris, writing the music. Da Ponte cannot have performed his celebrated conjuring trick after that date: it would have left too little time for Mozart and Martín to write their music. It is possible that Salieri sent da Ponte a copy of Beaumarchais's libretto from Paris, but somewhat more likely that the other two libretti were in an advanced state before *Tarare* reached him. The story comes down to size if we accept that da Ponte began adapting *Tarare* while Mozart and Martín were still requiring additions and alterations to the libretti that they were already setting to music against a September deadline. *Assur, rè d'Ormuz* had its Vienna première on 8 January 1788.

2

The first performance of Mozart's *Don Giovanni* was planned for the entertainment of the royal newly-weds during their stay in Prague on 14 October 1787. Mozart would be expected to send some of his score in advance for previous study, especially since he was acquainted, through the Prague *Figaro*, with some of the singers involved in the new opera. He would plan, if he did at all, on more or less finishing his composition by early September. Hermann Abert guessed that da Ponte gave him the libretto in June; Ernest Newman supposed that Mozart wrote his music between May and August—such of it as could be composed before his arrival in Prague. Christof Bitter* argues that Mozart's practice was to compose the music as fast as the poet could deliver the text, having surveyed the scenario and envisaged the total shape and the place of each musical number; therefore Mozart must have begun thinking about the music as early as March. This is a natural assumption. When Mozart returned to Vienna, about 12 February, he had no official position or duties, and little other work to do: a few appearances as pianist at concerts (Nancy Storace gave her farewell concert at the Kärntnertor Theatre on 23 February and may have included the first performance of a glorious concert aria *Ch'io mi scordi di te* which Mozart had written for her, with him as *obbligato* pianist and orchestral accompaniment, on 27 December 1786); a few pupils—Ludwig van Beethoven, aged seventeen, came to Vienna in April for three weeks, to study with Mozart. The surviving letters of the Mozart family tell us nothing about work on *Don Giovanni*; but the catalogue of completed compositions may offer a hint or two.

After arriving home Mozart wrote no music until 11 March when he entered the sublime A minor rondo for piano solo, perhaps a written-down version of something he improvised during his stay in Prague (it is one of his 'lonely' A minor pieces, see p. 23), in which case it would not take long to set on paper. Later in March he completed two concert arias: *Alcandro lo confesso* for Ludwig Fischer (see *Entführung*, p. 293), who gave a concert on a fleeting stay in Vienna and wanted to display his command of the Italian style; and *Mentre ti lascio*, a present for Mozart's friend Gottfried von Jacquin. Then creative silence until Mozart inscribed the great C major string quintet on 19 April. This will have taken some days to compose. Mozart could have been shaping *Don Giovanni* with da Ponte in late March and early April, as Bitter suggests. Da Ponte tells how, after the first evening's work, he gave Mozart the first two scenes of *Don Giovanni* (i.e. up to the first entrance of Don Ottavio). One can romantically imagine Mozart rushing to the desk to set them instantly; but he worked music out in his head before he wrote it down, and he was a great procrastinator, his father says, when getting to grips with music where manuscript paper was concerned.

Five days after the C major quintet was finished, the Mozarts moved house to

* *Wandlungen in den Inszenierungsformen des 'Don Giovanni' von 1787 bis 1928* (Gustav Bosse Verlag, Regensburg, 1961), p. 24—a splendidly informative volume.

a cheaper, quieter dwelling on the outskirts of the city, now the Landstrasser Hauptstrasse and very urban, though the apartments behind the huge shopfronts give an idea of the peaceful surroundings in which Mozart worked during this year (the actual dwelling was subsequently pulled down and was where No. 75 now stands). By 16 May Mozart had completed another string quintet in G minor, the most famous of all; he was preparing a set of three for sale to amateur chamber musicians—the third was a transcription of the C minor serenade for wind instruments (K.384a). Mozart had been unwell at the time of the house-moving; I do not suppose that he worked much at *Don Giovanni* during the gap between 28 April and 16 May.

In the latter weeks of May he completed four songs, and two more in June. They are some of his very best: *Die Alte, Lied der Trennung, Als Luise die Briefe ihres ungetreuen Liebhabers verbrannte* (an Elvira-esque song), *Abendempfindung*, which gives a foretaste of the Schubertian Lied. I suggest that this sudden corpus of songs represents Mozart limbering up for solid work on *Don Giovanni*; two of them, *Die Alte* and *Als Luise . . .* are almost operatic in nature. On 29 May Mozart finished the fine C major piano duet sonata, K.521, particularly enjoyable for its rondo finale which, fancifully, recalls Zerlina's *Vedrai carino*. I guess that Mozart had by 17 May read da Ponte's finished libretto for *Don Giovanni* and sent it back with a list of alterations required; while waiting for results he wrote the compositions just named.

There is now a further gap until 14 June. But on 28 May Leopold Mozart died and was buried the same day. The news will have reached his son, through a family friend Franz d'Yppold, the Court Minister of War, resident in Salzburg, a couple of days later (he wrote back to Yppold on 2 June). Romantics and psychoanalytics may believe that Mozart found therapy for sorrow in his work on *Don Giovanni*; on the other hand he may just not have felt like writing music at such a time, especially as his pet starling (which sang the rondo theme of K.453, the G major piano concerto) died on 4 June and was commemorated by a quite long and touching memorial poem written by Mozart that day. By 14 June he had snapped out of depression by composing *Ein musikalischer Spass*, 'A musical joke', which is a violently ludicrous parody of a serenade incompetently composed and executed, explicable (to me at least) only in the context of Mozart's bereavement. Some, including Alfred Einstein, have held that Mozart repented of this painful joke by quickly composing another truly masterly serenade, *Eine kleine Nachtmusik*, completed on 10 August, always one of his most popular and admired works. Its key and contents suggest that he may have been at work on the finale of Act I of the opera. Might he have devised the two serenades, comic and serious, for an unofficial party in Vienna in mid-August? Shortly after this he wrote one of his very finest violin sonatas, K. 526 in A major, inscribed in his catalogue on 24 August. He completed no works thereafter until *Don Giovanni* was entered on 28 October.

Mozart had to make some arrangements for the disposal of his father's effects during September, though he is not known to have travelled to Salzburg at all during 1787 and could rely on family friends. He may have sent part of *Don Giovanni* to Prague; when he got there he complained to Jacquin, in a letter, that 'few arrangements had been made in advance' (*so wenige Vorkehrungen und Anstalten*) and that the singers were lazy and poor learners. But he left quite a bit to compose on the spot: the duet with chorus, *Giovinette che fate*, because he did not know what sort of chorus would be available; similarly the demons' chorus in the second act finale. He seems not to have known Giuseppe Lolli, who doubled Commendatore and Masetto, since he left Masetto's *Ho capito* and the Statue's supper appearance until Prague. There he also placated Luigi Bassi, who complained that the title role included no major aria, with *Deh vieni alla finestra*. Gossip relates that Bassi made Mozart rewrite one number five times before the singer was content: gossip says this was *Là ci darem*, but Mozart had already written it in Vienna (so the paper attests) and he never allowed singers to interfere with the music of an ensemble, so the story, if true, can only refer to Don Giovanni's serenade No. 16, or to No. 17, *Metà di voi*. Mozart left the entire finale of Act II to be written down in Prague, and he also there converted the recitative which began Act II into the duet, *Eh via buffone*; it is a pity he did not do likewise with the opening of Act III in *Figaro*. Of course he also left the overture until last, as was his practice. If it is true, as Bitter★ claims, that Antonio Baglioni was the only singer in the *Don Giovanni* cast unknown to Mozart (he had been in Venice singing Don Ottavio in Gazzaniga's *Don Giovanni*) it is curious that Mozart composed *Il mio tesoro* in Vienna, but left much of Lolli's music for composition in Prague. I surmise that Mozart had met Baglioni on some other occasion unrecorded—he knew at least one other Baglioni (see *La finta semplice*, p. 38).

The foregoing pages are full of supposition. I apologize. Facts about the genesis of *Don Giovanni* are sparse, legends numerous but untrustworthy. Anybody interested in the work must be constrained to look further for hints between the lines of the unassailable facts. I have hazarded some deductions along such lines though they are only suppositions except where I have used the factual past tense.

At some time before October a libretto of *Don Giovanni* was printed in Vienna, surely for the scrutiny of the imperial censor. The opera was to be given in honour of the royal nuptials. Don Juan was at any time a subject liable to cause offence to nice minds—in Munich it was turned down by the censor who was nevertheless overruled by the Elector. Da Ponte submitted his libretto but without the latter part of the first act which ended abruptly with the quartet No. 8. It is conceivable that da Ponte had not yet written the first act finale which called for his unaided invention, though *Eine kleine Nachtmusik* suggests otherwise as, for different reasons, do Giovanni's words 'Viva la libertà' at the entry of the maskers.

On 1 October Mozart and Constanze took the coach to Prague—this was the journey which Eduard Mörike later fictionalized, beautifully if unhistorically, in his novella *Mozart auf der Reise nach Prag*. They arrived in Prague on 4 October. Before relating the circumstances of the rehearsals for *Don Giovanni* I shall briefly recall the history of the Don Juan saga which Mozart had to put to music.

3

The figure of Don Juan, the well born, randy young man who subordinates all conventional etiquette to his personal pleasure, was not invented by Tirso de Molina. This sort of character may be found in the mythology of all ages, at first as a god (e.g. Zeus, Jupiter, Odin, but also Pan), then as a more or less atheistic

★ Op. cit., p. 13.

man (though a band of heretics grew up in Holland, around 1625, who preached that nothing, of itself, is sinful). Icelandic saga tells of a licentious hero who appalled everyone by his amorous exploits. Spain in the sixteenth century claimed the credit for the creation of this modern libertine, significantly a country where family honour and female virginity were protected hardly less stringently than the cult of the Virgin and the Crucifixion. The wife was raised on a pedestal, says Marañón, the bedroom was a monastic chamber, marriages were arranged by parents, and matrimonial couples met only on the day of betrothal, in the presence of their assembled families. Young men sowed their wild oats in brothels; any girl who was not a prostitute was protected, as with a chastity belt, by family restrictions. So grew up the story of Don Juan, who defied these methods of protection and managed to pleasure hundreds of girls in his native Spain before he met divine condemnation and was plunged into hell. There was, it seems, a real-life seducer in Spain named the Conde de Villamedia who, in the sixteenth century, lechered a disreputable national reputation for himself. In 1630 a Spanish monk, Gabriel Téllez, published under the pseudonym Tirso de Molina a moralistic play on the subject, calling the reprobate Don Juan Tenorio, and entitling his drama *El burlador de Sevilla*, sometimes subtitled *Tan largo me lo fiáis* from Juan's catchphrase which may be translated 'Plenty of time for that!' The best English translation of 'burlador' is 'playboy'; Don Juan is something more than a mere philanderer, and it is for blasphemy of the dead that he is taken to hell.

Tirso had written *El burlador* long before 1630 (his dates were 1571–1648) and it had been often performed; the name part was associated with the actor, Roque de Figueras. Some drama of the kind, called *Il atheisto fulminato*, was known about 1600 to be performed in Italian churches for moral instruction. Tirso's play was supposed to take place at some time between 1312 and 1350. The situation, obviously, was Seville: part of the action is set in Dos Hermanas, a village just outside Seville on the Cadiz road. Music was included.

El burlador begins in Naples where Don Juan has successfully made love to Doña Isabela, he in the disguise of her fiancé Don Octavio. Juan is arrested as he leaves the house but released by his uncle, a court official, as is Octavio, but not Isabela! The scene changes to Tarragona where Juan and his servant Catalinón are cast ashore from a boat. They meet a peasant girl called Thisbe who is seduced by Juan and abandoned. (This will remind us of Mozart's Donna Elvira.) In the Alcázar at Seville the King rewards the martial exploits of Comendador Don Gonzago de Ulloa by betrothing the soldier's daughter Aña to Don Juan, whose parentage is immaculate. Aña is in love with the Marqués de la Mota. Juan inter-cepts a letter of assignation from her to Mota, borrows Mota's cloak, slips into the palace and adds her to his list. On the way out he is stopped by her father the Comendador whom he kills in a duel. Don Juan gives Mota his cloak back and escapes. Mota is arrested. The king erects a statue of Don Gonzago.

At Dos Hermanas Juan finds a peasant wedding party; he beats up the husband Batricio and seduces the wife Aminta. Now Isabela, arrived from Italy, meets Thisbe and both travel to Seville to narrate their wrongs. Don Juan finds Don Gonzago's statue in a church and invites it to supper. The meal takes place and Juan is obliged to return the invitation. The statue takes him to church, feeds him on scorpions, vipers, gall and vinegar and drags him, protesting that Aña is a virgin, down to hell. Catalinón observes all this and reports it to the king. The living parties agree to marry.

Several features of da Ponte's libretto are here already. The telescoping of Aña and Isabela was sensible and had been done before da Ponte set to work. The Marqués de la Mota was utterly dispensible; Thisbe more regrettably. The statue in Mozart is explained by *El burlador*.

The Don Juan story had taken hold in Italy quickly. In 1652 a *Confitato de petra* by Onofrio Giliberti was being played, and the extempore companies of *commedia dell'arte* regularly included this story, emphasis being given to the reprobate's servant Arlecchino, the statue who came to dinner, and the descent to hell. This was played in Paris, where *commedia dell'arte* was very popular in 1659, and found some French imitators. So in 1665 Molière clarified his ideas on the subject in his *Le festin de pierre*, a play in prose. Molière removed Donna Anna and Don Ottavio, but imported the character of Donna Elvira whom Don Juan had abducted from a convent, then abandoned. Her brothers pursue him for revenge, but she still loves him. Don Juan is a cold character, dominated by Spanish honour and French logic, full of epigrams. This play was unpopular in France but da Ponte knew it and borrowed some lines for his recitatives. Da Ponte's Zerlina is a blend of Molière's two country girls, Charlotte and Mathurine. His Masetto is called by Molière Pierrot, directly *commedia dell'arte*. Thomas Corneille and Thomas Shadwell both made popular adaptations of the story; John Fletcher's *The Wild Goose Chase* and George Farquhar's *The Inconstant* portray a lifelike hero; but the next version relevant to da Ponte is Goldoni's *Don Giovanni Tenorio* of 1736. This was designedly realistic and did without magic or status in motion; Don Juan is simply struck by lightning. The statue is erected, as a mark of honour, during the lifetime of the Commandant. Donna Anna clearly dislikes her arranged fiancé Don Ottavio and rather fancies Don Giovanni. The Elvira figure returns to the name of Isabella and pursues Don Juan, as Shadwell made her, in male disguise (interesting idea for Freudians who maintain that Don Juan is an over-compensated homosexual!). The Masetto character in this play is called Carino; did da Ponte intend to retain the name and fail to remove it from Zerlina's *Vedrai Carino*? In Goldoni we also find reference to the *padre e sposo* idea in da Ponte's Don Ottavio's No. 2.

The nearer history approaches 1787 the more versions of the Don Juan story accumulate, in Vienna as well as elsewhere. It was a familiar puppet-show, improvised with Hanswurst as chief comedian (he is usually translated into Jack Pudding, but English speakers know him as Punch), generally entitled *Das steinerne Gastmahl* ('Supper with the stone guest'). Gluck's ballet on the subject was given in 1781 and included features which Bertati borrowed, and after him da Ponte. In 1776 Righini composed a *Don Giovanni* which mixed serious and comic characters; it was first played in Prague, a year later in Vienna. It ended in D minor; Mozart could have heard of it.

Don Giovanni as a comic opera was new to nobody. But in February 1787 Giovanni Bertati, a hated rival of da Ponte (who described him as 'a frog blown up with wind'), produced in Venice his own *Don Giovanni*, set to music by Giuseppe Gazzaniga. It formed the one-act second part of an opera, *L'impresario in angustie*, nothing like *Der Schauspieldirektor* by Mozart, though dealing again with an opera manager's troubles. It had first been presented in 1775, where the second half was

L'italiana in Parigi. A libretto, which has *Don Giovanni Tenorio ossia il convitato di pietra* as its second part, is in the Bibliothèque nationale, handwritten dated 1787. Scholars assume that this was da Ponte's source.

Bertati's *Don Giovanni*, in one act, began with Pasquariello, then Giovanni and Anna, closely followed by the Commendatore, who is slain. Next comes Elvira (all this as in da Ponte), after her Ximena, then Biagio and Maturina. Giovanni seduces Ximena and Maturina (Biagio is beaten up). Elvira causes trouble for Giovanni, first with Ximena, then Maturina; all three have been promised marriage; each expects to be preferred. The scene switches to the cemetery where Ottavio is supervising the inscription on the statue. Then the invitation to supper, the meal including a concert, Pasquariello's secret feast, and Elvira's plea for reform, but also a song of praise for Venice. The statue arrives and removes Giovanni to hell. Afterwards the remaining characters sing an ensemble mimicking orchestral instruments; Mozart would not quickly have adopted this as a finale. Donna Anna doubled Maturina in this opera.

It will be recognized that da Ponte had some solid foundation for a *Don Giovanni* libretto at a time when he was already busy with *L'arbore di Diana* (if not already *Tarare*). He removed Donna Ximena and Giovanni's cook. And from Zerlina's seduction (an aria in Bertati, replaced by the gorgeous Mozart duet) to the cemetery scene da Ponte had to invent anew. He did; it is obvious padding but full of vitality, and it inspired Mozart so that none of us will object—in 1794, da Ponte revised Bertati's text for a London staging. Da Ponte's libretto for *Don Giovanni* has often been castigated for its incompetence. But if one compares it with the libretto of any other Italian comic (or serious) opera of the period, its poetic, dramatic, character-delineating virtues shine out like a laser-beam. Doubtless the demanding Mozart persisted until they did, but da Ponte responded obediently and like the brilliant creative artist which he had become. On his desk the Abbate had, for reference, Tirso de Molina, Molière, Goldoni and Bertati. He stole a little, but always repaid with more poetic language, here a new indication of character, there a new image, and in the middle of the opera line after line that could not but stimulate the creative imagination of a great composer.

Da Ponte reminisced that Mozart wanted to make *Don Giovanni* a serious opera, and da Ponte prevailed upon him to make it a comedy. He wrote his memoirs when Mozart was dead and sanctified, and when taste had become romantic. This, of all his recollections, makes good sense. Not that Mozart was inclined to write hysterical, personally inspired music. A composer is an actor: Mozart composed the A minor rondo and G minor string quintet in character, not his but the music's. He is as likely to have composed *Ein musikalischer Spass* after the deaths of his father and his pet starling as the trio *Ah soccorso*. This is why supposition, non-factual, can only deduce from keys and phrases, not from moods. We will best appreciate *Don Giovanni* if we suppose that da Ponte and Mozart wrote it as it came, sometimes very amusing, sometimes serious, but always about the characters, not about themselves. Of course they experimented with new forms and new methods of expansion. They were working for an immediate success, a job well done, performers well satisfied, and perhaps some performances elsewhere. They thought of posthumous fame not at all, probably regarded their work as ephemerally as today any journalist does. Mozart had the advantages of a super-brilliant inventive mind and a style exactly contemporary, even *avant-garde* ('too many notes', 'thick scoring', 'no meat for my Viennese', 'obsessed with elaboration'), yet endlessly fascinating and attractive, as well as masterly. We describe Mozart's musical contemporaries as 'rococo', but Mozart, like Haydn and later Beethoven and Schubert, as 'Viennese classical'. There is a difference between Dittersdorf's *Doktor und Apotheker* and Mozart's *Don Giovanni*. It is an abyss and the bridge across it is called classicism and exemplified by Mozart's work at this time.

4

Mozart and his wife arrived in Prague on 4 October 1787. At first they stayed at an inn: gossip relates that da Ponte lodged immediately across the road and could chat to Mozart, or discuss revisions to their opera, over the heads of passersby. Later the Mozarts stayed with their ex-Salzburg friends the Dušeks in the Villa Bertramka at Smichov, a suburb of Prague. The villa still stands and is sometimes used for public serenade concerts.

Ten days was regarded as a reasonable length of time for the study and production of a new opera. Mozart, experienced practical musician and man of the theatre, should have been aware how much time would be needed for rehearsal, and which parts of the score might create difficulties of learning for the performers. He had a quantity of music still to write, and he knew that da Ponte would be coming to Prague and could add to the libretto or make changes where necessary. Mozart had not been in Prague while *Figaro* was being prepared, so he did not know in advance just how slow the company were at learning new music. Nor had it occurred to him that, in such a small company, there were no alternative casts to perform another opera while *Don Giovanni* was rehearsed. The singers, all seven of them, had to take part in repertory performances on Monday, Wednesday and Friday evenings. On those days they, quite reasonably, refused to work all day as well. Coaching, stage rehearsals, and orchestral rehearsals were therefore restricted to Tuesday, Thursday and Saturday (perhaps Sunday in special circumstances—the première was planned for Sunday 14 October, and the postponed dress rehearsal took place on a Sunday too).

Mozart arrived on a Thursday and found himself with only five days, not ten, in which to prepare the première, i.e. on the 6th, 7th (if the company would oblige on a Sunday), 9th, 11th and 13th. For these last three he had the collaboration of da Ponte, who had been given a week's leave to see *Don Giovanni* on to the stage, and who arrived on Monday the 8th. It soon became clear that the new opera would not be ready in time for the royal couple on the 14th; they were bound to leave Prague on the following day to travel to Dresden for their official wedding on the 18th (the initial solemnization had taken place in Florence on 8 September with a proxy for the husband). Bondini proposed *Le nozze di Figaro* instead, conducted by the composer. One respectable and influential lady in Prague created a stir with her protests that *Figaro* was an altogether unsuitable opera for a royal wedding celebration: Bondini sent to Vienna for an Imperial recommendation. Joseph II, a decent friend to Mozart, returned word that if *Don Giovanni* was not ready, then *Figaro* must be performed.*

* All this and much else, paraphrased above or below, in Mozart's vivacious letter to Gottfried von Jacquin on 15 October 1787.

So *Figaro* it was, in a 'fully illuminated theatre'. The première of *Don Giovanni* was set back to the 24th, a Wednesday, which gave Mozart five extra rehearsals. The royal guests expressed their content but left early (was the Prince unwilling that his wife, who did not know the opera, should have to sit beside him and watch an aristocratic husband kneel to beg his wife's pardon in front of the servants?). Da Ponte had asked for extended leave but was sternly recalled to Vienna for further work on Salieri's *Assur*; he had to leave with the Royals, but travelling in the opposite direction. In his place there arrived in Prague da Ponte's old friend, and colleague in Don Juan's trade, Giuseppe Casanova, who had left Italy to live at Dux in Bohemia. Casanova's literary effects were found, after his death, to include some lines obviously written by him for the *Don Giovanni* sextet No. 19, though not printed in any authoritative text. We do not know whether he gave serious help to Mozart in the later stages of the opera's preparation: Mozart does not mention him in either of the extant Prague letters to Jacquin, though a third has been lost.

On 21 October it was decided further to defer the première of *Don Giovanni* because a singer, unspecified, was unwell. Mozart commented to Jacquin: 'Since the company is small, the impresario must always live in anxiety, and spare his people as much as possible, for fear that through some unexpected indisposition he will be put in that most critical of all situations where he cannot give any show at all.' Mozart thus gained two extra days' rehearsal before the final dress rehearsal on Sunday the 28th and the first performance on the 29th. It was not too much. The autograph manuscript, not quite complete in the library of the Paris Conservatoire, when compared with other contemporary copies, shows that Masetto's *Ho capito* was written down at a late stage. Mozart did not write down the overture to the opera until the night of 27–8 October, just in time to be copied before the dress rehearsal.

5

As always for Mozart the singers determined the nature of the music. We know a certain amount about the principals in the *Don Giovanni* original cast. Mozart had met, heard, and conducted some of them during his earlier visit to Prague to see *Figaro*. Three of these are known to have appeared in both operas.

Luigi Bassi had sung Count Almaviva and now took the name part in *Don Giovanni*. A contemporary engraving shows him singing a serenade, perhaps *Deh vieni alla finestra*—though he is not wearing Leporello's costume. He looks very tall and thin, beardless, not obviously a beefcake sex-symbol, though Beethoven later recalled Bassi as a 'fiery Italian' and Meissner as "very handsome and very stupid'. He was born at Pesaro in 1765 and was now only twenty-two, a credible age for the Don Juan of history and legend. He had studied with Norandini at Sinigaglia, and with Luisa Laschi's father (Mozart's intended Fracasso in *La finta semplice*) in Florence. Bassi joined Bondini's company in 1784 and became the acknowledged male star, euphonious of voice, handsome of person, but chiefly admired as the most accomplished actor there. He was thought 'masterly' in tragic parts, amusing but self-controlled in comedy. He was an excellent mimic, which perhaps encouraged Mozart to elaborate the scene in Act II where Giovanni and Leporello exchange cloaks. *Metà di voi* requires a Giovanni who can convincingly impersonate Leporello. Bassi was admired by audiences in Warsaw and Germany when Bondini took his company on tour there, and in Italy too on his own account. In 1795 his voice began to decline, at the age of only twenty-nine, but his skill kept him before the public. It was noted that his singing sounded 'hollow', but that his acting remained outstanding. He was still singing Mozart's Don Giovanni in 1814, though a year later he became a stage director at Dresden where he made some valuable comments about the supper scene in this opera. In 1787 he complained to Mozart that the leading male role was lacking in a substantial solo aria. Mozart had given him the brilliant *Fin ch'han dal vino*, and *Metà di voi*, and many excellent ensembles. Count Almaviva had been less generously served. But Mozart and da Ponte gratified him with an extra solo, the marvellous serenade, *Deh vieni alla finestra* which Mozart composed in Prague, and is supposed to have recast several times for Bassi's benefit.

The Leporello, Felice Ponziani, had been Mozart's Figaro in Prague. He had sung in Parma during 1784–5 and came to Prague in 1786. In 1792 he was singing in Venice. His voice was accounted even and ample but pleasing, not noisy. His enunciation of sung words was especially praised, and his ability in comedy. As a lover in serious parts he was rather a stiff actor; perhaps Mozart counted on this in the scenes where Leporello has to mime the part of Giovanni, Nos. 15 and 19, and their recitatives—a certain histrionic incompetence, if not exaggerated, makes the scene funnier.

The other listed singer in *Figaro* casts was Caterina Bondini, wife of the manager. She was the Susanna, here the Zerlina, and was accounted the *prima donna* of the company, a great popular favourite. Poems were written about her lovely singing and acting, and publicly distributed. Her position resembled those of Storace and Mombelli in Vienna; the first lady did not always have the loudest voice.

Mozart's first Donna Anna was Teresa Saporiti, born in 1763. She joined Bondini's company in 1782 when she was described as an unfinished singer and histrionic beginner, saved by her attractive appearance. Her elder sister Antonia, who (like Josepha Dušek) did not sing in opera, was thought musically her superior though she died quite young, just before the *Don Giovanni* première. Teresa, though not named in current playbills, must have sung Countess Almaviva in the Prague *Figaro*. Mozart wrote her music in Vienna which means he knew her vocal individuality already. Teresa Saporiti later sang in Venice, Parma and Bologna and died in Milan on 17 March 1869, aged 106. At the time of *Don Giovanni* she was a pretty young lady and sensitive singer.

Not much is known of Caterina Micelli, who sang Donna Elvira. Her voice was considered agile but not tonally pleasing. In 1793 she chiefly took soubrette roles. All her music in *Don Giovanni* was written in Vienna, so she must have been in the Prague *Figaro* cast. She might have sung Cherubino.

Giuseppe Lolli, who doubled Commendatore and Masetto, had most of his music written in Prague. In 1780–1 he sang in Parma and Venice. We may wonder if he sang Bartolo and Antonio in the Prague *Figaro*; but if so, why did Mozart leave *Ho capito* so late?

Antonio Baglioni was not among Bondini's company at the time of the Prague first *Figaro*. He was singing Don Ottavio in Gazzaniga's opera in Venice, and only joined Bondini's company during the summer. Mozart must have known him, though records are lacking, through his sister Clementine Baglioni for whom Mozart composed a role in *La finta semplice*. Later Antonio Baglioni was Mozart's first Titus at the Prague première in 1791. He had made an Italian reputation before this time and was admired for his purity of tone, persuasive expression and artistic refinement. Da Ponte remembered him as a singer of great taste and musicianship. Later his acting and singing were both admired. He sang in Venice in 1793–4 and in Vienna in 1796.

These were the singers for *Don Giovanni*. A small chorus was employed in three numbers. The orchestra was sparse in its string department: three first violins, four seconds, two each of violas, cellos and basses. The woodwind section were famous: Mozart made use of their skill in the second act supper scene—oboes, clarinets, bassoons, horns, an octet on stage, not the players in the pit before and after. Extra musicians were also required in the Act I finale. The stage production followed the standard practice of Bondini's company: excellent new scenery, fine new costumes, a carefully organized method of scene-changes whereby deep stage and shallow stage alternated so that no unduly long pauses occurred between scenes. Although the company was praised for realistic acting, the singers sang solos, and ensembles as well, directly to the audience, not to the character supposedly being addressed. Gossip says that Mozart persuaded Zerlina, in the Act I finale, to scream loudly by pinching her bottom at the required moment. Perhaps. He is also said to have made up to all three leading ladies: perhaps not, with his wife on the premises. Mozart was a nice ladies' man but not a Don Juan.

So *Don Giovanni* was given its first performance on 29 October 1787, beginning at 7 p.m., planned to end at 9.30. Mozart, on entering the orchestral pit, was greeted with three cheers by the audience, again when he left the rostrum. Guardasoni, the stage manager of the company, sent da Ponte in Vienna a florid congratulatory message. Newspapers reported in the same jubilant tone of voice. The run of performances was long: the programme bill shows that performing dates altered from week to week so that the singers always had a free day in between. On 3 November *Don Giovanni* was given its fourth performance for Mozart's benefit. He remained in Prague until the 13th. During this time he composed the concert aria *Bella mia fiamma* for Mme Dušek who shut him in his room until he had completed it—he made her agree to sightread it perfectly, then included some hair-raisingly difficult intervals in her vocal part. His friends in Prague were loath to let him go back to Vienna; he was offered a commission to remain and write another opera for Bondini's company. But he refused and on 13 November he and Constanze took the coach back to Vienna. It was in the big pond that he really needed to prove himself. The big pond, stinking and rotten as musically it was, did quite soon give him some small acknowledgement.

6

Mozart and his wife returned to Vienna, to be reunited with their small son Karl and their friends and not much work. But the success of *Don Giovanni* in Prague had not passed the Emperor by, especially since one of his court composers, the great Christoph Willibald Gluck (from whom Mozart had, rather unwillingly, learned something about musicdrama), had meanwhile died on 15 November, while Mozart was on the way home. Early in December the Emperor appointed

Mozart to fill the vacant post, at a much smaller remuneration. It was a mark of acceptance, the post of *Kammermusikus*, even if it required no more than the composition of dances for official parties. More important was the Emperor's command for a production in Vienna of *Don Giovanni*. This took place on 7 May 1788 in the Burgtheater, by which time Joseph II was already busy on the battle-field of the Second Turkish War. The Vienna production would require some extra comic business, the city's operatic taste being far from sublime. Mozart and da Ponte obliged with a scene, No. 21 B, in which Zerlina ties Leporello to a chair and threatens him with a cut-throat razor. Mozart had also to write some special music for his Vienna singers. The Don Giovanni himself was a new acquisition to Vienna, Francesco Albertarelli; Mozart did not require to compose new music for him, though he did write a concert aria for Albertarelli, *Un bacio di mano*, in the month of the Vienna production. The Don Ottavio, Francesco Morella, had only just made his Vienna debut and was not able to manage *Il mio tesoro* with its florid divisions; Mozart obliged with the expressive but less virtuoso *Dalla sua pace* in Act I. For the Vienna Donna Elvira, Catarina Cavalieri (his original Constanze), he wrote a new solo, *Mi tradì quell' alma ingrata*, really the summation of Elvira's characterization (Micelli in Prague, with her unpleasant voice, would not have managed the effect). As Donna Anna Mozart had his sister-in-law and ex-sweetheart Aloysia Lange who required no new music. Benucci was his Leporello, Bussani his Commendatore and Masetto. The Zerlina was Luisa Laschi (Countess in *Figaro*), now married (to the singer Domenico Mombelli) and preg-nant—the Emperor, at war, told Count Rosenberg 'the marriage of Laschi and Mombelli can take place without my return and I yield the *droit de seigneur* in this case to you'; Rosenberg was a noted womanizer. The salary list shows that Zerlina received the highest pay of all the female cast, and was thus accepted as the *prima donna*; later Zerlina was considered a much less important role than those of Donna Anna or Donna Elvira. Mme Mombelli had to give up her role, after seven performances, to Therese Teyber (Mozart's first Blondchen in *Die Entführung*) though she went on singing until shortly before she gave birth.

Mozart conducted the first three performances in Vienna; he and da Ponte were given an extra fee by the Emperor. Fifteen performances were given before the end of the year, then the opera was dropped from repertory. Joseph II had sug-gested, from the field of battle, to Count Rosenberg that the music was sure to be too difficult for the singers. When he did return to Vienna and saw *Don Giovanni* himself on 15 December, he told da Ponte that, with all its beauties, it was 'too much for the teeth of my Viennese'. Mozart later commented, 'Let them chew on it.' As usual in Vienna they didn't. *Don Giovanni* was not performed there again until Mozart was buried and at last accepted by Vienna as a great composer. The indefatigable and historically useful Count Zinzendorf attended many perform-ances of *Don Giovanni* in Vienna. At first he found it 'agreeable and very varied', some time later he confessed himself 'very much bored'. Twice in his diary he notes that 'il fût en robe de chambre'. I assume that this means the title role was informally costumed, in open-necked shirt rather than buttoned tunic; but Christopher Raeburn thinks the whole performance may have been acted, for some reason, not in costume at all, simply as a concert rendition. More information is needed on this point.

It has generally been accepted that, because new music had been added, Mozart agreed to end the opera with Don Giovanni's descent to hell followed by a concerted scream in D major on the part of the living characters who run into the room as the curtain falls. Christof Bitter has shown that this scream was deleted from the Vienna libretto and the final sextet included in full. The popular nineteenth-century ending with creepy flesh and D minor un-majorized is therefore unauthentic, as every good Mozartian suspected.

In theatrical production *Don Giovanni* is often given in the Prague version, more rarely in the Vienna version, omitting some numbers, including others. I shall discuss it, number by number, according to the chronological jumble most usually performed and published in Alfred Einstein's edition for Eulenburg. Not because I believe in it but because all the music of *Don Giovanni* is worth discussing and fits somehow into a ragged whole. Now and then I shall pause to consider one of these fascinating characters in what E. T. A. Hoffmann pleonastically yet justifiably called 'the opera of all operas'.

7

Mozart had a musically tidy mind. All his operas have a key-centre from which they start and to which they return: so we will instantly reject the legend (scornfully detailed by Dent, p. 119) that Mozart offered Bondini three alternative overtures to *Don Giovanni*. One was in D minor, which Bondini preferred; the next in E flat major (obviously that to *Die Zauberflöte*, written four years later), the third in C minor with an elaborate fugue. *Don Giovanni* is in the key of D, so its overture had to be in that key. I only mention this harum-scarum myth because I happen to have seen what may be the third candidate. It is the overture to an opera on the *Faust* story by Radziwill and, when I chanced upon a score in 1946,* I at once recognized the fugue as the one in C minor by Mozart for two pianos which I had often played at home. Mozart scored it subsequently for strings and added an introductory *adagio*. Radziwill borrowed it; it fits the drama of *Faust* quite well.

The next story is that Mozart composed the overture on the night preceding the première. His thematic catalogue disposes of this with the date 28 October; the first performance was on the 29th. Constanze Mozart may have remembered aright that she kept her husband awake, while he wrote this overture down, by plying him with coffee and telling him the stories of Aladdin and Cinderella, so as to keep his concentration going. Eventually he fell asleep: she awoke him at 5 a.m. and supplied him with hot punch until the task was complete. The story that the ink was wet on the parts when the first performance started, on the 29th, can be discounted, just as the story that Mozart left a party in Villa Bertramka in order to write this overture can be forgotten, since that was where he was living. His copyists had thirty-six hours to write out the parts, less if the overture was rehearsed.

What is true is that it was the first Mozart operatic overture to begin slow: *ouverture, andante* says the catalogue in which he notated the first bars differently from what he had written in the score.

* In the Pendlebury Library of Cambridge University Music School.

1 **Andante**

This is how they appear in the full score. In bars two and four of Mozart's catalogue the bass notes are crotchets, not minims. If you have heard them played as *tenuto* minims, you will never forget the menace that this groundbass conveys, the horrendous D minor prolonged.

There is a dramatic cause. The **Overture** to *Don Giovanni* begins with a fore-taste of the moment, in the second act finale, when the statue bursts into Don Juan's dining-room, the invited stone guest unexpectedly arrived. Being a skilled man of the theatre, Mozart left the harmonic blow of the statue's entry (see Ex. 90) until later, and simply started with a chill blast of pure D minor, for him a heavily loaded key, pregnant with dramatic menace. He left out the trombones which will be heard and explained later. For the moment the horns, trumpets and drums, and the shrill flutes, are enough to herald a new sort of entertainment. With them are pairs of oboes, clarinets and bassoons and the strings.

The two loud chords, aptly compared by Abert with the uncovering of the Medusa's head, are cut off. The woodwind softly outline a D minor theme, surreptitiously accompanied by strings with a furtive dotted rhythm related to the off-beat rhythm of Ex. 1. The orchestral texture expands but does not thicken. This too is a foretaste of the statue's arrival at supper.

2 Fiati

Comparison of the woodwind semibreves in Ex. 2 with the Commendatore's vocal line in Ex. 89 below will show that the latter is a filled-out version of the former. There follows a weird lurching passage, eerie treading bass, surreptitious semiquavers, more syncopated figuration (high romantic composers would have marked it *lamentoso*) punctuated by shock *sforzando* outbursts, a feature of this overture.

Then a pounding-heart figure on strings, again horrified by loud full chords. Anguished scales ascend *crescendo*, then fall softly, only to rise a chromatic step higher, straining upwards mysteriously. We who have seen the opera know that they belong in the ghostly supper scene. We are still, after hundreds of performances, shaken and moved by the passage, the wailing oboes, the wan flutes, the slithering scales that approach, hesitate, withdraw (in a sensitive performance) and are finally banished—for the moment—by a loud E flat chord in second inversion, the climax of this slow section, but not a static climax because of the chord's position, whereupon the horns and trumpets dispel the horrid vision.

Try to remember hearing this overture for the first time. You don't know the second act finale of Mozart's opera, but you do know the title *Don Giovanni* and perhaps the legend of the statue who came to supper, *Il convitato di pietrà*. This *andante* start to *Don Giovanni* is pretty thrilling (though Mozart, having written *andante*, did not mean *adagio*). Now imagine yourself a citizen of Prague in October 1787. The Don Juan story is well known, often performed as a horror-comic puppet show, sometimes as an operatic comedy. You have read the playbill where Mozart's opera is described as a *dramma giocoso*, a cheerful play. You probably saw his *Die Entführung aus dem Serail* and *Le nozze di Figaro*, two delightful comedies. The young maestro enters, you raise three cheers for him, and he brings in the orchestra. Woosh! It would be a surprise like a thunderclap two feet away (you have never heard any Beethoven or Wagner, let alone twentieth-century rock music), the loudest and most demanding music imaginable. And you would know almost at once that Mozart was putting you in a suitable frame of mind for a play which ends, as you know, with the ghostly statue who comes to supper and drags his naughty host down to red-hot hell through a trapdoor. The trapdoor is a familiar stage-property; the music suddenly brings the situation to life, before it has been shown to you on stage. What a *coup de théâtre* before the curtain has risen!

461

Don Giovanni is, nevertheless, called a *dramma giocoso,* and in 1787 romanticism was only preparing to knock at the door. So this evocation of divine justice and a violent death fades neatly into bright D major and an immensely energetic *molto allegro* sonata movement. E. T. A. Hoffmann (whose fantasy short story about *Don Giovanni* is readable and contains stimulating ideas)* led his followers into a labyrinth of romantic analysis showing how this *allegro* bears on Don Giovanni and his fellow-actors in da Ponte's libretto. They were half right. There is mercurial activity, a touch of noble pomposity (bars 38–9), a hint of melancholy (bars 41–3), bursting staccato jostled by woodwind cadences, like a crowd in a busy place. Then when A major the regulation dominant is reached, strings rush in scales, jostled still, and a gentler tune in thirds for oboes doubled by clarinets, pretty and cheeky (the flutes above sound more sad and philosophical). The dramatic shock chords intrude again and A minor results, with a determined cadence.

Now another idea in two parts: first determined, then soft and conspiratorial.

Romantics will think of the statue's thudding footsteps (even though he may be sculpted on horseback, he must walk to Don Giovanni's dining-room), followed by Giovanni's frivolousness; or they might liken this bipartite theme to Giovanni's masculine insistence answered by a girl's coy giggling. Music can suggest many emotions. This example can more confidently be said to summarize the *andante–molto allegro* contents of the overture and, in a larger sense, the serio–comic content of the whole opera. A description might be Destiny countered by Evasion. In terms of music the contrast is much less dubious. The first, insistent phrase of Ex. 4 is very important. At once it is taken up imitatively by various departments of the orchestra, and A major jumps through several related keys only to return to base and make a long determined cadence. Ex. 4 resumes in the development which unites both halves of that quotation. There is a false recapitulation in G major (sign that the home key is due), sent off into G minor, not for sad effects but so as to reach idealistic B flat major. G minor reasserts itself and Ex. 4 runs through other keys, relevant to the music of the opera (Mozart, writing the overture last, will have wanted to take his ideas through keys that are important in the opera, so as to tie musical threads together) before returning to D major for a solid recapitulation, not always Mozart's wont. At bar 251 there is a shift towards F major, a prophecy of No. 1 in that key, but D major returns and is reestablished. When the recapitulation is symphonically complete, one unquoted energetic theme rises to a flat seventh in D, very striking and reverting to the first part of Ex. 4 so as to switch into F major for the first scene. Mozart carefully added a concert ending which returns (much too suddenly and precipitately, like a schoolboy excuse) to D major and an unconvincing shower of concluding fanfares.

The opera ending is much more effective with its sleek, moonlit, conventional cadence for bassoon, flute, oboe, and violins on the verge of F major.

* Included in *The Pleasures of Music,* compiled by Jacques Barzun.

8

The orchestra pauses, with delicious quizzicality, on a chord of C major. Up goes the curtain. We see★ the garden of a very grand mansion at night, trees, monumental buildings behind, a superb sculptured front porch. This is the house of Don Gonzago de Ulloa, commander of the Spanish army recently returned victorious from some war. For his exploits the king has erected a statue in his honour as part of the Ulloa family catafalque, not necessarily on these premises.

It is late in the night, an hour or so before dawn. A cloaked figure is pacing angrily up and down in front of the porch. He is Leporello (it means 'Little Hare'), Don Giovanni's personal servant and unwilling partner in amorous escapades. He has borne many names, Sganarelle, Gracioso, Catalinón, Trivelin, Pasquariello, Lipperl ('little Philip'), Kasperle = Punch, Arlecchino = Harlequin, Hasenfuss = Coward = also Leporello. He resembles Cervantes's Sancho Panza and Casanova's famous servant Costa. He is the Plain Man, always necessary and, whatever name people give him, he is still the central character of every old comic drama, the fall-guy, not a hero but indispensible.

This musical number is *Notte e giorno faticar*, called **Introduzione, No. 1**, *molto allegro* in F major. There are flutes, oboes, bassoons, horns and strings—no sensuous clarinets, but shrill or mysterious flutes, shrill or plangent oboes, plump and piquant bassoons, insistent horns; the lower strings can sound eloquent, the violins bravura, when required.

Strings with bassoons announce a march theme. It should be at the same tempo as the foregoing overture's *allegro* and that of the trio soon to arrive: it is usually taken much slower.

5

The music says that Leporello is pacing angrily up and down outside the house. At the end of bars 2 and 4 he stops and looks for intruders, *forte* with a scrunch. At bar 8, after Ex. 5, he wheels furiously round twice and begins singing. He is keeping watch for his master who is inside the palace trying to seduce Donna Anna, daughter of the proprietor Don Gonzago de Ulloa. It must, for reasons to be described later, be about 3 a.m.

> Night and day I wear myself out for a man who appreciates nothing. I put up with rain and wind, eat badly and sleep badly. I want to be a gentleman myself, not a servant. What a charming cavalier! You're inside with a pretty girl, while I'm out here on sentry-go.

Leporello sings his first words, 'Notte e giorno faticar', to the tune of Ex. 5 (Beethoven later quoted it humorously in one of his Diabelli Variations). The

★ In the 1930s decors said to be based on Platzer's for the Prague première.

music shows that he is becoming progressively more annoyed (rising figures, furious scales). His ambition erupts with horns in thirds and a determined violin arpeggio: 'Voglio far il gentiluomo'. Its consequent is a copy of the bass line, but full of character, often used by Mozart for low-pitched roles.

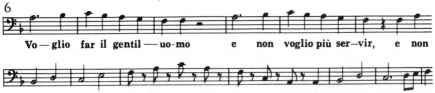

Strings produce a smarmy motif for Giovanni's pleasure—'O che caro galantuomo!' The contrast is Leporello's chilly duty, with equally frigid flutes.

Ex. 6 returns. Then Leporello hears a noise of people approaching and decides to seek a convenient hiding-place.

The key changes to more aristocratic B flat major and the solo becomes a trio. From out of the palace runs Don Giovanni, attempting to conceal his face, perhaps with his cloak, perhaps with a large floppy hat. Clutching him by the arm follows Donna Anna who promises not to leave hold, though he refuses to reveal his identity. Here, as in the overture, we have the stabbing *fortepiani*, the full, loud wind chords; and a violent, broken-chord figure for violins emphasizes Anna's cold fury (see Ex. 8 below where she sings 'Come furia disperata'). She is angry because she has been caught unawares. Don Giovanni, though well known to the Ulloa family as a nobly born citizen of Seville, and aware that Anna is betrothed to Don Ottavio, has determined to add her to his list of seducees. At dead of night he penetrated unobserved to her room and began to woo her. At first she supposed him to be Don Ottavio—it is important that they should be dressed identically —then some movement, perhaps a caress uncharacteristic of a noble fiancé, disclosed the mistaken identity. Fortunately for Giovanni it was too dark for her to see his face, though some words he murmured make it possible for her to recognize him later when she meets him in daylight. He has made his escape but she is dogging his heels, shouting for servants or family to come and help her. They carry out their recriminations in trio with Leporello's grumbling asides, as for example:

The descending violin scale, if it can be heard, keeps the music balanced towards picaresque comedy, as does a tiptoe theme for Leporello just before the first idea of this scene is recapitulated, now with Anna and Giovanni echoing one another in musical imitation to great purpose.

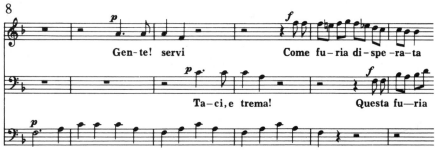

The situation is bound to remain unnaturally static (Giovanni and Leporello need to get away rapidly before Anna recognizes her would-be seducer) but this excellent trio is worth prolonging and its music is thoroughly dynamic.

At last the violins thunder out high Ds and the bass instruments rage from B flat major towards G minor. Don Gonzago storms out with drawn sword, calling on the miscreant to unhand his daughter and fight. Donna Anna releases her hold and runs back into the house. The angry runs for strings, suggestive of chivalry at the Commendatore's entry, persist between his exchanges with Don Giovanni who scorns to match swords with an old man, then return precipitously when he reluctantly consents to give satisfaction and throughout the nine bars of their duel in D minor, against shrill sustained woodwind chords.

The last bar is a sustained diminished seventh chord on B (the same to which the statue enters at the supper scene), with a pause on top. The Commendatore falls, mortally wounded. The tempo drops from *molto allegro* to *andante*, the key becomes F minor (though the key-signature is still only one flat). The dying man calls for help, Leporello fears the worst, Giovanni merely comments that the old man is dying, though he does so to a poignant phrase (interestingly similar to Anna's 'Come furia disperata' in Ex. 8), signifying that his braggadoccio has been momentarily checked.

The colouring of this trio, vocal and instrumental, is properly sombre, the plucked basses, low thirds for middle strings and bassoons, the horn dominant pedal, and the three bass voices—though their voices should be as different as their music, Giovanni's a bright baritone, Leporello's darker than the Commendatore's —as well as the muttered staccato triplets for first violins. Some suggest that these last inspired the opening movement of Beethoven's 'Moonlight' Sonata in C sharp minor for piano solo, op. 27 no. 2 (he copied out this passage, apparently, shortly before composing that work) but Mozart's triplets have a quite different expressive effect, perhaps the pouring-out of Don Gonzago's blood, perhaps the suspense and anxiety of the other two men, perhaps a more generalized tension on tenterhooks, none of them relevant to the Beethoven. In terms of music these triplets are the link which connects all the other conflicting ideas in the ensemble. Some music is specifically expressive, particularly about physical movement (e.g. *Notte e giorno faticar*, Leporello pacing up and down) but when internal personal emotions become involved (three of them here, at least) a great composer can turn one idea to several purposes.

The texture remains consistent, as the Commendatore, gasping for breath, expires. When he breathes his last the higher woodwind enter with a touching chromatic Requiem, added to the pitapat triplets.

10

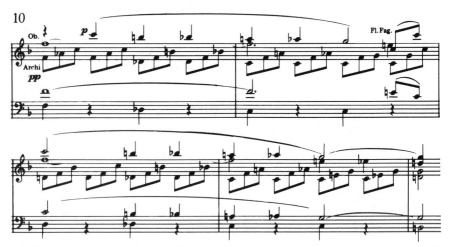

The orchestra stops. The old man is dead. Giovanni, in recitative, finds Leporello who congratulates his master on raping the daughter and slaughtering her father—he insisted, answers Giovanni. Did she, Leporello asks? Angrily Giovanni drags Leporello away.

Anna has collected her fiancé, Don Ottavio brandishing his sword, and some servants with torches, to search for Don Gonzago. Ottavio promises bravery. But alas! A sustained orchestral G and sounds of C minor lamentation (**No. 2**) show that Anna has espied her father's corpse on the ground.

11

This is **No. 2,** an accompanied **Recitative** and **Duet**, *allegro assai*, with flutes, oboes, bassoons, horns and strings, shrill and urgent. The loud descending minor seconds for orchestra are as important as evocative, like a beating of the breast. Ottavio addresses the body, without response. Anna remarks on the blood everywhere. She feels faint (descending violins) and loses consciousness. Ottavio's first thought (*maestoso*) is to have her revived by servants with brandy and smelling salts; then, when she shows signs of recovery, he orders them to remove the body and concentrates on consoling her. His behaviour is cool and positive.

She looks up at him, *allegro*, D minor, *Fuggi, crudele, fuggi!* and orders him away. She has confused him with the villain who tried to make love to her, and who then slew her dear father. Again it is clear that Ottavio and Giovanni must look moderately similar.

12

This is the beginning of their duet. Anna is hysterical, naturally. The corpse is no longer there, but she has it before her eyes. The figure for second violins has links with that in Ex. 3 from the overture, sinister and bloody. Ottavio reminds her who he is, and she at once apologizes. If Ottavio is not the villain, then where is her father?

13

The gentle, hopeful warmth of the violin figure at the beginning of the above example will be remarked, then the *crescendo* and Ottavio's firm insistence that, from now on, he must be both father and husband to her. The violent dynamic marks should also be noted. This duet is largely *piano* with some of the characteristic shock *fortes* of the opera. She repeats her questions twice, then breaks into accompanied recitative (strings only) insisting that Ottavio must swear to avenge the crime, which he does *adagio*. They compact their oath together in duet, *allegro* again, mostly in loving thirds and sixths, for formality's sake (tiresome for a producer) repeating the oath ceremony, and stepping up the noble florid promises, ending with loud orchestra. Later we may think them stiff, unspontaneous people,

467

noble Spanish to a fault. In this duet they show human, credible emotion for once, their aristocratic heroic reactions subtilized a trace by deep anxiety.

The next scene takes place in a street. While it is still empty we may consider the characters who have so far appeared on stage. About Leporello something has already been written. About the Commendatore Don Gonzago likewise a phrase or two: he was a soldier, commander of armies, and a royal knight. He died defending his daughter's honour. In the 'Don Juan in Hell' scene of Bernard Shaw's *Man and Superman* he frequently comes down to Hell from Heaven because he finds Hell less boring, and enjoys chatting with Juan to whom he insists that, being a superior swordsman, he would have won the duel if he had not slipped; the statuesque revenge gratified him not at all—though this is a later comment than any by da Ponte, and only relevant because Shaw, a knowing Mozartian, used Mozart's opera as incidental music for the scene and da Ponte's libretto as material for redevelopment.

Donna Anna, in the Bertati–Gazzaniga opera which was da Ponte's prime source, disappeared to a convent after the scene just described. Da Ponte fortunately expanded her character and activity, drawing a little on Goldoni who intimated that she did not much fancy Ottavio. Anna is an upper-class Spanish lady who has etiquette where her feelings and brains should reside. Duty and honour are her watchword. Towards all her fellow-creatures she presents a coldly correct personality. If she loves her father it is because the Bible told her so. Her censorious anger against others is a juvenile trait. All men, to her, are beasts, and it would be beneficial to her personal growing-up if she had been pleasantly raped by Don Juan (as some writers on Mozart's opera assume, I think optimistically). Her upbringing has made her afraid of other people, and she has given most of her sincere outgoing emotion to lapdogs or possibly horses. The idea that she is an incipient spinster, set in her maidenly ways, may be due to a casting tradition established by Wilhelmine Schröder-Devrient, a sizeable, established, but by no means frigid German opera singer, who appreciated the possibilities of the role and, having made it her own, persuaded posterity that Donna Anna is the *prima donna* in *Don Giovanni*. In Mozart's lifetime all principal soprano parts were potentially equal; the leading female role was the one in which the male audience would evince chief sexual interest. Anna is not such a character, though she has the advantage of some stunning and some beautiful music.

Don Ottavio is almost as cold to observe. He has been brought up to behave with perfect correctness in public, and to respect every other aristocratic person—he cannot believe that somebody as impeccably descended as Don Juan Tenorio, his friend from social clubs no doubt, could be a seducer and murderer, and so he is slow to take official action against the suspect. For such people women, after all, are a lower sex, a chattel after marriage; and they jump readily to emotional, irrational conclusions. Ottavio's ethic is irreproachability: Edwardian English ladies would have applauded him as S.I.T. (safe in taxi). The role, in Mozart's opera, will usually seem hopelessly dull and puppet-like. Virginio Puecher, in a famous production of *Don Giovanni*, emphasized the dislikability of all the other characters so as to display Ottavio as the one admirable and sympathetic person in the cast. Justice for Ottavio at last! But the whitewash is easily rained away and we enjoy Ottavio mainly for his two arias.

Giovanni (we should no more refer to him as 'the Don' than we would to Ottavio, or any university lecturer, or than we would speak of Herbert von Karajan as 'the Von'—Don is a Spanish respectful title like the now outmoded English 'Esquire'—though a friendly Spanish tradesman will be addressed as Don So-and-so) is much more interesting. Da Ponte and Mozart portray him in close detail. He is a healthy young male, proud of his virility, not at all class-conscious where women are concerned, nor yet idealistic in his search of the perfect woman (as Nikolaus Lenau later made him). For him every woman is a desirable object, old or young, pretty or ugly, queen or country-girl. He does not subscribe to the Spanish custom which instructed lusty males to use the brothel whenever they felt an onset of lasciviousness. Like Count Almaviva, Don Giovanni believed in winning by wooing; he did not mind taking advantage of his nobility in this pursuit but chiefly trusted to his personal allure and his erotic technique (like Almaviva he never talks down to a woman of lower class). His arrogance was personal rather than social; his pursuit of women is indeed anti-social, as Spain understood it, even self-destructive. A Spaniard set on a life of sin was only justified if the sinning was really extensive and monstrous. If fornication deserved hellfire, a few rolls in the bed were not adequate cause: the sinning must be grandiose, even blasphemous. Hence the slaughter in fair fight of an aged parent had to be topped by disrespect to that slain father's statue. Blasphemy of this kind was suitably mannish (*macho* in Spanish) to make the earlier profligacy worthwhile. Womanizers are men who have no other interest to divert them. Don Juan, a Spanish aristocrat, was bored by the company of other male grandees, found sport tedious (except bedroom sports), came to despise the ethical precepts of the priesthood, and so found his own goal in life, the satisfaction of the whole man, in association with as many women as possible. Later, more satirical generations found it piquant to cast a counter-tenor, even female sopranos, as Don Giovanni. Tenors sang the role (Gazzaniga's Giovanni was notated in the tenor clef), and nowadays many basses hubristically aspire to the part. But for textural balance the music requires a bright high baritone, 'the voice of a gentleman,' wrote Bernard Shaw. And a very young man, irresistibly good-looking, perfect in his manners, and in his sexual prime, under twenty-four years of age.

9

This street in which we have arrived is not further described in Mozart's score or libretto though it remains the scene until after Giovanni's No. 11. He mentions several times that his own villa is near by, and points to it: there may usefully be an entrance to it from this street. Donna Elvira at her first entrance is said to be in travelling clothes. Stage designers and directors have deduced that an inn is visible; from a front room window on (probably) the first floor Elvira will sing *Ah taci, ingiusto core* in Act II. The inn, if the kind with a downstairs bar and *al fresco* seating, makes an appropriate focus for the wedding celebrations of Masetto and Zerlina. Josef Platzer included a café of this kind in his design for the first Prague production, though it does not look like even a modest hotel and Platzer designed a different set, with a balcony, for the opening of Act II.

Here, at first daylight, come Giovanni and his servant on their way home.* They are conversing in recitative. Leporello, shaken by the débâcle of an hour or so ago, has a matter on his conscience. Having established that nobody is within earshot, and that his master promises not to take offence, he whispers loudly in his ear that Don Giovanni is leading the life of a villain. Giovanni forgets his promise and makes to assault Leporello who promises to say no more. The master therefore announces his next design: he has an assignation with a willing and pretty lady who is due tonight in his villa (since it is now 'l'alba chiara', Leporello might assume that 'questa notte' would mean in some fourteen hours' time—but Giovanni means now). Perhaps she is here even at this instant: Don Giovanni can smell woman. But it is not Donna Ximena; da Ponte had to omit her, for want of a fourth soprano. The new arrival, though heavily clad for a journey, looks attractive too. Giovanni and Leporello hide in order to 'prospect the territory', as Giovanni puts it.

Donna Elvira introduces herself with **No. 3, Aria and Terzetto**, *Ah! chi mi dice mai* in E flat major (a semitone above the previous number, i.e. tonally remote), *allegro* with clarinets, bassoons, horns and strings.

> O who will tell me where is that cruel man whom, to my shame, I loved and who broke faith with me? Ah, if I rediscover the scoundrel and he does not return to me, I will make a dreadful example of him; I will rip out his heart.

Mozart's dynamic music is often vividly suggestive of physical movement; so it is in the twelve bars of orchestral introduction to this aria, particularly in two of the ideas which I now quote as repeated with the addition of voice.

14

* Spanish drama tended to ignore the Aristotelian unities. But da Ponte was a classical scholar and observed them. The action of *Don Giovanni* can conveniently be fitted into a single day between about 3 a.m. and the following midnight, even if time passes, without change of scene, between episodes.

Donna Elvira is in a passionate rage, as can be heard in the violins' rising octaves at bar 5 of Ex. 14 (notice also the purposeful rhythm of the bass line below), and in her own outraged leaps later, accompanied by the typical *fp* pouncing chords, and the eloquent pause for effect before she completes her cadence.

15

vo' far—ne or-ren-do scem-pio, gli vo' ca-va—re il cor

gli vo' ca——va——re il cor.

Her anger has not the coldly trembling dignity of Donna Anna's outrage. Elvira is a warmer-blooded person, whence the choice of glowing E flat major with prominent clarinets. She is popularly supposed to be a more bourgeois lady than Donna Anna, and indeed the gait of her first theme, that for violins accompanying her first words in Ex. 14, is not quite dignified: if it applies to her flashing glances as she peers through the dawn light for a sight of her betrayer, she will look as extravagant a harpy as if we connect this figure, and the loud clump-clump between bars 2 and 3 of Ex. 14, with the way she walks. The more forward-moving the *allegro* tempo, the less comic her initial impression will be. Donna Anna and Don Ottavio, in No. 9, do instantly remark on her 'aspetto nobile' and 'dolce maestà' ('noble appearance' and 'gentle dignity') and in this aria Elvira has a pouncing theme, imitated through the string section, which connects with the noble rage of the Ulloa family.

16

However, the grand impression which Donna Elvira hopes to make with her exclamations of grievance is somewhat deflated by the comic asides of Giovanni, who determines to console her, and Leporello, who knows what sort of consolation it will be. One of these whispered exchanges forms the very short middle section of a neat binary structure. At the end of the second half Giovanni politely emerges to offer her his assistance. Too late (recitative now) he recognizes her and she him. He is the monster whom she has been seeking ever since he seduced and (so she claims) married her in Burgos, only furtively to leave her three days later. Da Ponte's Elvira forgets to mention what we know from Molière (who invented the part) that she was a nun in Burgos, abducted by Giovanni with a promise of marriage; having renounced her vows she cannot return to the nunnery and is obliged, by necessity as well as infatuation, to preserve her only link with the material world. Giovanni's excuse, in Molière, for abandoning this deconsecrated bride of Christ is that he recognized the blasphemy of his action and feared the wrath of heaven. In da Ponte Giovanni leaves Leporello to explain to Elvira. Behind her back Giovanni slips into his villa (there to dally with the unseen Donna Ximena) while Leporello covers his exit with some nonsense about quadrilaterals never becoming circular. She turns to protest, and finds herself yet again abandoned.

Leporello cuts short her lamentation with the cold comfort that she is neither the first nor the last lady to be victimized by Don Giovanni. For proof let him show her the book which he carries with him always. In it he has inscribed the name of every woman to whom his master has made love. Leporello's Catalogue **Aria, No. 4,** *Madamina*, in D major, beginning *allegro*, with flutes, oboes, bassoons, horns and strings, had become a favourite part of the *Commedia dell'arte* treatments of *Don Juan* long before Bertati wrote his version. (One could postulate that the essentials of this play were the death of the Commendatore, the catalogue, the churchyard invitation, and the death of Juan—the rest was embellishment and the test of a successful treatment.) The audience expected an impressive array of numbers and some newly invented varieties of conquest. To oblige in this respect was, for da Ponte, a duty of honour—how Casanova must have longed to write the text himself!

> Dear Madam, this is the list of the beauties my master has loved. It's a list I've made myself. Look at it, read it with me: 640 in Italy, 231 in Germany, 100 in France, 91 in Turkey; but in Spain there are 1003 to date. There are peasant girls and serving maids, ladies of the town, countesses, baronesses, marchionesses and princesses, women of every rank and shape and all ages.
>
> He likes the gentleness of golden hair and constancy of brunettes and the sweetness of ash-blondes. He prefers them fat in winter and slim in summer. Tall girls are majestic, but tiny ones are pretty as well. He makes elderly conquests too, for the pleasure of including them in the book. But his major passion is for young virgins. He doesn't worry if she's rich, ugly or beautiful; as long as she wears a skirt, you know what he'll do.

For Donna Elvira this must be an infernal recital of grounds for adulterous jealousy. Yet she must sit it out, since she has to sing a recitative afterwards (Bertati was kinder and added a duet at the end). When producers temper the wind to the shorn nun, and let her leave prematurely in disgust, we may sympathize. But why should Leporello, in such a realistic opera, continue his recital to the end without an audience? He knows the list almost by heart, hardly needs to refer to it—except that in No. 3 he assessed the conquests at 1800, whereas the tally of No. 4 is 2065.★

Mozart eases Donna Elvira's agony. The Catalogue Aria is too delightful to walk out on. It begins with incredible lightness, violins imitated by basses, Leporello reciting half in patter. Everything *piano* (Ex. 17).

When Leporello gets down to detail, two horns revel in *forte* cuckoldry, flutes and bassoons almost wolf-whistle with astonished delight. There are reverent

★ Alan Jefferson tells me of an Aphrodite Club at Montmorency in France, just before the Revolution, one of whose members, a lady of noble birth, listed 4694 male conquests over a period of twenty years. The *catalogue raisonée* makes impressive reading. But Spanish morals always were stricter than those in France, and women in those days much harder to seduce than men for whom a gift horse proverbially requires no oral inspection.

17

pauses when the total for Spain is reached, cheerfully counteracted by strings and wind as he repeats the amazing national yield. The light, delighted accompaniment is resumed for the categories ('V'han fra queste contadine'), and a joyful crescendo is stopped only by a return to the recitation of countries, with contrary motion scales by violins and basses (from every quarter of the world they flock to this super-lover, as it were).

18

Leporello keeps his glee going with ebullient repetition, then makes a firm, floridly accompanied cadence in dominant A major.

He has not finished. D major resumes, *andante con moto* (i.e., not too slow) for the second paragraph of text translated above with insinuating thirds for 'Nella bionda', richly doubled by *divisi* violas—a favourite Mozart touch.

19

Flutes are usually serious in effect for mature Mozart: here they sound radiant, almost ironical.★ For the majestic tall girl Mozart induces a grand *crescendo* in pompous style, only to collapse into exquisite filigree for 'la piccina'. A dark and sinister cloud of B flat major falls across the frank enjoyment of D major when Leporello comes to Giovanni's passion for untutored tyros in love—the *staccato* bassoons make it sound all the naughtier. The thrill of the pursuit is conveyed, too monotonously perhaps, in the trills of the sly theme at 'non si picca'—always the same, always new!

20

Leporello sums up his master's philosophy with a varied reprise of Ex. 19, elaborating and continuing it with leering *fioritura*—the last one traditionally hummed with many an innuendo.

21

In the library at Donaueschingen, whose score was copied in Prague almost under Mozart's eyes and the opera performed soon after the première, I copied an original embellishment for this passage. It grins even more evilly at Donna Elvira.

22

The orchestra gestures triumphantly as Leporello, flourishing his catalogue at Elvira, runs away.

Elvira remains only to express briefly her disgust and thirst for vengeance.

But as she leaves, perhaps to settle into the inn where Bertati says she is staying (with a personal maid whom da Ponte's Don Giovanni has rapaciously espied before the beginning of Act II), a crowd of country folk run to this spot. They are celebrating the forthcoming marriage of two among them, Zerlina and Masetto. The orchestra, flutes, oboes, bassoons, horns, strings, break into a joyful *allegro* G major **Duet and Chorus, No. 5**, *Giovinette che fate all'amore*, a bucolic six-eight dance extolling the delights of marriage. Apart from the cheerful chains of thirds at the beginning, the number's special charm is a touch of wistfulness when the singers contemplate matrimonial bliss: 'che piacer che sarà!' (Ex. 23).

Da Ponte has created two slight problems of timing here. It was about 6 a.m. when Donna Elvira entered. The text gives no indication of a gap in time between then and the conclusion of *Fin ch'han dal vino*. The peasants arrive as Elvira leaves.

★ There is an old tradition in Germany, I do not know how authentic, that Donna Elvira should wear a red wig, characteristic of a prostitute. It may have no bearing on Mozart's Elvira, but Richard Strauss in 1888 declared that his own Elvira theme must convey the colour of the lady's hair to any sensitive listener.

23

As soon as their chorus ends Don Giovanni returns, relieved to observe that she is no longer among those present. We must therefore assume that it is still no later than say 7 a.m.—rather early for the peasant carousal to begin. Perhaps they were on their way to church—Zerlina will tell Giovanni, 'I gave him my promise to wed him' ('io gli diedi parola di sposarlo'), and she is wheedled into accepting a proposal of marriage to Giovanni, therefore the wedding has not yet taken place. But by midnight of the same day (if we accept the opera's unity of time) Masetto and Zerlina are ready to go to their home and have supper. When do they have time to go to church? We must assume that, in a Catholic country, they propose to go to church before setting up house together—or have they taken the will for the deed?

Once again Don Giovanni's nose has scented femininity. Having established that Elvira is not in sight he makes himself pleasant to the gathering of countryfolk, establishes the identity of the bride and groom, compliments them both, and offers them all his protection. Squeals from a corner announce that Leporello too is offering his protection. Giovanni orders him to conduct the party to his palace, give them food and drink, show them the apartments and garden, and be particularly nice to Masetto. The host will reserve his special attention for the bride. Zerlina is not scared, knowing herself to be in the hands of a cavalier, but Masetto is unwilling to go off without her. Don Giovanni summarily dismisses him with a warning to know his place and respect a superior's sword.

Masetto, who is very young and very possessive, can recognize a bully and does not go without making his recognition plain in **No. 6, Aria**, *allegro di molto*, F major, *Ho capito*, with flutes, bassoons, horns and strings. It may have been transposed down from G major to accommodate Lolli.

I understand. Yes, sir, I'll bow my head and go. Since that's your pleasure I won't answer back. After all, you are a cavalier. I can't doubt it, can I? You've said you want to be kind to me.
(*Aside to Zerlina*) You hussy, you rascal, you always were my ruination.
(*To Leporello who is pulling him away*) I'm coming, I'm coming!
(*To Zerlina*) You're staying. The affair is quite open; now let this gentleman of ours make a lady out of you!

The aria begins with angry unisons, unnaturally subdued (Ex. 24).
They are its structural lynch-pin. But the music is largely sarcastic in tone of voice: the obsequious grovelling for 'chino il capo', the flippant, foppish trills for 'già che piace a voi', the exaggerated courtesy of 'Cavalier voi siete già'. The asides to Zerlina are curt. As Masetto turns furiously to Leporello Ex. 24 reappears, and

24

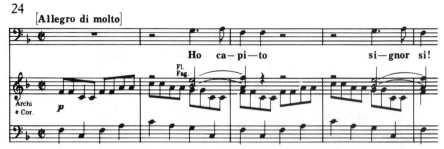

at 'faccia il nostro cavaliere' a new unison idea, mock-cheerful but rather sneering, is introduced; it forms the coda as Masetto is dragged off to the party in the *palazzo*.

Don Giovanni brushes away this remonstration as if it were a fly on his face and begins to exercise his practised fascination on Zerlina. The yokel is unworthy of such an exquisite creature. Her promises of marriage must not be held binding; she was destined for a more gracious way of life. She need have no fear; the tales about the fleeting licentiousness of noblemen are all plebeian slanders. See, he will make her his wife this very day in his villa there. And, the more to turn her bewildered little head, he begins the **Duettino, No. 7,** *Là ci darem la mano* in A major, *andante*, with flutes, oboes, bassoons, horns and strings—in some respects the most enchanting and probably most popular number in the whole opera (it is said to have been encored three times at the first performance). It shares its key and vein of voluptuous melody with the parallel duet in *Figaro* (the second part of *Crudel perchè finora*) but here the scoring is even more delicate: light strings, very few touches of wind until Zerlina's reserve begins to collapse ('Be quick, I can hold out no longer') and Giovanni returns to the tune, now shared with Zerlina, he doubled by flute, she by bassoon—nice touch of class-distinction.

25

Now he can press his desires more urgently, knowing that she will respond. Let us go, he begs; at last, over a momentous pause (though it need not last longer than a little flourish, sign of her new social status), she repeats his 'Andiam', accepting his proposal. They slip into a gentle six–eight, singing together in lilting thirds, and by the end the orchestra is dancing a little jig for them as they wander in an embrace towards Giovanni's villa.

The idyll is swiftly shattered by the arrival of Elvira who hurls herself upon Don Giovanni with expressions of thanksgiving that, by chance overhearing, she has saved another innocent from ruin. He whispers to her that he wanted only a little amusement; but this enrages her further. Giovanni tries to persuade Zerlina, in another aside, that he is the victim of this other lady's hopeless infatuation and, being kindly by nature, he cannot bring himself to undeceive her.

Elvira, however, turns firmly to Zerlina and delivers the following vehement, highly formalized address, her **Aria, No. 8,** *allegro* in D major, *Ah fuggi il traditor.*

Ah, flee from that traitor, let him say no more. His lips are liars, his eyes are false. Learn from my sufferings not to trust him, and let the perils that befell me start fear within you.

Donna Elvira is accompanied by strings alone, in an unusually strict contrapuntal manner full of exclamatory dotted (probably even double-dotted) rhythms. The total effect is, by Mozartian standards, old fashioned, even to the two spurts of floridity: we think of Handel, but Mozart may have looked back to the generation of Handel's stiffer, baroque successors, Hasse and Leo, for instance, whose operas were still to be heard occasionally in his boyhood.

26

In Gazzaniga's *Don Giovanni* Elvira recognizes a rival in Zerlina (or Maturina as, following Molière, she is called) and drives her away. Da Ponte softened the character, so that she takes Zerlina under her wing and, having harangued her in the equivalent of silent-film histrionic expression, sweeps her off to find Masetto.

Don Giovanni is left to curse the ill-luck that seems today, he says, to dog all his pleasurable exploits. They are all going badly. Da Ponte maliciously took over from Bertati's satirical treatment: Don Juan, the legendary amorist, fails in every seduction that we see him undertake. He who lived for conquests has evidently lost the knack, and so his downfall is due.★ Meanwhile he has landed himself with a large party in his villa, and his excuse has been wafted from under his nose. He needs a moment to plan. It is the moment chosen by Donna Anna and Don Ottavio (the last couple he wants to entangle with) to seek him out and ask him,

★ Some commentators, e.g. R. B. Moberly, argue that Don Giovanni does, indeed, have plenty of success during Mozart's opera. Do read Moberly's *Three Mozart Operas*, but he does not convince me and much of his reasoning is based on his English singing translations, not on the original texts. If Giovanni means what he says he did not presumably have his way with Anna, or with Ximena.

477

as a friend of the family, to help them in their need. Much relieved that he is not recognized as Anna's nocturnal visitor, Giovanni offers his all, but asks to what purpose he can serve them.

Before they can answer, Donna Elvira intrudes yet again, firmly convinced that this sedate little conversation is the prologue to yet another seduction. Addressing Giovanni as a perfidious monster she turns instantly to Donna Anna and begins **No. 19, Quartet,** *andante* in B flat major, *Non ti fidar,* with single flute, clarinets, bassoons, horns and strings. Elvira is now less manic, more tearful and appealing, as we notice from the warm sound of clarinets, the greater placidity and dignity of B flat major, and the demure cut of her melody as she begs these unknowns not to trust this scoundrel who has betrayed her and will treat them likewise.

27

Andante

Non— ti fi-dar o mi-se-ra   di quel ri-bal-do cor!

Me già tradì quel bar-ba-ro: te vuol tradi—re an-cor.

Elvira's last bar is repeated like a refrain, first by violins, then by Anna with clarinet, then by flute, then developed as Anna and Ottavio express surprise at Elvira's evident nobility of bearing and conviction of utterance which rouse their instant sympathy—the 'te vuol tradir ancor' phrase is again repeated three times; we can hear it as the bond of communication between them. Giovanni quietly tells Anna and Ottavio that Elvira is demented and may be calmed if they leave her to his understanding treatment. He has returned to a variation on Ex. 27 and as he speaks of calming, that refrain again recurs twice in the orchestra, rousing suspicions now ripened in the concerted quartet passage where Elvira insists on her case, growing more and more impassioned until, in between Giovanni's protests and the united doubts of Anna and Ottavio, she bursts repeatedly into florid patter about her anger and the rascal's perfidy, so much so that we others may believe her somewhat deranged. All the while the orchestra, especially woodwind, is speaking the language of sad consolation which stirs in Anna's heart: this unknown lady may be her means of finding justice for her father's death. Giovanni finds the situation distinctly embarrassing, whether he retreats or remains. Elvira is gaining ground: loudly she accuses him of falsehood. In an undertone of conspiratorial patter more suited to Leporello, he asks her to moderate her tone when people are near by. This only emboldens her to more heroic denunciation. The four characters mutter conflicting thoughts over a tense dominant pedal bass until Anna takes up Ex. 27 and once more its last bar is repeated again and again until, on flute and clarinet, it ends this superb number as Elvira walks sadly away.

Don Giovanni, anxious not to prolong this embarrassing encounter, pretends that he must follow and keep an eye on his unfortunate patient who may do herself some injury. He excuses himself: if he can be of service he will always be at home to them.

With a courtly farewell he hurries away. Something stirs inside Donna Anna's brain. Mozart uses the orchestra to suggest it.

28

It was for such moments of drama that he treasured the *Recitativo accompagnato*, and this is one, the introduction to **No. 10.** It is powerfully accompanied, by flutes, oboes (not clarinets who are for gentler music), bassoons, horns, trumpets and strings. They help Anna to analyse her fit of horror: that man Don Giovanni, she knows now, murdered her father. Giovanni's parting words just now reminded her precisely of the criminal . . . (she has dropped into *secco* recitative). Ottavio is shocked that a friend of the family should behave so disgracefully. More for our benefit than his, she retells the story of her attempted seduction; the strings help her, and Mozart takes a rare turn into the key of E flat minor. But I have told it already, on page 464. When she relates (twice) how she screamed for help, Ex. 28 on full orchestra is re-invoked, again when she recalls how her father ran to help her—the phrase is truthfully used to express a trauma.

She reaches the end of her narrative, with the discovery of the Commendatore's corpse, then bursts into the D major *andante* half of this number, *Or sai chi l'onore*, with oboes (faithful companions of Anna's determination), bassoons, horns and strings.

> Now you know who tried to ravish my honour, who was the traitor that took my father from me. I call you to vengeance, your heart calls you too. If ever your righteous anger grows weak, then remember the wound in his wretched breast, remember the ground drenched in his blood.

Less taxing than Donna Anna's final aria, this one is the more self-revealing, and a glorious showpiece for a great singer; not least because most of it is marked *piano*. Above the stealthy basses, the swirling tremolo chords of upper strings, Anna delivers her verdict confidently, but as a confidence. Oboes and bassoons mention revenge, but distantly (Ex. 29).

There is contrasted pathos at 'che il padre mi tolse', with the rising minor sixth, richly expressive. But the great moment comes at 'vendetta ti chiedo', where the urgent treble line is earnestly imitated canonically by the basses, and the voice hangs determinedly on to its top A—all this at a *piano* level, not shrieked out for the inhabitants of the inn or the merrymakers in Giovanni's garden. For the moment it is Anna's terrible secret. Compassionate D minor, followed by F minor (keys of Don Gonzago's death scene), enter the music as Anna recalls his corpse—violas and bassoons, also oboes, share her lament. The rising sixth, like an idée fixe, returns at 'se l'ira in te langue'; and then a full orchestral *forte* as passion released. But *piano* resumes with the reprise of Ex. 29 and the rest, slightly extended by a plangent anxious plea for 'rammenta la piaga', and an impetuous coda on

'vendetta ti chiedo', a call to heroic action which reaches *forte* but, characteristically, ends *piano*.

More formally than realistically, Donna Anna walks away, leaving Ottavio to express his incredulity that such a dastardly deed could be within the capacity of a gentleman. He intends to discover the truth: if Anna is his betrothed, Giovanni is his friend, and both have a call on his loyalty.

In the Prague version he follows her away. For the Vienna première Antonio Morella requested a less virtuoso aria than his No. 22, so Mozart wrote *Dalla sua pace*, **Aria, No. 10b,** and placed it here. It is *andantino sostenuto* in G major, with single flute, oboes, bassoons, horns and strings, in expression altogether innocent of the 'ira del giusto furor' which Donna Anna has charged him to nurture.

> On her peace my own depends. What gives her pleasure is life to me, what saddens her is death to me. If she sighs, I sigh too. Her anger, her sorrows, are mine, and nothing is good for me that is not good for her.

The aria begins in profound serenity, with soft, sustained string chords to support Ottavio's elegant melody.

The calm surface is ruffled by a crescendo (naïve or sly?) at 'quel che l'incresce', and at 'morte' the horns pound on the dominant. The melody completed, the music goes into G minor, for 'S'ella sospira' with plaintive sighs for wind and violins, then trembles with rage in B flat for 'è mia quell'ira', and languishes chromatically for 'quel pianto'. This is Mozart not thinking very hard (the anger music is still there when Ottavio gets to 'bene'), yet it all hangs together very beautifully, and the subsequent side-slip into B minor is sensuously done. The melody returns, back in G after a vocal flourish; a slightly more anxious episode starts but reverts once more to the main tune. The coda begins with chaste wood-wind harmonies and some surprising octave leaps for the singer and ends joyfully and positively, even though the singer's last words were 'morte mi da'. *Dalla sua pace* is an intrusion, written without dramatic engagement. Yet audiences will miss it when the Prague version is strictly adhered to—given a decent tenor.

Ottavio goes after Donna Anna. Leporello comes out of his master's villa—we are not sure how large it is, since Giovanni refers to it indifferently as 'palazzo', 'casino' (country house) and 'casinetto' (cottage)—to find and give his notice to the madman who has given him such a hectic morning: it must be about noon or 1 p.m. by now. Here is Don Giovanni indeed, looking very carefree, Leporello observes, delighted to learn that Leporello has been getting the peasant guests half tipsy and soothing Masetto's jealous breast. Nor is Giovanni surprised that Elvira arrived in his house with Zerlina. Leporello let Elvira throw a tantrum for a while, then led her through the garden out into the street and locked the gate in her face. Giovanni congratulates him on his resourcefulness in setting up a scene which the master can bring to fruition. His mind is full of the 'contadinotte' ('country wenches', with a jocular suggestion of 'nightbirds') whom he will now entertain until it is dark.

The orchestra plunges, *presto*, into his **Aria, No. 11** in B flat major, *Fin ch'han dal vino*, with flutes, oboes, clarinets, bassoons, horns and strings.

> Get ready for a feast that will go on till heads are buzzing with wine. If you find any girl in the square, bring her along too. We'll have dancing—the minuet, la follia, the almain, see that they dance them all. And I meanwhile will sing another song, making love to this girl and that. By tomorrow morning I should have ten more names for the catalogue.

This has long been known as the Champagne Aria, although da Ponte nowhere specifies what sort of *vino* is to be uncorked. The mystery is solved by reference to old German editions of the opera where the aria begins 'Treibt der Champagner'.* It is also traditional, though unauthentic, that Giovanni should brandish a glass of Champagne (not Spanish 'champagne', I hope—only palatable when spiked) as he sings *Fin ch'han dal vino*—not impossible if he is standing outside the inn shown in the supposed Platzer setting. The tempo is a fizzing one, the scoring full (often second violins as well as violas are *divisi*), the rhythm insidious and persistent.

* So it is sung by Heinrich Schlusnus on record. Modern German Don Juans are more likely to sing *Auf zu dem Feste*.

31

Fin ch'han dal vi——no   cal—da la te——sta   u—na gran   fe—sta   fà   pre-pa——rar.

Given such a good tune Mozart wisely casts the aria as something like a rondo with many reprises; yet though hard-driving in continuity it has time for attractive side-incidents such as the chromatics at 'teco ancor quella cerca a menar', and the woodwind hiccups from 'la danza sia', and the dislocation of the beat now and then, shown in the example below.

32

chi l'a—le——ma-na   fa—rai bal—lar, chi'il——   mi—nu——   —et—to   fa——rai bal—lar,

Then there is the sinister B flat minor passage at 'Ed io frattanto'—the point at which Liszt picked up this aria in the course of his *Don Juan Réminiscences* (because he wished to forge a link with the minor-key music of the Statue)—and the explosive *fp* chords several times.

Don Giovanni has a high-lying vocal compass in this aria, and his voice must project well to match the full scoring here and there. But he need not bawl or bark his music; and he must certainly not hurry if the characteristic rhythm of Ex. 31 is to remain clear. All too often it is deflated into sloppy triplets and the aria becomes a plebeian scramble.

Now the scene changes to a garden decorated with two arbours (like gazebos, perhaps) and surrounded by a wall with two gates locked—da Ponte scrupulously specifies—from outside. The country boys and girls are scattered about the garden, some asleep, some reclining on grassy banks. Zerlina and Masetto are among them. It is, I guess, about 3 p.m. They have, most of them, been drinking well since early morning and are ready for a siesta. Part of the palace—a window or balcony, or a porch—must be in view.

Masetto is still angry, and Zerlina is doing her best to appease him. She is a much meeker girl than Susanna or Despina, but she is young and very pretty and knows instinctively how to twiddle a man round her finger, cross though he may be. Masetto cannot bear even to be touched by a girl who left him on their wedding-day to go off by herself with another man. To an honest working chap her conduct is infamous. She insists that their host did not touch even a fingertip (with luck no one will tell Masetto about their loving embraces or her longing to 'ristorar le pene d'un casto amor innocente', as she most unchastely phrased her emotions of a few hours ago). If Masetto doesn't believe her, let him pummel her to pieces so long as he makes peace with her afterwards.

She elaborates her truly open-hearted submissiveness in her **Aria, No. 12,**

Batti, batti, o bel Masetto, which is *andante grazioso* in F major, with flute, oboe, bassoon (one of each), two horns, and strings, with an obbligato cello who is kept busy from start to finish without more than three quavers' rest all that long time.

> Dear Masetto, beat your poor Zerlina. I'll stand here, just like a lamb, to receive your blows. I'll let you tear my hair, gouge my eyes out, and then happily I'll kiss your darling hands.
>
> Ah, I see you haven't the heart to do it. Let's make it up, my sweetheart, let's live our days and our nights in happiness and contentment.

The first two and a half sentences of the above might lead one to expect violent music. Mozart knows Zerlina better. She exhorts Masetto in placid bucolic music, companionable with a hint of purling streams and grazing cattle.

33
Andante grazioso

Bat-ti bat-ti o bel Ma-set-to la tua po-ve-ra Zer-li-na sta-rò qui come agn-el—li—na le tue bot-te ad a—spet--tar,

Just so did Beethoven, twenty or so years later, depict his walk by the brook at Heiligenstadt in the Pastoral Symphony. Zerlina talks of wife-beating but to the music of her heart ('sentilò battere', as in No. 18, another sort of beating) which is about kissing and cuddling. The tune of 'starò qui' with its repetitions is delightfully pastoral and intimate; how curious to find it presaged in the early B flat major symphony K. 173dA, where it has more vigorous associations, relevant here but not evoked. Calmly the melody of Ex. 33 is sung again by the solo woodwind. For the pulling-out of all her hair, strings and wind approach C major with equal serenity and charm. The first hint of engagement between text and music (certainly deliberate) is at 'I shall kiss your darling hands'.

34

e le ca——re tue ma—ni—ne lie—ta poi sa-prò ba—ciar,
Vcl.

sfp

Here the voice's pairs of slurred semiquavers tell of quick repeated kisses to and fro, and the matching solo cello may suggest that its baritone voice is the loving murmur of a gentle husband, when she has placated him (not fiery, physical Giovanni but docile, quietly amorous Masetto). This idea is taken up in three-point counterpoint by woodwind, cello doubling bassoon (for euphony, doubtless more than thoughts of incipient parenthood) to bring back Ex. 33, Zerlina's vocal line now being tenderly ornamented. After the repeat, as before, rapid violin trills suggests Zerlina's secret amusement to observe that Masetto is weakening. She reaches a pause which she will decorate as gently and seductively as she knows how.

Having sensed that Masetto is won over, Zerlina moves, still with flowing cello, into an even more pastoral six-eight (still at the same pace, no faster or it will sound silly) for 'pace, pace'. Bucolic repeated phrases, almost recalling some *ranz des vaches*, enhance the charm. The cello's running semiquavers incite her to florid runs. Towards the end she teases him coquettishly with her 'sì, sì, sì' passages, again very tactile music, leading to chuckles which may be heard in the orchestra's concluding bars. They end *pianissimo*.

This aria can seem too long, but only when the Zerlina lacks vocal and personal charm, or when she exerts her fascinations too doggedly. Normally one should wish to hear at least the final six-eight again.

Masetto, for sure, is quite seduced by the little witch. But Giovanni's voice is heard from indoors, instructing his lackeys to be ready for the banquet. At this, Zerlina spoils her success by wishing to hide before he enters the garden. Masetto at once suspects and hides in an arbour, leaving her to be discovered by Mounseer Cavalier, as she has called him.

As he conceals himself, the first act's **Finale, No. 13**, begins, *allegro assai* in C major. The full orchestra is playing almost at once (timpani only at Giovanni's exit from the palace), but softly just now for Masetto's jealous design ('Presto, presto, pria ch'ei venga'). Zerlina begs him not to behave stupidly or he may get hurt; but he will not listen. They have a rapid duet at cross purposes. Now drums join the full orchestra in a noble fanfare. Giovanni, with four grandly clothed servants, walks into the garden, calling the couples on the grass to go inside and join the fun ('Sù, svegliatevi da bravi!'), and telling the servants to conduct his guests to the dance-floor and buffet. His injunctions, to joyous trills of entertainment as well as the fanfares of gracious living, are repeated in male chorus—by the servants according to Mozart's score, though the text clearly implies that it is the guests who lustily confirm that they are going to enjoy themselves greatly.*

The music grows softer as the peasants go inside, and now swiftly turns into F major, *andante*; clarinets, trumpets and drums have a rest. Zerlina is looking for a hiding-place and selects a tree (optimistically).

* Mozart wrote this music before arriving in Prague. He did not know if a chorus was available, but relied on a few male extras. In Prague he did find some choristers and wrote music for them in No. 5 and No. 24, but forgot to include them here or in the final ensemble of this first act where they can also contribute helpfully.

I quoted this so as to show how affectingly Zerlina's voice grows out of the violin phrase and into the cool nocturnal woodwind—typical *al fresco* Mozart. Giovanni spots her at once (by smell, no doubt, if not by sight) and catching hold of her leads her, most unwillingly, to one of the arbours. We are aware now that the tension is sustained by a succession of horn pedal-notes, just as the woodwind are keeping us aware of night-scented air (human as much as floral perhaps—for example:

each of these melodic strands enhances the fragrance of the anxiety of the moment). Of course Giovanni chooses the arbour where Masetto was hiding and is surprised into D minor when he finds him there. The horn pedal-notes were no whim; they now become repeated notes, at first menacing then, by a stroke of dramatic inspiration, comic with dancing *acciaccature* as Giovanni attempts to surmount an embarrassment by telling Masetto that Zerlina should not be left alone without him.

The joke is partly, at least, that something like these words was being said by Masetto to Don Giovanni a short while ago, before *Ho capito*. Masetto grimly sees the joke. Giovanni hears (*allegretto*) the distant sound of a dance band indoors, playing a *contredanse* (in English, country dance) of which more later. It inspires him to lead Zerlina and Masetto into the ballroom singing a cheerful concerted trio.

Another trio is at hand. F major turns into D minor, with violin scrunches and chill woodwind chords. Donna Elvira has made contact with Donna Anna. Don Ottavio has elaborated a plan to test the qualities of his old friend Giovanni. All three will disguise themselves as masked revellers (a common practice in da Ponte's Venice, I don't know about Spain, still less in the early afternoon) and here they are. The staccato violins indicate that the ladies' hearts are a-flutter, and they are exhorting one another to be brave and unmask the villain, though Anna fears a scandal that might tarnish their reputations. From within the house a dance band is heard playing a minuet in F major (suitable dance for people of their social pretensions). Leporello has opened a window to observe these gate-crashers. Giovanni instructs him to invite them to the party. The masqueraders could not be more pleased; Ottavio is deputed to accept on their behalf and answers gratefully.

But the orchestra, *adagio* in B flat major, joined by clarinets and emptied of strings, proposes more serious topics, and the three masqueraders pray for heaven's protection and assistance in their enterprise, to the strains of a solemn yet very florid trio with woodwind accompaniment ('Protegga il giusto cielo'). It is sublimely beautiful, infernally difficult, and of the utmost importance to the success of any performance. In Mozart's day, and much later, it was thought not inartistic to sing sensitively but *sotto voce*: this may be the way to bring off the exquisite phrasing and clean coloratura demanded by this trio and furthered by the subdued yet valuable woodwind support. Solo woodwind see these three avenging angels into the palace.

II

The scene changes to the ballroom of Don Giovanni's palace, brilliantly lit and peopled by the country guests who have just finished a dance and are being offered refreshments and chairs by Giovanni and Leporello and the other servants, ('Riposate, vezzose ragazze'). The music is *allegro* in E flat major; the oboes are now resting, with trumpets and drums, but the music is still festive and dancelike. Masetto warns Zerlina to behave herself and they both, in duet, fear that a nice party may end with tears. The music reaches B flat and the signpost to tears, Don Giovanni himself, arrives to fuss over Zerlina, rather to her taste. Leporello amuses the other guests by mimicking his master's antics to some girls called Gianotta and Sandrina. In short, they are all slightly mocking Masetto's lunatic jealousy, to extremely brilliant E flat major music.

Before Don Giovanni has time to live down to his reputation, the three masqueraders walk into the ballroom (*maestoso* in C major, with absolutely full orchestra, except for horns who have gone to join a stage dance band). Leporello welcomes them solemnly ('Venite pur avanti, vezzose mascherette'—thus rudely excluding Don Ottavio).

39 [Maestoso]

Ve—ni—te pur a—van——ti, vez—zo—se ma-sche-ret—te!

Don Giovanni announces that this is Liberty Hall—the only conceivable meaning, in seventeenth century Spain, for 'Viva la libertà', which the hosts and maskers repeat enthusiastically. Don Giovanni calls for the resumption of the dancing: Leporello will arrange partners.

Giovanni had ordered dances without restriction, in *Fin ch'han dal vino*. Now his command is obeyed. Leporello has engaged three dance bands.★ The first now begins a minuet in G major (oboes, horns, strings)—already overheard in the previous scene—to which Ottavio and an almost collapsing Anna bravely dance; Elvira has pointed out Zerlina to them, and she ought to be dancing too, though there is no obvious partner for her, Giovanni being busy with organization. Masetto, for a start, must be kept occupied. Leporello tries to jolly him into cutting a caper, without success. A second dance band of violins and bass is heard tuning up (literally, while the minuet proceeds) and soon begins a middle-class *contre-danse*—again as heard from the garden earlier. To this Giovanni and Zerlina dance, much to Donna Anna's fury, though she is restrained by her friends. A third orchestra, again of violins and bass, tunes up, and it plays a *Teitsch*, i.e. *Deutscher*, i.e. 'German Dance', which we call a quick waltz (supposedly plebeian). Leporello at last bullies Masetto into dancing with him. When these three bands on stage co-ordinate perfectly in their three dances, whose rhythms are quite different (minuet in three, waltz in three at double tempo, country dance in a four which achieves three bars to every two of minuet), the effect is intensely exhilarating.

40 Orch. I

Orch. II

Orch. III

This moment of contrapuntal gaiety, which provides exercise for guests of all ranks and tastes, is ideal for Don Giovanni's purpose. The *Teitsch* has hardly begun when he draws Zerlina forcefully away into an adjoining room. Masetto cries out with distress, as indeed does she. Leporello fears the worst and runs out. The three masqueraders observe with satisfaction that the criminal can now be caught red-handed. The dances have been proceeding cheerfully all this while. But when

★ This was not unknown in Vienna at the time, though the bands would play in different rooms: in the present scene the three dances have to be seen and heard going on at once before our eyes.

Zerlina is heard, from offstage, calling for help, the bands cease and the pit orchestra resumes *allegro assai* in E flat major, to swirling figures against the masqueraders' calls for action and Zerlina's shouts—now from the other side of the palace (she is not giving in without a chase). Masetto and Ottavio break the door down. (*Andante maestoso* in F major.)

After a pause Giovanni emerges from another room denouncing Leporello as the culprit. Zerlina, saved before the seducer had time to do much with her, is reunited with Masetto. Giovanni promises that Leporello shall die. Nobody is deceived. It is Don Ottavio, to the surprise of all, who draws a pistol and, unmasking himself, points it at his host. Elvira and Anna likewise unmask, each to the same phrase, the more telling on repetition, with varied instrumental doubling.

All denounce Giovanni as the traitor. Zerlina comes forward and leads a splendid ensemble in which they assure him that all is discovered.

This takes the music to the edge of C major for the closing *strepitoso- arcistrepitoso* of the finale, *allegro* to begin with. The full orchestra is now employed again, including trumpets and drums, appropriately for the solemn presage of justice with unison scrunches. The stage bands have departed, and the chorus of peasants is heard no more—though Mozart may have cued them in during the Prague rehearsals.

The accusers, led by Anna and Zerlina, promise to make Giovanni's baseness common knowledge, and prophesy that heaven's thunderbolt will strike him down this very day. Their principal phrase grows menacingly, and with a solemn touch of F minor which later features again.

43

Giovanni and Leporello, *sotto voce*, register confusion in between these threatening exclamations. As the tension grows, both resort effectively to patter scales. Don Giovanni's bravado finally exerts itself most jauntily in a soft violin phrase partnered by him.

44

This is the calm before the final storm of general noisy C major ensemble capped by orchestra alone as Giovanni and Leporello presumably fight their way out while the curtain falls—how they do it is left to a producer's ingenuity.

12

Da Ponte is regularly cursed for having messed up the libretto of *Don Giovanni* in the scenes where he had not Bertati to copy from. The judgment is unnecessarily harsh. After *Ah, fuggi il traditor* he sensibly developed the *imbroglio* of Elvira with Anna and Ottavio three times to strong dramatic effect—in the quartet *Non ti fidar*, in the Masquerade of the finale, and later in Act II the sextet *Sola, sola, in bujo loco*. He wisely removed Donna Anna's narration, No. 10, to a later, more effective dramatic position. He created Don Giovanni's party as a means of intensifying the involvement of Masetto and Zerlina, later of bringing the three other conspirators more positively into the action. He gave Giovanni another attempted seduction, and created one of his favourite *accelerando* finales. He gave his collaborator the opportunity to turn workaday comic incident into a blend of comedy and seriousness, with great virtuosity added, a real operatic finale. These dramatically relevant additions, enhanced by fine music, are not padding.

Da Ponte has likewise been stigmatized for his bungling of Act II up to the Cemetery Scene where at last he has Bertati to grasp again as a guideline. What he achieves here is a new development of character-confrontation. We do well to watch it, in Act II, suspiciously yet ready to applaud da Ponte's new ideas, as well as what Mozart made of them.

When the curtain rises on Act II we are back in the street from Act I. Leporello has been complaining indignantly about the public scene, at the end of Act I, when Giovanni threatened to assassinate him in his innocence for Giovanni's own crime. Giovanni protests that it was a joke ('Fu per burlar'). Leporello finds it no laughing matter, rather grounds for separation. The recitative first designed for this scene was wisely rejected in favour of a brilliant comic **Duet** for the master and his servant, *Eh via buffone* in G major, **No. 14.** This goes with great fire accompanied by oboes, horns and strings, and proves on examination to consist largely of orchestral unisons (for insistence), conventional *crescendi* and much rapid patter for both singers: polish and verve rather than original musical thought—the very spirit of Italian *opera buffa*.

Leporello is perfectly resolved to resign Don Giovanni's service—until he hears the clink of four doubloons,⋆ whereupon he withdraws his resignation on condition that his master and he leave women alone. Giovanni's reply, that they are as necessary to him as food and air, and that he would be faithful to one if that were not unfair to all the others, is sufficiently eloquent to convince Leporello of its sheer logicality. So they proceed to the next adventure, Donna Elvira's lovely maidservant for whose seduction it will be necessary for the adventurers to exchange clothes—no one is more class-conscious than a domestic servant; Giovanni speaks from great experience. Leporello tries to apply these scruples to himself, but Don Giovanni will not hear further argument. They withdraw into the shadow to swap hats and cloaks and Giovanni's sword (this episode descends from Tirso's play). Daylight is beginning to fade (perhaps 7 p.m.) and Donna Elvira chooses this romantic moment to appear at her window—a balcony is not specified but is usually supplied, following Platzer's original setting. In **No. 15, Terzetto,** *andantino* in A major, *Ah taci, ingiusto core*! she confides to the first breezes of night her weakness for the man she still loves, even though she knows him to be a villain, undeserving of her pity. Flutes, clarinets (as usual for Elvira), bassoons, horns and strings accompany this trio whose elegance and sensuous lyricism give little hint of the absurd situation which develops during its progress. The first subject is balmy serenade music for strings, answered by Elvira.

45

It continues to skittering violin scales which seem connected with the 'impious traitor' on whom Elvira's loving thoughts are unwillingly centred, since every return of these scales refers directly to her infatuation for him.

A sinuous shadowy phrase for bassoons follows Elvira's soaring cadence. It suggests conspiracy and at first indeed it is taken over by Leporello and Giovanni

⋆ The doubloon was worth a sovereign.

who, disguised as one another, have spotted Elvira. Don Giovanni envisages an opportunity here.

46

The phrase, as indicated, is repeated eight times in four bars, with few changes of instrumentation, yet growing more significant each time—as it will subsequently too. Gentle woodwind ease the music into E major for a repeat of Ex. 45, Giovanni singing instead of Elvira (because the change of key demands a lower *tessitura*). He has pushed Leporello into the street under Elvira's window and, hiding behind him, calls lovingly to her, begging forgiveness for past sins. When Ex. 46 returns it is Elvira who sings to it of the curious feeling his voice arouses in her—Leporello notes her credulousness.

The dominant section completed, the music moves amorously into C major for a middle section in which Giovanni passionately serenades Elvira, manipulating Leporello's arms into suitable (or unsuitable) gestures of pleading.

47

The resemblance to Ex. 48 below is clear, like a comic dress rehearsal for Giovanni's real serenade.

For a moment Elvira's credulity is conquered by reason. She refuses noisily to listen to him: stormy woodwind, sequential key-switches, string tremolos, and Leporello's mirth, all cloud the issue. But Giovanni's lyricism pulls the music back to A major for a reprise of Ex. 45 in which all three voices are united—though expressing divergent emotions: Elvira wondering what to do, Leporello praying to the gods that she will resist this liar (already he suspects that he is due to be the fall-guy in this adventure since he is impersonating the *barbaro*), Giovanni congratulating himself on his quick-wittedness. So the trio ends euphoniously with singers in harmony answered antiphonally by alluring wind and strings. It matches the trio for the same characters in Act I, but is more lyrical and dramatically more lively, as purely beautiful as any number in the opera so that, even if Leporello exaggerates for laughs, the music keeps the scales well balanced provided that the audience allows every note to be heard.

At the beginning of the opera Leporello was nurturing ambitions to 'far il gentiluomo'. His wish is now granted for, as he had begun to suspect ('Deh proteggete, o dei, la sua credulità'), his orders now are to field Elvira, when she emerges, butter her up nicely and take her off for a cosy stroll, thus leaving Giovanni a clear road to the heart of the chambermaid. The master is sure that Elvira will not penetrate the disguise if Leporello does not want her to.

Elvira duly appears and is quite taken in by the gusto of Leporello's impersonation which improves with exercise: he calls her his muse, his Venus, declares that her fire turns him to ashes, and kisses her voraciously on the hands and on the eyes.

Don Giovanni, who has been watching with amusement (it is a splendid opportunity for a basso buffo who is also an able mimic), decides to move the couple on. So he pretends, from his dark hiding-place, to be noisily slaughtering an enemy, whereupon they both take fright and run away. Giovanni, pealing with mirth, leaves his cranny to stand under Elvira's window and serenade the lady's maid in **No. 16, Canzonetta**, *allegretto* in D major, *Deh vieni alla finestra*, accompanied by mandolin (supposedly played by himself) and plucked strings.

> Come to the window, my treasure, come and console my longing. If you do not give me some solace, I will die before your very eyes.
> You, with a mouth sweet as honey, with sugar at your inmost heart, cannot be cruel to me, my joy. Let me at least see you, my fair love.

The two strophic verses of this love-song demand all the *bel canto*, smooth and sustained and elegantly phrased, as well as amorously interpreted, that a honeyed yet basically robust baritone voice can command. Yet the agile running semiquavers of the mandolin obbligato are no less important and rather more prominent. They make no use of the mandolin's characteristic *bisbigliando* but otherwise the part is aptly designed for the instrument and always sounds unconvincing when the mandolin is replaced by harpsichord or harp, or simply some extra plucked violins (nowadays the mandolin has resumed its old popularity and substitutes are even less condonable). I quote, for reference, especially to Ex. 47 above, the beginning of the first sung verse with its obbligato.

48
[Allegretto]

Deh vie—ni alla fi—ne—stra, o mio——— te-so———ro

Mand.

Archi pizz.

As his serenade ends, Don Giovanni sees somebody at Elvira's window; he makes 'psst' noises at her. But as usual on this day he is interrupted. Masetto and a posse of his fellow-farmhands come down the street, all as heavily armed as their resources allow. They are searching for Don Giovanni to murder him. Their prey suspects as much, so uses his disguise to hail them (Mozart and da Ponte expanded this recitative when they discovered Bassi's talent for mimicry) and promise to assist them in their design which he too considers a public benefaction. He gives them strategical advice in yet another **Aria, No. 17** (Bassi must by now have reckoned himself content!), *andante con moto* in F major, *Metà di voi quà vadano* with flutes, oboes, bassoons, horns and strings.

> Half of you go in this direction, (*to the right*), and the others along there (*to the left*) and quietly seek him out. He can't be far away. If you see a man walking across the square with a girl, or making love beneath a window, strike him down. It will be my master. He wears a hat with white feathers, a large cloak on his back, and a sword on his hip. Go on, be quick!

Mozart seems to have composed this in Vienna, before discovering Bassi's powers of mimicry. But the success of the aria depends entirely on a Giovanni who can ape Leporello's style of delivery, then forget himself for a moment and sing in his own character, realize his mistake (without written directions) and resume his comic servant impersonation.

The aria is also composed with scrupulous attention to musical and dramatic detail within a balanced structural frame. It begins with soft semi-comic stealth (for serious stealth look at No. 10, *Or sai chi l'onore*), as witness the sustained horn pedal, the offbeat violins, and the ceaselessly peering figure after 'vadano'.

49

The peering figure emerges in the second sentence of my English résumé: 'lontan non fia di quà'. Then comes a simultaneous representation ('If a man and a girl') of two people walking up a street and of the giggling girl.

50

Its consequent, of wide-ranging unisons for strings, is a perfect musical portrayal of violence, dumb and dull and brutal, followed by two lordly phrases with trills (bar 3 of Ex. 51), and a jocular cadence (bar 4).

51

The fake Leporello now describes his master's dress in some detail—his white-plumed hat:

52

his big cloak (Leporello's is short):

53

and his sword:

54

Here, as if impromptu, Giovanni's lordly self takes over from his impersonation of Leporello, and he has quickly to redeem himself with comic, non-*sostenuto* servant-type delivery. Ex. 50 and the brutal part of Ex. 51 return, then Ex. 49, subsequently a more urgent patter style, to send the yokels away. Giovanni has Masetto to himself.

You come with me alone. We must do the rest, and you'll see what.

The aria is not yet finished. The strategist is tranquillizing his victim with smiles and flattery.

55

While the orchestra elaborates on watchfulness and stealth, Giovanni leads Masetto down the street and back. The last six chords are loud, as if Masetto had taken sudden fright, or sudden courage.

Giovanni makes sure that murder, not merely mutilation or a good hiding, is Masetto's intention. He inspects Masetto's armoury, relieves him of each ramshackle item in turn, then belabours the poor fellow into near-insensibility, with insults to match, and rapidly makes off. He had given his sword to Leporello but would not demean himself to use even his dagger on a farmer.

Masetto is not unconscious. He is groaning and complaining noisily. His cries are heard by Zerlina who, knowing in advance what the escapade would lead to, has evidently been acting as rearguard, armed with a lantern. She inspects the damage in full detail and prescribes the appropriate remedy: return home, stop being jealous, and take the medicine she will now prescribe.

Her prescription is contained in her **Aria, No. 18**, *grazioso* in C major, *Vedrai, carino*, with flutes, clarinets (not for Elvira but for true love), bassoons, horns and warmly affectionate strings.

> If you're good, my dear, you'll see what a lovely medicine I'll give you. It's natural and doesn't taste nasty, and the chemist doesn't know the recipe. It's an ointment that I carry on me. I'll give you some if you'll try it. Would you like to know where I keep it? Feel it beating, touch me here!

Any reader who wonders why, in earlier days dating back to the first performance, Zerlina's was considered the star female role in *Don Giovanni* should read the text of this aria, in da Ponte's charming, sensual Italian if possible (the above English résumé is deliberately *naturale* and in Zerlina's character, yet it melts me to write it down because the sentiments are so sweet and persuasive in the Italian), and then listen to the aria as recorded long ago by Elisabeth Schumann who brought a voice of pearl and silver, a delicacy of expressive tenderness, and a poised musical style to the song that made me, as a boy, prefer it to all the grand heroics of Donna Anna and Donna Elvira. Nowadays the part of Zerlina is carefully cast, for gentleness and charm rather than *soubrette* flirtatiousness, and this aria is nicely sung, but seldom so as to make Zerlina obviously the most attractive of the three ladies in *Don Giovanni*. Mozart wrote it (like *Batti, batti*, which can easily outstay its welcome) as a vehicle for Caterina Bondini, the darling of Prague and the wife of his temporary employer. He knew her voice and musical quality and composed *Vedrai, carino* so that she and all her admirers would take it to their hearts.

The very simplicity of the first musical sentence is captivating: the lift in the second bar, the warm middle part at bar 4, the tender feminine cadence.

56

Trills in late Mozart are often flippant, but not those for 'È naturale'. Flutes are often used for chill displeasure, or sudden illumination, or celestial purity; at 'non lo sà far' (the chemist's ignorance) they convey secret healing love, as clarinets often do in Mozart elsewhere in this aria.

Until 'dove mi star', with its pause, the music could be thought over-sophisticated for a landgirl by those who have never left town. Now the pastoral heart begins to pound gently in the bass, the woodwind to play rustic unisons above.

57

Sen—ti —lo   bat—te—re,

Zerlina presses Masetto's hand to her breast (we see it, most appealingly, in an old print), and heartbeats are thereafter much prominent—heartbeat arias were a popular feature of Italian comic opera, e.g. Pergolesi and Logroscino, and we meet another one in *Così fan tutte*. There is a full reprise of the beginning and the end of the aria as Zerlina leads the hobbling Masetto away. He will recover and reappear sooner than anyone might imagine, so skilful a medicine-woman is she.

13

The scene changes to a dark and spacious courtyard in front of Donna Anna's house. Leporello has been leading Elvira as far as possible away from Palazzo Tenorio, but now he has seen a torchlight procession approaching. He knows this courtyard: he examined it closely last night when he was on sentry-go in the garden close by. It is usually empty and has three doors. To escape notice by the procession he draws Elvira in here, hoping to abandon her and escape by one of these doors as soon as possible. He whispers hifalutin' phrases of encouragement to her, then starts hunting for an exit. It is now about 9 p.m.

Elvira had expected a passage of love. Instead she finds herself left alone in this dark and cheerless place, **No. 19, Sestetto**, *andante* in E flat major, *Sola, sola in bujo loco* for full orchestra eventually. Flutes and bassoons in thirds portray her chill anxiety in unfriendly surroundings, she who needs warmth and encouragement more than anything in the world. The high violins are not smirking (as in the sextet of *Figaro*) but reflecting her fear.

58

A precipitate downward arpeggio just afterwards brings this fear even more forward ('m'assalle un tal spavento') so that she feels like to die—darkly murmurous strings. Leporello, meanwhile, is feeling for a door, to music of familiar stealth, oboes and clarinets to the fore. He finds the middle door; it is blind (part of a backdrop—this is one of Platzer's narrow-stage sets). Just as he reaches a side-entrance the music makes a brilliant modulation from B flat to D major, trumpets and drums enter, and with them through this door Donna Anna and Don Ottavio, both in heavy mourning, with servants bearing torches. After the disastrous masquerade they perhaps decided to visit the Commendatore's grave; theirs were the lights seen by Leporello. Now they have returned and once again Ottavio is attempting to restrain Anna's incessant weeping. The chilly flutes in sixths at his first words seem retrospective; they now fall silent while Ottavio sings a formal, heroic, long melody of exhortation, much like that of his forebears in Mozart's earlier heroic operas. Anna answers him, much more eloquently, in D minor (the key of No. 2), begging him to honour her sacred grief (self-pity, of course, but preferable to this dignified windbag who had a pistol and did not use it). She longs, floridly and sostenuto, for death in romantic, respectable C minor.

They have not seen Elvira or Leporello. Both are looking for an exit from this touching private scene. Elvira, in particular, is hunting for her husband.

This makes an apt and telling link from Anna to Elvira. She finds a door, so does Leporello. But through it enter Zerlina and Masetto, determined to tell Don Ottavio about Leporello's recent acts of assault and battery. Seeing the supposed Giovanni they pounce on him and exhibit him to Anna and Ottavio who respond vengefully. Elvira, to Ex. 59, pleads for her beloved husband, a status which surprises everybody. After a moment's confusion, suitably suggested by Ex. 59, the others all refuse mercy for Giovanni. The convoluted violin figure which punctuates their cries is unforgettable because so determined.

Again Elvira pleads, to a development of Ex. 59, again they deny her request.

So Leporello reveals his true face, without the floppy hat, very despondently—the descending woodwind sound like a deflated soufflée.

Fear for his life drives him into mournful descending diminished sevenths ('per carità').

The others are all mightily astonished. 'Goodness, Leporello!' they all cry hesitantly in full harmony with pattering orchestral heartbeats and fast-running bloodstreams. Ex. 59 makes a newly appropriate return, sad now because so bewildered.

E flat major, *molto allegro* with full orchestra, makes a decision; perplexed Leporello is pitted against a massed but equally perplexed throng of aggressors. He launches into terrified patter, they answer in livelier chorus, as for a grand finale (E. J. Dent deduced from this music that *Don Giovanni* was planned in four acts; I think it more likely that *Figaro* was planned in two acts, and this finale is for a scene, not the preparation for an interval). The harmonic movement is massive, slow, but tremendous, as at bar 178 where E flat major suddenly becomes D flat major with a heroic pseudo-cadenza for Donna Anna. Mozart keeps it going with repeats and new variations, including a stunned almost *a cappella* section for voices, with a hint of E flat minor, for a long time. Eventually Donna Anna sweeps out, followed by her servants, while the orchestra finishes grandly in E flat major.

It is a superlative ensemble number, not only for its music but for its dramatic action. If da Ponte had not included it, in his enlargements on Bertati's libretto, Mozart would have demanded it as an opportunity to draw personalities out in music, to extend the characters other than the already well delineated Don Giovanni.

Poor Leporello is now accused insultingly by Zerlina of causing Masetto's bruises, by Elvira for his allurements, by Ottavio for general delinquency—Ottavio is strong on strategy, weak in ratiocination. Leporello, even with a weak case, is a more eloquent counsel for his own defence, especially when four people show every sign of smashing him to smithereens. He defends himself in his **Aria, No. 20,** *allegro assai* in G major, *Ah pietà, signori miei*, with flutes, bassoons, horns and strings (violas several times richly divided). He has several parties to appease.

> Have mercy on me, my lords. You (peasants) and you (nobles) are right, I admit, but the guilty party isn't me. It was my overbearing master who robbed me of my innocence.
>
> (*Aside*) Do help me, Donna Elvira; you know yourself what happened.
>
> (*To Zerlina*) As for Masetto I know not a thing. This young lady (*indicating Elvira*)★ will tell you I've been walking about with her for the last hour or so.
>
> (*To Don Ottavio*) I've no explanation for you, sir. Partly I was frightened and partly it was mischance . . . light out there and dark in here. It isn't an excuse. The door, the wall, the . . . the . . . I came from over there, and then hid here. If I'd known how it was, oh, I'd have run away through that door, there!

Leporello suits action to word, and the others are not quick enough to stop him.

Leporello is an able *basso cantante*, we have several times discovered, especially in *Madamina*, but his characteristic diction is mostly semi-parlando, always musical whether fast or slow and always on the note. This is his most extensive aria, expressively, giving him greatest diversity of expression. He must begin *legato ed appassionato*, helped in pathos by the orchestra. At 'Do ragione' he adopts more *buffo* character but keeps on singing; then at 'ma, ma, il delitto' he can begin to play the musical clown, with detached tones. At 'Il padròn' he imitates his master, full and sonorous, only to collapse into self-pity for his robbed innocence. Violins

★ The word *fanciulla* should be enough to stop Elvira being cast as a middle-aged noble, or else hysterically comic, gentlewoman of *prima donna* pretensions. I would love to see a production of *Don Giovanni* in which each of the three principal sopranos exchanged roles at every performance. They would profit as much as their listeners.

help him to be taken seriously. With Masetto he speaks decisively in unison as an equal. He lapses darkly, with cheerful violin decoration above, into his memory of the innocent pitch-black walk with Elvira. His concentration goes as he sees a possible egress ('certo accidente'), and this is where he turns serious again, so as to impress his listeners.

62
[Allegro assai]

certo acci— den— te... di fuori chia—ro... di dentro o-scu—ro...

This searching idea helps him to get away. The others complain that he was too quick. Ottavio, always full of ideas, proposes that his companions stay in the house while he calls the police. Because he is going to sing a solo aria producers are inclined to send Zerlina, Elvira and Masetto off stage and leave him alone. But his **Aria, No. 21**, *Andante grazioso* in B flat major, *Il mio tesoro intanto*, directly addresses several people as friends ('Amici . . . andate') and we must assume that these three remain to hear him.

> Go meanwhile to my beloved and try to wipe away the tears from her lovely eyes. Tell her I have gone to revenge her wrongs and will only return when I can bring news of slaughter and death.

Don Ottavio is accompanied by clarinets (for affection), bassoons (for vigorous resonance), horns (for cohesion) and strings (muted at first for charm and confidentiality). In the Prague production this was his only solo. It is mellifluous, quite heroic (given his indecisive character), and technically demanding. In the early nineteenth century Rubini was famous for the top F which he introduced into it. Later John McCormack sang the florid runs with effortless virtuosity, and soon afterwards it became a delectably expressive, yet still perfectly poised, vehicle for Richard Tauber (whose interpretation, on the day before he was sent into hospital to his deathbed, remains unforgettable to one who had hitherto underestimated his artistry—records show how dapper a Mozartian he always was). *Il mio tesoro* is perfectly adjusted to the character of Ottavio: lovely music, lacking in tenderness, but fully expressive of an aspiring courtly love, the idol set in marble on a grand pedestal, the admirer determined to fight for her. Whether or not Mozart designed it so, it is much more Spanish than the gently sensuous *Dalla sua pace* (which suited Tauber even better, though he did not let on), and so more indicative of Ottavio's place in the drama.

14

The Prague original version now switched to the Cemetery Scene. But I am discussing the whole of *Don Giovanni* and must include some extra music composed for the first production in Vienna.

In this, Ottavio leaves with Donna Anna at the end of No. 20. Leporello, after escaping, is at once brought back by Zerlina who has caught him by the hair and has acquired a cut-throat razor of horrendous sharpness. The *recitativo* bass refers animatedly to the close of his aria No. 20 (compare Ex. 63 with Ex. 62):

This ostinato continues for twelve bars, switching between Zerlina and Masetto who can only plead for mercy ('Per carità'). Mercy is not on her list at present. She will cut off his hair, his head, gouge out his heart and his eyes. Leporello attempts wheedling. This makes her even angrier: she will pay him out for doing harm to young girls (this is obscure, as applied to Leporello). She drags him by the hair round the stage,* calling for Masetto who has somehow got lost, or for servants none of whom responds. During her travels she finds a seat and makes Leporello carry it to a spot indicated by her. She forces him to sit down ('Thanks, I'm not tired just now!'), binds his hands together behind his back, using a handkerchief, and with the aid of a passing farmhand (who never utters), ties him to the seat, and that to a window-frame, so that he cannot possibly escape. She intends to 'shave him without soap'. For Dent this denoted surgery *à la* Klingsor.

Leporello again begs for mercy, in the **Duet, No. 21b**, *allegro moderato* in C major, *Per queste tue manine*, with flutes, oboes, bassoons, horns and strings. He invokes her white and tender hands, her cool skin.

Coming from Leporello this solemn theme strongly recalls his reception of the masqueraders in Act One, Ex. 39; it is not characteristic of his usual musical diction. Indeed the rest of his opening plea sounds more like Giovanni—the servant using his master's winning tactics in an awkward situation. Likewise Zerlina, when she refuses all pity, likening herself to a raging tigress, a snake or lioness, adopts the tones we associate rather with Donna Elvira.

Leporello laments the cruelty of the gods, to grandly upsweeping string scales; Zerlina now sings in duet with him, applying 'barbaro' to him, wishing she might

* 'Absalom!' we almost expect her to cry (like Debussy's Golaud on a similar occasion).

cut out his master's heart at the same time, a thought which enlivens the orchestra as well. He now wails, in C minor with flutes in thirds, that she has bound him too tightly. Her glee soon pushes the music back into feathery, exhilarated C major in which, much less cheerfully, he has to join too.

66

Di gio-ia e di di — let — to   sen-to brillar mi il pet-to,   di gio-ia e di di—

che   scos————se. . .

-let — to   sen-to brillar mi il pet-to.

di. . .   tre — muo-to!

I quote this chiefly as an indication that the music of this duet is much less abysmal than commentators (who have probably never heard it) usually insist.★ The C minor passage is repeated with new and more expressive woodwind counterpoint, and the Ex. 66 section follows. Zerlina, in an access of Women's Lib ('this is the way to treat men'), bursts into a spate of comic patter—for all the world as if she were Leporello:

67

co-sì, co-sì, co—sì si fa,   co—sì, così, così, così, così, co—sì si

fa, così, così, così, così, co—sì si   fa, così, così, così, così, co—sì si fa,

—and then embarks on a syncopated figure, also on the word 'così', that looks back to the coda of Elvira's *Ah chi mi dice mai*. Considering that *Per queste tue manine* was only inserted to provide low Viennese taste with a moment of outright farce, it is a delightful piece that deserves wider circulation.

Zerlina, having established that Leporello cannot budge, goes off to fetch Masetto and Donna Elvira (they are not with Donna Anna: this is still the Vienna version of the opera). Leporello, in recitative, begs the farmhand for a drink of water, but he merely grins and goes away. The poor captive tries in vain to loosen the knotted handkerchief, so he prays for protection to Mercury, patron saint of thieves, and gives an almighty tug at the rope. It does not break but pulls out the window frame to which it was attached (much breaking of glass, no doubt). Leporello is now able to shamble away dragging the seat, still attached to his bottom, and the broken window frame.

Zerlina shortly reappears with Donna Elvira who looks forward to punishing

★ It is included in the recordings conducted by Leinsdorf and Barenboim. I am glad to see that Spike Hughes, in *Famous Mozart Operas*, also puts in a good word for it.

the fellow who exposed her weakness by dint of diguise. They have only just discovered his departure when Masetto enters with two of his farmhand friends. He tells them all how he has been rescuing a poor girl who was being ravished by a man—surely Don Giovanni from the description she gave, though the seducer fled on seeing Masetto approach. They decide to convey this news to Don Ottavio who must help to bring the criminal to justice. Off they go, leaving Elvira alone in the courtyard.

A small mystery attaches to the two recitative scenes summarized in the last two paragraphs above. In all scores of the Vienna version since the 1801 Breitkopf and Härtel edition, the first is given (with suspiciously faulty word-setting), but instead of the scene with Masetto there was a short dialogue in which Elvira tells Zerlina that Giovanni must have released Leporello—poor excuse for the outrage which she expresses in her immediately subsequent accompanied recitative. Mozart scholars long suspected that these two printed scenes were unauthentic, yet felt obliged to include them *faute de mieux*. One of these was Alfred Einstein who, after his edition for Eulenburg (still the most conveniently available pocket full score of *Don Giovanni*) had emerged, found in Florence one of Lausch's Viennese copies. This contained a different, obviously authentic version of the recitative for Leporello's escape, and the music for the second recitative with Masetto's narrative (the text of this had always been known from the printed Vienna libretto). The copy also included complete wind and brass parts for Act II, not in the Paris autograph.

Since 1938 reputable editions of *Don Giovanni* have included the authentic music for these two scenes. For the benefit of any reader unsure which Leporello recitative is Mozart's and which the forgery,* I quote the first bars of both versions. This is the one now attributed firmly to Mozart:

68

This is the forgery:

69

It may also be well to cite the beginnings of the later alternative scenes, since both begin with the same words sung by Zerlina. This is the one in Lausch's copy, made under Mozart's supervision:

---

* It stems from a revival of *Don Giovanni* in Prague in 1801. For full details see Einstein's *Essays on Music*, pp. 221–31 (Faber, 1958), or *Music and Letters*, xix/4, 1938, pp. 417 ff.

70

The version now disputed begins as follows:*

71

Even though the above are seldom performed, it seems necessary to discuss them in detail here, not simply for the sake of comprehensiveness. When Ottavio prefers not to sing No. 21, it is a good idea to give No. 21 B an airing. In either case the 'authentic' 'Andiam, andiam, signora', from Zerlina's 'Ah Masetto, Masetto, dove foste finor?' makes a more apt lead into Elvira's soliloquy—though for sensible motivation Masetto must run after Leporello, at the end of No. 20, perhaps after his one comment in the succeeding recitative, thus being absent for *Il mio tesoro*.

Let us return to Donna Elvira. Masetto's news of Giovanni's latest seduction, when added to the others of which she has knowledge, fills her soul with anxiety. Heaven is certain to punish such a wicked man at any moment; but he is the man whom she deeply loves. In the Prague first production Elvira had nothing to do between the sextet No. 19 and her interruption of the supper scene-finale No. 24. When the opera came to Vienna, Mozart was persuaded by Catarina Cavalieri, the Elvira there, that she needed an extra aria. She had an excellent part, but all its solos became ensembles. Cavalieri was the mistress of Mozart's official rival Salieri, but Mozart had always liked and admired the lady; he remained friends with her until his death (*cf. Zauberflöte*, p. 601) and she was closely linked with several of his operas. Her request fired him to the finest of all the 1788 additions to *Don Giovanni*: **No. 21c**, the B flat **Recitativo**, *In quali eccessi* with its **Aria** in E flat major, *Mi tradì quell' alma ingrata*. It is valuable because it reveals the true personality of Elvira more completely than any of her music elsewhere, a woman of genuine feeling at last able to express herself without being overshadowed by others or ridiculed by the nature of the *opera buffa* in which she finds herself. These other numbers have prepared us to recognize her true qualities (especially the trio, No. 15). Now we can concentrate on them. Since the music of No. 21c is superb, it follows that the opera loses something important if it is given remorselessly in the Prague original version.

* The distinction may be helpful since Erich Leinsdorf in his recording performs the 'authentic' Leporello scene and then switches to the 'fake' 'Andiam, andiam, signora'. In 1957 the 'authentic' version from Masetto's entry onwards was being performed by Carl Rosa Opera in Britain as a sensible introduction to *In quali eccessi*.

The Recitative, accompanied by strings alone, begins passionately with unison phrases:

72

The initial turbulence is mollified by the hint of compassion in the female ending of bars 2 and 4. Elvira has always felt in two minds about the man whom she still regards as her husband. Her words explain this dichotomy of heart and mind.

> O ye Gods, in what excesses, in what horrible, monstrous misdeeds has this wretched man implicated himself? Ah no! Heaven's wrath and earth's justice cannot tarry long. Methinks I see now the fatal thunderbolt which will crash upon his head, see the deadly abyss yawn wide. Wretched Elvira, what conflict of emotion stirs within your breast! Wherefore these sighs and these anxieties?

Ex. 72 suits five of these sentiments, the last two more economical in texture as if anger were tamed into objective anxiety. The 'fatal thunderbolt' induces a rushing instrumental figure. Her 'conflict of emotion' brings out a new phrase, poignantly melancholy.

73

This is a personal Mozart, reserved for profound emotion: I do not agree that it is proto-romantic; there is a prophetic Mozart (in *Die Zauberflöte* for example, even in *Batti, batti*, perhaps) but this expression is more backward than forward-looking. Those languishing appoggiaturas glance behind them to C.P.E. Bach, not forward to Beethoven or any romantic. Whichever way one looks, the recitative is deeply human, representative of a heroine to love and admire.

Elvira, having reached a spartan cadence in B flat, proceeds at once to her aria, *Mi tradi quell' alma ingrata*, in E flat major, *allegretto*, with single flute, clarinet and bassoon, two horns and strings. (Mozart allowed it to be sung a semitone lower.)

> That faithless soul betrayed me and made me unhappy. Yet I, betrayed and abandoned, still feel pity for him. When I feel my own torment, my heart calls for vengeance. But if I consider his plight, my beating heart forsakes me.

This is a sort of rondo where every new episode leads to a reprise of 'that faithless soul', a captivating expression of animated womanly love.

74

Allegretto

Mi tra—dì quell' al——ma ingra—ta, quell' al——ma in—grata:

The flavour and colour of the imitations by clarinet and bassoon will not pass unnoticed. In the first episode flute and bassoon vary the notes but not the rhythm of Ex. 74. Other instruments bandy this rhythm while the singer varies it, before resuming it for 'provo ancor', twice. The steady running quavers still persist—they do so almost throughout, in a hundred forms and nuances. The rondo theme is repeated. Then an E flat minor episode ensues, for 'Quando sento il mio tormento', melancholy but not frenzied; the one-bar phrases become two-bar by simple inventive extension: what was one sentence now requires two, though the thematic beat-count, an idea more than a rhythm, persists. G flat major (not a Mozartian tonality) is reached and quickly relinquished for G minor: 'palpitando il cor mi và' ('my beating heart'), still adorned by indefatigable woodwind, involves an eventful florid run, typical of the Elvira we have come to know.

75

pal———— pi—tan

do il cor— mi va,

'Palpitando' is broken up syllabically (for heart-palpitation), against the idée fixe on woodwind; the next rondo reprise arrives. The subsequent episode brings the orchestra even more expressively forward, and draws Elvira into even more florid divisions, always inspiring woodwind to like agility (easier for them than for a singer). The obsessive rhythm is lost in Elvira's final cadences, but regained in the orchestral coda, thoroughly active.

As she leaves the stage we may think back at this marvellous aria and perhaps conclude that, for all its springing musical invention and brilliant insistence on thematic rhythm, it shows Elvira as a woman who has to keep going, on no matter what tack, in order not to collapse of natural inanition. She is passionate, dynamic, determined, tireless, but motivated by an unreal life-force. She has to wind herself up, like a clockwork doll, otherwise she will cease to function, and flop to the ground. The dynamo is Don Giovanni: if she loses him she will be a dead battery as she was before he abducted her from the nunnery. This is her fear, the reason for her appearance in the final supper scene and her ultimate decision to return to convent life. Without *Mi tradì* we could believe that she might live happily hereafter. *Mi tradì*, an afterthought, puts a different complexion on the future of Donna Elvira.

This part of Act II is overburdened with static solo arias, as all have observed, even more than the last act of *Figaro*. Sometimes *Mi tradì* is interpolated into Act I. This is a practice originated by Friedrich Rochlitz early in the nineteenth century.

Textually it makes no sense. If *Mi tradì* is to be sung it can only be here where it is motivated.

15

We are back with the first Prague version of *Don Giovanni*, and da Ponte, after his necessary flights of original invention, is restored to his Bertati dramatic source. The scene is a churchyard.

It is an enclosed space in the form of a burial ground. There are numerous equestrian statues, one of them commemorating Donna Anna's father, the Commendatore. Don Giovanni jumps over a wall into this sanctuary, to find refuge from an unnamed female pursuer. He comments on the brightness of the night, just perfect for seduction, only two hours after sunset (perhaps 10 p.m.). He is wondering how Leporello got on with Donna Elvira when his servant's voice is heard grumbling outside. Giovanni calls Leporello into the cemetery and relates one of his adventures since they last met: the lady was one of Leporello's sweethearts who penetrated the disguise at the last moment, cried rape, and chased him to this sanctuary. Leporello is not amused: the lady might have been his wife. Even better, laughs Giovanni.

While his peals of mirth echo round the tombs, a solemn voice calls from one of the statues, reinforced by oboes, clarinets, bassoons and lower strings, but particularly by unearthly chords for trombones situated below the stage—or in modern theatres preferably in the wings as close as possible to the Commendatore's statue.★

You will be done with laughter before daybreak.

Giovanni draws his sword and seeks the owner of the voice, striking several of the statues as he perambulates. Again the statue speaks, similarly accompanied:

Rash ruffian, leave the dead in peace!

Don Giovanni pays scant attention but he does recognize the statue of Donna Anna's father, and forces Leporello to read the inscription: 'I wait here for revenge on the villain who put an end to my days.' Giovanni is delighted and orders Leporello to invite the statue to supper at his house.

Leporello, quaking with fear at the statue which seems to him almost alive, obeys in the **Duet,**† **No. 22**, *allegro* in E major, *O statua gentilissima*, with flutes, bassoons, horns and strings.

After a brief introduction, suggestive perhaps of deep bowing, Leporello addresses the statue politely, but instantly takes fright.

76

Pa—dron... mi trema il co-re; non pos-so, non posso, termi—nar.

★ Mozart had used trombones in *Idomeneo* but they were generally associated only with church music. He added the wind parts in Prague, finding neat ensemble difficult.
† So entitled though three voices are heard.

The falling sevenths are typical of Leporello's fear. Giovanni is not at all scared, and the music expresses his delight with cheerful semiquavers as he orders his servant to proceed or taste his master's swordpoint. Leporello is aghast with terror (addressing a dead man was tabu in Spain) and begins again, in the dominant, accompanied by shivering trills. After further hesitation, quaking and threats, he finally manages with great embarrassment to convey Giovanni's invitation. I quote the moment, preceded by an instrumental passage elaborated from a timid motif some bars earlier and characteristic of the musical tension lightly yet firmly sustained, and followed by a moment of quivering dread as Leporello sees the statue nod its head in assent.

Leporello's terror at this moment is realistically portrayed in the music, but Mozart never forgets that the scene is a comic one: the solemnity of the cemetery and the shivers of communication with the dead, are masterfully balanced with the cheerful nonchalance of Giovanni, and with Mozart's amusement at the ludicrous situation. The music therefore moves effortlessly from grave wood-wind chords, supported by tremulous strings, straight into brilliant jovial *buffo* scales for Giovanni's scornful comment. Leporello insists, with his falling sevenths, that his master must watch the statue nod its head. The statue obliges and Giovanni is suitably impressed. The head-nodding cadence (flutes and horns) is repeated but in interrupted form so as to reach C major instead of E: Giovanni good-humouredly asks the statue to accept his invitation verbally. The statue answers 'Yes', supported by horns. A moment of darkness overtakes the music, though Giovanni will only admit to finding the situation 'bizarre'. His high spirits quickly dominate the music, as he determines to prepare for his dinner guest, while Leporello grumbles his longing to be elsewhere as soon as possible. Spirited runs in semiquavers for strings chatter away, descending and growing softer until the last chord.

The scene changes to a dark room in Donna Anna's house where Don Ottavio is busy, as usual, consoling his tearful betrothed. He has evidently been to the police, since his first words to her are that, 'We shall shortly see the grave excesses of this scoundrel punished, we shall be revenged,' which in Ottavio's contorted verbal style means, 'An arrest can be expected at any moment.' He is emboldened by his *coup* to suggest that they should get married tomorrow. Anna begs him not to touch on that delicate topic at such a sad moment. He replies that to postpone the wedding with further delays is cruel of her. At once the strings jump into action, *risoluto*, for Anna's **Recitativo**, the first part of **No. 23**, *Crudele? Ah no, mio bene.*

> Cruel? Ah no, my dear one. It pains me to postpone a blessing that both our souls have long desired. But, O God, the world.... Do not undermine the loyalty of my susceptible heart. My love for you is eloquent enough.

The initial *risoluto* is quickly abandoned for *larghetto* and a tune of unearthly sweetness such as we have not associated with Donna Anna before.

78

It is, many readers will recognize, the first theme of the forthcoming aria *Non mi dir*, played a fourth higher. During this recitative the theme is repeated in its subsequent F major form, and forward reference is also made to another theme from the aria, Ex. 80 below, but at first in D minor. At 'my susceptible heart' the strings murmur a non-thematic phrase, dark and tender. It may be quoted as leading to the vocal phrase which perfectly summarizes Anna's nature, highly strung, melancholy, serious, not unloving but unawakened to love.

79

Still *larghetto*, but now in F major, clarinet, bassoon and first violins, with a flute from the second bar, announce Ex. 78 *sotto voce* as the opening of Anna's **Aria**, *Non mi dir*. The orchestra includes two clarinets, bassoons and horns, as well as strings, but only the one flute.

> Do not tell me, my dear one, that I am cruel to you. You know well how much I have loved you; you know my faithfulness. Calm your anxiety if you would not have me die of grief.
>
> Perhaps one day heaven will yet take pity on me.

This is cast in two sections, the second faster, as in later romantic operatic arias (the so-miscalled *cavatina* and *cabaletta*). In the first *larghetto* part we observe at once the tender orchestral colours, delicately softened (almost blurred) by the Alberti semiquaver accompaniment; the sensuous warmth of the clarinet (Anna as vengeful fury was always accompanied by oboes), the loving intimacy of violin and bassoon doubling, and then the virginal candour of the flute. When Anna begins to sing she has to start softly, and uncomfortably, on F at the top of the stave, in the soprano's *passaggio* or gear-change: the *tessitura* of this aria lies consistently in that 'uncomfortable' region, I believe deliberately for portrayal of her character as she tries to convince Ottavio that she feels love for him but is not yet ready to marry him.

At 'tu ben sai quant' io t'amai' ('you know how much I have loved you'), the violin phrase, three times repeated, again conveys this slightly stiff graciousness.

80

It sounded more personal, more committed, in its earlier D minor guise during the recitative. When Anna reminds Ottavio of her constancy she does it to elegant florid music. The subsidiary subject group begins with a duet for clarinets in thirds, suggestive of the true love that Ottavio feels more easily than Anna, whose ideas correspond more nearly to the second phrase for flute and bassoon almost two octaves apart! She is more herself when she can sing about dying of grief with hints of C minor and on the dominant minor ninth chord in F. A pause offers the singer a doubtless high-lying cadenza, or at least bridge-passage, after which the opening of the aria is repeated concisely, moving through F minor, D flat major and B flat minor to another pause and flourish.

Now the *allegretto moderato*, not too animated second half begins with antiphonal strings and wind. Anna is trying to dry her eyes and sound more cheerful ('Perhaps one day'):

81

This still has a high *tessitura*, and it involves a very long and intricate florid division which mortally offended Berlioz but seems completely in Anna's character and is lovely to listen to when the soprano has the artistry as well as the technique for it. The later music of this section is also florid and high-lying, with suitable touches of involuntary self-pity or melancholy.

Just as Electra in *Idomeneo* had to have her *Idol mio* to demonstrate a gentler streak in her nature, so Donna Anna needed *Non mi dir*, and I have tried to indicate how judiciously Mozart responded to this expression of loving sentiment so that it does not totally contradict the Donna Anna we have come to know in the earlier part of the opera. To romantic nineteenth-century Mozartians Donna Anna was the grand tragic heroine of this 'opera above all operas', noble and passionate in her grief, admirable in her insistence on extended mourning for her dearly beloved and murdered father. For such enthusiasts Berlioz spoke truly when he castigated Mozart for giving her this florid and optimistic conclusion to 'an aria of intense sadness, full of a heartbreaking sense of loss and sorrowing love'. We in the twentieth-century respond differently: as post-Freudians we diagnose Anna as frigid and hysterical, the victim of noble birth and puritanical upbringing in a home where all her love was lavished on her father; we assume that she is an only child whose mother is dead (but only because other members of the family are not mentioned). As students of history we will try to approach *Don Giovanni* in an eighteenth-century frame of mind, unswayed by romantic sentimentality or romantic ethical uplift. There is no evidence that anybody, even Mozart or da Ponte, regarded the Donna Anna of *Non mi dir* as a comic character; the evidence suggests that she is a *parte seria* in a *dramma giocoso*, a noble lady who behaves in character and gives balance to other farcical or picaresque characters. For the audience at the Prague première, we suppose, *Non mi dir* confirmed what was expected of Donna Anna as a relic of baroque opera who must sing arias in varied moods, the more completely to exhibit her art. History tells us that Zerlina was the prima donna but that Donna Anna, as the most aristocratic of the three leading ladies, is the one expected to beguile us with gratifying florid music. She does so, and it is more closely unified with its musical surroundings than Berlioz suspected. Let us start in the middle of the florid passage which roused him to anger.

I have regretfully omitted the beautiful sustained accompaniment to this passage. I suspect that Berlioz always heard it performed at top speed as a circus act for the agile soprano. Perform it *allegretto moderato* and you can feel the pathos in those repeated notes, the tender sentiment in the descending scales.

The scales have grown from a truly serious phrase earlier, optimistic even in melancholy.

The scale starting on top A is taken up afterwards:

Violins resume Ex. 83 and Anna ends with the same jump as in Ex. 84. She now picks up the beginning of Ex. 83, slightly varied but still distinctive, and develops it chromatically and pathetically.

This is the very essence of Mozartian personal musicdrama. After a high-lying vocal cadence the orchestra ends the aria very optimistically with a variant of the repeated-note figure in Anna's florid division Ex. 82.

Non mi dir is dramatically and musically worthy of its position, true and beautiful.

As a serious person Donna Anna leaves at this point. Don Ottavio only remains to observe that his company may eventually ease her suffering.

16

The scene changes, officially for the last time, to Don Giovanni's banqueting hall (it may be that used for the Finale of Act I—only one original setting survives for either scene, though there is an extra one for the final sextet). The supper table is laid ready for eating. Some producers choose to include numerous scantily dressed women as fellow-guests at the supper-table. This is not in character. Giovanni expects the statue to share his meal, in any case; but he is also psychologically a man who keeps food and women apart, and he deals in one woman at a time, pleasures her, then forgets her: as Ernest Newman perceptively remarked, he does not put sugar on an orange which he has already sucked.

This **Finale, No. 24,** begins *allegro vivace*, with flutes, oboes, clarinets, bassoons, horns, trumpets, drums, and strings, most majestically and festively in D major. 'Già la mensa è preparata', sings Don Giovanni ('The table is ready'), and he calls on an attendant wind band to supply entertaining music while he eats. Mozart wrote this finale in Prague, waiting to discover what choral possibilities there were, how much could be expected of Bassi and Lolli, if a stage wind band could be afforded (Prague woodwind were famous, as today Czech string players are), how efficient the stage equipment was. The rather vapid musical content of Giovanni's opening solo in this finale suggests that Mozart was not as yet trying very hard: the test was ahead.

The wind band begins while Giovanni demolishes his antipasto.

'Bravo!' calls Leporello, 'it's *Cosa rara*', a recent opera by Martín which had proved more popular than *Figaro* in Vienna the year before; this is from the first act finale. Giovanni pronounces his dish a 'piatto saporito': I have always wondered, knowing that this finale was written in Prague, whether 'saporito' was a pun on the name of the Donna Anna, Teresa Saporiti.* The band continues;

* Leporello's words at this juncture are not printed in the Prague libretto. It was reported that Ponziani as Leporello improvised them during rehearsal. Many years later in Dresden Luigi Bassi, the first Giovanni, told his colleagues that in the rehearsals this scene was never played twice the same, and that Mozart encouraged freedom of dialogue so long as it was musically in tempo.

Leporello comments on his master's voracious appetite, joined at some length by his hungry employer.

Giovanni calls for the next course. The music changes to Mingone's aria *Come un agnello* from Act I of Sarti's *Fra i due litiganti il terzo gode*.

88

'Long live the Litiganti,' notes Leporello. Giovanni calls for wine and praises the Marzimino, a red wine from the Trentino, da Ponte's native district—might it have been spotted in a Prague shop? Leporello filches a slice of pheasant (it should be lamb, 'agnello') from a sidetray and devours it with gusto, but Giovanni notices and decides to trick his servant.

Now the band changes to *Non più andrai* from Mozart's own *Figaro*, already the rage in Prague. Leporello, with mouth full, observes that he knows this tune much too well (Ponziani had sung Figaro in many Prague performances). Giovanni teases him by ordering him to talk, or whistle, both impossible for a chock-full mouth. Leporello has to confess that he has been acting as food-taster, so skilful is Giovanni's cook (called Lanterna in Bertati).

B flat major interrupts, *allegro assai*; flutes have returned after a decent rest, trumpets and drums are still on leave. Donna Elvira, urged by love for Giovanni, runs in and begs him to change his way of life. Her music is frenzied, in 3/8 time, but essentially empty and stiff. She cannot think of a good reason why Giovanni should suddenly be converted; yet she persists, noisily and on her knees. Giovanni sympathetically joins her in this position, he says out of sincerity not mockery, and then invites her to join him at supper. He tells her and us his Credo:

89

Women and wine are the sustenance and glory of manhood. The vocal trio takes fire in B flat major, full of accompanimental detail. Elvira runs away in despair, returning immediately with a shriek and escaping through another door. Leporello is sent to investigate but he too emerges shouting noisily about heavy footfalls. *Molto allegro* he describes the experience in F major with cautious stepwise movement. He has seen the statue walk (therefore it is not on horseback), with huge steps, towards Giovanni's banqueting hall. They hear a knock on the door; their duet is still bold and cheerful. Leporello, miserable, hides under the table. Giovanni opens the door himself (Ex. 90).

There stands the statue, framed in the doorway. Mozart's orchestra, now with trombones added, repeats the start of the overture, harmonically more terrifying. The statue speaks. He was invited to supper, and here he is. Leporello grumbles to himself but Giovanni orders him to lay an extra place at once—all this to music

90

Andante

Don Gio-van—ni, a cenar te—co m'in-vi—ta——sti, e son ve—nu——to.

familiar from the overture. Leporello makes to leave the room but is called back by the statue which needs no mortal food. The eerie rising and falling scales, remembered from the overture, have reappeared. A vocal trio (parallel to that of the Commendatore's death scene, but now more dynamic) is built up: Leporello feels feverish in sluggish triplets, Giovanni demands to know the statue's will; the Commendatore announces that time is up and Giovanni must listen. The eerie scales continue; Mozart's woodwind section excels itself in shrill, horrendous harmony.

The statue speaks clearly, grandly harmonized: he has accepted Giovanni's invitation, therefore Giovanni in turn must come and dine with him. Leporello entreats his master to excuse himself but Giovanni refuses to play the coward. The shock forte chords of the overture find verbal motivation in the exchanges of Giovanni and the statue, both equally determined and strong-willed. The orchestra settles on a G. The statue demands Giovanni's hand in acceptance. It is offered fearlessly. But the handshake is an agonizing pledge of infernal destiny. The music grows faster and harmonically tortuous. Giovanni is urged to repent, but he refuses, in a phrase of monumental courage. D minor is now established, sustained woodwind chords, surging basses, rolling drums. The statue insists on repentance, Giovanni again and again replies, 'No!' In a last hush the statue pronounces the running out of time. Giovanni is doomed (Lolli, the first Commendatore, had to disappear now so as to costume himself as Masetto for the final scene).

Allegro in D minor, Giovanni finds himself already in Hell. Flames rise about him and earthquakes, evil spirits. He feels his spirit torn to pieces. The music is dark and blindingly bright at once, sombre trombones and shrill flutes, rapid violin scales and sullen static basses, to counteract the threats of the below-stage choral devils and the surprise of the condemned villain. At structurally the precisely right moment the harmony draws Giovanni down below amid rising flames, though the tension and volume accumulated in the music need some time afterwards to reach their proper conclusion. Molière's Leporello beatified this moment by running to the trapdoor, crying, 'My wages, my wages!'

For Victorian opera-goers *Don Giovanni* ended here and romantics gladly spread the rumour that Mozart had ended it here when it was produced in Vienna—on the grounds that Mozart made a cut, then deleted it. But the libretto and the manuscript did go further: it was Mozart's pupil Süssmayr who suppressed the last sextet in 1798. For an eighteenth-century audience (as for a twentieth-century audience) what follows is absolutely necessary. Don Giovanni has descended to the everlasting toasting-fork, hellish to southerners who spend the best hours of the day taking a siesta indoors, perhaps alluring to northerners without central heating. But he is not the only character in this drama. How unsatisfactory to go home without knowing what happens to the others! How dreary to end a *dramma giocoso* like a hellfire sermon!

Mozart and da Ponte ended *Don Giovanni* properly and tidily. Hardly have the flames died down and the trapdoor shut when Giovanni's supper room is invaded by Zerlina and Masetto, Anna and Ottavio, Elvira, and a crowd of policemen ('ministri di giustizia'), all crying for the reprobate whom they have come to arrest. Donna Anna in particular, strangely accompanied by flutes and bassoons in frivolous thirds, wishes to see him bound in chains so that she may be released from trauma. Leporello tells them that his master has passed yonder. Their surprise draws his explanation that a Colossus . . . he cannot continue, he confides in fearful descending sevenths. When they do finally keep quiet his explanation is none too lucid: smoke and fire, a stone man, a great blow, the devil. Elvira understands what he is talking about—she met the statue. All the others echo her words, though none of them was there; still, it makes a good ensemble for those who do not understand Italian! Mozart here organized a cut to the final sextet.

Ottavio most needs to take the initiative. *Larghetto* in G major he asks Donna Anna to marry him, since all is avenged. His solo is beautifully lyrical with flutes and bassoons now in rapturous thirds. She insists, very charmingly, on a year's formal mourning (what new excuse will she find then?). They duet blissfully and at length on love's deference. Elvira announces that she will go back to the convent. Masetto and Zerlina remember that supper is waiting for them. Leporello will go to the tavern and look for a new master. The three plebeians sharply observe that Don Giovanni has gone to the realms of Proserpina and Pluto, a prospect that turns the music very cheerful on the edge of D major, and reminds them all of a wise old saw which they will now sing. Flute and violin expound its jolly common sense.

91

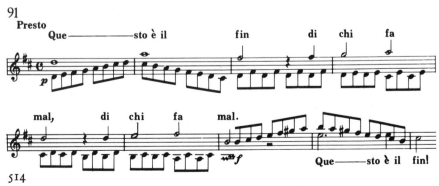

The saw is inaugurated not by any of them, but by Donna Anna and Donna Elvira in unison, as a fugue subject with rushing countersubject for second violins. Zerlina follows suit, but after that the counterpoint is forgotten in general pleasure. The words may be inaudible so I append my own doggerel version, chiefly because I fancy naughty old da Ponte believed in it as much as I do.

> This is how a bad man ends;
> how the scoundrel makes amends.
> In the finish, have no doubt,
> death will equal all things out.

The fugue was soon forgotten but counterpoint prevails gloriously and vivaciously. The orchestra continues cheerfully on its own before making for the final cadence and curtain.

17

For the nineteenth-century romantics *Don Giovanni* was self-evidently Mozart's greatest opera; for them it pre-echoed their own romanticism as no other opera of the eighteenth century did. There had been picaresque novels and plays but none that swashbuckled so outrageously, blasphemed so heartily, wrung the withers so thoroughly. The comic elements were distressing but could be underplayed or omitted. When Grand Opera became popular, *Don Giovanni*, by the divine daemonic Mozart, transformed itself, with little assistance, into the proto-grand-opera. A dashing hero, doomed to a grisly end, two noble and variously passionate heroines, a spectacular *deus* (or, at least, *miles gloriosus*) *ex machina* who precipitates doom, several sumptuous festive scenes, and music that was at once vocally demanding and orchestrally grandiose. While early eighteenth-century *opera seria* fell into obsolescence (*La clemenza di Tito* clung on for some time), *Don Giovanni* acquired more monumental trappings and was performed with the utmost splendour.

While the taste of the *ancien régime* endured, *Don Giovanni* had its detractors. It was translated into German and much performed even in Mozart's lifetime. At Mainz in March 1789 the music was considered 'though great and harmonious, difficult and artificial rather than pleasing and popular'. Dittersdorf in Vienna remarked that Mozart 'gives one no time to catch the breath and think about what has been heard: he goes straight on, and in the end one remembers nothing' —this from the composer who had just stolen the beginning of the *Figaro* overture for the main theme of an operatic ensemble!

Don Giovanni was produced in Frankfurt, Mannheim, Bonn, Passau, Hamburg, Graz, Brno, Munich, and many other places, while Mozart was yet alive. It was officially considered too noisy and too artificial (viz, not sufficiently naïve for untutored listeners), but it was popular. In Prague it remained standard repertory, greatly loved, for at least twenty years after the première. To diehard aristocrats it was even more reprehensible than Mozart's *Figaro* since it is a nobleman who disrupts society in *Don Giovanni*. The public enjoyed the eventfulness of the drama, the glamour of the characters, the homely humour of the comic parts, and also the spooky spectacle of the penultimate scene.

The monumental, larger-than-life view of Mozart's *Don Giovanni* minimized the comedy and its subtle relationship with the serious incidents; it inflated and depersonalized the principal roles, Zerlina as much as Donna Elvira. It also diminished the strength of Mozart's music, so much that the usually enlightened Bernard Shaw could write of Mozart 'revealing the hero's spirit in magical harmonies, elfin tones, and elate darting rhythms as of summer lightning made audible'.

It was as well, perhaps, for Shaw to insist that Mozart should not be conducted as if he were Wagner. A more robust Mozart style, freed from elfin delicacy, ensued; but so did psychoanalysis. Twentieth-century productions of *Don Giovanni* tend to fasten on one marginal feature of the drama and blow it up, like a photographic enlargement, so that one or another character becomes particularly sympathetic and dominates the action. Shaw, in *Man and Superman*, made Don Juan the hunted prey of women, not the hunter; in 1972 Stephen Oliver produced a semi-pastiche in which Don Giovanni was presented as a drooling moron, virtually inarticulate after all his debauchery. We were almost back to Tirso de Molina and his sermonizing play about the dangers of licentiousness.

The *Don Giovanni* of da Ponte and Mozart follows their success in *Le nozze di Figaro* by emphasizing character and realistic action in given situations. Da Ponte made a determined and intelligent attempt to bring all his chosen characters together, here or there, the better to construct dramatic tension and to make them all fuller and more credible persons. Each of their solo arias develops a character significantly: Elvira in *Mi tradì*, Anna in *Non mi dir* (structural excrescences, dramatic illumination); Zerlina and Masetto, mere dialect clowns in Molière, become real, likeable people, even Ottavio displays brains. Giovanni is more than a naughty boy, Leporello more interesting than his Arlecchino prototype. It is dangerous to read too much, psychologically, into them. Da Ponte hurriedly assembled them, Mozart injected them with life. We have learned, through many performances, to look deeper, and will continue to do so because of Mozart's music. My own analysis may have drawn too much out of Mozart; I would hesitate to infer more.

Yet when we compare this opera with *Figaro*, we may agree that, although the architecture is wobbly, all the characters and their musical portrayal are stronger, less formal, more communicative (even Anna and Ottavio). Nobody in Figaro makes so positive an initial impression as Elvira in *Ah chi mi dice mai*, or develops that impression so positively through her later ensembles to *Mi tradì*. No character in Mozart, not even Vitellia in *Tito*, rounds out determination with such a circumscribed yet completely expressed affection as does Donna Anna in *Non mi dir*. None of Mozart's servant girls, not even Susanna, is so gentle and lovable as Zerlina. Leporello is a Figaro more debased, less appreciated, no heroic mastermind, but musically a complete personality, who will run rings round the new master he finds in the tavern after curtain-fall. And Giovanni is the legendary anti-establishment young hero beloved in our century as in all previous ones: we find in him what we seek and what each one of us lacks. He is unsuccessful on this day but he has pursued remorselessly for several years and enjoyed his prey by the thousand. Men will not like nor admire him, though they will be jealous; no woman can resist a man who sings *Là ci darem* or *Deh vieni alla finestra* to her, or even *Discendi, o gioja bella*.

The appeal of *Don Giovanni* even when we have forgotten romantic heroic naughtiness (skilfully modernized in a British film entitled *The Knack*), is in the natural vivacity of its music. It is not a social drama like *Figaro*; nor an examination of the man–woman war like *Così fan tutte*, nor a tale of idealism like *Die Zauberflöte*. Compared with it Mozart's earlier libretti, even *Die Entführung*, were so many bedtime stories. It is a drama of the unsatisfied, endlessly challenging, never convention-accepting human spirit. A romantic subject, of course. Unromantic people can perhaps accept Don Juan's 2065 female conquests as a symbol for the new ideas that we would like to put into operation while we yet have energy and time to do so.

COSÌ FAN TUTTE

ossia
La Scuola degli Amanti

(All Girls Do It *or* The School for Lovers)

Dramma giocoso★ in two acts

Text by
LORENZO DA PONTE

K. 588

FIORDILIGI } DORABELLA } sisters from Ferrara,† living in Naples		SOPRANO
DESPINA, their serving maid		SOPRANO
GUGLIELMO, army officer, in love with Fiordiligi		BARITONE
FERRANDO, army officer, in love with Dorabella		TENOR
ALFONSO, an old philosopher		BASS

The action takes place in Naples

★ *Opera buffa* in Mozart's catalogue, *komisches Singspiel* in the poster for the première.
† Ladies from Ferrara had a loose reputation; but this may have been da Ponte's private joke about Adriana Ferraresi.

The year following *Don Giovanni* was an unlucky one for Mozart. He had little work, few pupils, an ailing wife, and not enough to make ends meet despite his imperial post which brought him almost as little cachet as money. During the summer of 1788 he planned a series of subscription concerts at a casino in Vienna, and wrote three symphonies (presumably) for them, his last and greatest three, Nos. 39–41. But the concerts did not draw enough subscriptions and had to be cancelled.

In January 1789 the Emperor Joseph II, now returned from the Turkish war, decided to suspend the Italian opera in Vienna altogether; it was losing too much money. Mercifully Lorenzo da Ponte elaborated a subscription scheme which convinced the Emperor not to disband his company.

In April Mozart was invited by his pupil and friend Prince Karl Lichnowsky (later a friend to Beethoven too) to travel with him to Berlin. On their journey they halted in Prague, where Guardasoni commissioned a new opera from Mozart (it was *La clemenza di Tito*, not written until 1791 when Guardasoni's troupe returned to Prague from a season in Poland); in Dresden and Leipzig, where Mozart made new friends and gave concerts; then to Potsdam where King Friedrich Wilhelm II at last welcomed the composer from whom he had long desired a visit. Mozart played for him, was commissioned to write six string quartets which would do justice to the King's excellent cello technique (he completed three), and six easy piano sonatas for Princess Friederike (only one, K. 576 in D, a difficult work, was finished).

The king is said to have offered Mozart a post as Kapellmeister, which Mozart refused out of loyalty to Joseph II. This is hard to believe: Joseph had given him little work (some dance-music), little salary, and not much appreciation though he was a good man and kindly employer in a city where Mozart enjoyed living. In Berlin Mozart made an enemy of the Court Chamber Music Director, Duport, by criticizing the Royal Orchestra's ensemble and the playing at the opera. Prussia was a stiffer place to live and work than Vienna, but it would have offered appreciation and gainful employment. Mozart, though still in his early thirties, turned down this offer, and offers to work in Prague, and the chance to visit London. Vienna did not appreciate his work, but it had become his home. He was an early Aquarian, strong-willed but not ambitious or pushing; he preferred to work at leisure, spurred only by the imminence of a deadline. If he had moved, with his family, to Prague, Berlin, or London he could well have lived to a ripe age. Mozart was dogged about his roots, his conditions of work, the society around him. Vienna did not favour him but he preferred Vienna. We must lament his destiny, but he chose it.

He was reunited on 4 June with his much-missed wife in Vienna (one of his letters to her about his sexual longing for her is most moving, if you are not too prudish), and settled down to his commissions. By July the Emperor had ordered a revival of *Figaro*. On 29 August it took place, as related earlier, very successfully. The Emperor decided to commission a new comic opera from Mozart for Vienna. Da Ponte was again to be the librettist. Gossip, written down much later, says that the Emperor proposed the subject, a comedy of couples in which the men are persuaded to test the faithfulness of their future brides by trying to seduce the other lady and succeeding—it had been a recent topic of Viennese gossip, we are informed. However Abbate Casti (see previous chapters) had in 1785 already provided Salieri with a libretto, *La grotta di Trofonio*, on a similar story in which a magician invites two loving couples into his cave and enchants them into changing partners. Before that in 1753 Jean Joseph Vadé had written for Antoine Dauvergne the libretto *Les troqueurs*, hailed as the first French plot worked out in Italian comic manner; here too a pair of couples indulge in a genteel equivalent of wife-swapping.

Da Ponte has been credited with creating the libretto of *Così fan tutte* out of his own head. He may have believed so, but no dramatic plot is new, only some of the topical features. The idea of couple-swapping was, it seems, a standard *lazzo* in improvised *commedia dell'arte* plays; and the notion of disguise to test the chastity of a wife goes back to the myth of Cephalus and Procris in Ovid's *Metamorphoses* (copied by Ariosto). Art and life reproduce one another; truth is what matters. Da Ponte accepted the subject, as did Mozart who had fallen in love with Aloysia Weber and then married her sister Constanze on the rebound. The story is a natural one, even without disguises: the same subject served Frederick Lonsdale in *On Approval* and indeed Shakespeare in *A Midsummer Night's Dream*.

The autograph manuscript of *Così fan tutte*, formerly in the Berlin State Library, is now apparently hidden somewhere in Poland by the Soviet regime which purloined it in 1945 and will not as yet admit to its location for study by serious students. Part of Act II in Mozart's hand is possessed by the University of Tübingen. Until the complete manuscript is available for study we will not know if it is true, as pre-1939 scholars stated, that Mozart's autograph was hastily written, full of musical abbreviations. Between early September, when he first worked on the scenario with da Ponte, and the end of December, when he invited Haydn and (Mozart's regular, loyal, source of much-needed money) Baron Puchberg to hear it, Mozart had plenty of time to elaborate the plot with da Ponte to his own complete creative satisfaction. He had very little other work: the major composition of this time is the clarinet quintet, K. 581, completed on 29 September. A sketch for its finale became Ferrando's *Ah lo veggio*.

Mozart's singers were all in Vienna. Louise Villeneuve, the Dorabella, had recently arrived there but between August and October Mozart had composed three arias for her to interpolate in other operas. The character of Dorabella shows how fully he appreciated this singer's qualities. For Vincenzo Calvesi, the Ferrando, Mozart had composed in 1785, the year of this tenor's arrival in Vienna, two additional numbers for *La villanella rapita*, a vocal quartet and trio. Calvesi had partnered Michael Kelly as the Antipholus twin in Stephen Storace's *Gli equivoci*. He had a reputation in Italy as well as in Vienna, and for once Mozart wrote a fine tenor heroic role in comic opera.

Fiordiligi was composed for Adriana Ferraresi del Bene who was da Ponte's current mistress. She was ugly and not a talented singer, but admired by some for her eyes and her pretty mouth. Burney had heard her as a girl in Venice and much admired her high E 'on which she dwelt for a considerable time in a fair, natural voice'. We cannot, however, be certain that Mozart wrote Fiordiligi for the voice applauded by Burney in 1770. There were two sisters, also called Ferraresi, daughters of a Prince Gabrielli's cook, and they also sang; one of them, Caterina Gabrielli was very famous. Mozart's Dorabella was neither of these, though O. E. Deutsch assumed that Fiordiligi's real name was Francesca Gabrielli.

In the rest of the cast the Despina was Mozart's first Cherubino, Dorothea Sardi-Bussani, wife of the company's manager and a favourite young singer in her own right. Guglielmo was sung by Mozart's first Figaro, Francesco Benucci, his Don Alfonso by the manager, Francesco Bussani. He was thus familiar with all six members of the cast. In December he had already composed a long and brilliant aria for Benucci as Guglielmo, *Rivolgete a lui lo sguardo*, too long for its dramatic context and entered separately into his private catalogue—it will be discussed in context. Also another aria *Donne vaghe* in E flat major which Alfred Einstein presumed to be intended for Despina.

Mozart thus had four months, seldom interrupted by other work, in which to prod da Ponte into making a libretto which suited all his purposes, for singers all familiar to him. We know that both he and da Ponte were procrastinatory creative artists, and that Mozart always required many alterations by a librettist. We can see that *Così fan tutte* is an exquisitely manoeuvred and polished libretto, and we can hear that Mozart lavished on it a quantity of the finest operatic music he ever composed. In no way does it sound like hurried workmanship. He must have spent October and November on it, even while playing skittles or going on excursions.

In December 1789 Mozart may have given his singers their music and rewritten an aria each for Dorothea Sardi and Benucci, so that they would know their parts in time for the run-through, with piano presumably, at Mozart's apartment on New Year's Eve. During January orchestral parts were copied, study proceeded. On 21 January the first rehearsal with orchestra took place in the Burgtheater: Haydn and Puchberg were also invited to this. Mozart mentioned in a letter that Salieri was plotting against *Così fan tutte* but that his plots were being completely undermined. Nobody has left reports of the rehearsals, and there are few accounts of the première in what was then called the Burgtheater on 26 January 1790 (the eve of Mozart's thirty-fourth birthday). Count Zinzendorf found the music 'charming, and the subject rather amusing'—high praise from him, but not as rare as some commentators believe. The *Journal des Luxus und der Moden*, published in Weimar, announced 'an excellent work by Mozart. . . . That the music is by Mozart says, I believe everything'—this could have been taken as uncomplimentary by reactionary music-lovers in Germany where Mozart's music was already thought too complicated and noisy, lacking popular charm. In this respect it may be significant that the copyist Lausch, who had brought out most of *Figaro* only a few days after the première, this time waited until 20 February and then offered for sale only the overture and one vocal number, the duet No. 23 *Il core vi dono*. It may be supposed from this that *Così fan tutte* roused little interest in Vienna. But there were further performances on 28 and 30 January, and on 7 and 11 February. On 20 February Mozart's protector Joseph II died. His successor Leopold II showed no interest in Mozart at all. One might almost date the start of Mozart's decline from Leopold's arrival in Vienna on 13 March.

Così fan tutte was resumed in Vienna on 6 and 12 June (this last performance conducted by the composer—though he is liable to have conducted some early performances as well), then on 6 and 16 July and on 7 August. After that it was dropped until long after Mozart's death.

On May Day 1791 the first performance elsewhere was given: it was by the Mainz company in Frankfurt-am-Main, in German as *Liebe und Versuchung*; the only extant criticism is scornful of such complicated music. Guardasoni's company played it in Leipzig and then in Prague, always in Italian of course. On 5 October it was also performed in Italian at Dresden.

There were many German performances, increasingly with altered libretti and plots, since the post-French-Revolution attitude regarded womanhood as almost sacred. *Così fan tutte* was given in Italian at the Haymarket Theatre in London in 1811 and 1819. But throughout the nineteenth century its contents were considered very distateful, unworthy of Mozart, therefore altered. It was not until 1896 that Hermann Levi in Munich presented *Così* more or less as da Ponte and Mozart wrote it. In 1900 Mahler in Vienna followed suit. London in 1910 realized with surprise what a delightful and charming opera *Così* was, when Thomas Beecham presented it. *Così* became a great attraction in Germany and Austria after this, particularly as conducted by Richard Strauss, who played the harpsichord continuo in the recitatives himself with many a witty turn of musical phrase. In 1934 *Così* became a cornerstone of England's new Glyndebourne Opera: its production there, under Carl Ebert and Fritz Busch, was generally hailed as a more distinguished and perfect interpretation of the opera than had been seen and heard anywhere in living memory. In 1944 almost as much was claimed for the Sadler's Wells production in English in London, where Dorabella as well as Fiordiligi was a soprano, as intended by Mozart—mezzos are usually assigned to Dorabella. Memory regards this as the inauguration of a new, more realistic attitude to *Così fan tutte*, nowadays accepted as standard practice.

Così fan tutte was being written while the Bastille was being stormed and the *ancien régime* expelled or killed. For a while it survived as an entertainment in that pre-revolutionary manner, elegant, enchanting, and totally unrealistic. As late as 1935 Eric Blom, a discerning Mozartian, could refer to it as 'a world of enchanted artificiality'. This is not the approach of the 1970s. We see the comedy as far more serious, far more personal, though not less amusing, even though its words and music are deliberately formalized in the manner of 1789.

2

Towards the end of the opera, in No. 30 to be precise, Don Alfonso justifies the behaviour of the two soldiers' fiancées with the words of the opera's title 'All women act that way', *Così fan tutte*. He makes Ferrando and Guglielmo repeat the words after him. The musical phrases to which these words are set appear first in the *andante* introduction to the overture; and they reappear at the climax of the conspiratorial *presto* which follows.

This is not quite the full extent of the self-quotation in the overture, though no other music from *Così* is prefigured here. The amount of quotation is about the same as in *Zauberflöte*, less than in *Entführung* or *Don Giovanni*, more than in *Figaro* (where the amount is *nil*).

Mozart begins with his full orchestra, two each of flutes, oboes, clarinets, bassoons, horns, trumpets, drums and violins, plus violas, celli and basses. He first proposes a Mannheim loud–soft alternation: loud C major chords with a grand, masculine, perhaps rather martial, rhythm for everyone, then a soft, aspiring, perhaps rather amorous oboe solo with woodwind accompaniment. This antiphony is repeated formally in G major as dominant of C; none of it is thematic, in that the ideas do not reappear. Yet the alternation and not-quite-repetition are appropriate to an opera about couples. Without collapsing into romantic fancy one can explain (the explanation works for Mozart's Jupiter Symphony and hundreds of other works in this period, because it is a basic human principle): *forte* in C major, behold Ferrando; *piano* in C major, he is thinking of Dorabella.

Then *forte* in G major, similarly though dropping a fifth instead of an octave, *ecco Guglielmo*! The oboe answers again, on the dominant seventh, and there is Fiordiligi in his thoughts. All four are different, but the males are as similar as the females: *così fan tutti/tutte*.

The *presto* is a nicely worked-out sonata movement, with the special feature that, as in Mozart's Haffner symphony and many symphonic movements by Haydn from which Mozart learned, all the material is exposed at once, requiring no new idea, merely variation, for the statutory section in the dominant. The ideas are also rich enough to dominate the development section which takes them through new circus-hoops of tonality. The first idea is conspiratorial for strings:

It is answered by full C major plagal chords for all—note the non-conformist drum rhythm.

At once the third idea, passed from one woodwind soloist to another, sometimes doubled. The swapping, characteristic of this next theme throughout, and the animation look forward to the overtures of Rossini who knew and idolized Mozart. It is a theme of supressed, secretive amusement.

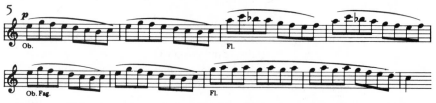

Bars 7–8 of the above example look back, perhaps coincidentally to Ex. 15 in my chapter on *Figaro* where Don Basilio sang much the same notes in just the same mood, though a tone lower, to the words 'così fan tutte le belle'.★

These three themes upon repetition and variation push the music towards the dominant. On the brink Ex. 4 becomes a syncopated accompaniment, for woodwind, to a variant of Ex. 3–5 with an identity of its own, slightly more sinister or sarcastic than the foregoing.

When this explodes into G major it is with Ex. 4 now slightly more dynamic in harmony, and confirmed in cadences which might be thought humdrum but for the luminous woodwind scoring. Out of this dominant cadence comes the development section, still intent on these few themes which rove into new keys and back to G, then away again. There is no time for other ideas and the pace can only just be halted for a return to Ex. 1 in *presto* tempo but with twice the note-values (so that *presto* must be exactly twice the speed of the introduction). The overture ends with a long Mannheim *crescendo* on the chord of C major.

Many writers have deplored the banality of the ideas in this overture. Hermann Abert was sufficiently kind as to admit that they have 'more temperament than character', meaning that he enjoyed the piece but could not find much to say about it. For me the *presto* main part is pure and perfect *opera buffa*, inexhaustibly galvanic in effect, and with its *andante* introduction the perfect overture to the perfect opera.

★ This subconscious echo was first pointed out, I think, by Harvey Grace in the *Daily Telegraph* on 15 July 1939 but surely known to musicians much earlier.

3

The curtain rises on a coffee house in Naples where Don Alfonso, an elderly philosopher, has evidently just been lecturing his friends, two young army officers called Ferrando and Guglielmo, on the naturally and irresistibly polyandrous nature of womankind, their own sweethearts not excepted. If his lecture had been translated into music it would have sounded very like the overture to which we have just been listening. Alfonso is experienced in the ways of women, and he is a thinker, but too affectionate to have become cynical, let alone misogynistic, diabolical or sadistic, as some have supposed. From the outset we must put out of mind the received theory that he is the puppet-master who will control the other five characters in all their actions during the next twenty-four hours: that way lies a sure misappreciation of the opera's charm and truthfulness. He is a teacher of philosophy in the old tradition, and his intention, following his lecture, is to rid his four young, love-infatuated, friends of their sentimental notions about true love at first sight and unshakable constancy. A can spend a long and happy life of matrimonial contentment with B, C, D, or any other symbol in the alphabet, so long as the chosen lady determines to cling to him only. But perils lie in wait for the pretty young ladies, as for handsome young men, and it is no use pretending that anyone, however strong willed, can hold out against them indefinitely.

Alfonso was quite serious about this, though he expressed himself wittily and vivaciously, as a man who has come to terms happily with the facts of life. His discourse has ended controversially but with a hangover of great cheerfulness, including pugnacity.

7

Allegro

La mia Do—ra—bel—la ca—pa—ce non è,   ca—pa—ce non è,

This is **No. 1, Terzetto,** *allegro* in G major, *La mia Dorabella capace non è,* with oboes, bassoons, horns, and strings, Mozart's standard *opera buffa* orchestra, capable of varied expression but not intrinsically loaded in any particular emotional direction. Audaciously Mozart constructs this first scene as a series of three vocal trios for the same three singers, though he does vary the scoring.

The young men, first Ferrando then Guglielmo, defend their sweethearts: their own two women are the exception to Alfonso's rule, as faithful as they are beautiful. This is the message of Ex. 7. Alfonso insists that he knows women better than they do; the two young men reply that he must prove his sweeping statement or else fight a duel with them both (all three wear swords, being of noble birth). It is a nice touch that they challenge him to the cheerful, unhostile Ex. 7. The duel itself is proposed to rushing scales as in *Don Giovanni.* They challenge him, but there is no hint of friendship broken. It may be noted that, in the score, Guglielmo is considered a lower bass than Alfonso: most of us would suppose Guglielmo (Mozart's Figaro) to be a light bass-baritone, Alfonso (Mozart's Dr Bartolo) a riper, more incisive basso.

In recitative the young soldiers again challenge Alfonso to a duel or to prove his case. He prizes his intelligence too much to indulge in duels—except at table (with knife and fork). As for fidelity he continues his argument in **No. 2, Terzetto** in E major, *allegro*, virtually a solo with comments from the two soldiers, *È la fede delle femmine*, with solo flute and bassoon, and strings. Alfonso, with a plushy underlay of strings, tells them that female fidelity is like the Phoenix of Araby: everybody has heard about it but no one has actually located it. Da Ponte borrowed the text from Metastasio. The high spirits of No. 1 are followed by Alfonso's assumed severity.

8

The young men insist that their girls are both phoenixes of this type, and able to be located. Alfonso responds with a theorem like his Ex. 1: 'Nobody knows its whereabouts.'

9

This is quite short, mostly accompanied by strings; the flute and bassoon contributions are rare but very telling, usually in octaves for confirmation. The young soldiers' answers, 'Dorabella' ... 'Fiordiligi', are especially attractive.

Don Alfonso now wagers that their perfect phoenixes are no more reliable than other women. They accept his bet to the tune of a hundred sequins.* Alfonso makes two conditions: they must not breathe a word about it to their Penelopes (she was the wife of Odysseus, grass-widowed for twenty years, but she survived persistent courtship by others until her husband returned); and they must obey all his instructions implicitly. They agree in duet (a feature of *Così* recitatives) and discuss how they will spend their winnings in **No. 3, Terzetto**, *allegro* in C major, *Una bella serenata*, with oboes, bassoons, trumpets, timpani and strings. Mozart uses trumpets more freely in *Così fan tutte* than was his *buffo* practice. Two principal characters are soldiers, of course, which is why the trumpets figure in this trio; but they do not only contribute to the music of Ferrando and Guglielmo.

Ferrando will spend his share on hiring an orchestra to help him serenade his sweetheart Dorabella.

* The sequin, or *zecchino*, was worth about twelve livres or nine shillings. In 1772 Mozart expected the equivalent of a hundred sequins for giving a concert in Vienna.

Guglielmo intends to give a banquet in honour of Cytherea (Venus); since he is singing a version of the bass line the tune goes to the violins and is more jaunty.

A shyly questioning phrase for strings asks if Alfonso will be invited to the party. Certainly, answer the soldiers in sixths of remarkable, almost pastoral placidity, doubled pleasantly by oboes and bassoons.

All three gentlemen announce that they will repeatedly toast the god of love—to a demure and dapper little tune, at first for violins with simple accompaniment for bassoons doubled by violas.

This will end the scene in a grander version with trumpets and timpani added.

The repeated toasts also involve a delicious musical representation of 'beaded bubbles winking at the brim'. In the second bar, woodwind and trumpets sustain a C major chord.

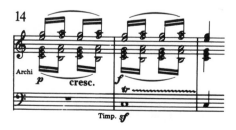

Off they saunter down the street in highest good humour, to Ex. 13, each of them convinced that the bet is already won. Don Alfonso has some work to do at Naples harbour and at the military barracks—bribery will be expected in both places—before he arrives in the seaside garden of the villa occupied by the sisters Fiordiligi (her name means 'flower of loyalty' or *fleur de lys*, the lily of the valley) and Dorabella who are the sweethearts of, respectively, Guglielmo and Ferrando.

We go there at once. The two sisters, very young and pretty, are sitting in, or wandering round, their garden, each gazing at the portrait of her lover contained in a locket hung from her waist ('al fianco'). Each points out the beauty of her lover's features to her sister in **No. 4, Duetto,** *andante–allegro* in A major, *Ah guarda, sorella,* with clarinets, bassoons, horns and strings.

The 3/8 *andante* should move easily, faster than the 3/4 that performances often suggest. As the curtain rises the violins in octaves take a graceful dive down and up the A major scale and the introduction ends with delectable chromatic sighs. Fiordiligi★ draws attention to Guglielmo's mouth and aspect in a repeat of Ex. 15, ending with a brief transport of floridity. Woodwind take the initial theme a stage further into E major while Dorabella dwells on Ferrando's flashing eyes to music a shade more flippant and kittenish, though she too cadences decoratively. Fiordiligi finds her man's face both warlike and amorous; Dorabella senses delight (a touch of wistful A minor here) and menace in the likeness of her sweetheart. How happy they both are! They sail into a spirited duet of thirds and sixths as they promise (all too prematurely) to live in torment if ever they suffer a change of heart. The off-beat accents of their melody here are full of character and confidence.

★ Mozart confused the sisters' names throughout Act I, giving Dorabella the higher line. But he knew perfectly well for which singer he was writing at any moment.

Clarinets and bassoons are again prominent, the bassoons (with cellos) giving agile support to the blissful roulades in thirds on the name of Love ('amore'). The highlight of this duet is perhaps the passage in which each sister in turn rises to a held note below which the other wreathes arpeggios in the rhythm of Ex. 16.

17

Se questo mio co—re mai

A—mo—re mi fac—cia vi—ven—do pe—nar ——————

cangia de—si-o, A—more mi faccia vi—vendo pe—nar,

Dorabella is doubled by clarinet, Fiordiligi by bassoon; when they repeat the feat a fourth higher the woodwinds swap parts for comfort. It will be observed that Fiordiligi is required to sing as low as Dorabella (this extended compass was a speciality of Adriana Ferraresi). The warm euphony of this *allegro* section is enhanced by *divisi* violas, a favourite effect of Mozart's youth, more sparingly used in his later works but frequently in *Così fan tutte*. Horns and first violins leap with delight in the orchestral coda.

Fiordiligi admits that she feels mischievous this morning, eager to play tricks on Guglielmo (wrong: she will be tricked); Dorabella senses the approach of Hymen and on having her hand 'astrologized' (as her sister puts it) discovers a clear M and P, obviously signifying 'matrimonio presto'. In that case, what the devil ('che diavolo', very emancipated language for a genteel young lady) do their fiancés mean by such late arrival. It is noon already ('le sei' means six o'clock, since Italy then still used clocks which struck no more than six, four times a day—they can still be heard in some parts of Europe—we can hardly suppose sophisticated young ladies would be receiving their sweethearts at 6 a.m.) Fiordiligi sees somebody approaching. It is not their betrothed but the boys' friend Don Alfonso. Fiordiligi welcomes him. His 'Riverisco' deflates their cheerfulness by tracing the outline of G minor; at once they know that something untoward has kept their dear ones.

Don Alfonso explains, or rather mumbles, unhappy non-explanations, in a very short 38-bar solo, **No. 5, Aria**, *allegro agitato* in F minor, *Vorrei dir, e cor non ho*, with strings alone (but divided violas).

I wish I could say, but I haven't the heart. My lips stammer, I can't project my voice; it's stuck in my throat. What will you do, what will I? What a great disaster! It couldn't be worse. I feel pity for you and them.

If we except Alfonso's No. 2, which is called a terzetto, this is the first aria so far;

there will be others later, but *Così fan tutte* is about couples and therefore tends always to the vocal ensemble.

F minor is quite a rare key in Mozart (he tended to avoid keys with more than three accidentals in the key-signature) but always strongly expressive, here of extravagant grief breathlessly expressed by accompanying violins as well as by the singer who takes little time to say nothing in a good many words. There is no sign of insincerity or play-acting; the music might almost have come from the death of the Commendatore in *Don Giovanni* (same key and one almost identical phrase). The flow of the aria is sustained throughout by the long notes of the two violas, natural voices of melancholy.

Alfonso keeps the girls in suspense for as long as possible. Their lovers are, he admits, not actually dead, nor wounded, not even sick. But—the royal command has posted them to battle, and they must leave at once. The girls again react in duet recitative. Alfonso adds that the boys, too wretched to break the news themselves, are here to say goodbye if their sweethearts wish. He calls them into the garden; they are dressed for going on a journey.

They have hardly the heart to walk towards their ladies, as Guglielmo at once confesses, and as Mozart suggests in the opening bars of **No. 6, Quintetto,** *andante* in E flat major, *Sento, o Dio*, with clarinets, bassoons, horns, and strings. E flat major has always been the key for solemnity, as the first four chords recall.

18

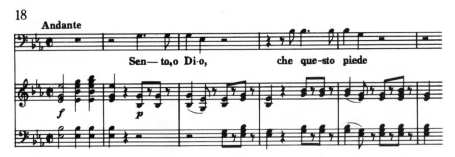

Strings with Guglielmo, answered by woodwind, tell us that the men are giving a perfect impersonation of numb grief with a stiff upper lip. Ferrando follows suit in his higher register. Alfonso encourages them to the courage of heroes in stark octaves. The girls collapse into tearful quavers (answered by writhing woodwind semiquavers) and, in the parallel thirds of complete solidarity which move towards B flat minor, they beg their lovers to plunge their swords bravely into the bosoms of their forsaken brides. The men blame destiny stiffly in B flat major, also in perfect duet, to which their ladies respond singly and hysterically that they must not go.*
Softly the strings chortle aside, and the soldiers turn and whisper to Alfonso their complete confidence. He replies, 'Finem lauda', a Latin tag which may be rendered 'Don't count your chickens before they're hatched.'

The quintet now develops the tones of completely convinced grief, in which Alfonso joins Guglielmo while Ferrando allies himself with the melodiously duetting sisters. Miserable they may be but the music remains anchored in major

---

* Many published libretti jump the gun by making the ladies address their future suitors, not the ones to whom they still claim eternal attachment. A scribe's error has been perpetuated here.

keys, though eventfully so and with increasing bursts of floridity from the ladies, even a poignant explosion from Ferrando. The quintet ends with consoling clarinets and bassoons as the lovers, we assume, fall into one another's arms in suitable attitudes of tragedy.

The men attempt consolation in recitative; their girls talk only of suicide and death of heartbreak. This drives the soldiers into duet recitative about protective deities (da Ponte, though a Catholic priest, seldom mentions the Christian or even his native Jewish god, preferring classical, usually plural divinities), and so to **No. 7, Duettino**, *andante* in B flat major, *Al fato dan legge*, with clarinets, bassoons, horns and strings (divided violas again):

> Your lovely eyes control destiny. Love will
> protect them; barbarous stars will not dare to trouble
> their repose. Look at me calmly, my dear; I hope
> to return happy to your breast.

This is, in the circumstances, a brave exhortation in almost regimented duet; Ferrando once breaks into a florid division, and Guglielmo follows him dutifully three bars later. The cheerfulness of the music is welcome and, on the rare occasions when it is performed, it looks forward curiously to the German moralizing of, for instance, the two priests in *Die Zauberflöte* and that opera in general.

Don Alfonso is delighted by the persuasiveness of his comedian-pupils. In the distance a drumroll is heard, signal for departure. Alfonso sees a boat approaching. The girls are distraught. From the distance, very gradually, a military march is heard, **No. 8, Coro**, *maestoso* in D major, *Bella vita militar!* The orchestra probably remains in the pit, flutes, oboes, bassoons, trumpets, timpani and strings; later a chorus (perhaps off stage) extols the delights of military life, travel, variety, inspiration—just like a recruiting poster.

Grand Opera devotees wish to see all the soldiers and bystanders in the chorus as well as the boat. Realism suggests that Don Alfonso bribed an idle boat to sail past the garden, and some local folk with a band to sing out of sight in the vicinity, so as to convince the distraught sisters that manoeuvres really were afoot.

In the subsequent recitative Alfonso tells the officers not to delay. Their regimental ship has already sailed; they will have to travel in a smaller boat with some friends. The lovers say goodbye in **No. 9, Quintetto**, *andante* in F major (again a major key for a touching scene of farewell), *Di scrivermi ogni giorno*, with clarinets, bassoons and strings. F major is a bright key, but here greatly poignant with the stammered pleas for frequent letters and the tearful assurances. Now and then the rapid heartbeats and hesitating avowals are interrupted by longer, smoother phrases, urgent and memorable. Fiordiligi comes out with the most eloquent of these, so memorable that Mozart subsequently put it into a sacred motet, *Ave Verum*, just before his death.

19

The only sign that F major is not the ideal key for lachrymose lovers' farewells is the *sotto voce* persistent undercurrent of Alfonso's bass figure to the effect that he will die if he is not allowed to let his laughter out. The situation, we know, is comic, the music cruelly sad (the boys would not tolerate it if they were not, like all southern Italians, dedicated gamblers).

The military march with chorus is resumed. The military lovers depart. Dorabella, who thought it appropriate to stage a faint for the occasion, makes her recovery, asking where the men have gone. Alfonso points to the boat where their sweethearts are waving goodbye; he brings out a pocket handkerchief and waves it, to add colour to the hoax. The girls follow his example and together they sing **No. 10, Terzettino,** *andante* (putative) in E major, *Soave sia il vento*, with flutes, clarinets, bassoons, horns, and strings.

Alfonso joins Fiordiligi and Dorabella in their prayer for a safe, pleasant journey, as though he believed in it too. He knows the boat will come to shore almost at once but he is acting, as Mozart is, in the mood of the sisters who have momentarily abandoned hysteria for religious optimism and prayer.

During the early 1970s this trio became wellknown to filmgoers all over the world as a musical *Leitmotiv* in the long-drawn but moving film *Sunday, bloody Sunday*. That film was set in urban London. This trio is set beside the Mediterranean Sea. The music matched the film's atmosphere of farewell but the setting ignored the major enchantment of this trio which is the evocation of placid water undulating beneath the visible boat—as in the A major duet No. 4 in this opera, and the chorus *Placido è il mar* in *Idomeneo* (again E major, many similar features). In the absence of the autograph manuscript, *andante* is an assumed tempo mark; I would think *larghetto* more suitable, since this is not a dynamic number at all. The united strings murmur serenely, the voices join in lyrically congealed harmony.

20

Woodwind arrive just after this. The singers touch lightly but eloquently on a dominant ninth at bar 15 and then go into an elaborate concentrated trio unaccompanied except by cool woodwind. Their cadence is interrupted by a soft yet fierce dissonance pointed by the first entry of flutes (bar 22) who carry the music upwards to a held third the resolution of which is more easily quoted than described.

21

Flutes and divided violas contribute gorgeously to the close of this magical trio.

The scene is not quite over. Fiordiligi and Dorabella leave the stage. Alfonso remains to congratulate himself on his histrionic ability, think of his champions dedicated to Venus and Mars, reflect on the extravagant emotions he has witnessed, and the folly of the friends who bet a hundred sequins on the virtue of women. His observations rouse a string orchestra in D minor, *allegro moderato*, stormy and wild as usual with this key in Mozart, for a tiny *arioso* (not so called) in which Alfonso compares trust in a woman's heart with building on sand or trapping the wind in a fishing-net. His remarks are in quotation marks; but nobody has identified the quote. He ends in C major and the scene changes.

5

We have moved into the living-room of the villa, furnished with chairs and a small table and entered by three doors, one on each side, the third in the far wall. Chocolate, a refreshing lunchtime drink, is being made for the ladies by their chambermaid Despina who complains that she has been stirring for half an hour and is supposed to smell but not taste it. Bacchus take it! ('Per Bacco' is another strong expletive), she *will* have a sip, and delicious it is.

Despina is the last of the *dramatis personae* to appear. She comes from the same drawer as Susanna and Zerlina and Blondchen, not to mention Ninetta in *Finta semplice*, and Serpetta in *Finta giardiniera*, a drawer originally labelled *Colombina* (cf. my chapter on *Opera buffa*). Mozart made individuals of all these nice girls though singers and opera producers sometimes tend to blur the distinctions and present each of them as a saucy café waitress who relies on arch poses and provocative *moues* rather than on character and real singing. All have vivacity and sexual allure in common. Zerlina is the simplest and most tenderly affectionate; Susanna combines affection and brains; Blondchen has pride and determination. Despina puts on no airs, but relies on peasant common sense and wit, together with a flair for running the establishment which she will shortly use for adept stage-management. She is hard and go-getting, and no respecter of persons. Humankind, for her, consists only of fools and confidence tricksters. She is no fool, but she will be honest as long as it pays, and while she is fairly treated. Like all her colleagues in the trade, but notably Susanna and Leporello, and particularly Vespina in Haydn's *L'infedeltà delusa*, she is a versatile mimic and impersonator.

After supping the chocolate she has to wipe her mouth quickly for here are her mistresses, making the most of their sorrows. When Despina offers them their luncheon*, Dorabella throws the tray to the ground. Both ladies rip the jewels from their persons and call for instruments of suicide. Despina's advice is cut short at the outset by Dorabella who orders her, in a string-accompanied recitative, to close the shutters, go away and leave her alone in the darkness with her grief—all this in high-flown theatrical rhetoric with rushing violin scales and peremptory rhythmic chords and, for one moment, a suggestion of inward misery.

Passages in *Così fan tutte* such as this are the chief stumbling blocks to many sensitive people. They recognize that Dorabella is indulging her emotions and that she is about to sing an extravagant aria of frenzied grief, more suited to Electra in *Idomeneo* than to a frivolous young lady in a comic opera. The effect is absurd and raises smiles of amusement. Then along comes Ex. 22 which is like the 'true' wretchedness of Constanze or Pamina, characters that we take seriously. Is it not unfair of Mozart to throw genuine pathos into a splendid exhibition of comic hamming? What, these searchers for truth ask, are we supposed to think? My own reply is that we should take everything at its musical, human face-value. Dorabella was, for Mozart at least, neither a doll nor a *commedia* type but a person, and a woman too. At thirty-three Mozart was not too young to know that women always mean what they say and do, in the moment of speech and action, even though they may not have reasoned beforehand, and are quite likely to decide otherwise a moment later. (Men have precisely the same temptation when they behave too hastily, but their inborn masculinity leads them either to rationalize earlier weaknesses, or to build them up into some disastrous dogma.) Dorabella truly believes in her own wretchedness though she can only communicate most of it in terms of what she has read or seen at the theatre. To us, outside her susceptible and mixed-up teenage, Ex. 22 is unbelievably mature, Ex. 23 the

* Many translations confuse *collazione*, the midday meal, with *prima collazione* and thus make Despina serve breakfast, which puts Alfonso's timescheme wildly adrift.

credible, hysterical reaction to her situation. To her the situation is incredible but her reactions are all sincere, however incoherent or inconsistent. There will be more to say about this later: enough, for the moment, to insist that Mozart was not cynical about female emotion when he composed for sopranos, witness Susanna's *Deh vieni* and the terzetto No. 15 in *Don Giovanni*. His last operas, particularly the three with da Ponte, centre on the ambivalence, indeed multivalence (I borrow this word from the *Mehrwertigkeit* of Karlheinz Stockhausen) of human emotion, none more than *Così fan tutte*.

Dorabella, ablaze with sincerity, launches into her **Aria, No. 11**, *allegro agitato* in E flat major, *Smanie implacabili*, with flutes, clarinets, bassoons, horns, and strings.

> Implacable frenzies, continue to disturb my soul until anguish brings about my death. If I remain alive, the horrible sound of my sighing will give the Furies a wretched example of deadly love.

The aria begins with a restless, tossing-and-turning figure in triplets for violins and this dominates the whole number, ceasing only towards the end for a few bars after which it is resumed till the conclusion. Dorabella's initial phrases in Ex. 23 show not only her tune, for identification, but the breathless word-fragmenting which is an expressive feature of the aria (compare it with Alfonso's No. 5, rather similar in several respects though Dorabella does not think she is acting, whereas Alfonso deliberately is). Only strings are involved at first.

23

Horns add a sustaining pedal note, then bassoons an incisive sustained chord, to this restlessness, then clarinets shed extra euphony on thoughts of death. The first loud entry of flutes in harmony with other woodwind, after 'wretched example' (*esempio misero*—Mozart gets through the text quickly, then repeats while developing da Ponte's data), is a powerful moment, harmonically too. 'Deadly love' turns the music towards B flat minor, only momentarily, since mention of the Eumenides (the Greek Furies were always referred to as "Kindly Ladies', out of superstitious euphemism) brings on a lengthy bout of *crescendo* tension and more breathless articulation, ending in the dominant B flat, quickly exchanged for its minor mode and other keys. Chill flutes are noticed, but also bassoons and clarinets in this second binary half which sweeps irresistibly forward through repeats and new material (n.b. flutes and bassoons imitating Dorabella on the Eumenides, all three taking wing as her thoughts rise aloft). Dorabella makes an interrupted cadence, perhaps flourishes, then descends to bare woodwind unisons, frosty as yells of pain from Cocytus, before the busy triplets resume and end. Both sisters have inspired this outburst, and both collapse into chairs at the end.

Despina knew her place too well to go away ('Ah! Scostati!') during this aria which was intended to put her in the picture. She seeks an explanation. The boys gone away? They will return. To war? They will come back loaded with medals.

They might die? In that case there are other men, just as attractive. The sisters are sure that they would die of love if they lost their fiancés. It's never been known, answers Despina. She expounds the quintessential moral of *Così fan tutte*: one man has just as much to love as any other, and is just as worthy of your love. Forget about remote mischance: the boys will return eventually; meanwhile amuse yourselves while they are away, making love like murderesses just as your sweethearts will do while they are away.

Dorabella is extremely shocked that her paragon of virtue and his equally soulful friend might be thought capable of infidelity at any time. Despina has to tell her mistresses that such ideas are too stupid even to be told to children.

She dismisses the idea of fidelity in men, let alone soldiers, in **No. 12, Aria**, *allegretto* in F major, *In uomini, in soldati*, with solo flute, oboe and bassoon supported by strings (the oboe's piquant tone has been missing for a while).

> Do you expect men, soldiers, to be faithful? For pity's sake, make sure no one's listening. They're all made the same. Swaying leaves, changeable winds are more stable than men. Their chief characteristics are crocodile tears, insincere eyes, deceitful voices, meaningless endearments. They only love us for their pleasure, then they despise us and refuse affection. No use begging such savages for pity. We women must pay this unkind, profligate mob in their own coinage. Let us make love at our convenience, to flatter ourselves.

Her ideas are excellent and she expounds them with great sense of humour as well as conviction. Mozart's music bears this out to perfection, neither Almaviva's proprietorship, nor Giovanni's hunting tactics, but mutual pleasure. Despina sermonizes with featherweight lightness. The first nine bars convey longing as well as flirtatiousness.

24

There is a passage of bubbling triplets, then a quasi-recitative followed by the meat of the sermon, distinctly pastoral, fragrant with sukebind.

25

This is a much more rustic, happy-go-lucky notion of love than we have learned from Mozart's other servant-girls, though later there is a curious and credible echo of Zerlina at bar 39. Despina's laughing philosophy is summed up in the trills of her coda.

26

amiam per co-mo-do,per va-ni—tà,   la ra la,   la ra la, la ra la   la,

She makes less than no impression on her mistresses who walk out on her: well, she is only a common servant, untutored in gentility. Despina walks out as well: they are repressed gentlefolk who will learn as soon as she can bring them to their senses.

Evidently Don Alfonso has the entrée to the house. He walks into the living-room and is surprised to find it empty, though he realizes why. The girls need the comfort he will bring them when their lovers return in disguise. As for Despina Don Alfonso has some qualms (the recitative bass moves to indicate emotional disturbance): she might recognize the boys. A bribe and a small share in the secret will secure her help. Alfonso knocks on her door and makes up to her. Men of his age are no fun to a young girl unless—yes, Alfonso drops a gold coin into her hand, and she evinces co-operation. If she helps him to infiltrate two admirers into the house to console her mistresses she will get a further twenty scudi (a sum well known to fans of *L'elisir d'amore* as the wages for a military commission). Despina is willing to assist so long as Alfonso's friends are young, handsome and loaded with money. Assured of these qualifications she is ready to inspect them.

Don Alfonso has persuaded Ferrando and Guglielmo that, in order to win their bet, they must disguise themselves heavily as foreigners, penetrate the sisters' villa, court one another's sweethearts and win their love. The young men are sure of their case, but they are also gamblers so they swallow the unpleasantness of the deception which they imagine only to be a joke; neither intends seriously to woo his best friend's beloved.

After organizing the boats and attendant soldiers and cheering crowd, Don Alfonso has taken Ferrando and Guglielmo to a theatrical costumier and hired for them disguises as Albanians (we learn this during the fake marriage ceremony in Act II), huge false moustaches, baggy and highly coloured costumes, floppy hats. Thus garbed they walk into the drawing-room, to a rather martial strain which introduces **No. 13, Sestetto**, *allegro* in C major, *Alla bella Despinetta*, accompanied at first only by strings, later with oboes, clarinets, bassoons, trumpets and drums as well (no flutes or horns). The introduction to Despina is as formal as the martial entrance; woodwind gradually join in while the men sing in impersonal duet, the trumpets implementing their pleas last of all, equally stiffly. Violins collapse into running scales in G major as Despina giggles at the aspect of these oddly garbed and bewhiskered dagos who lavish kisses upon her hand, and wonders whether they come from Wallachia (in present-day Romania) or from further Turkey. For her they are the very antidote to love. But at least she does not recognize the men beneath their fancy dress; Mozart keeps this tension going with a dominant pedal and slow chords, most impressive, for oboes, bassoons and trumpets. The ensemble becomes more intricate though still lightly deployed until the two sisters, roused by the noise, call out a complaint to Despina and enter to investigate (Alfonso retires to a corridor).

The key changes to F, the tempo to *allegro*. The mistresses berate Despina for entertaining camp-followers. Insinuating clarinets and bassoons support the two strangers (and Despina), as they beg the sisters to receive them as suitors, in bland C major with poignant chromatic touches and an even more lachrymose Neapolitan cadence in A minor. The ladies are appalled: the two boys are pleased by this reaction, not so Despina and (peeping from his hiding place) Alfonso. Abandoning C minor the sisters voice their indignation, *molto allegro* in C major, with active oboes and clarinets. The air is ripe for a finale *alla napolitana*. Vocal counterpoint, full of conflicting emotion and variegated texture, promptly appears as the ladies prematurely beg their sweethearts' pardon while the others wonder at such fury. The ladies indulge in runs, then they all converge in unison and the orchestra closes noisily in C major. It is to all intents a finale and there ought to be a curtain. But the scene is nowhere near finished.

6

Don Alfonso now steps forward, amazed at the noise. Dorabella explains the scandal but Alfonso recognizes these weird dagos as his best friends (recitative here accompanied by strings). After a nudge they back him up in dry recitative though the cause of their arrival is enough to bring back the string accompaniment. They were brought here by love.

At this point (bar 32) I have a strange suspicion that da Ponte and Mozart originally planned a duet in which the two pseudo-Albanians press their courtly suit. It would have been in D minor. In the finale of Act II the soldiers return, discover what has happened, and recover their disguises. As they confront their mistresses Guglielmo quotes his loving duet with Dorabella, No. 23, and both unmask Despina as the Mesmeric doctor. But before this Ferrando sings a passage which seems understandable only as a quotation—except that the quoted passage does not occur earlier in the score of the opera (there is something like it in the D major Divertimento K. 320b).

27

Allegretto

A voi s'inchina bella da-mi—na il Ca-va—lie-re dell'Al— ba— ni—a!

This is the only moment when Ferrando declares his Albanian nationality, except in the marriage contract. It is also music quite unlike any other in *Così fan tutte*. The specific content of the words makes it unlikely that Mozart was alluding to a Viennese popular song. These bars must have occurred in an early draft of the opera, perhaps before Guglielmo's Nos. 15 and 15a. Its location here is a piece of joint detective work by Stanley Sadie, R. B. Moberly and me.*

The accompanied recitative from here ('vista appena la luce') is exceptionally expressive and even duet-like, and ends firmly in G minor, after which a duet in D minor would begin appropriately. And this is the only place in the opera where such a sentiment might once have been placed by the authors.

Probably this will for ever remain a mystery. Ferrando and Guglielmo lecherously press their two suits with much sensuous string accompaniment. Dorabella asks for guidance in such a crisis. Fiordiligi takes the initiative, still in theatrical string-accompanied recitative, *Temerari, sortite* (only Despina does go, much startled). Her mood is determined but less wild than that of Dorabella in *Smanie implacabili*. She knows her love to be totally impregnable, proof against death and destiny. The recitative includes some tender, expressive music, and a big jump of a tenth; but they are so short as to sound unpuzzling.

Fiordiligi proceeds to her **Aria, No. 14**, *andante maestoso – allegro – più allegro*, in B flat major, *Come scoglio*, with oboes, clarinets, bassoons, trumpets (but no drums), and strings.

> As a rock remains motionless against winds and storms, so my soul is strong in love and constancy. For us a flame was born that gives pleasure and comfort; only death can change my heart's feelings. Thankless souls, respect this example of fidelity and do not let savage hope further your boldness.

Come scoglio is the grand vocal exhibition of the whole opera, so designed by Mozart for his *prima donna*. It begins with 'great solemnity (whence the trumpets) and an elaborate Metastasian simile which offers scope for monumental broken-chord figures and huge vocal leaps as shown.

Some Mozartians have suggested that these leaps in Fiordiligi's part should be filled in, like the ones for pianoforte in the slow movement of the A major concerto K. 488. I once found an early copy of Fiordiligi's part, with all the graces written in for an ill-schooled soprano (it is in the library at Donaueschingen); there were numerous bravura flourishes and cadenzas for both her arias but nothing added to Ex. 28 until a flourish in the last bar; similarly with the tenth jumps in bars 38–40 and even in bar 43, where a *fermata* suggests a cadenza, the leap was unadorned (though the pause-mark in the previous bar *was* filled in). It was evidently recognized that these monster leaps were a special effect, to be reproduced even

---

* Desmond Shawe-Taylor and the Earl of Harewood had both drawn attention to this enigma before I found it. So had Dennis Arundell who pragmatically located the original in the second act finale.

when the singer was not Adriana Ferraresi who prided herself on her extensive vocal compass. Mozart did not care for her and, being required to display this speciality of hers, made her expose her gear-change from head- to chest-register, and back, as violently as possible. It is also said that Mozart was playing on Ferraresi's technique of ducking her head for low notes and throwing it back for her top register, so that in these bars she would look as well as sound undignified.★

Immediately after Ex. 28 the tempo quickens to *allegro* and the music loses its sternness, becoming quite cheerful.

29

At 'E potrà la morta sola' ('only death', etc.) the hectoring tone is resumed. There is a florid cadence in F major and a triumphant orchestral intermezzo which concludes with dramatic scrunches and a varied return to *Come scoglio* and the passage from which Ex. 29 is quoted—now the scoring includes low trumpets. After a further F major cadence and pause the tempo becomes *più allegro* and the music more hectic for 'Thankless souls' (the wordsetting of Fiordiligi's first line, 'Rispettate, anime ingrate', needs adjustment for correct accentuation), gradually achieving *buffo* exhilaration and a sizable division of rapid triplets. There is also a remarkable passage in which Fiordiligi sings the bass line of the music.

30

The aria ends jubilantly and Fiordiligi is about to make a formal exit, followed by Dorabella. They are stopped by their two suitors—but the young men don't know what to do next and appeal to Alfonso for help. He suggests that the ladies might, out of charity to foreign gentlemen and friendship to him, show a little more courtesy.

Guglielmo sees a cue here for a request that the ladies open their hearts a moment to the words of love. This leads him to an aria in which he extols the handsome qualities of himself and his friend—or rather two arias since Mozart replaced the original one, *Rivolgete a lui*, by a shorter, more naïve number, *Non siate ritrosi*.

The text of the **Aria, No. 15a**, *Rivolgete a lui lo sguardo* had already been printed in the Vienna libretto, though Mozart removed it from the score and inscribed it separately in his catalogue (it is K. 584 in Köchel's catalogue). We do not know if

★ Ferraresi's previous role in Salieri's *La cifra* included similar vocal switchbacks, Peter Branscombe informs me.

he found it too long for the proportions of the act or the patience of the two sopranos, or if da Ponte's text seemed too absurdly full of literary allusions for the simple soldier Guglielmo. Either Mozart or da Ponte may not have wished so soon to show who is courting whom. As an extended comic aria for a great *basso buffo*, Benucci can hardly have turned down such a magnificent vehicle. I shall describe both arias, in order of composition.

In *Rivolgete* Guglielmo is accompanied by oboes, bassoons, trumpets and drums, and strings (Mozart wrote horn parts too, then deleted them). The aria is in D major.

> (*Allegro*) Turn your eyes (*to Fiordiligi*) on him and see him as he is—freezing, burning, adoring, begging for pity. And you (*to Dorabella*) look for a moment at me and you will find in my eyes what my lips cannot express. Orlando (Roland de Roncevalles) was no lover compared with me, and Medoro's wounds (also from Tasso's *Orlando furioso*) were nothing like my friend's. My sighs are made of fire, his desires of bronze; our eloquence is unmatched from Vienna to Canada.
>
> We are as rich as Croesus, as beautiful as Narcissus; as lovers we make Mark Antony look like a clown. We are stronger than Cyclops, and as literary as Aesop. When we dance, Picq grants us superiority, so elegant and agile is our footwork. When we sing trills, nightingales admit their incompetence. We have other skills that nobody knows.
>
> (*Allegro molto*) Hurray, they are faithful; I'm delighted they have walked out. They are heroic in constancy, mirrors of fidelity.

The words, lengthy as they are, deserve to be quoted even in translation, for their wit and verve. The music too is vastly spirited and effective, though its invention may be thought not more than pleasantly ordinary. More interesting, the musical structure is narrative, without reprises. Guglielmo's first phrase should be quoted for identification.

31

Ri—vol—ge—te a lui lo sguardo   e ve – dre — te   co—me   sta:

His vocal line is more expressive than melodious. After drawing attention to Ferrando (I should really refer to them as Sempronio and Tizio but, since this would confuse readers absolutely, they will remain Ferrando and Guglielmo, as in the libretto) his music turns to laughing semiquaver runs for violins. Some loud scrunches introduce his allusions to Tasso ('Un Orlando', etc.) which are more melodious and mark the second subject group.

32

Un   Or——lan-do   in — na ———— mo——ra—to   non è

nien-te, non è nien-te in mio con—fron—te,

This is repeated for Medoro, Orlando's rival in love (as the Albanians are to the soldiers). The bit about fiery sighs is a good but not important melody, less thematic than the unison tune about Vienna and Canada.

che gli u—gua—li non si trovano da Vi—en—na al Ca—na—dà,

The central intermezzo for orchestra in A diverts charmingly into F for the references to Croesus and Narcissus. Mark Antony induces G minor, Cyclops E flat, Aesop C minor. Carlo de Picq, the principal male dancer in Mozart's *Gelosie dei seragli*, the ballet in *Lucio Silla*, is commemorated here in a striking B flat major section, quite different in style (oboe and bassoon to the fore). For the virtuoso singing Guglielmo offers a slow trill *accelerando*, notated throughout. The lovers' secret techniques are for wind with trumpets and drums against a repeated top A on violins, very invigorating. There is a pause; the sisters angrily walk out. The violins' A drops an octave on to violas, the tempo increases to *allegro molto* and Guglielmo exults jubilantly, going up to top F sharp, about the girls' fidelity.

e—ro—i——ne di—— co—stan—za, spec-chi

son—— di fe————del—tà,

If this aria were to be sung in a performance of *Così* there would be a sparsely scored modulation from firm D major to the dominant of G, with sparkling oboes and strings while the suitors burst out laughing.

This passage was changed when Mozart wrote the replacement **Aria, No. 15,** *andantino* in G major, *Non siate ritrosi* with solo flute and bassoon added later to the basic string orchestra.

> Pretty eyes, do not be shy; shine a little in our direction. Be loving and we will make you happy. We are muscular and handsome: our feet, eyes, noses are worth touching, and our moustaches are triumphs of manhood, the plumage of love.

The replacement aria at once sounds more tuneful.

[Andantino]

Non sia-te ri—tro-si, oc—chiet—ti vez—zo—si due lam—pi a—mo-
-ro-si vi—— bra-te un po quà.

This melody is sung thrice with woodwind colouring the third time. After the ladies' exit Guglielmo can hardly sing for giggles. Almost at once **No. 16, Terzetto** intervenes, *molto allegro* in G major, *E voi ridete?*, with flutes, oboes, bassoons, horns, and strings. Don Alfonso asks why they are laughing; if the ladies hear, the enterprise will be ruined. The boys laugh out of assurance that their sweethearts are true. Alfonso is inclined to laugh because he foresees another conclusion, tearful for some. This trio is chiefly attractive for its irrepressible triplets and the nicely diversified rhythm of the vocal laughter.

In recitative the young men suggest that Don Alfonso should abandon his wager and pay half, or a quarter. He sticks by his bet, accusing them of childish ignorance and swearing them further to complete secrecy and obedience until next day. He will give them their next instructions in the garden shortly. Guglielmo is longing for a good meal. Ferrando encourages him to hold his appetite until the battle is over. For the moment love will give their hearts all the sustenance they need, he advises in **No. 17, Aria**, *andante cantabile* in A major, *Un aura amorosa*, with clarinets, bassoons, horns and strings (violins muted).

> A breath of love from one of our beloveds will sweetly sustain our hearts. A heart fed with the hope of love needs no extra nutrition.

The subject-matter sounds more beautiful in da Ponte's fluent and liquid Italian, beautifully matched by music in a favourite amorous key for Mozart. At the beginning Ferrando is hugging his love to himself in stepwise intervals.

36

He is accompanied only by gentle strings for the first half of this eventful aria whose musical highpoint is a run doubled and echoed by orchestra, strings at first, wind as well in the reprise.

37

The chromatic changes to the initial melodic idea exquisitely suggest the nutritious effect of the food of love. The middle section is more light-hearted with an idealistic cadence, floridly prolonged. After a pause Ferrando returns, gracing discreetly, to Ex. 36, now with magical new and balmy wind accompaniment, the exact musical suggestion of the bouquet of love for a lover. (One new gracing looks back to the slow movement of the E flat piano concerto K. 449.) In the reprise Ferrando has two opportunities for flourishes. The orchestral coda is more martial than amorous (we may think of Fiordiligi's 'guerriero ed amante') with strong dotted rhythms and prominent wind band.

Often this glorious aria is followed immediately by the finale. But there is still another scene in recitative and it is quite important. Ferrando and Guglielmo retire. Alfonso returns to the drawing-room, annoyed to find that, in a world peopled by inconstant women, he has chosen to bet on two who seem cursedly faithful. He holds a council of war with Despina who, totally convinced of her own amorous ethics, is sure that her mistresses will think likewise when pushed to the point. Love must always be a pleasure, never a burden. Alfonso asks her to admit that this first round was a failure. Despina proposes to take over the stage-management and bring the design to success, so long as the Albanian suitors have plenty of money. She fancies the prestige of a successful production, but she will insist on a handsome management fee.

7

We move into the garden, not the seaside portion but something more kempt and ornamental with grass couches at either side.

Fiordiligi and Dorabella moved out here after *Non siate ritrosi* for a breath of fresh air. Evidently it proved beneficial. This **Finale, No. 18**, *Ah, che tutta in un momento*, begins *andante* in D major calmly and cheerfully with an elegant string melody.

Solo flutes echoed by bassoons propose an even more frivolous idea (Carl Ebert has made us associate it with gaily twirling parasols).

There is more of charm and felicity in this orchestral introduction (horns are added discreetly) before the sisters sing, most inappropriately, of the torment and grief they claim to be undergoing, even with Ex. 39 to cheer them up; back it comes, to everybody's pleasure, and Ex. 38 afterwards. Their enchanting duet ends in D major. The tempo becomes *allegro*. Trumpets are added. The Albanians are heard behind the scenes crying for death, Alfonso trying to calm them in G minor. The sisters express concern. Now in B flat major their distracted suitors rush in, brandishing phials of arsenic which they proceed to drink, reproaching the cruelty of these hard-hearted ladies. We may notice that the hunters and the hunted always sing together in duet, like extra pairs of the woodwind who give so much variety of colour to the music. As the men writhe on the grass, apparently at their last gasp, the G minor music becomes heavily loaded with emotion. There are the poignant augmented triads at 'd'un disperato affetto', darkened by bassoons, the texture at the cadence spotlit ('abbiate almen pietà') by soft flutes; then swirling strings for the sisters' wails of 'O tragico spettaccolo', and a vocal quintet of block harmony, extremely tense, pierced by chill woodwind chords supported (as in

Come scoglio) by a low trumpet pedal. The shrill lamenting of 'Tremo, le fibre e l'anima', and the distracted interchanges of 'nè può la lingua', come close to the wronged dismay of Donna Anna, especially when Fiordiligi takes over Ferrando's line in the latter passage.

40

The quintet ends, G minor moves into E flat major, and the boys impersonate comatose symptoms. Alfonso reckons that, under the circumstances, the two sisters had better take some notice of these poor fellows. Instead of ministering to the corpses they call loudly for Despina who diagnoses imminent death; Don Alfonso explains the cause, and the music slips back appropriately to G minor for a moment. Despina, of course, is full of sensible advice. The patients both show signs of life. The ladies must therefore tend them with kindly hands while she and Don Alfonso fetch a doctor with an antidote for the poison. Mozart has now, since the G minor scene, got his eye on the target and consistently, even prodigally, finds the apt musical idea for each new turn of events; even conventional cadence passages, such as Despina's about going to the doctor, are temptingly quotable, as is the next passage where the sisters gingerly approach their task while the pseudo-corpses relish the *commediola*, the four converging in a quartet passage dominated by Ferrando as much as Fiordiligi. The girls are still teetering some way away from the moribund remains of their *inamorati* so the boys give a deathrattle groan to encourage some action from their recalcitrant nurses. Two contrasted ideas in C minor here will be brilliantly elaborated in what follows, so they are quoted now.

41

This provokes the ladies into individual comment and characterization, strengthened by their gormless dialogue and the working-out of Ex. 41 on bassoons and strings in open, polyphonic textures. Dorabella is the first to admit that the corpses' faces are interesting; Fiordiligi suggests that they should approach and investigate for temperature and pulse-rate—both unpromising. They fall into woeful duet, strongly supported by clarinets and bassoons. The men note their increasing involvement, in a duet passage very darkly scored with bassoons and violas. All four conclude this scene with a concerted quartet in hushed, chromatic C minor with honeyed clarinets to help.

The sisters' embarrassment is relieved by the return of Don Alfonso with a doctor—*allegro* in G major, with flutes, oboes, bassoons, horns and strings—whom the corpses instantly identify as Despina in disguise. Alfonso's introduction is quoted not only as a signpost but also a reminder that this scene is constructed largely on the example's broken chord of G major.

Doctor Despina (opportunity for disguised voice) addresses the company in mongrel-Latin (e.g. 'bones puelles') but condescends upon request to adopt the vernacular—Greek, Arabic, Turkish, Vandal, Swabian, Tartar, she speaks them all. Alfonso diverts her from linguistic prowess to medical diagnosis. The sisters and Alfonso give her the medical history in a trio from which the learned medico deduces a cure with a 'piece of iron'; it is a magnet as invented by Dr Mesmer (the inventor of Mesmerism was a Mozart family friend) in Austria, and publicized in France—Ex. 42 is still the basis of all the themes, though when she draws this magnet along the bodies of the poisoned lovers, the strings, answered by woodwind, shake violently in cadential trills. This causes the corpses to vibrate in sympathy much to the girls' relief; they are glad to hold the heads of the resurrected strangers, even commenting that this medico is worth all the gold in Peru.

The young men slowly raise themselves up; the music becomes *andante* in B flat major, rather hesitant, full of the galant rhythm from Lombardy which English-speakers call the Scottish snap. Uncertainly but in perfect duet the boys believe themselves in classical Olympus, being handled, rather uncertainly, by Pallas Athene and Venus Cytherea. Again their duet is supported by sustained trumpets in the middle. Quickly they admit recognition of their best beloveds, embrace them and kiss their hands, which the doctor and philosopher confidently ascribe to the after-effects of arsenic, though the sisters are afraid of what the neighbours may say. They all join in a sextet of three pairs, ladies, suitors, and Despina with Alfonso, still to the Scottish snap figure, much in evidence on violins. The sisters find it difficult to resist the kisses of their suitors. Despina and Alfonso assure them that the effects of the paroxysm will soon wear off; the two boys are almost helpless with laughter, though thoughts of gossip drive Fiordiligi into bouts of florid bravura from top B flat down to middle C.

For the concluding section of this finale the music returns to D major and increases pace to *allegro*. The boys plead for a kiss, much too forward for the faithful sisters ('Stelle! un bacio?') whose outrage ignites the final ensemble of the act. The suitors are partly convulsed, partly anxious lest real love should result as Despina and Alfonso foresee it will. Again the trumpets (now with drums) enhance the sound, again excursions to the submediant (B flat major) heighten the tension and sense of occasion, again Fiordiligi adds florid excursions to that tension. As an about-face, the duet patter which, in *Don Giovanni*, we associated with two basso leading characters, is here taken over by the two leading sopranos ('disperati, attossicati'). The appeal for a kiss formally returns with horrified pauses and repeated explanations. The sextet is resumed with some repetition and extra runs for the sopranos and indeed Ferrando, and a final unison passage for all six before a brilliant and animated orchestral coda (especially woodwind) concludes the act. The sisters surely leave in disgust, the soldiers are delighted, Despina and Alfonso have mixed feelings. It should already be stressed that, now and throughout, Despina has no idea of the Albanians' identity. And at this half-way point Fiordiligi and Dorabella are still cypher characters, though Ferrando and Guglielmo have begun to display personal characteristics.

8

The second of the two acts begins in the shared dressing-room of Fiordiligi and Dorabella. Like the second half of *Figaro* it begins informally with dry recitative. As Alfonso with the boys in Act I, so Despina here has been explaining common sense to her ladies and they regard it as offensive. Are they, her noble mistresses, to ape her loose morals? Despina explains how strict hers are, and how moral: gain experience, avoid danger, treat love lightly, behave as your sweethearts will on the battlefield. In this particular case, flatter the rich strangers who were willing to die for love. Girls can do without love, not without lovers. Fiordiligi is again worried about gossip, but Despina can spread word that the foreigners are chasing her. Both sisters are cautiously willing to receive the Albanians again, but wonder how to treat them.

Despina answers in her **Aria, No. 19**, *andante – allegretto* in G major, *Una donna a quindici anni*, with flute, bassoon, two horns and strings.

> From the age of fifteen a girl should know how to behave fashionably, where the devil's tail is, what is right and what is wrong.
>
> She must know how to catch lovers, listen to a hundred, speak to a thousand, learn to conceal and lie and get her own way.

Despina begins in conventional rustic mood in 6/8, doubled by bassoon, then flute, very pretty and insinuating. Her aria quickens to *allegretto* for a haunting pastoral section which is the real main theme.

43
Allegretto

It returns several times even after the music has stopped and the audience probably applauded—as if Despina were granting an encore. Despina makes her formal exit. The sisters are both appalled by the idea of free love, let alone rumour. Dorabella suggests that Despina is a good excuse, and that their sweethearts need never learn about a flirtation which will, in any case keep them both from tedium. Fiordiligi is persuaded to fraternize at a cool level. But which of the two young men? Dorabella has chosen already.

She explains, in **No. 20, Duetto**, *andante* in B flat, *Prenderò quel brunettino* with oboes, bassoons, horns and strings, that the dark-haired man is her choice, Guglielmo as we know him.

44

They agree, with some sensuous florid gracing, in agile duet too, that flirtation need not mean a change of heart. The reprise of Ex. 44 is deliciously canonic and nicely ornamented, emotional gasps of delight included.

Alfonso at once comes to bring them into the garden where singing, music and pleasure await them. The scene changes to the seashore part of the garden, presumably as for No. 4. Two stone tables are now prescribed and a flower-decked ship, with a band on board, has been moored here. On shore are a chorus, several smartly dressed servants, Despina, and the two Albanians ready to sing their serenade, **No. 21, Duetto con coro,** *andante* in E flat major, *Secondate aurette, amiche,* with flutes, clarinets, bassoons, horns, and no strings at all. It is, in fact a wind serenade, like old K. 375 and 388, its serenading music typical of a vein often cultivated by Mozart in other music. The wind band has a quite long, and very beautiful, introduction in which flutes are absent, clarinets omnipresent.

45

Ferrando and Guglielmo sing their beautiful serenade to this tune, about the message of love which they have taught the breezes to carry to their loves. A chorus briefly repeats the contents of Ex. 45, and the wind band makes a conclusion. It is a heavenly moment in an opera full of such things.

Fiordiligi and Dorabella, conducted by Alfonso, arrived in time to hear it all, and to receive baskets of flowers brought to them by servants from the boat which departs at once. Despina tells the young men to start talking, but they have lost their voices. Alfonso, recognizing their embarrassment, invites Despina to join him in a rehearsal of what men and ladies now should be telling one another. It is the **Quartet, No. 22,** *allegretto grazioso* in D major, *La mano a me date,* with flutes, bassoons, trumpets (again!) and strings. Soft, lightly articulated trumpets are a special feature of this number, and give it a particular expressive vivacity. There is a suggestion that Mozart planned this as a solo aria for Don Alfonso.

Alfonso takes Dorabella's hand, Despina Fiordiligi's. Speaking for the tongue-tied men, he tells the ladies how sorry he is for the trouble he caused them, how much he would like to demonstrate what they both desire. The tone of the music is as light as possible, as if the suitors wished only to touch the hands of their beloveds; not only flutes, but trumpets too, have to fall in with this featherweight mood. There is a smoother, more *cantabile* passage at 'Perdono vi chiede', though it is answered spikily by violins. The suitors repeat Alfonso's words now and then, like slow pupils in school. Nor do they take his instruction seriously—it is not in their own interest. Despina answers for the two ladies (who do not echo her words), and soon requires an *allegro* tempo: forget the past, accept the present, and be happy. Despina and Alfonso adopt a *presto* tempo for a rapid review of the situation which promises well but needs careful invigilation by them both.

If I had not already blown the gaff and explained who was to court whom, working from knowledge of Guglielmo's *Rivolgete* aria, nobody would have realized that the two soldiers have to court each other's sweethearts; though in No. 20 the ladies made up their minds to the same purpose. Girls and boys have sung almost always in pairs of the same sex. Now they have to pair off, and we see that Ferrando chooses Fiordiligi while Guglielmo takes Dorabella (there would be no point in courtship the other way round; the girls would penetrate the disguise at once).

At first both couples remain tongue-tied, smiling, the men sighing, all looking at one another. Dorabella has courteously taken Guglielmo's arm, Fiordiligi not so, though it is she who breaks the silence, commenting on the fine weather which Ferrando finds a trifle warm for him. Dorabella draws attention to the pretty bushes in the garden—more leaves than fruit, notices Guglielmo. Fiordiligi suggests a stroll along one of these charming paths; Ferrando is very ready, but whispers to Guglielmo on the way past that this will be the moment of truth—Dorabella did not quite catch the words, she says, and is told that he was asked to entertain her nicely. Dorabella also suggests a constitutional and they begin but, after a pause marked by emotional movement in the bass of the recitative, he begins to groan that he feels as ill as if he were at the point of death. Dorabella recognizes to herself the feebleness of the excuse and suggests that it is the after-effects of the arsenic. Guglielmo mentions the stronger poison of love, fiery as Mount Etna ('Mongibello'). Dorabella advises him to cool off, which he takes as cruel mockery (he notices apprehensively that the other two are now out of sight). Full of fine words and ardent sighs he begs a token of Dorabella's compassion. Two if you wish, is her answer (does she mean lips?); tell me what I must do and you'll see (the language of this recitative is surprisingly outspoken to a post-Freudian). Guglielmo changes tactics and offers her the locket from round his neck, heart-shaped. Guglielmo hates to do it, but he has pledged a soldier's honour. Dorabella is greatly impressed and soon accepts the gift.

Guglielmo, in **No. 23, Duetto**, *andante grazioso* in F major, *Il core vi dono*, with clarinets, bassoons, horns and strings, explains that she must exchange his heart for hers. The musical representation of heartbeats was already a feature of Zerlina's *Vedrai, carino* in *Don Giovanni* and earlier of Belmonte's *O wie ängstlich* in *Die Entführung*.

The first subject group is concerned with the giving and receiving of tokens, with the rhythm of the first whole bar, and the rising fourth in the second. Next to Guglielmo's idea I quote Dorabella's reply which includes three and a half different variants (the third one harmonically most affecting):

46a
Andante grazioso

Il co—re vi do—no,

46b

Mel da—te lo pren—do, ma il mio non vi——ren—do in—

—van me'l chie——de—te, più me-co ei non è.

Dorabella accepts his heart but cannot return the gift since hers has been given away already. He touches her on the bosom and asks what is beating there; she responds in kind. A staccato cadence figure on violins quickly grows into a heart-beat theme which introduces woodwind to the texture when they first sing together.

47
che mai bal-za, bal-za, bal-za lì?

per-chè bat-te bat-te bat-te quì?

A gentle, Zerlina-like C major cadence suggests a combination of Ex. 47's palpitation and Ex. 46's rhythm—the rising fourth becomes a rising sixth. But there is a pause: the heartbeat figure is diversified and put out of synchronization (two hearts are *not* beating as one).

48
ei bat—te co——sì,

Clar.+Fag. 8bassa

Viol.+Vla. 8bassa

552

The duet returns to F major. Dorabella has admitted that her heart beats for Tizio/Guglielmo: while they exchange idle phrases (high violins have the melodic interest) he exchanges her locket for his pendant, resorting to subterfuge when she resists. She feels a Vesuvius (this volcano, unlike Etna, may appropriately be visible on stage) pounding within her—the rhythm of Ex. 48 is augmented in her vocal line, a delicate touch. When the exchange is completed, and Dorabella is allowed to turn round, Ex. 46 returns on two adulterous horns. They duet happily together, much in the rhythm of Ex. 46 while high violins suggest their secret passion, and caressing woodwind thirds their pleasure.

This whole passage is repeated, and they return to Ex. 46 with the rising sixth and cadence to its repeated rhythms, wandering further into the garden arm-in-arm while a clarinet writhes an ecstatic coda.

Fiordiligi just misses them when she hurries to this spot for refuge from Ferrando who is pursuing her in high-mettled string-accompanied recitative. She is just as determined herself and refers to him as a snake, a hydra and a basilisk. The rushing string scales settle into a poignant *adagio* as she asks him to leave her in peace. First he wants her to look more kindly on him. When she does so, it is with an appended sigh from which he draws optimistic conclusions. He is particularly asked to sing very cheerfully (*lietissimo*) in his **Aria, No. 24**, *allegretto – allegro* in B flat major, *Ah lo veggio*, with clarinets, one bassoon, trumpets and strings.

> Now I realize: this lovely nature cannot resist my pleas, cannot rebel against her compassion. That glance, those sighs kindle my heart. You respond, you yield to my longing.
>
> What, silent, pitiless, evasive, deaf to my longing? I must give up my deluding hopes. She cruelly condemns me to death.

This sounds as if it could have been called a rondo, from the nature of the theme (which Mozart also sketched as a finale to the clarinet quintet K. 581), garrulous, exposed almost in one breath, as it were.

It does return rondo-fashion, each time more drastically varied. After fourteen bars of melody, including two of Mozart's passionately aspiring sixths, a transition passage, notable for the syncopated accented passing-notes in the violins (curious effect), moves towards F major for another tune in running quavers.

The last phrase quoted is a familiar Mozart tag (from the contemporary clarinet quintet, indeed). This idea is pulled up by a pause, then repeated. After another pause Ex. 50 returns, lightly decorated and, at last, doubled by the first clarinet which until now has listened silently to its own music; second clarinet quietly oodles away at an Alberti accompaniment, as in the trio of K. 543's minuet. This reprise ventures further into the flat side of the key but returns, with a solemn dominant middle pedal for trumpets (another old friend), to B flat and a reprise of the transition and Ex. 51 (now in the home-key) significantly varied and again repeated.

The cadence is dramatically interrupted for distraught groans on bassoon and viola, with Ferrando's discovery that Fiordiligi is not, after all, so cooperative. Another pause, and then the *allegro* coda, again based on Ex. 50, or a fragment of it thrice repeated. Ferrando's threats of suicide do not divert the music from animated and joyous B flat major.

Ah lo veggio is often omitted from performances, partly because Mozart (timorously after the final dress rehearsal, maybe) indicated the possibility in his score, chiefly I suspect because it lies uncomfortably high for most tenors and demands a long breath control. It is architecturally important to the scene and Mozart would not have composed the aria if it had been beyond Calvesi; he had known the singer for four years.

Ferrando leaves Fiordiligi, as she asked him to. He has no intention of killing himself, and he is still *lietissimo* because he can report joyful news to Guglielmo of Fiordiligi's fidelity.

Fiordiligi, still in accompanied recitative, is not so sure of herself. The foreigner's ardent entreaties have jolted her composure. At first she is tempted to call him back ('Ei parte'), but determines to hold fast to her lovers' vows with Guglielmo, though now she is aware that she executes them in despite of the mad, guilty passion (rapidly pattering strings) she has begun to feel for another man, not out of demure and untroubled virtuous love. She is becoming a more interesting, profound creature than the light-hearted girl of this morning.

She begins, with spare and subdued string accompaniment, to sing a prayer of apology to her absent Guglielmo.

This is her **Rondo, No. 25**, *adagio – allegro moderato* in E major, *Per pietà, ben*

mio, which will also involve flutes, clarinets, bassoons, and especially horns almost *obbligato*.

> Have mercy, my dear, forgive the error of the one who loves you. It shall remain concealed among these dark trees. My love and faith will forget this shameful weakness. To whom was my wicked heart unfaithful? Dear one, your purity deserved a better reward.

Fiordiligi begins, in Ex. 52, with a solemn obeisance to her absent lover; Mozart made a point, in this rondo (rather less rondoesque than No. 24), of exhibiting Adriana Ferraresi's chest register and only takes her up to G sharp (except once to touch top B) so as to let her lower tones glow appropriately. Again he treats Fiordiligi to great leaps, the first one heralded by the first entry of flutes and horns; the rest of the woodwind are soon added.

There is a short episode, with some liquid clarinet phrases and more leaps. At once Ex. 52 returns, now with prominent interludes for horns and bassoon (the effect is of three horns, whence the three for which Beethoven, imitating this aria, wrote in Leonore's *Abscheulicher* from *Fidelio*), the first horn part very florid, and for clarinets with bassoon (again effectively for three clarinets).

The reprise concluded, Fiordiligi thinks about the pure young gallant whose trust she has almost let down. The strings become more cheerful with her.

53

Allegro moderato

Viol. I *p*

A chi mai mancò di fede que-sto va—no, ingra—to cor, si do—vea mi-glior merce—de, ca-ro bene, al tuo can—dor, ca—ro be—————————ne al tuo can——dor.

The horns have joined in the general pleasure, at the end of Ex. 53. Almost at once solo clarinet leads Fiordiligi and other woodwind into an exhilarated phrase dealing with the *gruppetto* (the singer's is not written out, but must be added for conformity). This section is repeated with extra elaboration. The music yields for an affectionate passage in florid triplets given to the singer, then resumes the *allegro* pace for long rising trills accompanied by surging woodwind and horn runs and a final burst of virtuosity for Fiordiligi who leaves the stage confidently during a joyful orchestral coda.

Meanwhile Ferrando has found Guglielmo and he is still *lietissimo*. Ferrando had worked carefully on Fiordiligi, given her his arm, chatted, broached the topic of love, stammered and wept. To this she laughed and teased, pretended to show sympathy, then ran away calling that she was preserving her chastity for her dear Guglielmo. Having thanked Ferrando with an embrace, Guglielmo is forced to admit that Dorabella was not quite so adamantine in chaste resolve: in fact she gave Guglielmo a love-token, Ferrando's own portrait.

Ferrando draws the string orchestra into his furious receipt of this disclosure: he must find this false doxy and tear out her heart (Guglielmo's heart?). Guglielmo, in a desperate attempt at diplomacy, advises him not to worry about a girl worth only pocket-money. Ferrando remembers the happy moments with Dorabella that will always be worth more than a king's ransom (aspiring wisps of strings, *andante*). What (determined *allegro* in D flat major) shall he do?

Mozart first meant to end this recitative in C minor followed at once by Guglielmo's aria which might have been in F or A flat (less likely), or have begun in G with the tune. The join was ineffective, so Mozart added some extra bars and started Guglielmo's **Aria, No. 26**, *allegretto* from a D major chord working gradually towards the tonic key of G; this chattering approach from dominant to tonic is a cardinal feature of *Donne mie, le fate a tanti* which confirms Guglielmo's role as principal comedian in this comic opera and is scored for flutes, oboes, bassoons, horns, trumpets, timpani and strings.

54

My ladies, you behave this way to so many men that, truth to tell, I begin to sympathize when your lovers grumble. I love your sex, as you know and everybody knows; I prove it daily. But when you behave like that to so many, many men, I get put off. I've drawn my sword a thousand times to save your honour, defended you as often with my mouth and heart. But you do it to so many men, it's boring. You are lovely, graced by heaven from top to toe. But you maltreat so many men one can't believe it, and when they complain they have their reasons.

This is a real rondo where Ex. 54 returns many times after episodes of brilliant variety, cocky, martial, sad, astonished, angry. With its spirit and movement and integrity it does not call for closer description. It is related superficially to *Aprite un pò* in *Figaro*, in subject though not musical content. A young Mozart might have thought of Ex. 54 and made this a patter aria. The grown-up Mozart uses no patter sequence at all here. Da Ponte had indicated an angry Guglielmo; Mozart's singer is vexed but still charming—he has, after all, made the first conquest even if it cost him half the wager. He will vent his annoyance later.

Ferrando watches him go and at once continues in recitative accompanied by strings (*In qual fiero contrasto*) who persist with a theme of nagging inward perplexity.

55

Ferrando cannot advise himself nor take another's advice. Angry with Alfonso, who has half proved his point, Ferrando is set on revenge—though he still loves Dorabella.

His **Cavatina, No. 27**, *allegro* in C minor-major, *Tradito, schernito*, with oboes, clarinets, bassoons, horns and strings (violas sometimes *divisi*), is a short piece, as its title suggests—a *Cavatina* is properly a brief aria for the entry of a principal character—but manages to combine two moods. The first is aggrieved and recitative-like. The woodwind follow with a consoling melody. These ideas are alternated and the movement ends with a short but brave florid passage.

Betrayed, disparaged by her traitorous heart, I still feel that I have lost her, hear voices of love for her.

There is more drama and legato than bravura in this aria, which is perhaps why it is less often suppressed than *Ah lo veggio*, musically more attractive but also more difficult. The most pleasing feature of *Tradito, schernito* is the woodwind scoring, as in the second idea, later repeated in C major.

56

During this cavatina Guglielmo has brought Alfonso to eavesdrop on Ferrando who does *not* leave the stage at the end. Instead Alfonso compliments him on his constancy, and Guglielmo provokes his virility by suggesting that Ferrando is maybe less valiant a lover. For a Ferrando these are inflammatory words, but Alfonso tells both his young friends that they are still under oath to obey his commands.

9

The scene changes to another room in the sisters' villa, furnished with doors, a mirror and a small table. Despina congratulates Dorabella on behaving like a woman of the world, and commiserates with Fiordiligi on her long face. Fiordiligi confesses that she has fallen all too deeply in love with the fairhaired gallant. The other two encourage her to persevere with him and be happy. Fiordiligi cannot help thinking of the poor boys to whom they have promised fidelity and who are now far away at war. That's just it, answers Dorabella: they may get killed and then we're stranded. By the time they return, if they're still alive, we shall be married and a thousand miles away. Fiordiligi still intends to subdue her inclinations, but her sister asks her to respect the dictates of Cupid, in **No. 28, Aria**, *Allegretto vivace* in B flat major, *È amore un ladroncello*, with flute, oboes, clarinets, bassoons, horns in high B flat, and strings.

Love is a little thief, a little snake. He gives our hearts peace or takes it away as he fancies. He opens the pathway to passion and at once binds your soul in chains. If you humour him he'll bring you pleasure, but if you try to oppose him he'll fill you with disgust.

If he settles and gnaws within you, do whatever he tells you as I shall.

The special feature of this aria, which is in rondo form, is the prominence of wind band without strings. There they are in the introduction, flute entering late and positively, due to figure again subsequently. The high-pitched horns, common in early Mozart opera, are a special effect here. I quote Dorabella's entry.

57

È a—mo—re un la—dron—cel——lo,   un ser—pen—tel—lo è a—mor—,

A feature of this aria is of questioning pauses as if our confident Dorabella were something given to doubts. When strings enter they include divided violas but not for long. Wind resume and bring back a reprise about felonious Cupid. At 'porta dolcezza' the strings have another chance, something like a waltz in E flat major; but, for pugnacity and disgust, tremolos and abrupt dynamic switches intrude. Pastoral and rage are again contrasted. Then Ex. 57 returns once more with woodwind accompaniment alone, second clarinet's Alberti accompaniment very prominent. After another pause, 'come gli piace' induces spasmodic giggles on violins (staccato repeated notes as in *Figaro*, No. 18) then oboes, subsequently other instruments. The passage about love gnawing at the heart turns the orchestra to figures like the heartbeats in *Il core vi dono*. Ex. 57 is again repeated with woodwind accompaniment, then the whole orchestra ends with a variant of it.

Do you remember that this lady was, only a short while ago, babbling about implacable frenzy and the Eumenides? She has now reverted to her real self. But Fiordiligi is going to put up a defence of her own against her weakness. She decides to disguise herself (and Dorabella if persuadable) in military uniform and follow their old lovers to war; fortunately Ferrando and Guglielmo left some spare uniforms in the girls' villa (this invites leading questions never answered). Fiordiligi finds that Ferrando's fits her perfectly (some would find this highly psychological) and she is about to put it on in **No. 29, Duetto**, *adagio* in A major, *Fra gli amplessi*, with oboes, bassoons, horns and strings, when Ferrando (observed through a niche by Guglielmo and Alfonso) wanders in and renews his courtship (*con più moto*). Rushing string figures precipitate Fiordiligi's downfall, especially when Ferrando draws his sword. (O Siegmund, O Freud!) She carries resistance into a C major passage which Ferrando gratefully echoes. They begin to duet happily. Fiordiligi has a last qualm. Ferrando banishes it in a marvellous A major cantilena, *larghetto*. It persuades her totally; she admits defeat. *Andante* in A major they rejoice in mutual love, to some florid purpose, and leave together.

They have been overheard, remember, by Guglielmo and Alfonso. Guglielmo is out of his mind with rage, even more when Ferrando returns with the news. This Fiordiligi—'flower of loyalty'—is a devil's moll, 'flower of Satan'. Ferrando throws back Guglielmo's taunts of unmanliness. How to punish these perfidious bitches? Alfonso's answer is to marry them. Rather, reply the disappointed soldiers, marry Charon's boat or Vulcan's smithy. Alfonso insists that, if they love the girls, they should be philosophical and wed the ones whom they have just conquered.

Don Alfonso's plan, from the beginning, was instructive in purpose. He knew that his military friends and their brides had walked into a relationship without thinking properly about its significance once infatuation had vanished. He had to persuade not only two men, but two girls as well, that they were wrongly coupled. Ferrando is much better suited to Fiordiligi now that she has come out of her shell and is demonstrating positive emotions; Dorabella likewise will live more happily with Guglielmo who won her heart so quickly because he lived on her wavelength.

A double wedding is the perfect answer. They must not despise their ladies for flirtatiousness: it is a characteristic of the female sex. This is the message of Alfonso's **No. 30, Andante**, another solo with trio confirmation, accompanied only by strings in C major, *Tutti accusan le donne*.

> Women are not to be blamed; their instincts are fine. Only men who complain of cuckoldry are guilty of weak activity in courtship. Necessity of heart dictates that all ladies act the same, whether old or young, lovely or ugly.

They are made to repeat Don Alfonso's Ex. 1 (but note that one chord is changed, to less poignant effect: misgivings would be out of place here).

Despina, full of enthusiasm, joins the men and announces that the dear ladies are ready to marry them. She has sent for a notary to perform the ceremony (heavy winks at Alfonso) and told her mistresses that they will leave Naples with their husbands in about three days' time. The men pronounce themselves *contentissimi* in loud but partly insincere threepart harmony and Despina assures them that none of her enterprises is ever ineffective.

For the **Finale, No. 31** the scene changes to a richly illuminated banqueting room with a table set for four persons. It must be in the sisters' villa which is larger than we may have supposed. Four servants are lighting the silver candlesticks. An orchestra is making ready to play at the far end of the room; Mozart does not indicate where, if at all, they play but they and the servants do have a quantity of choral music to sing so their instruments are probably mute stage properties.

Allegro assai in C major, *Fate presto, o cari amici*, with oboes, bassoons and strings, Despina is organizing the finishing touches for the marriage feast, ensuring that the table and lighting and musicians are ready for the entry of the bridal couples. The servants and orchestral choristers repeat her instructions; trumpets and drums add festive splendour to their chorus, then rest while Don Alfonso enters, applauds the arrangements, and promises that the bridegrooms will tip them suitably. While he is singing the band is supposed to tune up; but Mozart did not play his tuning-up trick as in *Don Giovanni*, indicating that the stage orchestra is not a real one. Despina and Alfonso leave the room by separate doors, remarking on the deliciousness of the *commediola* that they are stage-managing.

A fuller orchestra (oboes, clarinets, bassoons, horns, trumpets, drums and strings) joins the chorus in welcoming the bridal quartet, *andante* in E flat major, *Benedetti i doppi conjugi*, as they enter the banqueting room. Da Ponte prescribed an orchestral march here, but Mozart did not write an extra one. While they are uplifting their voices in a prayer that the couples may be "as prolific as hens" (delightful metaphor), we may recall No. 3 in which the boys promised to spend their wager-winnings on a serenade and a banquet: Don Alfonso has kindly granted both these wishes; he is not a guest at the banquet—but he will have the consolation prize of 200 sequins.

The chorus have finished and the solo vocal quartet, with clarinets and bassoons, begins what musical analysis describes as the trio section of this Wedding Hymn: it includes grateful thanks to Despina who brought these four together—the gratitude sends Fiordiligi into a florid run and a Ferraresi tenth leap which Ferrando at once (impudently?) repeats. The instrumental part of the chorus returns prematurely while the soloists are still singing other music; when they have finished, the chorus is repeated. *Pizzicato* strings sink into A flat major; clarinets and bassoons in thirds announce a warm and cheerful melody for antiphonal duet by grooms and brides. They suggest a toast. It is proposed in canon, *larghetto*, still in A flat major, *È nel tuo, nel mio bicchiero*, by Fiordiligi.

In this sumptuous melody she asks that all thoughts and memories of the past may be drowned in their glasses. Well may she and Dorabella hope so. Ferrando takes up the tune, then Dorabella while the others add countersubjects (this quartet is a prototype of many more or less canonic ensembles, *Mir ist so wunderbar* in Beethoven's *Fidelio* being only more famous than similar examples by Rossini, Bellini and Donizetti). When it is Guglielmo's turn he restricts his contribution to muttered asides about dishonourable vixen and sooner poison than wine, while Fiordiligi returns to the melodic line. The explanation usually given is that Ex. 58 lies outside Guglielmo's compass; but only one note of it—and Mozart could have fudged that if he had wanted. The reason is surely less pseudo-practical, more psychological and dramatic. The boys are disgusted by this charade; furthermore they know they have just lost a hundred sequins each, and perhaps the respect of the girls whom they truly love. One of them must be seen and heard to voice this undercurrent of feeling, and it is Guglielmo who was the first to capture a victim and the last to lose his bet, therefore the more aggrieved of the two. As if to make up for his non-participation in Ex. 58 the strings are joined at this point by clarinets and bassoon, with a dominant middle pedal on horns.

This quartet completed, the music becomes *allegro* in E major (a rare key for Mozart like A flat major, but relevant to *Così fan tutte*). Flutes return to the orchestra which now has oboes, bassoons and strings as well. Don Alfonso hurries in, *Miei signori, tutto è fatto*, and announces the Notary Beccavivi who is, of course, Despina in a new disguise and assuming a nasal voice and a stage cough. Beccavivi reads out the details of the marriage contract: Fiordiligi is to marry Sempronio, Dorabella's groom is called Tizio; they ask for details of dowry to be suppressed, and the ladies sign the contract (trumpets are added here). The music has arrived at A major. A flute runs up that scale; the orchestra, with timpani added and an off-stage chorus, strikes up No. 8, *Bella vita militar* in D major, *maestoso* as before.

The lovers at first comment vaguely on the noise outside: the girls have forgotten the associations of this song. Alfonso pockets the contract which the men have not signed, and volunteers to investigate. The music jumps loudly into E flat major, *allegro* (flutes, clarinets, bassoons, horns, strings) and Alfonso returns, *Misericordia, Numi del cielo*, explaining that the ladies' other spouses have returned and are just landing on shore. The servants clear the table, the band disappear furtively. Alfonso leads Beccavivi into an adjoining room, the two Albanians are pushed into another one. The girls are tortured by G minorish fears, though Alfonso promises that all will be well if they trust him.

With a comfortable *andante* tune in B flat major Ferrando and Guglielmo, now cleanshaven again and in their pristine military uniforms (have they taken back the ones Fiordiligi was trying on?), breeze in to greet their sweethearts.

Alfonso, with clarinets, bassoons and horns, pretends surprise and delight. They explain that the royal order to battle was countermanded and they are home again. Their loved ones seem stunned and unwelcoming. Perhaps it is the unexpected shock. Let them stow their baggage in this ante-room. Who is the man hidden in that room? A notary? Despina reveals herself, *con più moto*, pretending that she has just returned from a fancy-dress ball and was about to change back into cap and apron. Suddenly the ladies realize that all has not been above board. In a minute they will realize that their marriage contract cannot be binding. But before that penny has dropped, Don Alfonso has let the document in question slither to the floor. Ferrando instantly picks it up. Guglielmo reads it. A marriage contract? They are appalled: 'Giusto ciel' in G flat major, *allegro* with oboes, trumpets and drums as well as clarinets, bassoons and strings (horns are given a rest). Their brides have betrayed them and blood will have to flow in torrents, like the strings' semiquavers.

They move towards the other anteroom. The ladies stop them, *andante* in C minor, with anguished thirds about guilt and just execution. They ask the cruel Alfonso, and the pander Despina, to speak in their defence. Alfonso, to cheerful active music in or around F major, unkindly remarks that the proof will be found in the anteroom. The sisters are distraught, on the verge of B flat minor.

The soldiers investigate and re-enter with some of their Albanian gear. Ferrando quotes his mysterious Ex. 27, bowing absurdly to Fiordiligi. Guglielmo, singing Ex. 46, returns Ferrando's portrait to Dorabella. Pouncing on Despina they reveal her as the magnetic doctor, trills and all. The ladies are nonplussed, Despina pretends likewise (she does not want to lose her job if it can be helped). They point to the vile trickster Don Alfonso. Blandly, *andante con moto* in D major, *V'ingannai ma fu l'inganno*, he explains that his confidence trick was for the education and illumination of Ferrando and Guglielmo who will no longer expect women to be less human and fallible than men. He makes the four join hands and embrace, and asks them to laugh it off as he did all the time.

The sisters beseech their lovers to forgive them in imploring thirds. The soldiers gladly do so. Despina admits that she too was tricked (but to what extent? Perhaps only the identity of Tizio and Sempronio).

They have returned to the verge of the opera's homekey, C major. The reconciliation has been effected. A full wind section, *allegro molto* without strings, introduces the final ensemble, *Fortunato l'uom che prende* which extols reason and the calming influence of being able to laugh when unreasoning folk would cry. All six characters join in preaching this moral. Eight bars of orchestral music bring down the curtain.

10

Whenever a performance of *Così fan tutte* comes to an end I begin to wonder, if not before, whether Ferrando will really live happily ever after with Dorabella, and Fiordiligi with Guglielmo. Will not Ferrando find Dorabella too unchallenging to his own temperament, and similarly Fiordiligi, now that her individuality has so greatly developed, begin to henpeck Guglielmo who is no match for her strength of character? Can they all revert to the *status ante quem* without hankering for the excitement of those temporary, delusive but much more ardent affairs wished on them, in the name of self-knowledge, by Alfonso–da Ponte? The libretto pushes them back, governess-fashion, into their original pairs. If this were a play we could laugh, as instructed by Alfonso, and applaud. But Mozart with his music has deepened the unwilling involvement of Fiordiligi and Ferrando, and heightened the resentment of Guglielmo. Of the four, Dorabella has been least changed: one hopes that, after this traumatic experience she will never again be tempted to put on such an unconvincing act as *Smanie implacabili*, beautifully as Mozart wrote it.

Is it strange to ask such questions and wonder about the subsequent fate of these lovers? Only if you insist on categorizing and pigeon-holing, and refuse to regard these six characters on the level generally accorded to those of *Figaro* and *Don Giovanni*, and beyond *Die Zauberflöte* to our own time. Such of our ancestors as unfashionably revolted against textual re-hashes of *Così* were still unwilling to regard it as a truthful document about sexual relations out of bed; they loved its irony or its charming puppetry. Irony is a dangerous but, in the right hands, powerful weapon; puppetry is a valid symbol of the influences which mould most people's behaviour and thought. *Così* could work at this level above the non-realism of the Punch and Judy show. But it was not Mozart's level: he wrote too much serious music. And I doubt if da Ponte thought of marionettes: he was writing about women and men whom he had met by the dozen during his adult life. His libretto mocks stupidity and conventionality now and then; and it is a lovely libretto, beautifully constructed and phrased, in Despina's arias, as in the extravagant Act I arias for Dorabella and Fiordiligi and, only just less extravagant, Ferrando's *Un aura amorosa*. The biggest send-up of all is Guglielmo's *Rivolgete a lui*, and I would not be surprised if da Ponte asked for it to be withdrawn and published separately. As a librettist he excelled in dramatic understanding and tact.

For a classicist, which da Ponte was, this is a greatly satisfying libretto to have written. It is fairly novel, observes all the unities, restricts itself to six characters. The scene is contemporary (very rare in eighteenth-century opera), the content purely enlightenment, concerned with true human emotions, equating female with male. The disguises are old hat, but for humanly revealing purposes and not just spectatorial amusement. All his three libretti for Mozart work towards the persuasiveness of human realism rather than the hallowed suspension of disbelief. *Così* is, I unfashionably believe, the least theatrical, most human and frank of them all, as is Mozart's completely non-artificial music, (e.g. in the *Sento, o dio* quintet and the two subsequent numbers). Mozart set it to music, as da Ponte wrote it: a comedy about thoughtless idealism conquered by commonsense. Men are expected to philander before they settle down: why not women too? In monogamous societies all lovers and spouses protest fidelity: do they really have no struggle to uphold it, no record of failure? Are women more constant than men? *Così fan tutte* applies literally to the ladies, but not to the credit of men who are expected to be naturally attracted to new conquest.

Così fan tutte has another subject. Boys and girls form partnerships instinctively. Sometimes these are transformed into ideal lifetime unions. More often the couples are too hastily married, then grow apart. Don Alfonso foresaw this disaster in the betrothal of the sisters with his two soldier-friends. Hence the wager. An infatuation is delightful: but it must be fed and nurtured before it ripens into abiding love. Da Ponte and Mozart demonstrated something of the kind in Ferrando's pursuit of Fiordiligi. It developed both characters, and this makes me wonder realistically how easily they will return to their original partners. Shakespeare's *A Midsummer Night's Dream* made the same point and resolved it effortlessly. Mozart's music has rendered the return more problematic.

The libretto is a masterpiece of exposition, development, resolution, and of lovely detail throughout. Above all it is active, dynamic; cuts always remove something of ultimate significance. Beside it, the texts of *Figaro* and *Giovanni* are untidy. Mozart responded with music which is not grand at all, but intimate, seldom exhibitionist or vainglorious, full of chamber textures, always concerned with character. The score is less venturesome than that of *Don Giovanni* but often bold within a context of perfectionism.

It is the summit of Mozart's quest for the all-embracing whole of communicative musical style which we call classicism. Mozart's handling of keys and scoring and construction here far surpasses any music he composed at other times in his short life. This does not mean that *Die Zauberflöte*, or *Don Giovanni* or *Idomeneo*, or indeed *Die Schuldigkeit des ersten Gebotes* are not to be enjoyed. From these, and everything Mozart ever composed, comes an understanding and appreciation of his quest. He most nearly approached the discovery of music's Grail in the un-sacred but totally human and all-perceiving *Così fan tutte*, in which he penetrates human nature while mocking it. *Così* is gloriously comic yet unfathomably profound, the whole story of the attraction between women and men, a subject which deserved and was granted the most captivating music ever composed.

21   LA CLEMENZA DI TITO

LA CLEMENZA DI TITO

dramma serio per musica

Libretto by PIETRO METASTASIO revised by CATERINO MAZZOLÀ

K. 621

VITELLIA, daughter of the Emperor Vitellius	SOPRANO
SEXTUS (Sesto), in love with her, Titus's friend	SOPRANO
ANNIUS Amnio), his friend, in love with Servilia	SOPRANO
PUBLIUS (Publio), prefect of the Pretorian Guard	BASS
TITUS VESPASIANUS (Tito), emperor of Rome	TENOR
SERVILIA, Sextus's sister, in love with Annius	SOPRANO

Chorus of senators, foreign ambassadors, guards, lictors
and populace

The scene is Rome

Once more the citizens of Prague, who had commissioned *Don Giovanni* and made a success of *Le nozze di Figaro*, called on Mozart for an opera. Bondini had left the Italian opera in 1788 and was succeeded as impresario by Domenico Guardasoni, an ex-singer who had been this company's stage director since 1785. In April 1789 after he became impresario Guardasoni discussed with Mozart, who was passing through Prague, plans for the next Prague opera by Mozart. It was due for performance that autumn. But by then Guardasoni and his opera company had left Prague for Warsaw. They returned to Prague on 10 June 1791. Almost at once they brought *Così fan tutte* into their repertory and took the production to Leipzig during their regular summer season there. It is not known whether Guardasoni had meanwhile negotiated further with Mozart for the new opera but it may be significant that hardly had his company returned to Prague before Mozart received a commission from the Bohemian Estates to compose an opera for that company to give during the festivities in September of the same year when Leopold II was to be crowned King of Bohemia. A castrato and a female soprano from Italy would be expressly engaged for the roles of hero and heroine.

Leopold had ascended the throne on 13 March 1790 and had pointedly ignored Mozart on musically important occasions, preferring Joseph Weigl when a new *Kapellmeister* was chosen, presenting Haydn, Salieri and Weigl to King Ferdinand of Naples who visited Vienna in September—but not Mozart. Nor was Mozart among the musicians invited to contribute to the coronation festivities at Frankfurt in October 1790, though he travelled there at his own expense and gave concerts with almost no material profit though much success. Mozart had no reason at all to honour the new King of Bohemia, and in any case the summer of 1791 found him busy completing *Die Zauberflöte* and embarking on the *Requiem* which had just been commissioned anonymously. But Prague held happy memories for him and he was greatly in need of money: Constanze was pregnant again and her ill-health necessitated treatment in Baden where she spent part of the summer—the baby, Franz Xaver Wolfgang, was born on 26 July and survived to become a pianist, composer and music-teacher.

The libretto chosen for the occasion, at Guardasoni's suggestion (surely because he had already agreed upon it with Mozart?), was Metastasio's *La Clemenza di Tito* originally written in 1734 for Antonio Caldara to set in honour of Karl VI's nameday, and subsequently put to music by, among others, Leonardo Leo, Hasse, Gluck and Wagenseil; at a time when monarchy was insecure, and now especially after the French Revolution, Metastasio's libretto which stresses the benevolence of royalty was obviously a favoured choice for opera companies owned by or giving command performances for royalty. It has always been assumed, for want of contradictory evidence, that the Metastasio text was wished upon Mozart in June or July of 1791 simply because it was appropriate to the occasion; assumed too that Mozart could not conceivably have wanted by this time to write an *opera seria* because he had, since *Idomeneo*, discovered how to create music drama of a much more realistically human order, part-comic and part-serious in a judicious balance. Assumptions were hard-hit by the discovery that on 26 April 1791 in Prague Josepha Dušek sang a Mozart rondo with basset-horn obbligato played by Anton Stadler: this sounds like *Non più di fiori* from *Tito*; and the text of *Non più di fiori* is not by Metastasio (with whose libretti Mozart had been familiar since his boyhood) but by Caterino Mazzolà who adapted the opera for Mozart's requirements and the changed taste of 1791. Tomislav Volek (in *Mozart Jahrbuch*, 1959) believes that the Mazzolà adaptation of *Tito* was made earlier, following Mozart's conferences with Guardasoni. Could Mozart have voluntarily agreed to write an *opera seria* for Prague? Metastasian subject-matter was no longer in vogue; but it is just credible that Mozart, remembering the power of *Idomeneo*, might have expressed a wish to return to *opera seria* so long as the libretto gave him opportunities for ensembles, choruses, and accompanied recitatives, and that *Tito* was chosen as an appeal to Joseph II. The possibility cannot be ignored that Stadler and Dušek performed a now lost concert aria expressly written for the occasion—but Mozart's catalogue makes no mention of such an aria and the autograph of *Non più di fiori* looks more worn than the rest.

Stadler, for whom the clarinet trio and quintet had been designed, was, to be sure, much involved in the première of *Tito*. On about 25 August Mozart left by coach for Prague: with him were his wife (their new baby was left behind), his pupil Süssmayr, and Stadler—who was given an obbligato part in two of the longest arias in the finished score, played in a performance of *Don Giovanni* during his visit, and for whom in September Mozart wrote his last major composition, the clarinet concerto. Long-standing rumour, nowadays masquerading as history, has it that during the journey Süssmayr was busy composing the recitatives. He was talented, they are not inspired, and the supposition accordingly may be believed. Mozart could not compose the arias until he had met their singers, but there was much concerted music for him to write on the way. We can believe that, in the month since he received the commission, he had little time to devote to it, with *Zauberflöte* and the *Requiem* to think about.

The journey to Prague took three days. The opera was completed by 5 September: quick work, but most of the musical numbers are short, especially by the accepted standards of *opera seria*. It earned Mozart 200 ducats, a fee agreed in April 1789.

Caterino Mazzolà, resident theatrical poet at the Dresden Opera, a long-standing and valued friend of da Ponte, may have been chosen to adapt Metastasio's libretto for *La Clemenza di Tito* because Dresden was Mozart's next stop on his journey from Prague in April 1789, though by July 1791 Mazzolà was in Prague. He had reduced Metastasio's three acts to two, removing only one scene, and he had turned some solos into ensembles which would please audiences as well as the composer. Mozart noted that Mazzolà had 'edited it into a true opera' ('ridotta a vera opera')—the nature of this operatic veracity may be the addition of ensembles or, bearing the word 'ridotta' in mind, the division into two acts rather than three. Mozart was presumably content with Mazzolà's work. He required but four alterations to the libretto as he received it, and at no time expressed disparagement of *La Clemenza di Tito*, Why should he? Its weakness is the Metastasian plot, by our standards undramatic. Mozart accepted it and supplied Mazzolà's revision with music as inventive and imaginative as any he had written. Perhaps he did not find it so undramatic; nor did audiences, to judge by the number of performances and published editions produced in the opera's first twenty years.

2

The Mozarts reached Prague on 28 August and divided their time between the town and the Dušeks' villa on the outskirts. Leopold II arrived in Prague next day, his empress Maria Louisa on 30 August. On 2 September they attended a performance of *Don Giovanni* with all but two of the original cast. If, as supposed, it was conducted by Mozart he was taking time he could ill spare from the feverish process of completing *Tito*. By then he had met the Italian guest-singers who were to perform his new opera. In the name part was Antonio Baglioni from Venice who had taken Don Ottavio in the première of *Don Giovanni*. It was later declared by Ignaz von Seyfried, reputedly one of Mozart's pupils, that Baglioni was offended because Mozart, and not an Italian, had been chosen to compose the opera, and Mozart repaid Baglioni with a dull part. But Seyfried was fifteen at the time and referred to Baglioni as a castrato; his story does not ring true. The *prima donna* was Maria Marchetti-Fantozzi, aged twenty-four, already esteemed in Milan and Naples for her good looks, pleasing voice, musicality and dramatic talent; she went on to make careers in Venice and Berlin. Mozart's music for Vitellia indicates that he was impressed by her ability, interpretative as well as technical— though Erik Smith suggests that Mozart was writing it for Josepha Dušek before the commission arrived. Fantozzi seems, from report, to have done justice to the role. Mozart had planned the part of Sextus for a tenor (and sketched the Duet No. 1, with a different opening, as well as the Duet No. 3 and the Trio No. 14) certainly before July 1791, when the commission specified a *castrato*. Domenico Bedini, whose arias suggest a strong, flexible singer, was eventually engaged. None of these but Carolina or Anchulina (? Angelina) Perini, 'the famous Italian' soprano who took the travesty role of Annio,* was chosen to sing at the Coronation banquet earlier on the day of the première. The two other principals, Gaetano Campi (Publio) and Signora Antonini (Servilia) were given one aria apiece. That for Servilia is slightly more extended; both are melodious, apt for pleasing ornamentation, but quite unspectacular—the written-out flourish, *in tempo*, at the end of Publio's aria may only indicate that no cadenza is required.

Mozart noted in his thematic catalogue that he completed *La Clemenza di Tito* on 5 September. The first performance was given on the following day. This means that, during the nine days since his arrival in Prague, the opera must have been copied (for solo singers and chorus as well as orchestra) learned, and rehearsed, as well as the music completed by the composer. At a conservative reckoning Mozart had twelve arias to write. One of these may have been the rondo sung by Josepha Dušek on the earlier occasion mentioned above; an aria for Titus in Act II, scene vii does not survive and was doubtless left unset by Mozart for want of time. If all the accompanied recitatives, ensembles and choruses had been completed before Mozart met the cast, we may expect that he had to alter some of the

* The roles assigned to Perini and Bedini are confused in many books including the NMA.

individual vocal lines to suit his singers. He had also to compose the opera's overture—it was his practice to leave this till last. Add to all this his obligatory social engagements in Prague (e.g., a party given by Prince Rosenberg on 1 September when 'the music from Don Juan' was performed) and one questions when Mozart ever found time to sleep, unless much of the music had been composed earlier, when the opera was first mooted.

The first performance on Coronation Day was a gala with free entry on production of invitation card. The Empress won eternal scorn for judging the opera a 'porcheria tedesca' (German piggishness)—by which I take it she was displeased to find so many ensembles and so much orchestral detail in an *opera seria* where an Italian expected only solo arias lightly accompanied.* Count Zinzendorf described *Tito* as a 'most tedious spectacle' but noted the superiority of Mme Marchetti who roused the Emperor to 'raptures'. Others enjoyed the opera. The Prague Coronation Journal maintained that the music did Mozart 'much honour', noting also that he was suffering from an illness. Franz Alexander von Kleist, who attended the performance with his nephew Heinrich (the famous poet), wrote that Mozart's melodies were 'so beautiful as to entice the angels down to earth'.

Later performances in Prague were enthusiastically received but drew poor houses though they picked up towards the end. Guardasoni lost money over the enterprise. After Mozart's death his widow mounted a series of concert performances of *La Clemenza di Tito*. In the Kärntnertor Theatre, Vienna, on 29 December 1794 (repeated in the Burgtheater the following March) the part of Sextus was sung by a soprano, Constanze's sister Aloysia Lange. Publius in the March performance was sung by Johann Michael Vogl, later to win immortality as Schubert's favourite song interpreter. In the entr'acte of this performance Beethoven played a Mozart piano concerto. Further performances were put on by Constanze in Graz, Berlin (where Ludwig Fischer† sang Publio) and Linz. The staged première in Germany took place at Cassel in 1797; Vienna followed in 1894 using a German translation, orchestrally accompanied recitatives throughout and some musical interpolations devised by Ignaz von Seyfried. *La Clemenza di Tito* was the first Mozart opera to reach London when, on 27 March 1805, Mrs Elizabeth Billington chose it for her benefit performance at the King's Theatre in Haymarket; the principal male singer was John Braham. The text was revised, and the music probably altered too (a newspaper report refers to the 'duets' sung by these two singers—no two characters in Mozart's score sing more than one duet together). Billington will have sung Vitellia, Braham Sextus. The opera was revived in London six years later for Angelica Catalani. That by this time it had won wide popularity must be assumed from the existence of fifteen different editions published before 1810.

3

The **Overture** makes instantly clear that *La Clemenza di Tito* is to be a grand festive opera for a splendid occasion. The orchestra is large, with clarinets among

---

* She may however have found it uncivil that, while her husband could happily identify with the kindly Titus, she herself could only find an opposite number on stage in the villainess Vitellia (a name which, for an Italian, suggests veal—hence perhaps her reference to pork).

† See *Entführung*, p. 293. But his eponymous son was also a singer.

the woodwind, trumpets and drums among the brass. No slow introduction is needed: the overture begins *allegro* in C major with pompous fanfare figures in the Jupiter Symphony vein.

1

The figure marked A recurs a good deal, especially in the bass under scales in sixths or thirds. Figure B is motivic right through the opera, suggesting courtly pomp.

Symphonic development concerns the soft–loud phrases following this fanfare.

2

This occurs continually. The second subject, for wind in pairs, with dry string punctuation, is still courtly and regally gracious; the prominent duet for bassoons is a bold touch. The need for haste did not prevent Mozart from working out themes scrupulously though we shall see that it affected his scoring. As in some earlier overtures he creates a false reprise effect, here in G major, recapitulates the second subject in the tonic and then proceeds to the first subject's true recapitulation whereby the tension is maintained unbroken to the end, with quantities of Ex. 1.

Act I opens in Vitellia's living quarters. She, the daughter of the Roman Emperor Vitellius, is in love with Titus, now Emperor and son of Vespasian who seized the throne from Vitellius. And she is furious because Titus has chosen for his bride Berenice, daughter of Agrippa I of Judea. She is therefore trying to persuade her young, infatuated admirer Sextus to kill Titus and set the Roman Capitol ablaze. Sextus's loyalties are split between the lovely Vitellia and his great friend Titus: he has promised to execute this criminal plan for Vitellia, and persuaded one Lentulus to help him; but he cannot bear to harm Titus, kindly paternal protector of his people, example of goodness to all the world, a man who counts each day lost when he has not made somebody else happy. Vitellia who, it will already be seen, is the dramatic mainspring of the work, the Lady Macbeth of eighteenth-century opera,★ is only rendered angrier by Sextus's qualms. Titus robbed her father of his throne, deluded Vitellia into falling in love with him, then threw her over for a dusky foreigner, a refugee at that—not very clement where the Vespasian family, flower of the purest Roman race, is concerned. Sextus's protests are cut short with Vitellian venom. We expect a jealousy aria at any moment. What we get is something, for her part, much more decorous and dramatically less credible (though since this opening recitative is often cut in order to start the act with a musical number, the dramatic volte-face is avoided).

Sextus asks Vitellia to give him precise instructions (**No. 1, Duet,** F major,

★ D. F. Tovey called her 'the horridest female that ever disgraced a libretto': he probably did not know Abigaille in Verdi's *Nabucco*, though he must have discovered Ortrud in *Lohengrin*—both these are just as nasty as Vitellia.

andante – allegro, flute, oboes, bassoons, 2 horns, strings, *Come ti piace, imponi*). Kill the miscreant before sundown, is her answer. Sextus, in this duet where Mazzolà reworded Metastasio's lines, sounds virile and heroic, Vitellia more like Donna Elvira than Donna Anna, let alone Electra in *Idomeneo*—though a soprano blessed with interpretative fire could do something cogent with this typically Mozartian phrase:

sai ch'egli u—sur—pa un re—gno,   che in sor—te il ciel mi diè.

A lively *allegro* follows (*Fan mille affetti insieme*) and this injects drama into the situation. Mozart must have remembered the first Anna–Ottavio duet in *Don Giovanni*, so similar in context; but his music is even more stately, less impulsive, an impression enhanced by the dominance of strings until the short postlude. An inventive duet, all the same.

Annius enters calling Sextus to the Emperor's presence. A sneer from Vitellia about Berenice prompts Annius to tell them that Titus has called off his marriage with Berenice because she was unpopular with his subjects. She has already left Rome, heavy-hearted but dignified. Vitellia's hopes of regaining the throne are revived and she tells Sextus to postpone the execution of their plan. He speaks of the torment he is experiencing: he is being used as a tool either to kill his best friend Titus or to engineer a marriage between that friend and the object of his own love.

Vitellia consoles him in **No. 2, Aria**, *larghetto–allegro*, G major, flutes, bassoons, horns, strings, *Deh se piacer*: this is Metastasio unaltered. In the *larghetto* Vitellia drops her harpy image:

> If you want me to love you, forget your suspicions and do not worry me with your tiresome doubts.

The flutes in thirds at the beginning give the music a pale, gentle quality, and Vitellia's vocal line, otherwise almost entirely supported by strings, is calm and dignified, as apt for Don Ottavio as Donna Anna. One of her vocal divisions is contextually interesting:

la———————————————scia i sospet—ti   tuo-i:

The pattern in bar 2 of this example bears a distinct resemblance to one in the slow movement of the D major piano concerto, K. 537.

This, it may be recalled, was the concerto Mozart took to the Coronation festivities of Leopold II in Frankfurt in 1790, now known as his Coronation Concerto. Mozart had composed it in 1788 and performed it before the coronation. But he may unconsciously have recalled that coronation while writing an opera for another coronation of the same monarch.

With the *allegro* Vitellia and her orchestra acquire fresh energy, not unlike that of Fiordiligi in *Come scoglio*, though the violin melody quoted below recalls Despina more than either of her mistresses.

6

The vocal continuation of this melody is one of the most memorable and characteristic ideas in the opera.

7

Trust breeds trust: whoever fears deceit is an easy prey to it.

Vitellia makes her routine exit after this aria. You might expect Sextus also to hurry to the Emperor, but he stays behind with Annius who asks him to get Titus's official permission for the wedding of Sextus's sister Servilia with Annius, a bond which Sextus has already approved and now re-confirms. Sextus and Annius join in a brief **Duettino, No. 3**, C major, *andante*, with clarinets, bassoons, horns and strings (divided violas) *Deh prendi un dolce amplesso*. The conjunct movement of the voices and gentle 6/8 lilt, the warmth of clarinets and bassoons and violas in thirds and sixths, all set this duet in contrast with the formal world of *opera seria*. The firm yet rounded cadences suggest German folksong, but in performance the music sounds perfectly Italian (I have already indicated that Mozart, an able linguist, preserved different styles for music in Italian or German; here we are near to *Così fan tutte*, not *Die Zauberflöte*).

It will be remarked that so far we have heard no unbroken voice: two of the characters have worn male clothes, but all three are sopranos.

The scene now changes to the Forum in Rome. Triumphal arches, obelisks and trophies are in evidence, in the background the Capitol from which we see Titus descending the steps, with senators, ambassadors, the Pretorian Guard under their prefect Publius, and a throng of the Roman populace. All this takes place during **No. 4, Marcia**, *maestoso*, E flat major, for full orchestra beginning with trumpet and timpani fanfares. The predominance of dotted rhythms as in Ex. 1 B and repeated chords gives the march a character of pomp and dignity appropriate to the scene (and, of course, to the occasion of the opera's performance). Mozart seems to have written it at a late stage, perhaps to accommodate the scene-shifters.

The same key is retained for **No. 5**, the *allegro* **Chorus** which immediately ensues, *Serbate o dei custodi* (using flutes, clarinets, bassoons, horns and strings), and the musical imagery is similar as well. The text is Metastasio's.

> Guardian gods, watch over Rome's destiny, and over Titus the just, the strong, the glory of our age.

The choral writing is solid and functional, but the orchestral part bristles with splendour and virtuosity, especially in the dashing runs for violins.

They prepare the way for Roman compliments to the Emperor. Publius tells Titus no populace has been so glad of its ruler, Annius wishes Titus to be worshipped in a temple as a tutelary god, and Publius draws his attention to the rich tributes sent in gratitude by the outposts of his empire. Titus expresses thanks but wishes the tribute to be handed over for the relief of suffering in Naples after a ruinous eruption of Vesuvius—the restoration of his people will be his temple. The crowd acclaims his selflessness with a repeat of No. 5. Titus then tells Sextus and Annius to remain while everyone else departs, to a repeat of No. 4.

In the recitative for Titus, Annius, and Sextus which follows, the Emperor declares his intention of marrying a wife who will (unlike Berenice) meet Rome's approval. Since he is not in love with anybody else he must marry out of friendship. He has therefore decided to choose Sextus's sister Servilia. Throughout the scene Annius and Sextus exchange *sotto voce* confidences or asides (rather comic to modern ears) especially since they had intended at this moment to seek Titus's approval for the wedding of Annius and Servilia. Sextus is nonplussed by Titus's decision but Annius, with true aristocratic altruism (for the benefit of this noble audience) declares that Titus could not have chosen more ideally; Annius is therefore told to inform Servilia of her good fortune, while Titus will further disclose his plans for Sextus's future. The only pleasure a monarch can know is the rewarding of fidelity, the conferring of favours on those who deserve them.

He expounds this philosophy in his first **Aria, No. 6**, *Del più sublime soglio* (words by Metastasio), in G major, *andante*, with flutes, bassoons, horns and strings.

> This is the only fruitful achievement for the loftiest monarch. All the rest is torture and slavery. What would remain if I were to lose these, my only hours of happiness, helping the oppressed, encouraging my friends, giving presents to deserving cases and virtuous people?

This is a simple, mellifluous *a–b–a* number, emphasizing Titus's mildness, connecting him in our minds with lovesick Ferrando or Ottavio, idealistic but not yet active Tamino, rather than with the authoritative Idomeneo. The smooth vocal writing makes no heavy demands on his technique, even his breath control, though the suave phrases, most eloquent when descending, invite musicianly moulding and shading. The accompaniment, mostly for strings, includes (twice) a more vigorous passage of rising scales in imitation between first violins and basses, and the two bars that conclude the first and last parts of the aria do suggest a determination elsewhere absent. The aria as a whole is not that of a *primo uomo* nor of a dramatic hero.

Titus and Sextus leave together. Annius has not yet departed. In recitative he wonders how to break to Servilia this, for him, dreadful news. She enters and, with many a sorrowful aside, he tells her that she is now his Princess, no longer his beloved. She tries to discover what has brought this sudden change; he finds it hard to explain, can only beg forgiveness for having loved her.

He does this in the first strain of **No. 7, Duet**, *andante*, A major, with flute, oboe, bassoons and strings, *Ah perdona il primo affetto*, the most beautiful melody in the opera.* It evokes the bare-nerved sensibility of innocent young love. His attempt at a farewell only fans the flames of the love they share for one another. And Mozart, a married man and father of a family at thirty-five, had not forgotten the shy stirring of young love: he blessed his memories (still fresh, who knows?) with a generously outgiving tune in his love-key of A major, and with tender, hesitantly short-breathed amorous phrases. Significantly the woodwind parts are prominent here, bassoon with Annius, flute with Servilia, and violas are divided when they sing together. This was doubtless one of the duets that Billington and Braham filched for their own glory at the opera's British première: if so, one can hardly blame them. The touches of subdominant harmony in the orchestral epilogue only enhance the twilit glow of this marvellous piece.

The scene changes to the imperial garden on the Palatine hill. Publius is about to show Titus an anonymous letter which reveals the names of those who are plotting against the throne. Titus does not wish to see the document: he either despises or feels sorry for the conspirators, but in any case forgives them.

Publius is about to mention . . . (surely the name of Vitellia, perhaps of Sextus). But Servilia runs to kneel at Titus's feet, confessing that she cannot, grateful as she is for the honour, be his consort, since her heart is given to Annius. Titus applauds her frankness, equally with Annius's self-sacrifice. Of course the lovers' bond will be blessed by him. He much prefers hurtful truth to pleasing falsehood. In this scene Metastasio allows us to recognize Titus as a genuinely good and heroic character, worthy of admiration, not a flabby goody-goody. We can only appreciate his positive goodness if we understand the Italian text properly, or hear a translation which faithfully renders that Italian. Jibes at Titus's role have been due to ignorance or mistranslation. If Mozart had composed the music for this recitative he would surely have made it stronger: this is a vital dramatic moment.

He did, however, content himself (at a late stage, perhaps to placate Baglioni) with writing the compact **Aria** that follows, to Metastasio's words, **No. 8**, *allegro*, D major, *Ah se fosse* (oboes, bassoons, horns, strings—separate cello and bass parts at the beginning).

> If only everyone at court were so frank-hearted, my vast empire would give me happiness instead of torment. Monarchs ought not to put up with such trouble to distinguish truth from polite deception.

This is a more heroic vehicle for Titus, even if the explosive dummy bass at the start sounds apoplectic rather than convinced. Again the florid music for the singer

* It was as a lyric to this melody that Shelley wrote his poem 'I arise from dreams of thee'.

is much restrained. An interesting feature is the martial theme introduced after the second half has begun as a reprise.

Titus having left the stage Servilia, in her delight, is joined by Vitellia whose mocking compliments are quickly parried by Servilia's hints that Vitellia is likely to take the throne at any moment. Servilia flounces confidently out. Vitellia assumes she is being done by as she did. When Sextus appears she rounds on him for laggardliness in executing her orders. Let him kill Titus: the throne will be hers and Sextus her consort. He meekly offers to obey at once, rather than be branded coward, feeble in love, passive in rivalry. In the text of this recitative, too, we see Vitellia in her true colours: shame, again, that Mozart did not write the vivid music for such a moment.

Sextus accepts her challenge and takes his leave in **No. 9**, (more Metastasio) **Aria**, *adagio – allegro – allegro assai* in B flat major, *Parto, parto,* scored for solo (basset) clarinet, oboes, bassoons, horns (in B flat alto) and strings.

> (*Adagio*) I am going, so be at peace with me; I will do what you desire. (*Allegro*) Look at me and, forgetful of all else, I will revenge you. (*Allegro assai*) O gods, what power you have bestowed on beauty.

In the opening section we note the stiff formal octaves for orchestra; the descending arpeggio which they trace is concluded by Sextus's first word, 'Parto'. His plea to Vitellia is urged in wheedling thirds, and through the instrument often used by Mozart as a symbol of human love, the clarinet which enters gently and sensuously, wriggling voluptuously to its first cadence. Determination in the strings ('quel che vorrai farò') is similarly followed by the clarinet's first major idea which could easily have found its way into the clarinet concerto a month later.

8

This section features the clarinet in bold downward and upward rushes, a standard resource of the instrument as all composers for it have realized; but here they descend to (written) low C below the standard bottom E, because Stadler was using his own extended instrument nowadays called the basset- or Stadler-clarinet. At the time of writing (1976) the obbligato was usually played on a conventional clarinet, and the lowest tones transposed up an octave; but the Stadler clarinet has been reconstructed, has displayed its advantages of tone-colour as well as compass in recordings and public performances by such champions as Alan Hacker, and will, perhaps during the lifetime of this book, come into general use for Mozart's late clarinet works.

Sextus's determination to do Vitellia's bidding gears the music up to an *allegro* in which the clarinet writing becomes more energetic and even cheerful. Perhaps even too cheerful: is not this tune too bland and debonair for a hero preparing to slaughter his friend and benefactor and set fire to his own city? Or does it represent hysterical zeal?

9

[Allegro]

dolce

Just before the return of the above theme Sextus has two dramatically gripping cries of 'Guardami!' (look at me!'), one loud, the other soft: with the imaginably strong yet flexible sound of a male soprano, and the added expressive ornamentation implied by the written *fermate* they must make a compelling moment.

A frenzied uprushing sequence introduces the *allegro assai* last section in which the clarinet plays suspenseful broken arpeggios against Sextus's vocal melody, then duets with him in writhing triplets, ending with transports of ecstasy.

The length of the aria, in three sections, and the superb quality of its invention incline some to believe that *Parto, parto* must have been written by Mozart some time earlier, like *Non più di fiori*, though conceivably he may have composed it during a stop on the coach ride to Prague with Stadler (but he had not met Bedini). He seems, in any case, to have found a special stimulus in the aria with solo instrumental obbligato: think of *Ch'io mi scordi di te* (soprano and piano), *Vorrei spiegarvi* (soprano and oboe), *Per pietà* (Fiordiligi and horn), *Per questa bella mano* (basso and double bass), *L'amerò, sarò costante* (soprano and violin), *Tuba mirum* in the *Requiem* (basso and trombone). Operatic arias with clarinet obbligato were a particular favourite of the Neapolitans. Mozart, knowing this, may have hoped to please the Naples-born Empress—little did he know her musical taste.

Sextus has gone to set fire to the city of Rome. Vitellia is rubbing her hands with glee at the estrangement of Titus's friends, if not his downfall, when Publius and Annius enter, surprised to find her away from her home to which Titus is proceeding. He has decided to ask her hand in marriage; she must be there to receive her Emperor and future husband.

Here is a promising dramatic moment. Mozart and Mazzolà made it an *allegro* vocal **Trio, No. 10** in G major, *Vengo! aspettate!* Flutes, oboes, bassoons, horns and strings accompany the voices. Vitellia as *prima donna* is kept in the foreground torn between triumph and guilt and longing that Sextus shall not execute their plan. Her wild outbursts are mistaken by the two men for delirious joy and, in sedate block harmony, they remark on this.

Vitellia's cries are fundamentally declamatory; the principal musical interest is in the first violin part which obsessively digs away at this dynamic yet oxymoronic idea:

10

Allegro

One might expect that Mozart, his mind still full of *Die Zauberflöte* (a really original project, his latest, still unproduced and not quite finished) would have automatically have turned to Queen of Night idioms. He does take Vitellia up to top D at the end, and above the stave increasingly, with one superb jump from middle F sharp to top B flat (her music elsewhere in the work lies lower). But as usual his Italian operatic music is couched in a different language of tones and phrases from his German, and so Vitellia recalls, if anybody else, Fiordiligi and Donna Anna, not the Queen of Night. The orchestra, especially when flutes contribute, is nearer to the music of *Don Giovanni*.

Without any intervening recitative the scene changes to a square in front of the Capitol, and the orchestra (oboes, bassoons, horns and strings) plunges into a C minor *allegro assai*, **No. 11**, which is like a hectic nightmare version of the march in the first movement of the C major piano concerto K. 503, crossed with the beginning of K. 415 in the same key.

High drama is being heralded. Mozart makes it felt but, exercising an architect's restraint, withholds the concerted finale and makes this a preliminary accompanied **Recitative** (words by Metastasio) for Sextus, who has just committed arson and is about to murder, his heart full of guilt and doubt (*Oh dei, che smania è questa*). The bracketed figure in Ex. 11c is developed obsessively through this exceptionally tense recitative as symbol of Sextus's plot and his anxiety in undertaking it—even, against off-beat violins, when he determines to get the deed done ('Ma compirla convien'). Towards the end of the recitative, during a further outburst of Ex. 11c, flames become visible in the background, and he realizes there is no turning back. The recitative ends in B flat.

Now the **Finale, No. 12**, can begin, *allegro* in E flat major, and with it the climax towards which the act has been moving musically since *Parto, parto*, No. 9. The full orchestra is scored for, though not immediately. A full chord launches Sextus on his prayer that Titus may be saved, or he perish with the Emperor; Sextus's initial phrase is a soaring musical rocket:

Annius enters, but Sextus can only talk brokenly of his shame, and hurry to the Capitol (brisk key-change to G flat major) much to Annius's bewilderment. Servilia joins him distraught, and a distant chorus is heard uttering cries. String-scrubbing (usually miscalled *tremolando*) and a purposeful bass typify this section, as well as the discordant choral harmonies. Publius strides forward determinedly—so the string basses suggest—fearing sabotage; and the choral cries off stage are echoed by more harmonious laments on stage. Vitellia enters too, looking for Sextus, and a big ensemble texture of horror and fear (much alternation of *forte* and *piano*) gathers force until the return of an appalled Sextus (first entry of drums with a bloodcurdling roll, as the rest of the orchestra suddenly turns soft) calling on the earth to open and hide him—a striking vocal line descending over an octave and a half at the words 'nel tuo sen profondo':

13

e nel tuo sen pro—fon———do   rin—ser—ra un tra–di——tor,

Sextus's wish to be enclosed in earth is vividly portrayed in the alternating wind and string chords of the phrase which follows Ex. 13.

He tells the company that Titus is dead—they react in a poignant *andante* burst of G minor harmony—and is about to admit his guilt when Vitellia orders him to hold his tongue. At once the pace drops again to *andante* and that earlier hint of harmony is confirmed in 'l'astro è spento', heavy with woe, and further weighed down with the distant cries of the off-stage populace ('O nero tradimento!'). At first the harmony moves glacially forward, numb with grief. The choral entry brings forward a strongly characterized instrumental bass with solemn funeral dotted figures for woodwind (masonic in suggestion). The soloists on stage, and the orchestra supporting them, tighten the screw of chromatic harmony while the distant chorus repeats 'tradimento' in octaves to a cogent rhythm. The perspective is switched as the crowd far away sings melancholy phrases in block harmony (again in Mozart's masonic mood—how much Victorian hymnologists owe to such passages!) which the on-stage singers punctuate with cries of 'Oh!'. The loud antiphonal cries of 'tradimento' give way to awesome murmurs that sink gently to rest in E flat major. Here we may, perhaps, recall the musical language of *Die Zauberflöte* (e.g., In *diesen heil'gen Hallen*), though it is being used in quite foreign territory.

14

di— do———lor,   di— do———lor!

It was unusual to end an act of *opera seria* quietly, and highly unconventional to do so with soloists and chorus in antiphonal, on- and off-stage, block harmony without a trace of prominence for the leading singers (Vitellia and Servilia are even singing the same vocal line). Mozart hoped to move his audience profoundly with pity and terror; if his conventional-minded noble listeners at the première failed to respond we need not be surprised, but can be sure that at later performances the music-lovers of Prague received the message in full. This is very dramatic music.

4

Act II opens in the Imperial garden where Annius and Sextus are discovered. Sextus is hardly able to believe that Titus, whom he had seen pierced by hostile weapons, escaped death and that Annius has just left the Emperor alive and well. Sextus confesses that he was the instigator of the fire and attempted murder: as a traitor he must flee the country, leaving Annius to defend Titus from his desperate foes. Annius assures him that the fire must have been an accident, no plot having been discovered. He begs Sextus to remain in Rome.

His **Aria, No. 13**, *allegretto* in G major, *Torna di Tito a lato*, is accompanied by strings only.

> Return to Titus's side, and make practical amends for your misdeed.

The raised-eyebrows string introduction suggests gentleness and hesitancy; once Annius has warmed to his sermon the idea does not need to return. Annius's opening phrases are worth quoting.

15

The initial wriggle is exquisite, a vivid musical image for a *volte-face*. The repeats of 'torna' in bars 3 and 4 recur later in the aria, imploringly and as a characteristic, touching refrain. The mood of the aria is suave and fluent, thoroughly boyish-enthusiastic—even though sung by a female soprano—and surely a true memory of Mozart's character as a boy, with a richer intensity at 'che di virtù'. The return to the beginning is especially felicitous. So is the high violin decorated version of bars 3 and 4 above in the orchestral postlude. I do not understand why Hermann Abert thought poorly of this delectable number.

Annius makes his official exit. Sextus is debating whether to run away or boldly remain in Rome. Vitellia now appears, urging him to fly so as to save his life and her honour. He insists that her secret is safe with him, but Vitellia knows Sextus's reverence for Titus and fears the omnipotence of the Emperor's famous clemency. If Titus behaves amiably, she fears that Sextus will tell all.

At this moment Publius appears with guards and arrests Sextus. The man whom Sextus stabbed was his fellow conspirator Lentulus; he did not die but named his assailant. The senate even now is assembled to try Sextus's case. Publius orders Sextus to follow him. Vitellia still fears that her complicity may be revealed in the course of the trial, and with it her chance lost of dominating Rome. Her reactions are entirely self-centred; even Sextus calls her 'ingrata' as he says farewell.

In the **Terzetto, No. 14**, (*Se a volto mai ti senti*) which follows (oboes, bassoons, horns and strings) in B flat major, there are two but not three contrasted emotions since Publius's contributions ('Follow me' and 'The lady's sorrow moves me, but pity is valueless') add nothing to the situation, though his music is quite inventive. Vitellia is all remorse, for herself, not for what she has done to Sextus; he bids her goodbye, sadly yet bravely, and asks her to remember him.

The trio begins *andantino* with serenading woodwind, and Sextus's first phrases do recall the scansion of Don Giovanni's *Deh vieni alla finestra* serenade—perhaps it sounds nowadays as if Giovanni's place has been taken by Zerlina, but we must blame the decline of the male soprano voice, not Mozart. For Vitellia's first entry ('He is going to his death for my sake; where shall I hide?'—perfectly in character) the music moves into B minor with faster note-values for the singer; woodwind are still commenting relevantly—this is worth mentioning in an opera where, for speed of composition, Mozart relied largely on strings for his orchestra. At Publius's first entry the strings introduce a new, more urgent, rather airy texture of choppy semiquavers. This bridges the way to the *allegretto* half of the trio, *Rammenta chi t'adora*, which begins almost bucolically (woodwind again have the tune repeated by Sextus). We are quite close to the quick half of Fiordiligi's and Dorabella's first duet (see p. 530).

16

Rammen—ta- chi— t'a —do—ra   in ques–to sta–to an–co—ra,

Here Vitellia's dotted rhythms are helpfully contrasted with the smoother phrases for Sextus and Publius—the latter's music is unusually positive in tone, and we may think of him as Almaviva to the two sopranos Countess and Susanna, as in *Susanna or via sortite* in *Figaro* (see p. 396). This part of the trio is very rich in musical invention, not harmonic (it does not range beyond near neighbours of B flat major) but linear and textural and dynamic (e.g. the unusual *mfp* just after Vitellia's reiteration of 'Che crudeltà' which, leading back to a reprise, ought to involve a cadenza though none is suggested). Strings and wind have thoroughly eventful parts, and Vitellia's dotted rhythms parade the orchestra more and more. A superb number.*

Publius and Sextus exeunt to one side, Vitellia to the other. The scene changes to a large room whose furniture includes a chair and writing table. During the **Chorus, No. 15**, *andante* in F major, *Ah grazia si rendono* (flutes, clarinets, bassoons, horns and strings—violas sometimes divided, especially effective at the very start), Titus and Publius enter with a chorus of patricians and pretorian guards.

The chorus gives thanks for the salvation of Titus's life. Their harmony is warm and loving—even the notes suggest character. The last phrase for flutes and violins has the ease and intensity of total understanding and total confidence. Titus regards himself as far from unfortunate (there must have been a textual cut here, since no one suggested that he was 'sventurato') as Rome favours him so much; the chorus repeats its thanksgiving.

This sort of number, a chorus with highly detailed orchestral invention framing a middle solo, is Gluckian by inspiration, most connectible in Mozartian terms with *Idomeneo* and chronologically to be contrasted with, if not likened to, the priestly scenes in *Die Zauberflöte*. Structurally it is simpler than the examples in *Idomeneo*, though atmospherically reminiscent. The detail ('porcheria tedesca'!) is unparalleled, especially the violin thirds and concerted wind in Titus's solo, the rising figures for flute and violins towards the end. Music of such sublime beauty needs no further pleading. Those who do not know it have only to listen to it.

---

* This trio is said to have replaced a solo aria for Titus, *Se mai senti spirati* (now lost, if ever composed). Obviously it belonged in the next scene, not this one in which Titus does not appear.

The chorus fades out of sight. Publius tells Titus to go and attend the festive games but the Emperor needs first to know that Sextus, all-faithful, has been acquitted by the senate. He cannot believe Sextus disloyal. Publius remarks that others are less good-hearted than Titus.

Now Publius has his solo **Aria, No. 16**, a C major *allegretto* with oboes, horns and strings, *Tardi s'avvede*. This is a short, lightish C major piece.

> The truly loyal person cannot err in his actions.

Publius gets no display passage until the scale at the end; Campi's speciality was evidently *legato* singing.

Annius calls for clemency, but Publius returns to say that Sextus has been adjudged the guilty party and been condemned with his accomplices to be thrown to wild beasts in the arena. The deed has only to be signed by the imperial hand. Titus wishes to meditate before signing and tells Publius and Annius to leave him. But Annius, as Sextus's promised brother in law, insists on a last plea.

This is Annius's solo moment, as No. 16 was Publius's—curiously both begin with the same vocal phrase (one would assume that the arias were mutually exclusive were it not that, for protocol, both had to be included). Annius's **Aria, No. 17**, *Tu fosti tradito* in F major, *andante* (oboes, bassoons, horns, strings) is an earnest, uplifted plea.

> You have been betrayed, and he deserves to die. But the heart of Titus gives me cause for hope. My lord, take your heart's advice; consider our grief.

Its music is for a female voice as much as Sextus's is for a male soprano. It is quite ornate and high-lying. The string writing is highly detailed. Mozart suggests, for example in the initial string figures and in the dynamic contrasts, a determined man; but the voluptuous harmonies and triplet cadences belong to a female singer, a voice with sensuous appeal. This is travesty, not castrato music.

Annius and Publius leave. Titus is alone, meditating in an *allegro* accompanied recitative (strings only: text by Metastasio) whether or not to sign the death sentence. High-pitched diminished seventh chords indicate the Emperor's rage and amazement at Sextus's perfidy. The punctuating string chords take the music ever flatter until, with a unison theme in D flat major (another heavily loaded flat key), Titus decides to sign. Pen in hand he reflects that it would be unjust to send Sextus to death without a chance to speak. He orders Sextus to be brought. Titus's thoughts stray (a wayward, melting five-note phrase for strings) to a consideration of the carefree happy existence of the rustic peasant, so much more desirable than a monarch's. The accompanied recitative is about to end in E flat, and we expect an aria for Titus at this point, presumably on some pastoral or imperial topic. However the cadence is interrupted and the recitative reverts to *secco*. Publius returns to reassure Titus that Sextus is on his way. The Emperor steels himself to adopt a demeanour suitable for the reception of an attempted regicide.

Sextus is led in by guards. He stops in the doorway, filled with dread at the stern aspect of Titus. The **Terzetto, No. 18** in E flat major is another two-speed number (*larghetto—allegro*) and involves flutes, clarinets, bassoons and strings.

Sextus's dread (*Quello di Tito è il volto*) is suggested by the shuddering figure in the introduction, repeated at his words 'or ei mi fà tremar' (the cool woodwind harmonies above this are superbly dramatic). In the introduction the shudders are followed by a soft dotted figure (Ex. 1B in fact), for horns then wind, expressive of Titus's solemn sternness; it returns *forte* when Titus orders Sextus, 'Avvicinati' ('Draw near').

Titus's first entry ('Eterni dei!') is an aside, like Sextus's, and he too comments on the change in his friend's face; Titus assumes that Sextus's amazement is the hardened criminal's look of hatred (wistful chromatic dialogue for strings). Tension increases, with rushing string scales, in Publius's entry ('Mille diversi affetti'), commenting on the passions at war in Titus's heart.

The splendid *allegro* section begins with an old friend:

The music matches the dramatic context in setting Sextus apart from society, represented by Titus and Publius who share the same words and musical material, often singing in imitative counterpoint. Sextus's vocal music is predominant and freely florid, much as was Vitellias's in the first terzetto, No. 10. Towards the end woodwind and strings exchange a more urgent pattern of chords.* The soft ending of the number, two flutes in chilly unison at the top of the last chord, is mightily effective, and characteristically Mozartian.

Titus dismisses Publius and the guards so as to question Sextus alone, to find an explanation for his crime so that he may be pardoned. Sextus, in a frenzy of remorse and grief, denies that his motive in attempting the Emperor's life was lust for the throne. Yet he cannot bring himself to incriminate Titus's chosen consort: he stops short of naming her, and begs only for a speedy death to end his misery. Titus, rendered increasingly impatient and offended by Sextus's secretiveness, now furiously dismisses him, refusing to let Sextus kiss his hand in parting.

In an A major tripartite **Aria, No. 19**, *Deh per questo istante*, sometimes described as rondo, (*adagio – allegro – più allegro*) Mozart gave Sextus yet another glorious solo.

> Remember, at this moment I beg, how I used to love you. It is your scorn and sternness that make me sorry to die. I do not deserve pity, truly, but only a terrible death. Yet you would be less stern if you could see my heart.
> (*Allegro*) I go despairing to my death. I do not fear to die, but the thought tortures me that I betrayed you. This is the madness of a heart that dies of grief.

The instrumentation features flute doubled two octaves below by bassoon, and oboes in harmony with horns. Only one flute is used but pairs of the others and strings. The aria is quite long by comparison with others in this opera (except the

* Compare it with *Ich folg dem inneren Triebe* in Fidelio's *Abscheulicher*. Beethoven presumably knew *La clemenza* (see p. 570 for a performance in which he took part).

two Stadler arias), does without brilliant written-out divisions but includes dramatic leaps and arpeggios, and considering its verbal content is curiously placed in Mozart's love-key of A major (but clarinets, the love-instruments *par excellence* for Mozart, are significantly absent). The initial descending scale in thirds for violins and violas augurs well, and the *adagio* section, with its tender, short phrases and melodic beauty—anguished harmony, too, just before the reprise of the first theme—confirms our expectations.

The *allegro* ('Disperato vado a morte') begins à la *Figaro* Overture, and is less remarkable, and the new melody for 'Tanto affanno' is surprisingly debonair:

18
[Allegro]

Tan—to af-fanno sof—fre un co-re, nè si mo—re di do——lor,

Just after this there is a dramatic turn into F major to heighten interest. The melody quoted above recurs in the *più allegro*—there is no indication that the tempo should revert for it.

Sextus is led away by the guards, and Titus again sits down to sign the death warrant. Much as he despises vindictiveness he forces himself to sign and thus taint himself with the blood of a citizen-subject and indeed friend. But when he ponders posterity's verdict he decides to abide by his policy of kindliness, and tears up the document: better be accused of compassion than of sternness.

However on Publius's return Titus (without telling an untruth) lets him think that Sextus is to die in the arena to which they will now go. In his **Aria, No. 20,** *Se all'impero* (by Metastasio), however, Titus is talking to himself and us, not to Publius.

> O gods who are my friends, if an emperor needs a stern heart, then take my empire from me or give me a different heart.
> (*Andantino*) If I cannot by love be sure of my subjects' loyalty, I care nothing for a loyalty born of fear.

This is another tripartite aria but a *da capo* one with a more florid repeat of the first section, like many in the early operas but more concise. For all the modesty of the sentiments the music is grand and brilliant in B flat major, with flutes, oboes, bassoons, horns (B flat alto) and strings. The energetic main *allegro* stands out for its bright instrumentation, fizzing start with offbeat second violin accompaniment, jaunty turns in the instrumental melody, and firework display for violins at the end of the ritornello and the start of the F major group. Titus himself has a little burst of fioritura before the fireworks conclude the *allegro*. The *andantino* middle section ('Se la fè de' regni miei') adopts 3/4 and F major with an uncomfortably abrupt switch towards C minor; the musical expression rather recalls Don Ottavio's 'Or che tutti' in the second finale of *Don Giovanni*. In the *da capo*, as well as extra florid runs, there is a reappearance of the stately dotted rhythm figuration for woodwind much in evidence throughout this opera.

Publius is following Titus to the arena when he is stopped by Vitellia who learns that Sextus has spoken long in private with Titus. She is convinced that Sextus has given her away. But Annius and Servilia now beg her to save Sextus, before he is the 'pasto infelice' of wild beasts, by pleading with Titus who will not refuse her since before sunset she is to become Empress. This news convinces her that Titus must therefore know nothing of her guilt. She promises to save Sextus but asks them to go on ahead. Servilia sees that Vitellia is weeping. In *S'altro che lagrime* (with eloquent text by Metastasio) **No. 21**, an **Aria** in *tempo di minuetto*, Servilia advises her.

If you have only tears with which to plead for him, all your weeping will be in vain. The pity you feel for him is as useless as cruelty.

This is a short, simple, *a*-mini *b-a* song, consoling rather than pleading, in a superbly ripe, introspective D major. Its most obvious single point of interest is this eloquent phrase—

which Mozart had used already in a slightly different form, to start the slow movement of his clarinet quintet K. 581; the connection is nonetheless unmistakable. There are other typical phrases, for instance this one, which recalls Zerlina's 'Sentilo battere' in *Don Giovanni*:

And it may be noticed that, although in this opera Mozart, to save time, scored mostly for strings, touching in his woodwind seldom and for special expressive effect, yet this aria includes much subtle woodwind writing (flute, oboe, bassoon— one each—two horns and strings). Also remarkable is the appealing effect of the supertonic penchant towards the end of the aria. No falling away here from the greatest operatic Mozart.

But now, if the opera is not to be rejected by our century, communication has to be made at some empathetic level: Vitellia, not Sextus, or Titus or anybody else, is the character who can make that communication. They are all much too virtuous. She, supposedly all jealousy and baseness, has manifested a trace of what we call human feeling. Because she was so horrible we are the more ready to understand her secret remorse.

Her self-questioning takes the form of an accompanied recitative (strings only). The initial instrumental phrase is nothing much, though it does convey a certain tension and anxiety (the trill and the rests), especially since the phrase is several times repeated. She is asking herself if she can face marriage to Titus when she has persuaded his friend, her admirer, to commit a crime for which he will have been sentenced to a cruel death—all this for her own sake. Not only would she feel his presence afterwards; she would fear that rocks and trees, all nature, would blurt out her guilty secret (here the violins burst into violent activity for a moment). She decides to save him or else say goodbye to all her hopes of marriage or influence.

This *volte-face* is effected largely by Metastasio and, especially since it is not the first in which his oratory is expressively persuasive (Titus's interview with Sextus was equally vivid), we should give him credit. He was not a hack dramatist but a poet of some power—and it may be in recitative more than in formal aria that we today may best appreciate his quality as he deserves.

The **Rondo** which follows, **No. 23**, should be the musical climax of the opera since it is extended, really telling for the artistry of the prima donna, and directly affecting. This is the famous *Non più di fiori* with basset-horn obbligato. It is marked *larghetto* increasing to *allegro*, and is in F major, with some subsidiary excursions to F minor and A flat major. It is quite carefully written, though the instrumentation, mostly for strings with basset-horn occasionally supported by other woodwind (flute, oboes, bassoon and horns), does imply that their parts might have been added later, when the rest of the opera was composed.

> No more will the goddess of marriage descend to scatter lovely wreaths of flowers. I see cruel people hurrying to put me to death.
> (*Allegro*) Unhappy Vitellia! Horrible fate! What will people say about me? Anyone who saw my grief would feel sorry for me.

The theme of the rondo is very plain, wan (especially at its first statement doubled by first violins) and inexpressive, one might think. But we hear it nowadays with post-Victorian ears. If it were played in an eighteenth-century style, with tasteful gracing, it would acquire the character Mozart certainly intended. This is one of Mozart's most advanced pieces (like some in *Die Zauberflöte*) that look towards the century whose musical ideals removed all character from music such as this. Can we admire a *prima donna* whose great moment is portrayed in this feeble tune?

21
Larghetto

Yet anybody familiar with the world of Mozart's music will readily read into this skeleton (as into the music of the D major Coronation Concerto) the grace and pathos that belong to it; it is like *Verdi prati* in *Alcina* which is either the dreariest or the most touching tune that Handel ever wrote, depending how much the singer adds to it of relevance and artistry.

The dummy accompaniment underneath this tune is exquisite. When the melody moves further there are delicate touches, indications of inevitable ornamentation, ravishing colours (e.g., the Alberti accompaniment for basset-horn, at first in triplet semiquavers then in demisemiquaver fours). For anybody familiar with the clarinet concerto that Mozart had already sketched for basset-horn (and was, only a few weeks later, to complete for basset-clarinet) the beginning of the *allegro* is adorable home territory:

22
Allegro

At bar 78 of the concerto's first movement we find:

23
[**Allegro**]
K.622

the same musical statement.

There is a spacious string texture in A flat major just after this, and then the basset-horn introduces a new, characteristic melody:

24

This is adopted as thematic, and the rondo theme too returns in common time and elevated to B flat major (with nice doubled wind accompaniment). A strange moment occurs when voice and basset-horn duet alone in counterpoint. *Non più di fiori* is a puzzling piece (perhaps even if properly ornamented) though one cannot help admiring it as superb vintage Mozart—an indication of what Mozart would have become if he had survived into the age of Schubert. It should be noted that Vitellia's compass descends to low A, though it has risen quite high earlier. Marchetti-Fantozzi was a true soprano with a compass from middle C to two octaves above. Josepha Dušek, on the other hand, was famous for her low register. This may add weight to the idea that *Non più di fiori* was written earlier, if not more of Vitellia's music.

The end of Vitellia's rondo, after her exit, keeps the orchestral music going through the change of scene, a procedure familiar in *Idomeneo* but uncommon here. The final cadence is interrupted, the solemn imperial rhythmic pattern for wind reappears, there are precipitous scale passages, the music moves from F to the dominant of G major.

We are now in, I suppose, the Coliseum, a large amphitheatre or circus, in the middle of which a collection of condemned criminals is waiting to be some wild beast's 'unhappy dinner' while a huge throng watches.

During **No. 24**, *Che del ciel*, a joyful **Chorus** in G major, *Andante maestoso* (for the whole orchestra excepting clarinets), Titus enters with Annius and Servilia and all the imperial following. This is a solemn piece full of thematically dotted rhythms, block harmonized, with an ending that recalls Handelian fervour and with some careful touches of woodwind colour.

Titus announces in recitative that before the start of the 'joyous entertainments' (viz. men and women being devoured alive by lions and tigers, if that is your idea of a 'lieto spettacolo') the guards must bring Sextus to him. Annius and Servilia beg for mercy but Titus tells them that pleas are useless: Sextus's fate is already decided. When Sextus enters the Emperor reminds him of his crimes and of the senate's sentence. Before he can go on to exercise clemency Vitellia rushes forward, kneels and confesses her guilt: she conceived the murderous plot and seduced her admirer, Titus's best friend, into attempting it. Her reason was her desire to share the imperial throne and her annoyance at being twice passed over.

Titus bursts into string-accompanied **Recitative, No. 25**. Just as he is about to pardon one criminal he is faced with another: it is as if fate were goading him into exercising severity. However he has determined to rule benevolently and so he will pardon all the conspirators and reprieve Lentulus and his followers from an uncomfortable doom.

Sextus promptly renders gratitude and in so doing launches the **Finale, No. 26**, which is marked *allegretto* and is in C major. It involves full orchestra and all the cast including chorus. The start is serene and low-pitched emotionally with strings alone (subdominant pull in the harmony to indicate the approaching end), supporting Sextus's protestation that though the Emperor pardons him (*Tu, è ver, m'assolvi Augusto?*) he cannot forgive himself. The music is rather stiff (a less enthusiastic version of *Una bella serenata* in *Così fan tutte*); but with the entry of oboe and bassoon in octaves the music begins to thaw. Titus adds a second verse, to a different, more moving melody in G, again accompanied by strings. Vitellia, Servilia and Annius add what seems like a trio-refrain, more chromatic with generously undulating violin arpeggios and pleasing woodwind support. The orchestra in C major resumes the imperial *Leitmotiv* of dotted rhythms; and in grandiose mass euphony all except Titus call on the gods to watch over the Emperor's life ('Eterni dei'). Titus responds to this somewhat formal hymn of praise with a more ingratiating verse, mostly supported by strings and with invigorating harmony produced by a descending bass line, asking the gods to cut short his life if ever he ceases to care first and last for his Roman people. The hymn of praise is resumed, but this time Titus interrupts at the end of each line with his 'Troncate i giorni mei', and eventually we have the people's 'Vegliate' ('Watch over him') answered by Titus's 'Troncate' ('Let me die'). This complex, a vivid representation of the Emperor as leader and father of his kingdom, is extended and the orchestra adds a stately epilogue of syncopations against dotted rhythms, ending with the same scrunches that began the overture—though this time we may fancy they depict the roaring of the lions deprived of their succulent promised luncheon.

5

I have done my best to explode the received idea that in writing *La Clemenza di Tito* Mozart was untrue to himself, forced himself to compose in a style he knew to be no longer valid, ceased to bother about dramatic construction, courted approval by simplifying his musical language, and in general thought only of earning a fee he needed.

The twentieth century opera-goer may be convinced that, for the composer of *Don Giovanni* and virtually complete *Zauberflöte*, opera seria was a lost cause. Mozart was not convinced of this nor, after the gala première, were opera-goers, even those who might be expected, after the French Revolution, to applaud Vitellia as the Madame Defarge of the opera stage and demand that Titus, be he ever so clement, be thrown to his own lions in the Coliseum. The people of Prague, when royalty had departed, enjoyed the opera, so did the Austrians, Germans, Italians and British.

As drama it is no great shakes. But Mozart's last initiated operatic project is musically as rich as the description implies: he was at the height of his powers, even though ill and working against an imminent deadline. Haste never worried Mozart who could write a new symphony in three or four days. He did not regard *La clemenza di Tito* as an *opera seria* but, thanks to Mazzolà's work, as a *vera opera*. And it was *vera opera* that he wrote. There is some stiff music, and many of the musical numbers (not to their disadvantage) are short. The orchestration is less elaborate than we expect, and we miss the linking of numbers that distinguishes *Idomeneo*. But the ensembles are superb (e.g., the chorus with Titus's solo, No. 15, and both finales), several solos are extended and magisterial, and the structure of the two acts is carefully designed to increase tension by the juxtaposition of musical numbers which grow more intense and inventive (Nos. 9–12 in act one, for instance). The Emperor Titus (by no means an Idomeneo) did not much inspire Mozart as he had Metastasio, but Vitellia is a real woman, vile in some respects but with genuine human feeling long before *Non più di fiori*. And Sextus is presented as a weak but good character. The lesser characters emerge in focus through their arias and ensembles, including the choruses.

If he had reverted to the old *opera seria* form of *da capo* aria (still favoured in Naples, home town of the Empress) he would have been untrue to his achievement. The shorter two-tempo aria, borrowed from French opera, was better suited to the taste of 1791 and to Mozart's personal genius. It is a pity that he had no time to write all his own recitatives and to orchestrate more elaborately. But as it stands *La clemenza di Tito* can command our affection as well as our admiration and it should certainly be accepted into the Mozartian operatic canon together with *Idomeneo* and the five favourite comic works, plus *La finta giardinera*. Recent revivals have indicated the liveliness and theatrical worth of *La clemenza di Tito*, not least the 1975 Covent Garden production which conquered Milan a year later, with Dame Janet Baker as Vitellia. The production by Anthony Besch combined *opera seria* style with human, realistic behaviour, and may be regarded as exemplary. The casting of a mezzo-soprano as Vitellia was bold, but Mozart's score suggests that Marchetti-Fantozzi was, like Dame Janet, the sort of mezzo with a reliable top register that the French call a 'Falcon', after the singer of that name. A successful production of *La clemenza di Tito* will depend on scrupulous casting of each part, physically and vocally. Sextus must look and sound like a man; Annius too. Titus must sound heroic as well as clement, and he must look a credible emperor. Vitellia must be a riveting stage personality, with a voice of unusual range. All this is not easy but the rewards will be great, as they are in a fine *Idomeneo*.

22   DIE ZAUBERFLÖTE

DIE ZAUBERFLÖTE

A German Opera★

Text by
EMANUEL SCHIKANEDER

K. 620

SARASTRO (priest of the sun)	BASS
TAMINO (a foreign prince on his travels)	TENOR
SPEAKER (a priest of Isis and Osiris)	NON–SINGING ROLE
1st Priest	NON–SINGING ROLE
2nd Priest	TENOR
3rd Priest	BASS
QUEEN OF NIGHT	SOPRANO
PAMINA (her daughter)	SOPRANO
1st Lady	
2nd Lady (in Queen of Night's service)	SOPRANOS
3rd Lady	
PAPAGENO, a birdcatcher	BASS
An old woman (later PAPAGENA)	SOPRANO
MONOSTATOS, a Moor	TENOR
Three boys	TREBLES
Three slaves	SPEAKING PARTS
Two men in armour	TENOR, BASS

The action takes place in Egypt

★ The playbill calls it a Grand Opera (*grosse Oper*). I adopt Mozart's entry in his *Verzeichnis*.

Mozart's fortunes in Vienna had not been particularly favourable under the monarchy of Joseph II. But at least he had an official post with a small salary, even if it involved duties of small and infrequent responsibility. And Joseph II had treated Mozart's operas kindly even if, having commanded their performance, he expressed himself unfavourably about them. His successor Leopold II, who arrived in Vienna on 13 March 1790, was no friend to Mozart: Leopold was opposed to everything that his progressive predecessor had championed. This included Mozart's music, and also Freemasonry, a movement, popular in Vienna, which their mother Maria Theresa had tried to suppress and against which Leopold began to take action, though not very stringently.

After the accession of Leopold II Mozart applied in May 1790 for an official post as assistant Kapellmeister in the cathedral, without salary. The honour was worthless to Mozart: he needed money but also the expectation of a senior well paid job. He had few pupils, no official work, and his wife was both pregnant and ailing. His best friends were Freemasons who lent him money, or secured jobs for him. During 1790 he composed some string quartets and sketched piano sonatas for the Prussian Emperor who had commissioned them. He reorchestrated some Handel choral works, probably for his academically minded friend Baron van Swieten. He paid visits to Marinelli's comic opera in the Kärntnertor Theatre, and to the much more bourgeois Theatre auf der Wieden, now run by an old Salzburg friend Emanuel Schikaneder with a remarkably accomplished company for whom Mozart wrote some additional music. In late September Mozart, with his violinist brother in law Franz Hofer and a servant, began a journey to Frankfurt am Main, where Leopold was crowned on 9 October. Mozart gave a concert there and in Mainz, called at Mannheim to look at a new production of *Figaro*, moved to Augsburg (his father's home), then Munich where he took part in a court concert.

On 10 November he arrived back in Vienna and completed several works including his last piano concerto (K. 595 in B flat major), another string quartet and the E flat quintet, and several works for a mechanical clock, nowadays played on the organ or as piano duets. He wrote much dance music as well as the concert-aria *Per questa bella mano*, and several songs with piano accompaniment.

He was thus in a strongly creative mood when Schikaneder suggested that he and Mozart should collaborate in an opera for Schikaneder's theatre. Mozart had long wanted to write a German opera again, he needed the work, knew Schikaneder's company and the Freihaus Theatre. He accepted the offer and the subject, adapted by Schikaneder from a book of oriental fairy-tales. The source-story was called *Lulu, or The Magic Flute*. The opera was finally entitled simply *The Magic Flute*, or in German *Die Zauberflöte*.

2

The author of *Die Zauberflöte* was born Johann Josef Schikaneder on 1 September 1751 at Straubing on the Danube in lower Bavaria. His parents were very poor and his education meagre but he learned to play the violin and, as a boy, scraped a living as an itinerant musician. By 1773 he had become an actor in the strolling company of Andreas Schopf whose fosterdaughter Eleonore Arth he married. By 1775 Schikaneder was already well known as an actor, particularly of tragedy, nationally renowned for his Hamlet, Macbeth and King Lear. In 1777 he was invited to make a guest appearance as Hamlet in Munich where his performance was so applauded that he had to repeat Hamlet's last scene; the annals of the theatre recorded this as a rare event. In that same year Schikaneder—having enjoyed his first success as an author and composer with *Die Lyranten* ('The Strolling Musicians'), which was given by Schopf's company in Augsburg and remained popular—moved with his wife to the better known travelling company of Joseph Moser, where he had more opportunities to act, sing, write, compose, direct ambitious and spectacular productions, and influence Moser in the choice of serious classical repertory: Gluck's operas, and plays by Lessing, Goethe, Shakespeare and Voltaire. In 1778 Moser's wife died and he decided to sell his company to Schikaneder who had just been offered a permanent engagement on the acting strength of the Munich Court Theatre. Schikaneder threw up the Munich offer, bought his own company and toured it throughout South Germany and Austria. During the winter of 1780–1 they played in Salzburg where Schikaneder made friends with Leopold Mozart and his family, was entertained in their home, played bowls and did target practice with them, and became on familiar *Du* terms with Wolfgang (before his departure for Munich in November). *Die Entführung aus dem Serail* was taken into the Schikaneder repertory in 1784. By then Schikaneder's troupe was in Pressburg, doing rather less well; but Joseph II saw two of the company's shows there and invited Schikaneder to Vienna where he took the Kärntnertor Theater in co-direction with Johann Friedel, an actor and author, and Hubert Kumpf. The company was admired in Vienna especially for the scenic grandeur of the productions and Schikaneder's attention to dramatic detail, uncommon in the work of a travelling company. Perhaps I have laid too much stress on the serious items: their repertory included ballets and orchestral concerts, farces and *Singspiele*, foreign comic operas in German, as well as Gluck and Shakespeare. The German Opera in Vienna had been virtually disbanded (though officially it continued until 1787). Schikaneder had no competition to fear from any performances there, and if he was sensible he would not attempt rivalry with the Emperor's Italian Opera, since his company was chosen for versatility, and the standard of *bel canto* was not high.

In February 1785 Schikaneder's Vienna season ended and his company split; his wife left him for Johann Friedel who in due course became director of the Freihaus Theater auf der Wieden on the outskirts of Vienna. Schikaneder played for a while with the National Theatre in Vienna, and during this time made friends with the Gottlieb family whose eleven-year-old daughter Anna was next year to sing Mozart's first Barbarina in *Figaro* and in 1791 his first Pamina. Schikaneder did apply for Imperial permission to build his own theatre for *Singspiel* in Vienna, and Joseph II approved; but when permission was given, Schikaneder could not raise the required money. So he returned to the road and in 1786 formed another company of his own: he recruited Benedikt Schack and his wife—Schack was a composer and flautist as well as actor and singer; when this company revisited Salzburg in the same year Leopold Mozart wrote enthusiastically about Schack's excellent singing. A year later, in 1787, the Schikaneder company played in Regensburg, at that time the parliamentary centre of Germany, and formerly Schikaneder's youthful residence in his itinerant musician days. It was here that he joined the Masonic Lodge, a step of historic importance, much greater than he imagined, since it brought him immortality as the librettist of *Die Zauberflöte*. He was by no means a respectable mason, and seems to have been expelled from the Regensburg Lodge for some philandering adventure. He remained an active Mason elsewhere, partly because the connection was commercially useful. In 1789 Johann Friedel died and Eleonore Schikaneder asked her husband to return and run the Theater auf der Wieden which she had inherited from Friedel. Schikaneder was willing to return to his wife. He brought his company back to Vienna in June and at once relaunched his forces there on a challenging and broad repertory in competition with Karl Marinelli's *Singspiel* company which since 1781 had been playing a repertory of popular and somewhat primitive *Singspiel* at the Leopold-stadt Theater. A Viennese Freemason, Joseph von Bauernfeld (he later translated Shakespeare into German for Schubert) gave Schikaneder financial help.

The Theater auf der Wieden had been built two years earlier as a temporary play-house (its replacement, the Theater an der Wien, opened on another site in 1801, by which time *Die Zauberflöte* had become so famous that the exterior decoration includes a figure of Papageno). It held a thousand spectators, had a wide and deep stage, and included numerous dwellings on the premises. Schikaneder soon discovered that in order to prosper in Vienna he must ration his serious and classical repertory in favour of the comic and romantic *Singspiele* which were best favoured by Viennese audiences. In the realm of low farce the hallowed Viennese Punch-like figure, Hanswurst, had changed his name in the Leopold Theater to Kasperle. Schikaneder created his counterpart, Dummer Anton or Silly Tony, whose exploits ran to seven plays. Also popular in Vienna was the *Zauberoper*, a comic rescue play which gave rise to splendid scene changes, involved the appearance of animals on stage and sundry magical objects whereby heroes could conquer villains. Thus in November 1789 Schikaneder produced *Oberon* (the same story of Sir Huon and his squire Sherasmin which Weber was to set for London as his last opera) with music by Paul Wranitzky to a text borrowed and faintly rewritten by Karl Ludwig Gieseke, one of Schikaneder's actors, from the story by Christoph Martin Wieland as already adapted by F. S. Seyler. The hero here is given a magic horn which will release him from troubles in his task of rescuing the captive heroine; a March by Wranitzky in this *Oberon* also helped Mozart at a difficult moment in the composition of *Die Zauberflöte*. Another magic opera presented by Schikaneder in September 1790 was *Der Stein der Weisen* ('The Philosopher's Stone'), to a text by himself, with music by Benedikt Schack: one duet, in which the heroine can only miaow, was scored if not composed by Mozart. The source of *Der Stein der Weisen* was the book of oriental fairy-tales mentioned above: it was called *Dschinnistan* and had been collected by Wieland. The scene was set in Egypt, and the hero had to undergo a trial by fire and water in order to rescue the heroine—features of *Die Zauberflöte*. There were two pairs of lovers, as well as a good and bad genie. Much of all this came from a tale by A. J. Liebeskind in *Dschinnistan* called *Lulu, oder die Zauberflöte*, but Schack's opera involved no magic flute, even though Schack was himself a flautist. Schikaneder regarded the coincidence as too good to be ignored. Having looked further into *Dschinnistan* he sensed a new *Singspiel* centring on a hero-rescuer armed with a magical flute. This was his proposal to Mozart in or about March 1791.

3

The plot of *Lulu, oder Die Zauberflöte* may be summarized as follows. Prince Lulu, son of the King of Khurasan, is sent by Perifirime, a good and radiant fairy, to rescue her daughter Sidi from the wicked wizard Dilsengbuin who has abducted her together with a fiery sword which is Perifirime's principal magic wand. To help him in this task she gives him a magic flute which can transform him into any shape he chooses (like Alberich's *Tarnhelm* in Wagner's *Ring*) and will also win the sympathy of all who hear it, man and beast, exciting or calming their passions as the player chooses. Lulu finds the wizard's stronghold. The wizard tries to nullify the flute's magic power, by encouraging Sidi to fall in love with Lulu. But Lulu is able to play his flute to Dilsengbuin and enchant him and his retinue into magic sleep. He and Sidi escape. Perifirime plays the flute while hovering over the wizard's castle, and reduces it to nothingness.

This is, with one major exception, a recognizable source for Schikaneder's *Die Zauberflöte* as set by Mozart. Schikaneder had to find a good comic part for himself—he was said to exaggerate in comedy but, like every famous Hamlet, he loved a clown's part—so he borrowed Sherasmin's squire role from *Oberon* and invented Papageno the birdcatcher, drawing on the bird disguises of Marinelli's Kasperle, and one of the Italian comedies by Carlo Gozzi which his company found successful, *Il rè cervo**, where Truffaldino is a birdcatcher: contemporary drawings often show *commedia dell' arte* comedians dressed in feathers and masked with a bird's beak. The Italian *commedia* influence can be seen in the Italian endings of the characters' names, though Papageno must derive his from *Papagei*, the German for 'parrot'—an early *Zauberflöte* drawing shows parrots perching in Papageno's birdcage. If the names really were Italian we would call the birdcatcher 'Papa-jay-no'; the Viennese, however, have always pronounced Italian carelessly and, with *Papagei* as source, 'Papa-gay-no' is quite a convincing pronunciation.

The chief difference between the *Lulu* story, summarized above, and that of Mozart's *Zauberflöte* (apart from the sensible alteration of the hero's name which in the west has female connotations, as witness the Wedekind dramas set by Alban Berg as his second opera *Lulu*) is that the radiant good fairy and the wicked magician have swapped virtues: kindly Perifirime has become the malign Queen of Night: dastardly Dilsengbuin has changed into the virtuous and idealistic Priest of the Sun, Sarastro, with whose band of initiates the hero and heroine decide to remain. Some other literary sources were behind these variations from Liebeskind's *Lulu* story. The three magic boys who guide and advise Tamino and Papageno come from another story in *Dschinnistan* called *The Three Boys*: in it they advise the hero to be

* The same made into an opera by Hans Werner Henze.

'steadfast, patient and taciturn', much as in *Die Zauberflöte*. Tamino's love at first sight on beholding Pamina's portrait may go back to *Zaide* (see p. 238) or to Naumann's opera *Osiride* whose libretto was being written by Mazzolà in Dresden while da Ponte was lodging with the poet. Declarations of love to portraits were stock theatrical property in any case (see *Così fan tutte*, No. 4, for example). So were frustrated suicides such as Pamina and Papageno attempt. The scenes for the priests and initiates in the temple of the sun had no part in *Lulu*; but they had been part of several operas, not only *Osiride* but Wenzel Müller's *Das Sonnenfest der Brahminen* staged by Marinelli in 1790. Sarastro's Palace of Truth or Wisdom (recalled in Pamina's idealistic cry of 'Die Wahrheit' in No. 8) is to be found in *Dschinnistan*, and doubtless other details of Schikaneder's text. In connection with the snake, which looms large in the first scene of all, I was interested to read of the Indian myth whereby a dead man returns in serpentine form to guard his own riches; this explains not only the monster which terrifies Tamino and is so zealously dispatched by the Queen's Ladies (did Schikaneder know?), but also *Fafner als Wurm* in Wagner's *Siegfried*.

As an extra source Schikaneder, above all, drew on the French novel *Sethos* by Jean Terrasson, 'histoire ou vie tirée des monuments anecdotes de l'ancien Egypte', published in Paris, 1731, and in German translation by Matthias Claudius in 1777–8. Terrasson pretended that he was translating a Greek text from the time of Vespasian. He was really interested in forging a link between the Freemasonry of his time and ancient Egypt from which Masonry claimed its original derivation. *Sethos* gives us the text of the rubric on the pyramid solemnly read out by the Two Armed Men in No. 21 of *Die Zauberflöte*, the serpent, the Three Ladies, the Queen of Night as Villainess (she is called Daluca), the initiation rites in some detail with the trials by fire and water, the trial in which men have to resist the temptations of forthcoming women, the possibility of initiates marrying rejected female candidates, and the existence of low-class semi-initiates. Sethos, incidentally, was the hero of Gebler's Egyptian drama *König Thamos*, for which Mozart wrote incidental music (see pp. 247 ff).

All the dramatic materials of Mozart's *Die Zauberflöte* are here, except for Monostatos. Shortly after Mozart's death rumours began to be published (a) that Schikaneder was not the author, nor even sole author of his other works; (b) that the plot of *Die Zauberflöte* had been switched, indeed turned upside-down, after Mozart had begun to write the music, to be exact at the beginning of the first act finale, No. 8. For the second supposition there is some justification. Mozart's *Zauberflöte* begins, and goes on, as if it were a version of Liebeskind's *Lulu*, as summarized above. Monostatos makes sense at this point (especially if it had been he who abducted Pamina). With the entry of the Three Boys at the beginning of the first act finale, a different, newly solemn numinous tone of voice suddenly emerges; it strikes you from the orchestra pit, before the voices enter, announcing that all the foregoing has been a blind (though not the overture which should have prepared you to disbelieve in the opera's opening scenes) and that truth is now for the first time being admitted. Tamino sees the three temples and henceforward morality is the principal topic and Freemasonry is the clue to the action, though non-Masons will find the action highly enlightening as well. We are asked to believe that Schikaneder and Mozart changed their plot drastically in June 1791 when Marinelli produced a new magical comic opera in Vienna called *Kaspar der Fagottist, oder Die Zauberzither*, also based on *Lulu*. The characters have different names and some extra incidents are introduced, but the action closely resembles that of *Lulu*. Mozart saw an early performance, while he was in the middle of composing *Die Zauberflöte*, and told his wife that *Kaspar* was noisy and stupid.

I do not believe that Schikaneder and Mozart altered the plot of *Die Zauberflöte* from fear that their story had been anticipated by *Kaspar der Fagottist*. Nobody at that time objected to the same subject being treated by other writers or composers: even the ethics of borrowing were sensibly lax—whoever borrows must justify himself by improving on what he has borrowed. Schikaneder's *Zauberflöte* had borrowed copiously from his company's recent successes. But the plot of *Die Zauberflöte* did change during that summer. How, otherwise, explain Monostatos's employment in Sarastro's kingdom, or the Three Boys provided by the Queen of Night but always servants of Sarastro, or the magic instruments given by the villainess but used only to Sarastro's advantage?

The story-line was altered, I fancy, long before either Schikaneder or Mozart saw *Kaspar der Fagottist*. Mozart wanted his German opera to be something more uplifted, more interesting to compose, than a Viennese farcical magical puppet show. He was capable of writing excellent comic music; but his abundant creativity had recently been moving into regions where charm and innocence were expressed with a depth touching on profundity, and where the seriousness of his Italian comic operas was very much at home. He was also a concerned and committed Freemason who had found in the Craft a superior adjunct of his inborn Christian and Catholic faith (undermined perhaps by the violent break with Colloredo). He had been composing Masonic music before he became a Mason. Since his initiation much of his music was touched with Masonic imagery (the slow movement of K. 595, all three of his last symphonies, and parts of all three da Ponte operas, as well as less ambitious works, use musical symbols that can be identified with his Masonic music and with what can be read about the beliefs and practices of eighteenth-century Freemasons—I am not a Mason and am sure that Masonic private language has changed since 1791; in 1956 my father, a loyal Mason, admitted that *Die Zauberflöte* had special relevance for him but not as much as people suggested).

Mozart, I imagine, proposed that the plot of *Lulu* should be given a healthy injection of seriousness to heighten the Papageno element. He and Schikaneder were both Masons, Mozart committedly so, and Vienna was a flourishing Masonic centre, threatened by the new and anti-Freemason Emperor, its morale in need of exhortation at a discreet ('verschwiegen', as the Boys advise) level. Schikaneder, an initiate at a Papageno level, saw the box-office advantages at least. One of them laid hands on *Sethos*; it may have been through Carl Gieseke, another Freemason, who had brought Schikaneder to *Dschinnistan*. Gieseke may even have read Schikaneder's libretto and pointed to suitable episodes in *Sethos*, or in other quasi-Masonic operas, which could find a telling place in *Die Zauberflöte*. Gieseke's subsequent claim, after Mozart and Schikaneder were dead, that he was the actual librettist of *Die Zauberflöte* was taken seriously but does not bear comparative examination of his librettos and Schikaneder's, and especially that of *Zauberflöte*, whose greatest solemnities are expressed in pure Schikaneder simplistic, however idealistic language. I do not like to believe Gieseke a liar, even though some questioned his honesty in calling himself Sir Charles Louis Gieseke when he was a Professor of Mineralogy at Dublin University. He may have given helpful advice to Schikaneder, perhaps altered a word or two, and much later exaggerated his assistance into sole authorship. The libretto of *Die Zauberflöte*, for those who can read German, is more than decent: it is simple in diction and inspiring, and confirms Abert's judgment, 'waschechter Schikaneder', straight off the laundry-line.

Schikaneder watched over it, gloried in it, kept the production new, brought it to his new Theater an der Wien. Papageno rather than Hamlet was his visiting-card for immortality when he died in 1812, after ten years of insanity which Papageno never deserved. He left 300 Gulden to Wieland in his will as a thank-offering for *Dschinnistan*.

4

In early June 1791 Constanze Mozart, pregnant and ailing, went off to Baden near Vienna to take the cure. Mozart wrote constantly to his Constanze, begging her to be careful about the cure, begging her not to behave too freely in sociable company. He travelled out to be with her quite often. While he was in Vienna Schikaneder put a little summerhouse at his disposal in the courtyard of the Freihaus Theater: Mozart could work comfortably there and remain in instant contact with his librettist (who could also make sure that the composer was not too frequently distracted). Legends declare that Schikaneder kept Mozart nourished on oysters and wine (oysters are out of season between May and September and would not be fresh by the time they reached Vienna, but Michael Kelly, a keen gastronome, maintained that Germans and Austrians only enjoyed old and rotting oysters), and dragged him off to riotous parties, not really in Mozart's line. We do know, from letters, that he ate and stayed the night with other friends: Baron Puchberg, Baron Montecuculi, Ignaz Leitgeb the horn virtuoso and cheese-seller, as well as Schikaneder. He also stayed during this time for some periods on the Kahlenberg in a tavern where his room is still pointed out to visitors. He was writing *Die Zauberflöte* in June, his letters show, and by 2 July was ready to score the first act which his pupil Süssmayr had taken off to Baden.

On 18 June Mozart composed the short motet *Ave verum corpus* for his choir-master friend Anton Stoll in Baden; it includes a poignant phrase from *Così fan tutte* (see p. 583). By mid-July he had written enough of *Die Zauberflöte* to enter it, with the incipit of No. 1, into his personal catalogue. The music was written out in vocal and bass lines and was being studied by the cast; Süssmayr may have been told to fill in passages of dummy accompaniment before Mozart broached the full score.

He now had to concentrate on *La clemenza di Tito* (see Chapter 21), though he also composed his *kleine deutsche Kantate*, K. 619, in this month. Constanze's baby was eventually born in Vienna on 26 July (Mozart had brought his wife home from Baden) and christened Franz Xaver Wolfgang. He, with his older brother Karl, alone survived of all Wolfgang's seven children; Franz Xaver Mozart became a solo pianist and composer and died in 1844. The Mozarts went to Prague for *Tito*, as already related, and returned to Vienna about 12 September when Mozart sat down to complete the remaining *Zauberflöte* music: the second act finale, the chorus No. 18 *O Isis und Osiris*, and Papageno's solo songs—these details are based on later recollections. On 28 September Mozart entered the *Zauberflöte* overture and Priests' March No. 9, as well as the A major clarinet concerto, in his catalogue.

The first performance of *Die Zauberflöte* took place on 30 September in the Theater auf der Wieden. Mozart conducted it from the keyboard of course, and the second performance on 1 October. Süssmayer turned the pages for him. J. B. Henneberg, regular Kapellmeister of the company, played the magic bells (a keyboard Glockenspiel, like Mustel's later celesta) and after 1 October took over the conducting.

Sarastro was sung by Franz Xaver Gerl, the company's chief basso (Mozart had composed the concert-aria *Per questa bella mano*, K. 612, for him with double-bass obbligato for Herr Pichlberger, a member of Schikaneder's orchestra), who was also a straight actor and a composer. Gerl's wife, née Barbara Reisinger, sang Papagena; she had been a child prodigy in the 1770s and was said to have had an affair with Mozart, improbably. Josepha Hofer, née Weber, Constanze Mozart's sister, sang the Queen of Night: she was the company's principal soprano, and only occasionally acted in plays. Something has already been said about Schack, who came from Bohemia and took Tamino, playing the magic flute himself. By now he had become a close friend of Mozart's. His wife, née Weinhold, sang Third Lady. Anna Gottlieb has also been mentioned earlier; Schikaneder chiefly used her as an actress. It is not true that she lost her voice on hearing of Mozart's death; she had a full and successful career as a singer thereafter. Schikaneder, of course, was Papageno. His elder brother Urban, an actor, was First Priest. Herr Kistler, a tenor, sang Second Priest; Herr Moll, Third Priest, was a bass. The priest named *Sprecher* was played by Herr Winter, the company's stage manager and official transcriber of Schikaneder's manuscript texts. The Old Priest (as Mozart describes him in the score), who interviews Tamino in No. 8, is a bass. The libretto does not mention him in the cast list, and though modern performances almost always call him the *Sprecher* (which means Speaker) I am sure that he was sung by Herr Moll, and that Urban Schikaneder and Herr Winter had only the speaking parts allotted to them in Act II (though Winter did sometimes appear in *Singspiele*). Kistler and Moll will also have sung the Two Men in Armour. Confusion is chiefly caused by the tenor–bass duet No. 11 which Mozart assigned to First and Second Priest; he meant Second and Third who were the professional singers, whereas First Priest and Sprecher were basically actors, for this was not a large opera company but a team of actors and singers who took what roles they could.

Of the others, First and Second Lady were Mlle Klöpfer and Mlle Hofmann. Monostatos was Johann Joseph Nouseul, primarily an actor. The Three Boys were sung by Nanette Schikaneder, small daughter of Urban, and by two real boys, Matthias Tuscher and Master Handlgruber. In modern productions they should, when possible, all be boys. The three slaves were Gieseke (see above, p. 598), Wilhelm Frasel and Herr Starke. All these names were not included on the playbill, which is nevertheless unusually informative. We also know that the monkeys, who appear in No. 8 at Tamino's *Wie stark ist nicht dein Zauberton*, in the first performance included Ignaz Castelli, a poet who wrote his memoirs, and a housemaid in the home of the young Grillparzer's parents. The scenery and costumes were the work of Joseph Gayl and Herr Nessthaler, and formed a special attraction of the production mentioned favourably by everyone who commented on the première. A member of the orchestra later reported that the opera was coldly received at first, until the duet *Bei Männern* after which enthusiasm began to spread. Mozart, the reminiscences record, was disheartened by the lukewarm applause, unwilling to take a call at the end, and had to be dragged on stage by Schikaneder. *Die Zauberflöte* was repeated almost daily throughout October. By 7 October Constanze Mozart had returned to Baden-bei-Wien for the cure, and her husband wrote that he had just returned from a performance; 'it was as full as ever. The duet *Mann und Weib* [*Bei Männern*] and the bell-playing in Act I [*Das klinget so herrlich* in No. 8] were repeated as usual, likewise in the second act the Boys' Trio [No. 16]. But what gives me most joy is the *silent applause*! One really sees how much, and ever more, this opera is catching on'. And in the same letter Mozart recalls the evening 'when my new opera was performed for the first time with so much applause'. Knowing the unenthusiastic Viennese reception of earlier Mozart operas we may give credence to the orchestral player's memories; but Mozart himself, little more than a week after the première, remembered hearty applause.

He attended a performance next day, 8 October, when a Bavarian acquaintance in the same box (the Freihaustheater had two tiers of boxes) annoyed Mozart by laughing and applauding even in the serious scenes; as a result Mozart left the box, went backstage and played Papageno's Glockenspiel. 'So I played a trick. At one point where Schikaneder has a pause I played an *arpeggio*—He was startled—looked into the wings and saw me—when it came the second time—I didn't play one— then he stopped and refused to continue—I guessed his thoughts and played another chord—then he hit the Glockenspiel and said, 'Shut up!'—everybody laughed at this—I believe that many people, as a result of this joke, realized for the first time that he does not play the instrument himself.'

Mozart took his mother-in-law, Frau Weber, to see *Die Zauberflöte* on the following night and again on 13 October when his party also included his young son Karl, Franz Hofer (Josefa's husband and Mozart's companion on the trip to the coronation in Frankfurt), Antonio Salieri and his mistress Catarina Cavalieri (the first Constanze in *Entführung*) both highly enthusiastic about this *operone*, as Salieri called it, 'fit to be performed before the greatest monarchs at the greatest festivities' —Mozart was evidently flattered by such praise from an ex-rival, and by Salieri's insistence that he and Cavalieri would return to it many times. This party is of interest inasmuch as Salieri has often been supposed to have poisoned Mozart, and to have confessed as much at the end of his life when he was mentally distressed. Mozart also told Constanze in this letter that the party were obliged to take their seats in the theatre at 4 p.m. though the performance did not start until seven o'clock. This is confirmed by other later reminiscences: patrons were obliged to do so, at four or five in the afternoon, or the seats would be taken over by other people, so great was the demand. That helpful diarist Count Zinzendorf attended the twenty-fourth performance of *Die Zauberflöte* on 6 November, noting that 'the music and décors are pretty, the rest an incredible farce. Huge audience'. In several subsequent entries he recorded pleasure at hearing the music of *Die Zauberflöte*. On 5 November Lausch the copyist had announced the availability of several numbers from the opera; other publishers soon followed him. This had not happened after *Così fan tutte*.

There is no surviving report of the *Zauberflöte* première in a Viennese newspaper. On 9 October the critic of the Berlin *Musikalisches Wochenblatt* reported that 'the new comedy with machines, *Die Zauberflöte*, with music by our Kapellmeister Mozart, which is given at great cost and with much magnificence in the scenery, fails to have the hoped-for success, the contents and the language of the piece being altogether too bad'. This does not square with Mozart's letters about the success of the piece.

To complete the story: on 15 October Mozart brought Constanze home from Baden; he intended to accompany her to another performance of the opera, sitting in a box near the stage where the music sounded much more effective than from the gallery where she sat on the first night. For the composition of *Die Zauberflöte* he is said to have received 100 Ducats, which would be a normal fee, though rumour also had it that he was never paid. O. E. Deutsch could find no authoritative statement on the subject.

On 18 November in one of Vienna's Masonic lodges Mozart introduced his Freemason's Cantata, K. 623; the text may have been by Schikaneder, or perhaps Gieseke. On 20 November Mozart took to his bed for the last time. On Monday 5 December at 2.55 a.m. he died. *Die Zauberflöte* remained popular in Vienna; in November 1782 Schikaneder announced the hundredth performance—this was only a slight exaggeration. It remained in his company's repertory throughout the 1790s, with new productions in 1794 and 1798, and again 1802 when, on 4 January, a further new production graced Schikaneder's Theater an der Wien and the playbill announced two unpublished musical numbers by Mozart. During the 1790s Schikaneder had kept a sizeable Mozart repertory: *Figaro* and *Don Giovanni* in 1792, *Così fan tutte* in 1794, *Schauspieldirektor* in 1797, and *La clemenza di Tito* in 1798. *Entführung*, which had been his first show in Vienna in 1784, had a new production in 1794. I can believe the legend whereby, to the end of his days, Schikaneder's eyes filled with tears when anybody mentioned the name of Wolfgang Mozart.

5

The **Overture** to *Die Zauberflöte* is in E flat major, traditionally a key of stability and solemn brilliance, as earlier chapters of this book have indicated. It is also a key for Masonic music, with its three flats in the key-signature, though the overture does not use a triple time-signature. Three was an important number to eighteenth-century Freemasons. *Die Zauberflöte* is full of trinities: Ladies, Boys, knocks at the door or trumpet-signals (the Threefold Chord hereafter), Priests, musical instruments on stage (pipes, flute, Glockenspiel). There are three grades of Masonry, three temples in No. 8, three initiatory visits to the altar, three major Egyptian deities. . . . you can read about them at length in Jacques Chailley's masonic interpretation, though many of his ideas seem far fetched to me. The number three has also, been significant to non-Masons from the beginning of civilization: one, two, three, go (as in Papageno's suicide ritual), the Holy Trinity, the days of Jonah's residence inside the whale and of Jesus's burial between death and resurrection, Portia's boxes, the heads of the Brahmin god, the Fates, the Furies, the

Graces, the Harpies, the Christian virtues (see Brewer's *Dictionary of Phrase and Fable* for further examples). But three is not the only number in *Die Zauberflöte*. There are two Men in Armour, and the other characters are often linked in pairs: Tamino–Pamina, Sarastro–Queen of Night, and so on. There are four elements, and masonic initiation involved trial by all four, though in *Zauberflöte* we only see two (Chailley explains the other two). Jews and Masons alike revere the five-pointed star of David; Chailley tells us that five is the significant number for female Freemasons and concludes from this that the opening chords of Mozart's *Zauberflöte* overture, being five in number, refer to the role of womankind in this opera. As a musician I have always experienced these introductory bars as three chords, because they are three harmonies: E flat–C minor–E flat six-three. They may be compared with the chords which open No. 2 of *König Thamos* (see p. 248).

This, it will be seen, is an *adagio* introduction to the overture. It is scored for two flutes, oboes, clarinets, bassoons, horns, trumpets, drums, three trombones and strings. Trombones had been used by Mozart for the voice of Neptune in *Idomeneo* and for the statue of the dead Commendatore in *Don Giovanni*, otherwise in church music where trombones had been chiefly at home. They are at home in *Die Zauberflöte* because it deals with a religion, the priesthood of Isis and Osiris in ancient Egypt, as a symbol of the super-denominational religious Craft of Free-masonry in Catholic-dominated eighteenth-century Vienna.

This *adagio* is very much in earnest, its searching melodious phrases, gracious yet sometimes melancholy, punctuated by solemn three-part harmony for trombones. It is not surprising if the first audience was puzzled to hear church music instead of the expected overture to a knockabout farce. Cheerfulness intervenes after fifteen bars with the irruption of an *allegro* in the same key.

Some listeners in 1791 would be reminded of a piano sonata by Muzio Clementi (opus 43, no. 2 in B flat) and Mozart certainly knew it since Clementi had played it on the occasion when these two virtuosi had a competition in 1781. Mozart alters the third and fourth bars and uses the theme for quasi-fugato treatment, highly invigorating to us, perhaps rather heavily intellectual for lighthearted Viennese tastes. Eventually a solo flute (I doubt if this is connected with the title of the opera) breaks away from the strings' development of Ex. 2 for some chromatic scales which lead to a new idea mostly for woodwind, with Ex. 2 in the accompaniment (a wily, very Haydnesque idea).

3

With loud interruptions of Ex. 2 on full orchestra this continues to a full close in the dominant, the overture's half-way mark.

Instead of a development (we have heard some already, a feature of fugal texture), the *adagio* resumes for a first announcement of the sacred fanfare known as the Threefold Chord when it reappears during the priestly scenes of Act Two.

4

These chords differ from those of Ex. 1 in that the harmony remains static: only the flutes add extra degrees to each chord of B flat. I have notated Ex. 4 as shown in Abert's edition (published by Eulenburg). Some scholars are convinced that the minim chords should be tied across the barlines, thus linking them with the rhythm of Ex. 1. They are supposed to represent the Masonic Initiate's knocking on the temple door before he is admitted. Only a Freemason, or perhaps even a masonic historian, could know whether the knocks are iambic or short-long-long. Musically the pairs of chords seem preferable; and musical ties are supposed to represent masonic fraternal links, according to Alfred Einstein.

The *allegro* is resumed, now without written-in *forte-piano* marks, rather the level of *piano* is indicated as norm. Trombones in soft octaves lead to a loud *stretto* on Ex. 2. On the verge of G minor, key of dramatic sad tension for Mozart, there is a bar's pause. Antiphony on the lines of Ex. 3 seems to lead to the woodwind theme of that example but actually induces a recapitulation beginning with Ex. 2 which has never been far away. It is a straight recapitulation with a rather menacing coda dominated by the figure D flat–B natural–C *fortissimo*, as if referring to some threat, like the machinations of the Queen of Night. But this is subsumed in jubilant E flat major, ending with three chords in that key.

The first act begins with a scene that shows a rocky landscape partly overgrown with trees. To right and left there are mountains, used for entrances and exits. In the middle, slightly removed, is a circular temple.

A young man runs down one of these mountains. He is grandly attired in an oriental costume (*japonisch* or *javonisch* according to which text you read, though

Mozart omits the direction—he is a foreigner nevertheless) and carries a bow but no arrows. He is pursued by a snake, a very large and angry snake intent on devouring him. The snake was originally a lion, metamorphosed because lions are connected with Sarastro. The man is Tamino. He is evidently a noble young aristocrat in the middle of the Grand Tour, completing his education by broad travel. He has found his way to Egypt but lost his servants as well as his arrows. The music of **No. 1, Introduction**, *allegro* in C major *Zu Hülfe!*, with oboes, bassoons, horns and strings, shows that he is very much afraid—tremolos, abrupt dynamic contrasts, the minor key—before he opens his mouth. The orchestra is actually playing the music to which he soon sings about his terrible plight. At 'schon nahet sie sich' the orchestra portrays the fearsome lolloping along the mountain of this monstrous predatory beast. Tamino faints from fear, and his C minor cadence is diverted into A flat major as three veiled ladies, armed with silver javelins, emerge from the little temple and stab the serpent dead. An early picture shows that the beast is cut into three pieces: presumably one javelin hit it between the eyes or in the heart, and then the other two did the chopping for ternary purposes (three is a musical number as well!). The instruction is printed in Abert's Eulenberg score but does not appear in the first libretto or the musical autograph.

The Ladies, who are servants of the Queen of the Night, rejoice in solemn E flat on wind and brass, (flutes, clarinets, trumpets and drums, not all in the early scores), interrupted by brilliant violin runs, congratulating themselves on their heroic activity and rescue of the young man. They then pause to observe the unconscious object of their heroism. This takes them into mellow A flat major, rather questioning and investigatory (a rare key for Mozart in any case): each lady in turn remarks on his handsomeness, and all three declare their readiness to fall in love with him. To serious minded commentators these Ladies represent Unenlightenment or the Roman Catholic Church or even female Freemasonry. One might have believed such theories during their E flat music about 'Heldentat' and 'Tapferkeit'. But now we hear that they are romantic womanhood yearning for a man.

The Third Lady, who has the bass line in the second half of Ex. 5, even sounds a touch saucy when she remarks that the boy is as pretty as a picture. The rhythm of the first bar rather suggests Papageno.

All three Ladies take a cheerful view of the situation in determining to apprise 'the Princess' of the news.

The handsome stranger may cheer her up. So, to Ex. 7, each lady tells the others that they must go to the *Fürstin* while she nurses the patient. A jealous tiff develops and goes to the edge of G minor. But it collapses into a cheerful G major *allegretto*, Papagenoesque again with jolly bassoon and flute thirds.

Exs. 6 and 8 will both reappear for Papageno in No. 6. The Ladies agree, to a marchlike *allegro* in C major with plentiful vocal imitation (a serious effect used comically), that, since none will leave another here, they must all go together. They bid farewell, very tenderly in a harmonious trio, to their heart's desire. The thought of seeing him again rouses their spirits and the music is jubilant, with trumpets and drums, as they walk to the temple whose doors open, and close behind them, of their own accord.

Tamino regains consciousness, looks fearfully about him and is astounded to find himself still alive. The snake is dead at least; but who has killed it? He talks to himself: this may be entitled a Grand Opera, but it is still *Singspiel* and has spoken dialogue, not dry recitative. Hearing the sound of panpipes (Schikaneder calls them variously 'Waldflötchen' und 'Faunenflötchen') offstage he hides behind a tree, still commenting on the strangeness of the place while the orchestra (oboes, bassoons, horns and strings) plays the extensive introduction to **No. 2 Aria**, *andante* in G major, *Der Vogelfänger bin ich ja*. During this a man strolls down a mountainous footpath towards the temple. He is Papageno, a birdcatcher, dressed very like a bird and carrying on his back a huge birdcage that towers above his head and contains numerous birds. The original printed libretto included an engraving of Schikaneder in his Papageno costume to supplement what the stage-directions omitted. From time to time he blows his panpipes to lure birds.

9

When he reaches the centre of the stage he begins to tell us about himself in a song of easy-going popular Viennese cut: it quickly attained folksong status.

10

Der   Vogel—fän——ger   bin ich ja stets   lu—stig hei—ßa hop-sa—sa!

Yes, I'm the birdcatcher, always cheerful, well known to young and old everywhere. I go about, piping and setting traps, and all birds are mine. If only I had a girl-trap I'd snare them by the dozen and they would all be mine. I'd pick my favourite and feed her on sugar. She'd kiss me and sleep beside me, and I'd rock her like a child.

Papageno's song has three verses, all sung to the same melody, as in Ex. 10. A quantity of pipe-playing is allowed for, to the tune of Ex. 9, and one gathers that Schikaneder used to play it during dialogue as well. Gagging had a prominent part in Schikaneder's comic performances: he complained that Mozart had ruined Papageno for him by leaving so little room, in the musical numbers, for extempore jokes. When a modern Papageno introduces crisp topical gags (Sir Geraint Evans is a perfect example in the late 1970s) we should not turn up our scholarly noses but be thankful that Schikaneder's quick wit is not extinct. Even in an Egyptian setting Papageno traditionally talks broad Viennese.

The third verse of No. 2, 'Wenn alle Mädchen wären mein', does not appear in the original libretto or musical autograph but seems perfectly authentic. After his last verse Papageno blows a couple of blasts on his *Faunenflötchen* and makes for the temple. Tamino comes from behind his tree and grasps Papageno by the hand (a means of restraint, not a Masonic greeting, not yet). During their extensive conversation we learn that Tamino is a Prince, son of a monarch who rules over many lands and people; Papageno is fascinated to learn that other inhabited countries exist—scope for bird-selling—and knows nothing of his parentage except that he was brought up by a jolly old man and that some said his mother was a servant to the Nocturnal Starbright Queen ('nächtlich sternflammende Königin'); he now lives in a straw hut and lives by bartering birds, to the Queen and her Ladies, in exchange for food and drink. This Queen is veiled, never seen by him nor anybody. Tamino has heard tell of her from his father; he wonders if this curious fellow may be some unearthly genie in her service. Papageno becomes uneasy and boasts of his gigantic strength from which Tamino deduces that Papageno was the killer of the snake. After making sure that this monster is really dead, Papageno takes the credit for slaughtering it with his own bare hands.

The Three Ladies have heard his boast and call out his name menacingly: he is stealing their thunder. Papageno tells Tamino that the Ladies take his bird booty in exchange for wine, sugarbread and sweet figs. He does not suppose them to be lovely, else why veil their faces? Again a call of remonstration: the Ladies were hoping to win Tamino's love. Papageno senses that the Ladies are in a bad mood and quickly corrects himself: of course they are the most beautiful creatures he has ever seen. Again a remonstration (that makes three). Now the ladies approach. Papageno hands over his catch for the day (the pretty birds, it seems, are destined to be cooked for the Queen's supper—are we meant to understand now that she is a nasty character, eating shish-kebab of parrot and cockatoo, or was 1791 Vienna used to such delicacies?) His rewards for today's offering are not the usual goodies, but an elegant carafe of water, a stone, and a golden padlock for his mouth as a punishment for telling lies to strangers. They explain to Tamino that the *Heldentat* which laid the serpent low was theirs. The great *Fürstin* has sent them to bring the portrait of her daughter to Tamino. If it moves him he will be destined for fame and happiness. With some barbed witticisms to Papageno the Ladies withdraw.

Papageno is amusing the audience with padlock business (it had masonic significance in those days). Tamino has paid no attention since he clapped eyes on the portrait. The enchantment of the girl portrayed inspires his **Aria, No. 3** (in Germany regularly called the *Bildnisarie*) which is marked *larghetto* in E flat major, *Dies Bildnis ist bezaubernd schön*, and scored with sensuous clarinets, bassoons, lowlying horns and strings.

> This portrait is enchantingly beautiful; no one has ever seen the like. I can feel this divine image filling my heart with new excitement. I cannot put a name to it, though it burns like fire. Can it be love? Yes, it must be. O, if only I could find her! If she were here in front of me! I would—what, then?—press her to me, and she would be mine for ever.

The strings begin with pride muted into perplexity. Tamino's first phrase, repeated a tone lower, is typical *Zauberflöte* aspiration and wonder, and will recur later; the rising sixth has been noted in earlier chapters as an archetypal vocal opening which Mozart regularly used for such moments of spiritual illumination.

11

At 'Ich fühl es' Mozart resorts appropriately to a telling and nonconventional idea which Ilia had used in No. 11 of *Idomeneo*.

12

Jacques Chailley claims this aria as a form new to Mozart, but it is a fine example of the compact *a-b-a* which we have examined ever since *Idomeneo* and before, ever since Mozart broke free from the extended *da capo* and full concerto first movement aria structures which he inherited. The A section closes with a stylish, elegant phrase varied on repetition so as to refer back to the rising sixth of Ex. 11.

13

mein Herz—— mit neu-er Regung füllt, mein Herz— mit neu-er Regung füllt.

The B section, B flat major in fact, begins with voluptuous clarinets in thirds and a tune which Tamino repeats. The second idea ('Soll die Empfindung Liebe sein?') asks the question hesitantly, with a florid violin adjunct. In the third idea (clarinets and bassoons in encouraging thirds) it is positively answered, though a fourth idea ('Die Liebe, die Liebe') still raises astonished eyebrows at the realization of love at first sight.

In late Mozart (as in nineteenth-century opera) arias tend to fall into two parts, the second being faster. Here the sensation is suggested but the tempo remains constant and the main musical idea is designed to lead back from B flat to E flat, dominant to home tonic. The dominant pedal theme that effects this process does suggest a faster pace, though I am sure there must be no true *più mosso*—it is in the music—and it is neatly linked to the E flat last section. Here is this bridge passage.

14

O wenn ich sie nur fin-den könn——te!

And here is the return to E flat major, the violin part and vocal line obviously derived from Ex. 14. I append an affecting consequent, also related to Ex. 14.

15

p cresc.

Ich würde sie   und e-wig wä-re sie dann mein,

After this the aria returns unequivocally to Ex. 13 and makes a jubilant cadence with a soft, female-ended coda that is typical of Mozart's *Zauberflöte* music.

Tamino makes to leave, by exit-aria rules, but is restrained by the Three Ladies, so excited that they continually interrupt one another in mid-sentence. Their Sovereign has heard Tamino's every thought, and resolved to make him the happiest man in the world. He will rescue her daughter—the Original (as Tamino unforgettably puts it) of the portrait. The Ladies explain that she was abducted by a powerful and wicked demon while she sat, one beautiful day in May (forget about Schumann), all alone among the cypress trees that she loved (is necrophilia suggested?). The demon transformed her into some easily portable shape and made off with Pamina, this being the Original's name.*

Tamino fears the worst for Pamina but the Ladies assure him her virginity is impregnable. The magician lives near by in a splendid fortress set in a lovely valley. Tamino, soon roused to deeds of valour, implores the Ladies to lead him to the villain's stronghold. He vows to release Pamina. At this moment, according to Schikaneder, 'a violent, awe-inspiring chord with music is heard', thunder as well. The Ladies know that their Queen is approaching.

Mozart did not react obediently to the stage directions. **No. 4, Aria**, begins softly and only gradually makes a *crescendo* as the mountains separate† to reveal a splendid room in which the Queen of the Night sits on a throne decorated with transparent stars.

The music is marked *allegro maestoso* in B flat major, with oboes, bassoons, horns in high B flat for brilliance and tension, and strings. This introduction to the Queen's first solo builds from syncopated *piano*, perhaps representative of terror, to loud tonic–dominant grandeur with dramatically agile bass line.

The Queen's solo falls into three sections.

> (*Recitative*) My dear son, do not tremble. You are guiltless and wise and pious, best able to comfort a mother's careworn heart.
> (Arie, *larghetto*, G *minor*) I am doomed to suffer because I am without my daughter. A villain absconded with her. I can still see her terror, hear her cries of, 'O, help me!' But my help was too weak.
> (*Allegro moderato, B flat major*) You will be her saviour. And when I see you victorious she will be yours for ever.

The recitative refers twice to the orchestral prelude. Note that, even in a *Singspiel*, orchestrally accompanied recitatives are in order for characters of heroic stature. In the finales they are inevitable; in the rest of *Die Zauberflöte* this is the only example. They were scarce too in *Die Entführung*. Note also that Mozart never persevered with the melologue innovation of *Zaide*.

The Queen's aria, *Zum Leiden bin ich auserkoren*, expresses pathos and then exhortation (a standard recipe as we have seen in earlier chapters). She begins in a rather stiff G minor with a pseudo-academic hint of thematic imitation between top line and bass, and a *staccato*, startled or peremptory end to the first line (compare *Tradito, schernito* in *Così fan tutte* or Almaviva in *Vedro mentr'io sospiro*).

---

* Schikaneder confused the male and female names, Egyptologists say. Min is the name of the god. Pa is the male, Ta the female prefix. They were given Italian name-endings and so Pamino should be the hero, Tamina the heroine. But our hero Tamino is not an Egyptian. He has travelled from a far oriental country. It is only Pamina who has been incorrectly named, by the Queen of Night who probably wished her to be an heir of the Sun-trophy. Observe the fantasy involved in Pamina's abduction: Sarastro is no magician; quite incapable of turning anybody into some other shape. This is part of the old magic scenario.

† E. M. Batley has shown that Schikaneder borrowed this stage direction from Philip Hafner's *Megära oder die förchterliche Hexe*.

16

Zum Lei—den bin ich auser—ko-ren,

She continues with a plaintive phrase doubled by oboe and bassoon; the effect is plaintive in this key and at this tempo, but not quite apt to the sovereign of the starry heaven, more reminiscent of momentary sadness by a non-aristocrat in an *opera buffa*.

17

durch sie ging all' mein Glück ver—lo—ren, durch sie ging all' mein Glück ver—lo—ren,

She flares up impressively at mention of the 'Bösewicht', or criminal, who ran off with Pamina. The Queen's narration of the abduction is also convincing, with a poignant melodic middle part for bassoon doubling viola, and melancholy chromatic vocal line. Ex. 17 returns, and Pamina's cries for help, as reported by her mother who was too weak to render adequate help, are genuinely touching.

Rapidly the Queen snaps out of self-pity into her *allegro moderato* no-nonsense, and far from weak, instructions to Tamino. She has recovered her royal and magical composure, and also the voice and style of a *prima donna* in an *opera seria*, even to a big florid division of scales and arpeggios demanding powerful notes above the stave up to top F, a speciality of Josepha Hofer (as Ignaz Castelli remarked); this extreme of the soprano compass is again exploited in the Queen's second aria. In *Die Entführung* Constanze was asked to soar up to top D and move around, and Blondchen to run up to top E (like Faunus in *Ascanio*) but this is higher still. Ernest Newman felicitously described her as 'a vulture with the throat of a nightingale'.

18

e —————————————————————wig dein,

Having delivered this volley the Queen and her Ladies leave, or are perhaps rendered invisible since the mountains close again, leaving Tamino and Papageno alone in front of the temple. Tamino, hardly crediting what he has experienced, prays for strength in his quest.

He has been completely won to the cause of the Queen: naturally, since he is infatuated by the portrait of her daughter, and has been encouraged by her mother to go out and win Pamina for his wife. She is, herself, a mightily impressive lady with her violent dramatic exclamations and high-mettled bravura promises; she must sing Ex. 18 (not to mention Ex. 37 below) in the rock-like Fiordiligi manner and not, as we too often hear, like a dear little chirping bird. Do we, nevertheless, obtain such a favourable impression of her character from No. 4? I think not. She began quite graciously in her recitative, almost the female Sarastro that she would wish to be. But the G minor part of her Aria, where she acts the helpless and distraught little woman, does not ring true, and the clues have been discreetly laid in Mozart's music, as I have suggested. Brigid Brophy wants us to believe that the Queen was originally to represent the goddess Isis, the Queen of Heaven, *regina coeli*. A case could also be argued, on Robert Graves lines, that she is the White Goddess, the original Matriarch, a figure at once inspiring and destructive, the goddess of air and darkness, known formerly as Astarte and as Luna.

The 'sternflammende Königin', starblazing Queen, 'Astrafiammante' as she was known to nineteenth century audiences of Mozart's *Il flauto magico*, is white, silver, infinitely bright, the more because she is so surrounded by darkness. If there was an earlier Schikaneder libretto she would have been ruler not of the dark sky but of bright light; the wicked magician would have dwelt in subterranean darkness. Presently, in the extant *Zauberflöte*, the temple of the sun will be reached, and then it will be obvious that Night and Day are opposed forces, Evil and Good. But already Mozart had implied in No. 4 that the starry Queen is not necessarily on the side of the angels.

At her first appearance in Act II she will tell Pamina the nature of the struggle between her and the abductor of Pamina. If we are to view the whole drama in perspective we had better learn it now. Our Queen of Night was the wife of the Priest of the Sun. As such she expected that the sovereignty would descend by matrilinear succession, that is according to the old tradition of husband-sacrifice, characteristic of myths in which all men were subservient to the mother-goddess. The Old Law prescribed that, upon the death of Pamina's father, Astrafiammante would take other husbands who in turn would have to die after a term of office until eventually Pamina finally succeeded her mother. But in all these myths the second stage of civilization arrives when one husband rebels and establishes male succession, abolishing the rite of husband-sacrifice. Pamina's father has evidently prepared for this palace revolution, just before his death, by giving the emblem of his sovereignty, the sevenfold circle of the sun, into Sarastro's keeping. The Queen very naturally wished to counter this revolution; but Sarastro took Pamina, heir to the throne of Night, under his own wing so that she would in due course serve as consort to his own successor, thus re-establishing the old link between night and day on a new patrilinear and patriarchal footing.

All this is not wild guessing, even though Sir James Frazer and Robert Graves wrote their books long after Mozart and Schikaneder were dead. *The Golden Bough* and *The White Goddess* were constructed from source-material already printed and known in 1791 Vienna. Schikaneder, self-educated and intellectually inquisitive, was always looking for useful ideas. Mozart, more carefully educated, knew about classical mythology; antique lore was studied, to a greater or lesser extent, by all educated persons until the middle of the twentieth century. Carl Gieseke may have helped with a reference or more. The real authority in Mozart's Vienna on rites in ancient Greece, and on antique scholarship, was Ignaz von Born, supposedly the prototype of Sarastro in *Die Zauberflöte*, a prominent Freemason who died during the summer of 1791, and whom Mozart had known since 1784, the time of his initiation into the Craft. In that year Born produced *The Mysteries of Egypt*, a work based on classical sources. In 1787 he inscribed Mozart's autograph book with a mysterious prayer to Apollo which may yield esoteric meaning to Freemasons. The

Queen of Night's behaviour can be given a further motivation, not only masonic: women are always jealous of any activity in which their men engage without them.

There are a few wild inconsistencies in the plot of *Die Zauberflöte* which strongly suggest that Schikaneder altered it drastically. But the foregoing paragraph is to explain why I think Mozart was aware of the new libretto before he composed No. 4.

We left Tamino intent on his quest. Papageno was with him throughout this vision of the 'star-blazing Queen'. Now he reminds Tamino of the frustrating padlock through which, doubled by bassoons, he tries to converse at the beginning of **No. 5, Quintet**, *allegro* in B flat major (the same as No. 4). Papageno's attempts are at once amusing and memorably tuneful, consistent with all the music in his role. Oboes, clarinets, bassoons, horns in high B flat, and strings are involved, not all at once.

Now it is Tamino's turn to echo the Queen's words and confess that he is too weak to help. The music turns to F major as the Ladies return and remove the padlock by the Queen's compassionate order (not entirely altruistic, it will be discovered). The five characters unite in one of the prim moral stanzas that abound in this score: the world would be a happier place if all liars had their mouths padlocked. Oboes mellifluously punctuate this wise saw.

The orchestra moves back to B flat major and the first Lady gives Tamino a golden flute (actually it is made of oak and gilded, we learn in the second act finale); the presentation is made to a phrase which reappears, barely noticed, at the end of this quintet. This should be a solemn moment, for earnest commentators, yet it is set to thoroughly Papageno-type music.

The cheerfulness is mellowed for another moralizing quintet with gentle descending scales for violins. It may pass unnoticed that Mozart, with a musician's innate tact, does not include the flute in this ensemble. Some have opined that it was because he hated the flute as a musical instrument, but that was in his young Paris days. In all his late works the flute is sparingly but most eloquently used.

After the moral—such a flute is priceless, since it can increase human happiness (the Ladies have already promised that it has protective powers and can change sadness into joy in those who hear it)—the music chops its way into G minor and Papageno takes his leave, but is told by the Ladies that he must accompany the Prince to Sarastro's fortress. Now we hear the name of the magician; it derives from Zoroaster and Zarathustra. Papageno is not at all pleased: the Ladies them-selves have told him that this adversary eats Papagenos for breakfast and throws the remains to his dogs.

21

Nein, da—für be-dank' ich mich.

The semiquaver figure at the end of this example is much used, and connects with Papageno elsewhere in the opera, perhaps rhythmically even with the panpipes of Ex. 9.

The Ladies promise Papageno that the Prince will protect him and, in E flat major, give him a ring of bells which, according to Schikaneder, resemble 'wooden laughter': Mozart again forbears to bring them into the music. Another quintet of moralizing and farewell appears to terminate the current proceedings. Hindsighted knowledge picks on one musical phrase in the leavetaking.

22

Le——bet wohl, auf Wie—der——sehn!

The violin figure in semiquavers will recur in Act II, very aptly.

The two men and three ladies are about to separate on their several ways when Tamino and Papageno, as an afterthought, ask for some instruction about how to get there.

Now the clarinets join the orchestra, *andante*, still in B flat, with plucked violins and high bassoons, a serene yet not static colour. *Sotto voce* the ladies explain that three boys, young, fair and clever, will guide them on their journey and give them directions. The musical colouring of this final section is magically beautiful and strange; the effect recurs, always varied but identifiable, whenever these Boys appear, usually in an aerial car. So this quintet ends in a haze of tranquil optimism.

The scene changes to a splendid Egyptian room. Later we gather that it is part of Sarastro's fortress. Two slaves bring cushions, carpets and a splendid Turkish table ('prächtig', which I translate 'splendid', is Schikaneder's favourite word, as it was his spectacular ideal). A third slave joins them, highly delighted at the prospects of violent death in store for their hated master Monostatos. His charge, Pamina, has escaped. Monostatos was lusting after her as usual when she cried aloud the name of Sarastro. In terror the Moor turned round. Pamina promptly ran to the canal near by, jumped into a gondola and rowed off towards a forest of palmtrees, perhaps farther to her mother's kingdom.

These slaves are sometimes presented as blackamoors, like Monostatos. But they are no friends of his and are more likely white second-class initiates of the Sun Temple, as described in *Sethos*. Now the voice of Monostatos is heard calling for his slaves to bring fetters. All three slaves, seeing that he has Pamina by the hand, are appalled and run away. But other slaves are dragging Pamina into the room, led by a triumphant Monostatos. He is a black, often so described, and as such destined eventually to find his own element in the kingdom of Night. Schikaneder refers to him as a Moor, but he lacks the pride and nobility of an Othello, or the spirituality of the Afro-American negros that we in the twentieth century admire as Black. He is a golliwog, the sort of comic black doll much adored by white European children, except that, looks apart, Monostatos is not lovable at all. In our racially sensitive age Monostatos is a problem for operatic producers. He is lecherous, ambitious and totally dishonest. I have seen a *Zauberflöte* in New York with a black Pamina and a white Monostatos: it made perfect sense except when Sarastro says, 'Your soul is black as your face.' At this point one was reminded that there are wicked blacks as well as wicked whites. For Schikaneder there was no colour problem—the blackest man he ever saw was probably an Italian chimney-sweep; this has been worked into a theory that *Die Zauberflöte* was a diatribe against Italian opera (the Queen of Night sings Italian florid divisions, remember), but not even an all-black *Zauberflöte* will persuade me that this theory is worth consideration. Monostatos is a wicked golliwog; the Queen of Night is a wicked white woman; they belong together, and racialism is as far away as Betelgeuse. Mozart even equated Monostatos with Turkish music, as can be faintly sensed now in **No. 6, Terzett**, *allegro molto* in G major, *Du feines Täubchen, nur herein*, with flutes, oboes, bassoons, horns and strings. It begins noisily and could well involve cymbals and bass drum in Turkish style. Monostatos is promising Pamina instant death for her escape; she only regrets the pain that her death will cause her dear mother. She swoons on a sofa and Monostatos dismisses the slaves.

Mozart makes a pretty transition here. At this moment Papageno looks through a window into the room and his theme is very close to that which accompanied Monostatos's command to his slaves.

23

Papageno cheerfully walks into the room, having seen nothing untoward, only people.

24

The tune is pure Papageno though close to the Three Ladies' Exs. 6 and 8, likewise the twiddle for flutes. Papageno's song about the pretty lady white as chalk is probably addressed to the portrait which he has in his hand (Brigid Brophy's sensible suggestion). At this moment he and Monostatos see one another: the golliwog and the parrot-man. Both are horrified, each convinced that the other must be the devil. They stammer fearful exclamations and run away in opposite directions.

We know that Papageno is timid and unheroic by nature. Monostatos has presented a more boastful front but he too is scared by the unknown, a natural ally of the pre-Enlightenment court of Astrafiammante. He is corrupt and malevolent, but powerless—superior forces always prevent him from accomplishing his evil designs, however petty they are. What is he doing in the courts of Goodness and Light, as we shall discover them to be? What, for that matter, was friendly, kind-hearted Papageno doing in the female court of Chaos and old Night? If we pretend that the plot of the opera was *not* changed (and this is necessary for enjoyment of a live performance in the theatre) then they must be the misfits who find their own level in the end, Monostatos with the defeated Queen of Night, Papageno living happily among the second-class initiates of wisdom and goodness. It makes sense that Monostatos represents the traitors in the Viennese Masonic Lodge who denounced their Brothers to the police as anti-monarchical revolutionaries.

Pamina recovers from her swoon, calling for her mother in vain, regarding her loneliness as more bitter than actual death. Papageno returns: if there are black birds, then why not black men? He turns and sees the sitter for the portrait he is holding. She does not recognize him though she admits her identity. He tests it by the portrait, feature for feature. It is a persuasive likeness except that the hands and feet are missing. He relates how he came to assist Tamino, the lover-rescuer, and how they have been held up in their rescue-operation by the non-appearance of the Three Boys who were supposed to be their map-readers. Pamina warns Papageno that he risks torture and death by his presence here. She asks him the time; he answers 'close to midday'—this is apparently of strong masonic significance, meaning that positive action is due.

They are about to leave together when Pamina conceives reasonable doubts as to Papageno's genuineness. He protests his affection for the family, even though he has no Papagena to love. Pamina sweetly counsels him to patience.

Together they sing about the inevitability of perfect human love, in **No. 7, Duet,** *andantino* in masonic E flat major, *Bei Männern welche Liebe fühlen*, with clarinets, bassoons, horns and strings. This was the piece which won the hearts of the opera's first audience, and no wonder. It is another moralistic number, about how love makes the world go round.

25

The warmth and intimacy, even among two characters who have never met and are not in love with one another, are very German and purely typical of this opera: it is short-phrased, very diatonic, but naturally *bel canto*. The second verse is lightly decorated and followed by a vivid and variegated coda in which Pamina's vocal line becomes progressively more florid and ecstatic as she thinks about this ideal emotion. Papageno accompanies her in this love-duet, not as lover, but as another seeker after love, another class but for the moment at one with her.

Legend has it that Mozart made an earlier setting of this duet which Schikaneder rejected. After the composer's death Schikaneder announced a performance including two unpublished numbers. This may have been one. As the other Hermann Abert proposed a duet for Tamino and Papageno in B flat major, *Pamina, wo bist du*, the music of which was found in the Theater an der Wien. It occurred before the Quintet No. 12 in Act II.

The scene changes again for the **Finale, No. 8**. It represents a grove in which stand three temples dedicated to Wisdom, Reason and Nature, all three connected by pillars. The promised helpers, The Three Boys, each carrying a silver palm twig, have led Tamino here and now give him a word or two of advice about his mission, *larghetto* in C major, with flutes, clarinets, bassoons, muted trumpets, three trombones and muffled drums as well as strings. He is to be steadfast, tolerant, and discreet, and then he, a young lad, will conquer like a man.

The orchestral introduction to this scene is most unconventionally scored: it looks odd on the page and the sound is unlike anything heard so far. The first bar sets the scene of the temples, with two rhythms, variously notated: the rhythm of five notes looks back to Ex. 1, the opening chords of the overture, and is given evocatively to two trombones, bassoons and cellos; the muted trumpets are used, like the other instruments, to underline the strong beats. Then the melody of the Boys' trio floats along in sixths, buoyed up by the dominant pedal above and in the middle of the tune, with brass punctuation to enhance solemnity and a light sustained bass on bassoons and cellos. It is at this moment that Mozart reveals the emotional centre of the opera, for which the foregoing scenes were an almost irrelevant preparation.

The continuation of this melody is more conventional and pompous. But then the Boys begin the melody again, adding their own unoperatic treble voice quality (it is essential that they be boy trebles, not adult sopranos, if the strangeness of the effect is to be felt). Tamino, with strings and a triplet accompanying figure above the dotted bass rhythm of Ex. 26, asks them if he will be able to rescue Pamina. They answer, almost mechanically, that they cannot tell him; he must be 'standhaft, duldsam und verschwiegen', in short he must behave like a man. They walk away to Ex. 26.

Tamino is left alone, with string accompanied recitative as befits the situation.

He approves the Boys' advice but is puzzled that they have led him, not to a wizard's palace, but evidently to some holy sanctuary, a residence of the gods. The very portals and pillars signify that cleverness and hard work and the arts live here. The pace of the music increases to *allegro* and he breaks into a snatch of *arioso*; bassoons, sustaining the harmony, are added to the strings. The inscriptions on the temples have surprised Tamino into a loftier tone of voice: where action rules and idleness slinks away, vice will not easily gain control. He himself must take action, *allegro assai* with flutes and oboes as well as the instruments already playing. He will boldly enter the portals, since his intentions are noble, frank and pure. The criminal shall tremble, and Pamina be rescued (her name rouses Tamino to unwritten, nowadays usually unsung, vocal flourishes); it is his duty.

He walks over to the temple on the right, with fairly jaunty steps in D major (they recall the first orchestral bars of No. 5). He opens the door and is about to enter when a bass voice from within orders him to retreat ('Zurück!'). Slightly taken aback he decides to try another door, the left-hand temple; his walk is in G minor now, more cautious perhaps; but here too the response is the same. He approaches the third door in C minor, and this time he knocks. Strings and bassoons slide into A flat major, *adagio*; first violins creep up the arpeggio and an old man, dressed in priestly garments, opens the door and inquires the impetuous stranger's purpose within this temple. This Priest, as explained above, is in modern cast lists referred to as *Der Sprecher* ('The Speaker'). But in this, his principal scene, he only sings, most eloquently with a mature bass-baritone voice, and though it is a scene in recitative (accompanied by strings with occasional and significant intrusions by woodwind) everybody acknowledges it as a scene of prime musical importance in which the Old Priest must be sung superbly—by someone like Ludwig Weber or Hans Hotter or Dietrich Fischer-Dieskau. Maybe Mozart thought less ambitiously and settled for Herr Winter, but having troubled to write great or at least impressive music for a company whose work he knew well, he insisted, I reckon, on a real bass singer, who was Herr Moll. Mozart was used to high musical standards.

Tamino, *andante* with woodwind in E flat major, discreetly forgets to mention his quest for Pamina. The awe-inspiring interlocutor impels him to answer that he is seeking love and virtue. The Priest has seen through him: fine words, but useless to one who is enflamed by thoughts of death and vengeance (a menacing unison in C minor). Tamino only wants revenge on a criminal: but criminals are not to be found in this temple. Impetuously Tamino mentions Sarastro and learns that this man is the ruler of Wisdom's Temple. The bottom drops out of the vessel carrying Tamino on his sacred quest: with a protesting diminished seventh chord on strings *tremolando* he declares that all is hypocrisy, and he begins to walk away. The Old Priest keeps the conversation going, politely and gently, so that Tamino does not actually move out of earshot. The young man is clearly mistaken in his information and must explain himself. If he hates Sarastro, then why, and what is his proof? Tamino gives the evidence of a sorrowing woman. The Priest (and by now it is plain that he knows the full story, even the latest details through the three aerial messenger boys) warns Tamino that female gossip is not to be trusted; Sarastro could provide a true and convincing defence. The Priest admits that Sarastro removed Pamina from her mother's control, though oaths and duty prevent him from revealing her present whereabouts. Tamino's bewilderment will only be enlightened 'when the hand of friendship leads him into the eternal bond of sanctity'. This long conversation has been conducted in accompanied recitative, but every exchange has been set to music of a speaking eloquence close to *arioso* such as opera was only to know in the later works of Wagner and Verdi where aria and recitative are equally striking, in Debussy's *Pelléas* and in Richard Strauss's conversational operatic music, inspired by this very scene. The level of musical intensity is set in the Old Priest's first question, an invitation to *bel canto*.

27

Wo willst du, kühner Fremdling, hin? Was suchst du hier im Hei—ligtum?

(I have given him the *appoggiatura* that such a noble soul deserves.) His scene with Tamino, much of it quotable for its superb music-drama quality, ends with this glorious statement of hopeful idealism.

28

So—bald dich führt der Freundschaft Hand ins Heiligtum zum ew'———gen Band.

It is underlined by cellos and sometimes basses. A minor has been reached, a blank and lonely key after strongly emotional and thoughtful flat keys, one after another.

Having impressed Ex. 28 on the young man's intellect (if everybody in the world were to observe its teaching, our planet would be a better place to live in; let me rephrase it: 'your life will cease to be blinkered when you and all your friends decide to work together for an ideal society') the Old Priest shuts the door.

Tamino is left alone in the A minor of eternal night. When will day dawn? He is answered at once by the orchestral cellos with Ex. 28, above which voices from within the temples, supported by soft trombones for churchly solemnity, murmur, 'Soon, young man, or never.' Tamino hears them and is emboldened to ask these distant voices whether Pamina still lives. To the same music they answer that she is alive. Tamino reverts to joyful recitative, full of gratitude and accompanied by strings. He takes his magic flute and plays a hymn of thankfulness to the immortal gods, *andante* in C major, *Wie stark ist nicht dein Zauberton*. Now for the first time we hear Benedikt Schack play his magic flute.

29

The effect of his flute-playing is Orphean: as he plays Ex. 29 wild beasts of all sorts emerge to listen to the music; the birds even chirrup with him. When he ceases playing, either at a rest or when he sings, they run away, to reappear when he plays the flute again. Schikaneder's repertory used animals on stage, usually children dressed as animals, as often as possible since audiences adored to see them. An early print suggests that they were all monkeys looking pathetically like misshapen golliwogs. But they are not Monostatos, and the more diverse and charming the fauna available, the more effective.

Tamino is really trying to enchant Pamina here by his fluting but (C minor) she does not arrive, however beguilingly he plays. His *arioso* peters out, and in despair he runs up the G major scale. Its last five notes correspond with those of Papageno's panpipes, and these answer him from the distance, repeatedly. The answer excites a *presto* (oboes, bassoons and strings, no flute) of ecstatic joy stopped only for delightful pauses at 'perhaps' ('vielleicht'). Tamino runs after the sound of Papageno's pipes.

But in the wrong direction. No sooner has Tamino gone than Pamina (now rid of her fetters) and Papageno hurry on (*andante* in G major, *Schnelle Füsse, rascher Mut*), to a very Viennese popular sort of tune. Unless they find Tamino soon they will be caught and slaughtered. The orchestra is still oboes, bassoons, horns and strings. Pamina, with triplet accompaniment, calls for the handsome young man. Papageno shushes her and uses his panpipes; they hear Tamino's flute to their delight and hurry in its direction. The orchestral flute returns to the pit orchestra.

But they are intercepted by Monostatos who mocks their last words and calls his slaves to tie them up, with typical patter music full of gesticulation. As a weapon against this rigid music Papageno dares the cheekier enchantment of his magic bells. The strings are playing the tune before the *stromento d'acciajo* starts up in the wings.

30
[Allegro]

The magic works. Monostatos and his slaves with all their instruments of imprisonment are captivated by the sound and dance away as they hear Ex. 30, almost a march rather than a dance. There is a full pause (Mozart's stage direction is enigmatic), perhaps filled with jubilant Glockenspiel, or hearty laughter by Pamina and Papageno. These two moralize again in a folkish duet, like the Ladies' farewell to Tamino in No. 1, like Schubert's *Heidenröslein* some years later, probably like some well known Viennese song. If every brave man had such bells he would lose his enemies; harmony between friends helps everyone in trouble.

Now trumpets and drums by themselves play a fanfare, *allegro maestoso* in C major, and an off-stage chorus salutes Sarastro. Papageno wishes he were a mouse and could crawl into a hole—what can they tell Sarastro? Pamina's answer is one of the great affirmations, Nietzsche's Yes-statements, in all music; *Die Wahrheit*—'the truth, even though to tell it were a crime'.

31
[Allegro maestoso]

Die Wahr-heit, die Wahr-heit, sei sie auch Ver—brechen!

Here Schikaneder wrote another moralizing quatrain about Truth and subservience to rulers. Mozart did not set it: he had made his musical stand, and the Masonic rule of discretion and ethical compromise with strict truth did not fit here. He moved straight into the grand triumphal entry of Sarastro in C major, with oboes, bassoons, trumpets, timpani and strings.

A procession enters and completes its salutation to Sarastro. Although this is a Brotherhood along masonic lines it includes sopranos and altos. They do not have to be choirboys, in my belief are not: they are not priestesses either but the lay wives and children of second-class initiates. With their men, and the bachelor priests, they are praising their model and idol Sarastro in strong harmonious C major. As the orchestra completes the paean Sarastro himself enters in a triumphal chariot drawn by three-plus-three lions. He dismounts, I think (though the libretto does not mention it), to a repeat of the Ex 1 chords, now in F major, *larghetto*, with the new addition of Masonic bassett-horns to the woodwind section—they sound mellow but rather straitlaced. Pamina kneels and begs Sarastro's forgiveness. It was to evade the Moor's unwelcome attentions that she was forced to escape. She too sings in a sort of exalted recitative, a special feature of *Die Zauberflöte*. Sarastro answers likewise (in what Bernard Shaw called the only music which might without blasphemy be put into the mouth of God): he knows her loving heart (oboes and basset-horns in yearning thirds), her love for another man (marvellous flute colouring). He will not forbid her to go freely. To fluttering C major music Pamina protests her longing for her mother. The wind section stops still; Sarastro interrupts: Pamina's mother would ruin her chance of happiness if given an opportunity. With an affecting rising sixth, doubled poignantly by woodwind, Pamina puts her case for the loyalty she feels towards her mother. Another orchestral freeze: the Queen is a proud woman. Pamina must be guided by masculine wisdom if she is not to wander from the boundaries of her best potential. (He is trying to tell her that she will be Queen in his dominion when she acquires her King.)

Abruptly the music switches into F major, *allegro*. Monostatos fussily conducts his prisoner Tamino before Sarastro. Pamina and Tamino, with heartfelt string arpeggios, recognize one another at first sight, and fall into a passionate embrace, much to the surprise of the chorus. Monostatos is shocked and tries to separate them. He kneels to Sarastro reminding him of his loyalty and his prisoner's naughty plan to abduct Pamina with the aid of the weird birdman. His fluttering, quasi-Turkish music continues. Sarastro rewards him with seventy-seven strokes of bastinado. Monostatos is led away while the chorus approves of Sarastro's unprejudiced justice (but what wrong had Monostatos done, unless Sarastro knew about his lecherous designs, in which case why was he allowed to look after Pamina?).

In plain, accompanied recitative Sarastro announces that the two strangers will be conducted, with cloaked heads, into the temple of initiation. Papageno, let alone Tamino, had not applied for initiation, but sacks are shoved on to their heads and off they are led while the chorus, trombones, basset-horns, and the rest of the orchestra, praise virtue and justice, mankind's way to heavenly life, in a firm but rather stiff concluding C major chorus, during which Sarastro himself leads Pamina away.

6

The second act deals with the initiation of the new candidates and the conquest of Pamina's power-motivated mother. Tamino has quite willingly accepted Sarastro's suggestion that he submit to the trials which will make him an initiate of the Sun Temple; his candidature, supported by true love and the magic power of music, is bound to succeed. His companion Papageno showed no willingness to undergo any sort of trial at all; but he was pulled into the trials nevertheless. Even with the promise of a bird-wife, and the assistance of two musical instruments, he is, we know, sure to be ploughed.

Before we condemn Schikaneder, for embroiling Papageno in this sacred ritual, as an impious vulgarian, we should consider that Sarastro's philosophy embraces both high and low, eternal and transitory. The Three Boys have told us that stability and tolerance and discretion are the virtues of a successful questor; but the aim of all philosophy is to know yourself—as Papageno certainly does. Even in the Temple of Wisdom life proceeds on several levels. Papageno and his family will have a useful place in it. If the Queen of Night and her entourage are overthrown, in Sarastro's dominion you can be fairly hopeful that they will not be killed but merely converted unto useful and contented citizens.

Act II begins in a forest of silver palmtrees with golden leaves (the Three Boys were carrying sprays of them at their first entrance in No. 8). In the centre, where the tallest trees grow, stands a great pyramid. Round it can be seen eighteen (i.e. three plus three times three) thrones for the eighteen priests of the sun. Each throne is surmounted by a pyramid and a large horn (or is it a trumpet?) of black and gold (damaskeen?).

Sarastro and his fellow-priests enter in a solemn procession; each is carrying a palm branch. 'A March with wind instruments accompanies the procession,' writes Schikaneder. This is the Priests' **March, No. 9,** *andante* in F major, with one flute, basset-horns, bassoons, horns, three trombones and strings, all marked *sotto voce*, which Mozart wrote out only just before the overture, two days before the first performance. Then in his hurry he resorted to a march from Wranitsky's *Oberon* (as E. J. Dent shows with musical illustrations in *Mozart's Operas*) though Mozart did repay the loan with inventive musical interest and two preliminary sketches, both of which he rejected. He also added strings to Schikaneder's specified wind band. I quote the first eight bars for identification.

32

They take their seats. After a pause Sarastro addresses the initiates of Isis and Osiris in tones of greatest earnestness. Their assembly today is of momentous importance. Tamino, twenty years old and the son of a King, is waiting at the northern gate of their temple,* eager to be initiated into their rites. It is their solemn duty to tender the hand of friendship to him.

Three Priests rise in turn to ask if this candidate is virtuous, discreet, beneficent (the Boys' 'tolerance' has here become a more active quality); Sarastro reassures them. If they approve the Prince's application, let them follow Sarastro's example. He raises his brazen musical instrument to his lips, the others all do likewise, and

---

* This geographical detail, seemingly unimportant (except to Jacques Chailley who construes it as a point of blank darkness), is a direct loan from Terrasson's *Sethos*.

together they sound the Threefold Chord ('dreimalige Akkord'), as shown in Ex. 4 and discussed there. Sarastro is moved by, and grateful for, their unanimity: this is because Pamina's father bequeathed the Kingdom of the Sun to Sarastro as regent until Pamina was ready to succeed with her chosen husband. Tamino is a sort of godson or Isis-son to Sarastro, and the rightful succession is his concern and responsibility. Sarastro prays that the initiates may be spared the censure of prejudice, even though wisdom and reason could annihilate it as if it were some spider's web, and it could not shake the columns of their temple. Nevertheless this prejudice does exist, and will be dispelled as soon as Tamino has attained full initiation. The gods have destined gentle, virtuous Pamina for Tamino—wherefore Sarastro removed her from the influence of her mother who, in her *folie de grandeur*, hopes to trick the populace, by superstitious and crafty propaganda, into destroying their temple. Her evil design will be frustrated when Tamino joins the initiates, fortifies their building with his assistance, rewards virtue and punishes vice. His oration is greeted with another blast of Ex. 4.

Now the Speaker-Priest makes his first contribution. He questions whether such a young man, of royal and cosseted upbringing, can withstand the tests of initiation. Sarastro answers that Tamino, above princedom, possesses the gift of humanity. If he dies in the ordeal he will enjoy the company of Isis and Osiris, and divine joy, sooner than the rest of them. Again his eloquence is applauded with the threefold blast of Ex. 4. Sarastro orders the prince and his companion to be led into the courtyard of the temple. The Speaker must then fulfil his sacred office and instruct the newcomers in the duties of wisdom and the power of the gods.

The Speaker, with another priest, departs. The remaining initiates cluster together for a hymn to the gods, sung by Sarastro with choral refrain. It is *O Isis und Osiris, schenket*, **No. 10, Arie mit Chor**, *adagio* in F major, with basset-horns, bassoons, three trombones, two violas and cello, another example of unconventional, powerfully evocative instrumentation in this opera. No string-bass, no violins, but low-lying textures all the time. It is a binary hymn, with a choral refrain at the end of each half. Schikaneder thought of it purely as a chorus; Mozart saw the effect of a noble solo for a *basso cantante* whose melody would, as in much early music, trace the bass line of the music, for example here:

33

stärkt mit Ge—duld   sie   in   Ge—fahr.

The text is partly translated from Terrasson's *Sethos*.

> O Isis and Osiris, grant the spirit of wisdom to this new pair. Strengthen them in danger, let them see the fruits of their trial and, if they should descend to the grave, take them to your mansions.*

> * 'Isis, ô grande déesse des Egyptiens, donne votre esprit au nouveau serviteur qui a surmonté tant de périls et de travaux pour se présenter à vous. Rendez-le victorieux de même dans les épreuves de son âme en le rendant docile à vos loix, afin qu'il mérite d'être admis à vos mystères.'

Some people, even good Mozartians, find this scene a trial as painful as any witnessed hereafter in *Die Zauberflöte*. They find the two musical numbers, 9 and 10, slow and dark and dreary, the long spoken ritual scene interminably heavy. Certainly the whole scene is solemn: the spectator must not be alienated. It is essential that Nos. 9 and 10 be played not fast but with a powerful underlying pulse, that No. 10 be sung at least as beautifully as Wolf's *Michelangelolieder* or Brahms's *Vier ernste Gesänge*, and that the dialogue be spoken as if spontaneously, not like prepared speeches. The scene is a rite, like Anglican Holy Communion; but the Bidding in that service is only tolerable when the Priest says it as if he had just invented it. The solemn sentences, 'Who in the same night. . . .', can make a religiously inspiring effect when properly spoken, or they can be parrot-gabbled and turn away the more thoughtful in the congregation. So with this first scene of the second act in *Die Zauberflöte*. It should, in short, sound new and uplifting, not familiar and mind-blurring.

Sarastro leads his priests away. The scene changes to a small courtyard of the Temple. There are pyramids, pillars, lofty doors in the Egyptian style, many in ruins; and there are thornbushes. It is night-time. Thunder is audible in the distance. The Speaker and his fellow-Priest lead Tamino and Papageno into this courtyard, remove the sacks from their heads and withdraw. Tamino wonders where they are, on this dreadful night. Papageno is terrified out of all conscience by the noisy thunder. Be a man, recommends Tamino. Papageno answers that he wishes he were a girl.

The Speaker and two other Priests (singers) return, carrying torches. The Speaker formally asks their intentions in the temple. Tamino is driven by Friendship and Love for which he is willing to give his life and undertake every sort of ordeal in the pursuit of wisdom: his reward, he knows, will be Pamina. He gives his hand to the Speaker in promise. Second Priest makes similar inquiries of Papageno who will not fight, does not value wisdom, desires only sleep, food and drink, and if possible a wife. The Priest insists that he must undergo the trials, facing death, to obtain his desire. Papageno would rather stay single, even in the knowledge that Sarastro has found a female counterpart for him, his own Papagena. If death is a risk, he will still remain a bachelor, though he is willing to remain silent while she appears before him. Tamino and Papageno shake hands on the pact of silence, the beginning of their ordeals. The two singing Priests embark on a **Duet, No. 11,** *andante* in C major, with (curiously) full orchestra. *Bewahret euch vor Weibertücken* is quite cheerful and mellifluous, a moralizing hymn about the importance of not talking, and the painful death which has befallen all who, during this ordeal, were tempted to converse with gossipy women. For the sake of the drama's oath of silence it must be sung; yet it is not musically out of Mozart's top drawer, at least not until the *sotto voce* sprightly coda about 'Tod und Verzweiflung'.

The Priests leave Tamino and Papageno alone in this dark place, Papageno extremely concerned about the darkness. Almost at once the stage trapdoors open and up come the Queen's Three Ladies. **No. 12, Quintet,** *allegro* in G major, with full orchestra except for clarinets, *Wie, wie, wie?*, gives us women at their most gossipy. What, they ask, are the Queen's expeditionary forces doing in this dreadful place? They will never get out alive.

34

Allegro

Wie? wie? wie? ihr an diesem Schreckens—ort?

Strings double this three-part close harmony. The passage can be sung haughtily and insistently, but considering the texture and the key, and what follows, it may be as well to maintain the lighter characterization of the Ladies as we met them in Nos. 1 and 5. A flute is added to the strings for interludes between the concerted vocal phrases—here, though by no means always, it may refer to Tamino's magic flute.

Papageno, on being told that all is lost for him, begins to comment optimistically. Tamino urges him to keep quiet. The three phrases knit so nicely together that the Ladies must, by musical deduction, be presented non-seriously.

35 *3 Dam.*

Du, Pa—pa—ge-no! bist ver——lo—ren! Nein, nein, nein, das wär' zu

viel. *Tam.* Pa—pa——ge-no schweige still!

The Ladies warn these men that the Queen has secretly made her way into the temple, and that rumour reports scandalously about these priests and their un-savoury practices which lead the doer straight to Hell. Mozart sets these items of gossip in pattering quavers, with much vocal imitation between the Ladies, a vivid suggestion of female tittle-tattle. Tamino treats it with the prim contempt it deserves and contrives also to restrain Papageno's answers to a minimum. The Ladies are nonplussed by their failure to provoke conversation and conclude that the attempt had better be abandoned. The quintet can now get going in earnest: Papageno and Tamino, *sotto voce*, observe with delight that the Ladies have been shamefully routed, the Ladies sadly that they have failed.

36

Wir müs-sen sie- mit— Scham ver———las———sen:

Wir müssen sie mit Scham ver——las—sen:

Sie müssen uns mit Scham ver——lassen:

First Lady's vocal line is particularly memorable; it draws on the same melodic vein as Mozart's late clarinet music (though clarinets do not feature in this number). All five characters unite in a block-harmony moral: men are firm of purpose, and think before they speak—a joke where Papageno is concerned. As they reach the end of this chirpy concerted passage a chorus of Priests off-stage calls out that women are profaning the sacred precincts (loud unison in C minor). The Ladies are further terrified to hear 'a frightening chord with all instruments, thunder, lightning and percussion, as well as two loud claps of thunder'—Mozart now brings in the trumpets, trombones and timpani for *fortissimo* diminished sevenths by everyone, as the Ladies cry, 'Alas!' and disappear down their trap door. Papageno echoes their cry, in G minor, and falls to the ground in terror; his last 'Weh' is sustained after the orchestra has finished, according to the libretto's prescription.

The Threefold Chord, Ex. 4, is sounded and the Speaker, with two Priests bearing torches, comes to tell the initiates that they have passed this test. Tamino is hooded again and led to his next trial by the Speaker. Second Priest has to rouse Papageno from his pretended faint and encourage him to continue his pilgrimage— all this eternal walking could turn a man away from love, Papageno reckons.

8

The scene changes to a pretty garden with trees in horseshoe formation and an 'arbour of flowers and roses' in which Pamina is sleeping, her face lit up by the moon. A grassy bank is at the front of the stage.

Monostatos has found his way here. Was it for this tender plant that he was due to be thrashed on the soles of his feet? Luckily he was spared this time and his passion for his foreign flower is mounting again. He fans his ardent face with his hands, makes sure that nobody is about, and decides to try again, if only for one harmless little kiss. But first he will sing a song about it. His **Aria, No. 13**, *allegro* in C major, *Alles fühlt der Liebe Freuden*, with one piccolo, one flute, two clarinets and bassoons, and strings, is to be sung and played, directs Schikaneder, as softly as if the music were heard from far away. In character, with its flood of busy semiquavers and with a prominent piccolo, it is like the Turkish music then popular in Vienna, though there is no Turkish percussion. For Schikaneder and Mozart, I suspect, Moors and Turks were much the same, dark-skinned foreigners.

> Everyone enjoys the pleasures of love, flirting, hugging, kissing, except I who am hateful because black. Have I not got a heart, am I not flesh and blood? To be womanless for ever would be sheer hellfire. So I flirt and fall in love, because I am alive. Pardon me, Moon, and hide for a while. I am captivated by this lovely white woman and must kiss her, so shut your eyes.

There are two verses, quite short and low-lying in vocal compass; Nouseul was really an actor. The aria is very cheerful and charming (thematically not far from the finale of the E flat piano concerto, K. 271, itself perhaps sparked by a C major symphony by Mysliviček, heard by Mozart in 1770), and encourages us to regard Monostatos sympathetically and consider him harshly treated, even if he does fancy the ladies (Sarastro has, most negligently, omitted to provide him with a pretty Monostata). Before he can reach Pamina's side there is a clap of thunder, and the Queen of Night pops up through a trapdoor close to Pamina's floral couch and repels Monostatos with a word, 'Zurück!' He recognizes the newcomer as the Queen of Night, is fascinated to hear Pamina address her as Mother, and decides to eavesdrop. Mother, in high dudgeon, comes straight to the point: where is that young man? Pamina's answer tells the Queen that her matriarchal power (which she explains in a speech already summarized by me) is finished, unless—either Pamina persuades Tamino to escape before sunrise, through a trapdoor into the subterranean passages which lead to Astrafiammante's realm, or she plunges this dagger into Sarastro's heart. Pamina tries to defend Sarastro but the Queen is in no mood for argument. Full of unrighteous wrath she bursts into her most famous solo, the warhorse of every soprano who even hopes that she can reach top F.

It is **Aria, No. 14**, *allegro assai* in D minor, *Der Hölle Rache*, with flutes, oboes, bassoons, horns, trumpets, drums and strings—the orchestration tells us that the Queen must have a big, powerful voice, and the words confirm that she must sing with all the vehemence of a vitriol-thrower.

> Hellish revenge is boiling in my heart. Death and despair [*Schikaneder repeating No. 11*] blaze all around me. If you do not inflict a painful death on Sarastro, you are not my daughter. You will be outcast, for ever rejected. Gods of revenge, hear a mother's oath!

Mozart altered Schikaneder's text of which the last four lines rhymed neatly. Here, more than in No. 4, he draws on the *opera seria* type of *furibondo* aria. After a characteristic blast of initial D minor the Queen begins unmelodiously, as if in accompanied recitative, and does not launch into melody until 'Fühlt nicht durch dich' in F major. The Queen is too dramatic a person for pleasant tunes: she has a message to deliver at once. So it is all the more surprising when she gets to 'nimmermehr' and embarks on a huge and astronomical florid division.

37

[Allegro assai]

meine Tochter nimmermehr,

This sounds out of character only when it is sung in the chirpy manner described above. Delivered with righteous indignation under pressure Ex. 37 will convey the message intended by Mozart. The Queen sings Ex. 37 twice (Friede Hempel used to put the Fs up an octave the second time, with stunning effect, and I suspect the repeated notes should also be decorated on repetition). The quasi-recitative character is retained in the second half ('Verstossen sei auf ewig') because the words are essentially declamation not contemplation, not persuasive but insistent. This half also includes a florid division, in D minor and in triplets, with an allusion to the broken chords of Ex. 37. She ends unequivocally in eloquently accompanied recitative and promptly descends through the earth, having deposited a dagger in Pamina's astonished hand.

Pamina is certain that she could not contemplate such an act of violence upon a man so benevolent (and a friend of her father, as well). Now Monostatos, who has found the Queen's message a savoury contribution to his supper, sidles up to

Pamina and, revealing that he has heard it all, threatens to betray her unless she will let him make love to her. One word from him, and her Mother will be drowned by Sarastro in the subterranean initiatory waters. She continues to reject him (he protests too much that it is because he is black—perhaps in 1791 Vienna the sexual attractions of black men were unknown to the white female inhabitants) and he menaces her with the dagger which he has seized. She remains constant to Tamino.

He is about to stab her when Sarastro enters. At once Monostatos protests his innocence (the words 'Herr, ich bin unschuldig', often spoken, are not in Schikaneder's libretto, nor in Mozart's autograph), indeed his concern for the High Priest's safety. Sarastro answers that he knows the whole story, that Monostatos's soul is as black as his skin, and that he may only go unpunished because Pamina is the virtuous daughter of an unprincipled mother. Monostatos creeps away remarking that, if he cannot make the daughter, he had better try the mother (Goethe, in his unfinished sequel to *Die Zauberflöte*, had Monostatos married to the Queen of Night).

Sarastro tells Pamina his intentions. Tamino must survive the ordeals of initiation, and win her as his wife; her mother will return in disgrace to her fortress from the sewers in which she is at present roaming. The temple of wisdom is not vengeful, as he explains in his **Aria, No. 15**, *larghetto* in E major (rare Mozart key), *In diesen heilgen Hallen*, with flutes, bassoons, horns and strings.

> We do not know revenge in this holy place. If someone falls, he is raised up by love and friendship to better things. Traitors cannot survive when all people love one another and treachery is forgiven. Anybody who does not appreciate this is unworthy to be a human being.

This two-stanza strophic song is essentially the creed of Sarastro's temple and of the Freemasonry which Mozart and Schikaneder embraced. It is, I hope, the basic creed of everybody, no matter what ethical faith they subscribe to. It is also the positive answer to the negative, vengeful statement of No. 14.

The very short orchestral introduction calls a tune of benevolent comfort, and then Sarastro begins his smooth melody of idealism. Flutes are discreetly but pointfully added, again to suggest virtue. For the journey to a better land Mozart uses the conventional motif of walking in different directions with unchanging support. It occurs in music of all periods but this example is the most obvious, and possibly the most famous.

38

The last bars of each verse bring the solo voice on to the bass line, as often in Mozart's music for *bassi*. In the nineteenth century it was customary for a Sarastro to exploit his bottom E when he had one. This can be a boring or a sublime aria.

Sarastro leads Pamina away. The scene changes to a hall, again with roses and flowers and grassy banks, but with a door as well. Tamino and Papageno have been relieved of their hoods and are led in by the two priests for their next ordeal. It still involves total silence; they are to await the 'rattling trombones' ('röchelnde Posaune'—good old Ex. 4, it will turn out to be). The Priests depart, promising that they will meet their initiates again. This does not necessarily mean that they are the Men in Armour. They also reappear in Nos. 18 and 19.

Papageno is as talkative as ever and has to be shushed by Tamino continually. He longs for a drink: even water would be better than nothing. Immediately an ugly old woman enters, carrying a big mug of water which she offers to Papageno who at once strikes up a most indiscreet conversation with her. She admits her age to be eighteen years and two minutes, and she is in love with a man ten years older, called Papageno. The birdcatcher, horrified, throws the water in her face; this is not what he has endured ordeals for. Her name is ... she descends through a trapdoor before she can disclose it. Papageno once again promises to keep quiet.

Now a sort of aerial railway-carriage floats on. It contains a table laid for supper, the magic flute, Papageno's jingle-bells, and the Three Boys, who address the initiatory candidates in **No. 16, Terzetto**, *allegretto* in A major, *Seid uns zum zweiten Mal willkommen*, with flutes, bassoons, and strings, arguably the most ravishing musical number in the entire opera. At the beginning of No. 8 the Boys behaved like automata. Now they are allowed to behave naturally and they are natural as well as airy.

39

In close harmony, with strings alone, they welcome the initiates to Sarastro's kingdom; the Boys did not belong to the Queen at all (unless there was a plot-change, as of course there was). They have brought back the magic flute and the ring of bells which Sarastro has allowed them to use in their trials as well as a meal to fortify the candidates. They will reappear when the ordeals are over. Tamino must be brave, Papageno silent. Their hovering phrases, with copious trills and hardly any bass, high violins and floating woodwind, are unique. They bring their table of food out of the aircraft and set it on the floor, then fly away again in their aerial car.

Tamino is too idealistic to eat; he plays his flute instead. Papageno gladly tucks in, and congratulates Sarastro's excellent cook whose food encourages oaths of silence, as does his cellar. Pamina has followed the sound of the magic flute, but Tamino will not talk to her, and Papageno's mouth is too full. She, like the Three Ladies, is part of the Silence Ritual, and therefore partly a hallucination. So we will only half believe in the tragic **Aria, No. 17**, *andante* in G minor, with flute, oboe, bassoon (all solo) and strings—Nannina Gottlieb was still very young with an unformed mature voice.

> Ah, I feel that the joy of love is vanished for ever. Tamino, see my tears! If you feel no longing, then I must find repose in death.

The emotional power of this aria is partly in its chromatic harmony, partly in the carefully expressive soul-searching use of woodwind, especially flute and bassoon, partly in the magically eloquent vocal line. This is, beyond question, the most affecting aria Mozart ever wrote for any voice. When one thinks of G minor, other works or movements may spring to mind, but *Ach ich fühl's* goes automatically to the front of the queue, rightly. It begins most discreetly, in G minor for strings. Pamina enters almost at once. The word for 'feel' sharpens the minor third, like a twinge. The bassoon entry at bar 4 adds to her pain, as does the plangent oboe in the next bar, and then the melancholy flute (not Tamino's). For her memories of bliss she goes into B flat major and her vocal line becomes painfully chromatic, each half-step a dagger in the heart; the exploration of feeling makes her bolder, to dare arpeggios, divisions, expressive florid phrases touching and, like pressure on an aching open wound, retouching top B flat. Flute and oboe tempt her upward; bassoon and second violins suggest a false relation. She sticks by her chromatic grief-loaded vocal line; if the orchestra suggests something apt, she decorates it more eloquently. At her thought of death ('So wird Ruhe') she becomes calm and cool. Woodwind incite her to dramatic outcry but only for a moment. Her appeal to Tamino is concentrated on her expression of repose in death.

She follows this with a Ferraresi-style jump and a florid cadence. The orchestral postlude mixes six and three metres confusingly, because Pamina is confused. If you are following this chapter with a record, put the needle back and play it again, several times. G minor is the most intimate key for Mozart, and this his most intimate statement about G minor (compare it with K. 550, the Symphony No. 40, much more impersonal though very splendid and emotional too).

Pamina, distraught, wanders away. Papageno congratulates himself on his silence. The Threefold Chord (Schikaneder's 'röchelnde Posaune') is sounded; this ordeal has been survived. Tamino makes ready to move on but Papageno wants to feast further. Tamino leaves. Papageno's banquet must be finished, even if Sarastro's lions come to enjoy it. At once these lions appear; Papageno is appalled. Tamino returns, blows his flute and the lions vanish. The brass section again blows the Three-fold Chord, twice, between conversation. They both go, Papageno still unwillingly.

The scene changes to the priestly grove with pyramids as for No. 9. The priests enter solemnly, carrying illuminated pyramids of lantern size, Sarastro with them. They sing the **Chorus No. 18**, *adagio* in D major, with full orchestra barring clarinets, *O Isis und Osiris, welche Wonne*, its melody and texture strongly hymnological (in fact close to ecclesiastical hymns of the period), and decidedly static. It ends with an orchestral reminiscence of No. 15.

Tamino, hooded, is led on, and told by Sarastro that he has acted bravely, will proceed to win Pamina and, one day, rule wisely in this temple. Pamina, brought on wearing a hood, as an initiate all of a sudden, is told to bid him a last farewell. They do so in the **Terzetto, No. 19,** *andante moderato* in B flat major, *Soll ich dich, Teurer, nicht mehr sehn?* This has oboes, bassoons, and strings, and is as curiously scored as the beginning of No. 8. The dummy broken-chord accompaniment for bassoons, violas and cellos is unusually dark. It sets off the transparence of the vivid singing voices. Tamino tends to sing in close duet with Sarastro, Pamina commenting separately. At one stage Tamino quotes a whole, eloquent phrase from the clarinet quintet K. 581. A strange feature is that the names of Isis and Osiris have not yet been mentioned to the initiates, though the previous chorus was addressed to them.

Sarastro announces the hour of further initiation and farewell; the part-writing, Sarastro separated from the lovers, rather recalls J. S. Bach's in his Passion Music. The twelve strokes are musically portrayed. This trio must have been a late addition. When performed it renders Pamina's suicide scene unintelligible. The mood looks strongly forward to Beethoven, and particularly to *Fidelio*. In *Die Zauberflöte*, and some other compositions of the last period we do notice Mozart making for the nineteenth century, which he would have led as musician. Think only of his fiftieth symphony, thirty-fifth piano concerto, and his operas on Goethe's *Faust* and Shakespeare's *Tempest*.

The assembly disperses. Papageno, late in arrival, runs in, completely lost and blaming Tamino. He tries a door or two and is given the familiar 'Zurück!' with thunder and fire, as well as a noisy chord, not written down by Mozart. The same happens at the other door (Papageno is repeating Tamino's first test). He is tired and bored. Now the Speaker, with attendant Pyramid, comes to tell him that he will never be a first-class brother. Papageno only longs for a glass of wine. Magically it is produced from the ground. The Priests have departed. Papageno drinks the wine. It is fabulous and inspires him to recognize his ideal wish—a wife. He expounds it in **No. 20 Aria,** *andante* in F major, with flute, oboes, bassoons and horns (in verse 3), strings and glockenspiel. *Ein Mädchen oder Weibchen* is a three-stanza strophic aria that has become a German folk song, deservedly. Generations of musical people have agreed that, if a ring of bells could make music of its own accord, this is what would automatically emerge.

> Papageno would like a wife; a tender dove would be bliss. I'd enjoy food and drink, and rank myself among princes. If I don't get one I shall fret myself to death and burn in my own flames. But if a girl would kiss me I should be cured.

This, the most popular song in the whole opera, has a tune older than Mozart though best known nowadays as a radio identification signal. It was certainly aimed at the great Viennese public who adored it like every audience anywhere since. The three central verses are often performed in an order organized by Mozart against Schikaneder's wish. Schikaneder's third verse is 'Wird keine mir Liebe gewähren'. The Glockenspiel, named in the score as *stromento d'acciajo*, has a newly graced part for each refrain, normal eighteenth-century practice for once written out, because Mozart himself was not playing the instrument every night and could not rely on the invention of the player.

Papageno's prayer is answered: the ugly old lady reappears, dancing to his tune and supporting herself as best she can upon a walking-stick. She has discovered his longing and now binds Papageno to a bargain: either he will love her for ever as his wife; or he will be condemned to a diet of bread and water for all eternity. Papageno, inventing as many excuses as he can think of, consents. The old crone is transformed into a young girl dressed exactly like him. He has hardly time to stammer her name, Papagena, before the Priests remove her, because he is not yet worthy of her. 'Let the earth swallow me up,' says Papageno in despair. It does.

9

The **Finale, No. 21**, of the second act begins in a small garden (*kurz* because the full depth of the stage is required for the next scene, and audiences always grumble about slow scene-changes). *Andante* in E flat major, with clarinets, bassoons, and horns alone (no strings) the Three Boys arrive in their aerial car and descend, to music of weightless solemnity. This time they are alone on stage as they hail this day of triumph (strings have now been added), then observe the approach of Pamina who, almost beside herself with grief, has taken back her mother's dagger (Sarastro took charge of it, surely) and is addressing it as her bridegroom to whom she will shortly be married. The Three Boys warn her that suicide is a crime, but she pays no attention to them. Tamino has left her and her mother's curse pursues her; she will be better dead. The Boys clasp her hand as she is about to stab herself: Tamino (*allegro* in E flat major), they swear, is faithful, and loves her alone. They cannot divulge the reason for his silence in the scene of *Ach ich fühl's* (it is here that we realize the later addition of the Trio No. 19 which ended with an optimistic temporary farewell) but they can take her to him, an offer she gladly accepts. Together the four of them sing another *Spruch*: human weakness cannot separate two loving hearts since the gods watch over them. Pamina's music, of radiant eloquence throughout this scene, is particularly lovely here, with a sustained top B flat followed by a gleaming downward scale; the solo and concerted woodwind writing has remained as elegant and expressive as in the opening bars of the scene. The Boys lead Pamina away in a joyful and energetic coda which ends with four firm E flat chords, like No. 7.

The place to which they are bringing her is now seen. It is the meeting-point of two large mountains. Inside one is a raging waterfall, in the other a fiery furnace, both visible through iron grilles. On the fiery side the sky is bright red, on the watery side it is black with clouds. Between the mountains stands a pyramid with an inscription in transparent writing. The flats to each side represent crags and iron gates. Tamino, lightly clad and unshod (a reference to the clothing required for masonic initiation ordeals), is led here by two men in black armour, with lighted torches on their helmets.

This scene begins *adagio* in C minor, with three knocks on C by trombones and strings, answered plaintively by a hymnlike phrase for flutes, oboes, bassoons and cellos. The exchange is repeated on the dominant.

41

The knocks, it may be remarked, are in a different rhythm from those in Ex. 4, more like the beginning of Ex. 1. The woodwind responses slightly recall the Masonic Funeral Music K. 479a, and the phrases in major-mode form will return later. The strings now begin a fugato as accompaniment to the Two Men's recitation of the inscription. The melody which they sing is that of the German Lutheran chorale on Psalm XI, *Ach Gott, vom Himmel sieh darein*. Mozart sets it in the manner of J. S. Bach as a fugato chorale-prelude. This will seem perfectly reasonable to any modern listener. But in 1791 J. S. Bach was hardly more than a name in musical history, and in catholic Vienna the chorale-prelude meant nothing. Mozart had discovered and studied J. S. Bach's music through a Viennese friend, Baron Gottfried van Swieten, who gave Sunday morning parties at which Bach and Handel and their baroque contemporaries were discussed and performed. For a Viennese audience the chorale-prelude would sound solemn and antique, appropriate to the reading of this inscription. Mozart did not have to scour libraries for a book of Lutheran chorales: he could have found *Ach Gott vom Himmel* quoted in his own copy of Kirnberger's standard treatise on composition. He made an eighteen-bar sketch of a four-part chorale-prelude on this tune, but in B minor, during his work on *Zauberflöte*, not necessarily intending it for this scene (the key does not fit at all) but perhaps in connection with a pupil's contrapuntal studies. The imitative point here is also scalic.

42

Here is the first line of the men in armour's chorale, showing the chorale tune with its original form played in minims by woodwind, in crotchets by trombones. The imitative point is played by basses in the first whole bar, then by first violins.

43

633

The inscription on the pyramid, as read by the Two Men, is as follows:

> He who walks this difficult road will be purified by fire, water, air and earth. If he can conquer the fears of death he will soar from earth towards heaven. Then he will be illuminated in his position to dedicate himself wholly to the mysteries of Isis.

Schikaneder borrowed this from the equivalent moment in Terrasson's *Sethos*:

> Quiconque fera cette route seul, et sans regarder derrière lui, sera purifié par le feu, par l'eau et par l'air; et s'il peut vaincre la frayeur de la mort, il sortira du sein de la terre, il reverra la lumière, et il aura droit de préparer son âme à la révélation des mystères de la grande Déesse Isis.*

The movement ends in C major, Picardy-style (C minor continues). Tamino declares himself undaunted and asks the Men in Armour to open the gates of dread ('Schreckenspforten') so that he may enter. The music has reached a brave, not melancholy, F minor. He is stopped by Pamina's voice offstage; she pushes the key for a moment into D flat major. The Men confirm that it is she, that they can undergo the two ordeals together and may converse freely. Tamino's delight finds expression in a most un-solemn trio for the three men whose accompaniment especially, for violas and cellos and for offbeat wind, might belong to a comic operetta sixty years later or so.

This cheerful outburst ends with a little *Spruch*: 'A woman who does not shrink from death is worthy and will be initiated.'

The doors are opened. Tamino and Pamina fall into one another's arms. The music turns into F major, *andante*, for their reunion in a passage of moving lyrical beauty.

* Only three purifying elements are named by Terrasson as against Schikaneder's complete four. In this scene we watch two of them. What are the ordeals by earth and air? Jacques Chailley has an interesting theory about them in his book, but my own opinion is that Schikaneder simply omitted showing them on stage so as to keep the opera at reasonable length.

Pamina's first phrase may recall Tamino's No. 3 Aria. Students of conventional harmony will observe that Mozart happily commits consecutive octaves between melody and bass, twice in five bars.

The strings set up one of Mozart's ravishing palpitation accompaniments (another example is the slow movement of the C major piano concerto K. 467) with repeated quavers in the upper strings, a steady plucked string bass, and sustained notes for bassoons and horns. Tamino shows her the gates of dread. She offers to lead him through the two caverns while he plays his magic flute. Love will strew their path with roses as well as thorns—here she seems to quote Ex. 45. She relates the story of the flute's construction by her father (I have told it earlier; Chailley finds all four elements present in the ceremony). A fine bassoon solo accompanies the tale. Together, and with the Men in Armour, they vow to survive death through music's power—another passage, simple, even repetitive, but totally compelling.

46

Wir wan——deln durch des To——————nes Macht

Wir wan——deln durch—— des To————nes Macht

Ihr wan-delt durch—— des To————nes Macht

They enter the fiery cavern whose gates close. Crackling flames and roaring wind, distant thunder and rushing water are heard, as well as Tamino's flute and muted drums who play a march, *adagio* in C major, accompanied by horns, trumpets and trombones.

47

Here is another piece of curious orchestration—perhaps designed to penetrate the noise of Schikaneder's stage effects. At the end of this march Tamino and Pamina emerge from the cavern, embrace, and sing a short stanza of thanksgiving in smooth thirds and sixths.

48

Wir wandelten durch Feuerglu-ten,

They then pass into the watery cave while Ex. 47 is heard again. They have here to walk down some steps. The ordeal is not further described: in Terrasson it involved swimming the length of a sewer filled with water, not exactly feasible for a flute-player. After the March they come out again and repeat Ex. 48 in shortened form. A door opens to reveal a brilliantly lit temple, the most blinding light yet seen in the opera. Then trumpets and drums, *allegro* in C major, launch a chorus, *Triumph, Triumph, du edles Paar*, welcoming Tamino and Pamina to the company of the initiates. Presumably the chorus sings from within the brilliant temple, though neither score nor libretto includes the commonly printed *von innen* stage direction, and in fact at the end of the chorus there is a direction *exeunt omnes* (*alle ab*) which may imply that the chorus is sung on stage.

Tamino and Pamina have earned their right to live happily ever after. But the story is not yet finished. We return to that little garden whither Papageno has come in search of his promised wife (*allegro* in G major, flute, oboe, bassoons, horns and strings). He blows his panpipes as in No. 2, and calls her name, rather as if out of breath.

49

But he gets no response, and he knows it was his own fault for chattering during the oath of silence. Yet how he has longed for his 'Herzensweibchen' (Mozart changed the text so as to include his private pet-name for Constanze) ever since he tasted the wine. He decides (G minor) to end his days by putting a rope round his neck and decorating a tree—this was a standard *lazzo* in the *commedia dell' arte*. First he will give the audience a chance to save him by taking pity on him. One musical phrase has been frequently returning since the introduction to this scene.

50

Nobody replies, even when he counts to three, blowing his pipes at each count (much opportunity for comic effect with the pipes and with extra gags such as 'half-past two', 'five to three', '2.59 and 59 seconds', etc.). So *andante* in G minor, and with real melancholy on the woodwind, he gets into the noose, saying good night to the false world. Luckily the Three Boys are travelling past in their aerial car, and call out to him to desist (*Allegretto* in C major), using a phrase from Act I where Papageno prepares to use the magic bells on Monostatos and the slaves. It is just this instrument that the Boys advise him to play now if he wants his bride. Their carriage has landed on the ground. While Papageno plays his jingle-bells, *allegro* in C major, and sings an earthy ditty—

51

Klinget Glöckchen, klin—get, schafft mein Mädchen her.

the Boys run to their car and fetch out Papagena who was hiding in it. Papageno ends his song and the Boys tell him to turn round (Schikaneder gave them four lines of *Spruch* which Mozart rejected).

There is Papagena. The strings play a comic farmyard-type melody to which the two lovebirds perform a fantastic dance of courtship.

52

There is a tradition, effective though not authorized, that this should begin slowly and hesitantly, gradually gathering speed until the two are delightedly looking forward to the arrival of a numerous brood of little Papagenos and Papagenas. They include in their duet, of course, a *Spruch* about large families belonging to the loftiest of emotions (no good for the population explosion age). With torrents of stammering patter they run joyfully away.

Out of the trapdoor into this garden come the Queen of Night, her Three Ladies, and their new ally Monostatos. They all carry black torches in their hands, and are about to make their assault on the temple, *più moderato* in C minor, with catlike tread.

53

Before Monostatos lets them in by his secret backway he makes the Queen renew her promise that, if they are successful, he will marry Pamina. Thunder and rushing water can be heard, rather to their discomfiture; Monostatos interprets this to the effect that the Initiates are in the hall of the Temple where the Queen and her assistants will destroy them all at once. In impressive concerted harmony the Ladies and Monostatos vow allegiance to the Queen. But as they do so, 'the loudest chord' (a diminished seventh on full orchestra) is heard, 'thunder, lightning, tempest'. The conspirators are precipitated down their trapdoors into endless night. The musical sky clears sublimely.

54

The stage, says Schikaneder, is transformed into a sun. Sarastro stands on a dais. Tamino and Pamina are dressed in priestly garb. Beside them on both sides are the Egyptian priests. The Three Boys, holding flowers, are there as well. In an orchestrally accompanied recitative (the whole orchestra) Sarastro briefly announces the Sun's victory over the forces of Night. *Andante* in E flat major the chorus (female as well as male, though second-class female initiates are not mentioned) hymn the success of Tamino and Pamina, to Ex. 41 in the major (it also occurs at a similar point in the last chorus, *Höchste Gottheit*, of *König Thamos*), and offer thanks to Isis and Osiris. The grandeur of this chorus is much enhanced by the first violins' soft descending scales.

The final chorus of all is a jubilant dancelike *allegro* in E flat major.

55

The choral treatment here somewhat recalls *Es lebe Sarastro* in the first act finale after Monostatos had been sentenced to bastinado. Ex. 55 is extended to suitable dimensions and has a specially eloquent phrase about beauty and wisdom near the end.

56

In character this is related to Mozart's clarinet music of his last years, and appropriately the repeat is doubled by that instrument; it also recalls Ex. 46, another moment of quiet joy and the March of Ex. 47. But it is Ex. 55 which rings down the curtain with proud fanfares for the victory of Beauty and Wisdom.

10

Die Zauberflöte was for a long time considered a puzzling opera for a great composer to have written, particularly in full mastery at the end of his life. Much of it seems superficially quite trivial, parts of it are deliberately sublime. It suited the early nineteenth century very well when popular taste encouraged managers to add comic numbers to tragedies and serious numbers to farces, so as to balance the entertainment; *The Magic Flute* contained both, and music of all sorts, *opera seria*, streetsongs, hymns. With romanticism came pigeonholing and a revived puritanism. *Die Zauberflöte* could not easily be pigeonholed: there were the Priests and the moralizing proverbs which I have called by the German name of *Sprüche*, but there was also Papageno and his farcical exploits, rather blasphemous for those who looked on Sarastro and his Priests as a symbol of the Established Church. For opera-lovers *Il flauto magico* did hold some opportunities to hear great singing, especially in the arias for the Queen of Night and Sarastro, in Pamina's *Ah, lo so* and Tamino's Portrait Aria; but the rest was a vulgar hotchpotch and required new recitative music besides. As early as 1794 serious folk began to ignore the tomfoolery and elaborated complicated, earnest interpretations of the opera's hidden meaning; they are still busy, now that psychology has given them a new shot in the arm. These interpreters are not Gadarene Swine even when one of them sometimes rushes over a cliff: Schikaneder and Mozart did deliberately include serious matters in *Die Zauberflöte*. Schikaneder, like his predecessor Philipp Hafner (but unlike Karl Marinelli), quite often introduced new subtleties into his dramatizations of well known stories. And Mozart had almost made his reputation on an ability to combine serious themes and musical pleasantries into integrated works of art. It would be foolish to pretend that there are no allusions to Freemasonry in the libretto and in the music of *Die Zauberflöte*, and that Schikaneder and Mozart did not introduce them in a spirit of commitment. For years Mozart had wanted to write serious opera which would not be just a mummified Italian *opera seria*—he contemplated turning *Idomeneo* into something of this kind. And he wanted to write an opera that was German, not Italian or French. His achievement in the operas written with da Ponte had shown him how serious music-drama could be found in texts that were overtly comical. *Die Zauberflöte* was just such another libretto, but in some ways musically more viable. Schikaneder was not a sophisticated poet: his diction was extremely simple, short on polysyllables and elaborate images, free from the sophisticated poet's ideals of varied metres which hamper a composer's musical invention. Schikaneder's words are instantly intelligible and allow a composer to set similar stanzas to quite diversified musical metres (no poem in *Die Zauberflöte* constrains Mozart to a particular rhythm as do da Ponte's *Fin ch'han dal vino* and *No sò più cosa son*). Schikaneder had, for Mozart, another virtue as librettist, highly sympathetic. He was a great and experienced Shakespearian actor. *Die Zauberflöte* shows how thoroughly Schikaneder had digested Shakespeare's dramatic recipe of mixing comic and sublime ingredients into a convincing dramatic integer, drawing effect by violent juxtaposition of the sublime and the ridiculous. This technique is the great virtue of the libretto for *Die Zauberflöte*. It could well end after the ordeal by fire and water. But the ends must be tied up. One is farcical, Papageno's frustrated suicide and reunion with his wife; the other is blood-and-thunder, the vain assault of Astrafiammante on the Temple of Wisdom. These two scenes make the Finale all the more effective and conclusive and brilliant. Mozart, his letters show us as well as his music, was a true disciple of Shakespeare, relishing all these contrasts and creating music of emotional genuineness for each character and situation that would make the diametrically opposed character seem all the more impressive. Without Papageno as relief, Sarastro could be a pompous bore. Without the Temple of Initiates Papageno would outstay his welcome long before two acts were drawing to an end. They set one another off dramatically and by their contrasted music, perfectly appropriate in both cases thanks to Mozart's character, both antipoles are united in the play of humanity.

Some commentators emphasize the plainness of the music in *Die Zauberflöte*, the reliance on diatonic harmony and uncomplicated melody, as if to stress the opera's reliance on essentials. It is true that Papageno and Monostatos, and to some

639

extent the Ladies, are comedians and the Boys, though they may seem intellectual youngsters, sing music close to folk and popular song, the LCD of the Wieden audience. The priestly hymns are also simple and straight, because they are hymns, for musically untutored congregations, in a masonic lodge so to say. But much of *Die Zauberflöte* is chromatically forward-looking, not only the music for Pamina and Tamino, but that for the orchestra. This is no nursery music-drama: attention has been drawn to oddities of rhythm and harmony and texture and instrumentation. In these respects *Die Zauberflöte* is the most experimental of all Mozart's operas. It is also very advanced in its use of instruments: muffled drums, trombones, basset-horns, lightly touched strings, flutes and clarinets (always cautiously employed by Mozart), lyrical bassoons, protean oboes—but these in earlier operas too, as are trumpets (especially in *Così fan tutte*). It is hardly necessary to mention the special use of panpipes and Glockenspiel, for Papageno.

Die Zauberflöte, as Mozart's last opera, is a helpful guide to his feelings about tonality. E flat major, his inherited key of solemnity, is the tonic of the opera, though one very solemn aria, No. 15, is in E major with an extra accidental and a traditional image of greater brightness. G major is the key of frivolity for the Ladies as well as Papageno. C major is for brilliance, the radiance of the sun and the frank lechery of Monostatos. A major, Mozart's key of romantic love, occurs once in No. 16 for totally unromantic effect. A flat major is obviously very solemn; C minor sad and menacing, B flat rather bright, even when muted as in No. 19; G minor reserved for wretchedness, real or fictitious. F major is solemn as well as cheerful, D minor anxious and dramatic, even furious in the Queen's second aria. The hierarchy of tonalities is fairly consistent like the scoring.

For Mozart it was 'a German opera', the fulfilment of the longstanding wish. Wagner agreed that it was the beginning of German opera where there was nothing to admire before *Die Zauberflöte*; and in our own century Abert explained how typically German all the virtues of *Die Zauberflöte* are—though, being a careful scholar, he admitted the Italian musical influences; the Shakespearian element did not strike him.

Die Zauberflöte could so easily have become a ritual drama, without opportunity for momentary improvised illumination. Two other authors would have weighed it down with ethical meaning. Not, fortunately, in 1791, and not with Schikaneder and Mozart, ideal partners. They impress us, stretch our minds, cheer us up, and confirm us in respect and love for all sorts and conditions of people. If Sarastro's solemnity is emphasized to the detriment of Papageno, or Papageno's entertainment value at the sacrifice of the Initiates, *Die Zauberflöte* suffers. When a performance, in its totality, enables us to see Sarastro look in a mirror and find Papageno reflected in front of him, we know that *Die Zauberflöte* is being interpreted aright and that Mozart did not live in vain.

BIBLIOGRAPHY

ABERT, Anna Amalie. 'The Operas of Mozart' in *The New Oxford History of Music:* Vol. VII. Oxford U.P., London, 1973.

ABERT, Hermann. *W. A. Mozart: Neubearbeitete und erweitete Ausgabe von Otto Jahns Mozart.* 2 vols. Breitkopf & Härtel, Leipzig, 1923.

ANDERSON, Emily. *The Letters of Mozart and his Family.* Chronologically arranged, translated and edited with an Introduction, Notes and Indexes. Second edition prepared by A. Hyatt King and Monica Carolan. 2 vols. Macmillan, London, 1966.

ANHEISSER, Siegfried. *Die Gärtnerin aus Liebe.* Comic opera in 3 acts by Wolfgang Amadeus Mozart. Trans. from Italian by Siegfried Anheisser. Deutscher Musikverlag in der NS-Kulturgemeinde, Berlin, 1934.

APOCRYPHA, THE.

ARUNDELL, Dennis. *The Critic at the Opera.* Ernest Benn, London, 1957.

—— Introduction to *'Le nozze di Figaro' and 'Così fan tutte'.* Cassell Opera Guides, Cassell, London, 1971.

AUDEN, W. H. and KALLMAN, Chester. *The Magic Flute.* English version Faber & Faber, London, 1957.

BAKER, G. P. *Sulla the Fortunate: the great Dictator.* John Murray, London, 1927.

BATLEY, E. M. *A Preface to 'The Magic Flute'.* Dennis Dobson, London, 1969.

BEARD, Harry. 'Figaro in England' in *Maske und Kothurn.* Böhlaus, Graz, 1964.

BEAUMARCHAIS, Pierre Caron de. *Théâtre choisie.* Robert Laffont, Paris, 1959.

BIBLE, THE HOLY.

BITTER, Christof. *Wandlungen in den Inszenierungen des Don Giovanni von 1787 bis 1928.* Gottfried Bosse Verlag, Regensburg, 1961.

BLOM, Eric. *Mozart* (The Master Musicians series). J. M. Dent, London, 1935.

BLUME, Friedrich. *Classic and Romantic Music.* Faber & Faber, London, 1972.

BROCKETT, Oscar T. *The Theatre.* New York, 1964.

BRODER, Nathan. *The Great Operas of Mozart.* Essays with Libretti of *Die Entführung, Figaro, Don Giovanni, Così fan tutte,* and *The Magic Flute.* English versions by John Bloch, Auden and Kallman, and R. & T. Martin. Schirmer, New York, 1962.

BROPHY, Brigid. *Mozart the Dramatist.* Faber & Faber, London, 1964.

—— Introduction to *'Die Entführung' and 'Die Zauberflöte'.* Cassell Opera Guides, London, 1971.

BURGESS, Anthony. Introduction to *'Idomeneo' and 'Don Giovanni'.* Cassell Opera Guides, London, 1971.

CARSE, Adam. *The Orchestra in the Eighteenth Century.* Heffer, Cambridge, 1940.

CHAILLEY, Jacques. *La flûte enchantée, opéra maçonnique.* Robert Laffont, Paris, 1968.

CHAUCER, Geoffrey. *The Parlement of Foules.*

CICERO. *De Republica.* Liber VI. *Somnium Scipionis.* Latin text with English translation by E. H. Blakeney. Fortune Press, London, 1927.

CORRI, Domenico. *The Singer's Preceptor.* London (?) 1810.

DA PONTE, Lorenzo. *Memoirs*. Trans. Elisabeth Abbott. Dover, New York, 1967.

DENT, Edward Joseph. *Mozart's Operas: a critical study*. Rev. ed. Oxford U.P., London, 1947.

—— *Die Schuldigkeit des ersten Gebotes: an Introduction* (in programme of Royal Festival Hall, London, 3 July 1952).

—— *Il rè pastore: an Introduction* (in programme of Royal Festival Hall, London, 19 May 1952).

—— *The Marriage of Figaro*. English version. Oxford U.P., London, 1937.

—— *Don Giovanni*. English version. Oxford U.P., London 1938.

DEUTSCH, Otto Erich. *Briefe Mozarts*.

—— *Mozart: a documentary biography*. Trans. Eric Blom, Peter Branscombe & Jeremy Noble. A. & C. Black, London, 1965.

DICK, Kay. *Pierrot*. Hutchinson, London, 1960.

EINSTEIN, Alfred. *Mozart: his character; his work*. Trans. Arthur Mendel and Nathan Broder. Cassell, London, 1946.

—— *Essays on Music*. Faber & Faber, London, 1958. (Includes material on *Die Entführung*, *Figaro* and *Don Giovanni*.)

FORSYTH, Cecil. *Orchestration*. Macmillan, London, 1914.

FRAZER, Sir James. *The Golden Bough*. Macmillan, London, 1962.

GARCIA, Manuel. *Traité complet de l'art du chant*. Paris, 1847.

GRAVES, Robert. *Greek Myths*. Cassell, London, 1958.

—— *The White Goddess: a historical grammar of poetic myth*. Faber & Faber, London, 1961.

GREITHER, Aloys. *Die sieben grossen Opern Mozarts*. Verlag Lambert Schneider, Heidelberg, 1956.

GROUT, Donald J. *A Short History of Opera*. Columbia U.P., New York, 1956.

HILDESHEIMER, Wolfgang. *Wer war Mozart?* Suhrkamp Verlag, Frankfurt-am-Main, 1966.

HIRSCH, Paul. 'The 1906 Mozart Festival in Salzburg' in *Music Review*.

HUGHES, Spike (Patrick Cairns). *Famous Mozart Operas*. Robert Hale, London, 1957.

HYATT KING, Alec. *Mozart in Retrospect*. Oxford U.P., London, 1955.

—— (ed.). *Peter Prelleur, the Modern Musicmaster or the Universal Musician*. 1731. Modern edition Bärenreiter, n.d.

JAHN, Otto. *W. A. Mozart* (see ABERT).

JOUVE, Pierre Jean. *Mozart's 'Don Juan'*. Trans. Eric Earnshaw Smith. Vincent Stuart, London, 1957.

KERMAN, Joseph. *Opera as Drama*. Oxford U.P., London, 1957.

KNAUER, *Knauers Lexikon A–Z*. Droemersche Verlag, Munich, 1956.

KNOCH, W. J. G. *Short History of Austria and the Habsburgs*. Kunstverlag Wolfrum, Vienna, 1960.

KOBBÉ, Gustave. *Kobbé's Complete Opera Book*. Ed. and rev. by the Earl of Harewood. Putnam, London, 1976.

KÖCHEL, Dr Ludwig Ritter von. *Chronologisch-thematisches Verzeichnis sämtlicher Tonwerke W. A. Mozarts*. 3rd edn. ed. Alfred Einstein. J. W. Edwards, Ann Arbor, Michigan, 1947. 6th edn. ed. F. Giegling, A. Weinmann and G. Sievers. Breitkopf & Härtel, Wiesbaden, 1964.

KUNZE, Stefan. *Don Giovanni vor Mozart*. Fink Verlag, Munich, 1972.

LANDON, H. C. Robbins. *The Viennese Classical Style*. Barrie & Jenkins/Cresset Press, London, 1970.

—— (ed.). *Studies in Eighteenth Century Music: a tribute to Karl Geiringer on his 70th birthday*. Allen & Unwin, London, 1970.

LANDON, H. C. Robbins and MITCHELL, Donald (eds) *The Mozart Companion*. Faber & Faber, 1956. (Chapter on the operas by Gerald Abraham).

LANG, Paul Henry (ed.). *The Creative World of Mozart*. Norton, New York, 1963.

LEMPRIÈRE, J. *Classical Dictionary*. Routledge, London, 1908.

LIEBNER, Janos. *Mozart on the Stage*. Calder & Boyars, London, 1972.

LOEWENBERG, Alfred. *Annals of Opera 1597–1940*. Heffer, Cambridge, 1943.

/ MACKERRAS, Charles. 'Sense about the Appoggiatura' in *Opera*, October, 1963.

—— 'Appoggiaturas Unlimited?' in *Records and Recordings, c.* 1964.

MANCINI, Giambattista. *Pensieri e riflessioni pratiche sopra il canto figurato*. Vienna, 1774.

MANFREDINI, Vincenzo. *Regole armoniche*. Venice, 1775.

MITCHELL, Donald. 'The Truth about *Così*' in *Tribute to Benjamin Britten*, ed. Anthony Gishford. Faber & Faber, London, 1963.

MOBERLY, R. B. *'Figaro's Wedding': English translation and commentary*. Travis & Emery, London, 1965.

—— *Three Mozart Operas: 'Figaro', 'Don Giovanni', 'The Magic Flute';* an altogether new approach to Mozart's scores. Gollancz, London, 1967.

MOBERLY, R. B. and RAEBURN, Christopher. 'Mozart's *Figaro*: the plan of Act 3' in *Music and Letters*, April, 1965.

MOLINA, Tirso de. 'El burlador de Sevilla', in *Don Juan Tenorio*, Temas de España 4. Taurus Ediciones, Madrid, 1967.

MOZART, Wolfgang Amadé. *Briefe und Aufzeichungen*. ed. Wilhelm A. Bauer and Otto Erich Deutsch. 7 vols. Bärenreiter, Cassel, 1971.

MOZART in the British Museum. Trustees of the British Museum, London, 1956.

MOZART-JAHRBÜCHER. Salzburg.

Music Review. Articles passim.

Musical Times. Articles passim.

NETTL, Paul. *Mozart in Böhmen*. Prague, 1938.

Neue Mozart Ausgabe. Bärenreiter, Cassel.
  Die Schuldigkeit des ersten Gebotes: ed. Franz Giegling, 1958.
  Mitridate, rè di Ponto: ed. L. F. Tagliavini, 1966.
  Betulia liberata: ed. Tagliavini, 1960.
  Ascanio in Alba: ed. Tagliavini, 1956.
  Thamos, König in Ägypten: ed. Harald Heckmann, 1956.
  Zaide: ed. Friedrich-Heinrich Neumann, 1957.
  Le nozze di Figaro: ed. Ludwig Finscher, 1973.
  Don Giovanni: ed. Wolfgang Plath and Wolfgang Rehm, 1968.
  La clemenza di Tito: ed. Giegling, 1970.
  Die Zauberflöte: ed. Gernot Grube and Alfred Orel, 1970.

NEWMAN, Ernest. *Opera Nights*. Putnam, London, 1943.

—— *More Opera Nights*. Putnam, London, 1954.

—— 'Beaumarchais and the Musicians' in *Fortnightly Review*, October 1909.

OSBORNE, Charles (ed.). *Opera 66*. Alan Ross, London, 1966. (Includes an intelligent non-singing translation of *Zauberflöte* by the editor, and a characteristic essay on Countess Almaviva by Boris Goldovsky.)

Österreichische Musikzeitschrift. Articles passim.

PLEASANTS, Henry. *The Great Singers*. Gollancz, London, 1967.

PLUTARCH. *Lives*. Trans. Dryden, revised by A. H. Clough 1864. 3 vols. J. M. Dent, London, n.d.

RADANT, Else. *The Strange Demise of W. A. Mozart*. High Fidelity, U.S.A.

643

RAY, Cyril. *The Wines of Italy*. Penguin Books, London, 1971.

ROBINSON, Michael F. *Naples and Neapolitan Opera*. Oxford U.P., London, 1972.

—— *Opera before Mozart*. Hutchinson, London, 1966.

ROSEN. Charles. *The Classical Style*. Faber & Faber, London, 1971.

ROSENBERG, Alfons. *Die Zauberflöte: Geschichte und Deutung*. Prestel Verlag, Munich, 1964.

ROSENTHAL, Harold. *Two Centuries of Opera at Covent Garden*. Putnam, London, 1958.

—— *Opera at Covent Garden: a short history*. Gollancz, London, 1967.

ROYAL MUSICAL ASSOCIATION. *Proceedings*: passim.

RUSHMORE, Robert. *The Singing Voice*. Hamish Hamilton, London, 1971.

SACKVILLE-WEST, Edward. 'Mozart's Operas in England'. (In Royal Opera House, Covent Garden bicentenary souvenir programme, 27 January 1956.)

SADIE, Stanley. *Mozart*. Calder & Boyars, London, 1965.

SCHENK, Erich. *Mozart and his Times*. Secker and Warburg, London, 1960.

SHAW, G. Bernard. *Music in London*. Constable, London, 1932.

SMITH, Erik. '*Così fan tutte*: Introduction' (in Philips record album, 1975).

SMITH, Patrick J. *The Tenth Muse: a historical study of the opera libretto*. Gollancz, London, 1971.

STENDHAL. *Vies de Haydn, de Mozart, et de Métastase*. P. Didot l'Aîné, Paris, 1814. (Modern edition ed. Daniel Muller, Librairie ancienne Honoré Champion, Paris, 1914.)

TOSI, Pier Francesco. *Observations on the Florid Song*. Wilcox, London, 1743. Modern reprint, Reeves, London, 1967.

TOVEY, Donald Francis. *Essays in Musical Analysis*. 6 vols. Oxford U.P., 1935-9.

—— *Essays and Lectures on Music*. Oxford U.P., 1949.

VANCEA, Zeno. *Stand und Ergebnisse der rumänischen-musikwissenschaftlichen Forschung über die Beziehungen der Werke Mozarts zu Rumänien*. Verband Tschechoslowakischer Komponisten, 1956.

WELLESZ, Egon and STERNFELD, Frederick (eds.). *The New Oxford History of Music*, vol. VII: *The Age of Enlightenment 1745-1790*. Oxford U.P., London, 1973.

WESTRUP, J. A. 'Cherubino and the G minor Symphony' in *Fanfare for Ernest Newman*, ed. Van Thal. Arthur Barker, London, 1955.

WYZEWA, T. de and ST. FOIX, G. de. *W A. Mozart, sa vie musicale et son œuvre*. Descleé de Brouwer et cie, Paris 1937-58.

YORKE-LONG, Alan B. *Music at Court*. Weidenfeld & Nicolson, London, 1954.

INDEX

Titles and figures in **bold** type indicate whole chapters devoted to operas discussed in detail. *Italics* are used for other musical works, and SMALL CAPITALS for non-musical works. Opera houses, theatres, etc., are under the names of their towns or cities.

Hofer, Franz, 593, 601
Hofer, Josepha (soprano), 230, 600, 611
Hoffmann, E. T. A., 459, 462
Hofmann, Mlle (soprano), 600
Holcroft, Thomas, 366
Holzbauer, Ignaz, 230
Hornung, Joseph (bass), 39
Horvath, Odön von, 365
Hübner, Beda, 10n
Hughes, Spike, 501n
Hunter, Rita, 425

Idomeneo (Mozart), **251–88**; origins, 253, 257–9; libretto, 253, 254 *and n*; composition, 253–6; rehearsals, 255–6; title role intended to be rewritten, 256; first performance, 256, 281, 284; later performances and versions, 256–7, 270n, 273, 279; Mozart's score, 257; use of trombones, 284, 506n, 603; as Mozart's supreme *opera seria*, 286–8; treatment of characters, 288
  Overture, 259–60; **Act I**, 260–9 (*Scene 1*, 260–6; *Scene 2*, 266–9); **Act II**, 269–77 (*Scene 1*, 269–75; *Scene 2*, 275–7); **Act III**, 277–85 (*Scene 1*, 277–81; *Scene 2*, 281–2; *Scene 3*, 282–4; *Scene 4*, 284–5)
  Other mentions, 21, 22, 43, 67, 70, 71, 141, 177, 190, 230–1, 235, 293, 370, 509, 534, 536, 587, 589
Impresario in angustie, L' (Cimarosa), 354
INCONSTANT, THE (Farquhar), 452
Incontro improviso, L' (Haydn), 236
Incoronazione di Poppea, L' (Monteverdi), 355
Iphigénie en Tauride (Gluck), 38, 231n, 248

Jacquin, Gottfried von, 448, 454n, 455
Jannequin, Clément, 356
Jautz, Domenik, 293
Jefferson, Alan, 472n
Jommelli, Niccolò, 70, 96n, 111n, 211, 360
Jonson, Ben, 333
Joseph II, Emperor, 37, 38, 211, 255, 291, 295, 320, 345, 346, 347, 353, 366, 368, 372, 373, 374, 422, 441, 447, 454, 457–8, 521–2, 523, 568, 593, 594
Jugement de Midas, Le (Grétry), 231n
Jünger, F. J., 349

Karl Theodor, Elector Palatine, 230, 231
Kaspar der Fagottist (Müller), 598
Kaufmann von Smyrna, Der (Vogler), 292
Kelly, Michael, 346n, 370, 372, 373, 415, 416, 522, 599
Kistler, Herr (tenor), 600
Klebe, Giselher, 365
Klein, Herbert, 11
Kleine Nachtmusik, Eine (Mozart), 296, 311, 449, 450
Kleist, Franz Alexander von, 570
Klöpfer, Mlle (soprano), 600
König Thamos (Mozart), 62, 177, 235, 237n, 247–9, 603, 638
Kumpf, Hubert, 594

Lampugnani, Giovanni Battista, 76 *and n*
LANASSA (Plümicke), 248
Lange, Aloysia (soprano), 212, 230–1, 232, 254, 293, 346 *and n*, 353, 458, 522, 570
Lange, Joseph (actor), 254, 346n, 347
Lanterna di Diogene, La (Draghi), 356
Laschi (later Mombelli), Luisa (soprano), 38, 373, 391, 414, 458
Laschi, Signore (tenor), 38, 42, 52
Le Grand, Pierre, 254
Lehmann, Lilli, 409
Leigh, Adèle, 19
Leinsdorf, Erich, 501n, 503n
Leipzig, 248, 521, 524, 567
Leitgeb, Ignaz, 599
Lenau, Nikolaus, 469
Leo, Leonardo, 95, 358, 360, 477, 567
Leopold II, Emperor, 523, 567, 569, 573, 593
Leppard, Raymond, 357n
Levi, Hermann, 524
Lewis, Richard, 273
Lichnowsky, Prince Karl, 521
Liebeskind, A. J., 596, 597
Linz, 324, 570
Lipp (later Haydn), Maria Magdalena (soprano), 11, 39
Lippert, Friedrich Karl (tenor), 293
Lisbon, 78
Liszt, Franz, 247, 482
Loewen, Jan van, 325
Loewenberg, Alfred, 127, 257, 356 *and n*
Logroscino, Nicola, 360
Lohengrin (Wagner), 571n
Lolli, Giuseppe (bass), 450, 456, 475, 513